DREAMS OF HAPPINESS

DREAMS OF HAPPINESS

SOCIAL ART AND THE FRENCH LEFT, 1830–1850

Neil McWilliam

PRINCETON UNIVERSITY PRESS

Published by Princeton University Press, 41 William Street,
Princeton, New Jersey 08540
In the United Kingdom: Princeton University Press,
Chichester, West Sussex

Library of Congress Cataloging-in-Publication Data

McWilliam, Neil.
Dreams of happiness : social art and the French Left,
1830–1850 / Neil McWilliam.
p. cm.
Includes bibliographical references and index.
ISBN 0-691-03155-X (alk. paper)
1. Aesthetics, French—19th century. 2. Art—Political aspects—
France. 3. Saint-Simonianism. I. Title.
BH221.F83M39 1993
111'.85'094409034—dc20 92-38222

This book has been composed in Linotron Galliard

Princeton University Press books are printed
on acid-free paper and meet the guidelines
for permanence and durability of the Committee
on Production Guidelines for Book Longevity
of the Council on Library Resources

Printed in the United States of America

1 3 5 7 9 10 8 6 4 2

Que restera-t-il d'un mouvement si profond? Quelques livres, quelques manuscrits curieux pour servir à l'histoire de l'esprit humain au dix-neuvième siècle. Est-ce là, mon cher ami, ce que nous avions rêvé?

Charles Duveyrier, former Saint-Simonian,
to Charles Lambert, July 1854

Contents

Illustrations

Acknowledgments

DURING THE course of the academic *rite de passage* that extends from doctoral thesis to published monograph, one inevitably contracts many debts of gratitude, which it is a pleasure to acknowledge here. Due to the following, production of this book has been an object lesson in what Fourier would have described as "travail attrayant"—at least most of the time.

In Oxford, where I first embarked upon the study of *art social*, I would like to thank Jon Whiteley, my supervisor, and Professor Francis Haskell for their constant encouragement and support. In the Department of the History of Art, Noelle Brown and Régine Page both provided exceptional help in unearthing photographs of obscure art works from often uncooperative museums.

A number of friends and colleagues have been unfailingly generous with their time and expertise; in particular I would like to thank Andreas Broeckmann, Marie-Claude Chaudonneret, Olga Grlic, Frances Jowell, Ralph Locke, Christopher Parsons, Iain Pears, Vera Schuster, Raymond d'Unienville of the Société de l'histoire de l'Ile Maurice, and Martha Ward. Special thanks are due to Ruth Harris for her scrupulous critical reading of the final text. Both my parents and my sister, Alison McWilliam, have provided long-term moral and material support, for which I am deeply grateful.

Among the librarians encountered along the way, I would single out the staff at the Bibliothèque de l'Arsenal for their kindness and courtesy during my work on the Saint-Simonian archive, and the personnel of the Bibliothèque municipale in Douai, where I encountered the formidable archive of the sculptor Théophile Bra. I would also like to thank Brian R. MacDonald, my copy editor, for the exemplary care with which he prepared my manuscript for publication.

It is a pleasure to record my thanks to the Université de Paris IV, which welcomed me on an exchange scholarship with Oxford during my doctoral research, and, above all, to the J. Paul Getty Trust, which awarded me a postdoctoral fellowship in the history of art and humanities in 1988–89, crucial to the completion of this project.

At the University of East Anglia, I should like to thank Michael Brandon-Jones for his valuable help with illustrative material. My late colleague Nicholas Green was always challenging and stimulating in sharing his ideas on the nineteenth century. More generally, I thank my colleagues in the School of Art History and Music for providing a supportive environment for research in a political atmosphere increasingly antipathetic to scholarly work.

Abbreviations

D.P.	*La Démocratie pacifique*
J.P.	*Le Journal du peuple*
L.A.	*La Liberté. Journal des arts*
Nat.	*Le National*
Phal.	*La Phalange*
O.S.S.E.	*Oeuvres de Saint-Simon et d'Enfantin*, 47 vols., Paris, 1865–78
Org.	*L'Organisateur*
Prod.	*Le Producteur*
R.E.	*Revue encyclopédique*
R.P.	*La Revue du progrès*
R.R.	*La Revue républicaine*

DREAMS OF HAPPINESS

CHAPTER 1

Introduction

IN THE prospectus to his *Journal de la Société de 1789*, issued in the summer of 1790, the philosopher Condorcet called for the elaboration of an *art social*. Coined as part of a trinity completed by a social science and a social mathematics, the term was used to evoke the rational organization of collective life according to the principles of human nature in order to afford greatest happiness to the greatest number.[1] Some hundred years later, in November 1891, the phrase had been promoted to the masthead of a new monthly review sponsored by the "Club de l'Art social," an organization with anarchist leanings dedicated to forging a cultural alliance for revolutionary change. Arguing that "the artist must make an effort to study the social environment, he must incline toward everything concerning science, enlightenment, reason, justice, humanity,"[2] its supporters shared Condorcet's faith in rationalism as a key to social progress, a commitment that survived their very different ideological sympathies. In the intervening century, however, their understanding of the nature and scope of an *art social* had undergone radical transformation, acquiring a specifically cultural resonance at the expense of the term's more abstract designation in the language of late Enlightenment political science.[3] What survives, however, is a concern for the reorganization of collective experience, related now to the artist's intervention in social life as a champion of progressive ideals and catalyst for fundamental change.

It was during the 1830s that the notion of *art social* had come to the fore in radical circles, denoting the ideological appropriation of culture as an active element in the struggle for a new political order.[4] Though drawing on a well-established practical and theoretical understanding of art's contribu-

[1] See K. M. Baker, *Condorcet: From Natural Philosophy to Social Mathematics* (1975), 201, 273–74.

[2] "L'artiste doit s'efforcer d'étudier le milieu social, . . . il doit tendre à tout ce qui est la science, la lumière, la raison, la justice, l'humanité." A. Tabarant, "Le Club de l'Art social," *La Revue socialiste* (January 1890): 102.

[3] For subsequent examples of the use of the term in Condorcet's sense, see F.-A. Boissy d'Anglas, *Essai sur les fêtes nationales suivi de quelques idées sur les arts; et la nécessité de les encourager* (an II), 1, and Abbé H. Grégoire, *Plan d'association générale entre les savans, gens de lettres et artistes pour accélér les progrès des bonnes moeurs et des lumières.* (n.d., c. 1816), 14.

[4] For an early example of the term's cultural application, see T. Thoré, "L'Art social et progressif," *L'Artiste*, 1st ser., 7 (1834): 39–42.

tion to statecraft, advocacy of social aesthetics was galvanized under the July Monarchy through its championship by some of the regime's most implacable and articulate opponents. In this regard, *art social* forms an integral part not only of mid-nineteenth-century cultural history, as a vital stimulant to radical initiatives in literature and the visual arts, but also of our understanding of developments in political theory at this decisive moment in the formation of the modern capitalist state. As the present study will show, this apparently peripheral field offers a fertile starting point for reevaluating the meaning and aspirations of those figures—Saint-Simon and his followers, the Fourierists, and the Republicans—who laid the foundations of post-Revolutionary progressivism. Relating as it does to the metaphysical underpinning to these ideologies, an investigation of social aesthetics forces us to confront their conceptions of nature, of individual subjectivity, of man's relationship with God, and of the ethical foundations upon which social equity had to be based.

First and foremost, however, this study sets out to offer a critical account of ways in which the visual arts could be assessed and understood in the middle decades of the nineteenth century. Its central focus is on the relationship between two apparently disparate forms of writing: political theory and art criticism. We shall be concerned to explore not only how the arts could be designated a specific range of social responsibilities and potentialities within largely abstract theoretical discourse, but also with how this language was adapted to the practical task of evaluating contemporary cultural production. To this end, we shall examine the strategies developed by differing political groups in approaching the Paris Salon, an exhibition whose preeminence ensured its centrality not only to debates on the nation's cultural health but also to broader speculations on the contemporary artist's capacity to mold opinion and thus contribute to securing radical change. As we shall see, the tensions that frequently underlay such calls reveal limitations in a project all too often constrained by an incapacity to break with inherited cultural expectations and question the ideological ramifications of the institutions of fine art itself.

Though particular groups' initiatives at enlisting and exploiting the skills of painters and sculptors will be discussed in detail, it is not our intention to offer a seamless art-historical narrative of a protorealist "radical art." As the present study suggests, any notion of a coherent practice reducible to a set repertoire of preoccupations and themes overlooks radical theorists' complex, often contradictory, understanding of what such a cultural practice might mean. It also underestimates artists' persistent difficulties in giving concrete expression to often highly abstract critical injunctions, particularly in the increasingly competitive commercial environment in which they were obliged to operate. As we shall see, understandings of what constituted a social art defy any attempts to impose reductive stylistic definitions. When one is confronted by what, in fact, turns out to be the disconcertingly polymorphous array of imagery noted by critics for its ameliorative potential, restricting analysis to art-historical categorization seems not only inappropriate but futile. If calls for a social art during the 1830s and 1840s are to be understood at all, we must be prepared to look beyond a diffuse, at times confusing, assemblage of objects to the theoretical debates within which they were circulated and to the historical moment within which both object and ideology were generated.

Despite Léon Rosenthal's groundbreaking survey of radical criticism in *Du romantisme au réalisme*,[5] art historians have done little to investigate the theoretical ramifications of mid-century social aesthetics. Although individual artists and commentators have attracted attention,[6] a pervasive unease at the overt conscription of visual art for political ends has inhibited more synthetic analysis. Significantly, perhaps, it has been left to literary historians to explore the conceptual underpinning of radical art criticism more systematically,[7] and preliminary investigation has grown out of a well-established tradition of inquiry into the theory and practice of social romanticism. H. J. Hunt's *Le Socialisme et le romantisme en France: étude de la presse socialiste de 1830 à 1848* remains an essential starting point for any study of the cultural politics of groups such as the Saint-Simonians and the Fourierists, and has more recently been enriched by Paul Bénichou's magisterial study of post-Revolutionary thought, *Le Temps des prophètes*, which effectively situates radical cultural perspectives within a broader intellectual spectrum. Since Marguerite Thibert's seminal study in 1927, it is the Saint-Simonians who have consistently sustained greatest scholarly interest as the progenitors of social romanticism, most significantly providing the focus not only for Ralph Locke's fascinating survey of their use of music as a propaganda tool,[8] but also for Philippe Régnier's definitive exploration of their literary philosophy.[9] While Régnier's subtly argued and exhaustively documented inquiry sets a new benchmark for any understanding of radical poetics, some earlier commentators have succumbed to treating advocates

[5] L. Rosenthal, *Du romantisme au réalisme* (1914), 365–77.

[6] See, for example, the excellent work on Thoré by Grate and Jowell, and Rousseau's thesis on Jeanron, Horaist on Besson, and Amprimoz on Papety.

[7] See, in particular, D. Kelley, "L'Art: l'harmonie du beau et de l'utile," *Romantisme* 5 (1973): 18–36, B. Juden, "L'Esthétique: 'l'harmonie immense qui dit tout,' " ibid., 4–17, and, more recently, the special issue of *Lendemains* 37 (1985), containing articles by K. Biermann, W. Drost, and H. Stenzel on the Saint-Simonians, Christian Socialists, and Fourierists.

[8] R. P. Locke, *Music, Musicians and the Saint-Simonians* (1986).

[9] P. Régnier, "Les Idées et les opinions littéraires des Saint-Simoniens (1825–1835)," 3 vols. (1983).

of *art social* with a mixture of irritation and disdain. Asserting the incompatibility of art and politics, cultural historians have inclined to recoil from the aesthetic ideologies they explored, and to denigrate the social ideologies sustaining them as fanciful and absurd.[10]

It is, of course, sometimes hard to come to terms with the more outlandish ideas of an Enfantin or a Fourier, or to keep incredulity under control as the Saint-Simonian adventure runs its extravagant course. Yet, however eccentric, the ideas and initiatives attending the birth of socialism in France responded to very real needs and ambitions in the culture that sustained them. Only through sympathetic, though critical, analysis will the historian decipher this subterranean sense and reconstruct the hidden logic of desire which makes these movements more than marginal curiosities in a rapidly changing, volatile society. With their appeal to artists, radical theorists offered assurance in an environment of vertiginous cultural transformation, promising eminence and authority in exchange for the precariousness of survival in a market economy. More generally, they addressed a nation polarized by decades of political conflict, holding out the prospect of harmony and progress, underwritten by the resolution of psychological, social, economic, and religious tensions embedded in the moribund order of a decaying world. In the pages that follow, we shall attempt to reinsert mid-nineteenth-century radical ideologies into their cultural milieu, focusing on their treatment of the aesthetic as a socially revivifying force. Our account will challenge the common equation of *art social* with a narrow and reductive didacticism to emphasize instead the varying strategies developed to exploit the formal properties of visual representation, rooted in the imagination's response to sensual experience rather than in the more measured apprehension associated with reason. As we shall see, the differing ideological complexions of the groups under discussion fostered distinctive, often contrasting, understandings of art's role as a catalyst for change and guardian of a regenerate polis. Yet, beyond these variations, the contours of a common project emerge, visible still in the writings of Proudhon, Kropotkin, Jaurès, and Zhdanov. The vitality of *art social* in its successive manifestations, modulated by changing ideological circumstances, underscores the importance of understanding this moment in the often troubled history of art's political career.

As a means of approaching such an understanding, we must first explore the ideological and aesthetic cultures out of which *art social* emerged in the early years of the July Monarchy.

10 See, for example, B. Tolley, "The Social Role of Art and Literature according to the Saint-Simonians 1825–1833" (1968), 24: "Saint-Simon's insistence on the value of art and literature as propaganda gives an aridity to his aesthetic ideas which can only be attributed to his lack of imagination and to his defective powers of appreciation."

RADICAL PERSPECTIVES

"A new generation is growing up, which was born in the midst of skepticism":[11] Théodore Jouffroy's diagnosis of the spiritual malaise left by the fall of Napoleon and the trauma of revolution identifies a sense of disorientation and loss, which echoes through political commentary across the early decades of the nineteenth century. As successive regimes vainly attempted to consolidate their authority by redefining the rights and duties of the citizen, so the search for new, more resilient foundations on which to secure legitimate rule took on increasing urgency. Such conditions provided fertile ground for wide-ranging speculation on the nature of human organization and on the metaphysical beliefs upon which civil society forged its ethical codes. Bénichou's characterization of the period as "l'âge des prophètes" emphasizes the prevalence of totalizing explanations of humanity, its past, its collective existence, and its relationship with God. In an age preoccupied by its lack of belief, new ideologies vied to fill the vacuum left by a monarchy deprived of mystique and a church whose doctrines no longer commanded the untroubled reverence accorded by previous generations.

The movements that form the focus of this study were centrally involved in attempts to provide a comprehensive blueprint for post-Revolutionary society. Though their perceptions of the state of the nation and its concommitant needs varied in detail, they were united in their sense of living through an era of momentous change, which called for decisive theoretical guidance to ensure that the remnants of the old order were comprehensively superseded by institutions and beliefs appropriate to new challenges and opportunities. It is this all-encompassing vision, in which political intervention forms merely one facet of a philosophical program embracing epistemological, scientific, psychological, and religious concerns, which marks out the groups whose aesthetic systems will preoccupy us here. Rather than a liminal interest, feebly reflecting a body of thought forged in response to more pressing ideological demands, the aesthetic takes its place as an integral element in these systematic world views, engaging in intensive dialogue with the broader social and philosophical aspirations upon which radical thinkers based their claims to succeed the outworn institutions inherited from the ancien régime. Any understanding of the significance and objectives of *art social* must thus be undertaken within the framework of an examination of those doctrines that sustained it, an examination made all the more compelling by the long-standing controversy surrounding the historical meaning of early nineteenth-century radical movements.

[11] "Une génération nouvelle s'élève, qui a pris naissance au sein du scepticisme." T. Jouffroy, "Comment les dogmes finissent," in *Mélanges philosophiques* (1833), 20–21, reprinted from *Le Globe* (24 May 1825).

Commentators have traditionally distinguished two broad currents dominating the French left in the years leading up to the 1848 revolution, broadly identifiable as republican and "utopian." This dissymmetry between a value-free description of ideological affiliation and an inherently pejorative term suggesting impracticality or frivolousness immediately points to a central problem in assessing the historical significance of these contending traditions. There has been a tendency, originating at least with the *Manifesto of the Communist Party* and amplified by Engels in *Socialism: Utopian and Scientific*, to equate the ideas of figures such as Saint-Simon and Fourier with an "immature" phase in the unfolding class struggle.[12] It has also been habitually supposed that the two thinkers and their respective followers were impelled by sufficiently similar ambitions to merit congruent assessment. While both assertions demand reexamination, even more fundamentally, the appropriateness of bracketing their ideas together as utopian, let alone of regarding their commitment as unproblematically socialist, raises questions which disrupt efforts at neat ideological compartmentalization.[13]

There is, of course, an undeniable contrast between the generally limited social and political concerns of republican thinkers active under the July Monarchy and the more global ambitions associated both with full-fledged "utopians" and with thinkers profoundly affected by them, such as the Christian socialist Philippe Buchez and the democratic socialist Pierre Leroux. Just as striking, however, are the radical discrepancies, affecting not only philosophical first principles but also the social programs they inspired, which frequently gave rise to violent polemics between competing factions. Efforts at distinguishing clear-cut oppositions between two distinctive camps are thus frustrated by the very diversity and inclusiveness of vision characterizing individual positions across the ideological spectrum. In view of this, it is perhaps most fruitful to explore the underlying preoccupations that transcend apparent theoretical differences, and attempt to identify common—or contrasting—structures that disclose the premises shaping early nineteenth-century radical discourse. Such a strategy will help us identify the needs to which oppositional thinkers attempted to respond and account for the appeal their ideas held out to many of their contemporaries.

Though intended as a grand gesture of historical closure neutralizing the

[12] See K. Marx and F. Engels, *Manifesto of the Communist Party* (1848; reprint, 1968), 70, and F. Engels, *Socialism: Utopian and Scientific* (1880; reprint, 1975), 51–52. Robert Owen, the third thinker discussed in these texts, falls outside the scope of the present study. The Icarian leader Etienne Cabet, whom both Marx and Engels largely ignore, will be treated only briefly, due to his school's general indifference to artistic questions.

[13] See, for example, M. Larizza-Lolli, " 'Socialisme' et 'utopisme': deux catégories à méditer? Quelques considérations à partir du cas du *saint-simonisme*," in *Romantismes et socialismes en Europe (1800–1848)*, ed. A. Billaz and U. Ricken (1987), 137–50.

previous quarter century of conflict and change, the restoration of the Bourbon dynasty in 1815 served for many to confirm the irreversibility of the process unleashed in 1789 and to expose the ideological impasse in which the nation had become trapped. Across the political spectrum, from the theocratic right centered on Bonald and de Maistre to the liberal opposition grouped around Guizot and Cousin, the need was felt for a solution more decisive than the mere refurbishment of regal power with Bonapartist institutions and constitutional trappings. In the eyes of many, the attempt to suture past and present on the basis of dynastic succession could never adequately bridge the divide isolating post-Napoleonic France from the assumptions and beliefs of the ancien régime. As even a monarchist such as the philosopher Ballanche was obliged to recognize, turning the clock back was not an option: "We have reached a critical age, an era that marks an end and a renewal; society no longer rests on the same foundations, and the people need institutions relating to their future destiny."[14]

Such a realization opened up the vertiginous prospect of wholesale institutional renewal in a nation already divided and confused by the social experimentation of recent years. Though ambivalence, if not outright hostility, toward this period of upheaval was widely shared, so too were doubts as to the adequacy of a superannuated monarch foisted on the nation by foreign invaders.[15] It was this sense of being denied the social and spiritual certainties on which previous generations had based their lives that fueled a *mal du siècle*, which sought in subjectivity and the exploration of emotional intensity the consolation civil society was unable to provide. It fueled, too, what Alan Spitzer has described as an "epidemic of conspiracy,"[16] transmitted among a liberal intelligentsia impatient with efforts to reassert archaic ideals in a society no longer prepared to lend them credence. Both currents would, in their different ways, inflect the more far-reaching attempts being made to take up the challenge outlined by Ballanche. As embodied by thinkers such as Fourier, Saint-Simon, and their followers, this response situated a radical critique of existing institutions, and the power relations they sustained, within a fundamental reexamination of the nature of man and of the deity in whom the significance of human existence was invested.

In challenging the received doctrines of the Christian faith, the Revolution had bequeathed a sense of anxiety and doubt central to all subsequent

[14] "Nous sommes arrivés à un âge critique, à une époque de fin et de renouvellement; la société ne repose plus sur les mêmes bases, et les peuples ont besoin d'institutions qui soient en rapport avec leurs destinées futures." P.-S. Ballanche, *Essai sur les institutions sociales dans leur rapport avec les idées nouvelles* (1818), 66, cited in P. Barbéris, *Balzac et le mal du siècle. Contribution à une physiologie du monde moderne* (1970), 1:53.

[15] On the attitudes toward the Bourbon restoration among the young, see A. B. Spitzer, *The French Generation of 1820* (1987), 38–41.

[16] Ibid., 67.

attempts at social reconstruction. A broad consensus traversed the ideological divide that some form of shared belief was essential to guarantee the integrity of society and to underwrite the ethical system upon which its effective functioning depended. Just as Traditionalist writers regarded faith as the essential prerequisite for a cohesive, organic society responsive to the authority vested in institutions tested over time,[17] so thinkers as varied as Mme de Staël and Saint-Simon concurred in treating religion as the fundamental guarantor of stability and virtue. Though Catholicism had enjoyed a revival under the Empire, fostered by publicists such as Frayssinous, Chateaubriand, and La Harpe,[18] and benefited from aggressive official support under the Restoration, its continuing credibility was widely questioned. The proliferation of often fanciful and short-lived "new" religions throughout the first half of the century[19] points to a *théomanie*[20] prompted by the need to fill the void left by Catholicism's perceived demise.

This crisis in belief is integral to understanding radical schemes in the first half of the nineteenth century. With the exception of Philippe Buchez, most major thinkers on the left contended with what they believed to be Christianity's obsolescence and the need to devise new structures of belief responsive to the demands of the modern world. On one level, their claims to initiate a new era of faith smack of sheer political opportunism, as with the "Physicist" religion explicitly introduced by Saint-Simon as a device for subduing the masses, or of an authoritarianism that undercuts more democratic claims, a feature of Leroux's "Religion nationale," with its denial of freedom of conscience. Yet, more fundamentally, the obsessive religiosity of groups such as the Saint-Simonians points to a real need for a metaphysic on which to formulate, and indeed justify, conduct in a society deprived by the Revolution of former spiritual certainties. Claims that Saint-Simon stood in direct succession to Moses and Christ, or that his disciple Prosper Enfantin was the new Messiah,[21] seem quite characteristic of a doctrine whose religion of love and social concord all too evidently underwrote a desire to legitimate an essentially authoritarian social creed. Yet even a thinker such as Fourier, hostile to organized religion and committed to an anarchistic indulgence of individual instinct, could place himself unambiguously in the revelatory tradition in claiming to be the *postcurseur* of Christ, charged with the salvation of society.[22] This pervasive religiosity is a recurrent theme in

[17] See, for example, D. G. Charlton, *Secular Religions in France 1815–1870* (1963), 10.

[18] See F. P. Bowman, *Le Christ des barricades 1789–1848* (1987), 37ff.

[19] See Charlton, *Secular Religions*, esp. 130–35, and A. Erdan, *La France mystique; tableau des excentricités religieuses de ce temps* 2 vols. (1858).

[20] The term was coined by contemporary alienists to describe a putative psychological condition; see Bowman, *Christ des barricades*, 242.

[21] See ibid., 176–77.

[22] Ibid., 181.

radical discourse. Though in many instances oppositional ideologies presented themselves as moving beyond the Christian tradition, for a figure such as Buchez, as for an early communist like Cabet or the apostles of a *Christ révolutionnaire* before 1848, existing theological models remained capable of meeting the challenge of social renovation. Transcending such distinctions, however, and crucial in providing these diverse movements with a common ideological foundation, was a commitment to the importance of faith as an adhesive force bonding individuals together in a network of duties and commitments.

If the Revolution had bequeathed a legacy of skepticism with which all subsequent ideological initiatives had to contend, its political inheritance proved no less fatal to preconceptions over the organization and governance of society. The crisis in theories of natural rights, precipitated by the Terror, was compounded by a major shift away from egalitarian models of human capacity upon which much Enlightenment political theory had been predicated. The coincidence of these factors persuaded many of the need to reformulate the basic principles upon which the revolutionaries had attempted to reorganize the state and to devise governmental structures more responsive to the irreducible diversity of the nation's citizens. Liberal thinkers such as the Idéologues critically reassessed the Declaration of the Rights of Man as embodying a belief in the innate equality of individual capacities inherited from a materialist such as Helvétius.[23] This understanding of the citizen—conceived as developing uniformly in response to stimuli absorbed from a common environment—stood accused of abstraction, a charge reiterated by Traditionalists like de Maistre, for whom the rationalist contract theory of government, promoted by the Revolution, negated all sense of the organic development of national institutions over time.[24]

These dual crises—concerning the role of history in the formation of government, and the nature of the individual as a political (and ultimately a physiological) subject—remained decisive for post-Revolutionary radical thought. With the notable exception of Fourier, whose perspective tended to be cosmic rather than retrospective, theorists cultivated a profoundly historicist understanding of social development, which shaped their vision of the need for institutional renewal. The prevalence in their work of analogies between the development of civilization and human growth and maturation also testifies to the importance accorded to the natural sciences as a foundation upon which new social systems could be elaborated. The pivotal role played by physiology, both as an epistemological model and as a funda-

[23] See, for example, C. B. Welch, *Liberty and Utility: The French Idéologues and the Transformation of Liberalism* (1984), 34.

[24] See M. T. Bovetti Pichetto, "L'influenza di Joseph de Maistre sul pensiero di Saint-Simon," in *Joseph de Maistre tra illuminismo e restaurazione*, ed. L. Marino (1975), 103.

mental predicate in approaching the problem of collective organization, points to a repudiation of the abstract egalitarianism of Enlightenment political science in favor of an awareness of variations in human potential and need.

Sensitivity to individual difference—underlying Saint-Simon's categorization of distinctive classes comprising artists, scientists, and *industriels*, as well as Fourier's anatomization of human passion—reflects a major reorientation of physiological investigation, which, as we shall later see, proved particularly decisive for radical cultural theory. Most closely associated with the seminal medical inquiries of Cabanis and Bichat, this current modified sensationalist theories of cognition inherited from Locke to emphasize instead variations in individual response to external stimuli, and to posit innate differences in human aptitudes and ability. As the image of man as malleable *tabula rasa*, callibrated emotionally and intellectually by the accumulation of sensory experience, gave way to a more complex equation involving temperament as well as environment, so the elaboration of institutions designed to optimize individual potential and secure collective welfare seemed less amenable to the totalizing sweep of pure reason. As physiology laid claim to displacing the traditional ethical role of philosophy and theology, offering the man of science an organizing role in society far surpassing established professional demarcations,[25] so political thinkers sought in the insights of medical science the basis of an ontology upon which to found a polity infallibly suited to human need.

Not only did human physiology provide theorists such as Saint-Simon, Buchez, and Leroux with a basic component from which they could extrapolate new systems of collective organization, it further offered an epistemological model for conceptualizing the workings of an organism as complex as human society. Barbara Haines has spoken of Saint-Simon regarding government as "an applied science of man,"[26] and indeed both he and such disciples as Enfantin and Buchez continually returned to the analogy between the individual body and the social body as one possessing more than a loose metaphorical resemblance. Though what Saint-Simon styled as his *physiologie sociale* echoes comparisons elaborated by such conservative thinkers as Bonald,[27] the investment in medical science both he and his disciples were to make far surpassed other contemporaries. Crucially, for

[25] See L. S. Jacyna, "Medical Science and Moral Science: The Cultural Relations of Physiology in Restoration France," *History of Science* 25 (1987): 116–18.

[26] B. A. Haines, "Henri de Saint-Simon and the Idea of Organism" (1969), 45.

[27] For Bonald's authoritarian variant on the body/society metaphor, which also reasserts mind-body dualism in the face of the monist theories of figures such as Cabanis, see *Recherches philosophiques sur les premiers objets des connaissances morales*, in *Oeuvres complètes* (1838), 8.1:305–17. See Jacyna, "Medical Science and Moral Science," 131–32.

Saint-Simon, developments in physiology held out the promise of a revolution in theories of knowledge which would herald a positivist epistemology allowing future decisions in all areas of life to be taken according to objective criteria.

Saint-Simon's ambitions for epistemological unity point to a widespread conviction among radical thinkers in the epochal consequences resulting from the discovery of a common basis to human knowledge. These totalizing ambitions, reiterated by figures such as Buchez and Leroux, indicate a desire to overcome the perceived fragmentation and conflict in the modern world to secure a regime from which all sources of friction had been eliminated. Both Saint-Simon and Fourier, who claimed his analysis of human passion followed strict mathematical laws, invested their hopes in specific areas of investigation unlocking the secret of social concord and individual happiness. Themselves pretending to the status of scientists who had succeeded in discovering the fundamental principle governing human interaction, each looked to Newton's theory of gravity as a unifying force operating in the social as well as the physical domain. In this respect, both thinkers—despite conspicuous differences in rhetorical style—cultivated positivist ambitions shared by such contemporaries as the Idéologues and Auguste Comte.

This preoccupation with epistemological unity is most strikingly echoed across the left in the pervasive calls for a synthesis of knowledge transcending historical antinomies hitherto responsible for frustrating human progress. Inflecting such theoretical concerns as the Saint-Simonians' ambitions for a religious reconciliation of Christian spirituality and pagan materialism, or Leroux's pantheistic conception of *humanité*, this theme renews and exceeds the encyclopedic project of the Enlightenment to equate the ideal of synthesis with a quasi-mystical resolution of millennial conflicts alienating man from man and sundering the psychological integrity of the individual. Its centrality to all levels of post-Enlightenment thought is confirmed by the spiritual outpourings of Saint-Simonian converts and in such eccentric fringe religions of the 1840s as Louis de Tourreil's *fusionisme*, with its evocation of the androgynous demiurge "Evadam," or claims by Ganneau to embody male and female deities in his incarnation as the "Mapah."[28] In the context of radical ideologies of the period, this obsession with synthesis and the neutralization of conflict highlights a com-

[28] On Tourreil and Ganneau, see Charlton, *Secular Religions*, 132–33; P. Bénichou, *Le Temps des prophètes. Doctrines de l'âge romantique* (1977), 429–35; Erdan, *La France mystique*, 2:183–88. According to the entry in the *Larousse du XIXe siècle*, 10.2:1111, Ganneau's disciples included Thoré and Félix Pyat. A sculptor by training, Ganneau produced bas-reliefs illustrating the new faith; see the description of the monstrance depicting "la synthèse religieuse la plus complète et la plus absolue" in Erdan, 2:185.

mon aspiration to develop organic structures uniting all levels of society and eliminating recourse to coercion as an instrument of statecraft.[29] In virtually every instance, the groupings who form the subject of this study sought a means of rallying all sectors of society behind a leadership enjoying the unqualified obedience of the masses. A contributory factor to the priority accorded the arts, this goal helped to promote epistemological synthesis not merely as the bedrock of an irrefutable positivism but as the metaphor and guarantee for a regime that had successfully transcended the sources of former social antagonism.

Such ambitions attracted the scorn of Marx and Engels in their comments on utopianism in 1848. Accusing Saint-Simon and Fourier of treating the proletariat as "a class without any historical initiative or any independent political movement,"[30] they condemned their attempt to stand apart from class conflict as delusory and derided their efforts at winning support among all levels of society. Their remarks implicitly assume that the "utopian" theorists' avowed desire to ameliorate the material conditions of the working class provides sufficient justification for characterizing their enterprise as "socialist." The variegated nature of radical theory in France prior to 1848 should caution against such assumptions. The central impetus behind Saint-Simon and his disciples might best be characterized as technocratic, predicated as it is on the governance of society by a managerial elite whose control over the flow of capital, through the establishment of a central credit bank and abolition of inheritance rights, reinforces central authority over economic activity. Though in some respects prefiguring the economic machinery of state socialism, Saint-Simonianism can equally be regarded as an inherently inegalitarian initiative, reinforcing the power of the state while simultaneously claiming to limit its jurisdiction to the *administration des choses*. Its inegalitarianism is shared by Fourier and his followers, whose commitment toward relocating society in the communal setting of immense *phalanstères* seemed ill-equipped to confront the increasingly complex nature of material production. The sexual libertarianism of both groups displays less of an interest in the moral and material emancipation of women within a society offering economic opportunity to all its members, than a preoccupation rooted in psychological and epistemological assumptions much less disruptive of dominant distribution of gender roles than is often assumed.

The most characteristic feature of radical economic theory before 1848, uniting thinkers such as Buchez and Leroux with a socialist like Louis Blanc

[29] On the elimination of coercion as a theme of Saint-Simonian theory, see E. Durkheim, *Le Socialisme. Sa Définition—ses débuts. La Doctrine saint-simonienne* (1928), ed. M. Mauss 1978, 166ff.

[30] Marx and Engels, *Manifesto*, 70.

or the incipient French communist movement, is a commitment toward workers' cooperatives, in which small-scale producers would each have a stake in the means of production and enjoy a share of collective profits. Though such a proposal apparently corroborates Engels's remarks on the "immaturity" of the class situation and the corresponding solutions offered by early reformists,[31] research by economic historians underlines its appopriateness for prevailing conditions. In a period characterized by low levels of mechanization and increased industrial output based on intensified labor exploitation, high levels of competition tended to proletarianize traditional artisans at the same time as enhancing the power of merchants and holders of finance capital[32]—precisely those economic agents most fiercely attacked by radical polemicists. Such a situation contributed to an understanding of social class—most conspicuous within Saint-Simonianism—in which a determining distinction was drawn between small entrepreneurs and artisans on the one hand and such *oisifs* as middlemen and *rentiers* on the other. Though the cooperative movement attempted to eliminate dependence on these ancillary groups, it was incapable of resolving the problem of internal competition between workshops, and could at best offer only provisional protection from the encroaching effects of industrialization.

These varying economic perspectives should caution against too inclusive an understanding of the groups under discussion here. First and foremost, they must be understood as a product of what Pierre Barbéris has described as the period's *ardeur systématrice*,[33] with its passion for all-encompassing intellectual programs—made all the more alluring by the apparent ideological vacuum inherited in 1815. In their often intemperate anti-individualism, they reveal at once a yearning for authority and certainty at the same time as apprehension at the threat of force, from whatever quarter it might come. A common concern with the systems of belief upon which social legitimacy could be consolidated testifies to a desire for social organicism and the pursuit of material progress free from conflict far more compelling than any commitment toward egalitarianism or democracy. In this respect, currents represented by Saint-Simon, Fourier, Buchez, and Leroux are perhaps most aptly understood as "secular religions," impelled by a vision of the world more grandiose than the comparatively pragmatic concerns of the republican movement. As we shall see, many of the master themes identified as integral to the radical enterprise are represented in the particular inflections each group applied to the notion of *art social*. In according a significant role to the arts within their overall philosophical system, each reflects the emer-

[31] Engels, *Socialism: Utopian and Scientific*, 51–52.

[32] See E. Berenson, *Populist Religion and Left-Wing Politics in France, 1830–1852* (1984), 26–33.

[33] Barbéris, *Balzac*, 1:120.

gence of aesthetics over the course of the previous century not simply as an isolated study of beauty and affect but as an anatomization of emotion carrying ultimately political consequence.

THE AESTHETIC DIMENSION

The crystallization of the aesthetic has come to represent a privileged moment in the history of bourgeois individualism. Critics regard the theorization of imaginative experience as private, subjective, disinterested, and inwardly directed as auguring the retreat of artistic utterance from the public sphere and extending a domain in which the myth of autonomous selfhood could be given free rein.[34] The dominant history of aesthetics, from Kant to Fry, focuses on the exaltation of art as a cornerstone of liberal humanist values. Yet a countervailing genealogy, within which radical theories of social art are pivotal, extends down from the birth of aesthetics as a discrete area of inquiry in the eighteenth century, shadowing its evolution and sharing many of its presuppositions, while insisting on art's capacity to further political goals by appealing to collective sentiment. Paradoxically, these apparently contrasting perceptions of art concur in the central role they accord its capacity to arouse intense emotional feeling. Yet what in liberal humanist discourse serves to reaffirm the uniqueness of individual identity, social aesthetics regards as contributing to the sublimation of selfhood in the collective being of the polis.

This rerouting of subjectivity into the public domain draws theoretical sustenance from transformed understandings of the nature of sentiment, crucial to challenging rationalist classicism and to speculation by philosophers and physiologists that objective laws of sensory response, allowing precise manipulation of behavior and beliefs, awaited discovery and potential exploitation as an instrument of statecraft. The simultaneous, and interrelated, reconfiguration of visual art less as an imitative than an expressive medium facilitated the promotion of its creator, again in two apparently irreconcilable, though fundamentally analogous, directions. The artist's accreditation within liberal humanist discourse with a heightened sensibility distinct from the more materially oriented mentality of polite society assumes a psychological particularity also central to his elevation by advocates of *art social* as a prophet or guide, enjoying privileged insight. The constellation of circumstances that produced agitation for a social aesthetic thus grew out of a longer-term shift in understanding, affecting artistic production and reception as well as the place of culture within the public domain. Investigation of this change, which serves to qualify more familiar readings

[34] See, for example, T. Eagleton, *The Ideology of the Aesthetic* (1990), 3.

of the nature of the aesthetic, will help clarify our understanding of the broader sociocultural implications of radical theories in the 1830s and 1840s.

Nineteenth-century thinkers' ambition to channel individual response to sense impressions for socially beneficial ends stood in sharp contrast to the mistrust that had surrounded imagination and sensory perception before the Enlightenment. For Pascal's generation, imagination distorted moral discrimination, promoting error and folly through its appeal to blind instinct, while Descartes maintained that the very intensity of affective response stimulated by such faculties as vision compromised their reliability as a source of judgment.[35] Precisely those characteristics which later thinkers were to regard as most potent in art's capacity to mold collective opinion and transform patterns of behavior—namely its appeal to sentiment and imagination—here demand the moderating check of rational precept to forestall potentially damaging consequences. The rehabilitation of noncognitive modes of perception during the Enlightenment, made possible by Locke's insistence on the role of the senses in forming ideas, brought about a new understanding of instinctual feeling, valued now as complementary to reason, rather than as subordinate to it and necessitating vigilant control.[36]

Reversing earlier epistemological models, eighteenth-century thinkers increasingly identified moral discernment less with the measured intellectual calculations of reason than with the intuitive response of emotional sensibility, rooted in the body's spontaneous reaction to external stimuli. Though Catholic apologists resisted the materialist implications of such a construct, upholding Malebranche's identification of sentiment with the soul,[37] sensationalists and spiritualists concurred in according it an immediacy and lucidity reason was unable to match. In the words of the Jesuit *Dictionnaire de Trévoux*: "Through sentiment, the mind suddenly and spontaneously discovers truths which it would develop only gradually by deliberate thought process."[38]

Understood as the basis of the human impulse to enter social relations,[39] in the aesthetic sphere the promotion of sentiment eclipsed the equation of

[35] See R. G. Saisselin, *The Rule of Reason and the Ruses of the Heart: A Philospohical Dictionary of Classical French Criticism, Critics, and Aesthetic Issues* (1970), 102–7; R. Descartes, *Les Passions de l'âme*, article 85, "De l'agrément et de l'horreur," in *Oeuvres*, ed. S. S. de Sacy (1966), 2:565–66.

[36] See P. Bénichou, *Le Sacre de l'écrivain 1750–1830* (1973), 30–32; P. Gay, *The Enlightenment: An Interpretation* (1970), 2:187–207.

[37] See A. Becq, *Genèse de l'esthétique française moderne. De la raison classique à l'imagination créatrice* (1984), 1:173ff.

[38] "Les vérités de sentiment sont celles où l'esprit découvre tout d'un coup et par la première impression, les mêmes marques de vérité qu'on développe peu à peu par des réflexions expresses." Cited in ibid., 2:508.

[39] See the discussion of Mercier in ibid., 2:576.

beauty with truth in favor of a more overtly moral, socially oriented identification with goodness.[40] Such a liaison encouraged increasing insistence on art's ameliorative power, based on a belief in sentiment's receptivity to the representation of edifying action and its ability unconsciously to absorb moral meaning valuable to the conduct of everyday life.[41] At its most extreme, this valorization of art's capacity to excite feeling authorized a total rendering of self-control in a pantomime of emotional excess allegedly beneficial to refined moral understanding. This reversal of Descartes's cautioning against the unreliability of intense emotion failed to persuade all proponents of art's ethical effect, however. Diderot, relating the physiological phenomena of *sensibilité* to the circulatory system, questioned the efficacy of a process in which somatic forces so comprehensively overwhelmed the brain's powers of discrimination, and counseled a less violent understanding of aesthetic reception.[42] His advocacy of art as a stimulant to moral conduct, given practical expression in the *drames bourgeois* and his championship of Greuze and Richardson, abjured the histrionic self-indulgence of *sensibilité* in favor of a measured appeal to sentiment of lasting effect. While maintaining that "it is only the passions at their grandest which can raise the soul to accomplish great deeds,"[43] Diderot understood art less as a self-indulgent catharsis than as a refined, though intense, modulation of feeling for edifying ends. Given his theoretical belief in vision's superior efficacy as a channel for emotional response,[44] it was to painting and the theater that he turned to find his didactic conception of art fulfilled most completely. As he argues in the *Essai sur les règnes de Claude et de Néron*:

> Let us exhibit paintings of virtue, and we will not want for copyists. Not only does that form of exhortation which addresses the soul by way of the senses have a permanent effect, it is also more accessible to ordinary men. The people use their eyes better than their understanding. Images preach continually without wounding their pride.[45]

[40] See E. Schiefenbusch, "L'Influence de Jean-Jacques Rousseau sur les beaux-arts en France," *Annales de la Société Jean-Jacques Rousseau* 19 (1929–30): 25.

[41] See J. A. Leith, *The Idea of Art as Propaganda in France, 1750–1799: A Study in the History of Ideas* (1965), 30–70; T. M. Mustoxidi, *Histoire de l'esthétique française 1700–1900* (1920), 58–76.

[42] See A. Vincent-Buffault, *Histoire des larmes* (1986), 51–52. On *sensibilité* in painting, see A. Brookner, *Greuze: The Rise and Fall of an Eigthteenth-Century Phenomenon* (1972), 37–53.

[43] "Il n'y a que les passions et les grandes passions qui puissent élever l'âme aux grandes choses." D. Diderot, *Pensées philosophiques* (1746), in *Oeuvres complètes*, ed. H. Dieckmann, J. Fabre, J. Proust, and J. Varloot (1975), 2:17.

[44] See D. Diderot, *Lettre sur les sourds et muets* (1751), in ibid. (1978) 4:185–87.

[45] "Exposons les tableaux de la vertu, et il se trouvera des copistes. L'espèce d'exhortation qui s'adresse à l'âme par l'entremise des sens, outre sa permanence, est plus à la portée du commun des hommes. Le peuple se sert mieux de ses yeux que de son entendement. Les images prêchent, prêchent sans cesse, et ne blessent point l'amour-propre." D. Diderot, *Essai sur les règnes de Claude et de Néron* (1778–82), in ibid., 13:503.

The promotion of sentiment within aesthetics has been identified by Annie Becq with attempts by an ascendant bourgeoisie to naturalize those ethical impulses central to its emerging ideology. As she has noted, the intimate relationship between *sentiment* and the somatic processes of *sensibilité* "allows an immediate identification of sentiment with the reactions of attraction or repulsion associated with physical feeling, and thus provide[s] physiological roots for the impulses on which the moral and social order are based."[46] The overdetermination of sentiment by the moral ends it was charged to serve led to its conscription in promoting normative values in private and public life, extolling domestic harmony and the patriotic duties of the virtuous citizen. In the view of Johann Sulzer, the Swiss aesthetician whose ideas featured extensively in the *Encyclopédie*, their control over sentiment enabled the arts to surmount resistance to ethical injunctions and "in moments of crisis to exert a subtle violence on our hearts and chain us through a sort of pleasure to the most disagreeable duties."[47] Conscious of its potential value as an instrument of social hygiene, Sulzer called for the elaboration of a science to study the precise effect of aesthetic sensation on the emotions, in order eventually to harness art's moral influence over the population at large.[48] Similar ambitions informed the investigation of the psycho-physiological foundations of cognition by Idéologue thinkers such as Cabanis and Destutt de Tracy in the late 1790s. While Tracy's ambitions to develop a positive science of understanding promoted interest in grammar as the basis for communicating ideas,[49] Cabanis's concern for "modifying existing human characteristics in a radical way"[50] found one outlet in a discussion of aesthetics, where he stressed the need for a "methodical understanding of intelligent and sensible nature"[51] as a means of elaborating a formal vocabulary capable of acting on consciousness with infallible efficacy.

Though such ideas had already gained implicit endorsement with the ancien régime's promotion of patriotic and moralizing art in the 1770s and 1780s,[52] it was only following the Revolution that more overt attempts

[46] "Permet de parler de sentiment, dès les réactions d'attraction ou de répulsion de la sensibilité physique et donc d'ancrer dans la physiologie les impulsions génératrices de l'ordre moral et social." Becq, *Genèse*, 2:771.

[47] "Dans les moments de crise faire une douce violence à nos coeurs, et nous enchaîner par une sorte de plaisir aux devoirs les plus pénibles." J. Sulzer, "Beaux-Arts," in *Supplément à l'Encyclopédie* (1776), 1:589–90.

[48] See J. Sulzer, "Esthétique," in ibid., 2:872–73.

[49] See E. Kennedy, *A "Philosophe" in the Age of Revolution: Destutt de Tracy and the Origins of "Ideology"* (1978), 126–31; B. W. Head, *Ideology and Social Science. Destutt de Tracy and French Liberalism* (1985), 45–54.

[50] Welch, *Liberty and Utility*, 46.

[51] "Connaissance méthodique de la nature intelligente et sensible." P.J.G. Cabanis, *Lettre à M. T**, sur les poèmes d'Homère*, in *Oeuvres complètes* (1825), 5:359.

[52] See Leith, *Art as Propaganda*, 72ff., and R. Rosenblum, *Transformations in Late Eighteenth Century Art* (1967), 50–74.

were made to articulate the theoretical principles underlying state cultural intervention. Spearheaded by the Société populaire et républicaine des arts, initiatives were launched to enlist artistic production behind the new order, recording decisive moments in the revolutionary struggle, elaborating a symbolic repertoire to enshrine its values, and representing exemplary public and private actions for popular emulation. Endorsing an art designed to "stimulate great deeds, and thus contribute to the happiness of mankind,"[53] the Revolution's leaders contended with ideological instability, economic scarcity, and artistic hesitancy in their attempts to institute a coherent cultural policy.[54] Across the Revolutionary decade and its shifting political configurations, the discourse of official art proposed an intimate alliance between artists and the state, focusing on the modification of the citizen's consciousness in the interests of collective unity and well-being. Though artistic allegiance was generally understood to result from judicious government encouragement and institutional reform, initiatives were made to restrict public exhibition to patriotic works[55] and to subordinate artistic production to official control. Thus in 1798, Allent, winner of a prize competition on the moral influence of painting, suggested close government supervision: "Since painting speaks to people's imaginations, it is for the Legislator to ensure that it offers them only useful lessons; it is up to him to make it uphold morality and spread those virtues which should make up the national character."[56]

Given new urgency in a nation attempting to reconstruct the private and public spheres *ab novo*, this appropriation of interior life demanded cultural forms capable of embodying abstract ideas in an immediately engaging and accessible way. In its absorption of the individual into a spatiotemporal realm set apart from the contradictions of everyday life, the Revolutionary festival offered the citizen privileged access to a promised land of unalienated being, and the state covert control over "the sphere of imagination

[53] "Exciter aux grandes actions, et contribuer ainsi au bonheur du genre humain." Speech by Vergniaud to members of the Académie, cited in Leith, *Art as Propaganda*, 101.

[54] See ibid., 99ff.; D. Kelder, *Aspects of "Official" Painting and Philosophic Art 1789–1799* (1976); W. Olander, "'Pour transmettre à la postérité': French Painting and Revolution, 1774–1795" (1983); and E. Pommier, *L'Art de la liberté. Doctrines et débats de la Révolution française* (1991).

[55] The idea was mooted by the artist Balzac in 1793, though rejected by the Société républicaine et populaire des arts. See Leith, *Art as Propaganda*, 115. Similarly, A. C. Quatremère de Quincy argued that the legislator should allow only "des monuments, des tableaux ou des statues capables de jeter dans l'âme des jeunes gens les principes de l'harmonie, les images du beau et les éléments de la perfection" (*Considérations sur les arts du dessin en France* [1791], 56).

[56] "Puisque la peinture parle à l'imagination des peuples, c'est au Législateur à faire en sorte qu'elle ne lui donne que d'utiles leçons; c'est à lui de la faire servir à la conservation des moeurs, à la propagation des vertus qui doivent composer le caractère national." Cited in Leith, *Art as Propaganda*, 133.

and sentiment."[57] Although Mona Ozouf has remarked on the organizers' relatively rudimentary interest in the psychological processes triggered by these mass events,[58] their faith in the mind's susceptibility to permanent transformation through the sentimental appeal of spectacle reconstitutes Enlightenment social aesthetics in a more overtly political sense. Thus Cabanis reiterates familiar antitheses in explaining how the festival is able to leave an indelible impression on the citizen's psyche:

> It is less a matter of . . . convincing than of moving him; less of proving the excellence of the laws governing him than of making him love them with feelings of strong affection, whose traces he would try to efface in vain and whose omnipresence presents him continually with the fatherland's beloved and venerable image.[59]

For radical theorists in the 1830s and 1840s, the Revolutionary festival offered a paradigm of noncoercive control over individual will. These highly choreographed spectacles, most readily associated with David and culminating in Robespierre's histrionic Festival of the Supreme Being in June 1794, set out to channel consciousness through their rigorously structured rituals of collective affirmation. Though contemporaries evoked the talismanic precedent of the Greek Republic,[60] their roots lay more nearly in the liturgical rites of the Catholic church—a source ideologically uncongenial to the 1790s,[61] but one openly embraced by thinkers such as Saint-Simon, more explicitly preoccupied with society's need for organic institutions. Nor does the regimentation of sentiment, whether in the festivals or in the Revolution's broader promotion of social aesthetics, accord with the precepts of one of its greatest mentors, Rousseau, whose antipathy toward the artifice of civilization fostered a dissenting model of culture largely suppressed after 1789 but revived in Fourier's more libertarian social philosophy in the early nineteenth century.

For Revolutionary theorists, as for later proponents of a radical aesthetic, culture is essentially a manifestation of the state. The artist's civic duty is to advance progressive beliefs consonant with national interest, defined by the political leadership, and to calibrate popular sentiment accordingly. Culture thus operates as an organic institution, helping bind the individual to the

[57] "Le domaine de l'imagination et du sentiment." P.J.G. Cabanis, "Travail sur l'éducation publique trouvé dans les papiers de Mirabeau, fait et publié par Cabanis," in *Oeuvres complètes* (1823), 2:444.

[58] M. Ozouf, *La Fête révolutionnaire: 1789–1799* (1976), 243.

[59] "Il s'agit . . . moins de le convaincre que de l'émouvoir; moins de lui prouver l'excellence des lois qui le gouvernent, que de les lui faire aimer par des sensations affectueuses et vives, dont il voudrait vainement effacer les traces, et qui, le poursuivant en tous lieux, lui présentent sans cesse l'image chère et vénérable de la patrie." Cabanis, *Travail*, 2:451.

[60] See ibid., 457; Boissy d'Anglas, *Essai*, 145.

[61] See Boissy d'Anglas, *Essai*, 39.

collectivity through an awakening of moral sense, which permeates every facet of private and public life. Within this model, institutions such as the Revolutionary festival of necessity follow a predetermined structure appropriate for inculcating a desired instinctual repertoire, and the formal organization of culture acts to consolidate the moral vitality of the state. Such an understanding had animated the pre-Revolutionary utopias of Morelly, Mercier, and Restif de la Bretonne,[62] and was to inspire most subsequent thinking on *art social*. As invoked by Rousseau, however, art represents less the organized expression of refined moral feeling than a symptom of social corruption. Though alert to the mobilizing force of sentiment[63] and to vision's particular influence over the imagination,[64] Rousseau regarded complex cultural forms as stifling the emotional mechanisms upon which unmediated social contact could be based. His ideal of absolute psychological and interpersonal transparency generated antipathy to the "vile and deceptive uniformity" of a culture that instilled "the appearance of all the virtues without possessing any."[65] His notion of the festival accordingly departs from the more formalized spectacles organized in the 1790s to endorse instead a fluid, open-ended communion of citizens, mounted "without pomp, luxury, or artifice."[66] Rousseau's vaunted hostility to the theater, with its onanistic dissipation of affect on a fictive object capable of inspiring only fleeting moral sympathy, shapes his vision of a spectacle from which all meaning extrinsic to the pure act of participation has been eliminated. "What will be shown there?" he asks, to declare—in an assertion of immediacy as foreign to David or Robespierre as it would later be to Saint-Simon or Enfantin—"Nothing, if you wish";[67] the "expansive transparency"[68] of a people united becomes an end in itself.

The guileless simplicity of human contact of which Rousseau dreamed in ancient Sparta and planned for modern Poland[69] abolishes the distinction between actor and observer more radically than anything achieved after 1789. His evocation of such merrymaking as the *fête champêtre* accompany-

[62] See B. Baczko, *Lumières de l'utopie* (1978), 238–49.

[63] See, for example, J.-J. Rousseau, *Emile, ou l'éducation* (1762), in *Oeuvres complètes*, ed. B. Gagnebin and M. Raymond (1969), 4:645.

[64] See ibid., 647.

[65] "Vile et trompeuse uniformité"; "les apparences de toutes les vertus sans en avoir aucune." J.-J. Rousseau, *Discours sur les sciences et les arts* (1750), in *Oeuvres complètes* (1964), 3:7.

[66] "Sans pompe, sans luxe, sans appareil." J.-J. Rousseau, *Lettre à M. d'Alembert sur les spectacles* (1758), ed. M. Fuchs (1948), 181.

[67] "Qu'y montrera-t-on?"; "Rien, si l'on veut." Ibid., 168.

[68] P.E.J. Robinson, *Jean-Jacques Rousseau's Doctrine of the Arts* (1984), 265. On this theme, see J. Starobinski, *Jean-Jacques Rousseau. La Transparence et l'obstacle* (1971), 116–21.

[69] See D. Leduc-Fayette, *Jean-Jacques Rousseau et le mythe de l'antiquité* (1974), 128–37, and J.-J. Rousseau, *Considérations sur le gouvernement de Pologne* (1771–72), in *Oeuvres complètes* (1964), 3:959–66.

ing the grape harvest in *La Nouvelle Héloïse* crystallizes a Golden Age of innocence in which leisure and labor become one and the same.[70] Yet the permissive nature of Rousseau's fête is more apparent than real, contained as it is within a projected technology of power which inducts the individual into virtuous citizenship from childhood. This appropriation of consciousness, replicated in aspects of Jacobin culture, stimulated attacks on what Mme de Staël described as "the despotism of liberty."[71] Contemptuous of a state-controlled propaganda machine she regarded as employing a psychological coercion incapable of forming independent citizens,[72] Staël challenged the primacy of passion as the basis of social virtue, proclaiming: "that impulsive force which drags man along despite himself, that is the real obstacle to individual and political happiness."[73] Yet while this liberal critique focuses on the authoritarianism implicit in Rousseau and amplified in Revolutionary social aesthetics, a countervailing libertarian tradition links the *philosophe* to Fourier and currents within fin-de-siècle anarchism. Here, the challenge to social demarcations sustaining art as a discrete professional enterprise envisages unalienated labor, once achieved, releasing creative energies in the population at large. The artist—so profoundly mistrusted by Rousseau—becomes redundant as distinctions between art and life lose their meaning.

This dilution of creative authority runs counter to a powerful tide, originating in the mid eighteenth century,[74] which exalted the artist as a privi-

[70] J.-J. Rousseau, *Julie, ou la Nouvelle Héloïse (1761)*, in *Oeuvres complètes* (1964), 2:604–11. The passage may be related to Boissy d'Anglas' evocation of a harvest festival in which there is "point de cette joie préparée d'avance et calculée avec plus ou moins d'art," in *Essai*, 55. In terms of revolutionary mythology, this moment was perhaps most nearly realized in the collective preparations for the Fête de la Fédération on the Champ de Mars in July 1790. See Ozouf, *Fête*, 44–74.

[71] "Le despotisme de la liberté." G. de Staël, *Des circonstances actuelles qui peuvent terminer la Révolution et des principes qui doivent fonder la république en France* (1798–99), ed. J. Viénot (1906), 278.

[72] "On ordonne d'aller à telles fêtes, de pratiquer telles institutions, parce que ces institutions persuadent ceux qu'on y envoie de l'excellence du gouvernement républicain, et par cela seulement qu'on commande et qu'on menace, l'effet de l'évidence même est détruit." Ibid., 277–78. See also Constant's critique of revolutionary propaganda in A. Jardin, *Histoire du libéralisme politique. De la crise de l'absolutisme à la constitution de 1875* (1985), 233, and J.-B. Say's "liberal" theory of the festival in *Olbie, ou essai sur les moyens d'améliorer les moeurs d'une nation* (1800), in *Oeuvres diverses*, ed. C. Comte, E. Dairet, and H. Say (1848), 610–11.

[73] "Cette force impulsive qui entraîne l'homme indépendamment de sa volonté, voilà le véritable obstacle au bonheur individuel et politique." G. de Staël, *De l'influence des passions sur le bonheur des individus et des nations* (1796), in *Oeuvres complètes* (1821), 3:9. For a contrary standpoint, unifying ethics and aesthetics within the ambit of sentiment, see crucially P.-S. Ballanche, *Du sentiment considéré dans ses rapports avec la littérature et les arts* (1801), 44–55. Ballanche argues that "Le sentiment est la seule source du vrai et du beau; le sentiment est le grand type, l'unique type des productions de génie" (44).

[74] Bénichou, *Sacre*, 27, dates the rise in the writer's status to the 1760s.

leged being, possessing attributes others lacked. Intimately related to the reconceptualization of creative activity as an imaginative outpouring of feeling rather than a rational process of invention,[75] this cult of the artist shaped perceptions of his social role on left and right well into the nineteenth century. As traditional institutions found their supremacy challenged by broad changes in the nation's socioeconomic structure, so championship of the artist as a source of truth and enlightenment intensified, allowing the writer Félix Pyat to comment in 1834: "Art has almost become a cult, a new religion which is arriving just in time, when gods and kings are disappearing."[76] The term itself simultaneously contracted—to end a long-standing association with artisanal labor—and expanded, denoting at its most extreme creative activity of any type, from rhetoric and philosophy to poetry and painting. What came to define the artist above all was a particular temperament whose instinctive vision could generate insights of prophetic intensity. Thinkers such as Saint-Martin and Ballanche traced the poet's genealogy back to primitive religion and to the foundation of human society around the Orphic bard, whose inspired utterance drew on a language of pure presence, uncorrupted by the contingency of meaning which succeeded the Fall.[77] For Sulzer, the artist's foundational role as priest or secular guide exploited a capacity to transmit enthusiasm, rooted in sentiment, and to rupture temporal barriers, releasing his audience from the restrictions of practical existence to glimpse an alternative realm of being. In such a state,

> Since understanding is no longer able to distinguish the real from the imaginary, what is merely possible seems already to exist and even the impossible appears possible; the relationship between things is no longer assessed by judgment, but by sentiment; what is absent seems present, and the future exists in the here and now.[78]

Though challenged by thinkers as diverse as Bonald and Mme de Staël,[79] and staunchly opposed by Saint-Simon in his early writings, this exaltation

[75] See G. Matoré and A. J. Greimas, "La Naissance du 'Génie' au dix-huitième siècle. Etude lexicologique," *Le Français moderne* 25 (1957): 271. More generally on this well-documented phenomenon, see Bénichou, *Sacre*, and G. Matoré, "Les Notions d'art et d'artiste à l'époque romantique," *Revue des sciences humaines* 16, nos. 62–63 (April–September 1951): 120–37.

[76] "L'art est presque un culte, une religion nouvelle qui arrive bien à propos, quand les dieux s'en vont et les rois aussi." Cited in Matoré, "Les Notions," 131.

[77] See Bénichou, *Sacre*, 99–102, 163–66.

[78] "Comme l'entendement n'est plus en état de distinguer ce qui est réel de ce qui n'est qu'imaginaire, le simple possible paraît actuel et l'impossible même semble possible; la liaison des choses n'est plus évaluée d'après le jugement; elle l'est d'après le sentiment, ce qui est absent devient présent et l'avenir existe actuellement." J. Sulzer, "Enthousiasme," *Journal littéraire* 6 (June 1773): 138, cited in Becq, *Genèse*, 2:579.

[79] See L. G. de Bonald, *Recherches philosophiques sur les premiers objets des connaissances morales* (1818), in *Oeuvres complètes*, (1838) 8.1:369. On Mme de Staël, see Bénichou, *Sacre*, 240.

of the artist as seer gained wide currency and proved central to radical aesthetic programs under the July Monarchy. Their assumption of a profound interrelationship between the artist and his historical milieu won acceptance across a broad ideological spectrum,[80] though many were unwilling to envisage any explicit subordination of culture for politically contingent purposes. For Idealists such as the philosopher Victor Cousin, as for Mme de Staël, art's edifying qualities relied on intrinsic formal characteristics, rather than on the artist's exploration of extrinsic themes drawn from the contemporary world. It was thus his command over the technical resources of his medium which allowed the artist to communicate feelings ultimately beneficial to the prevailing moral climate. As Mme de Staël asserts in *De l'Allemagne*, in relation to Kant:

> Everything of beauty must doubtless give rise to generous feelings, which themselves stimulate virtue; but as soon as the exposition of a moral precept becomes one's aim, then the liberty of feeling generated by great works of art is inevitably destroyed; for when one has a recognized goal, whatever it might be, the imagination is inhibited and made uneasy.[81]

Such sentiments inform Cousin's attribution of divine characteristics to art, a facet of his wider quest for a system of thought capable of filling the void opened up by the apparent demise of religious faith. While repudiating any instrumental role for art, Cousin invested an ethical dimension in aesthetic experience through his Platonic identification of beauty with goodness. His assertion that "the aim of art is the expression of moral beauty through the aid of physical beauty"[82] evades any subordination of the aesthetic to didactic ends by investing nature itself with a moral eloquence manifest to the creative imagination. As with later proponents of *l'art pour l'art*, a phrase he is often thought to have coined, there is no question of Cousin absolving the artist of concern with anything other than form as an end in itself; rather, the exaltation of form offers a glimpse of the divine.

The remarkable appeal during the Restoration of Cousin's synthesis of

[80] See Bénichou, *Sacre*, 227, on liberal historicism under the Restoration and, more generally, H.A. Needham, *Le Développement de l'esthétique sociologique en France et en Angleterre au 19e siècle* (1926).

[81] "Sans doute tout ce qui est beau doit faire naître des sentiments généreux, et ces sentiments excitent à la vertu; mais dès qu'on a pour objet de mettre en évidence un précepte de morale, la libre impression que produisent les chefs-d'oeuvre de l'art est nécessairement détruite; car le but, quel qu'il soit, quand il est connu, borne et gêne l'imagination." G. de Staël, *De l'Allemagne* (1813), ed. J. de Pange, (1959), 4:223.

[82] "La fin de l'art est l'expression de la beauté morale à l'aide de la beauté physique." Cited in F. Will, *Flumen Historicum: Victor Cousin's Aesthetic and Its Sources* (1965), 80. On the pervasiveness of such ideas in the early decades of the nineteenth century, see Bénichou, *Sacre*, 226–27.

the Platonic tradition with German Idealism[83] highlights the anxieties provoked by the inexorable entanglement of cultural activity in a developing market economy. While Cousin proposed a value for art immune to the vitiating taint of materialism, the far-reaching commercial and institutional changes that had transformed artists' relationships with the public in the previous half century radically questioned the social function of the work of art and the status of its creator. For the visual artist in particular, hard-won acceptance as a figure of learning and skill, invulnerable to the pejorative stereotypes of ignorance and poverty common in the eighteenth century,[84] was destabilized by evolving class relations, which gradually elevated a mercantile bourgeoisie as the nation's effective cultural arbiters. In a market where a burgeoning middle-class clientele was serviced by a growing community of artists, often from comparable social backgrounds, former distinctions between patron and painter tended to diminish. Market structures further reduced the interpersonal aspect of patronage to the relative anonymity of a cash nexus, attenuating the art object's perceived difference from comparable luxury items available on the open market. As artists increasingly resembled the clients for whom they worked—both socially and as producers of material goods—so the practical basis on which they could lay claim to superior professional standing was eroded. The irrelevance of academic tuition to the range of imagery where demand was most buoyant, and the decline in the prestige and conspicuousness of large-scale public commissions, pointed to a privatization of culture inimical to claims for art's authority as an embodiment of collective value. By the mid 1830s, with mounting critical attacks on cultural commercialization and widespread disenchantment with the flagrant opportunism of official patronage,[85] the very purpose of art as anything other than a source of inconsequential gratification or crude manipulation seemed increasingly open to question.

It was these circumstances that produced a need to renegotiate the role accorded to the artist and his work within society. The Idealist aesthetic popularized by Cousin pointed toward a mystification of the material base of artistic production, retrieving an aura of disinterested imaginative endeavor distinct from the more instrumental associations with which other forms of labor were freighted.[86] A more radical, aggressive variant emerged out of the "Jeune-France" movement in the early 1830s, particularly in the

[83] On Cousin's influence as a teacher, see Spitzer, *French Generation*, 71–78. Bénichou (*Sacre*, 241–42, n. 182) points to the indirect knowledge in France at this date of Kant and Hegel, neither of whose aesthetic treatises were translated before 1840.

[84] See G. Levitine, *The Dawn of Bohemianism: The "Barbu" Rebellion and Primitivism in Neoclassical France* (1978), 9–32.

[85] See N. Hadjinicolaou, "Art in a Period of Social Upheaval: French Art Criticism and Problems of Change in 1831," *Oxford Art Journal* 6, no. 2 (1983): 29–37.

[86] For a distinction between beauty and utility, see Cousin's disciple, T. Jouffroy, *Cours d'esthétique* (1843), 25–29. Jouffroy's course was initially delivered in 1822.

polemical defense of *l'art pour l'art* mounted by Théophile Gautier. A persistent *bête noire* of advocates of social art, this formalist current espoused a noninstrumental understanding of art reminiscent of Cousin, which scorned any subordination of pictorial effect to ethical or narrative ends. Thus, in 1834, the novelist and critic Jules Janin extols "painting that paints, and which has confidence in itself, and itself alone, to produce its effect; painting that plays neither melodrama, tragedy, nor idyll; that plays at being nothing but itself, since it is all it wants or is able to be."[87] Yet, like the Eclectics, formalism saw art as standing less outside morality than as constituting its own morality: the pursuit of beauty enshrines spiritual values, which can only be tarnished by the intrusion of extraneous concerns. As Gautier argues in 1845: "Art for art's sake means not form for form's sake but form for the sake of beauty, excluding any extraneous idea, any exploitation on behalf of a particular doctrine or any direct usefulness."[88]

Creative labor thus becomes the one pure form of human endeavor, apparently transcending the narrowly material concerns motivating activity among all other sectors of society. This denial of art's status as anything other than the disinterested pursuit of beauty segregates the artist from other groups, whom Gautier explicitly denigrated for their occluded imaginations and mundane concerns. By claiming for the artist an inherent "sixth sense"[89] offering privileged receptivity to beauty, and elaborating an enticing vision of a mysterious world of creativity and pleasure inaccessible to outsiders, Gautier and others restored a sense of artistic particularity rooted in an ostentatious rejection of bourgeois mores. In doing so, they jettisoned the rationalist model of artistic creation, upon which claims to professional eminence had been mounted within the academic tradition, to embrace instead the artist's identification with sentiment, a psycho-physiological distinction implying inherent, rather than acquired, difference from other social groups. Yet while radical theorists equated sentiment with the artist's imputed capacity to respond instinctively to collective need, formalists recast the concept to denote a form of inwardly directed sensuous intuition, given expressive form in the autonomous act of disinterested creation.[90]

[87] "De la peinture qui peint, et qui se fie à elle-même pour produire son effet; de la peinture qui ne joue ni le mélodrame, ni la tragédie, ni l'idylle; qui ne joue rien en elle-même, car elle est tout ce qu'elle veut être, ce qu'elle peut être." J. Janin, [Untitled article], *L'Artiste*, 1st ser., 7 (1834): 295.

[88] "L'art pour l'art veut dire non pas la forme pour la forme, mais bien la forme pour le beau, abstraction faite de toute idée étrangère, de tout détournement au profit d'une doctrine quelconque, de toute utilité directe." T. Gautier, "Du beau dans l'art," in *L'Art moderne* (1856), 153. Reprinted from the *Revue des deux mondes* (1845). Gautier goes on to state: "Le beau dans son essence absolue, c'est Dieu. Il est aussi impossible de le chercher hors de la sphère divine, qu'il est impossible de trouver hors de cette sphère le vrai et le bon absolus" (160).

[89] See ibid., 132–33.

[90] See I. Singer, "The Aesthetics of Art for Art's Sake," *Journal of Aesthetics and Art Criticism* 12 (March 1954): 345–47.

The proclaimed self-sufficiency of art served as symbolic repudiation to a society accused of sacrificing everything to material advance. The myth of Bohemia—predominantly a literary construct promoted in the early 1830s by texts such as Gautier's *Albertus*—provided a space in which the perceived tensions between creative imagination and capitalist individualism could be played out. Infinitely flexible, Bohemia refracted complex, often contradictory, projections of the artist's place in a nascent industrial society, setting up a resonant dialectic of subversion and containment in which critiques of bourgeois values could ultimately be deprived of their more corrosive implications. As pursued in the popular press, the bohemian image helped to define the outer limits of individualism, providing an alter ego for the financier or merchant whose own, differently directed, sense of self-sufficiency was attracting increasing—and often adverse—notice by social observers.[91] It offered, too, an opportunity at once to assert or to question the credibility of artists' claims to superiority, pitting exemplary martyrs such as the poets Chatterton and Gilbert against arrant charlatans like the painter Oscar in Louis Reybaud's *Jérôme Paturot* or Murger's genial mediocrities in the *Scènes de la vie de Bohème*. Yet, however apparently trite or self-serving, the elaboration of a paradigm of artistic difference and alienation from established values reflected broader unease at the cultural implications of material progress. While some anticipated only benefits from the commercialization of cultural exchange,[92] others—from across the political spectrum—looked to the example of other industrial societies with some trepidation. As proponents of technological advance such as the Saint-Simonians were to discover, liberals and conservatives alike feared that the price of greater equality and affluence would be a deadening uniformity fatal to imaginative endeavor. In the words of Gustave de Beaumont, Tocqueville's companion on his visit to America in 1831, "What harmonies will the modern poet find in shop counters, stills, steam engines, and bank notes?"[93] From this perspective, assertions of the nonutilitarian, spiritually directed nature of the artistic enterprise could help stiffen resistance to the tightening grasp of bourgeois materialism.

Yet, for all their posturing against middle-class values, adepts of bohe-

[91] See, for example, Tocqueville's discussion of individualism and democracy in *De la démocratie en Amérique* (1840), in *Oeuvres complètes* (1864), 3:162–63, and, more generally, K. W. Swart, "'Individualism' in the Mid Nineteenth Century: 1826–1860," *Journal of the History of Ideas* 23 (1962): 77–90.

[92] See, for example, S.G.L., "De l'avenir des arts," *L'Artiste*, 1st ser., 2 (1831): 254, and A. de Saint-Chéron, "De la position sociale des artistes," ibid., 1st ser., 4 (1832): 50–53. For a refutation of this defense of the cultural benefits of capitalism, see the reply by "Un Artiste," *L'Artiste*, 1st ser., 4 (1832):79–81.

[93] "Quelles harmonies le poète moderne puisera-t-il dans les comptoirs, les alambics, les machines à vapeur, et le papier-monnaie?" G. de Beaumont, *Marie, ou l'esclavage aux Etats-unis. Tableau de moeurs américaines* (1835), 1:242. See also Tocqueville, *De la démocratie*, 62ff.

mianism largely rejected direct political engagement as compromising their pose of aesthetic disinterestedness.[94] To this degree, formalism's ideology restricted opposition to symbolic dissent from dominant values, acted out in a cultural domain whose esoteric, elitist connotations underwrote its rhetorical effect. This refusal to engage infuriated radical critics, for whom *l'art pour l'art* epitomized the bankruptcy of contemporary culture. Yet, beyond the polemics, distinctions between the two seem less clear-cut. The idiosyncratic republicanism of "Jeune-France," evident in Pétrus Borel's iconoclastic contributions to the oppositional art journal *La Liberté*, encouraged a truculent disdain for authority carrying unmistakable political resonance.[95] The movement's medievalism, generally reckoned a merely stylistic inspiration, could encourage one of its leading adepts, Jehan Duseigneur, to rally behind the Christian Socialist Philippe Buchez before enlisting in the Confrérie de Saint Jean, a brotherhood of Catholic artists, in 1839. Conversely, on the left, *art social* signified far more than an uncompromising commitment to overt didacticism, embracing instead a complex understanding of form which frequently recalls the idealism of its proclaimed opponents. Crucially, both currents invested in the figure of the artist an authority and distinction that set him apart from his fellows, whether as disengaged aesthete or prophetic guide.

Those critics and theorists under the July Monarchy for whom such an investment demanded of the artist an explicit act of ideological dedication looked back over recent history with guarded optimism. The Revolution, however uneven its cultural legacy, had bequeathed a powerful mystique of political engagement, despite ample evidence of opportunistic trimming by artists anxious to gain favor from subsequent regimes. The precocious bohemian initiative launched around the turn of the century by a minor pupil of David, Maurice Quay, also indicated a nascent messianic streak such as later theorists hoped to channel for their own ends.[96] Quay's cultivation of what his fellow student Etienne Delécluze later described as "humanitarian utopias"[97] and his establishment of a communal group dedicated to vegetarianism, illuminist philosophy, and the rediscovery of the Golden Age[98]

[94] Thus Joseph Bouchardy comments to Gautier, his former comrade in "Jeune-France": "Tandis que les fouriéristes faisaient des phalanstères, les saint-simoniens de nouveaux contrats sociaux, les démocrates des projets, sourds à tous ces bourdonnements d'alors, nous n'entendions que le murmure de l'art qui s'agitait dans l'enfantement d'un progrès." Cited in Bénichou, *Sacre*, 430.

[95] See, for example, Borel's attack on the radical Academician David d'Angers, "Les Fourberies de Scapin," *L. A.*, 3 (August 1832): 13–16.

[96] On Quay and the "Barbus," see Levitine, *Dawn of Bohemianism*, 45ff.

[97] "Utopies humanitaires." E.-J. Delécluze, *Louis David, son école et son temps* (1855), 89.

[98] Charles Nodier describes the group as "ces artistes qui portaient l'habit phrygien, qui ne se nourrissaient que de végétaux, qui habitaient en commun, et dont la vie pure et hospitalière était une vivante peinture de l'âge d'or," cited in J. Larat, *La Tradition de l'exotisme dans l'oeuvre*

suggest a dawning sense of the artist's intuitive capacity to assume a social authority far surpassing any literal definition of his professional competence. Though the strict regimentation of culture under the Empire, and its antiheroic denouement under the Restoration, reputedly indicated a period of crisis and introspection, romantic philhellenism and early calls for social responsiveness[99] fueled growing interest in art's capacity to mobilize mass opinion. It was this wave that radical thinkers attempted to channel after 1830 in a climate of cultural and political upheaval which was to generate vigorous debate and inspire a number of practical initiatives to harness art to the cause of social change.

---

de Charles Nodier (1780–1844) (1923), 23. Aspects such as the symbolic dress code, the conventual existence, and the orientalist leanings of the "Barbus" bear striking, if fortuitous, parallels with the Saint-Simonians.

[99] See particularly F. Flocon and M. Aycard, *Salon de 1824* (1824).

CHAPTER 2

Saint-Simon and the Promotion of a Social Aesthetic

ALTHOUGH a number of commentators during the eighteenth century had revitalized traditional notions of the moral influence of art, advocacy of a social aesthetic on the left during the mid nineteenth century owed much to the example of Count Claude-Henri de Rouvroy de Saint-Simon. An impecunious former soldier and sometime speculator under the Revolution, this descendant of a long and distinguished aristocratic line played a pivotal role in the development of French socialist thought. If his ideas on social organization and industrial expansion were to enjoy brief but spectacular exposure by an avid group of disciples during the late 1820s and early 1830s, his conception of the artist's potential authority within society proved no less seminal. This legacy appears paradoxical from examination of much of Saint-Simon's work; his early preoccupations in particular seem incompatible with any serious appreciation of the arts and only in his later writings does the artist emerge as a prominent element in the social equation. As the present discussion will suggest, Saint-Simon's elevation of the artist's status during the Restoration depended on a shift of theoretical priorities attendant on an increasing consideration of the practicalities of social change and the development of conditions favorable to industrial growth. As attention toward the interplay of class groupings convinced him of the need for a mechanism capable of rallying all sectors behind the enlightened guidance of a ruling elite, so Saint-Simon temporized his initial commitment to reason through an appreciation of the value of sentiment, embodied in the arts, as a vital catalyst in securing universal acceptance of progressive reform.

In order to appreciate the significance of this reassessment of art's social role and to highlight the fundamental interrelationship between the aesthetic and the political within Saint-Simon's thought, we must first examine his initial concern with intellectual synthesis and the possibility of achieving an epistemological revolution through methodological innovations in the life sciences. This exploration reveals inherent regard for the intellectual status of the artist at the same time as displaying theoretical priorities that prevented the emergence of any clear account of his practical contribution to social life. In a series of texts produced during the Empire, Saint-Simon not only shows concern at the danger of class antagonism important to his subsequent philosophical evolution but also investigates issues of scientific development which inform the emphasis on industry in his later work. Consideration of the ambiguous and ill-defined attitude toward art within this constellation of interests demonstrates his ambivalence toward the potential influence of intellectuals and his desire to forestall their emergence as rallying points for social dissent.

SCIENCE, PROGRESS, AND THE INTELLECTUAL

In common with such thinkers as Bonald and de Maistre, Saint-Simon's intellectual formation was profoundly affected by the upheaval of the French Revolution. His interests in the early years of the nineteenth century show a central concern with the means of achieving progress while avoiding a repetition of social conflict. Much of his effort at this period was devoted to an investigation of science, whose methodological refinement he hoped would presage the extension of rational modes of thought possessing infallible validity into all aspects of social life, from individual morality to political organization. In such a way, Saint-Simon looked to research within the natural sciences to provide the foundations for a social science, under whose aegis far-reaching change could be secured without the risk of revolutionary violence. After initially turning to Newton's gravitational theory as a possible source of a unifying social and epistemological principle, Saint-Simon came to believe that the study of physiology would provide the key to a momentous breakthrough. If physiology could shake off its speculative and metaphysical aspects and emerge as a positive science, he maintained, the ground would be laid for an intellectual synthesis capable of uniting two fragmented scientific traditions—the inductive current dominated by Descartes and the deductive, empirical strain associated with Newton and the *philosophes*. Saint-Simon saw himself at the junction of these two forms of thought, and advocated publication of a new *Encyclopédie* to act as a comprehensive repository of human knowledge. Such an endeavor was designed to provide the tools for epistemological synthesis and to foster the development of a positivist methodology which he thought would yield immeasurable social benefits.

Belief in the broad advantages to be gained from independent research informed the proposals set out in Saint-Simon's first major work, the *Lettres d'un habitant de Genève* of 1803. Here, plans are outlined for the construction of a series of temples to commemorate Newton, over which a *conseil* of leading scientists and artists would preside, pursuing their work for the general benefit of humanity. In emphasizing the social value of an intellectual elite, the *Lettres* initiate a theme that was to feature throughout Saint-Simon's career and provide a structural core to his later conceptions of government within industrial society. In its early form, however, his ideas are firmly rooted in a tradition extending back to Bacon's "Salomon's house," described in the *New Atlantis*, and to the more recent advocacy of "une société perpétuelle pour le progrès des sciences" in Condorcet's unpublished *Fragment sur l'Atlantide*.[1] Unlike the newly established Institut de France or its academic predecessors, Saint-Simon stressed the need for complete freedom from official control and for the coordinated pursuit of learning in all areas as a means of achieving the intellectual synthesis essential to future progress. Given such priorities, the inclusion of nine artists amongst the ruling council of twenty-one *hommes de génie* comes as something of a surprise, as there is little in Saint-Simon's work at this stage to suggest any sensitivity toward the social value of imaginative endeavor. On one level, their presence may be related to an all-embracing regard for intellectuals as "the beacons who enlighten humanity, the rulers as well as the ruled,"[2] though such admiration scarcely accounts for the quantity of artists co-opted onto the Conseil de Newton. Rather, their inclusion seems to testify both an awareness of art's didactic impact and a deep-seated suspicion toward the subversive potential of disaffected intellectuals.

Some indication of interest in utilitarian aesthetics emerges in Saint-Simon's description of the temple itself, an edifice whose conceptual similarities to Boullée's *Cénotaphe à Newton* are not reflected in its interior design:

> The temple will be divided into two parts: one, containing the mausoleum, will be embellished by every means that artists can devise; the other will be built and decorated in such a way as to give men some idea of the eternal fate awaiting those who harm the progress of the sciences and the arts.[3]

In a setting described as "majestic and brilliant," the artist would contribute to glorifying "every service rendered to humanity, every action valuable in spreading the faith,"[4] a didactic function consistent with the role projected for the arts under the Revolution. Yet this conviction in art's capacity to modify attitudes and behavior stands in isolation in Saint-Simon's work at

[1] M.J.A.N.C. Condorcet, *Fragment sur l'Atlantide*, in *Oeuvres* (1847), 6:611.

[2] "Les flambeaux qui éclairent l'humanité, les gouvernants aussi bien que les gouvernés." *Lettres d'un habitant de Genève*, in *Oeuvres de Claude-Henri de Saint-Simon* (1966) 1 (*O.S.S.E.*, 1):13. [All volume numbers relating to the works of Saint-Simon refer to the six-volume "Impression anastaltique" published in 1966. Reference is made in parenthesis to the corresponding volume numbers in *O.S.S.E.*, the original Dentu edition of Saint-Simon's work from which the first five volumes of this partial reprint were made.]

[3] "Ce temple sera divisé en deux parties; l'une contiendra le mausolée, sera embellie par tous les moyens que les artistes pourront inventer: l'autre sera construite et décorée de manière à donner aux hommes une idée du séjour destiné pour une éternité à ceux qui nuiront aux progrès des sciences et des arts." Ibid., 51.

[4] "Majestueux et brillant"; "tous les services rendus à l'humanité, toutes les actions qui auront été grandement utiles à la propagation de la foi." Ibid., 52.

this period and fails adequately to explain the prominence of painters, writers, and sculptors on the proposed *conseil*. Their place within the overall scheme can perhaps be related most convincingly to Saint-Simon's belief in the inherent antagonism of class relations and to his fear of the intellectuals' power in fomenting social unrest.

This current in Saint-Simon's work owes much to his interpretation of the French Revolution, an event that, despite early enthusiasm, had instilled in him a commitment to a social model that enshrined certain basic inequalities while eradicating the danger of class discord. Arguing by analogy from the laws of Newtonian physics, Saint-Simon came to the pessimistic conclusion that social conflict formed an inevitable reflection of the wider opposition of forces within the universe. He thus aspired to limit the scope of this antagonism, and displayed unequivocal sympathy for the property-holding classes whose inherent intellectual superiority over the propertyless he regarded as justifying their more eminent status.[5] Yet just as conservatives such as de Maistre castigated the *philosophes*' reformist zeal for provoking revolutionary violence,[6] so Saint-Simon believed that intellectuals, if unsympathetic to the prevailing social structure, could pose a fundamental threat to the property holders' dominant position. A note of intimidation is struck in conjuring up the specter of social conflict fanned by a group attracted toward exerting its influence over the disaffected and the dispossessed as a means of surmounting its own marginality:

> Avoid getting into dispute with these people, gentlemen, for you will be beaten in any war that you give them chance to declare against you; you will suffer more than they during the hostilities and peace terms will be unfavorable to you; have the good sense to give freely what sooner or later the intellectuals, artists, and men of liberal opinion, united with the propertyless, will take from you by force.[7]

The Conseil de Newton thus serves a dual role. While providing optimum conditions for socially beneficial scientific research, it simultaneously reconciles all classes of intellectuals—including the artist—to prevailing power relations by elevating them from their formerly marginal rank. Such a mechanism forges an implicit alliance with the property owners and the menace of insurrection is diminished. In the absence of any explicit explanation for

[5] See ibid., 30, n. 1.

[6] See P. Bénichou, *Le Sacre de l'écrivain 1750–1830*, (1973), 116–28.

[7] "Evitez, Messieurs, d'avoir querelle à ces gens-là, car vous serez battus dans toutes les guerres que vous leur laisserez l'occasion d'engager avec vous; vous souffrirez davantage qu'eux pendant les hostilités, et la paix vous sera désavantageuse; donnez-vous le mérite de faire de bonne grace une chose qui tôt ou tard les savants, les artistes et les hommes ayant des idées libérales réunis aux non-propriétaires, vous feraient faire de force." Ibid., 31–32.

the artist's incorporation within the *conseil*, it would appear that his enlistment is largely a preventative measure provoked by suspicion of his potentially disruptive power.

This strategy is confirmed by examination of the *Introduction aux travaux scientifiques du 19e siècle* of 1807–8 where Saint-Simon abandons his former insistence on the independence of the *homme de génie* and advises his incorporation into the governmental system in the interests of social stability. Arguing that unrest is fostered by the exclusion of able individuals from positions of influence, Saint-Simon maintains that a resilient social structure depends on the ruling class assimilating intellectuals into its ranks. Rejecting his former equation of property with intellectual superiority, he now acknowledges that men of ability may emerge from outside the propertied elite and proposes a flexible meritocracy ensuring the perpetuation of existing power relations through recruitment of artists and intellectuals from all social strata.[8]

The shift here is significant. Not only has the cardinal principle of intellectual independence been jettisoned in favor of strategic reinforcement of the ruling class, the proposed function of the *homme de génie* has also been expanded. Rather than directing his efforts toward specialized professional research, the intellectual is now offered an extensive field of action in the more practical areas of government. While including the artist—here as elsewhere defined in broad, generic terms—Saint-Simon fails to offer a precise explanation of his potential contribution. If forestalling intellectual disaffection is still a consideration, more positive assessment of the *homme de génie* prompts the unsubstantiated assertion that his natural abilities qualify him for influence within civil society. The meritocratic emphasis of such beliefs mirrors changes within contemporary bureaucratic structures, with Napoleon's introduction of "la carrière ouverte aux talents." Indeed, Saint-Simon points to the emperor as an exemplary administrator, particularly admiring the tricameral legislative system in the recent Italian constitution, where a "collège des savants et des artistes" ensured that the ruling class should draw on all men of ability, irrespective of background.[9]

A diffuse respect for genius, complemented by a desire to foster stability by accommodating potential sources of discontent, thus seems to underlie the persistent regard for the artist in Saint-Simon's early work. If the incorporation of *savants* and *artistes* into the ruling structure prefigures his later philosophy, the rationale behind their presence, spelled out in the 1820s, remains unclear at this stage. This ambiguity is an inevitable corollary of his early methodological ambitions; emphasis on the life sciences and the priority accorded to the development of a positivist epistemology favored con-

[8] See *Introduction aux travaux scientifiques du 19e siècle*, in *Oeuvres*, 6:190.

[9] Ibid., 189–90.

centration on reason as a spur to social change and promoted a dismissive attitude toward the value of imagination.[10]

In justifying this rationalist bias, Saint-Simon looked to history and physiology, presenting human progress as a constant refinement of mental processes whose ultimate outcome would be marked by the achievement of positivism. Comparing the evolution of humanity to the development of the individual, Saint-Simon equates imagination with infancy and with the polytheistic cultures of the ancient world, while regarding the prevailing monotheistic stage of civilization as a transitional phase in a historical trajectory culminating in positivism.[11] In common with the distinction between *conjectural* and *positif* thought advanced by his precursor Turgot, Saint-Simon values deductive reason over conjectural, inductive systems and equates progress with man's gradual maturing as a rational being. Both men, however, recognize the superiority of the ancient world in the imaginative field of the arts. Arguing that "as the human spirit ages, so its rational faculty grows and its imaginative faculty declines,"[12] Saint-Simon acknowledges that the benefits accrued by progress toward reason are won at the expense of the inferior value of imagination and entail a gradual diminution of artistic creativity. Echoing Ballanche and Mme de Staël,[13] he expresses a belief in the imaginative spontaneity of ancient societies, likening classical Greece to a period of adolescence, whose freshness and inventiveness can never be recaptured. Yet Saint-Simon regards the Greeks' achievements as being confined to accomplishments of superficial value and, in a fictional dialogue between Socrates and his pupils, presents the philosopher endorsing his own dismissal of imagination as a cultural asset of limited worth:

> [The Greeks] allow themselves to be dominated by their imagination and direct their attention almost exclusively to the arts. They are so good in this field that I doubt whether their successors will be able to match them. But is this the most important field? I think not, and see it only as a form of pleasure. Philosophy seems to me the most important of all the sciences.[14]

[10] Thus, he writes dismissively on the value of literature in 1813: "Je vois les choses telles qu'elles sont; mon âme n'a point été amollie, amoindrie par la littérature, qui est une manière superficielle d'envisager et de traiter les questions les plus importantes." *Mémoire sur la science de l'homme*, in *Oeuvres*, 5 (*O.S.S.E.*, 11):57–58.

[11] On the influence of Condorcet and the physiologist Vicq d'Azyr on this model, see H. Gouhier, *La Jeunesse d'Auguste Comte et la formation du Positivisme* (1936), 2:316ff.; P. Ansart, *Sociologie de Saint-Simon* (1970), 40; and M. Collinet, "A propos de l'idée de progrès au 19e siècle," *Diogène* 33 (January–March 1961): 116–17.

[12] "A mesure que l'esprit humain vieillit, sa faculté de raisonner augmente, et sa faculté d'imaginer diminue." *Introduction aux travaux scientifiques*, 131.

[13] See G. de Staël, *De la littérature* (1800), in *Oeuvres complètes* (1836–38), 4:65.

[14] "[Les Grecs] se laissent dominer par leur imagination, leur attention est presque entièrement absorbée par les beaux-arts. Ils sont dans ce genre tellement forts, que je doute que leurs successeurs puissent les égaler. Mais, ce genre est-il le premier? je ne le pense pas, je ne le regarde

If Saint-Simon regarded reason as a sign of superiority consequent on historical maturity, he also imposed a further demarcation in distinguishing between a progressive move toward positivism and a retarded reliance on imagination, this time couched in social terms and related to his conception of religion. In line with Dupuis's *L'Origine de tous les cultes* of 1795, Saint-Simon identified successive religious systems with the prevailing level of scientific knowledge; in examining contemporary society, he argued that the prevalence of deism amongst the popular classes suggested their relative immaturity, testified in inductive beliefs that demanded strong imaginative investment amongst the faithful. His own commitment to scientific rationalism convinced Saint-Simon of the need for a new religion whose positivist tenets would respond to the intellectual requirements of the more enlightened sections of society. His proposed Physicist faith, supplanting the notion of the rule of God with that of a supreme physical law governing the universe, is conceived as appealing to this elite minority, while the less advanced groups continue in their established beliefs—a two-tier system is thus proposed, "Physicism for the educated, and Deism for the ignorant."[15] As with many thinkers of the previous century, Saint-Simon valued religion amongst the lower classes as a buttress to social order and it is on this basis that he envisages the preservation of their anachronistic faith. For the more advanced, however, Physicism offers a rational belief whose validation by the laws of science is embodied in the replacement of the traditional priest by the scientist, whose superior analytical capacities justify the pivotal role imagined for him.

This commitment to scientific rationalism thus promotes an attitude toward imagination inherently incompatible with any sympathy for art. In investing his expectations for social transformation on an epistemological revolution fueled by scientific advance, Saint-Simon accords privileged status to the *savant*, extending consideration to other groups only later in his career. It is under the Restoration that this process occurs, and at this stage two further categories—the *artiste* and the *industriel*—emerge to take their place alongside the *savant* as agents for change within society. The shift that allows this promotion to take place marks not so much an abandonment of Saint-Simon's earlier train of thought as a move away from a predominantly abstract interest in the value of science toward a preoccupation with the practical benefits it could offer and with the social reforms needed to take

---

que comme un amusement. La philosophie me paraît la plus importante de toutes les sciences." *Mémoire sur la science de l'homme*, 253. The point is also made by Bonald in 1818, *Recherches philosophiques sur les premiers objets des connaissances morales*, in *Oeuvres complètes* (1838), 8.1:352. Bonald shares Saint-Simon's relative depreciation of imagination, which he regards as primarily visual and associates with women, children, and savages (368).

[15] "Le Physicisme pour les gens instruits, et le Déisme pour la classe ignorante." *Introduction aux travaux scientifiques*, 170.

full advantage of technical innovations. This new focus not only allowed the *industriel* a more prominent role as epitomizing the generation of wealth through labor, but also offered an exalted place to the artist, whose power to influence popular opinion by firing the imagination now acquired more positive connotations. In revising his opinion of the artist, Saint-Simon accords him a central place in the imagined social structure through his ability to transcend the popular classes' intellectual limitations by manipulating their responsiveness to sentiment. Rather than an unfortunate impediment to rational enlightenment, imagination, and the associated faculties of passion and sentiment, are now valued as mechanisms whose cultivation can hasten popular acceptance of far-reaching change.

ART, SENTIMENT, AND THE PROMOTION OF INDUSTRY

The reorientation of Saint-Simon's interests around 1817 toward the practical details of forging a social system responsive to the economic opportunities offered by industry echoes concerns voiced by other commentators of the period. Republication of Jean-Baptiste Say's *Traité d'économie politique* in 1814 and 1817 stimulated discussion over the development of commercial activity, and such contemporaries as de Laborde and Constant explored issues of political and administrative reform that proved crucial to Saint-Simon.[16] It is in this context that his former preoccupation with the scientific talents of the *savant* was supplemented by regard for the two classes seen as pivotal to the emergence of a new social order—the *industriel* and the *artiste*.

Conviction in the pivotal value of labor had been a consistent feature in Saint-Simon's writing; indeed, the injunction "tous les hommes travailleront"—"all men will work"—had been attributed to no less an authority than God in the *Lettres d'un habitant de Genève*.[17] As the promotion of industry emerged as a growing priority, so Saint-Simon reassessed the social role of those groups who fulfilled this divine command. Abandoning his earlier commitment to the interests of the *propriétaires*, under the Restoration he displays increasing concern for the "amélioration des conditions de la classe la plus pauvre" ("improvement in the condition of the poorest class") and consequently sees government not as the preserve of a propertied elite but as a body whose legitimacy depends on mass support[18] and upon its regard for the well-being of the productive classes. Jettisoning the demar-

[16] See Gouhier, *Jeunesse* (1941), 3:31–33.

[17] *Lettres d'un habitant*, 55.

[18] See *Du système industriel* (1820–22), in *Oeuvres*, 3 (*O.S.S.E.*, 5):167.

cation of social groups on the basis of property ownership, Saint-Simon now classifies individuals according to their productive capacity—a distinction already adopted in Say's liberal utopia *Olbie* of 1800. Within this new framework, the productive *industriel* is promoted at the expense of the *oisif* class of aristocrats, *rentiers*, and clergy, who stand accused of inhibiting industrial growth and upholding an anachronistic governmental system incompatible with progressive needs.

Dedicated to facilitating industrial advance, the new order's social structure was designed to optimize its general benefits. Saint-Simon imagined three main classes in society. The majority of the population would be made up of *industriels*, a term having two distinct meanings in his thought. Though on one level the class comprises individuals engaged in all forms of productive labor, artists included,[19] more narrowly, it is identified with an elite group of "entrepreneurs de travaux scientifiques,"[20] granted administrative preeminence through their superior appreciation of social and economic needs. The class of *savants*, though still regarded with sufficient respect to be offered the new priesthood in a regenerated industrial society, figures less prominently in Saint-Simon's later thought, as his earlier concern with methodological innovation was superseded by more practical interest in generating wealth. The artist—who makes up the third class of the new triumvirate—emerges as the clearest beneficiary of Saint-Simon's revised social philosophy. This promotion, which coincides with the group's assimilation into the projected ruling elite, relates to Saint-Simon's continuing commitment to eradicating conflict in social relations and to an emerging conviction that art's appeal to popular sentiment could help secure this aim.

Such an understanding grew out of an appreciation of sentiment informed by developments in contemporary physiology. In a reformulation of the sensationalism of the *Encyclopédie* and Condillac, medical theorists at the end of the eighteenth century had begun to challenge the belief in a fundamental identity of ability and looked to variations in individual formation to explain the diversity of human character and aptitudes. Cabanis's lectures to the class of moral and political sciences at the Institut and the work of his Idéologue colleagues pointed up innate differences in human capacity,[21] a belief seemingly corroborated in an exploration of the infinitely varied contours of the human skull by the phrenologist Franz-Joseph Gall. This investigation of individual particularity coincided with the inegalitarian tenden-

[19] See, for example, *Le Politique* (April 1819), quoted in M. Rose, *Marx's Lost Aesthetic: Karl Marx and the Visual Arts* (1984), 12.

[20] *Du système industriel*, 3 (*O.S.S.E.*, 5):116.

[21] See M. S. Staum, *Cabanis: Enlightenment and Medical Philosophy in the French Revolution* (1980), 207–43.

cies advanced by such thinkers as Necker, Bonald, and de Maistre, who all shared Saint-Simon's commitment to the development of an organic society accommodating individual difference in a stable hierarchical structure.[22]

More particularly, Saint-Simon looked to Bichat's *Recherches physiologiques sur la vie et sur la mort* of 1800, which argued that all men were not inherently equal and of undifferentiated abilities but could be characterized within three specific categories, identified as "brain," "motor," and "sensory." Saint-Simon equated these with his three social groups: the rational brain type was that found in the *savant*, the motor type that of the *industriel*, and the sentimental and imaginative sensory type that of the *artiste*.[23] In such a way, medical science was used to endorse an ordered hierarchy that inscribed in nature the distinctions that the ancien régime's categorization of three estates had invested wholly in social function and birth. It was the artist who emerged as pivotal in this system, through his perceived capacity to forge social cohesion by an appeal to sentiment—a universal attribute that the artist possessed to an exceptional degree. He was thus delegated the socially essential role of countering the egalitarian and atomistic tendencies that Saint-Simon believed to be particularly acute in the modern world, firing the popular imagination toward fulfilling its preordained goal and buttressing social organicism.

This ability gave the artist a special place in Saint-Simon's blueprint of an ideal society. Convinced that the extension of a positivist epistemology to the social sphere would permit decisions of objective validity to be made by a rational elite, he asserted that enhanced administrative skills would lead to the state's disappearance as an oppressive force.[24] His conception of individual disparity meant, however, that the unimpeachable wisdom of particular measures could be implicitly understood only by the small minority enjoying enhanced faculties of reason. For the masses, a different path had to be followed if endorsement for the administrative elite's proposals was to be won.

It is here that the artist's ability to appeal to popular sentiment takes on its strategic role. Transforming the hermetic rationalism underlying the administrators' proposals into the varied languages of art, he uses the immediacy and universality of sentiment to enthuse the masses and win their undivided commitment to the leadership's ideas. Class antagonism ostensibly disappears, as receptivity to the artist's presentation of the leaders' deci-

[22] See F. E. Manuel, "From Equality to Organicism," *Journal of the History of Ideas* 17 (1956): 62–65.

[23] On Saint-Simon's indebtedness to Bichat, see B. Haines, "Social, Biological and Medical Thought in Saint-Simon and Comte," *British Journal for the History of Science* 11, no. 1 (March 1978): 30–31.

[24] Thus, in a Saint-Simonian society "le peuple n'a plus besoin d'être gouverné, c'est-à-dire commandé. Il suffit pour le maintien de l'ordre que les affaires soient administrées." *Lettres à ses concitoyens* (1819), in *Oeuvres*, 2 (*O.S.S.E.*, 4):144–45.

sions forestalls the danger of popular resistance and obviates any need for coercion. The place accorded to sentiment thus enables Saint-Simon to reconcile a perception of individual inequality with an open and progressive social structure, allowing him to share a belief in human disparity with such Traditionalists as Bonald and de Maistre without following the overtly authoritarian implications of their political stance. While conservative thinkers hankered after a return to the hierarchical organization of medieval society, Saint-Simon could look to the artist's imagination as facilitating radical change without endangering the equilibrium of class relations. Though such manipulation carries its own authoritarian implications, it nonetheless apparently removes the need for more concrete forms of control while eradicating the specter of conflict. Saint-Simon thus secures his ambition for social organicism by deploying sentiment both in the cohesive sphere of religious belief and in the artist's intervention among the people as an agent of the administrative elite.

Appreciation of the artist's social value first emerges in the *Lettres à ses concitoyens*, issued in the journal *L'Organisateur* in November 1819. Though only recently he had been vaguely classed among the progressive elements in society, contributing "la force de l'imagination" to the coalition of scientists, industrialists, and artisans,[25] a much more concrete perception of his potential influence now appears. Discussing proposals for transforming the prevailing social hierarchy, Saint-Simon speculates how a broad base could be won for the reforms he envisages. He argues that recent shifts in economic power and political influence necessitate a concomitant change in governmental structures, and maintains that only two factors frustrate the adoption of his ideas—the need for the active participation of artisans and scientists and for popular endorsement of change:

> Let the arts, through the power of imagination which they possess, exert sufficient influence on the common masses to persuade them irrevocably to follow this direction, and support their natural leaders in this great cooperative enterprise.
>
> *Let artists transport the earthly paradise into the future, presenting it as the consequence of the new system's foundation, and this system will be established without delay.*[26]

[25] "Le Parti national ou industriel comparé au parti antinational," *L'Organisateur* (November 1819), in *Oeuvres*, 2 (*O.S.S.E.*, 3):205. The artist is also classed with this group in the political fable "Sur la querelle des abeilles et des frelons," published in the same journal (ibid., 211–34).

[26] "Que les beaux-arts, par la force de l'imagination qui est entre leurs mains, exercent sur la masse commune l'action suffisante pour la déterminer à suivre irrévocablement cette direction, et à seconder ses chefs naturels dans cette grande co-opération.

"*Que les artistes transportent le paradis terrestre dans l'avenir, qu'ils le présentent comme devant être le résultat de l'établissement du nouveau système, et ce système se constituera promptement.*" *Lettres à ses concitoyens*, 165–66. Italics in the original.

As described here, the artist is essentially conceived as a propagandist, exploiting his skills to win over mass support. His own commitment to the future, and enhanced vision of it, are the raw material from which he elaborates a promise of progress and felicity to entice and rally the people. In such a way, Saint-Simon envisages radical transformation occurring in an entirely pacific way, as reform takes place with universal compliance and enthusiasm.

Despite variations in emphasis, the artist's eminence in the *Lettres à ses concitoyens* is reflected in virtually all of Saint-Simon's subsequent work. Some indication of the priority he is now granted emerges in the *Lettre à MM. les jurés*, published some six months after the earlier text, in March 1820. While Saint-Simon had previously argued that only positive scientists—physiologists, physicists, and chemists—were capable of evaluating his scheme,[27] he now revises his opinion, arguing that "fresh consideration has convinced me that it should be the artists who come first, followed by the intellectuals, with the *industriels* only after these first two classes."[28] The artist is given precedence in order to prepare the ground for the practical innovations to be introduced by the *savants* and the industrial elite since, as Saint-Simon asserts in *Du système industriel* of 1820–22, "every great intellectual movement necessitates a comparable transformation in feelings."[29]

Both in this extensive discussion of the contemporary social malaise and in the *Catéchisme des industriels*, published as a sequence of brochures in 1823–24, the proclaimed need to secure artistic endorsement seemingly remains a dead letter. The incomplete state of both works helps explain this apparent reticence, however. Concentration on the means of ending the political impasse of the Restoration, on which discussion focuses in *Du système industriel*, forms only one aspect of a projected triptych also comprising a ""travail scientifique" and culminating in a "travail poétique," intended to "passionner les hommes, et particulièrement les artistes" ("enthuse men, and artists in particular") for the practical proposals detailed earlier in the work.[30] Similarly, a discussion of the power of sentiment, to be included in the fourth *cahier* of the *Catéchisme*, remained unwritten at the time of Saint-Simon's death in 1825.

Despite the incompletion of both of these works, it remains clear that the role of sentiment and its practical application in an ethical code emerge as

[27] Ibid., 239.

[28] "De nouvelles méditations m'ont prouvé que l'ordre dans lequel les choses devaient marcher était les artistes en tête, ensuite les savants, et les industriels seulement après ces deux premières classes." *Lettre à MM. les jurés*, March 1820, in *Oeuvres*, 6:422.

[29] "Tout grand mouvement dans les idées en exige un semblable dans les sentiments." *Du système industriel*, 3 (*O.S.S.E.*, 5):21.

[30] *Travaux philosophiques, scientifiques et poétiques, extrait du système industriel*, in *Oeuvres*, 6:470.

increasing preoccupations at this period. Emphasis on fostering social concord through philanthropy and Christian principles of brotherly love promotes consideration of the artist as an individual whose enhanced sentiment best qualifies him to draw up moral guidelines to be observed by all groups.[31] Such a function is given formalized status in the *Catéchisme*, with the proposal to establish an Académie des sciences morales charged with elaborating a "code des sentiments." Explicitly inspired by such contemporary institutions as the Société libre de la morale chrétienne, Saint-Simon's projected organization further recalls both the Institut's Classe des sciences morales et politiques, abolished by Bonaparte in 1803, and the Abbé Grégoire's scheme for a "General Association between intellectuals, men of letters, and artists to expedite the progress of good behavior and enlightenment," first broached in 1796.[32] Overlapping the Conseil de Newton in its emphasis on epistemological synthesis, Grégoire's institution reveals a common concern with elaborating a comprehensive moral code and shares Saint-Simon's preoccupation with sentiment, and the artist's potential as an ethical guide. It is on the grounds of their practical insights into the manipulation of sentiment that Saint-Simon includes "the most distinguished poets, painters, sculptors, and musicians" within the ranks of his academy, arguing "theoreticians should not be separated from those who play a leading role in practice."[33]

Culminating in the promotion of an altruistic faith of love and fraternity in *Le Nouveau Christianisme* of 1825, Saint-Simon's later work accords increasing priority to the ethical foundation of social relations. Within such a process, the artist is set to work in conjunction with the *savant* who, as "the new spiritual power,"[34] takes on responsibility for an educational system which in itself is heavily weighted toward the inculcation of moral principles. Ensuring "the triumph of intelligence, genius, and moral force over animal force and numerical superiority,"[35] such an alliance indicates the

[31] In *Du système industriel*, Saint-Simon thus looks to the artist and the savant to undertake "l'organisation d'un système de morale et de politique, suffisamment clair et assez positif pour que les gouvernants se trouvent forcés de le suivre de même que les gouvernés." *Oeuvres* 3 (*O.S.S.E.*, 6):78.

[32] Grégoire's scheme was presented to the Institut in 1796, and published in the *Mémoires de la classe des sciences morales et politiques* in 1798 (1:552ff.). It was reprinted as an undated pamphlet, signed "G," around 1816, under the title *Plan d'association générale entre les savans, gens de lettres et artistes pour accélérer les progrès des bonnes moeurs et des lumières*.

[33] "Des poètes, des peintres, des sculpteurs et des musiciens les plus distingués"; "Les faiseurs de théories ne doivent point être séparés de ceux qui se distinguent dans les principales applications." *Catéchisme des industriels* (1824), in *Oeuvres*, 5 (*O.S.S.E.*, 10):28.

[34] "Le nouveau pouvoir spirituel." *Du système industriel*, 3 (*O.S.S.E.*, 6):116.

[35] "Le triomphe de l'intelligence, du génie et de la force morale, sur la force animale et sur la supériorité numérique." *L'Artiste, le savant et l'industriel. Dialogue (1824)*, in *Oeuvres*, 5 (*O.S.S.E.*, 10):216.

resilience of Saint-Simon's earlier fears of popular volatility. Associated with the formulation of moral principles designed to forestall such unrest, the artist thus finds himself assimilated into ruling circles as an authority on sentiment. More important, however, it is to his role as a propagandist, intervening directly among the people and tailoring his work to socially beneficial ends, that the artist owes his prominence within Saint-Simon's later thought.

ART AS SOCIAL EXHORTATION

As his growing regard for the value of sentiment led Saint-Simon to incorporate the artist within his administrative projects, so he turned his attention toward art's practical function as a spur to change and a buttress to social solidarity. Though his analysis of history pointed to the imminent adoption of the industrial system he advocated, his explanation of the concrete measures needed to achieve this transformation remained vague, relying at worst on such devices as a monster petition to win regal support.[36] His perception of social class excludes anything resembling the historical explanation of change later advanced by Marx, and his commitment to preserving order and hierarchy denies recourse to violent revolution. It is in such a context that the artist helps to bridge the seemingly impassable abyss separating the present from a new world of industry and brotherly love. His control over sentiment serves to generate pacific enthusiasm for abandoning the prevailing order and forges common dedication to a new regime whose benefits his work so vividly portrays. Thus, in *De l'organisation sociale* Saint-Simon describes the germination of a regenerate industrial system:

> In this great enterprise, men of imagination will lead the way; they will proclaim the future of mankind, they will transport the Golden Age from the past to enrich future generations; they will enthuse society for the enhancement of its well-being, by offering a rich picture of new prosperity and showing that every member of society will soon share in those pleasures which have hitherto been restricted to a very limited class; they will sing of civilization's benefits and exploit every aspect of the arts—eloquence, poetry, painting, music—to achieve their goal: in a word, they will develop the poetic aspect of the new system.[37]

[36] See *Du système industriel*, 3 (*O.S.S.E.*, 5):32 and the *Catéchisme des industriels*, in *Oeuvres*, 4 (*O.S.S.E.*, 8):113. Here, Saint-Simon's argument that the adoption of his ideas by an elite minority will inevitably lead to their universal acceptance renders the artist's mediation redundant.

[37] "Dans cette grande entreprise, les hommes à imagination ouvriront la marche; ils proclameront l'avenir de l'espèce humaine; ils ôteront au passé l'âge d'or pour en enrichir les générations futures; ils passionneront la société pour l'accroissement de son bien-être, en lui présen-

In presenting art as a catalyst in this way, Saint-Simon formulated a conception of its psychological and social influence of seminal importance to subsequent advocates of *art social*. The power of imagination, operating on individual sentiment, is accorded a dynamic force in generating progressive consciousness and fostering consensus for change. Emphasis on the predictive capacity of art conceives its sensual appeal lending an irresistible tangibility to the evocation of a hypothetical future and thus hastening its realization in fact.

This appreciation of art receives fullest expression in the dialogue *L'Artiste, le savant et l'industriel*, published as part of the *Opinions littéraires, philosophiques et industrielles* in December 1824. Probably written in collaboration with Léon Halévy, one of a number of young men who assisted the philosopher toward the end of his career,[38] the dialogue takes the form of a conversation in which the artist predominates and where his position within society emerges as the central issue. This prominence marks the artist's promotion from his subordinate role to the *industriel* in the *Catéchisme* to a full-fledged partner in the administrative elite represented by the two other protagonists in the dialogue. Thus the artist asserts that social progress depends on their mutual collaboration: "without any one of the three classes of which we are part, the social body would suffer and be in imminent danger, and . . . if it were suddenly to be denied the sciences, arts, and industry, it would instantly fall dead."[39]

Taking up Saint-Simon's belief that in a fully developed industrial society government would be rendered redundant, the artist argues that it is the

tant un riche tableau de prospérités nouvelles, en faisant sentir que tous les membres de la société participeront bientôt à des jouissances qui, à ce jour, ont été l'apanage d'une classe très peu nombreuse; ils chanteront les bienfaits de la civilisation, et ils metteront en oeuvre, pour atteindre leur but, tous les moyens des beaux-arts, l'éloquence, la poésie, la peinture, la musique, en un mot, ils développeront la partie poétique du nouveau système." *De l'organisation sociale*, in *Oeuvres*, 5 (*O.S.S.E.*, 10):137.

[38] Although volume 10 of the 1867 edition of Saint-Simon's works ascribes the dialogue to Olinde Rodrigues, another disciple of the 1820s, the burden of evidence suggests that Saint-Simon and Halévy collaborated on the text. Halévy's "Souvenirs de Saint-Simon," published in *La France littéraire* in March 1832 (and reedited by G. Brunet in 1925), confirms this attribution, as does Henri Fournel's *Bibliographie saint-simonienne* of 1833 and a note by Enfantin in volume 1 of the "Archives saint-simoniennes" (Arsenal Ms. 7643), also of 1833. Ill health following an attempted suicide in December 1823, in conjunction with Saint-Simon's recognized preference for developing ideas in conversation rather than on paper, further strengthens the credibility of this attribution. P. Régnier, "Les Idées et les opinions littéraires des Saint-Simoniens (1825–1835)" (1983), 1:35, favors attribution to Rodrigues; R. P. Locke, *Music, Musicians, and the Saint-Simonians* (1986), 37, emphasizes Halévy's independent contribution. Irrespective of authorship, the ideas expounded in the dialogue are entirely consistent with the philosopher's views at this period.

[39] "Sans l'une des trois classes dont nous faisons partie, le corps social serait en état de souffrance et dans un immanent danger; que privé tout à coup des sciences et des arts et de l'industrie, il tomberait frappé de mort subite." *L'Artiste, le savant*, 209.

triumvirate of progressive capacities who best understand popular needs and whose destiny it is to administer the state. Only suspicion and misunderstanding prevent them from assuming this role and bringing about sweeping change in the moral and political order. The remarks placed in his mouth signify the artist's final admission into ruling circles as the peer of both *industriel* and *savant*. His newly recognized powers transform him from an independent professional into a public figure whose work must be dictated by broad considerations of polity. In this respect, Saint-Simon robs him of the autonomous exercise of moral judgment demanded by such eighteenth-century commentators as Diderot and La Font de Saint-Yenne; in return for social eminence, he is obliged to direct his talents toward propagating ideas that emerge from the deliberations of the administrative triumvirate. From this perspective, the artist in the *Dialogue* foresees his colleagues taking on decisive responsibilities:

> It is we artists who will serve as your vanguard, since art's power has greatest immediacy and rapidity. We have arms of every sort: when we wish to spread new ideas among men, we inscribe them on marble or canvas; we make them popular through poems or melodies; we use in turn the lyre or the flute, odes or songs, stories or the novel; the dramatic stage is also open to us, and it is there above all that we exert an electric and victorious influence. Since we speak to man's imagination and sentiments, we must always exert the strongest and most decisive effect. If today we seem to have no role, or only a very minor one, this is because the arts lack what they most need for their energy and success, a common impulse and a unifying idea.[40]

[40] "C'est nous, artistes, qui vous serviront d'avant-garde; la puissance des arts est en effet la plus immédiate et la plus rapide. Nous avons des armes de toute espèce: quand nous voulons répandre des idées neuves parmi les hommes, nous les inscrivons sur le marbre ou sur la toile; nous les popularisons par la poésie et par le chant; nous employons tour à tour la lyre ou le galoubet, l'ode ou la chanson, l'histoire ou le roman; la scène dramatique nous est ouverte, et c'est là surtout que nous exerçons une influence électrique et victorieuse. Nous nous adressons à l'imagination et aux sentiments de l'homme; nous devons donc exercer toujours l'action la plus vive et la plus décisive; et si aujourd'hui notre rôle paraît nul ou au moins très secondaire, c'est qu'il manquait aux arts ce qui est essentiel à leur énergie et à leur succès, une impulsion commune et une idée générale." Ibid., 210.

For a discussion of this passage, see D. D. Egbert, "The Idea of 'Avant-Garde' in Art and Politics," *American Historical Review* 73 (December 1967): 343–50; M. Thibert, *L'Art social selon les Saint-Simoniens* (1927), 10; and N. Hadjinicolaou, "Sur l'idéologie de l'avant-gardisme," *Histoire et critique des arts* 6 (July 1978): 51–53. Egbert's suggestion that the phrase *avant-garde* prefigures its later usage in the sense of an artistic vanguard is entirely misleading. Rather than referencing formal or thematic experimentation, the context in which the term is habitually used within modernism, its deployment here refers exclusively to the political relationship the artist sustains as mediator between the leadership and the people. Valuing the artist only insofar as his talents contribute to the progressive amelioration of society, Saint-Simon restricts his discussion to a range of functional priorities entirely indifferent to any formal characteristics intrinsic to the various media embraced within the term *beaux-arts*.

Though the artist's mediating role essentially transforms him into the mouthpiece of the elite, his function is now regarded as in no way inferior to the intellectual process of administration. Without the artist, his rationalist colleagues are severely impaired, since their proposals exert little direct appeal for those on whom they depend as active agents of social and industrial transformation. To this degree, Saint-Simon's evaluation of the artist has acquired new depth; whereas in *Du système industriel* he was merely a *vulgarisateur*,[41] lacking the methodological penetration of the *savant* and *industriel*, now he is projected as their partner and equal, possessing complementary skills crucial for achieving social advance.[42]

The new-found conviction that "reasoning merely convinces, while feeling persuades and excites"[43] leads Saint-Simon to adopt an exalted attitude toward the artist, whom he now describes as fulfilling "a positive power, a true priesthood."[44] In endowing the creative process with sacramental overtones, he makes a point frequently repeated by his disciples and indeed echoed in the heightened self-consciousness and self-regard of the romantic generation of 1830. The conditions Saint-Simon imposes for acknowledging this superiority are rigid, however. Contemporary art, like society itself, stands condemned of egotism—"this bastard fruit of civilization,"[45] nurtured in the corrupting soil of economic individualism. Rather than entertaining the narcissistic pretensions current in artistic circles, Saint-Simon sets the tone for later advocates of *art social* in demanding a thorough purging of the creative imagination to allow new priorities to emerge:

> The arts would risk losing all of their importance, . . . if they persisted in following a direction where nothing remains to be discovered—that of imagination without purpose, of retrograde imagination. On the contrary, if they endorse the general movement of the human spirit, if they too show themselves willing to serve the common cause, contribute to the increase in general well-

---

In emphasizing his designation of the artist as being in the avant-garde, Egbert ironically overlooks the term's appearance in Saint-Simon's earlier work, where he speaks of a scientific avant-garde in a sense closer to modern usage, albeit in the context of a different discipline. In discussing the history of nonorganic and physiological sciences in the *Mémoire sur la science de l'homme*, for example, he writes "c'est alternativement que les brutiers et les physiologistes ont occupé le poste de l'avant-garde scientifique, pour pénétrer dans le pays des découvertes" *Oeuvres*, 5 (*O.S.S.E.*, 10):37.

[41] See *Du système industriel*, 3 (*O.S.S.E.*, 6):59. This resembles Comte's restrictive conception of the artist in the third *cahier* of the *Catéchisme des industriels*.

[42] See *Du système industriel*, 3 (*O.S.S.E.*, 6):60.

[43] "Les raisonnements ne font que convaincre, tandis que les sensations persuadent et entraînent." *L'Artiste, le savant*, 207. Thus he speaks of the artist's role as being to "s'élancer en avant de toutes les facultés intellectuelles" (216), exploiting the more responsive nature of sentiment in conveying his didactic message.

[44] "Une puissance positive, un véritable sacerdoce." Ibid., 216.

[45] "Ce fruit bâtard de la civilisation." Ibid., 215.

being, stimulate fruitful feelings in man, appropriate to his developed intelligence, and, with the help of these feelings, spread ideas that are altruistic and CONTEMPORARY, then no sooner will they see an immense future of glory and success opening up before them.[46]

The anti-individualism of Saint-Simon's political philosophy, with its emphasis on social organicism, is thus echoed in his aesthetic attitude. In the same way as he proposes the cooperative exploitation of nature through industry to remedy the egocentric pursuit of personal gain, so he relates the moral regeneration of art to the development of a new sense of responsibility among its practitioners. In abandoning self-gratification for an awareness of the tangible social benefits his work can instill, the artist directs imagination toward specific rational goals: it is in this sense that Saint-Simon demands of art common sense, "du sens commun"[47]—a strategic, outward-looking attitude that exploits the power of sentiment to confront issues of contemporary concern.

Practical indications of how such a revolution is to be achieved are rare in the philosopher's work, though two precedents—the use of art in the Catholic church and during the French Revolution—do provide some insight into Saint-Simon's precise visualization of the moral potential of art. From this evidence, it is clear that, far from implying prosaic restraint, the call for common sense is entirely compatible with extravagance and sensory gratification. Saint-Simon turns on several occasions to the example of Catholicism and seems particularly sensitive to its value as a precedent for his own belief in the artist's didactic role. Thus he attacks the austerity of Protestantism in the *Nouveau Christianisme* and argues that all of the arts have an essential place in religion as a means of reaffirming the effect of doctrine through an appeal to the senses, and hence to the emotions.[48] The decorative and dramatic example provided by Catholicism acts as the spur—and, indeed, the closest model—for an aesthetic rooted in the affirmation and

[46] "Les arts risqueraient de perdre toujours leur importance, . . . s'ils s'obstinaient à suivre une direction où ils n'ont plus rien à exploiter, celle de l'imagination sans objet, de l'imagination rétrograde. Mais, au contraire, s'ils secondent le mouvement général de l'esprit humain, s'ils veulent aussi servir la cause commune, contribuer à l'accroissement du bien-être général, produire sur l'homme des sensations fructueuses, telles qu'il convient à son intelligence développée d'en ressentir, et propager, à l'aide de ces sensations, des idées généreuses qui soient ACTUELLES, aussitôt ils verront s'ouvrir devant eux un avenir immense de gloire et de succès." Ibid., 212–13.

[47] Ibid., 212. Saint-Simon's emphasis on the artist's social obligations and his opposition to individualism is strikingly reflected in the work of such Traditionalists as Bonald, whose similar commitment to social organicism is accompanied by suspicion of the subversive potential of art. See Bonald's *Réflexions sur les questions de l'indépendence des gens de lettres* of 1805, in *Oeuvres* (1819), 10:65–103.

[48] See *Le Nouveau Christianisme*, in *Oeuvres*, 3 (*O.S.S.E.*, 7):161.

fortification of faith. Just as the painters, musicians, and architects employed by the papacy used their skills to glorify God and indoctrinate the faithful, so too the artist in Saint-Simon's scheme works to uphold the ideological system within which he operates. Though the example of Catholicism, which was to be further developed by Saint-Simon's disciples and more generally provided an important precedent for radical art theorists, was currently favored in traditionalist circles, Saint-Simon himself is important in elevating the Middle Ages as a period of exceptional creative achievement. This relatively precocious reevaluation grows out of his understanding of history, which promoted the Middle Ages as an organic period during which social harmony was secured through the unifying force of shared religious beliefs. Saint-Simon's emphasis on social cohesion, and on the centrality of faith in guaranteeing stability, fostered a sympathy for pre-Reformation Catholicism as a temporal institution and for its art as a potent ideological auxiliary. Enthusiasm for the social and ethical impact of medieval art thus endorses culture's role in buttressing unequal power relations and establishes an alternative paradigm to the progressive depiction of antiquity which the Revolution had exploited to represent its less stratified conception of citizenship.

A more immediate source of inspiration was possibly provided by the Revolution itself, both in its appropriation of the arts for morally and politically didactic purposes and in its use of the popular *fête* as a collective event in which the masses were exposed to prevailing ideological ideals. Saint-Simon's comments on the role of the artist during the Revolution, made in the *Lettres à ses concitoyens*, reveal his belief in the mobilization of the arts at this period in reaffirming the course of political events. Under the Revolution, "artists abandoned their imaginative work relating to the improvement of social life to redouble the strength of our armies by uplifting the souls of those citizens who had now become soldiers."[49] In a small way, Saint-Simon himself had entered into this process of stimulation in 1794, with his design for a set of playing cards (plate 1) for the engraver Jean-Démosthène Dugourc, conceived as a "manuel de la révolution."[50] By substituting the revolutionary virtues of liberty, equality, and fraternity for the court cards, Saint-Simon had set out to combine entertainment and edification, transforming an idle game into a course of political instruction. The replacement of such figures as the king of hearts and jack of spades, with their reactionary monarchist overtones, by the "Génie de la guerre" and the

[49] "Les artistes ont abandonné leurs travaux d'imagination rélatifs à l'amélioration du sort de l'homme social, pour doubler les forces de nos armées exaltant l'âme des citoyens devenus soldats." *Lettres à ses concitoyens*, 228.

[50] Prospectus dated 13 nivôse, an III (3 January 1795), cited in E. Fleury, *Les Cartes à jouer du Comte Saint-Simon* (1874), 6.

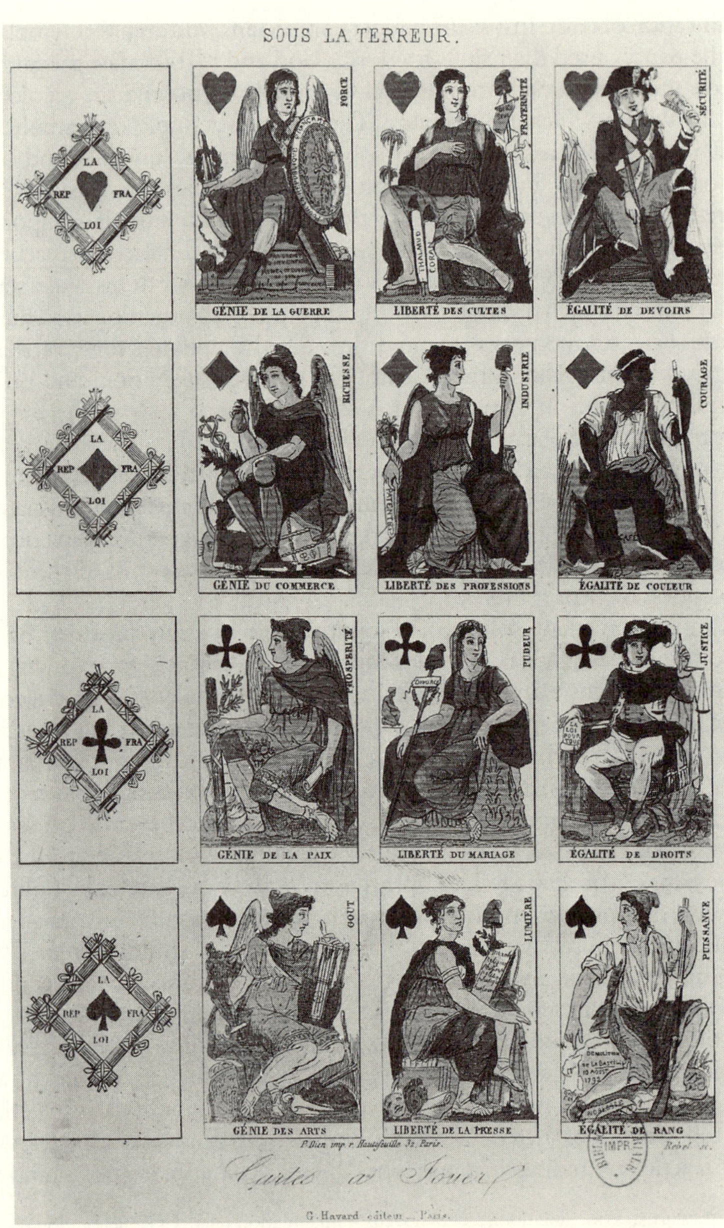

Plate 1. J.-D. Dugourc: Set of Revolutionary playing cards, designed by Saint-Simon. Reproduced from Augustin Challamel, *Histoire-Musée de la République française,* vol. 2, 1842. Bibliothèque nationale, Paris.

"Egalité de couleurs," provides a symbolic repertoire incorporating values central to revolutionary ideology.[51] On a much more ambitious scale, the *fête* contributes to a similar end, providing a ritualized space in which abstract virtues are paraded before the people with a drama and immediacy equaled only by the rites of religious belief. As a secular counterpoint to church ceremonial, Saint-Simon valued the festival's address to a vastly extended congregation. In its abolition of the distinction between spectators and participants, it provides a model of organic sociability, consolidating the individual citizen's dedication to the extended national family of which he forms an integral part. The resources it combines further serve to enhance its emotional appeal; drawing upon drama, music, and the visual arts, it solicits all of the senses in a spectacle of overwhelming richness and inspirational power. This collaboration of media seems to underlie Saint-Simon's particular attention toward the festival; like his followers, whose limited initiatives to develop a distinctive form of artistic propaganda focused around quasi-liturgical ceremonial, Saint-Simon conceives art enjoying its greatest emotional force in a form of *Gesamtkunstwerk*, the breadth of whose range is directed toward political edification rather than pure aesthetic delight.

It is in the *Lettres à ses concitoyens* that Saint-Simon pays greatest attention to the festival. Here he proposes the establishment of a tricameral administrative system largely composed of scientists and industrialists. In one branch, however, designated as the "Chambre d'invention," painters, poets, sculptors, and musicians figure prominently. Working in collaboration with civil engineers, they are given responsibility for elaborating public works programs and are also empowered to organize festivities to strengthen popular devotion to national progress. Three forms are prescribed: *fêtes d'espérance*, which look to the future and are used as a vehicle for presenting proposed reforms; *fêtes consacrées aux souvenirs*, which provide an opportunity for appreciating the improvements within society under the new regime; and *fêtes* devoted to particular classes and groups, such as children, farmers, or the old. At each event, orators will figure prominently who "will make a speech on the social duties of those in whose honor the festival is celebrated."[52] The *fêtes d'espérance* provide a particularly rich opportunity for the orator to secure the people's sanction for measures taken on their

[51] J. Dautry, "Nouveau Christianisme ou nouvelle théophilanthropie? Contribution à une sociologie religieuse de Saint-Simon," *Archives de sociologie des religions* 20 (July–December 1965): 16–17, points to the cards' sacralization of the state, and the religious synchretism of the "Liberté des cultes" card, with its references to the Gospels, Talmud, and Koran.

[52] "Feront un discours sur les devoirs sociaux de ceux en l'honneur de qui la fête sera célébrée." This schema recalls proposals outlined by Mathieu and Robespierre in 1794, and enshrined in modified form under the Directory in the Law of Brumaire, year IV. This initiated such moral festivals as those to "La Jeunesse," "La Vieillesse," and "L'Agriculture."

behalf: "[They] will set out for the people works projects decided by parliament and encourage citizens to labor enthusiastically by persuading them how greatly their lives will be improved once these projects are completed."[53] The didactic purpose of such celebrations is thus clear, with the inherent moral enshrined in the event underlined by the orator, whose speech concentrates and distills the ideology infusing the festivities. The collective efforts of painters, poets, musicians, and sculptors create a participative spectacle that carries along the people in willing endorsement of the prevailing social structure by celebrating the present, welcoming the future, and spurning the past. Through such a ritual of dedication, a new cult of the state, embracing every citizen, is given ringing affirmation.

Saint-Simon's emphasis on overt didacticism underlines the transitional status of his ideas. While the disciples who took up the banner of industry following the philosopher's death in 1825 were to cultivate a mystical religiosity where sentiment was given pride of place, Saint-Simon's own attitude toward imagination and the arts remained qualified by an underlying commitment to reason. Positivist leanings provide a continual bedrock to his thought, surviving, and indeed justifying, the modifications in his practical outlook. In this respect, Saint-Simon displays epistemological convictions that grow out of the rationalist tradition of Enlightenment philosophy. His promotion of a utilitarian aesthetic, too, has eighteenth-century antecedents, not only in the Revolution but also in ancien régime interest in the morally inspiring impact of art. Yet, in certain respects, Saint-Simon makes a break with the Enlightenment. His perception of contemporary medical theory, with its repudiation of the egalitarian connotations of sensationalism, prompted an acknowledgment of the inherent limitations of reason as a faculty found in developed form only among a small minority. It is in this context that sentiment, whose organic origins apparently guaranteed more universal appeal, acquires a pivotal role in the political equation and leads to the artist's promotion in Saint-Simon's later work. Such an appreciation of sentiment, while sharing some of the characteristics advanced in eighteenth-century texts, fundamentally deviates from this earlier tradition in its overall place within an explanation of aesthetic response and differs markedly from the essentially élitist conception of *sensibilité*.

Saint-Simon's attitude toward art is, moreover, unambiguously functional in tone. Beauty is a concept entirely foreign to his concerns; art achieves significance in his eyes only insofar as it can be justified on strictly utilitarian lines. Symptomatically, his aesthetic speculations remain on an exclusively abstract plane, eschewing any reference to specific works of literature, painting, or sculpture. Nor did Saint-Simon make conspicuous

53 "[Ils] exposeront au peuple les projets de travaux qui auront été arrêtés par le Parlement et ils stimuleront les citoyens à travailler avec ardeur, en leur faisant sentir combien leur sort se trouve amélioré quand ils auront exécuté les projets." *Lettres à ses concitoyens*, 56.

attempts to acquaint himself with contemporary practice. While he had gone to elaborate lengths to cultivate leading scientists, even contracting a short-lived marriage in 1801 as a means of establishing a fashionable salon in his home near the Ecole de médecine,[54] his familiarity with artists of the period remained slight—though the painter Ary Scheffer briefly entered Saint-Simon's circle in 1816, through friendship with his young collaborator Augustin Thierry.[55] This isolation confirms the general indifference with which the artistic community responded to Saint-Simon's promise of unprecedented social eminence, a promise all too apparently qualified by a highly instrumental understanding of culture as subservient to priorities determined through the superior insights of reason.

The rationalist ballast that holds Saint-Simon's aesthetic in place was largely jettisoned by his disciples. As the following chapter will demonstrate, their cultivation of pronounced religious overtones had far-reaching implications not only for their interpretation of Saint-Simon's philosophy of social organization but also for their understanding of art and of the artist's status, which far surpassed anything their mentor had been willing to allow. In this respect, the movement cast aside much of the Enlightenment inheritance in Saint-Simon's philosophy and forged an understanding of *art social* that moved beyond his utilitarian commitment to exert a far more potent appeal on the artistic community in the years after 1830.

[54] See Gouhier, *Jeunesse*, 2:102–4, who mentions that a number of unnamed writers and musicians frequented the salon.

[55] See ibid., 3:133.

CHAPTER 3

From Positivism to Sentiment: The Aesthetics of Saint-Simonianism

THE EVOLUTION of Saint-Simonianism in the years following the master's death amplified elements discernible in the writings of Saint-Simon himself, moving from an initial emphasis on positivism toward the cultivation of a mystical antirationalism. This trajectory allowed the development of an aesthetic endowing the artist with a superior vision and potential social influence far surpassing anything envisaged in the doctrine inherited by the new group. Their assertion of these enhanced powers informed a complex theory of art expounded in the Saint-Simonian press, through special lectures and in exhortatory texts, culminating in the celebrated *Aux artistes* by the group's principal aesthetician, Emile Barrault, in 1830. Though, as we shall see, this initiative met with only limited success and provoked often hostile comment, it nonetheless marks a crucial turningpoint in the development of social aesthetics during the July Monarchy and Second Republic.

The movement itself had a brief, but meteoric history, spanning scarcely a decade. The small group that Saint-Simon had gathered around him in the years before his death was soon swelled by new recruits, most of whom had scientific or administrative backgrounds and a record of oppositional political activity. Prominent among this new generation were Saint-Armand Bazard and Prosper Enfantin, both of whom were to dominate the subsequent history of the "école saint-simonienne." Together with Philippe Buchez, another early disciple whose christian socialist aesthetic we shall explore in a later chapter, Bazard had played a leading role in Carbonarist opposition to Charles X. His liberal pedigree parallels that of converts such as Hippolyte Carnot and Hippolyte Auger, who cultivated Masonic connections and conspiratorial ambitions—the former, for example, had plotted against the Bourbon regime with Godefroy Cavaignac and the artists Decaisne and Drolling.[1] Enfantin's background was much more cosmopolitan. In common with many other converts, he had been educated at the Ecole polytechnique but had gone on to work for a banker in Russia, where he had developed an interest in economics. His domination of the fledgling school, which becomes perceptible in 1826, increased throughout the early 1830s

[1] See H. Carnot, *Sur le Saint-Simonisme* (1887), 15. For general histories of the movement, see S. Charléty, *Histoire du Saint-Simonisme (1825–1864)* (1896; reprint, 1965), and H. R. d'Allemagne, *Les Saint-Simoniens. 1827–1837* (1930).

and led to the transformation of a political grouping into a highly emotional religious sect.

This metamorphosis prompted a shift away from doctrinal dependence on Saint-Simon toward a hybrid system of thought combining economic analysis with metaphysical speculation on the nature of God and audacious rejection of prevailing sexual mores. The positivist legacy evident in the school's early journals, *Le Producteur* (1825–26) and *L'Organisateur* (1829–31), was slowly eroded as Enfantin elaborated an extravagant mystical creed, in which sentiment increasingly eclipsed the progressive value of reason. This process, which encouraged theocratic tendencies in the analysis of social relations, culminated in December 1829 with the declaration of Saint-Simonianism as a religious faith under the joint leadership of Bazard and Enfantin. The contrasting personalities and ideological propensities of the two *pères*—the former retaining liberal, rationalist commitments, the latter increasingly prone to a mystical authoritarianism—inexorably divided the group over the nature and aims of its political intervention. These tensions reached breaking point in November 1831, fueled by Enfantin's growing intolerance toward dissent and his advocacy of a libertarian sexual code, ostensibly attuned to human instinctual urges. The resulting debate, which dealt a major blow to the group's surviving democratic links, consolidated Enfantin's role as *Père suprême* by provoking Bazard's secession.

Under the two men's control, the school had accumulated a public following, both through the doctrinal lectures, which attracted audiences of up to five hundred until official action led to their suspension in October 1830, and through acquisition of the prominent journal *Le Globe*, whose editor Pierre Leroux declared his allegiance the following December. The split with Bazard was a severe blow, however, depriving the group of some of its leading members, including Leroux, whose subsequent theoretical evolution will be discussed in a later chapter.

Freed from these apostates, Enfantin consolidated his power by declaring himself pope of the Saint-Simonian religion in 1832. As sexual liberation increasingly displaced commitment toward economic transformation, so the group attenuated calls for emancipation of the proletariat, promoting instead a gospel of social conciliation, enacted in the rituals and structures of the school itself. These apostolic overtones were given full rein with the establishment of a retreat at Enfantin's home in Ménilmontant, where the disciples pursued a communal regime intended as a model for future social organization. The liturgical ceremonies organized there brought together members of the Saint-Simonian family and enthusiastic workers, whose hymns in praise of social concord and its new messiah attracted crowds of curious spectators and again prompted official action. Evicting the apostles from their monastic fastness, the state tried and imprisoned Enfantin and a handful of followers in August 1832, for contravening public order.

In a final effort to revive the apostles' flagging enthusiasm, Enfantin declared 1833 the "année de la mère," promising that the discovery of a female messiah—whose attributes would complement his own—would initiate a new moral millennium. Hopes for her discovery in Egypt, together with ambitions to advance the group's practical commitment to progress by supervising construction of a Suez canal, lured a small cohort of disciples. Yet the ill-starred expedition merely deferred the sect's collapse. The Egyptian authorities would lend their support only for a dam across the Nile to control flooding, and work on this, far from heralding the anticipated birth of a workers' army, proved slow and frustrating. As more and more of the remaining disciples succumbed to cholera or left for home, Enfantin had to admit defeat, returning to France, a leader without apostles, in January 1837.

Despite the overwrought, histrionic nature of the Saint-Simonian episode, the intellectual currents it represented concentrate and symbolize a broad spectrum of concerns enjoying wide currency in mid-nineteenth-century France. Though retrospectively dismissed by Flaubert as "a bunch of jokers who wanted to redo Catholicism,"[2] the Saint-Simonians undoubtedly struck a chord among many contemporaries. Their aesthetic philosophy, with its glorification of the poet as social seer, was not entirely foreign to a generation for whom the artist could be described as "the apostle of a certain truth, the servant and mouthpiece of the Almighty."[3]

In tracing the evolution of their aesthetic, we shall see that, far from maintaining a narrowly functional attitude toward *art social*, the Saint-Simonians developed a philosophy of art sensitive to questions of form. Previous historians' emphasis on dogmatic utilitarianism results from concentration on critical texts produced before 1832. After this date, however, investigations of the psychological impact of words, sounds, and color, rooted in a growing appreciation of the social value of sentiment, allowed a broader perception of the artistic enterprise that no longer entailed insistence on direct didacticism. In this respect, there develops a suppler—if highly speculative—aesthetic stance, which, as we shall see, bears similarities with Fourierist currents of the 1840s. Such ideas, however, could emerge only in the light of broader shifts within the movement, most particularly associated with Enfantin's religious musings. In the years immediately following Saint-Simon's death, such options had yet to be investigated, and the origins of the group's artistic philosophy remain within a positivist reading of their master's work.

2 "Un tas de farceurs qui voudraient nous refaire le catholicisme." G. Flaubert, *L'Education sentimentale* (1869), in *Oeuvres* (1952), 2:169.

3 "L'apôtre de quelque vérité, l'organe du Très-Haut qui se sert de lui." H. de Balzac, "Des artistes," *La Silhouette* 2, no. 5 (22 April 1830):34.

THE REASSERTION OF POSITIVISM: *LE PRODUCTEUR*

In many respects, *Le Producteur*'s stance marks a retreat from the direction Saint-Simon had taken in his later works to embrace a positivist ideology promoting reason, science, and industry. This retrenchment encouraged a return to the functional justification of religion as safeguarding social order and of art as facilitating popular acceptance of reformist initiatives. The extended domain offered to the artist in the *Dialogue* seems to have shrunk, reducing him again to the less exalted status of *vulgarisateur*. Like religion, so the arts are understood to inculcate an ideology emanating from the ruling elite, appealing to the same mechanisms of sentiment to achieve their effect. This circumscribed role is spelled out in an early discussion of art's role where the sciences are said to determine "the theory of natural laws on which are based 1) the form and extent of man's action on external nature; 2) the laws governing his moral and political relations," whereas the arts are to "determine actions by feelings, and focus intelligence through pleasure."[4]

Delegation of responsibility for moral and political concerns to the scientist derives from a reassertion of his unique rational penetration and a concomitant demotion of the sentimental perception of the artist. Although the *Dialogue* had suggested that the latter's characteristics could be profitably exploited through his active contribution to social management, Saint-Simon's earliest disciples generally subordinate both art and religion to science and restrict them to the auxiliary role of promoting popular receptivity toward rationally inspired initiatives. Though this mediating function is still deemed vital in securing progressive change, the artist now assumes a largely passive role as an agent of the *savant*, with most commentators explicitly rejecting any suggestion that he intervenes in the process of social innovation. Thus Adolphe Garnier states: "Let us not forget that literature and the arts are entirely passive; that they are incapable of representing a moral system before its foundation, or of anticipating a social form of which, in any event, they are only the reflexion or expression."[5]

This revised assessment informs the narrowly functionalist stance adopted by many of the journal's critics. Though literary reviews predomi-

[4] "La théorie des lois naturelles sur laquelle se basent (1) le mode et l'étendue de l'action de l'homme sur la nature extérieure; (2) les lois de ses rapports moraux et politiques"; "déterminer les actions par les sentiments, et de fixer l'intelligence par le plaisir." A. Cerclet, "Considérations philosophiques sur la littérature," *Prod.* 1 (1825): 60, 58.

[5] "N'oublions pas que la littérature et les arts sont entièrement passifs; qu'ils ne peuvent représenter un système moral avant qu'il soit établi, ni devancer une forme sociale, dont ils ne sont, dans tous les cas, que le reflet ou l'expression." A. Garnier, "Le Salon des industriels," *Prod.* 1 (1825): 524.

nate, some consideration is given to visual art[6] and here the need for contemporaneity and the promotion of international understanding are major themes. Arguing that the arts should be used to "encourage society down the modern route it must follow,"[7] early Saint-Simonian commentators castigate academic classicism[8] and call for a visual vocabulary capable of representing the problems, outlooks, and achievements of the present. Garnier, for example, proposes a reappraisal of natural beauty, which will break with eighteenth-century admiration for the sublime and the pastoral, and instead cultivate appreciation of landscape dominated by human industry. His assertion that "we must recognize that society too has its poetic side"[9] accords with the group's commitment to an art that will contribute toward fostering an industrial society of global dimensions, with the artist promoting popular regard for the progressive value of labor. In line with these priorities, the commemoration of "the heroes of peace and philanthropy"[10] becomes an important area of public edification, glorifying figures more truly devoted to general welfare than the monarchs and churchmen traditionally memorialized. In inspiring emulation of such benefactors, artists serving an industrial regime are seen as surpassing purely formal considerations to forge an art that is both contemporary and socially beneficial:

> Sculptors will then raise monuments to great men of peace; painting will reproduce their features and actions, since painters will appreciate that their mission is not to demonstrate their ability to produce a torso or draw a naked leg but to develop moral truths through the charm and influence of their talent; and they will no longer be afraid of using bourgeois dress in history paintings.[11]

Rather than representing a dynamic source of inspiration in itself, art is here alotted a didactic function entirely compatible with prevailing practice. Yet this restricted understanding of art's power encountered limited, though growing, opposition within the pages of *Le Producteur* as reason's preeminence over sentiment was challenged. Symptomatic of a more fundamental

[6] See J. Allier, "Exposition des ouvrages de David," *Prod.* 3 (1826): 252–64.

[7] "Encourager la société dans la route moderne qu'elle doit suivre." Garnier, "Le Salon des industriels," 509.

[8] See L. Halévy, "Première Lettre au directeur," *Prod.*, 1 (1825): 129.

[9] "Il faut reconnaître que la société a aussi son côté poétique." A. Garnier, "Du beau dans la nature sauvage et du beau dans la société," *Prod.* 3 (1826): 506.

[10] "Les héros de la paix et de la philanthropie." J. Allier, "Notices biographiques sur les industriels célèbres," *Prod.* 1 (1825): 26.

[11] "Alors les statuaires dresseront des monuments aux grands hommes pacifiques; la peinture reproduira leurs traits et leurs actions, car le peintre comprendra que sa mission n'est pas de montrer qu'il sait faire un torse et dessiner une jambe nue; mais de développer les vérités morales, par le charme et l'influence de son talent; et il ne redoutera plus de faire des tableaux d'histoire, avec des costumes bourgeois." Garnier, "Le Salon des industriels," 519.

doctrinal reorientation, this move credited the arts with the capacity to anticipate—and, indeed, initiate—change within society, an assertion that reveals a source of tension with the liberal positivists who had first claimed Saint-Simon's inheritance. Culminating in the movement's elevation as a new religion, this shift away from reason toward more intuitive modes of cognition was principally engineered by Prosper Enfantin, under whose guidance the positivist legacy was decisively rejected.

PROSPER ENFANTIN AND THE REHABILITATION OF SENTIMENT

In the months immediately following his adoption of Saint-Simonianism Enfantin's correspondence reveals a positivist bias and open skepticism over the mystical tone of Saint-Simon's later work.[12] At this stage, Enfantin prioritizes exploitation of the *savant*'s social potential and expresses uncertainty over the auxiliary role of religion and sentiment, confessing to Pichard, a sympathizer in the provinces, "since I don't really understand religious feeling, as the people might experience it, I don't know in what language they should be spoken to, to move them in society's interest."[13] While refuting accusations of materialism, and assuring his correspondent of the arts' unprecedented prestige in Saint-Simonian society, he nonetheless emphasizes their dependence on initiatives originating with the *savant*: "In order for artists, writers, and poets to popularize a doctrine, it must be clothed in the authority of the thinker; this is the first step."[14]

Signs of a change of heart emerge in the "Avertissement" inserted in the second volume of *Le Producteur* at the time of Enfantin's appointment as editor. Here the arts are identified with "the vivid expression of moral sentiments" and are accorded a potential ability to "contribute powerfully to tightening social bonds, or to increasing their strength by extending them."[15] This acknowledgment coincides with a more general rehabilitation of sentiment that alienated positivist sympathizers from the group. As this contingent disappeared, so Enfantin and Bazard took on increasing

[12] See letter to Pichard, 26 November 1825, Arsenal Ms. 7643:15, where, commenting on the role of religion in the *Nouveau Christianisme*, he comments, "je vous avouerai que c'est un sujet où je me sens peu de dispositions à suivre Saint-Simon."

[13] "Ne me rendant pas bien compte du sentiment religieux, tel que le peuple peut l'éprouver, je ne sais pas quelle langue il faut lui parler, pour l'émouvoir dans l'intérêt de la société." Ibid.

[14] "Pour que les artistes, les littérateurs, les poètes, popularisent une doctrine, il faut qu'elle soit revêtue de l'autorité des savants; et c'est le premier pas à faire." Ibid., 14.

[15] "L'expression vive des sentiments moraux"; "Contribuer puissamment à resserrer le lien social, ou à l'étendre pour augmenter sa force." P. Enfantin, "Avertissement," *Prod.* 2 (April 1826): 628–29. For attribution, see *O.S.S.E.*, 1:176.

power, formally recognized in 1829 with their elevation as *pères* presiding over a hierarchical following of disciples. This promotion marked the climax of a tendency, apparent in *Le Producteur* before its collapse in 1826, to cultivate religious overtones as a means of enhancing the movement's influence over sentiment. Rather than being considered inherently inferior to reason and useful only in facilitating acceptance of reformist initiatives, sentiment now acquires more positive connotations as religious pretensions supplant Enfantin's initial reserve over Saint-Simon's mysticism. On one level, this rehabilitation relates to changes in the group's propaganda methods; the lecture series, initiated in 1828, aimed to promote conversion through persuasive effect rather than rational appeal, thus apparently overcoming the obstacle that bourgeois self-interest had posed to the more abstract presentation of *Le Producteur*. More fundamentally, however, the elevation of sentiment must be related to the group's interpretation of ideas prevalent in contemporary physiological theory.

Though disputed by figures such as Bichat, claims by Cabanis and the Idéologues that the sentiments could be modeled and controlled by environmental manipulation had implications for social hygiene that the Saint-Simonians were quick to appreciate. In a series of highly complimentary articles for *Le Producteur* in 1826, Philippe Buchez introduced the ideas of Tracy and Cabanis and argued that closer investigation of man's behavioral patterns would allow elaboration of a positivist moral code.[16] Such speculation fueled a belief that scientific anatomization of the sentiments would enable the arts to attain the status of positive sciences, and allow the artist to manipulate particular effects with a sure knowledge of their power to modify actions and beliefs. As Léon Halévy predicted as early as 1825:

> The time is coming when the painter, musician, and poet, having reached the peak of their powers of feeling, will possess the capacity to move or to please with as great a certainty as today the mathematician is able to solve geometrical problems or the chemist to decompose a particular substance. It is then that the moral aspect of society will have been definitively established; no longer will there be provisionality or crisis in the fine arts or politics, since ethics will have finally attained the rank that the present state of the human spirit so imperiously demands and will have become a science like physics.[17]

[16] See P. J. B. Buchez, "De la physiologie," *Prod.* 3 (1826): 122–34, 264–81, 459–79, where he argues that physiology can "fournir une base positive à la morale individuelle" and help "organiser et à surveiller l'hygiène publique" (132).

[17] "L'époque approche où le peintre, le musicien, le poète qui sera parvenu à l'entier développement de sa faculté de sentir possèdera, d'une manière aussi certaine, la puissance de plaire et d'émouvoir qu'un mathématicien possède maintenant celle de résoudre un problème de géometrie ou un chimiste de décomposer un corps quelconque. C'est qu'alors la partie morale de la société sera définitivement constitutée; il n'y aura plus ni dans les beaux-arts, ni en politique de provisoire ni de crise, parce que la morale aura prise enfin le caractère réclamé

This highly instrumental attitude toward sentiment undergoes radical change as a result of Enfantin's intervention. Reversing earlier interpretations of psycho-physiological research, which retained a conviction in the superiority of reason, he promotes sentiment as an integral and equal aspect of human makeup. Epistemological commitment to deductive, a posteriori reasoning is now balanced by an elevation of inductive, a priori thought grounded in sentiment, a shift that, for example, allows Saint-Simon to be described as "even more a poet than a thinker."[18] Reason and sentiment are now conceived as operating in complementary domains, exploitation of which promises a new understanding of the nature of God, revealed at once through the empirical researches of science and the inspirational revelation of sentiment.[19] Ultimately, Enfantin foresees a synthesis of the two faculties, with science flourishing through the exploration of inductive forms of thought, while religion and art attain quasi-scientific understanding of human emotion.

This rehabilitation of sentiment crucially affected Saint-Simonian conceptions of the social domain and had a particular impact on their approach to religion and to art. In Enfantin's eyes, sentiment becomes the key to social organicism, its sympathetic mechanisms countering individualism and promoting an altruistic regard for general well-being upon which cooperative association could be built.[20] Enfantin's new-found conviction in religion's essential role in reinforcing social cohesion led the group toward a position far in advance of the humanitarian faith of Saint-Simon's *Nouveau Christianisme*, since, as Eugène Rodrigues observed, "the sacred fire of enthusiasm is not lit in the feeble hearth of philanthropy."[21] Christianity, moreover, with its rejection of worldly values, was judged incompatible with the materialism implicit in promoting industry. Identifying the Old Testament with matter and the New with spirit, the Saint-Simonians established a parallel between these two currents and the antithesis of sentiment and reason, and called for a new faith to synthesize the two. Such a synthesis was conceived

---

impérieusement pour elle par l'état actuel de l'esprit humain et sera devenue science comme la physique." L. Halévy, review of *Les Martyrs de Souli* by Népomucène Lemercier, *Prod.* 1 (1825): 83.

[18] "Poète avant d'être savant." *Doctrine de Saint-Simon. Exposition. Première année*, ed. C. Bouglé and E. Halévy (1924), 193.

[19] See P. Enfantin, "Lettre du Père à Bailly sur le sentiment religieux" (1827), in *O.S.S.E.*, 24:140–58.

[20] See Bazard, *Doctrine de Saint-Simon. Exposition de la deuxième année* (1829–30), in *O.S.S.E.*, 42:341–45.

[21] "Le feu sacré de l'enthousiasme ne s'allume pas au chétif foyer de la philanthropie." E. Rodrigues, *Lettres sur la religion et sur la politique* (1829), cited in introduction to *Exposition de la première année*, 22. On Rodrigues's crucial contribution to the religious evolution of Saint-Simonianism, see Régnier, "Les Idées et les opinions littéraires des Saint-Simoniens (1825–1835)" (1983), 1:146–47, 153–54.

as rendering meaningless any distinction between the sacred and the secular, so that in the future "not only will [religion] dominate the political sphere, but the political sphere will, as a whole, become a religious institution."[22]

This attitude, which prompted critics to liken the Saint-Simonians to such defenders of theocracy as Bonald and de Maistre,[23] highlights the role of faith in placing "*individual* wills in harmony with the *general* goal, to make them work together for this goal,"[24] and focuses on the figure of the priest in engineering this consensus. Identified through his heightened sentimental nature, the priest's privileged insight into the essence of God and his enhanced sympathy for mankind endow him with a superiority of vision that places him at the apex of society. The earlier mediating role between the *savant* and the masses gives way to broader responsibilities in which other administrative classes are subordinated to his surveillance; from this superior position, the priest oversees the direction of industrial endeavor and inculcates a morality inspired by love and social harmony.[25]

The functions and character ascribed to the priest correspond closely with the role and personality associated with the artist. Though their respective statuses remain open to considerable inconsistency and renegotiation, on occasions their similarity merges into total identity, with the terms *artiste* and *prêtre* being used interchangeably.[26] On one level, this fusion arises from a broad, generic definition of the artist not as somebody engaged in a particular profession, but as an individual whose passionate nature enables him to "enrich his thought with an expressive sympathy: his domain is the heart of other men, which he exploits masterfully for society's benefit."[27]

[22] "Non seulement [la religion] dominera l'ordre politique, mais l'ordre politique sera, dans son ensemble, une institution religieuse." *Exposition de la première année*, 405.

[23] See, for example, Constant's attack in the *R.E.* 29 (January 1826): 432, and—from a former disciple—Jean Reynaud, "De la société saint-simonienne," ibid., 53 (January 1832): 9–36.

[24] "Les volontés *individuelles* en harmonie avec le but *général*, pour les faire concourir sympathiquement vers ce but." *Exposition de la première année*, 402. Italics in original.

[25] "La mission du PRETRE est de rappeler sans cesse aux hommes leur destination, de la leur faire aimer, de leur inspirer les efforts par lesquels ils peuvent l'atteindre, de coordonner ces efforts, de les rapporter à leur fin. L'AMOUR a donc pour expression générale la MORALE, c'est à dire . . . la RELIGION, qui, considérée dans les institutions sociales auxquelles elle donne naissance, embrasse en son entier le système politique." *Exposition de la deuxième année*, 335–36.

[26] See, for example, Enfantin's "Note sur le prêtre de l'avenir," 1829, in *O.S.S.E.*, 17:231–40.

[27] "Enrichir sa pensée d'une expression sympathique: le coeur des autres hommes est son domaine; il l'exploite en maître pour le profit de la société." H. Carnot, "Discours sur les beaux-arts," *Org.* (25 December 1830): 145. The question is explored in P. Régnier, "Les Saint-Simoniens, le prêtre et l'artiste," *Romantisme* 67 (1990): 31–45.

Intention rather than form is thus the crucial identifying characteristic, enabling the Saint-Simonians to equate the artist with the priest through a constellation of shared psychological attributes and allowing the term to be extended to such figures as the orator, who exemplifies the archetype of the Saint-Simonian *artiste* by his persuasive command over his audience's collective will.

On another level, the artist and the priest are conceived as differing historical manifestations of the same phenomenon. During periods dominated by shared religious doctrine, it is the priest who elaborates and articulates the moral code observed by the faithful. In societies where collective belief has been undermined, the artist takes on this ethical role. Through reconciling the sacred and the secular, and resolving the conflict between the antithetical biblical traditions of spirit and matter, the Saint-Simonians hoped to end this historical dialectic and forge a social system in which the artist and the priest would become one and the same:

> Like the priest, the poet's mission has always been to impel the masses toward accomplishing the future of which they sang or preached, which both conjured up most powerfully since they were most enthused by it: in the future, these two functions will be combined, since the greatest *poetry* will also be the most powerful of *sermons*.[28]

The close relationship between artist and priest stresses both the Saint-Simonians' identification of the creative personality with heightened sentiment and their preoccupation with artistic utterance as a medium for transmitting moral and social imperatives. Like the priest, the artist acts as a vital intermediary between the rational *savants* and the *industriels*, ensuring that their more abstract priorities are constantly directed toward concrete social benefits for the greatest number. At the same time, his persuasive powers inculcate harmony and collective endeavor by stirring the masses' enthusiasm for reformist initiatives.

Like the priest, the artist is characterized by an ability to subordinate his personality to the broader interests of society. His work is conceived not as the outcome of a process of personal introspection, but as the result of immersion in and implicit sympathy for the needs and aspirations of others. Creativity constitutes an effacement of self since the sentimental nature of the artist is essentially social. Thus Philippe Buchez, in an article that introduces several points developed by later theorists, argues that the arts "are the

[28] "La mission du poète, comme celle du prêtre, a toujours été d'entraîner les masses vers la réalisation de l'avenir qu'il chantait ou qu'il prêchait, dont ils étaient l'un et l'autre les plus puissants interprètes, parce qu'ils en étaient les plus fortement animés: *l'avenir* confondra ces deux fonctions en une seule; car la plus haute *poésie* sera en même temps la *prédication* la plus puissante." *Exposition de la première année*, 453.

creation of passionate feelings; in other words of the least individual aspect within man."[29]

In this respect, the doctrine's *prédicateurs* themselves exemplify the artistic mentality, exercising persuasive skills in stirringly emotional performances intended to project not their own subjective feelings and beliefs but objective truths whose sentimental appeal should inspire and galvanize their hearers. The anti-individualism implicit in this conception of the artistic personality, consistent with the group's overall emphasis on the individual's subjection to the collective good, provoked accusations of authoritarianism in the contemporary press and, as the following chapter will show, nurtured antipathy toward the movement in artistic circles.

Yet if Saint-Simonianism apparently threatened contemporary glorification of creative subjectivity, it offered in return an exalted notion of the artist's inherent capacities. While Saint-Simon's notion of art as *sacerdoce* had been eclipsed by rationally inclined commentators in *Le Producteur*, their successors were prodigal in promising a "new career to art" in which its practitioners would become "teachers of the human race."[30] As a consequence of the rehabilitation of sentiment and inductive inspiration, the artist is no longer regarded as passively reflecting social currents but becomes a *prophète*, sharing the *savant*'s ability to penetrate the future.[31]

Assumption of this role depended on a radical reappraisal of art's place in the prevailing social structure. Saint-Simonian commentators repeatedly call upon artists to overcome present reliance on the bourgeoisie and to "make words of faith, love, and hope echo in a desolate society."[32] Such a move necessitated a more critical stance toward the *oisifs* on whom they currently depended and greater concentration on the people, whose exploitation they should expose and whose glorious destiny they should paint in enticing colors. In accepting their true social function, artists were promised

[29] "Sont les créations des sentiments passionnés, c'est-à-dire de ce qu'il y a de moins individuel dans l'homme." P. J. B. Buchez, "Quelques Réflexions sur la littérature et les beaux-arts," *Prod.* 4 (1826): 190. A similar point is made in 1828 by Hippolyte Auger in "Les Académies," published in the pro-Saint-Simonian *Le Gymnase*: "le vrai poète n'a pas d'opinion individuelle, il sent comme tous, il est l'organe de tous"; cited in B. Tolley, "A Saint-Simonian Writer: Hippolyte Auger (1797–1881)," *Australian Journal of French Studies* 11 (1974): 300.

[30] "Nouvelle carrière à l'art"; "précepteurs de l'humanité." E. Barrault, "Prédication du 1er mai: l'art," *Le Globe* (2 May 1831): 492; and E. Barrault, *Aux artistes. Du passé et de l'avenir des beaux-arts* (1830), 76, usually described by commentators as his *Appel aux artistes*.

[31] "Sentir le mal de son époque et l'exprimer, concevoir l'avenir, découvrir par inspiration ce que les sciences apprennent, et montrer au grand nombre cette voie de bonheur et d'immortalité, voilà ce qui appartient aux grands talents." Buchez, "Quelques réflexions," 204. As Régnier astutely observes ("Idées et opinions," 1:79–80) the article's inconsistencies regarding the artist's mediating role epitomize prevailing doctrinal tensions between positivism and more speculative projections of the relationship between reason and sentiment.

[32] "Faire retentir dans une société désolée une parole de foi, d'amour et d'espérance." Barrault, "Prédication," 209.

a wide and receptive constituency among the popular classes and an integral role in regenerating the modern world. It is in this light that they are commended by Buchez to "attack what is falling, hasten the destruction of what must perish, and cultivate everything that grows through science and labor."[33]

This renewed sensitivity to the social value of art was translated into a number of practical interventions designed to generate support in intellectual circles. Apart from regular articles in *Le Globe*, the group mounted a lecture series in 1831 specifically intended for artists. Assisted by Baud and Charton, the campaign was directed by the architect Charles Henri, who had made a special point of proselytizing among his colleagues since his conversion in 1830.[34] Henri's efforts were supplemented by Emile Barrault, a young teacher noted for his emotive oratorical style.[35] Barrault had entered the school in 1828 and soon emerged as its principal aesthetic theorist, publishing a detailed doctrinal study, the pamphlet *Aux artistes*, in March 1830.[36] Framed by a sweeping doctrinal interpretation of the history of Western culture and a bleak diagnosis of contemporary artistic ills, the work held out to the potential convert the promise of creative regeneration and future influence, emphasizing doctrinal sympathy for imaginative endeavor and refuting accusations of philistine materialism. Barrault ends with a histrionic appeal for the artist to realize his providential destiny:

> Come to us, then, all of you whose heart is capable of love, whose brow of burning with a noble hope! Let us join our efforts together to impel humanity toward that future, united like the harmonious strings of a single lyre. Let us today begin to sing those holy hymns which posterity will repeat; from now on, the arts are the cult, the artist the priest.[37]

[33] "Attaquer ce qui tombe, hâter ce qui doit périr et élever tout ce qui grandit par la science et le travail." Buchez, "Quelques réflexions," 209.

[34] See P. Enfantin to H. Fournel, 29 March 1830, *O.S.S.E.*, 27:71.

[35] See P. Enfantin to Bailly, April 1830, ibid., 80: "Barrault est notre *prédicateur*, car il n'*expose* pas, il REMUE; il ne se propose pas de *démontrer*, il veut faire SENTIR ce qu'il SENT; il veut faire AIMER ce qu'il AIME."

On Barrault's introduction to the group, see P. Enfantin to Rességuier, 30 November 1827, Arsenal Ms. 7643:134. On his conversion, see P. Enfantin to Rességuier, idem, April 1828, ibid., 154.

[36] An initial attempt was made to publish the *Aux artistes* in the *Revue encyclopédique*; see P. Enfantin to Rességuier, December 1829, *O.S.S.E.*, 26:194–95. The *Appel* had a run of fifteen hundred copies, all of which were sold; see H. Fournel, *Bibliographie saint-simonienne* (1833), 66. His lecture on art of 1 May 1831 was published, in a run of one thousand (ibid., 81).

[37] "Viennent, viennent donc à nous tous ceux dont le coeur sait aimer, et le front s'enflammer d'une noble espérance! Associons nos efforts pour entraîner l'humanité vers cet avenir; unis entre nous, comme les cordes harmonieuses d'une même lyre. Commençons dès aujourd'hui ces hymnes saintes qui seront répétées par la postérité; désormais les beaux-arts sont le culte, et l'artiste est le prêtre." Barrault, *Aux artistes*, 84.

Barrault did not rely on sheer force of rhetoric, however. Rather, the solicitation of artistic support, both here and elsewhere, was constructed around an analysis of cultural history, which formed an integral part of Saint-Simonian philosophy. It is to the group's interpretation of artistic tradition and to its views on the contemporary creative malaise that we now turn.

HISTORICAL THEORY AND THE SOCIAL HISTORY OF ART

Emphasis on the power of sentiment reinforced the theory of historical periodicity first advanced by Saint-Simon. His identification of two antithetical currents, classified as organic and critical periods, was expanded by his followers and used in cultural analysis to refute previous assertions of the steady decline of art caused by reason eclipsing imagination in the unfolding historical process. In an elaboration initiated by Philippe Buchez and extended by Barrault, the movement exploited the organic-critical polarity to examine the arts' changing influence on social practice and to suggest a reconciliation of this historical dialectic in which their persuasive authority could be harnessed to promote harmony and progress.

Organic societies—polytheistic Greece and early Catholic Europe provided the central examples—were characterized by social cohesion, stable political and economic stratification, and an ideological system, rooted in religion, commanding universal compliance. By contrast, the critical eras of the Roman Empire and the post-Reformation forfeited stability by challenging traditional orthodoxies. Society fragmented as dissent steadily gained ground; the political order crumbled as beliefs that had formerly provided the bedrock of ideological consensus were gradually undermined.

Within this process, the artist played a crucial role. Animated by sentiment during organic eras, his work served to "bind hearts and minds together,"[38] expressing and consolidating religion's popular appeal. In critical periods, however, rationalism and its perceived corollary, individualism, came to the fore, isolating the artist and severing his association with the church.[39] This repudiation of the fundamental tenets of an organic society explained for Saint-Simonian theorists the introversion and alienation characterizing current cultural production.

Commentators asserted that the distinction between artist and priest was most attenuated during organic periods, when their work exploited the

[38] "Relier les coeurs et les esprits." Carnot, "Discours," 146.

[39] On Barrault's refinement of this dialectical model, identifying the survival of organic elements in critical periods, and vice versa, see Régnier, "Idées et opinions," 1:204–5.

impact of aesthetic form on human sentiment to reinforce faith.[40] Parallels were drawn from the group's philosophy of religion to equate Greek idealism with an essentially materialist conception of deity, exemplified by classical preoccupation with the perfection of the human body.[41] The Christian tradition, by contrast, was related to a more abstract art consonant with the theological identification of corporeality with corruption. The Catholic church of the Middle Ages provided the Saint-Simonians with a paradigmatic instance of artists participating in a devotional system that served as the foundation of contemporary ideology. Gothic architecture is repeatedly presented as exemplifying a perfect concordance between form and meaning, the architectonic quality of the cathedral providing a physical metaphor for spiritual values and serving as a setting for the emotionally charged ceremony of the mass. As Barrault comments in *Aux artistes*: "At the sight of these Gothic structures whose daring architecture seems to carry our gaze, our hopes, and promises up to heaven, can we avoid feeling a holy enthusiasm?"[42]

This susceptibility to the Gothic as a style attuned to its social and religious setting and outstanding in its solicitation of the believer's emotions grows out of remarks made by Saint-Simon himself. Though the glorification of medieval culture underlines innate parallels with traditionalist currents, comparison with such a Catholic apologist as Chateaubriand points up significant differences in aesthetic stance. While *Le Génie du christianisme* prefigures Saint-Simonian emphasis on the sentimental manifestations of faith in art and literature, Chateaubriand displays a concern with individual experience at variance with the later group's emphasis on the social dimension of art. His aesthetic preferences, moreover, favor such baroque monuments as St. Peter's or Les Invalides, and his remarks on the Gothic are brief and relatively lukewarm.[43] In this respect, Saint-Simonian medievalism represents the enthusiasm of a younger generation, echoed in the work of such romantics as Michelet, Hugo, Nanteuil, and Delacroix, and anticipating growing interest in the period within Catholic circles, apparent in the investigations of Montalembert, Rio, Ozanam, and—emerging out of Saint-Simonianism itself—of Philippe Buchez and his school.[44]

[40] See Buchez, "Quelques réflexions," 194.

[41] See Carnot, "Discours," 147.

[42] "A la vue de ces édifices gothiques dont l'architecture hardie semble emporter jusqu'au ciel nos regards, nos voeux et nos espérances, pouvons-nous nous défendre d'une sorte de sainte ardeur?" Barrault, *Aux artistes*, 17.

[43] See F. R. de Chateaubriand, *Le Génie du christianisme* (1802; reprint, 1966), 1:399–401.

[44] Michelet's exaltation of the "mystère pétrifié" of the Gothic cathedral in his chapter "La Passion comme principe d'art au moyen âge" (*Histoire de France*) dates from 1831. Montalembert published his article "De l'état actuel de l'art religieux en France" in 1837, Rio his *De la poésie chrétienne* in 1836. See exhibition catalog, *Le "Gothique" retrouvé avant Viollet-le-Duc*, Paris, Hôtel de Sully (1979–80), 61–64.

Sympathy for the Gothic as a perfect expression of organic faith contrasts with the school's negative assessment of art produced during critical eras. The ideological fragmentation of these periods was identified with the artist's retreat from a mass public to cultivate a small group of cognoscenti. This loss of public purpose was blamed for the demise of such monumental forms as the epic and the impoverishment of art's conceptual vocabulary in the absence of commonly shared beliefs on which it could draw. No longer supported by a coherent social edifice, art reputedly became either a medium of dissent or an inward-looking expression of personal feeling whose ever greater technical proficiency scarcely concealed a dwindling capacity to communicate significant moral meaning. All of these problems were discerned in a particularly acute form in contemporary society, which was diagnosed as having entered a phase of terminal crisis since the Revolution, exacerbated by uncoordinated industrial expansion. In branding the current situation as one of senile decay in which tensions far surpassed those normally characterizing critical periods, the Saint-Simonians sought confirmation in a survey of the artistic climate. Examination of the literary scene in particular served to corroborate their pessimistic prognosis. Here a pervasive cynicism and morbidity were highlighted as evidence of a nihilistic perversion of sentiment, a repressed and introverted "sensibilité refoulée sur elle-même," which stood in stark contrast to the detached rationalism typical of critical periods.[45]

Symptomatic of this sense of impotence were the formalism and eclecticism that commentators identified as the most disabling features of contemporary production. While formalism signified the artist's retreat from moral engagement into solipsistic gratification, eclectic tendencies were interpreted as further proof of art's abandonment of its rightful social role. Saint-Simonian emphasis on the interdependence between specific artistic forms and prevailing ideological systems promoted profound hostility to the plundering of the past for creative inspiration. The "eclectic mixture, lacking in unity or character"[46] perceived in modern art was read as a stylistic counterpart to contemporary ideological incoherence, which compromised the very possibility of producing works of universal meaning. Incapable of discovering a conceptual repertoire or stylistic range adequate to the present, artists stood accused of indiscriminately exploiting the past in a way that testified their indifference toward art's specificity as a social phenomenon. Barrault points to the rise of museums to confirm this assertion, seeing their contents as petrified objects of curiosity deprived of their former capacity to communicate meaning: "Museums are veritable catacombs littered with artistic monuments which once upon a time touched the imagination; into

[45] See Barrault, *Aux artistes*, 62.

[46] "Mélange hétérogène, dénué d'unité et de caractère." Carnot, "Discours," 148.

them are emptied temples, churches, and public buildings where once these statues and paintings, wreathed in a sort of aura, excited intense enthusiasm."[47]

Antipathy toward eclecticism grew out of a perspective on cultural history which insisted on the artist's responsiveness to his social environment. Because of its enhanced sensibility, the creative personality was said to enjoy the capacity of anticipating the emergence of currents still dormant in the world around it. Reference to this prophetic gift allowed the Saint-Simonians to explain why the organic periods they identified with artistic excellence did not always coincide with the accepted canon. Thus the flowering of the High Renaissance, which in doctrinal terms marked the eclipse of medieval organicism and the birth of the modern critical era, was interpreted in terms of artistic anticipation, with the illusionistic virtuosity of Raphael and Michelangelo's physicality being seen as premonitions of approaching materialism.[48] The High Renaissance appears as a brief but fertile meeting between the spiritualism of a dying Catholic tradition and the more worldly concerns of the post-Reformation:

> Thus great artists, men whose prophetic gaze is ceaselessly cast toward the future, were among the first to display the need to abandon an incomplete doctrine through introducing into their works the element opposed to this doctrine; this also explains the more intimate harmony between material beauty and spiritual beauty which suffuses their compositions.[49]

This antithesis between spirit and matter complements and overlays the dichotomy between reason and sentiment in Saint-Simonian historical periodicity, the former identified with Christian civilization, the latter with polytheistic societies. Emphasis on muscular activities such as hunting and war in the pre-Christian world encourages theorists to identify their belief systems—and hence their art—with physicality as embodied in the human form.[50] By contrast, they interpret Christian asceticism as having inspired a rejection of the material world. Such an attitude serves as the basis for an attack on the Middle Ages' failure fully to exploit nature for human good

[47] "Les musées sont de véritables catacombes où gisent pêle-mêle tous les monuments des arts, qui autrefois ont remué les imaginations; là se vident les temples, les églises, les édifices où naguère ces statues et ces peintures, entourés d'une sorte d'auréole, excitaient un vif enthousiasme." Barrault, *Aux artistes*, 69.

[48] Carnot, "Discours," 146.

[49] "Ainsi, les grands artistes, les hommes dont le regard prophétique s'élance incessament vers l'avenir, auraient, des premiers, témoigné le besoin de quitter une doctrine incomplète par l'introduction dans leurs ouvrages de l'élément opposé à cette doctrine; et de là en même temps l'harmonie plus intime qui règne dans leurs compositions, entre la beauté matérielle et la beauté spirituelle." Ibid., 147.

[50] See Barrault, "Prédication," 491.

and as an explanation for the Primitives' anti-illusionism and the etheriality of the Gothic cathedral:

> Life was nothing but an unending battle between the *soul* and the *body*, *spirit* and *matter*, *spirit* and *flesh*. The *body*, *matter*, *flesh*, *riches* were all vile objects of contempt, were *sinful*, the devil's part. Christian perfection consisted in taming *matter*, in mastering the *flesh*, in freeing the *soul* as much as possible from its ties to the *body*.[51]

This antimaterialism ostensibly withered as the Reformation ushered in a more positive appreciation of the natural world. Both the commercial expansion of such societies as Holland and Venice and the sumptuousness of their cultures provided evidence of this change and allowed Saint-Simonian commentators to offer a social explanation for mutations in religious painting and the rise of landscape and genre during the seventeenth century.[52]

Such speculations demonstrate doctrinal attempts to forge a social history of style around the spirit-matter antithesis. Form, as well as content, is treated as reflecting, and sometimes anticipating, the broader evolution of civilization. In line with Saint-Simonian historical theory, all such changes stem from an understanding of religion as the basis of ideology, prevailing conceptions of God fundamentally affecting human perceptions of nature. As investigation of the group's later discussions of art will show, the spirit-matter antithesis, first elaborated by Barrault in May 1831,[53] became increasingly important in underwriting an aesthetic that moved beyond a commitment toward overt didacticism. In terms of their analysis of contemporary art, it also offered a theoretical framework for understanding the contrasting tendencies represented by classicism and romanticism.

Accused of "abstraction" and anti-illusionism, classicism represented a secular variant of the spiritual tradition, condemned for its tenuous appreciation of nature, its etiolated interpretation of human relations and its reduction of drama and conflict into a formal vocabulary lacking any sense of immediacy.[54] Attitudes toward romanticism were more ambiguous. Al-

[51] "La vie n'était qu'une lutte perpétuelle entre l'*âme* et le *corps*, l'*esprit* et la *matière*, l'*esprit* et la *chair*. Le *corps*, la *matière*, la *chair*, la *richesse* étaient choses viles, réprouvées, étaient le *péché*, étaient dévolus à Satan. La perfection chrétienne consistait à dompter la *matière*, à maîtriser la *chair*, à dégager le plus possible l'*âme* de ses liens avec le *corps*." Anonymous, "Le Salon," *Le Globe* (12 May 1831): 531.

[52] See *Le Globe* (11 June 1831): 649.

[53] In his *prédication* "L'Art" of 1 May 1831, published in *Le Globe* on 2 May 1831.

[54] "On a devant soi une *figure*, une *image*, mais point de *réalité*; des lignes, des ombres, disposées conformément à une convention arrêtée; mais des hommes, des édifices, la nature, point. Il faut pour comprendre un tableau, pour ne pas être trompé par la technique actuel, avoir subi une éducation particulière, fort simple à la vérité; être familier avec ces *signes*, avoir dressé les yeux à lire cette *écriture*." "Le Salon," *Le Globe* (12 May 1831): 531.

though certain literary currents were favorably received,[55] its doctrines and many of its preoccupations offended the Saint-Simonian sensibility. The cult of individualism, lyrical introspection, and stylistic archaism smacked of the artist's amoral refusal to acknowledge his social responsibilities. Romanticism was described as anarchic, justified insofar as it questioned an outmoded status quo, but blameworthy in its incapacity to offer any constructive alternatives—"Everyone acts as they see fit, following chance, rejecting all past rules without substituting new ones."[56] More positively, the movement won credit for initiating a reappraisal of nature, testified in the vogue for landscape, which ostensibly foreshadowed a resurgence of materialism favorable to industrial growth.

In contrast to Saint-Simonian literary criticism, writings on the visual arts tend to be predominantly theoretical, a distinction largely explained by the infrequency of Salon exhibitions before 1831.[57] Yet, as we shall see, commentary in the Saint-Simonian press did provide an opportunity to survey the state of contemporary art and to exploit its analysis in a critique of social deficiencies.

ASSESSMENTS OF CONTEMPORARY PRODUCTION

The Saint-Simonians' diagnosis of art during the early years of the July Monarchy is summed up by Marie-Camille de G. in her survey of the 1834 exhibition for the school's feminist journal *La Femme nouvelle*:

> On leaving the museum, a sad thought strikes one. Battles, shipwrecks, hangings, landscapes, portraits, thousands of paintings, and so little thought of the future! Unimaginable efforts of draftsmanship and color, a prodigious outpouring of talent to paint only outworn and sterile scenes.[58]

Such remarks were endorsed, with differing emphasis, by critics across the political spectrum throughout this period, yet for the Saint-Simonians

[55] See P. Régnier, "Les Saint-Simoniens et le mouvement romantique," in *Romantismes et socialismes en Europe (1800–1848)*, ed. A. Billaz and U. Ricken (1987), 207–23.

[56] "Chacun agit à sa guise, se laissant aller au hasard, rejetant toutes les règles du passé, sans y substituer aucune." Anonymous, "Le Salon," *Le Globe* (12 May 1831): 531. These remarks paraphrase Hugo's introduction to *Hernani* of 1830.

[57] The review of the 1831 Salon was suspended after two preliminary articles devoted to theoretical issues; Arsenal Mss. 15031, vol. 6, nos. 857 and 858, two rough drafts of an account of the exhibition by Alexis Petit, may suggest authorship of the published text.

[58] "En sortant du Musée, il vous vient une pensée triste. Des batailles, des naufrages, des échafauds, des paysages, des portraits, des milliers de tableaux, et si peu de pensées d'avenir! Des efforts inouïs de dessin et de couleur, une dépense prodigieuse de talent pour ne peindre que des scènes usées et stériles." Marie-Camille de G., "Salon de 1834," *La Femme nouvelle. Tribune des femmes* 2 (April 1834): 162.

failings in contemporary art took on particular social resonance. Though sharing a perception of the transitional status of current production with such bourgeois critics as Fabien Pillet and Louis Peisse—himself an early contributor to *Le Producteur*—the school's rejection of liberal reformism encouraged calls for radical artistic transformation, which echoed their advocacy of far-reaching political change. While liberal critics related art's lack of direction to the unsteady progress toward constitutional monarchy, and republicans asserted the need for a revolution in productive relations to resolve the social impasse affecting cultural life, the Saint-Simonians called for a more dramatic remedy, involving divine intervention channeled through the *Père suprême*.[59]

In line with their emphasis on the social integration of the arts during such organic periods as the Middle Ages, Saint-Simonian critics attributed current cultural decline to artists neglecting the edification of a mass public to divert a small and unrepresentative elite of *oisifs*. Financial pressures meant that many artists "abandon art for the production line"[60]—an accusation of commercial debasement, which, as we shall see, was widely voiced on the left and indeed often recurs in critical discourse throughout the period. Such material imperatives, consequent on an ill-organized and individualistic capitalist regime, are blamed for the modern artist's superficiality:

> He has to sell to live; he works to appeal to the presumed taste of the privileged, repressing his own inclinations. And he produces everything that clutters our exhibitions: those endless odalisques produced for the boudoirs of old lechers; those endless battle scenes, whose glittering uniforms are designed to pique the imagination of our mustachioed young idlers, veterans of Longchamp or the Parc de St Cloud.[61]

In an ironic deflection of accusations leveled at the movement itself, Saint-Simonian critics accused the bourgeois outlook of the monarchy of exacerbating this situation, fostering a narrow utilitarianism indifferent to all aspects of social life other than commerce and industry. Highlighting the monarch's traditional role in directing the arts toward the consolidation of social cohesion,[62] they argued that the budgetary constraints imposed in

59 See ibid., 159.

60 "Abdiquent l'art et se font industriels." Anonymous, "Le Salon," *Le Globe* (12 May 1831): 531.

61 "Il faut qu'il vende pour vivre: il travaille au goût présumé des privilégiés, laissant taire ses propres penchants. Et il produit tout ce qui encombre nos expositions: ces éternelles odalisques faites pour les boudoirs de vieux débauchés; ces éternelles batailles, qui par le brillant de leurs uniformes doivent exalter les imaginations de nos jeunes *oisifs* à moustache, qui ont fait la campagne de Longchamp ou du Parc de St Cloud." Anonymous, "Activité des oisifs," *Le Globe* (21 April 1831): 448.

62 See Anonymous, "La Liste civile et les beaux-arts," *Le Globe* (14 October 1831): 1148.

1830 with the introduction of the Civil List, together with the new king's characteristically bourgeois literal-mindedness, militated against the crown fulfilling its obligations as a cultural leader.[63] Though similar misgivings were frequently reiterated during the early years of the July Monarchy,[64] for the Saint-Simonian press the crown merely exemplifies a broader sacrifice of common values in the pursuit of individual wealth and factional interests.

Such sensitivity to the ideological debasement of art further informs the school's strictures on contemporary production. Commemorative monuments, in particular, provide a focus for attacks on the manipulation of art by successive regimes. The capital's streets come to symbolize the disorder paralyzing society, with their relics of contradictory political tendencies, ranging from the Restoration's attempted reassertion of *la monarchie féodale* in the Expiatory Monument to Louis-Philippe's accommodation of Bonapartism in his proposed memorial to Napoleon.[65] Arguing that such works were irrelevant to current concerns and merely served to incite popular disgust over the betrayal of the nation's leaders, Saint-Simonian critics recommended their relegation to a museum, where their noxious political connotations would be neutralized.

Such a remedy underlines the group's commitment to contemporaneity and its entrenched opposition to the exploitation of values deemed irrelevant to the modern world. Thus in 1831, *Le Globe* willingly endorsed proposals to pull down Saint-Germain-l'Auxerrois in order to widen the road, arguing "we should allow all the old monuments of the past to be demolished without sorrow; their destruction is as progressive and providential as the fall of Charles X."[66] Insistence on the relationship between the work of art and the society it addresses heavily qualifies admiration for Gothic architecture; emphasis on the historical specificity of style precludes the preservation or rehabilitation of forms out of keeping with current social need.

Preoccupied with the past and confused by the political aimlessness of the present, the arts stood accused of failing to offer any positive political inspiration and the artist castigated for his jaundiced outlook, which either gloried in exposing human weakness or shunned contact with the modern world entirely. Critics within the movement militated for a renewal of artistic engagement, calling for the treatment of themes directly related to

[63] See Anonymous, "De l'avenir des beaux-arts dans les gouvernements à bon marché," *Le Globe* (28 June 1831): 770.

[64] See, for example, A. Jal, *Salon de 1833. Les Causeries du Louvre* (1833), 103; A. Barbier, *Salon de 1836 (1836)*, 37.

[65] See Anonymous, "Des monuments publics de la Restauration," *Le Globe* (1 March 1831): 237; Anonymous, "Concours pour la statue de Napoléon," ibid. (12 June 1831): 656.

[66] "Laissons sans douleur démolir tous ces vieux monuments du passé; cette destruction est aussi progressive, tout aussi providentielle que la chute du trône de Charles X." Anonymous, "Saint-Germain-l'Auxerrois," *Le Globe* (18 July 1831): 800. Enfantin similarly endorsed plans to demolish one of the pyramids to construct a barrage across the Nile.

modern life and its injustices. Thus Marie-Camille de G. advocates a cultural initiative in support of female emancipation and directs the artist toward the miseries inflicted on the working class:

> Make your canvas weep, moan, and cry, so that we see this world in all its anguish, tortures, and wounds, concealed by civilization behind a deceptive smile! Let us hear the terrible scream of hunger, and the prostitute's weeping! Let your paintings be a mirror reflecting all the agonies of the poor, focusing them so sharply that they melt the iron that encases the rich man's heart, and chokes it so tightly that its beating is stifled.[67]

Saint-Simonianism offered itself as a creed allowing the artist to come to terms with the responsibilities he had so conspicuously shirked in current society. The appeals directed at him repeatedly echo Marie-Camille de G.'s demands in their calls for culture to endorse the progressive movement. Yet such advocacy of overtly didactic works constitutes only one aspect of Saint-Simonian aesthetics. Under the influence of Enfantin the movement gradually turned away from explicit moralism and evolved a more flexible understanding of form as an essential element in aesthetic effect. Such transformations were grounded in ideas emerging from the religious philosophy propounded by Enfantin in the early 1830s at the time of his dispute with Bazard and the retreat to Ménilmontant.

TOWARD A NEW CONCEPTION OF FORM

The crucial event coloring the development of Saint-Simonianism under the July Monarchy was its declaration as a new religion in December 1829. This move had direct implications for the group's aesthetic, both in the reduced role it reserved for the artist and in the revised understanding of form resulting from the rehabilitation of matter in its expanded theological program. In order fully to appreciate the ramifications of this change, we must first examine the conception of deity elaborated by the school in the early 1830s.

The group's conception of God owed much to Saint-Simon's distinction between organic and critical periods, upon which Enfantin and his followers isolated a series of antitheses running throughout human history.[68]

[67] "Faites . . . pleurer, gémir, crier votre toile qu'on y voie tout ce monde d'angoisses, de tortures, de déchirements que la civilisation voile d'un sourire menteur! qu'on y entende les cris terribles de la faim, et les sanglots de la prostitution! Que vos tableaux soient un miroir qui réfléchisse toutes les douleurs du pauvre, et les concentre sur un foyer qui fonde le fer, qui emboîte le coeur du riche et l'enserre si étroitement que tout battement soit étouffé." de G., "Salon," 164.

[68] This analysis is elaborated in the two series of doctrinal lectures of 1829–30 and modified by Enfantin in the *Enseignements* held between November 1831 and February 1832; see *O.S.S.E.*, vols. 14, 16, and 17.

Polytheism and Christianity provided the two poles for elaborating a network of oppositions which resulted from the partial understanding of God within each tradition. Polytheistic materialism was contrasted with the spiritualism of Christianity and this in turn related to the antithesis of industry and science—the former concerned with the exploitation of nature, the latter an abstraction of it. In the sphere of sexual relations, a similar disjunction between polytheistic worldliness and Christian asceticism had led to sexual inequality and the inhibiting system of monogamous relationships.[69] Finally, sentiment and reason had been historically opposed within conflicting metaphysical structures whose partiality was blamed for deferring an epistemological union capable of transforming human relations and ameliorating material conditions.

Neither pure matter nor pure spirit, God came to represent for the Saint-Simonians a pantheistic fusion of both these elements: "the UNION of *spirit* and *matter*" which would lead to "the future HARMONY between *ideas* and *acts*."[70] The Saint-Simonians founded their conception of God on the resolution of conflict in synthesis, promoting progress through recognition of the complementary nature of those elements—social, epistemological, sexual, and aesthetic—formerly regarded as incompatible antitheses. Matter and spirit, reason and sentiment, science and art—all were deemed equally essential for arriving at an understanding of God and for mobilizing such understanding in social practice. In God, perfect harmony would be achieved through the synthesis of opposites,[71] a process that, when applied to the concrete domain of politics and economics, ostensibly neutralized the threat of class antagonism.

Such a perception presented God in terms of a trinity—a synthetic element uniting two seemingly opposing forces. Arguing that this trinitarian structure was implicit in the *Nouveau Christianisme*, Enfantin emphasized its importance in perfecting an appreciation of the universal and the social order.[72] Elaboration of the trinity, increasingly prominent after 1829, broadly followed the pattern established by Saint-Simon in his discussion of the social triumvirate of the *artiste*, the *savant*, and the *industriel*. Sentiment, reason, and action, the attributes corresponding to each of these categories, provided the fundamental properties of the divine trinity, with sentiment enjoying pivotal status as the synthetic element uniting the two others. Within the social sphere, the trinitarian model elevated sentiment as a prime

[69] This matter is discussed by Bazard in the sixth lecture of the second series of the "Exposition de doctrine," in *O.S.S.E.*, vol. 42, and developed by Enfantin, notably in the "Premier Enseignement" of 28 November 1831, in *O.S.S.E.*, 14:1–40. This statement coincides with Bazard's secession following his defeat over the issue of sexual libertarianism.

[70] "L'UNION de l'*esprit* et de la *matière*"; "L'HARMONIE qui existera dans l'avenir entre les *idées* et les *actes*." Ibid., 35.

[71] As G. d'Eichthal says of God ("Notes sur le dogme," 1832, Arsenal Ms. 7641:233), "en lui l'*idée* et la *forme*, la *parole* et l'*action* sont harmonieusement confondues."

[72] See P. Enfantin, "Enseignements," 28 November 1831, in *O.S.S.E.*, 14:5.

synthetic force, upon which organicism depends, and allowed the promotion of art as a cardinal value. Thus Enfantin could construct a trinity of "BEAUX-ARTS, science, industrie," with the first element in the series embracing the other two.[73]

The implications of this theological system for the artist's place within society were twofold, not only enhancing his power through affirming his unifying role, but also demoting his social status, as theocratic tendencies in the movement were given full rein. This latter move relates to the authoritarian conception of hierarchy that Enfantin had promoted in the late 1820s and early '30s. Egalitarianism was incompatible with the group's approach to "l'amélioration des conditions de la classe la plus pauvre,"[74] since such improvement was deemed to depend upon an industrial mobilization which only a ruling elite could effectively direct. Emile Péreire, a leading disciple, argues in favor of a controlling *pouvoir spirituel* through reference to recent physiological research pointing to the fundamental disparity of individual capacities: "A spiritual power is necessary, indeed indispensable, since inequalities in mental makeup give rise to a general and hierarchical dependence between individuals who are organized among themselves."[75]

Promotion of a hierarchical social structure, reflected after 1829 in the organization of the school itself, culminated in 1831 with Bazard's secession and acceptance of theocracy as the political system best able to secure stability and cohesion. Enfantin's acclamation as *Père suprême* shifted focus to the priest as possessing an instinctive love of the people and understanding of their interests. His elevation gave formal recognition to an erosion of the artist's status as prophet and guide, which had been underway virtually since the moment Barrault's *Aux artistes* had conjured up its vision of creative preeminence. As religiosity eclipsed purely political aspirations, so the artist's imputed insight paled before the priest's enhanced understanding and persuasive power, which was deemed capable of inspiring total loyalty from the masses in a situation where "love is the principal BOND that unites the *superior* to the *inferior*." As the incarnation of sentiment in its highest form, the priest presides over a merging of the sacred and secular, relegating the artist to the role of popular intermediary:

> The PRIEST IMAGINES the future and provides the RULE linking humanity's *past* destiny with its *future* destiny; in other words, the PRIEST GOVERNS. The artist siezes the priest's thought, translates it into his own language and, incarnating it in every possible form, makes it universally understandable; he reflects

[73] Ibid.

[74] C.-H. de Saint-Simon, *Du système industriel*, in *O.S.S.E.*, 21:167.

[75] "La nécessité, l'indispensabilité d'un pouvoir spirituel résulte de l'inégalité des organisations produisant la dépendance générale et hiérarchique des êtres organisés entre eux." E. Péreire to Rességuier, 13 January 1828, Arsenal Ms. 7643:142.

within himself the world that the priest has created or discovered and, by concentrating it as a symbol, reveals it to all eyes . . . It is through the artist that the priest manifests himself; the *artist*, in short, is the *word* of the PRIEST.[76]

Despite this demotion, the heightened concentration on sentiment nonetheless allowed the artist a prominent role. "Je parle des artistes, c'est presque parler du prêtre," Enfantin announced in 1831,[77] and the school devoted considerable attention to elaborating an aesthetic system whose sway over sentiment would transcend pure didacticism and open up a vastly expanded emotional range to the creative imagination. This program relates directly to the school's metaphysical system and to the identification of contrasting spiritualist and materialist currents in the history of art. Recognition of God as a synthesis of spirit and matter was presented as allowing a reconciliation of these two incomplete traditions in an enriched formal vocabulary, revealing his spiritual presence in the physical aspect of nature. Thus, Barrault had promised in 1830, "henceforth, didacticism will be made more palatable by emotion and the ideal" and "truth and beauty will be reconciled";[78] armed with a complete understanding of God, the artist would learn how to cloak a spiritually elevating message in a physically enticing form.

More concretely, this spiritual synthesis was offered as a solution to the debilitating division between romanticism and classicism, each of which was held to be a complementary, though partial, expression of the same fundamental truth.[79] Present developments ostensibly heralded such a synthesis: a review of Heinrich Heine's 1831 *Salon* remarked approvingly on his appraisal of Léopold Robert as an artist whose work combined Raphaelesque idealism with a sense of physical immediacy.[80] The illusionism of

[76] "L'amour est le LIEN principal qui UNIT le *supérieur* à l'*inférieur*." "Le PRETRE CONÇOIT l'avenir et produit le REGLEMENT qui lie les destinées *passées* de l'humanité à ses destinées *futures*; en d'autres termes, le PRETRE GOUVERNE. L'artiste saisit la pensée du prêtre, il la traduit dans sa langue, et, l'incarnant sous toutes les formes qu'elle peut revêtir, il la rend sensible à tous; il réfléchit en lui le monde que le prêtre a crée ou découvert, et, le réduisant en symbole, il le dévoile à tous les yeux. C'est par l'artiste que le prêtre se manifeste; l'*artiste*, en un mot, est le *verbe* du PRETRE." "Exposition de doctrine," in *O.S.S.E.*, 42:355. Lecture delivered by Bazard on 21 April 1830. For further attenuation of the artist's prophetic power, see Barrault's lecture "Les Femmes," 7 November 1830.

[77] Enfantin, "Enseignements," 3 December 1831, in *O.S.S.E.*, 14:124.

[78] "Désormais le didactique sera vivifié par l'onction, c'est-à-dire par l'émotion et l'idéal"; "le vrai et le beau seront réconciliés." Barrault, *Aux artistes*, 76, 83.

[79] Thus Barrault claims in his "Prédication du 1er mai: l'art," 491: "l'une l'expression de l'intelligence, de la sagesse; l'autre l'expression de la force, de la matière, de la beauté; toutes deux répondent fidèlement aux deux faces sous laquelle Dieu et l'humanité se révèlent à nous, destinées à s'associer à leurs progrès et s'unir dans un art nouveau inspiré par l'amour le plus vaste."

[80] Anonymous, review of "*Gemaeldaustellung in Paris (Salon de 1831 etc.*) par M. Heine; extrait de plusieurs articles du 'Morgenblatt,' " *Le Globe* (2 January 1832): 8.

the diorama and the panorama was also interpreted as marking a rehabilitation of materialism in art and revealing heightened awareness of the natural world. Such trends were seen as premonitions of more far-reaching developments in the future when art would achieve "a representation of human nature and the outside world which is at once palpitating, sensual, and brilliant as well as meditative, dreamy, and contemplative."[81]

The Saint-Simonians promised that clearer understanding of God would help realize these tendencies, overcoming the precedence of abstract *science*, consequent on the Christian spiritualist tradition, and rehabilitating *faire*—the material aspect of artistic technique eclipsed by Catholic asceticism. The revelation of God is thus associated with a rehabilitation of form; understanding God as simultaneously spirit and matter allows the artist to advance pictorial technique through the reconciliation of theory and practice, of rational abstracted knowledge with manual dexterity.[82] In advancing such a prediction, the Saint-Simonians moved beyond any narrowly didactic interpretation of *art social* and foresaw the eventual abolition of distinctions between utilitarianism and formalism. In the future, art would fulfill its social role precisely through its unprecedented exploration of formal properties.

Delineation of the aesthetic realignment offered by an understanding of God as the reconciliation of antinomies focused around discussions held at Ménilmontant in 1832. In elaborating a catechism for the new faith, *Le Livre nouveau*,[83] the group explored art's role in strengthening social organicism and attempted to sketch out a theory of verbal and visual form drawing upon their religious synthesis. Integral to these investigations was the alignment of the spirit-matter dichotomy with male and female characteristics, the former identified with Christian rationalism, the latter with the emotion and spontaneity of polytheistic cultures. In the same way as Enfantin related social renovation to the reconciliation of sexual divisions, so aesthetic renewal came to depend on a fusion of formal elements identified with complementary sexual characteristics. Emphasis on the rehabilitation of feminine qualities, systematically suppressed by Christian spiritualism, gave added theoretical force to an aesthetic in which form played a vital role.

[81] "La reproduction palpitante, charnelle, brillante, en même temps que méditative, rêveuse, contemplative de la nature humaine et du monde extérieur." Anonymous, "Le Salon," *Le Globe* (11 June 1831): 650.

[82] The distinction between *science* and *faire* was first developed by Buchez in 1826 and elaborated in the review of the 1831 Salon.

[83] Notes for *Le Livre nouveau* are in two manuscripts in the Arsenal: the *Procès verbal de séances pour la confection d'un catéchisme* (Ms. 7793) is an account of the initial discussion on 14 July 1832. The text contains numerous corrections and alterations and appears in revised form in Ms. 7641, a transcription made by Enfantin in 1853 of the séances, the *Livre nouveau*, and other contemporary writings. The *Livre nouveau* has recently appeared in a critical edition by Philippe Régnier (1991). The following citations are based on my own transcriptions of manuscript sources.

The male-female antithesis informed doctrinal investigation of language, literature, and music. In their desire for a language possessing "le caractère de l'universalité,"[84] the group distinguished between the rational, spiritualist mode of poetry and the more active, materialist forms of prose. Identifying the former with the male and the latter with the female, a corresponding distinction was elaborated around verbal modes employed in the gospels and the Old Testament and a synthesis of the two traditions proposed.[85] A similar synthesis was sought in literature between the rationalism of classical drama and the emotive immediacy of rhetoric and the novel, and in music between the emotionally compelling *mélodie payenne* and the more abstract *harmonie chrétienne*.[86] In each instance, the fusion of apparently isolated traditions would ostensibly generate new forms capable of exerting a powerfully persuasive effect on both heart and mind.

Such ambitions also underlie consideration of the visual arts, where similar analytical procedures obtain. Here, the spirit-matter antinomy is equated with a dislocation between theoretical knowledge and practical technique, which has produced the antitheses between *dessin* and *couleur*, *peinture* and *décoration*. According to Barrault, the abstracted notion of art engendered by Christianity has promoted male qualities of reason and calculation at the expense of the female values of materiality and spontaneity:

> Women have not . . . been great *painters*, which points to the generally *Christian* character of modern *painting*. Until now, painting has exalted meditation, a tendency imposed by the place accorded to it in monuments and the majority of subjects it had to portray. . . . That is why women have not been tempted to express their inspiration in paint, a medium that also repelled them because of the long preparation it demands. Everything in the art calling for calculation, compositional deliberation, and precisely rendered detail, they have left aside for men.[87]

Barrault identifies the suppressed female aspect of art with the harmonious and decorative use of color in such areas as fashion, cosmetics, and interior design, which allow the "female sensibility" to explore the sensuous qualities of visual experience unconstrained by rationalist preoccupations

[84] Arsenal Ms. 7641:22.

[85] "La langue de l'avenir sera l'*harmonie* de ces deux formes; à cette condition elle sera universelle." Ibid., 23.

[86] Ibid., 43.

[87] "La *femme* n'a pas . . . été grand *peintre* et c'est l'indication du caractère généralement *chrétien* de la *peinture* moderne. La peinture a été jusqu'à présent très exaltante de méditation: la place qui lui était réservée dans les monuments et la plupart des sujets qu'elle avait à traiter lui ont imprimé cette tendance. . . . Aussi la femme n'a-t-elle pas été entraînée à exprimer son inspiration par la peinture dont les lentes préparations devaient d'ailleurs la rebuter. Tout ce qui dans cet art réclame du calcul, des combinaisons étudiées et une précision de détails arrêtés, elle l'a abandonné à l'homme." Ibid., 28–29.

with *sujet* and *dessin* characteristic of the male-dominated fine arts. The merger of these two visual languages promised new expressive possibilities in the plastic arts, with the appearance of techniques capable of encapsulating both aspects of God in forms of unprecedented richness and authority.

In common with Saint-Simon, the disciples' speculation over the visual art most suitable to future society concentrated on religious ceremonial and the secular *fête*, favored for their appeal to all of the senses and their enhanced emotional impact. Through the use of sound, light, color, and a panoply of visual and technical effects, such collective manifestations reputedly served as an unequaled means of galvanizing the people into a united body and sharpening their consciousness of the immanent presence of God. Public ceremony thus represents the site within which religious faith and secular ideology unite and are mutually reinforced in a way reminiscent of doctrinal interpretations of the social authority of medieval Catholicism.

Ecclesiastical precedent underlies the various liturgical ceremonies conceived at Ménilmontant. Here the plastic arts are incorporated into imagined settings, the physical proportions and sensual impact of which far surpass the majesty of the cathedral. Music and language add to the overall effect, transporting the congregation on an irresistible wave of enthusiasm. Past and future, theory and practice, reason and sentiment—all of these dichotomies find resolution in the synthesizing power of God. It is this eradication of conflict in a harmonious synthesis of social, sexual, and aesthetic dichotomies which Barrault highlights in describing the act of worship:

> [The church] will rise and open up its breast to the theater, the pulpit, the forum, and the novel, providing them all with a home. The harmony of these two forms will give birth to the new drama; tradition, the past, and convention will be solemnly praised there under the direction of the genius of *man*. But *prophecy* and the *future*, made *extraordinary* by the inspiration of *woman*, will cast about their dazzling colors and their holy vitality. Painting, music, choreography, speech, rythmical words, *decoration*, *dance*, *mime*, *improvisation*, and free verse will unite to fill all hearts with enthusiasm. Men of *thought*, *intellectuals*, *theoreticians*, and men of *action*, *industrial workers*, *practicians*, will *commune* together in this vast drama, acting simultaneously as spectators and *participants*. The fictions of memory and the fictions of *imagination* will take on an enormous illusionistic power through their *role* in blessing the work of the *present* and through the real presence of the *holy couple*, God's image on earth.[88]

[88] "[L'église] s'élevera et ouvrira son sein au théâtre, à la chaire, au forum, au roman en leur permettant de s'y déployer. De ces deux formes harmonisées naîtra le nouveau drame; la tradition, le passé, la convention y seront glorifiées solenellement, et le génie de l'*homme* y présidera; mais la *prophétie*, l'*avenir*, *extraordinaire* grâce à l'inspiration de la *femme*, y jetteront

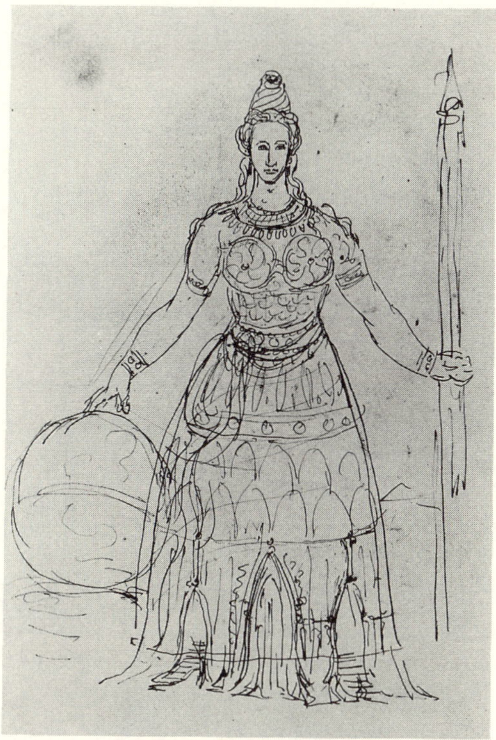

Plate 2. Philippe-Joseph Machereau: *Saint-Simonian Temple,* 1832. Ms. 13910, p. 9v., Bibliothèque de l'Arsenal, Paris.

Barrault's invocation of the splendors of the temple points to art's role in making tangible the spiritual aspect of God, while the materiality of the building itself and the act of worship taking place within its walls evoke his spirituality. Emphasis on physical scale and overwhelming visual effect also emerges in sketches by Philippe-Joseph Machereau (plates 2 and 3), which echo Charles Duveyrier's vision of the temple as a colossal female figure—"la femme Messie"—the pleats of whose skirt form the portals by which the

leurs couleurs éblouissantes et leur sainte pétulance. La peinture, la musique, le geste arrangé, le débit, le verbe rythmé, et le *décor*, la *danse*, la *pantomime*, l'*improvisation*, le verbe libre s'associeront pour verser dans tous les coeurs l'enthousiasme. Et les hommes de *pensée*, les *savants*, les *théoriciens*, et les hommes d'*action*, les *industriels*, les praticiens, à la fois assistants et *personnages*, *communieront* entre eux dans ce drame immense, où les fictions de la mémoire et les fictions de l'*imagination* recevront une puissance d'illusion énorme de leur *lien* avec leur consécration d'une oeuvre *actuelle* et de la présence réelle du *couple sacré*, image de Dieu sur la terre." Ibid., 36–37.

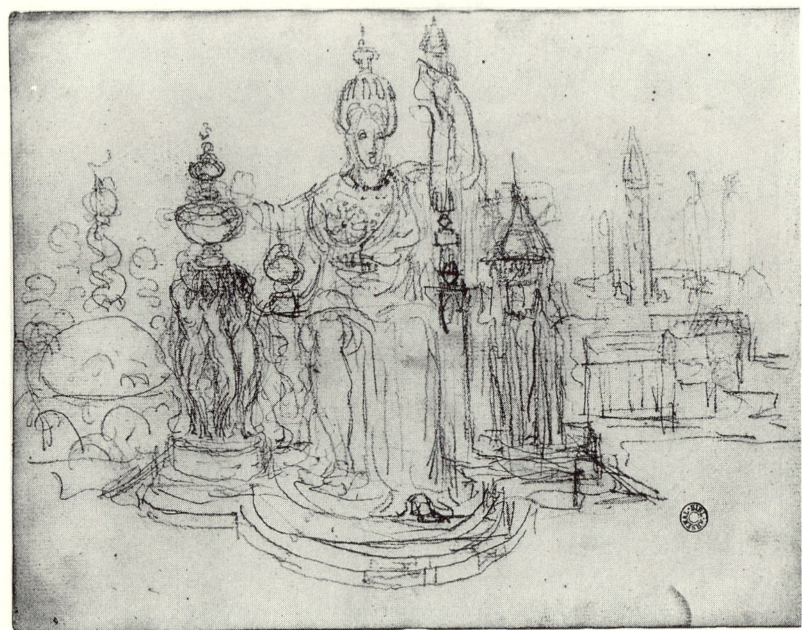

Plate 3. Philippe-Joseph Machereau: *Saint-Simonian Temple and City,* 1832. Ms. 13910, p. 38v., Bibliothèque de l'Arsenal, Paris.

congregation enters the towering structure.[89] Michel Chevalier, too, in his "Notes sur l'architecture," surveys the resources to be exploited for glorifying God. The edifice he describes is a technically advanced combination of architectural, chemical, and meteorological effects—"a raging orchestra," "a gigantic thermometer"—in which worshipers are exposed to a dazzling array of cosmic forces, revealing the divine presence with startling immediacy:

> A temple as a Voltaic battery, a temple built of colossal magnets, a temple through whose mechanism enormous lenses would throw shafts of warmth

[89] Duveyrier proclaims "Mon temple est une femme! Autour de son vaste corps, jusqu'à sa ceinture, montent en spirale, à travers les vitraux, des galeries qui s'échelonnent comme les guirlandes d'une robe de bal. . . . Le bras droit de la bien-aimée de ma ville est tourné vers les coupoles et les dômes industriels, et sa main repose sur une sphère au sommet de cristal. . . . Cette sphère forme en-dedans du temple l'emplacement de mon théâtre sacré, dont les décors sont des panoramas." Cited in P. Régnier, *Les Saint-Simoniens en Egypte 1833–1851* (1989), 40, who notes Illuminist and Masonic parallels with Revolutionary symbolism. Maurice Agulhon has drawn an analogy between this figure and the personification of Liberty, remarking too on radical preference for colossal figures at this period *(Marianne into Battle: Republican Imagery and Symbolism in France 1789–1880* [1981], 56–58). For a full transcription, see Régnier, *Livre nouveau*, 222–36.

and light, a temple in which at a given moment gas would overwhelm light and fire: the mysterious facet of earth's life revealed by magnetism and electricity, its majesty displayed by shining metals and cloth, by wondrous fountains . . .— the sun's life revealed in fire . . . the life of men revealed in all the arts, in the profusion of painting and sculpture, by panoramas and dioramas, bringing together in one place all of time and space: what an immense communion! what a vast means of moralizing an entire nation![90]

With this pyrotechnic spectacular, *moralisation* abandons restrictive notions of didacticism to reach out to the sublime. Concentration on emotional engagement is complete: in Chevalier's temple, the individual is held in a vortex of sound, light, and color which solicits a total rendering of individuality and galvanizes the collectivity behind its sacred and secular guides without any recourse to rational persuasion.

If the religious ceremony aims to promote social cohesion by placing the individual in direct communion with God, the secular festival exploits the arts to inspire class harmony and generate enthusiasm for industrial growth. Conceived as "the union of all hopes, the mixture of all fortunes and classes,"[91] the *fête* uses leisure as a means of refining the people's manners and reinforcing their allegiance to an industrial regime that promises to extend such agreeable diversions into everyday life. As outlined by the Saint-Simonians, the *fête* recalls such future public spectacles as the *exposition universelle* and the mass rally. Gymnasts, dancers, horseback riders, and balloonists entertain the assembled multitudes and provide evidence of the wealth and beneficence of the state, while the workers are enlisted in a more active capacity in *tableaux vivants* and parades in praise of labor.[92]

Such collective rituals are supplemented by visual spectacle, concerts, drama, and dance, provided to enable the people to "moderate themselves through the touching delicacy of all that is most refined in the arts." The rich will be encouraged to participate in these events, their wealth and elegance supposedly stimulating discipline and conscientiousness among the work force by displaying the comforts attainable through hard work. As the

[90] "Un orchestre rugissant"; "un thermomètre gigantesque"; "Un temple, pile de Volta, un temple bâti d'aimants colossaux, un temple à travers le mécanisme duquel d'énormes lentilles jetteraient des dards de chaleur et de lumière, un temple qui à un instant donné vaincrait la lumière et le feu par le gaz: la vie de la terre manifestée dans sa face de mystère par le magnétisme et l'électricité, dans sa pompe par l'éclat des métaux et des tissus, par des cascades merveilleuses . . .—la vie solaire manifestée par le feu . . . la vie des hommes manifestée par tous les arts, par la profusion des peintures et des sculptures, par les panoramas et dioramas, qui réunissaient en un seul point tout l'espace et tout le temps, quelle communion immense! quelle gigantesque moralisation de tout un peuple!" M. Chevalier, "Notes sur l'architecture," Arsenal Ms. 7641.

[91] "L'union de toutes les espérances, le mélange de toutes les fortunes et de tous les rangs." C. Duveyrier, "Travaux publics—Fêtes," *Le Globe* (16 April 1832): 425.

[92] See *Le Globe* (11 April 1832): 407.

people become "polite, elegant, and restrained" through familiarity with the "pleasures of high society,"[93] so the rich will identify more easily with them and feel reassured that the eradication of poverty has removed the danger of unrest.

In the context of the *fête* the arts are thus used to promote class harmony. The culture to which the working classes are exposed is that of their betters—the composers Rossini and Meyerbeer, and the dramatist Scribe are among the names mentioned—and the underlying assumption is that art's refining influence and the promise of upward mobility will encourage acceptance of remaining inequalities and foster a community of interests among differing classes. Beauty thus facilitates social pacification as culture provides a common language promoting the work ethic and uniting the *industriels* with the more affluent *grand monde*.[94]

This sensitivity toward the moral value of beauty contrasts sharply with the work of Saint-Simon, whose utilitarian aesthetic precluded any discussion of form. For Enfantin and his followers, however, form and content were inseparable—in historical terms, they equated formal change with change in meaning, while discussion of projected ceremonial gave precedence to form as a medium for emotional effect. Beauty thus became a primary concern in relation to the reassessment of matter that accompanied the school's promotion of a pantheistic conception of God. Yet even before the emergence of this new theological structure, Enfantin had shown an awareness of the importance of beauty in a way that marks a departure from Saint-Simon. His initial interest seems to have been stimulated by the work of his brother Augustin, a landscapist who trained under Bertin.[95] From his earliest comments, Enfantin shows a qualified approval of romantic naturalism and deprecates classicism for attenuating the physicality of nature.[96] In line with Platonic tradition, Enfantin insists on the moral connotations of beauty and elaborates an aesthetic correlation of *le bon* and *le beau*, which

93 "Se pacifier à la délicatesse touchante de ce que les arts ont de plus raffiné"; "poli, élégant, doux"; "plaisirs du grand monde." Ibid. A similar notion of moralization is expressed in E. Souvestre, *Des arts comme puissance gouvernementale, et de la nouvelle constitution à donner aux théâtres* (1832), 7. Souvestre, best known as an instructive novelist and playwright under the Second Empire, attended Saint-Simonian meetings at the rue Monsigny in 1832 (Charléty, *Histoire*, 74).

94 Receptivity to the *fête* as an instrument of social hygiene is already found in P. Enfantin, "De l'influence des fêtes publiques sur le bien-être de la société," *Prod.* 1 (1825): 168–79, and A. Garnier, "Des fêtes du carnaval," *Prod.* 2 (1826): 335. On high art as a vehicle of social conciliation, see G.-T. Doin and E. Charton, *Lettres sur Paris* (1830), 86–87.

95 See P. Enfantin, "Notice biographique sur Augustin Enfantin," *Catalogue de tableaux, études peintes à l'huile, aquarelles, dessins et croquis du feu M. A. Enfantin*, produced for the sale held by Petit on 3 March 1828, the year after the painter's death in Italy, aged thirty-four.

96 See P. Enfantin to T. Nugues, 23 September 1825, Arsenal Ms. 7643:73, where the relative merits of the classical landscapist André Giroux and the "romantic" Jacques-Raymond Brascassat are discussed.

later served as a central tenet in Saint-Simonian theology. In the same way as God represented a synthesis of spirit and matter, so Enfantin argued that beauty was the physical manifestation of goodness. Both the contemplation and the material exploitation of nature thus provide privileged access to God and artistic representation becomes an inherently moral act—in the future "the *fine arts* will no longer be profane pleasures, but the expression of divine *morality*, . . . industry will truly be an *act of worship* to the Eternal."[97]

Such a perspective evidently molds Saint-Simonian speculation on liturgical forms and inspires descriptions of the temple and festivities of the future. The group's sexual libertarianism arises from the same source; the rehabilitation of the flesh, as exemplified by the exaltation of female beauty, represents a putative acknowledgment of divine presence in corporeal form. In rejecting Christian asceticism, Saint-Simonianism presents the celebration of sensuality as a legitimate aspect of human nature and a fundamental facet of worship.

Enhanced appreciation of divine materiality is equated with more vivid realization of the presence of God in nature; the artist's particular sensitivity allows him to interpret the symbolic meaning of natural forms, reading them as a "divine hieroglyphic," which provides "a constant reminder of the WILL OF GOD."[98] His indication of the "moral" immanent in nature is conceived of as fostering popular regard for the social and spiritual hierarchy as an infallible and unassailable element in the "infinite hierarchy of worlds." As the celebration of beauty leads to the revelation of God, so recognition of the divine order serves to corroborate the validity of the social order. In the confines of the temple, as in the infinite variety of nature, the artist directs the people toward a more immediate perception of a God whose very essence is inscribed in and defined by the moral and ideological authority of his representatives on earth.

The mediating role accorded the artist operates on a number of levels: between God and man, as an auxiliary of the priest; between the upper echelons of the social hierarchy and the people, as a delegate of those charged with the administration of collective resources; between the present and the future, as an individual whose enhanced emotion grants instinctive understanding of the optimum evolution of society. The conception of art advanced by the Saint-Simonians is essentially concerned with communicating meaning—the aesthetic stands not as a self-sufficient domain but as an inextricable aspect of ideology. The group's contempt for formalism,

[97] "Les *beaux-arts* ne seront plus les plaisirs profanes, mais l'expression de la *morale* divine, . . . l'industrie sera le véritable *culte* de l'Eternel." P. Enfantin to T. Nugues, October 1829, in *O.S.S.E.*, 26:135.

[98] "Divin hiéroglyphe"; "un rappel constant de la VOLONTE DE DIEU." Enfantin, "Enseignements," 3 December 1831, in *O.S.S.E.*, 14:134.

echoed and indeed amplified by contemporary advocates of *art social*, arises from a conviction in art's potential as a catalyst for change and a tool for control. The overtures made to the artistic community underline this emphasis on the importance of meaning; cultural regeneration comes to depend on incorporating a precise body of doctrine into artistic production. Its acceptance implies not only fundamental change in the content of the work of art, but also a complete reorientation in the artist's understanding of his public and of his obligations toward them. The assertion of artistic authority was widely associated with abjuration of individualism and a readiness to respond to the changing needs of society as a whole. As the next chapter will demonstrate, the commercial pressures experienced by artists attempting to succeed in a highly competitive market lent some attraction to this vision of professional integration and heightened recognition. Equally, though, the accumulation of such pressures made it all too clear that fulfillment of the Saint-Simonians' ideals assumed a break with familiar practice of such proportions as to make their aesthetic program unconvincing to most of those at whom the *appel aux artistes* was directed.

Doctrinal emphasis on the social potential of art derives, as in the work of Saint-Simon, from a fundamental inability to provide a credible model of the mechanisms of social change. The group's pacifism, born of an insistence on the identity of class interests and an instinctive mistrust of popular militancy, prevented any concerted stand in July 1830 and was further accentuated following Bazard's secession. Under such circumstances, progress had to depend on mass indoctrination to the virtues of social, economic, and religious transformation. Insofar as all of these changes supposedly evolved from an irrefutable analysis of the immediate needs of society, their wholesale acceptance was theoretically inevitable. Acceleration of this process was seen to depend on generating a popular enthusiasm so overwhelming that all resistance would evaporate and power would be transferred into Saint-Simonian hands without demur. Building sufficient support around issues such as banking reform and abolition of inheritance rights seemed unlikely, however. The ontological system borrowed from contemporary physiology enabled the Saint-Simonians to present enthusiasm, stimulated by appeal to sentiment, as a decisive means of rallying support and building up an unstoppable impetus for change. Proselytization had to inspire rather than convince—the artist symbolized the potential offered by this religious fervor for the Saint-Simonian *âge d'or*.

Exaltation and religiosity rather than reason and restraint characterize much Saint-Simonian propaganda. Doctrinal statements become *prédications*, the movement's principal spokesmen—Enfantin, Bazard, Barrault, Chevalier—cultivate the persuasive, visionary style of ideological evangelists. The disciples' adoption of a distinctive costume and the open-air ceremonies held at Ménilmontant accentuate this pungent appeal to emotion[99]—indeed, the entire episode, together with the Egyptian adventure, can perhaps best be understood as elaborate forms of theater mounted to fire the popular imagination.[100] Publication of a lithographic portrait of Enfantin in 1832 appeared a decisive means of winning over the workers by inspiring them with instinctive love of the great man and elevating them to an understanding of the epoch-making nature of the new faith.[101] In a society dedicated to preserving "the holy inequality of virtue and merit,"[102] such strategies promised to eliminate the need for coercion by eliciting emotional compliance, a form of persuasion which supposedly reconciled liberty and organicism, since individuals' perception of freedom would be inextricably bound with their sense of insertion in the community: as Enfantin remarks "man is FREE when he LOVES what he MUST DO."[103]

The centrality of religion in Saint-Simonian philosophy reveals the priority afforded the government of opinion and the achievement of ideological coherence as the basis for stability. Ideas systems are perceived as central to social organization: societies that have flourished in the past are identified as those with firm roots in religious beliefs which provided strictly respected codes of behavior in all areas of life. A religion's viability is linked to its responsiveness to the needs of the socioeconomic regime; as this evolves, so the stability provided by religion crumbles and organic social organization gives place to conflict and dissent. A central preoccupation in Saint-Simonianism is the formulation of an ideas system appropriate to an industrial age. The religious structure established on this basis exploits a belief in the impressionability of human sentiment in elaborating a theocracy that elides the spiritual and the secular as a means of extending the willing compliance of the believer into the social domain.

Achievement of harmony and progress informs Saint-Simonian religion, while, on a broader level, reconciliation of tension provides the basic struc-

[99] Among several accounts of Saint-Simonian ceremonies, see particularly P. Enfantin, "Compte-rendu d'une cérémonie saint-simonienne" (Arsenal Ms. 7814:31–32), a letter dated 2 July (1832), which betrays a certain satisfaction at the successful manipulation of emotion during such manifestations: "Je donne la main à l'un d'eux [les travailleurs], Barrault les fait pleurer au fond de la scène, puis il s'avance et parle au peuple tandis que [Félicien] David remplit sur le piano les silences de sa parole ou prélude sur sa parole même, comme au mélodrame. Ceci était un essai qui a dû frapper bien des gens; Barrault était superbe."

[100] Thus Hoart remarks on the Egyptian undertaking *(Livre des actes*, January 1834, cited in Régnier, "Idées et opinions," 2:306), "on n'associe pas les hommes par des textes, des lois, des tarifs; il faut quelque chose de vivant qui fasse vibrer les coeurs, qui rallie les intérêts, qui enfante la gloire."

[101] See Cavel, "Portrait lithographié de P. Enfantin," *Le Globe* (27 March 1832): 345, where women and workers are seen as being particularly susceptible to the image's impact.

[102] "L'inégalité sainte de la vertu et du mérite." Ibid.

[103] "L'homme est LIBRE quand il AIME ce qu'il DOIT FAIRE." Enfantin, "Enseignements," 3 December 1831, in *O.S.S.E.*, 14:115. Enfantin is quoting Bazard from the thirteenth *séance* of the 1829 *Exposition de doctrine*.

tural motif for the political philosophy as a whole. Saint-Simonian analysis in virtually every area identifies a series of dichotomies—epistemological, sociopolitical, historical, religious, sexual—to which it offers resolution and hence the achievement of harmony. Historical analysis points toward a millennial dialectic finally to be ended by the attainment of synthesis under the guidance of Saint-Simon. Reason and sentiment, matter and spirit, male and female—all of these antitheses, blamed for perpetuating tensions in the past, are to be overcome in the harmonious order heralded by the new religion.

It is this fundamental commitment to synthesis, culminating in a social order that has abolished the discrepancy between act and desire, that underlies Saint-Simonianism's adoption of an aesthetic that overcomes explicit didacticism through unifying form and content. The theological foundations for this move allowed the material aspects of art a prominence equal to subject matter and suggested a solution to the antagonism between *art social* and formalism, a resolution that, as we shall see in later chapters, similarly inspired the aesthetic doctrines of Pierre Leroux and the Fourierists. Saint-Simonianism, however, failed to overcome widely voiced suspicions that its artistic philosophy implied abdication of creative independence in the interests of promoting official ideology in a direct and undiluted form. Such suspicions, which inevitably drew upon evidence in the group's doctrinal pronouncements and critical reviews rather than the less public formulations of the Ménilmontant period, significantly compromised support in the artistic community. The contradiction between theory and practice, between appeals for support and actual response, was one vital antithesis the Saint-Simonians were incapable of resolving. As examination of the fruits of the *appel aux artistes* will show, the exhortatory calls for allegiance and for the practical mobilization of an aesthetic vocabulary capable of seducing the masses found little resonance among the painters and sculptors whose talents the school valued so highly.

CHAPTER 4

Theory into Practice: The Frustration of Saint-Simonian Aesthetics

HISTORIANS of social romanticism rarely neglect the opportunity to reproduce the roll call of cultural luminaries attracted by the Saint-Simonians. We are reminded that Sainte-Beuve, Berlioz, Vigny, and Liszt attended doctrinal gatherings, while George Sand and Maxime du Camp were impressed by the philosophy in a more diffuse, though nonetheless profound, way.[1] Among committed disciples, Charles Duveyrier and Emile Barrault brought the group's ideas to the stage, while Félicien David set them to music.[2] Yet although the Saint-Simonians could claim some success in literature and music, their impact on the visual arts appears to have been slight. Their theoretical influence proved decisive in encouraging agitation for an art that would be both contemporary and socially committed, but in terms of practice, the school's appeals apparently fell on deaf ears.

The absence of anything but an occasional Saint-Simonian portrait in the Salons of the 1830s makes it easy to assume that the *appel aux artistes* failed to elicit any positive response. Raymond Bonheur might be cited as an isolated exception—though his reputation relies on his progeny rather than his pictures. Bonheur's standing as the token Saint-Simonian painter obscures the fact that he was by no means the only artist involved with the movement. Where he is typical is in his meager contemporary reputation and subsequent neglect. A further common denominator uniting Saint-Simonian artists is their failure to generate a distinctive body of work to

[1] On Saint-Simonianism and literature see H. J. Hunt, *Le Socialisme et le romantisme en France: Etude de la presse socialiste de 1830 à 1848* (1935); M. Thibert, *Le Rôle social de l'art d'après les Saint-Simoniens* (1926); P. Bénichou, *Le Temps des prophètes. Doctrines de l'âge romantique* (1977), 288–310; P. Régnier, "Les Idées et les opinions littéraires des Saint-Simoniens (1825–1835)" (1983). On Vigny, see *Journal d'un poète*, ed. F. Baldensperger (1928), which contains a "Chant d'ouvriers," dated December 1829 (p. 32). On Berlioz, see R. Locke, *Music, Musicians and the Saint-Simonians* (1986), 114–20. Locke provides a thoughtful general survey of the group's aesthetic philosophy, as well as a detailed discussion of its impact on musical life. For Du Camp, see P. Bonnefon, "Maxime du Camp et les Saint-Simoniens," *Revue de l'histoire littéraire de la France* 17 (1910): 709–835.

[2] Duveyrier's work includes *Clifford le voleur* (1835), *Le Monomane* (1835), and *Maurice* (1839). Barrault's *Eugène* (1839) provided a vehicle for Saint-Simonian feminist ideas. On David, see Locke, *Music, Musicians*, 82ff., and D. Hagan, *Félicien David 1810–1876: A Composer and a Cause* (1985).

propagate their cause, despite avid professions of readiness and vociferous encouragement from the group's ideologues. Who, then, were the Saint-Simonians' artists, and what attracted them to the movement? In answering these questions, we will necessarily also confront the striking discrepancy between theory and practice—the one endlessly voluble, the other strangely mute—and examine the adequacy of the Saint-Simonians' vision of a social art for the political and cultural climate of the 1830s.

THE SAINT-SIMONIAN CONSTITUENCY

Apart from a few popular songs, aimed at the working-class clientele of the *goguette* drinking clubs, and quasi-liturgical festivals incorporating music, rhetoric, and dramatic spectacle, Saint-Simonian propaganda was essentially discursive.[3] The brochures and journals produced by the movement appealed most readily to a middle-class public familiar with their historical references and sociopolitical vocabulary, and committed adherents were predominantly bourgeois. Though some provincial evangelical campaigns apparently excited broad popular interest, and special lectures and social services were established in Paris to cater for the working population,[4] evidence suggests that the success of such inroads was relatively limited.[5] Awareness of this limitation prompted Enfantin to speculate on the enhanced receptivity of women and workers to the emotional appeal of art, and helped to inform the group's increased concern for spectacle and other nonverbal forms of propaganda after 1832. Yet examination of correspondence to *Le Globe* and the *professions de foi* made by new converts[6] confirms

[3] On Saint-Simonian popular song, see C. Lodewijk de Liefde, *Le Saint-Simonisme dans la poésie française entre 1825 et 1865* (1927), and J. Vinçard, *Mémoires épisodiques d'un vieux chansonnier saint-simonien* (1878). See also Arsenal Ms. 7803, *Poésies saint-simoniennes imprimées*, which contains works by worker-poets produced on single-sheet *feuilles volantes* for distribution in working-class districts. See also Locke, *Music, Musicians*, 123–52 and 153–66, on ceremonial and *chansonniers* respectively. More generally, see J. Vidalenc, "Les Techniques de la propagande saint-simonienne à la fin de 1831," *Archives de sociologie des religions* 10 (July–December 1960): 3–20.

[4] At the end of 1831 special weekly lectures were held for workers. *Maisons d'association* were established in the rue Popincourt and the rue de la Tour d'Auvergne, providing material and moral aid, such as educational facilities, to the twenty-five families they sheltered (see *Le Globe*, 6 October 1831). Sympathetic doctors and pharmacists set up a medical scheme in each arrondissement (ibid., 14 October 1831). Raymond and Sophie Bonheur administered operations in the 8e arrondissement (Arsenal Ms. 7793:8, Liste des adhérents).

[5] A report by Henri Fournel and Claire Bazard set membership of the "degré des ouvriers" at 330 in October 1831. This group seems to have been predominantly artisanal; see Vidalenc, "Les Techniques de la propagande," 5, and J. Rancière, *La Nuit des prolétaires* (1983), 145ff.

[6] Correspondence to *Le Globe* is preserved in Arsenal Mss. 7601–9; *professions de foi* are in Ms. 7794.

that the movement remained strongest among the commercial middle class and liberal professions.

The leadership itself drew heavily on graduates of the Ecole polytechnique, many of whom later forged substantial careers in public life.[7] Important in attracting such figures seems to have been Saint-Simonianism's promise of unlimited industrial growth, with the technocrat enjoying a pivotal role in social organization. Though concern over capitalism's exploitation of the working classes was genuine enough, this underlying altruism was framed by—and, indeed, subordinate to—aspirations for pacific industrial expansion. The school's proposals for economic and organizational reform promised tangible rewards in terms of power and status for the administrators and technicians of the industrial Golden Age. In some respects, for the promising young technocrat facilitating the onset of this age represented a personal investment in a future free from the labyrinth of *concours* and provincial placements, which, together with the aristocracy's stranglehold on state bureaucracy before 1830, frustrated meritocratic ambitions.[8]

Appeal to professional interest offered some attractions to the artist. Saint-Simonian publicists repeatedly pointed to their degraded position; not only was their social potential squandered, they were also obliged to tolerate the indignities and hardships imposed by an unsympathetic market and inadequate state support. By contrast, the Saint-Simonians envisaged "a future where everyone will work according to their tastes and aspirations, without being in the pay of an exploiter."[9] Yet though such promises must have held undoubted appeal for the painter or writer attempting to establish a career in an increasingly competitive environment, the tantalizing vision offered by Saint-Simonian publicists seems to have proved largely resistible. An immediate explanation for this indifference can be found in the nature of the promises themselves and in the exigencies faced by artists more concerned with surviving in the present than in acquiring untold influence at some vague future date.

On the one hand, Saint-Simonian philosophy was much more concrete in its appeal to scientists and administrators than in the offers it held out to the artist. The ideas inherited from Saint-Simon made industrial expansion a central priority and any success could be anticipated on this level. Though winning over public opinion might not be an easy task, once the group had secured popular endorsement the rewards available to engineers, managers,

[7] On Saint-Simonians under the Second Empire, see H. R. d'Allemagne, *Prosper Enfantin et les grandes entreprises du XIXe siècle* (1935).

[8] On the broader problem of the perceived "excess of educated men" at the period, see A. B. Spitzer, *The French Generation of 1820* (1987), 225–58.

[9] "Un avenir où chacun travaillera suivant ses goûts, suivant ses aspirations, sans se mettre aux gages d'un exploitant." Anonymous, "Activité des oisifs," *Le Globe* (21 April 1831): 448.

and the like would be tangible and immediate. The same could not be said for the artist, whose future eminence seemed more an act of faith, depending on acceptance of a metaphysic far more ambitious, and less immediately credible, than Saint-Simonian visions of industrial revolution. Artistic allegiance thus required considerable commitment, whose rewards meant accepting a complex of propositions that entirely recast conceptions of human character and behavior. Few were prepared to make a long-range commitment on such speculative terms.

Investment in the present inhibited a number of artists from following through their interest in the group. However great their sympathy for critiques of the commercialization of contemporary art, their immediate livelihoods depended on negotiating the prevailing system. Artists prospering under such conditions had less motivation to endorse Saint-Simonian calls for change, while those still hoping for an eventual breakthrough were generally loath to pass up possible success for the promise of future fortune. Saint-Simonianism's appeal thus seemed most potent to those with little to look forward to and nothing to lose—artists whose careers showed meager promise and who felt bruised and frustrated by the pressures of an unsympathetic market.

MARGINALITY AND *MAL DU SIÈCLE*

Converts to the movement often articulated professional frustration in terms of wider personal malaise. Mediated through a rhetoric of emotional intensity learned from texts such as Chateaubriand's *René*, confessional statements repeatedly evoke the perceived crisis within society and the personal anguish it has caused. In all of this, religion and social injustice were key factors. The decline of Catholicism and the resulting spiritual vacuum were powerful motives in attracting many to Saint-Simonianism. Correspondents to *Le Globe* frequently evoke a sense of personal futility resulting from society's fragmentation, and exploitation of this features strongly in Saint-Simonian propaganda. The promise of renewed social cohesion and the restoration of faith exerted a powerful appeal to many for whom the century seemed tarnished by spiritual bankruptcy and economic exploitation.[10]

The group's equation of religious crisis with creative impotence struck a responsive chord in several artistic converts, allowing individuals to see in the proclaimed deficiencies of society the roots of their own sense of failure.

[10] See, for example, the letter of 1829 from Jean Reynaud to his mother, cited in D. A. Griffiths, *Jean Reynaud, encyclopédiste de l'époque romantique* (1965), 36: "Plus de vide! . . . Plus de spleen! O ma mère, une immense joie innonde mon âme! L'idée de Dieu m'est apparue, claire, sans nuage! L'idée de Dieu présent, personnel. . . . Le monde est maintenant rempli pour moi par un adorable ami."

The painter Jules Laure, attracted to the movement in 1830, conflates the personal and the social in a letter to Edouard Charton, written during a visit to Florence. Evoking the sense of disorientation and unbelief with which he had previously been afflicted, Laure writes of the "burning faith," the "enthusiasm such as I have never before experienced" provided by his discovery of Saint-Simon. Remarking that "the change that occurred within me had all the signs of a revelation," he continues:

> Without Saint-Simon, discouragement and despair would have overtaken my soul; I would have denied God and hated the world, which presented me only with chaos. Even today, I am not fully cured of my sorrows. In this city, so richly embellished by the Medicis, I am unsure how to take advantage of the wealth surrounding me: I am like a man abandoned without a compass in the midst of the ocean who does not know in which direction to strike sail in order to reach port. Oh! how I groan to see myself so ALONE and isolated, without anyone to love and enlighten me, to guide me in my studies and continually show me a clear goal to aim for. You, my dear sir, you, my father, whose poetic words reveal a generous heart, you will understand the sadness I feel as an artist; you will hurry to help me. Make haste, time is pressing. . . . It is because I am now so much more aware of how little use are my individual labors that I cry so loudly, "Help!"[11]

The interrelationship expressed here between religious doubt and personal despair is typical of outpourings by converts to the movement. Individual alienation frequently emerges as a central motive in inspiring allegiance to Saint-Simon. Frustration at unfulfilled promise, acute consciousness of the difficulty of social insertion, grievance over professional setbacks—all are explained in terms of a hostile social environment, dominated by egotism and greed. Unable to find acceptance in this network of conflicting interests and ambitions, the individual often turns to Saint-Simonianism for a social structure free of tension, where individual attainment would be given full due.

[11] "Foi ardente"; "enthousiasme tel que je n'en avais jamais eprouvé"; "le changement qui s'opéra en moi eut tout le caractère d'une révélation"; "Sans Saint-Simon, le découragement, le désespoir allaient s'emparer de mon âme; j'allais renier Dieu et haïr ce monde qui ne me présentait qu'un chaos. Aujourd'hui même je ne suis pas bien guéri de mes peines. Dans cette ville, que les Médicis ont embellie avec profusion, au milieu des richesses qui m'entourent, je ne sais comment en profiter: semblable en cela à un homme qu'on aurait abandonné sans boussole au milieu de l'Océan, et qui ne saurait de quel côté faire voile pour trouver un port. Oh! combien je gémis de me voir ainsi SEUL, livré à moi-même, de n'avoir personne qui m'aime, qui m'éclaire, qui me guide en mes études, en me montrant sans cesse un but certain à atteindre. Vous, mon cher monsieur, vous, mon père, dont la parole poétique révèle un coeur généreux, vous comprendrez ma douleur d'artiste; vous vous empresserez de venir à mon aide. Hâtez-vous, le temps presse. . . . C'est que je sens davantage maintenant le peu d'utilité de mes travaux individuels que je crie si fort 'Au secours!' " Reprinted—anonymously—in the collection *Religion saint-simonienne; correspondance. Articles extraits du "Globe"* (1831), 40–41.

This sense of frustration and failure is highlighted in the figure of Pol Justus. A young painter whose career seems to have experienced considerable setbacks,[12] Justus apparently had a turbulent personal life and volatile character, which occasionally provoked discord within Saint-Simonian circles. During early contacts with the group, he writes emotionally of his anguish and isolation. In a letter to Enfantin of March 1832, he describes himself:

> In the midst of agonizing pains with which the world has often struck my artist's soul; prey to the sadness of a young man who finds himself carried violently away by generous feelings and daring thoughts which no sooner well up in my head or heart than they expire without being given form by my pen or paintbrush; spending all my time deflecting the blows with which the heavy hand of prejudice strikes at my thirst for freedom.[13]

Justus projects his professional frustration onto a society whose shortcomings are testified by his own failure. Success and acceptance are of crucial importance—"how much pain and struggle, how much persecution and contempt it costs to be loved and admired." Yet both have proved elusive—"I should be someone today, but I am nobody, and I suffer for it."[14]

For such as Justus, Saint-Simonianism offered an alternative to the conflictual patterns of contemporary society. The ordered hierarchy, the stability and comradeship (more illusory than real as the violent dispute between Bazard and Enfantin revealed), the sympathetic figure of the *père* himself, all seemed to offer the moral support absent in the outside world. Enfantin appears as the supreme patriarch, omniscient and reassuring, worthy of the highest accolade: "In my faith as an artist and a Saint-Simonian I know of only one man today who is capable of equaling you: Monsieur Ingres."[15]

[12] Justus exhibited in the Salon only twice—in 1845 and 1846. In 1848, he emerged as an advocate of infants' vocational schools (see *L'Artiste*, 5th ser., 1 [1 July 1848]: 188–89) and of a series of international congresses to promote peace, industry, and the arts. Enfantin's failure to support the initiative, outlined in a series of pamphlets, provoked an angry response (Arsenal Ms. 7630:148–49). In July 1849, Justus founded the Société internationale des artistes, whose journal—*La Voix des artistes*—he briefly edited in 1850.

[13] "Au milieu de douleurs poignantes que le monde a souvent apportées à mon imagination ardente; en proie aux chagrins d'un jeune homme qui se surprend violemment entraîné par des sentiments généreux, par des pensées hardies, mais qui dans la tête ou le coeur ne surgissent que pour y expirer aussitôt sans qu'elles aient encore pu se faire jour par la plume ou le pinceau; toujours occupé à parer les coups que portaient à ma soif d'émancipation la main pesante des préjugés." P. Justus to P. Enfantin, March 1832, Bibliothèque nationale, N.A.Fr. 24610, f. 46r. Transcriptions of this and following manuscripts retain errors found in the originals.

[14] "Par combien de souffrances et de luttes, par combien de persécutions et de mépris on achète le droit d'être aimé, admiré"; "je devrais être quelque chose aujourd'hui et je ne suis rien, aussi je souffre." Ibid., f. 46v.

[15] "Je ne connais dans ma foi d'artiste et de Saint-Simonien qu'un homme capable aujourd'hui de se placer en face de vous: Monsieur Ingres." Ibid.

Laure's crisis of belief, Justus's crisis of confidence—both can be seen as a means of negotiating, indeed justifying, a sense of marginality. Both men emphasize their spiritual particularity as artists and relate their setbacks to the incomprehension of a corrupt society. Personal trauma marks several other artistic converts, not least Raymond Bonheur, whose enthusiasm for Saint-Simonianism coincided with a period of extreme poverty and professional frustration. Having left his wife and children in Bordeaux in 1828, Bonheur moved to Paris, hoping to improve his difficult circumstances. Such attempts proved fruitless, and when his family joined him the following year Bonheur was reduced to penury.[16] His contacts with Saint-Simonianism date from mid 1830. Following his *profession de foi* in December 1831, where he described himself as *peuple*, *prolétaire*,[17] Bonheur entered the convent at Ménilmontant in June 1832, where he remained for five months. Comments by colleagues constantly emphasize his poverty; as Alexis Petit writes to Enfantin in February 1833: "Illness and misery have haunted this family, which has always shown its undivided love for you."[18]

Yet to describe all Saint-Simonian artists as paupers and failures would be to distort the picture. Several of the more shadowy members of the group—the painters Cherot and Morazini, the architect Foilquin, and Baret, described simply as an *artiste*—made little public impact.[19] Some adherents did acquire substantial reputations, however, either on a local or a national level. The sculptor Jean-Baptiste-Jules Klagmann, a pupil of Feuchère and Ramey *fils*, is listed as a disciple in 1831.[20] His career was solid, if unremarkable, culminating in the award of the Légion d'honneur in 1853. His legacy to Saint-Simonianism seems to have been slender, however, and no material record of his adherence has survived.

Of two other figures, much more can be said. Pierre Hawke, an engraver living in Angers, and the sculptor Théophile Bra both met with some success in their respective careers—the former making a comfortable living in a provincial center, the latter enjoying a national reputation. Both men's involvement in Saint-Simonianism derives from personal dissatisfactions broadly similar to those experienced by Laure and Justus, whose insistent self-consciousness and highly charged language they echo in their intensely confessional mode of address.

Hawke was born into a Catholic family in Newport on the Isle of Wight

[16] See A. Klumpke, *Rosa Bonheur, sa vie, son oeuvre* (1908), 130–53.

[17] See "Enseignements—quatorzième séance," December 1831, *O.S.S.E.*, 16:219.

[18] "La maladie et la misère ont plané sur cette famille, toujours tout amour pour vous." A. Petit to P. Enfantin, 10 February 1833, Arsenal Ms. 15031:893, f. 4v.

[19] Baret, Cherot, and Foilquin—an "enfant des classes pauvres"—are listed as having made professions de foi (Ms. 7794, nos. 7, 29, and 48). Jules Morazini is mentioned by Cazeaux in a letter to Chevalier from Bordeaux of 4 May 1832 in Bibliothèque nationale, N.A.Fr. 24609, f. 302r.

[20] Arsenal Ms. 7793:8.

in 1801.[21] His father had trained for the priesthood in Douai, but had returned to England in 1793 before completing his studies. In an autobiographical letter to Michel Chevalier of August 1832, Hawke writes of a pious and sheltered upbringing which left him ill-prepared for the outside world:

> I was suddenly thrown on the stormy seas of today's society, unfamiliar with the elements that surrounded me and seemed about to drag me under. But my frail vessel didn't sink. My preconceptions about men were soon disabused, and so I enthusiastically dedicated myself to study. . . . Here too my expectations were destroyed and it was not long before I discovered the sterility of art and science, isolated as they were from any religious bond, and so I threw myself into the voluptuous pleasures of love.[22]

Love proved as treacherous as learning, when the object of his affections was "sacrificed by her cruel mother" in marriage to "a man who was wealthy but totally incapable of appreciating the treasure he had bought." Hawke's consequent resentment provoked a total loss of faith in society and a period of dissipation involving a series of affairs. His encounter with the world had left him "almost atheist" and indifferent to political life.[23] Having left Dinan, where he spent most of his youth, Hawke was in Paris at the time of the July Revolution—an event he describes as having interrupted his lethargy before further reinforcing his disillusionment:

> Intoxicated, I embraced the tricolor flag, believing that freedom for the nations was dawning. My illusions evaporated and I resumed my apathetic state until one of Saint-Simon's writings, the *Nouveau Christianisme*, fell into my hands and I discovered the fulfillment of all my hopes.[24]

Like Laure and Justus, Hawke presents his discovery of Saint-Simon as a revelation, allowing new personal assurance and confidence in the future:

[21] Célestin Port, *Dictionnaire historique, géographique et biographique de Maine-et-Loire* (1978), 2:277, gives his birth date as 18 January 1801. For Hawke's correspondence with the Parisian school, see Bibliothèque municipale, Angers Mss. 1367.

[22] "Je fus lancé tout à coup sur l'océan orageuse de la société actuelle, étranger aux éléments qui m'environnaient et qui semblaient sur le point de m'engloutir. Cependant ma frêle barque n'a pas sombré. Mes prévisions sur les hommes furent bientôt démentis, alors je me livrai avec ardeur à l'étude. . . . Là encore mes prévisions furent anéanties car je ne fus pas longtemps à découvrir la stérilité de la science et de l'art isolés comme ils étaient d'un lien religieux et je me précipitais dans les jouissances voluptueuses de l'amour." P. Hawke to M. Chevalier, 21 August 1832, Arsenal Ms. 7606:24.

[23] "Sacrifiée par sa cruelle mère"; "un homme riche mais totalement incapable d'apprécier le trésor [qu']il avait acheté"; "à peu près athée."

[24] "J'embrassai avec ivresse le drapeau tricolore croyant que l'aurore de la liberté pour les nations avait paru. Mes illusions s'évanouissaient et je devins dans mon état apathique jusqu'à ce qu'un écrit de Saint-Simon, le Nouveau christianisme, est tombé dans mes mains et là je voyais la satisfaction de toutes mes esperances."

> I was tossed on a stormy sea, without a compass to guide my frail vessel; you appeared like a sun resplendent in glory to bring it to shore on a coast of delights. Through the faith, I am crossing the promised land of the future. Oh! how beautiful it will be![25]

Significantly, Hawke uses the same image as Laure: both describe themselves as cast adrift without a compass. For both—as indeed for Justus and Bonheur—Saint-Simonianism is perceived as offering a sense of purpose in life, where previously only self-doubt existed. Hawke's melodramatic "confession d'un enfant du siècle" shares with Laure and Justus a highly colored prose style, emphasizing the conflict between the correspondent's acutely sensitive "artistic personality" and the indifferent, egocentric world he inhabits.[26] For all three, investment in the present has proved either fruitless or deceptive; all regard themselves as outsiders unreconciled to the values of a corrupt society. In all three, a self-conscious "otherness" emerges through the text, arising from a particular temperament whose values, though derided by their contemporaries, are more generous and "creative" than those obtaining in the world around them.

The histrionic tone affected by Laure, Hawke, and the others finds fullest expression in Théophile Bra, a quintessential *artiste maudit*, led into a number of arcane enterprises, including a brief flirtation with Saint-Simonianism, by an almost pathological sense of marginality and alienation.[27] Professionally, Bra achieved a success that eluded other artistic adherents to the movement. His father Eustache practiced as a sculptor in the provincial town of Douai and Théophile continued the family tradition, training under Bridan *fils* in Paris. Recognition came at an early age, with the award of a first-prize medal by the Académie in 1813, when the sculptor was only sixteen, and second place in the Prix de Rome five years later. Though never a *lauréat*, Bra established a thriving practice, specializing in

[25] "J'étais ballotté, sur une mer orageuse, sans boussole, pour diriger ma frêle nacelle: vous êtes paru comme un soleil resplendissant de gloire pour la faire aborder sur un rivage de délices. Par la foi, je parcours la terre promise de l'avenir. Oh! elle sera belle!" P. Hawke to M. Chevalier, 8 April 1832, Bibliothèque nationale, N.A.Fr. 24612, f. 380v.

[26] A further example is provided in the "Profession de foi" of the engraver P.-J. Machereau (*Org.*, 2d year, 29 [5 March 1831]: 227–28), whose narrative structure bears striking similarities to Hawke's and Laure's self-representations. Social disillusionment leads to frustrated love and dissipation (again interrupted by the false dawn of the July Days) before salvation is offered by Saint-Simon. Thus, in the beginning: "Je fus lancé au milieu d'une humanité que mon coeur se forçait de trouver aimante, généreuse. Je la vis égoïste, haineuse, jalouse. Désirant ardemment de me confier en elle, je fus trompé par elle; et moi-même, en me séparant de tout ce qui m'entourait, je fus égoïste, haineux et jaloux" (227). Since conversion, however: "J'ai trouvé des hommes de plus en plus aimants, et que j'aime toujours davantage, et SAINT-SIMON, par leur bouche, en me réconciliant avec mon passé, m'a dévoilé l'avenir!" (228).

[27] On Bra, see most recently A. Bigotte, "La Sculpture Bra. Eléments d'approche," *Amis de Douai* 9, no. 2 (April–June 1983): 20–7.

classical and religious works, and his professional standing was acknowledged with the Légion d'honneur in 1825. Nonetheless, Bra was a difficult, unstable character, whose eccentric behavior following his first wife's death in 1826 provoked a bitter custody dispute over his children in which the sculptor's sanity was questioned in the courts.[28] It was at this time that Bra became intensely involved in somnambulism, an obsession that fed on a penchant for mysticism fueled over the previous decade by voracious study of religion, world history, philosophy, and science. Between July 1826 and August 1829 Bra generated a vast quantity of drawings and writings, apparently produced in a suspended state of consciousness, in which he elaborated a hermetic symbolic vocabulary consisting of violently etched geometrical forms and obscure emblematic figures (plates 4 and 5). Encouraged by the Swedenborgian Emile Broussais and Christobalina Favières, a Spanish somnambulist to whom he was briefly married in 1829,[29] Bra used his trances to penetrate the secrets of human existence, though, as he admits of his drawings, "their character is so strange that nobody except their author could make anything of them."[30]

Like the Saint-Simonians, in his somnambular works Bra reveals anxiety over the conflicts in contemporary society—discerned on a personal as well as a collective level—and a yearning for a harmonious state free from contradiction. A highly individual, syncretic Christianity and an abiding preoccupation with *unité* are presented as the means of overcoming current social division and defeating the dangers posed by materialism. Such preoccupations eventually attracted the sculptor to the Christian socialism of Buchez, and remained central to his work during the 1840s and 1850s.

Bra's adherence to Saint-Simonianism dates from early 1830, when his enthusiasm was aroused by Barrault's *Aux artistes*, lent to him by the sculptor Duret. The new disciple was seen as much as a challenge as an asset by the group's leaders—Enfantin, Lechevalier, and Gustave d'Eichthal all comment on Bra's disordered personality and emphasize the importance of freeing him from the pernicious influence of Broussais.[31] Jules Lechevalier,

[28] See ibid., 22.

[29] Balzac described Bra's behavior following Favière's death in a letter to Mme Hanska in 1835 (H. de Balzac, *Correspondance*, ed. R. Pierrot [1962], 2:619): "C'est un homme curieux en ceci qu'il a été conduit au mysticisme par la perte d'une femme qu'il aimait et qu'il a été pendant deux mois l'évoquer sur sa tombe et qu'il m'a dit l'avoir vue tous les soirs."

[30] "Ils portent un tel caractère de singularité que personne excepté l'auteur ne pourrait y rien connaître." Manuscript cited in Bigotte, "La Sculpture Bra," 23. Hippolyte Fortoul remarked of the artist that he carried "l'intelligence jusqu'à la folie, et la rage du symbole jusqu'à la bêtise"; see F. Ambrière, *Le Siècle des Valmore. Marceline Desbordes-Valmore et les siens* (1987), 2:505.

[31] P. Enfantin to C. Duveyrier, 28 April 1830, *O.S.S.E.*, 2:164; J. Lechevalier to P. Enfantin, 1 May 1830, Bibliothèque nationale, N.A.Fr. 24610, ff. 93–94; G. d'Eichthal to C. Duveyrier, 15 June 1830, Bibliothèque nationale, N.A.Fr. 24609, ff. 378–82. The latter

who regarded Bra's salvation as a particular responsibility, wrote to Enfantin about the new convert, whom he describes as "bubbling over with enthusiasm":

> Though he has superb manners, this man is a somnambulist prone to hallucinations. He believes he has a mission, claims to be driven by Jesus, and draws an enormous number of mystical symbols while under trance in which he sees the entire history of humanity, but in which until now I have seen only some rather expressive heads in the most bizarre accoutrements. St. Simon has already been symbolized in this way—Artists think Mr. Bra mad and I am almost tempted to take M. Duret's behavior toward him as a mystification, which would be quite typical of the present day. I myself am not in the slightest mystified. The sight of this talented man, full of a great sense of sympathy, has touched me greatly. I shall devote myself to him, as to a sick man whom only the doctrine can revive. . . . I want M. Bra's cure to be my first Saint-Simonian miracle.[32]

Though Bra's adherence to the movement seems to have been short-lived, ending in late 1830, he appears to have retained some ties with the group. In April 1832 Barrault suggested that the sculptor's influence among the student population could be put to use in proselytizing in the Latin Quarter, and in March 1833 his bust of Saint-Simon formed the centerpiece of an elaborate ceremony commemorating the disciples' first year of celibacy.[33] Like many others who severed connections with the school, Bra seems to have been most repelled by its autocratic leadership. As he later wrote, "Enfantin wanted to be a father of humanity, a King of progress, a living absolute law. He broke all family ties and destroyed all individual dignity by monopolizing the dignity of the species himself."[34]

---

speaks of "ce fou de Bra" and describes Broussais as his "Méphistophèle" who has been attempting to intercept copies of *L'Organisateur* sent to the sculptor.

[32] "Tout bouillant d'enthousiasme"; "Cet homme a des manières superbes, mais il est somnambule et sujet aux hallucinations. Il se croit une mission, se prétend impulsionné par Jésus et pendant son sommeil magnétique il trace une énorme quantité de symboles mystiques où il vit toute l'histoire de l'humanité, mais où je n'ai vu jusqu'ici que quelques têtes assez expressives dans le plus bizarre accoutrement. Déjà St. Simon est symbolisé de la sorte—Mr. Bra passe pour fou parmi les artistes, je serais presque tenté de prendre la démarche de M. Duret auprès de lui pour une mythification, chose si digne de l'époque actuelle—pour mon compte je ne suis nullement mystifié; la vue de cet homme de talent, doué d'une grande capacité sympathique, m'a profondément touché. Je m'attacherai à lui comme à un malade que la doctrine seule peut guérir. . . . Je veux donc que la cure de M. Bra soit mon premier miracle Saint-Simonien." J. Lechevalier to P. Enfantin, 1 May 1830, f. 94.

[33] See Vinçard, *Mémoires*, 116, on the bust of Saint-Simon. On proselytization, see E. Barrault to P. Enfantin, April 1832, Bibliothèque nationale, N.A.Fr. 24609, ff. 31–35.

[34] "Enfantin voulait [être] un père de l'humanité, un Roi du progrès, une loi vivante absolue. Il brisait tous les liens de famille et détruisit toute la dignité individuelle en s'appliquant à lui-même toute la dignité de l'espèce." Bibliothèque municipale, Douai, Bra Mss. 1674, box 1.

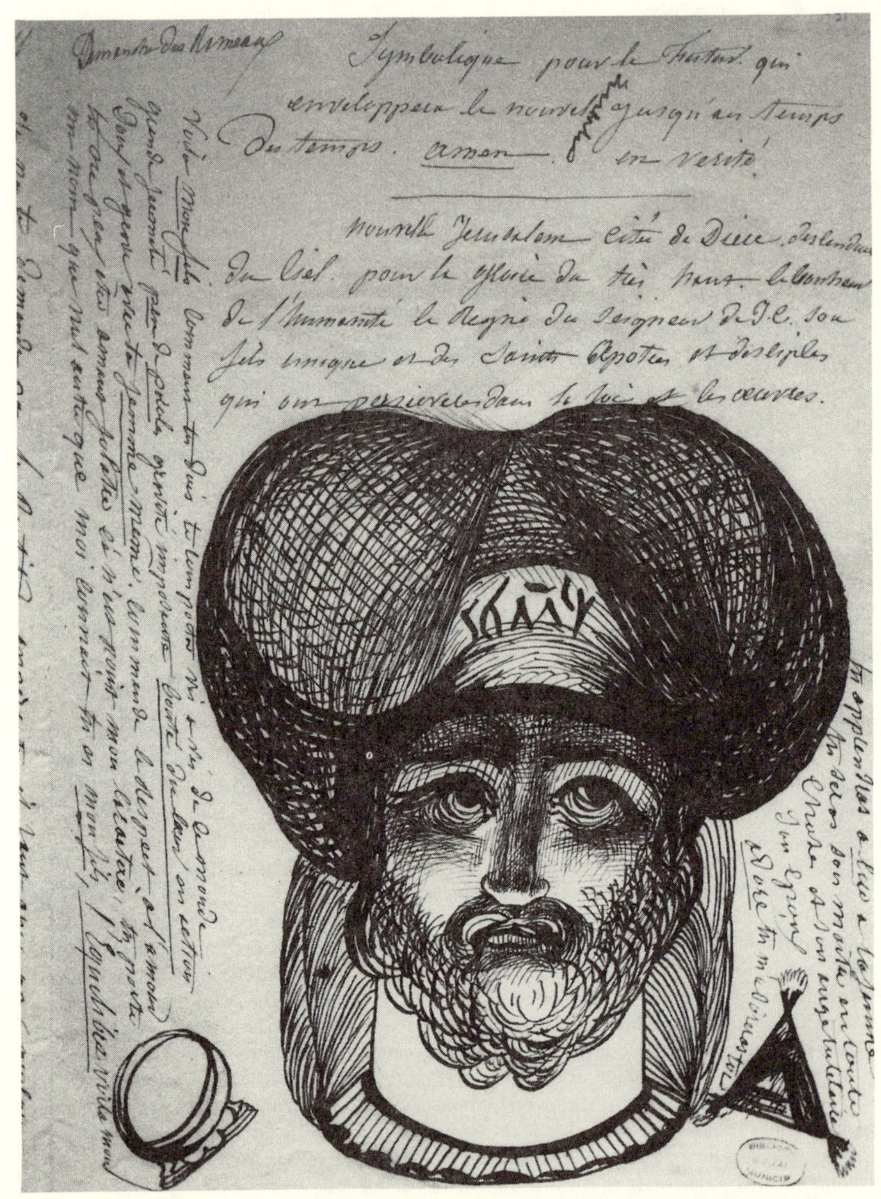

Plate 4. Théophile Bra: *Visionary Head*, undated (c. 1829). Ms. 1674/1, f. 431, Bibliothèque municipale, Douai.

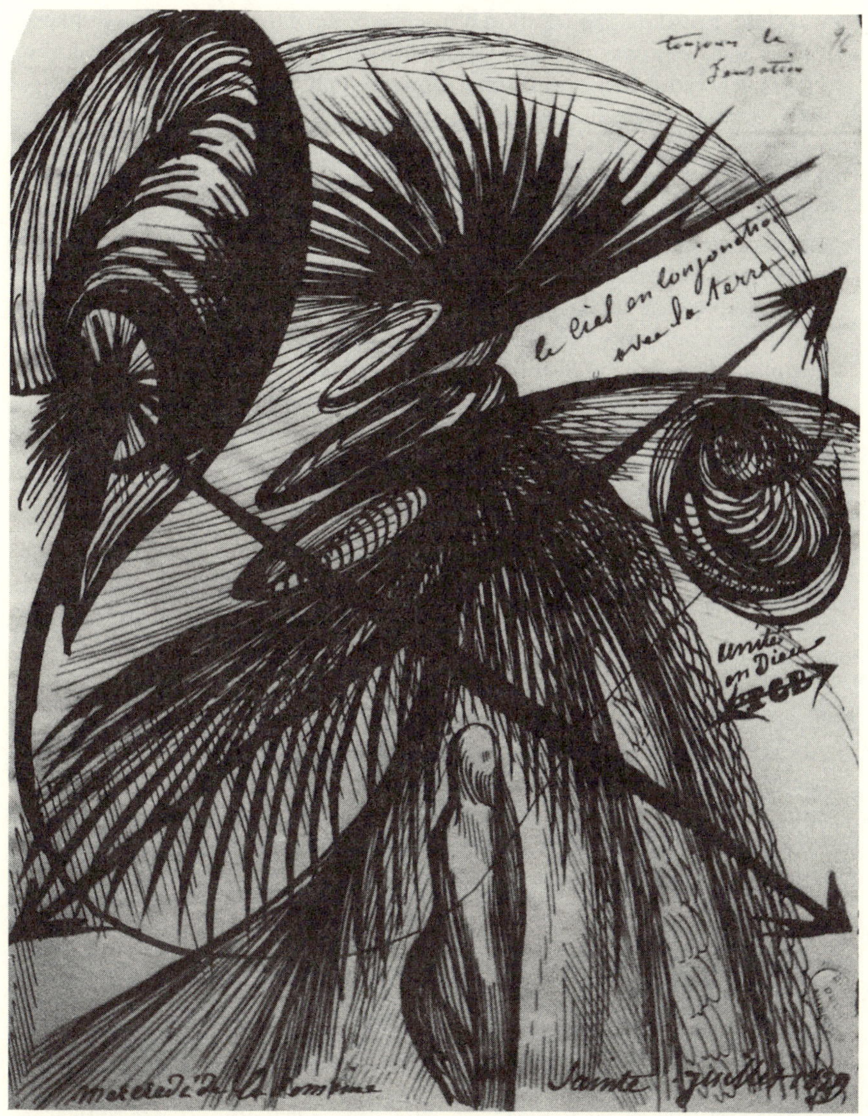

Plate 5. Théophile Bra: *Automatic Drawing,* July 1829. Ms. 1674/1, f. 96, Bibliothèque municipale, Douai.

While regarding Saint-Simon himself as "one of the most daring thinkers of his age," Bra was ultimately unconvinced by what he regarded as the excessively rationalistic, unsynthetic bias of a philosophy that "totally overlooked the fundamental laws of the moral world," and was capable of catering only to man's physical needs.[35] In transferring his allegiance to Buchez, however, Bra remained committed to reform and, as we shall see in a later chapter, devoted considerable energy to projects designed to foster the onset of a new era of social concord and artistic regeneration.

The sense of marginality and creative impotence we have encountered so far underlines the appeal of a movement that emphasized the need for social organicism and presented the artist of the future poised in the vanguard through his command over human emotion. For those denied access to the fruits of the contemporary market, these promises of quasi-sacerdotal power proved enticing.

A further factor uniting many of the artists connected with Saint-Simonianism is their youth.[36] Though individuals such as Hawke and Bra had already embarked upon their careers, others were still completing their professional training. In Paris, the future critic Théophile Thoré, who had abandoned the law and was meeting considerable frustration in establishing himself as a journalist, was briefly involved with the movement in 1832.[37] A small group of converts active in Rome around the time of Laure's visit in 1830 further illustrates Saint-Simonianism's appeal to those still unsure of the pattern their careers would follow.

Central to this group was François Cendrier, son-in-law of the architect Charles Henri who in 1831 initiated a series of special doctrinal lectures for artists in Paris.[38] Cendrier arrived in Italy in 1830, after repeated failure to win the Prix de Rome. Together with Laure, he began recruiting among the artistic community and attracted the architects Goury and Corbin, and the

[35] "Un des plus hardis penseurs de son époque"; "ignora totalement les lois primordiales du monde moral." Notes on Saint-Simon, ibid., box 3. In an undated fragment (ibid., box 6), Bra argues that Saint-Simon "n'est lui-même qu'un symbole," presaging broader social rebirth accompanied by the transfiguration of Christ.

[36] Bra was born in 1797, Cendrier in 1803, Justus and Laure in 1806. This age profile is reflected throughout the movement. Rancière estimates working-class converts' average age at thirty-three (*La Nuit*, 154).

[37] See P. Cottin, ed., *Thoré-Burger peint par lui-même* (1900), 15, letter to Mme Thoré, 7 December 1832, and references to Thoré in letters from Michel Chevalier in Arsenal Mss. 15031:39 (14 January 1833) and 70 (30 January 1833). Thoré was also a friend of Hawke, who visited him when he was imprisoned in 1840 (Cottin, p. 65). On Hawke, see also Thoré papers, Arsenal Mss. 7917, letter from Fournier, 25 September 1839. Thoré's first published article, "De la phrénologie dans ses rapports avec l'art," *L'Artiste*, 1st ser., 6 (1833): 122–25, 259–61, is distinctively Saint-Simonian in tone, though Fourier is also evoked sympathetically. On this phase, see F. S. Jowell, *Thoré-Bürger and the Art of the Past* (1977), 1–22.

[38] On Cendrier, see C. Bauchal, *Nouveau Dictionnaire biographique et critique des architectes français* (Paris, 1887), 620, and C. Henri to C. Duveyrier, 11–13 June 1830, Bibliothèque nationale, N.A.Fr. 24610, ff. 12–14.

sculptors Jules Alric and Antoine Etex.[39] Alric was to remain most committed to the movement, abandoning his training under Bartolini and joining the mission to Egypt in 1833.[40] Etex's enthusiasm proved more transitory. He had arrived in Italy on an official scholarship, granted following failure to win the Prix de Rome. A committed republican, he forged contacts with the Italian opposition, but experienced bouts of depression, prompting him to consider either suicide or a monastic existence in the company of his recent acquaintance Hector Berlioz. His interest in Saint-Simonianism was aroused while in Rome,[41] and during his return to France he encountered two former Polytechnique students, both converts to the group, and set out for Algeria with them. Here he met Christophe de Lamoricière, a soldier who was also an enthusiastic Saint-Simonian. Lamoricière was impressed by the sculptor's talent, and contacted Michel Chevalier, encouraging him to introduce Etex to the disciples on his return to Paris. Describing Etex as "a man of outstanding potential," Lamoricière recounted the circumstances of his conversion:

> The young man is self-aware; he is so devoted to art, feels such an irresistible calling, that he would still think himself fortunate were he to be locked up for life with blocks of stone and his hammer. In this frame of mind, he met an old architect friend called Sandrier [*sic*] who had become an enthusiastic St. Simonian. Through repeated contact with this man and reading the "Globe" Etex discovered the life of the future and the new role accorded to art; he felt it, he believed it.[42]

Lamoricière confidently affirmed "such is his need for a new order of things, which he sees so well defined and so attainable through St. Simonianism, that his faith will not flag before any sacrifice."[43] Unfortunately, such confidence proved misplaced, and Etex's newfound convic-

[39] Cendrier was also in contact with Berlioz, who arrived in Rome in early 1831 as a *pensionnaire* at the Ecole de Rome. See letter to C. Duveyrier, 28 July 1831, in *Hector Berlioz. Correspondance générale*, ed. P. Citron (1972), 1:476.

[40] See A. Cendrier to J. Alric, 2 March 1834, Arsenal Ms. 7702:23. See also J. Laure to M. Chevalier, 17 November 1831, Arsenal Mss. 7604:171.

[41] See A. Etex, *Souvenirs d'un artiste* (1877), 119. On this period, see A. Le Normand-Romain, "Le Séjour d'Etex à Rome en 1831–1832. Un Carnet de dessins inédit," *Bulletin de la Société de l'histoire de l'art français* (1981, pub. 1983): 175–88, which makes no mention of Etex's Saint-Simonian contacts.

[42] "Une virtualité de premier ordre"; "le jeune homme a conscience de lui-même, il est si dévoué à l'art, se sent appelé par une force si irrésistible qu'il se croirait encore heureux si on l'enfermait pour sa vie avec des blocs et son marteau. Dans cette disposition il a rencontré un nommé Sandrier [*sic*], architecte, son ancien ami qui était devenu chaud St. Simonien. Le contact répeté de cet homme, la lecture du "Globe" ont révélé à Etex la vie de l'avenir, le rôle nouveau que l'art était appelé à remplir; il a senti, il a cru." C. de Lamoricière to M. Chevalier, 14 August 1832, Bibliothèque nationale, N.A.Fr. 24611, f. 468.

[43] "Il a tellement besoin d'un nouvel ordre de choses et le voit si bien défini et si réalisable par le St. Simonisme que sa foi ne reculerait devant aucun sacrifice."

tions seem not to have survived the journey home. Like many other converts he remained politically active, however: a combattant in February 1848 for the republican cause, he participated in the repression of the June days, and was briefly involved with Auguste Comte following the 1850 coup d'état.[44]

The Rome episode is significant in bringing together artists who were still on the brink of their careers. Like the engineers and polytechniciens who gravitated toward the movement, it is probable that this younger generation saw Saint-Simonianism not only as a response to social inequality and fragmentation but also as a solution to the professional barriers imposed by the current political and economic regime, barriers that both Cendrier and Etex had experienced at first hand. Anticipating neither the amelioration of productive relations that underlay popular allegiance, nor the establishment of an industrial elite attractive to aspiring technocrats, the artists we have encountered here seem to have regarded Saint-Simonianism as a spiritual panacea, capable of overcoming personal anguish and heralding a moral order in which their creative potential could blossom. Examination of the work actually produced within the school, however, reveals a considerable discrepancy between such professions of enthusiasm and tangible achievement.

FROM MÉNILMONTANT TO CAIRO

Saint-Simonianism's promise of cultural regeneration ultimately depended on restructuring the social system, but artists such as Justus offered their services as a contribution to the campaign for proselytization in the present. Yet despite constant emphasis on art's didactic potential and repeated insistence on the need to attract converts through the power of sentiment, practical deployment of the arts seems to have been minimal.

Greatest concentration of activity occurred during the Ménilmontant retreat, initiated in April 1832 following the authorities' suspension of the "Exposition de la Doctrine" at the Salle Taitbout and the closure of *Le Globe*. Despite its rapid curtailment by official intervention, Ménilmontant forms a significant interlude in the movement's doctrinal and cultural evolution. Doctrinally, the episode consolidated a reordering of priorities in which religiosity and personal comportment eclipsed political intervention as central concerns. Evidenced in the establishment of a collective organization where each of the forty inmates was allotted a specific manual task in a *hiérarchie d'amour*,[45] this enhanced regard for interpersonal relations fundamentally affected cultural life at the retreat.

[44] On Algeria, see Etex, *Souvenirs*, 149–57. On 1848, see ibid., 240–45.

[45] The expression is Michel Chevalier's, cited in S. Charléty, *Histoire du Saint-Simonisme (1825–1864)*, (1896; reprint, 1965), 141.

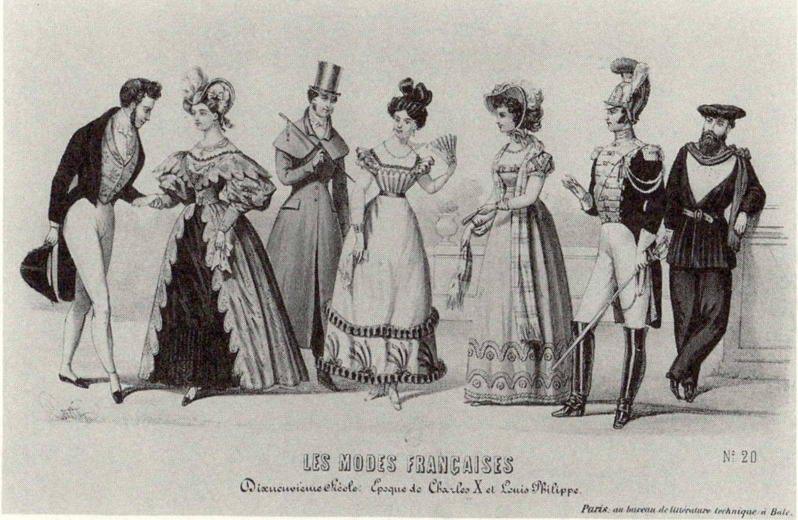

Plate 6. *Les Modes françaises,* number 20, showing Saint-Simonian dress on extreme right. Cabinet des estampes, Bibliothèque nationale, Paris.

Monastic parallels were assiduously cultivated. A specially designed costume (plate 6), which Enfantin claimed "efface la hiérarchie ancienne et consacre une égalité nouvelle,"[46] exploited putative symbolic associations in combining white trousers, red waistcoat, and blue tunic, respectively signifying love, work, and faith. The liturgical structure of everyday life generated a rich repertoire of music theater, as everything from meal times to collective labor provided a pretext for choral singing. Music, too, played a conspicuous part in the elaborate festivities mounted in the convent's grounds on such occasions as the taking of the habit (plate 7) or initiation of work on a new temple.[47] All of this indicates a redirection of theoretical and practical energies, intended to attract a broader following than had been possible through abstract ideological debate. Michel Chevalier outlines the centrality of art in this process, emphasizing its complete integration in life at Ménilmontant:

> The fact dominating life at present is the foundation of our cult, or in other words the widespread introduction of art into our public and private activities; song before and after our meals, song when the *Père* meets with the family in public, simple, standardized costumes, the elegant use of movement—all of

[46] Ibid., 143. This equality was symbolized in the design of the waistcoat; buttoned at the back, it could only be put on with the help of a fellow apostle. For a detailed discussion of Saint-Simonian dress and its symbolism, see P. Régnier, *Les Saint-Simoniens en Egypte 1833–1851* (1989), 16–21.

[47] The definitive account is provided in Locke, *Music, Musicians*, 123–52.

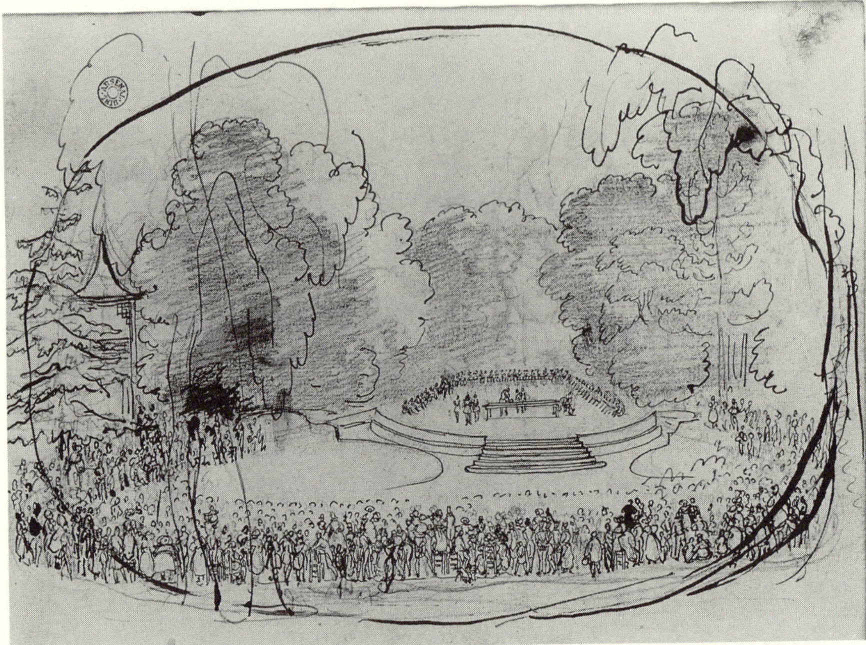

Plate 7. Philippe-Joseph Machereau: *Ceremony at Ménilmontant,* 1832. Ms. 13910, p. 34v., Bibliothèque de l'Arsenal, Paris.

> this is rich in its powerful appeal to the people and to women. Women, artists, the people—these are the ones who will come to us now: rational men will live off our past. The former know how to love, the latter only how to feel esteem: everything can be done with love, but little enough with esteem.[48]

Rather than exploiting social antagonisms, attempts to convert the Parisian working class were couched in terms of love and sentiment. The workers were to be shown the disciples' overwhelming benevolence and would pledge their allegiance in return. The paternalist connotations of such a strategy are revealed in the murals planned for the outer walls of the convent. The slogans mentioned in Chevalier's account of the project, reminiscent of Campanella's temple decor in the City of the Sun or Say's descrip-

[48] "Le fait dominant de la vie actuelle, c'est la fondation de notre culte, c'est en d'autres termes l'introduction large de l'art dans nos pratiques publiques et intimes; du chant avant et après nos repas, du chant quand le Père arrive en public dans la famille, des costumes simples et uniformes, des manoeuvres faites avec aisance, tout cela est riche de puissance de propagation populaire et féminine; les femmes, les artistes, le peuple, voilà ceux qui vont venir à nous maintenant: les hommes raisonnables vont vivre sur notre passé. Les premiers savent aimer, les autres ne savent guère qu'estimer: on fait tout avec l'amour, on fait peu avec l'estime seule." M. Chevalier to E. Humann, 2 July 1832, Arsenal Ms. 7814:36. For a transcription, see P. Régnier, ed., *Le Livre nouveau des Saint-Simoniens* (1991), 55–61.

tion of the moral injunctions decorating the liberal utopia of Olbie,[49] emphasize obedience and labor, values central to Saint-Simonian conceptions of an organic social hierarchy:

> Raymond Bonheur, a painter gifted with versatility, will probably paint the facade and boundary walls; we will cover the walls with inscriptions such as the following, which I give merely as examples: blessed are those who join together to labor in God's name—God loves the hardworking man, who cares for his body and soul—Education for the young, for the aged worker repose.[50]

Bonheur's efforts at Ménilmontant were supplemented by three other artists—Justus, the architect Henry, and the lithographer Philippe-Joseph Machereau, who was given particular responsibility for proselytizing the working classes.[51] An atelier was established principally for Bonheur's use, and some friction developed when the irrascible Justus attempted to interfere with his work.[52] Despite the facilities, however, production was limited, greater priority apparently being given to public events. Machereau's illustration to Félicien David's score *Ménilmontant* (plate 8) portrays one such occasion, while the artist's sketchbooks suggest he was planning a history painting of a group of apostles encountering their former comrade Jules Lechevalier on their way to Bazard's funeral in July 1832 (plate 9). Portraits of the leadership, which decorated the rooms at Ménilmontant, also seem to have been produced.[53] The meagerness of these results can scarcely be imputed either to indifference or lack of theoretical awareness—discussions concerning the *Livre nouveau* clearly testify to the importance accorded to aesthetics at this stage in the movement's history.

The artists at Ménilmontant were ambitious enough—as ever, Justus was most effusive in his professed willingness to develop innovative stylistic solutions to the doctrine's artistic needs:

> If I should work to imagine subjects, invent costumes, harmonize my artistic ideals with the doctrine and draw on yours for inspiration in order to have sketches ready for use when the time is right, if I should give new life on canvas

[49] See T. Campanella, *La città del sole: dialogo poetico* (1623), trans. and ed. D. J. Donno (1981), 32–36 for a description of the didactic illustrations on the temple walls, and J.-B. Say, "Olbie, ou essai sur les moyens d'améliorer les moeurs d'une nation," in *Oeuvres diverses* (1848), 614–15.

[50] "Raymond Bonheur qui est un peintre doué de facilité va probablement peindre la façade et les murs d'enceinte; nous allons couvrir ces murs d'inscriptions telles que celles-ci que je ne vous cite que comme indication: ceux qui sont associés au nom de Dieu pour travailler sont bénis—Dieu aime l'homme laborieux, soigneux de son esprit et de son corps—A la jeunesse éducation, retraite au vieux travailleur." Chevalier to Humann, 2 July 1832.

[51] See H. R. d'Allemagne, *Les Saint-Simoniens. 1827–1837* (1930), 314.

[52] P. Justus to P. Enfantin, n.d. (1832), Bibliothèque nationale, N.A.Fr. 24610, ff. 48–51.

[53] A number of largely unattributed portraits are in the Arsenal; see the manuscript *Inventaire sommaire (provisoire) des tableaux, dessins, gravures, objets divers de la collection Enfantin.*

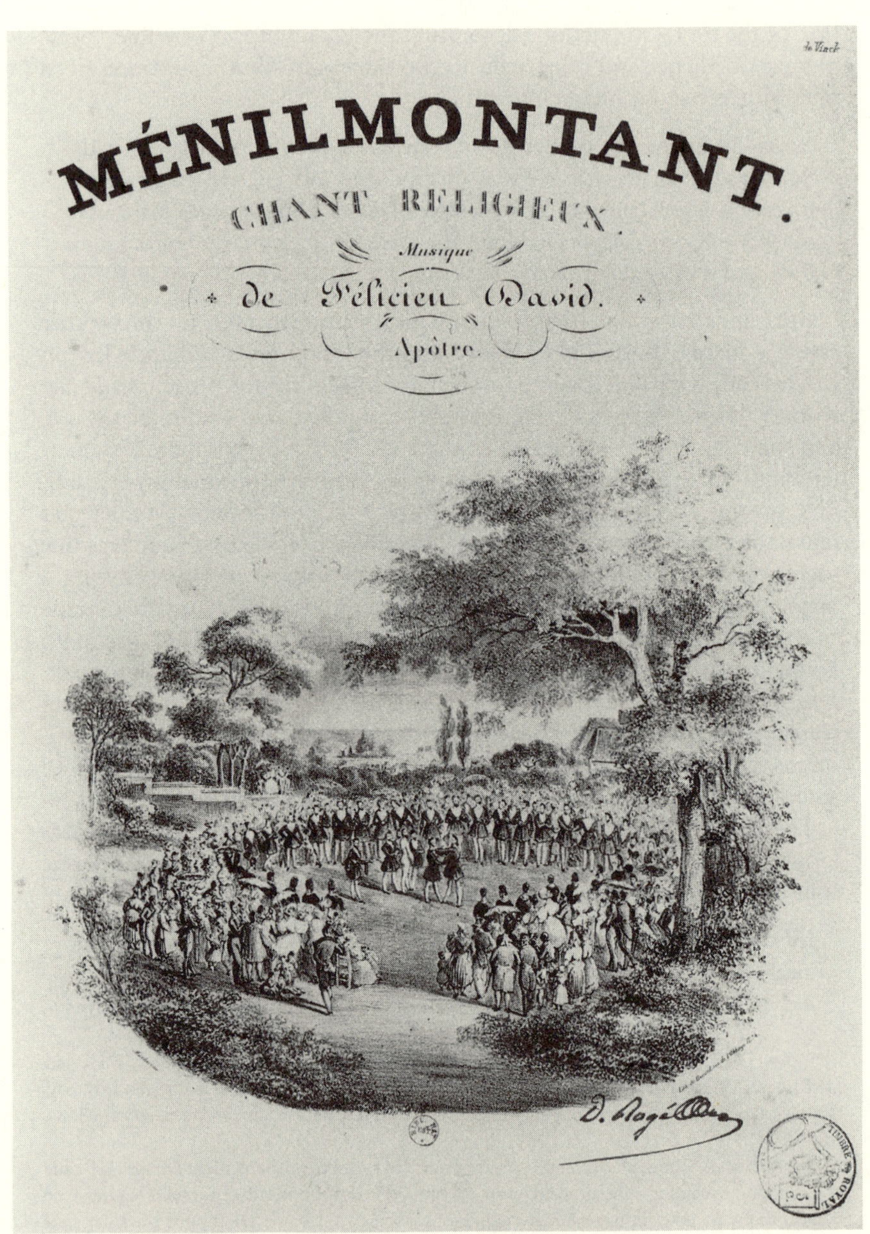

Plate 8. Philippe-Joseph Machereau: Cover to *Ménilmontant. Chant religieux* by Félicien David, 1832. Cabinet des estampes, Bibliothèque nationale, Paris.

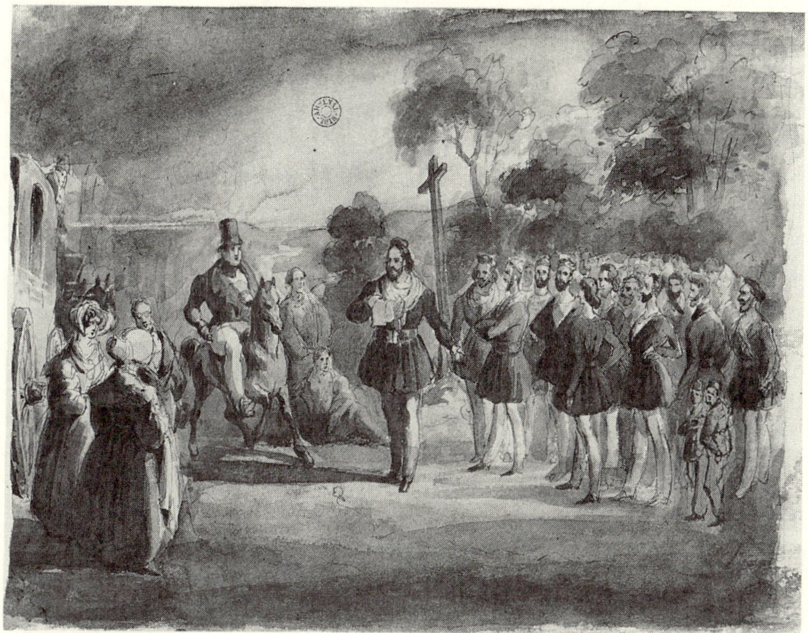

Plate 9. Philippe-Joseph Machereau: *Rencontre de Jules Lechevalier et des Saint-Simoniens à Courty, 30 juillet 1832,* 1832. Fonds Gustave d'Eichthal, Ms. 14410, p. 17, Bibliothèque de l'Arsenal, Paris.

> to the major events in the progress of humanity, plunge into the future to call society forward through works which carry it toward its goal. . . . If I should put on the chameleon coat of the artist, laughing or enraged by turn, sometimes joyful then, for no particular reason, sometimes somber and sad, then here is my life. Do you want it? I am giving it to you, my fathers.[54]

Such ambitious perspectives were never to be explored and the artists at Ménilmontant seem to have been relatively underemployed. Indeed, the movement tended to commission works from professionals outside the group and such works were themselves limited to the comparatively unexacting field of portraiture. A lithograph of Enfantin by Grévedon and a portrait medallion by Caunois were sold to believers in 1832, while illustra-

[54] "S'il faut travailler à créer des sujets, chercher des costumes, harmoniser mes idées d'art avec la doctrine et m'inspirer des vôtres pour disposer des esquisses à exécuter dès que le temps sera venu, faire revivre sur la toile les principaux faits qui caractérisent les progrès de l'humanité, plonger dans l'avenir pour y convoquer la société par des oeuvres qui la portent vers son but. . . . S'il me faut endosser le camélionique manteau de l'artiste tantôt riant ou se fachant, tantôt allègre puis après, sans sujet bien déterminé, quelquefois sombre et chagrin, voilà ma vie, la voulez-vous? je vous la donne, mes pères." P. Justus to C. Duveyrier, 26 April 1832, Arsenal Ms. 7606:99.

tions of the leadership were commissioned from Decaisne and Léon Cogniet and a portrait purchased from Bouchot.[55] The *art de l'avenir* so zealously promoted by the Saint-Simonians was apparently stillborn: portraits of Félicien David by Bonheur and of Massol by Jules Laure,[56] a few likenesses of the group's leaders—the achievement seems rather meager. One unidentified work does suggest a more ambitious initiative, however. The Swiss writer Juste Olivier, visiting Paris in 1830, describes a statue the prophetic overtones of which he identified as "doubtless Saint-Simonian":

> It is a virgin . . . (in other words a holy virgin, though they obviously modify the Christian idea). She is represented wearing an ornament on her head showing earlier forms of organization (I don't know whether they have two or three of them) while above the sculptor has placed a star, representing the new form of organization (Saint-Simon's doctrine).[57]

The Ménilmontant period marks a watershed in the movement's development. Beneath the seemingly feverish activity one senses a degree of lassitude following the internecine disputes of previous years. It is, indeed, precisely around this time that a number of artists associated with the group began to sever their ties—Bra had already forsaken Enfantin for Buchez, Hawke's correspondence gradually ends during 1833,[58] Bonheur reluctantly abandoned convent life and was later attracted to Fourierism and the Templar movement.[59] Others remained, however: Machereau joined an apostolic *Mission du travail* to Lyons in October 1832, while Justus and Henri left for the same destination the following month.[60]

[55] On Grévedon, see Cavel, "Portrait lithographié de P. Enfantin," *Le Globe* 27 (March 1832):345. The brochure *Religion saint-simonienne: Procès en la Cour d'assises de la Seine les 27 et 28 août 1832* contains lithographs by Cals after Cogniet—a group portrait of Barrault, Chevalier, and Duveyrier, together with a portrait of Enfantin. The *Procès en police correctionelle, le 19 octobre 1832* has a lithograph of Caunois's medallion of Enfantin by Cals and a portrait of Fournel by Cals after a drawing by Decaisne.

[56] Massol's portrait, misattributed, is now in the Arsenal collection.

[57] "C'est une Vierge . . . (. . . c'est-à-dire une Sainte-Vierge, mais il est clair qu'ils modifient cette idée chrétienne). Elle est représentée avec un ornement de tête qui figure les organisations précédentes (je ne sais s'ils en comptent deux ou trois) et au-dessus le sculpteur a représenté une étoile, qui figure l'organisation nouvelle (la doctrine de Saint-Simon)." J. Olivier, *Paris en 1830*, ed. A. Delattre and M. Denkinger (1951), 126, entry dated 21 June. The work was described to Olivier by Vigny's friend, Robert, a Saint-Simonian doctor who died the following year, aged twenty-five. See ibid., 67, n. 1.

[58] Hawke subsequently left for America, though he was in Paris during 1848, when he published Salon reviews in the *Représentant du peuple* and the *Voix des femmes*, and articles in *Le Lucifer*. He died in Tunis in 1887.

[59] See Rancière, *La Nuit*, 157; Klumpke, *Rosa Bonheur*, 152–60; C. Pellarin, *Souvenirs anecdotiques: médecine navale—saint simonisme—chouannerie* (1868), 176.

[60] For Machereau see d'Allemagne, *Les Saint-Simoniens*, 326; for Justus, ibid., 327, and *Le Livre des actes* 1 (1833). Justus was subsequently involved with the working-class Parisian group around 1835–36; see Vinçard, *Mémoires*, 126.

Though provincial proselytization expanded during Enfantin's imprisonment, tensions within the Lyons group began to surface early in 1833. At stake was the practical and theoretical prominence accorded to the artist. Resentment at their privileged status—most clearly articulated by the former army officers Hoart and Bruneau, and by Desloges, a butcher's assistant turned apostle—focused deeper ambivalence toward the movement's increasing individualist tendencies and its apparent abandonment of political concern for the inequalities suffered by the proletariat.[61] Having renounced his directive role within the movement, Enfantin declined to intervene as the artists split from the main apostolic group. In May 1833, Machereau embarked on a *mission d'art et de travail* with eight colleagues, all dressed in a special costume reserved for artists, arriving in Marseilles two months later.[62] Such initiatives were thought particularly appealing to workers and women, both regarded by Saint-Simonian theorists as essentially unresponsive to intellectual persuasion. The *dogme*, elaborated in the "Exposition" and *Le Globe*, was to be revivified through its presentation as a *culte*, exploiting music and theatricality in an immediate appeal to sentiment.[63]

Though the *mission d'art et de travail* focused on these more participative and dramatically engaging media, visual art retained an important place within the Saint-Simonian aesthetic, as is amply demonstrated in the final abortive attempt to rally artists during the expedition to Egypt. The mission to the east, encouraged by Enfantin from his prison cell in Sainte-Pélagie and coordinated by Barrault through the foundation of the apostolic group, the Compagnons de la Femme, was intended to fulfill several aims. Most important, the expedition signified rejection of the European rationalist tradition for a civilization believed to be more responsive to sentiment, through its mystical religious heritage. This was thought to augur well for the discovery of the *Femme-Messie*, whose appearance would complement the rationalism of the *Père suprême* and embody an epistemological synthesis capable of securing radical social transformation. Fournel also emphasized Egypt's industrial potential and encouraged Enfantin to press for the construction of a Suez canal. More pragmatically, the mission to the east forestalled the total collapse of the movement which, following Enfantin's imprisonment, seemed increasingly aimless and impotent.

The expedition was initiated by Barrault, who reached Constantinople in

[61] See Régnier's fascinating account in "Idées et opinions," 2:392–96.

[62] See Hoart to P. Enfantin, *Le Livre des actes* 3 (1833): 40.

[63] Thus, Enfantin writes to Hoart and Bruneau (26 October 1832, Arsenal Ms. 7646:353) of his conviction that, faced by such sensual appeal, "il n y aura pas d'âme forte qui ne s'ébranle et qui ne soit prête à répéter un amen." The new theatricality would prove particularly attractive to artists: "ce sera pour nous la forme des prédications adaptées au moment actuel. De là nos pièces auront un caractère plutôt prophétique que traditionnel, de là aussi une excitation pour tous les artistes qui comprenderont la puissance de cette innovation dans l'art; or, c'est sur elle que je fonde la force de notre enseignement actuel."

April 1833. His firm belief that the *Femme-Messie* was to be found in the city was frustrated, as the authorities expelled him within a week of his arrival.[64] Following this setback, Barrault moved to Egypt, where he was gradually joined by other disciples who had rallied to the *compagnonnage*. Among this group were two artists—Alric and Machereau. The sculptor was among the earliest to leave for the east, and in late 1833 set out on an apostolic campaign in the Greek Islands.[65] Machereau embarked for Egypt soon after the initial exodus, sailing from Marseilles in August 1833, having completed a grueling tour around the south of France with the *mission des artistes*.[66] With his release from prison, Enfantin arrived at the end of 1833 and took over control of proselytization and the public works programs the group had proposed to Egypt's rulers. Although the industrial initiative came to dominate activities, the arts were still considered a priority.

Barrault initiated lectures on aesthetics in Alexandria during November 1833, while Machereau improved the group's finances by giving drawing lessons and painting portraits,[67] and Alric received commissions for busts. A commission from the Egyptian viceroy Mohammed Ali was considered a particular achievement. The group regarded prohibition of representational imagery as symptomatic of Islamic antimaterialism, which had to be overcome if Egypt's industrial potential was to be realized and its repressive attitude toward women reversed. Barrault regarded Alric's commission as a promising step in this direction, but disagreement over pricing almost prevented the work's completion.[68] Both Alric and Machereau subsequently secured posts teaching drawing in schools at Abu Zabal and Giza, though Alric was not to remain in work for long; with a number of other disciples, he was struck down by cholera and died in April 1835. By contrast, Machereau thrived in Egypt; after his post at the cavalry school in Giza expired, he was commissioned by Soliman-Pacha to paint a mural of the battle of Nezib, and later decorated the Pacha's billiard room. Believing he had inhabited the Orient in a previous existence, Machereau changed his name to

[64] See Charléty, *Histoire*, 178.

[65] See J. Alric to X, 18 October 1833, in *Le Livre des actes* 10 (1833): 202–3.

[66] See P. Machereau to A. Petit, 24 June 1833, Arsenal Ms. 15031:145, and R. Fakkar, *Sociologie, socialisme et internationalisme pré-marxiste: l'influence de Saint-Simon* (1968), 222. On Machereau in Egypt, see ibid., 231; J. Carré, *Voyageurs et écrivains français en Egypte* (1932), 1:263–67; S. Voilquin, *Souvenirs d'une fille du peuple ou la Saint-Simonienne en Egypte* (1866), 271 and the fictionalized account by Charles Edmond Chojecki, *Zephyrin Cazavan en Egypte* (1880), where Machereau appears as the artist Gendel (see 112–18).

[67] On Barrault's lectures, see Fakkar, *Sociologie*, 247–48; on Machereau, see *Le Livre des actes* 10 (1833): 209, and E. Barrault to Prax, 13 April 1834, Arsenal Ms. 7691:9.

[68] See E. Barrault to J. Alric, 2 September 1834, Arsenal Ms. 7691:58; Alric's letters to the Egyptian viceroy, Arsenal Ms. 7680:1–3; J. Alric to Lamy, 22 August 1834, Arsenal Ms. 7680:11, and X to Lamy, August 1834, Arsenal Ms. 7680:9. See also P. Granal, "Choubrah et le buste du pacha," *Le Temps* (31 January 1838): cols. 48626–27.

Mohammed el Mahdi, became a Muslim, and married an Egyptian wife, remaining in the Middle East after his colleagues' return to France.[69]

Billiard rooms were not quite what Enfantin had in mind as the art of the future. Hoping to use Egypt as the base for a major artistic initiative, in 1834 he sent Petit and Duguet back to France in an attempt to enlist painters to travel east. Petit himself, a lawyer and agronomist by profession, seems also to have trained as an artist in the 1820s, and continued to paint at Ménilmontant and in Egypt. His correspondence with the artist Auguste Dorgemont, who had returned to his native Guadeloupe in 1830 after training in Paris, suggests that he may have retained some contacts in the artistic community and helps to clarify Enfantin's choice in sending him to France. A letter to Dorgemont, written during the journey home, explains why such an initiative was thought sufficiently important to merit this step. After describing the immense artistic potential of the Egyptian landscape, Petit continues:

> Egypt is reaching one of those solemn moments in the history of humanity when the future surges from the ruins of the past. . . . At such a time, art must have a role to play. First of all, the Mahometans' religious prejudice against images must be overcome. We have already made some attempt here. Alric, a distinguished sculptor, is producing busts of several generals. One of these busts will make the Pacha want his own; once the upper echelons have been attacked, this prejudice will quickly dissipate among the masses, and, as you know, all prejudices are interconnected.[70]

Petit spent much of the summer in Paris, returning to Egypt in November 1834. Despite ceaseless activity, involving personal lobbying, the insertion of an article promoting Egypt in *L'Artiste*,[71] and lectures to the Société libre des beaux-arts, he was unable to entice the artistic community to the Orient. Various individuals were contacted, some of whom, such as Cogniet, Laure, Etex, and Cendrier, had ties with the movement. Others, such as Alexandre Dumas, were canvassed more speculatively,[72] but in every instance the re-

[69] See Régnier, *Les Saint-Simoniens en Egypte*, 136–38.

[70] "L'Egypte touche à un de ces moments solennels dans l'histoire de l'humanité où l'avenir surgira du sein des ruines du passé. . . . Dans une semblable époque l'art doit avoir un rôle à jouer. Il faut d'abord déraciner les préjugés religieux des Mahometans contre les images. Déjà quelques tentatives ont été faits par nous. Alric, sculpteur distingué, fait les bustes de plusieurs généraux. L'un de ces bustes donnera au Pacha le désir d'avoir le sien; une fois attaqué dans les sommités, ce préjugé s'affaiblira vite dans les masses, et, vous le savez, tous les préjugés se trament." A. Petit to A. Dorgemont, n.d. (March 1834), Arsenal Ms. 15031:543. See also A. Petit to L. Cogniet, 29 April 1834, Arsenal Ms. 15031:792.

[71] See letter dated Cairo, 8 April 1834, in *L'Artiste* 7 (1834): 201–2. An anonymous introductory note describes the group as "des jeunes gens ardents, pleins de talent et animés de vastes pensées" and commends Petit's proposals as offering artists "un monde nouveau."

[72] See A. Petit to A. Dumas, 11 July 1834, Arsenal Ms. 15031:880.

sponse was either evasive or openly negative. In a series of letters to Enfantin, Petit expresses his disgust at artists' pusillanimity and his frustration at the obstacle imposed by their ambitions to succeed in the Paris market. His early impressions were relatively hopeful; several artists, including Cogniet, Barye, Etex, Antonin Moine, Laure, and Cendrier had promised to encourage younger colleagues to give Petit a fair hearing, though none had made any personal commitment.[73]

Initial optimism soon evaporated, however, despite the enthusiasm with which Petit projected the Orient as an infallible means of artistic regeneration. Europe, he argued, had exhausted its inspirational potential and any cultural renewal depended on infusing new elements from the hitherto neglected eastern civilizations. From such a synthesis an art of unsurpassed power would appear:

> It is from the arts of Asia and Africa, as well as from Greek or Christian Art—from the Egyptians' massiveness, the Arabs' diversity, and the Brahmins' refined compositions—no less than from the elegance of Rome and the Middle Ages' grave yet graceful austerity that the fertile breath of a new genius will bring forth the new art which will regenerate the world.[74]

The fusion of the West's spiritual tradition with the materialist sensuality of the East becomes a key to aesthetic renewal in the same way as unification of the two hitherto isolated civilizations now serves to underwrite social and religious regeneration. Petit's descriptions of the East highlight its sumptuousness, which he presents as equaling, if not surpassing, such traditionally favored areas as Greece and Rome. Italy in particular, he argues, had been exhausted by years of exploitation; the East offered new and stimulating possibilities: "Here art of form and color, whatever its type or purpose, finds numerous models and magnificent inspiration."[75]

This seductive vision proved entirely resistible to every artist whom Petit solicited, an obduracy he blamed on a number of factors. Many, including those sympathetic to the movement, cited prior obligations as a pretext for refusal, while others pointed to the dangers of the voyage and the uncertainties awaiting them in Egypt. After several months of fruitless persuasion, Petit, frustrated and contemptuous, wrote to Enfantin:

> There is still no one with a will powerful enough to free him from ties of family and the world, even for personal glory, no one seduced by the hope of a rich or

[73] See A. Petit to P. Enfantin, 3 July 1834, Arsenal Ms. 7614:98–101.

[74] "Des arts de l'Asie et de l'Afrique aussi bien que de l'Art grec ou chrétien, des masses Egyptiennes, de la variété Arabe, des savants combinaisons des Brames, non moins que de l'élégance Romaine et de la grave et légère austérité du moyen âge, le souffle fécondant d'un nouveau génie fera surgir l'art nouveau qui régénérera le monde." A. Petit to L. Cogniet, 29 April 1834, Arsenal Ms. 15031:792.

[75] "L'art de la forme et de la couleur, quelque soit sa nature et son but, trouve ici des modèles sans nombre et de magnifiques inspirations." Ibid.

> glorious life, impelled by the thought of artistic regeneration or the creation of a new art. . . . Even those who know and love us draw back and disappear. Cendrier can leave only by consoling his mother with the prospect of a good job. Laure is waiting for the next exhibition and the *completion of a painting* before coming. Others are busy learning and improving. As if their artistic education could not be completed beneath the sun which beats upon the *Père's* tent. As for the herd of *industriels* who call themselves artists, they ask what *guarantees* there are![76]

Evasiveness and careerism were only part of the problem. More fundamentally, Petit felt that the prevalent artistic orthodoxy underlay the general indifference to his proposals. He expressed surprise at the vitality of the academic tradition and artists' commitment to antiquity as the aesthetic norm. Eurocentrism was strengthened by Ingres's inflexible promotion of the Italian masters and by what Petit regarded as the more opportunist maneuvering of the Academy itself. By making concessions to those who had challenged its doctrinal preeminence, Petit argued that the institutional structure had successfully disarmed potential opposition and had absorbed putative rebels in a slightly more liberal orthodoxy. An improbable encounter with Ingres was forestalled by realization that for him, as for his devotees, the image of the Orient could do little to supplant the supremacy of Rome.[77]

Petit ended his mission in Autumn 1834, having failed to persuade any of the artists he met to return to Egypt with him. His campaign marks the final attempt to recruit artists to the cause; indeed the school was itself in a state of crisis,[78] and many demoralized disciples soon returned to France and the

[76] "Pas un homme encore qu'une volonté puissante dégage, même pour sa gloire, des liens de la famille ou du monde, pas un homme que séduise l'espoir d'une vie riche ou glorieuse, qu'entraîne la pensée de la régénération de l'Art ou la conception de l'art nouveau. . . . Ceux-là même qui nous ont touché, et qui nous aiment s'effacent et reculent. Cendrier ne peut partir qu'en consolant sa mère par l'appât d'une belle position. Laure attend pour venir la nouvelle exposition et la *fin d'un tableau*. D'autres s'occupent d'apprendre et de se perfectionner. Comme si leur éducation d'artiste ne devait pas s'achever sous le soleil qui brule la tente du *Père*. Enfin le troupeau d'industriels qui se sont qualifiés d'artistes demandent quelles sont les *garanties*!" A. Petit to P. Enfantin, 27 July 1834, Arsenal Ms. 7614:101–7, 101v.

[77] "J'ai fait sonder M.Ingres; l'art pour lui est dans Rome: j'ai vu ses élèves qui m'ont répondu: qu'il n'y avait point en Egypte ni de Raphaël ni de Titien. La Roméomanie emporte encore les écoles de Paris. L'Académie, que je croyais morte, est partout. Pour ne pas mourir tout à fait, elle a transigé avec le Romantisme. Delaroche y est accepté comme Berryer l'est par les républicains marseillais." Ibid., 102r.

[78] Encountering the group during a visit to Cairo in Spring 1835, the Swiss painter Charles Gleyre noted in his journal: "Leur air désillusioné, désoeuvré, me font de la peine. . . . Le Père assure que leur mission est accomplie. Ainsi soit-il." Cited in Winterthur, Kunstmuseum, *Gleyre ou les illusions perdues* (1974), 54. Enfantin was later an habitué of Gleyre's salon in the rue du Bac, and the subject of an unfinished portrait (C. Clément, *Gleyre. Etude biographique et critique, avec le catalogue raisonné de l'oeuvre du maître* [1878], 203). On Gleyre's Saint-Simonian sympathies, see *Gleyre ou les illusions perdues*, 102, and J. Salles, *Mémoires d'un vieil artiste* (1896), 205.

security of careers in the administrative and industrial system they had attempted to transform. The artist, on whom the doctrine had come to place so much emphasis as a partner in this process, had remained doggedly indifferent to all promises of social influence and formal regeneration.

WHY WERE THERE NO GREAT SAINT-SIMONIAN ARTISTS?

Though the absence of any significant Saint-Simonian cultural legacy has never much preoccupied art historians, there is no inherent reason why the group's attempts to win support should have been so conspicuously unsuccessful. Attacks upon the aesthetic propounded by the movement and the disciples' own refutations of accusations leveled against them throw some light on the issues contemporaries perceived as critical to the Saint-Simonian perspective on the arts and helps to illuminate the reasons underlying the failure of their initiative.

The proclaimed incompatibility of art and industry had been an issue refuted by Saint-Simon himself. Despite his denial that organized industrial exploitation would bring about the demise of art, critics such as Benjamin Constant continued to argue that Saint-Simonianism was a materialist ideology, antipathetic to creativity. The devaluation of art through the debilitating influence of commerce was attacked by a correspondent to the Saint-Simonian journal *Le Gymnase* in 1828; the arts were seen as being carried away by "the tide of industry" which had transformed the artist into an "ideas merchant"[79] more concerned with diverting his public than producing works of integrity and enduring value. A similar point was made by the journalist Alphonse Karr four years later. Fulfillment of material needs, he argued, would lead to "an absurd and boring world"—free from conflict, but equally free from excitement and artistic inspiration. Individuality would be attenuated as satisfaction of material wants introduced a passionless uniformity fatal to creative endeavor:

> No longer will you be able to show us faces on which suffering has written its tale, or the passions have left their mark. . . . The painter will be able to produce only pictures of flowers and the portait of Père Enfantin with his umbrella. . . . The sculptor will be able to produce only vases or basins.[80]

[79] "Le flot industriel"; "marchand d'idées." Anonymous, "Contre la tendance industrielle du siècle," *Le Gymnase* 9 (31 July 1828): 232–41. See P. Hazard, "Saint-Simonisme et littérature," *Neophilologus*, 23 (1937–38): 129–34.

[80] "Un monde absurde et ennuyeux"; "Vous ne pourrez plus nous montrer des visages où la souffrance a écrit toute une histoire, où les passions ont laissé des traces. . . . Le peintre ne pourra plus faire que des tableaux de fleurs et le portrait du père Enfantin, avec son parapluie. . . . Le sculpteur ne pourra plus faire que des vases ou des cuvettes." A. Karr, "Les Saint-

Underlying both critiques is the belief that true art can emerge only when the artist is a socially and economically marginal figure. While the *Gymnase* writer equates poverty with liberty,[81] Karr argues that marginality induces dissatisfaction with the present and inspires the artist to create an imaginary world by exploring his own subjectivity:

> Because he carries within himself intuition of a better life or is impelled by a sacred fire that purifies his soul, the poet is someone with needs that society and nature are unable to satisfy. Imagining that God would not put needs into men's hearts which did not carry a tacit promise of satisfaction, he starts out with beliefs only to see his illusions fall one by one like autumn leaves; with all the outpourings of his soul battered and betrayed, he withdraws and turns inward, his sadness expressed in bitter criticism of things as they are and touching regrets for what they ought to be.[82]

Both commentators arrive at differing conclusions from the same premise—the *Gymnase* writer equates marginality with romantic insouciance while for Karr creativity thrives on agony and introspection. Yet both concur in identifying art with isolation, a perspective forming part of a broader discourse most fully expressed in Gautier's assertion of formal autonomy and artistic independence. This tradition stands in direct opposition to the "humanitarian" current, first fully elaborated in Saint-Simonian theory. While this latter trend emphasized the desirability of artistic assimilation in a fully integrated, organic society, its detractors remain attached to an individualist construction of the artist. Both trends accept the particularity of his personality, though the Saint-Simonians regard him as an element within a social totality and argue that his talents can only be given full expression through regard to its needs. The artist must therefore address himself to the people in a way that is both accessible and consonant with their political needs, as prescribed by the ruling elite.

Such a perspective was anathema to the orthodoxy represented by Karr.

Simoniens: les arts," *Le Figaro* (17 April 1832), part of a bitingly hostile series on the movement. For a response, see P. Rochette, "Quelques mots sur l'art," *Le Globe* (18 April 1832): 435.

[81] "On disait autrefois gueux comme un peintre, c'était là le bon temps pour eux, indépendance, liberté d'esprit, absence d'embarras et de soins, insouciance et gaité, voilà la véritable loi des arts. Les soucis de l'industrie sont mortels pour eux." Anonymous, "Contre la tendance industrielle," 241.

[82] "Le poète est celui qui, ayant en lui le pressentiment d'une vie meilleure, ou animé d'un feu sacré qui épure son âme, a des besoins que le monde et la nature sont impuissants à satisfaire. D'abord plein de croyances, et imaginant que Dieu n'a pas mis au coeur de l'homme un besoin qui ne soit une promesse tacite de le satisfaire, il a vu tomber une à une toutes ses illusions comme les feuilles sous le vent d'automne; tout ce que de son âme il a mis en dehors a été heurté et froisé, alors il s'est replié et renfermé en lui-même, et ses douleurs s'exhalent en amères critiques de ce qui existe et en touchants regrets de ce qui devait exister." A. Karr, "Les Saint-Simoniens: appel au poètes," *Le Figaro* (9 April 1832).

Commitment to the autonomy of artistic creativity went hand in hand with an assertion of individualism directly at odds with Saint-Simonianism's collectivist tendencies. The artist was regarded as the paradigmatic individualist; though his preoccupations and life-style were presented as directly opposed to the perceived conformity of bourgeois values, he nonetheless paradoxically stood as guardian of those values. This common assertion of individualism presented the artist as the personification of liberty, standing outside the mundane considerations of the everyday world, but at the same time embodying in their most extreme form values of personal independence embodied in bourgeois mercantilism. This stance of artistic autonomy was attacked by the Saint-Simonians and their successors as vehemently as they condemned the fragmentation of contemporary social life. Their rejection of bourgeois values as egocentric and divisive is consistent with their critique of the artist's abdication of social responsibility. In the same way as the industrialist stood accused of a fixation with material advancement, irrespective of the common good, so the artist was taxed with solipsistic self-gratification, oblivious to social imperatives.

Saint-Simonian designs were frequently seen as incompatible with the preservation of individual liberty, and hence inimical to artistic creativity. Though, particularly after 1832, the movement itself revealed some apprehension of the dangers posed by excessive authoritarianism, this was not enough to stifle dissent within the ranks. The issue contributed to tensions within the *mission du travail* in Lyon, while in December 1832 Pol Justus proclaimed himself "Apôtre artiste de l'individualité" and subsequently denounced Saint-Simonianism's repression of individual freedom, calling for "respect and realization for all personalities, liberty, equality of rights, no more castes, no more aristocracy."[83] Similar misgivings colored Sainte-Beuve's attitude, as Vigny reported in 1830:

> Sainte-Beuve told me that he accepted the Saint-Simonians' idea for the abolition of inheritance, but that he detested their religion, feeling that it destroys the individual and spontaneity, but he believes—and he took me aside to say this—that they will take over the world and the sect will become a religion.[84]

[83] "Respect et développement à toutes les natures, liberté, égalité de droits, plus de castes, plus d'aristocratie." P. Justus, *Vie et liberté! Pol, apôtre, artiste de l'individualité à ses frères et soeurs en Siant-Simon* [*sic*] (1834). His attitude contrasts with Machereau's devotion to Enfantin, whom he described as a "Napoléon pacifique" (d'Allemagne, *Les Saint-Simoniens*, 248) and whose authority he unquestioningly accepted.

[84] "Sainte-Beuve m'a dit qu'il adoptait des Saint-Simoniens l'idée de l'abolition de l'héritage, mais qu'il répugnait à leur religion parce qu'il sent qu'elle détruit l'individu et la spontanéité, mais il croit—et il me l'a dit à part—qu'ils s'empareront de la terre et que la secte deviendra religion." A. de Vigny, *Journal d'un poète*, ed. J. Baldensperger (1928), 9 December 1830, 44.

Expression of such fears prompted denial that the doctrine compromised creative freedom in any way. The explicit response made by Barrault in 1831 suggests the frequency of such attacks, however, implying that the group was conscious of its failure to rally artistic support and wished to set the record straight.[85] Barrault acknowledged that the issue had discouraged artists, but argued that their fears derived from a misinterpretation of the group's motives and intent;[86] far from aiming to limit individual freedom, Saint-Simonianism wished to end the atomization of society and institute a coherent system in which the artist would direct his efforts to the general good rather than dissipating them in isolation. Arguing that "our religion does not stifle liberty nor subsume the sanctity of the individual," Barrault maintained that the Saint-Simonian regime safeguarded creativity; rather than enforcing conformity to a preordained ideology, the artist freely interprets the inspirations of the "chef légitime," who owes his preeminence to the fact that he is a "poète lui-même," an individual whose instinctive understanding of social need derives from his highly developed capacity for love. Under such circumstances, Barrault argues that the artist spontaneously responds to the leader's injunctions, which constitute "la révélation du progrès," and which are given aesthetic expression according to his "vocation, son goût, son penchant."[87] The artist's function, moreover, is not merely passive. Conscious of his refined sensibility and popular sympathies, the chief consults him on the needs and aspirations of society, treating him as a mediator between the people and the leadership.

Barrault thus attempts to reconcile the maintenance of personal expression with a fully integrated social function for the arts. The balance he strikes between independence and social responsibility recalls Saint-Simon's own distinction between "l'imagination sans objet"—and thus "rétrograde"—and an imagination serving "la cause commune."[88] In both instances, imaginative independence is endorsed, but the paths it follows must accord with externally validated criteria of utility. The reassertion of autonomy is thus only partial and still sets Saint-Simonian aesthetic princi-

[85] See, for example, A. Petit to *Le National*, 6 September 1832, Arsenal Ms. 15031: 864.

[86] "Effarouchés de l'ardeur avec laquelle nous nous efforcions à ramener à l'unité une société anarchisée, vous avez cru voir en nos mains, au lieu de la lyre nouvelle, un inflexible niveau sous lequel devaient se courber en s'alignant tous les inspirations; vous avez reculé à l'apparence d'un cercle étroit dans lequel vous avez craint d'être emprisonnés." E. Barrault, *Religion saint-simonienne. Cérémonie du 27 novembre* (1831), 16. See also E. Barrault, *Aux artistes. Du passé et de l'avenir des beaux-arts* (1830), 77–78.

[87] "Notre religion n'étouffe pas la liberté, n'absorbe point la sainte personnalité." Barrault, *Religion*, 17. By contrast see E. Souvestre, *Des arts comme puissance gouvernementale, et de la nouvelle constitution à donner aux théâtres* (1832), which advocates total official control of cultural production (5).

[88] *L'Artiste, le savant et l'industriel*, in *O.S.S.E.*, 10:213.

ples at odds with the more comprehensive endorsement of artistic freedom represented by Karr.

The movement's anti-individualism and materialism appear to have been crucial in limiting its appeal among artists. Related to these misgivings was the belief that the group had little real understanding of the arts and that their gradual drift from positivism to religiosity was merely strategic. Vigny expressed doubts in 1829, writing "its pupils are, above all, capable economists who adopt religion to seduce artists."[89] A review of Barrault's *Aux artistes*, possibly by Balzac, highlighted just how unseductive the group's presentation was and emphasized the disciples' need for "a language appropriate to the age and its attitudes," capable of "relying less on reason and more on emotion."[90] While admiring Barrault's analysis, the reviewer deprecated his arid tone, arguing that "to be an apostle is an artist's mission, and the pamphlet's author has shown himself unequal to this imposing character."[91] The journalist's critique corroborates Barrault's emphasis on the evangelical power of sentiment, and his demands for a more poetic presentation mirror, and in some ways outstrip, Saint-Simonian agitation for an art form capable of effectively articulating theoretical issues. From such a perspective, the Saint-Simonians had failed to develop such a communicative strategy, and hence severely compromised their ability to rally artistic support.

The evolution of new stylistic forms embodying doctrine in a way immediately accessible to the nonintellectual faculties remained an abiding problem. Increasing regard for emotion stimulated the search for a verbal and visual language whose sensual appeal could incorporate a progressive political message. Spectacle and song were apparently conceived as one avenue for exploration, while language and intonation provided a major topic for debate at Ménilmontant. Discussion of the plastic arts seems to have remained relatively abstracted and efforts to evolve a visual vocabulary were largely abortive. Portraits of Enfantin, emphasizing his benign character and drawing subliminal parallels with Christ (plate 10), are the effective sum total of public proselytization.

The group's difficulties in finding a workable alternative to overt didacticism were later to be faced by the Fourierists, who harbored similar ambitions. In both instances, the problem was one of exploiting a medium whose

[89] "Ses élèves sont surtout des économistes habiles et font les religieux pour séduire les artistes." Vigny, *Journal*, December 1829, 24.

[90] "Un langage approprié au temps et aux hommes"; "moins raisonner et d'émouvoir davantage." H. de Balzac [?], review of *Aux artistes* by E. Barrault, *Le Feuilleton des journaux politiques* (March 1830).

[91] "L'apostolat est une mission d'artiste, et l'auteur de la brochure ne s'est pas montré digne de ce caractère imposant."

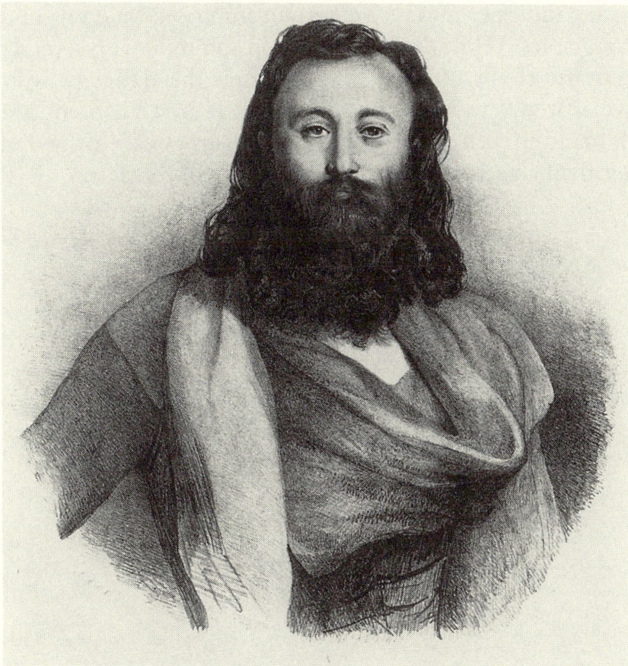

Plate 10. Aglaé Saint-Hilaire, after Léon Cogniet: *Le Père,* 1832. Bibliothèque de l'Arsenal, Paris.

potential range for articulating abstract ideas was limited, and to focus this articulation on the sensual, concrete properties of the image rather than conceiving it as a vehicle for cognitive forms. Emphasis on sensuality as a persuasive device supposed an aesthetic vocabulary not only at odds with dominant artistic codes, but also without precedent in recent practice. The earlier demand for a didactic art, appealing to reason rather than sentiment, was ambitious enough. Though parallel allegorical codes could be found, the ideas and properties specific to a hypothetical political future could borrow little from existing models. Projects such as Chevalier's imagined temple or Duveyrier's Vitruvian architectural projections[92] either lapsed into the fanciful or replicated past precedent without any overriding internal logic. To move beyond this relatively concrete stage and advance the need for an art that would elide the seemingly incompatible perspectives of

[92] See M. Chevalier, "Notes sur l'architecture," Arsenal Ms. 7825:3, and C. Duveyrier, "La Ville nouvelle ou le Paris des Saint-Simoniens," 6 November 1832, Arsenal Ms. 7825:5, published in *Le Livre des cent-et-un*, illustrated by Gros's pupil Chambellan, and transcribed in Régnier, *Le Livre nouveau*, 222–36.

formalism and didacticism was to entertain ambitions built on entirely new aesthetic principles. While the Fourierists, in common with several republican critics of the 1840s, attempted to overcome this difficulty by imputing progressive attitudes to works without overt political content, the Saint-Simonians made no such concessions; for them *art social* remained an imperative rather than an actuality, however imperfectly conceived.

CHAPTER 5

Sentiment and Faith: Philippe Buchez and His Circle

WITH THE secession of Philippe Buchez in December 1829, the Saint-Simonians lost one of their most prominent members.[1] Over the next two decades, culminating in his appointment as president of the National Assembly in 1848, Buchez acted as an important focus for a number of currents in the contemporary social movement. As the self-professed inheritor of Saint-Simonian orthodoxy, he attracted such dissidents as the playwright and critic Hippolyte Auger and the sculptor Théophile Bra, while his gravitation toward Catholicism in the mid 1830s brought an influx of young artists and writers onto his journal *L'Européen*, providing a link with the liberal Catholicism of Montalembert and Lacordaire, and establishing Buchez as a seminal figure in the growth of Christian socialism. Throughout the July Monarchy, Buchez also retained close contacts with the working-class movement, emerging as an early advocate of associationism and presiding over the foundation of a workers' journal, *L'Atelier*, in 1840.[2] Finally, Buchez stands apart from mainstream Saint-Simonianism in celebrating Jacobin republicanism—an enthusiasm deriving from his early Carbonarist involvement and given monumental expression in his *Histoire parlementaire de la révolution française*.[3]

Though aesthetic issues feature in Buchez's large corpus of historical, theological, medical, and political writings until his death in 1865, it was during the July Monarchy that his ideas received fullest theoretical formulation and practical application in art criticism. His lectures at the rue de Choiseul in 1830, directly competing with the Saint-Simonians in the Salle Taitbout, attracted such figures as Vigny, Béranger, and Raspail, while *L'Européen* provided a forum for doctrinal examination of contemporary art

[1] On Buchez's involvement with the Saint-Simonians, see F. A. Isambert, *De la Charbonnerie au Saint-Simonisme. Etude sur la jeunesse de Buchez* (1966); F. A. Isambert, *Politique, religion et science de l'homme chez Philippe Buchez (1796–1865)* (1967), 25–40; and A. Cuvillier, "Buchez et le Saint-Simonisme," in *Hommes et idéologies de 1840* (1956), 9–49.

[2] See A. Cuvillier, "Buchez, fondateur de l'association ouvrière de production," in *Hommes et idéologies*, 50–68, and his study *Un Journal d'ouvriers: "L'Atelier," 1840–1850* (1954).

[3] Published between 1834 and 1838, this forty-volume work was prepared in collaboration with Pierre-Célestin Roux-Lavergne, a fellow Saint-Simonian dissident.

following its foundation in 1831.[4] Through his association with painters, sculptors, and architects, such as Jean-Baptiste Besson, Louis Steinheil, and Louis Piel, Buchez also attempted to promote an art that embodied his social interpretation of the gospels, and played a key role in Gothic revivalism.

Previous commentators have been quick to denigrate Buchez's social aesthetic as reductively moralistic, amounting to little more than a religious variant on the basic didactic refrain.[5] Such a peremptory verdict disregards the doctrinal complexity of Buchez's position, however, and also fails to register the tensions inherent in his attempted reconciliation of Saint-Simon's positivist legacy with the tenets of the Christian faith. Insistence, within his political philosophy, on the centrality of social organicism fostered an authoritarian streak, reminiscent of Enfantin, which compromised egalitarian aspirations and invites comparison with such Traditionalists as Bonald and de Maistre. Unreconciled tensions exist too in the *science de l'homme* which, in the wake of Saint-Simon, Buchez predicated as the necessary foundation to his *science sociale*. It is here, above all, that the ideological consequences of his religious affiliations collided with his political progressivism, as Buchez found himself obliged to uphold spiritualist values more commonly associated with such conservative thinkers as Cousin, Jouffroy, and Royer-Collard. These contradictions necessarily affected Buchez's philosophy of art, rooted as it was in an understanding of human psychology and of a social teleology underwritten by faith. Our investigation of his aesthetic, and its adaptation and realization by sympathetic artists and critics, will confront these ambiguities, exploring the role of art in Buchez's theological and historical thinking and concluding with a discussion of his work on the psycho-physiological origins of aesthetic response. It will suggest that, while embracing a firmly utilitarian attitude toward the arts, Buchezian theorists avoided reductive moralism by developing a significantly modified understanding of *sentiment* within a framework provided by their conception of the centrality of religious faith to social life.

THE PRIMACY OF FAITH

Though Buchez's attitude toward religion superficially resembles Saint-Simonian tenets, albeit with more explicitly Christian overtones, the prominence he accords to faith evolved from a rationalist epistemology more akin

[4] On the rue de Choiseul see H. Auger, *Mémoires (1810–1859)*, ed. P. Cottin (1891), 378. Buchez's ideas on art reached a broader audience, in a dilute and covert form, through the work of his disciple H.-R. Feugueray, who contributed Salon reviews to the republican *Le National* in the 1840s under the pseudonym Henri Robert. See Buchez's biographical introduction to Feugueray's *Essai sur les doctrines politiques de Saint Thomas d'Aquin* (1857), xv.

[5] See, for example, H. J. Hunt, *Le Socialisme et le romantisme en France: Etude de la presse socialiste de 1830 à 1848* (1935), 92.

to Saint-Simon himself than to the stance elaborated by Enfantin in the late 1820s.[6] This intermixture of spiritualism and rationalism gives a particular inflexion to Buchez's subsequent doctrinal stance, stranding him between a Catholic tradition that, even in its more liberal manifestations, he found theologically uncongenial, and radical currents whose more heterodox or frankly secular convictions he was unable to share.

Buchez's rationalist bias is confirmed by the circumstances leading to the split with Saint-Simonianism. He had approached the group in 1825 a convinced materialist, having renounced Catholicism under the impact of studies at the Ecole de médecine and exposure to the work of Cabanis and the naturalists Cuvier and Lamarck.[7] Articles on physiology contributed to *Le Producteur* in 1826 refute dualist notions of an immaterial soul fashioned by God to preside over man's physical being, but discussions following the journal's closure obliged Buchez to revise his position. While Enfantin advanced the primacy of sentiment in asserting the necessity of religious belief, Buchez arrived at faith by a significantly different route. Arguing that any attempt to achieve a synthesis of the differing branches of science entailed acceptance of a first cause, Buchez called upon predominantly rationalist considerations to justify belief in a creation.[8] Enfantin's monist conception of God, with its strong pantheist implications, proved unacceptable to Buchez.[9] It was this, together with disagreements over the group's hierarchical organization and the role accorded to women, that prompted the final rupture with Bazard and Enfantin, and the establishment of a dissident school.

If Buchez's acceptance of religious faith was initially inspired by epistemological considerations, in succeeding years his ideas accorded a pivotal role to religion in human history and social organization. With his *Introduction à la science de l'histoire* of 1833,[10] Buchez arrived at a theory of progress

[6] See, for example, Bazard's repudiation of the Buchezians' claims to be the true inheritors of Saint-Simon and his dismissal of their promotion of reason in his letter to J. and A. Alisse and A. Boulland, 25 January 1830, Bibliothèque historique de la Ville de Paris, Buchez Papers, C.P. 3706:258–63.

[7] The extract from the manuscript *Ontognosie* of 1814 quoted by A. Cuvillier (*P.J.B. Buchez et les origines du socialisme chrétien* [1948], 8–9) clearly demonstrates Buchez's materialist position and the influence of Cabanis.

[8] See Isambert, *De la Charbonnerie*, 162–66. As he remarks in 1838, "toute construction véritablement encyclopédique est impossible en dehors d'une doctrine purement spiritualiste." Buchez, *Introduction à l'étude des sciences médicales* (1838), 65–66.

[9] See particularly Buchez's attack on Saint-Simonian pantheism in his contribution to P. C. R. . . x [Roux-Lavergne] et al., *Science nouvelle. Lettre d'un disciple de la science nouvelle aux religionnaires prétendus Saint-Simoniens* (1831), 48–60, dated October 1829, and the "Projet de lettre sur le panthéisme" (November 1829?), where he rejects promotion of the belief as opportunistic and inconsistent: Buchez Papers, C.P. 3706/257.

[10] A revised edition was issued in 1842; the remarks on art, cited later, appear unaltered in this text.

combining evidence drawn from geology, comparative anatomy, and embryology with a study of world religion to argue for the gradual transformation of life forms toward increasingly equitable social structures, culminating in the attainment of fraternity under the guidance of Christianity.[11] This teleological reading not only asserted a belief in human solidarity by establishing a network of historical interdependence between individuals and successive stages in humanity's progressive development,[12] it also accorded a central role to religion in this dynamic process. Building upon an elaboration of Saint-Simon's theories of historical periodicity begun while still within the group,[13] Buchez argued that religion proved decisive in shaping successive civilizations, with faith providing the moral foundations for individual and collective conduct within society and holding out a general goal for all its members. The attainment of this goal represented each society's contribution to the progressive evolution of humanity toward the ultimate aim of fraternity.

Dividing history into four epochs, each initiated by a revelation, beginning with Adam and Noah, and culminating in Christ's prophetic message of fraternity, Buchez adopted a strictly historicist evaluation of the religions characterizing each of these periods. Each age, he argued, generated a faith consonant with its place within historical evolution, drawing from its dominant system of belief a distinctive goal within the overall development of humanity. Successive concepts of God were thought to have generated a concomitant moral system, around which forms of worship and an organic system of social institutions had evolved.[14]

While sharing the Saint-Simonians' belief in the centrality of religion to an organic social system, Buchez and his followers rejected their assertion that Christianity had run its course and needed replacing by a new faith. Its egalitarian potential was thought to be far from exhausted, though this did not rule out its eventual abandonment once its providential function had been accomplished.[15] Although Buchez initially showed little sympathy for Catholicism as a vital Christian force, contacts with Lacordaire in the late 1830s prompted a rapprochement with the church, though this fell short of unqualified adherence.

[11] For Buchez's historical philosophy, see A. Ott, "Notice sur la vie et les travaux de Buchez," in *Traité de politique et de science sociale*, by P. Buchez (1866), 1:lxv ff., and B. P. Petri, *The Historical Thought of P.J.B. Buchez* (1958).

[12] Ott outlines the social and religious implications of this concept of *solidarité* in "Notice," lxvii–lxviii.

[13] See F. A. Isambert, "Epoques critiques et époques organiques. Une Contribution de Buchez à l'élaboration de la théorie sociale des Saint-Simoniens," *Cahiers internationaux de sociologie* 27 (1959): 131–52.

[14] See P. Buchez, *Introduction à la science de l'histoire* (1842), 1:332. This emphasis is shared with Saint-Simon. See, for example, *L'Industrie* 2 (1817): 32.

[15] See Isambert, *Politique, religion*, 153–58.

The determining influence ascribed to religion on all areas of social practice was crucial for Buchezian conceptions of art. In contemporary terms, this entailed commitment to art as a vehicle for Christian theology and morality. Buchez's interpretation of cultural history accorded precedence to religious institutions as the spurs to creation and change.[16] Emphasis on this close interdependence, and on the artist's doctrinal obligations, was reinforced when after a three-year break Buchez relaunched his journal *L'Européen* in 1835 with several committed Catholic artists on its staff. Thus the architect Louis Piel writes in his 1837 Salon review:

> To restore art's full power as an educational tool, we must seek inspiration in the Christian faith and, each in our own speciality, draw from the Gospels a firm will to accomplish the common duty assigned to us all: the fulfillment on earth of the reign of equality, fraternity, liberty, and devotion.[17]

This identification of art with Christianity's social mission also informed the work produced by Buchez's followers. A number of Buchezians, including Piel and his pupil Louis-Auguste Boileau,[18] together with the sculptors Jehan Duseigneur and Eugène Bion, the decorative artist Louis Steinheil, and the painter Jean-Baptiste Besson,[19] all concentrated on ecclesiastical themes. While Bion's holy-water basin (plate 11), warmly praised by Buchez in 1834,[20] adapts Catholic iconography in an allegory of the papal blessing consecrating the contents of the stoup, with the venial sins surrounding the base providing a warning to its users, other works produced within the school offered a more overtly political interpretation of the Christian message. Besson produced several popular images, issued in Paris by the

[16] See, for example, Buchez's intervention at the Congrès historique of 1836 in Institut historique, *Congrès historique européen. Discours et compte-rendu des séances* (1836), 1:261–64.

[17] "Pour rendre à l'art toute sa puissance comme instrument éducateur, il faut s'inspirer de la foi chrétienne, et puiser dans les Saints-Evangiles la ferme volonté d'accomplir, chacun dans sa spécialité, le devoir commun assigné à tous: la réalisation sur la terre du règne de l'égalité, par la fraternité, la liberté et le dévouement." L. A. Piel, "Salon de 1837," *L'Européen*, 2d ser., 2 (August 1837): 64.

[18] On Boileau, see B. Foucart, "La 'Cathédrale synthétique' de Louis-Auguste Boileau," *Revue de l'art* 3 (1969): 49–66.

[19] Bion was joint author with Baptiste and Besson of the 1836 Salon in *L'Européen*. On Besson, see E. Cartier, *Un Religieux dominicain: le R. P. Hyacinthe Besson. Sa Vie et ses lettres* (1865), and B. Horaist, "L'Oeuvre peint du R. P. Besson O.P. (1816–1861)," 2 vols. (1982). On Steinheil, see A. Darcel, "Louis Steinheil," *Gazette des beaux-arts*, 2d period, 32 (1885): 61–73. A further adherent to the group, Martin Sylvestre Baptiste, a pupil of Vincent and Guérin, specialized in military works in the style of Charlet—significant, perhaps, in the light of Buchezian nationalism.

[20] P.J.B. Buchez, "Salon de 1834," *R. R.* 1 (1834): 129. Much of this review was reproduced in *L'Européen*, 2d ser., 1 (1836): 218–25. Its attribution to T. Thoré in N. McWilliam, *A Bibliography of Salon Criticism in Paris from the July Monarchy to the Second Republic 1831–1851* (1991), no. 222, is erroneous.

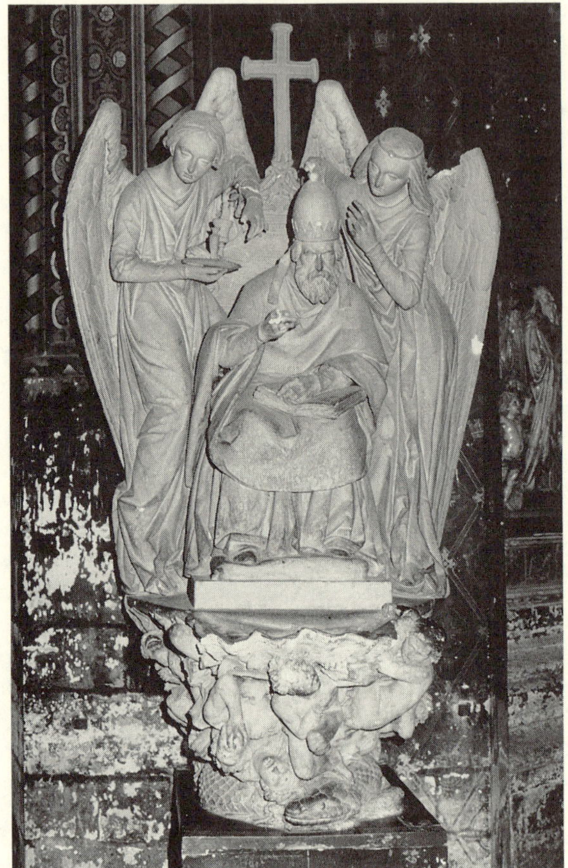

Plate 11. Louis-Eugène Bion, holy water stoup, Salon of 1834. Eglise Saint-Eustache, Paris.

Buchezian Eveillard and distributed as woodcuts from Metz, which conflate the Christian and the revolutionary traditions. *Prenez et lisez* (plate 12) superimposes the republican trinity of *Liberté*, *Egalité*, and *Fraternité* on figures of Christ and two angels wearing phrygian bonnets. Trampling a dragon, bearing the cardinal social sin *l'égoïsme* on its brow, Christ carries a scroll associating him with the spirit of fraternity, thus explicitly identifying the work with Buchezian theology.[21] Like the Saint-Simonian *feuilles volantes*, such an image addressed working-class viewers, exploiting a visual

[21] On this image, which was reissued in 1848, see M. Agulhon, *Marianne into Battle* (1981), 53. M. Reardon, "The Reconciliation of Christianity with Progress: Philippe Buchez," *Review of Politics* 33, no. 4 (1971): 532, connects the image to the opening passage in the *Histoire parlementaire de la révolution française*.

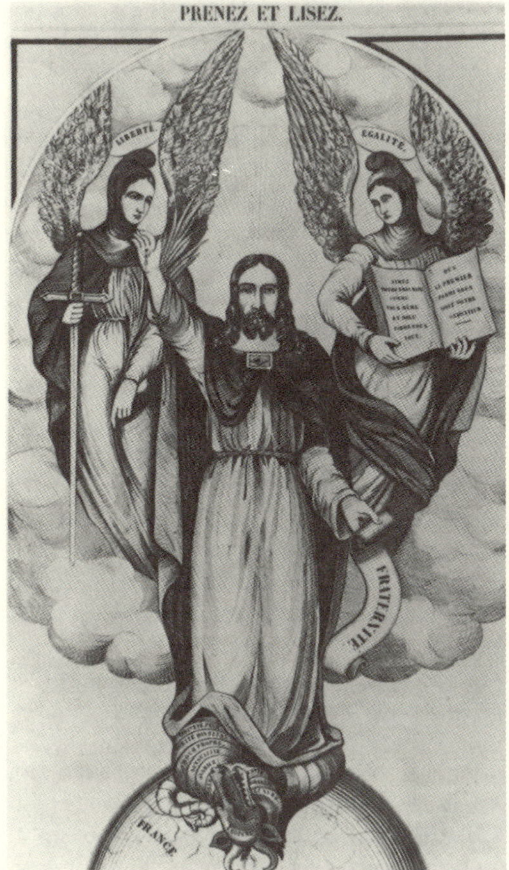

Plate 12. Charles-Jean-Baptiste Besson: *Prenez et lisez,* undated. Cabinet des estampes, Bibliothèque nationale, Paris.

idiom borrowed from the *images d'Epinal*, which circulated amongst the popular strata of society.[22]

Such an approach served as a logical extension to the critical stance adopted by the school in its assessment of the aesthetic enterprise and of contemporary production. The intimate association predicated by Buchez between prevailing systems of belief and ethical values encouraged an evaluative model insistent on religious sincerity and moral propriety. As he states in 1834: "In a word, this is our critical doctrine: in examining a work

[22] On the Buchezians' more open attitude to popular culture, see Régnier, "Les Idées et les opinions littéraires des Saint-Simoniens (1825–1835)" (1983), 2:322.

of art, it is its intention that must first be judged before turning to its stylistic merits."[23]

Similar sentiments inform the reviews published in *L'Européen* and recur in the moralistic tone adopted in *L'Atelier* during the 1840s.[24] Deficiencies in contemporary religious art provided a perennial source for complaint; Bion, Besson, and Baptiste dismiss virtually all such works in the 1836 Salon, blaming their superficiality on artists' lack of belief in the "moral needs of society."[25] Besson's political interpretation of the gospel offers some indication of how these imperatives could be satisfied, and indeed progressive works did elicit favorable remarks from Buchezian commentators. Piel's enthusiasm for Scheffer's *Christ consolateur* (plate 13) in 1837 focuses on the painter's treatment of such current concerns as gender inequality, slavery, and the plight of Greece and Poland. In demonstrating the immediacy of Christian teachings to the modern world, Piel extols Scheffer for adopting "a language that we all understand"[26] and commends his example to other artists.

By contrast, most painters of religious themes are seen as oblivious to such considerations, producing work incapable of inspiring faith or moral duty.[27] The school's emphasis on morality as the basis of social relations and the spur to progressive change provokes extreme intolerance toward infringements of propriety in contemporary art. Piel attacks those artists who "sordidly speculate on the nation's dissolution through the corruption of morals" and warns: "Every sensual statue or lascivious image poisons innocence by arousing passions in the adolescent and the virgin inimical to the family and society: passions that religion calms through morality, without destroying desire, which has provoked even the greatest saints."[28]

On an immediate level, therefore, Buchezian moralism must be understood as deriving from a particular conception of the interrelationship be-

[23] "En deux mots, voici notre doctrine critique: Lorsqu'on examine une oeuvre d'art, c'est son but qu'il faut juger d'abord pour prononcer ensuite sur le mérite de l'exécution." Buchez, "Salon de 1834," 126.

[24] See, for example, Anonymous, "Salon de 1841," *L'Atelier* 1, no. 7 (March 1841): 55.

[25] "Besoins moraux de la société." E. Bion, J.-B. Besson, and Baptiste, "Salon de 1836," *L'Européen*, 2d ser., 1, no. 6 (25 March 1836): 191.

[26] "Une langue que nous entendons tous." Piel, "Salon de 1837," *L'Européen*, 2d ser., 2 (July 1837): 27. See also the Buchezian Auguste Boulland's presentation of Scheffer as a model Christian painter in *Mission morale de l'art* (1852), 515.

[27] See, for example, Piel's attack on Delaroche's *Sainte Cécile* as a "nullité absolue" displaying a "défaut d'inspiration et de pensée" in his "Salon de 1837," 32.

[28] "Spéculent sordidement sur la dissolution de la patrie par la corruption des moeurs"; "Tout marbre charnel, toute image lascive empoisonne l'innocence en réveillant dans l'adolescent et la vierge des passions ennemies de la famille et de la société: passions qu'assoupit la religion par la morale, sans détruire la concupiscence dont les plus grands saints ont senti l'aiguillon." L. Piel, "Déclamation contre l'art païen," in *Notice biographique sur Louis-Alexandre Piel, architecte*, by A. Teyssier (1843), 268.

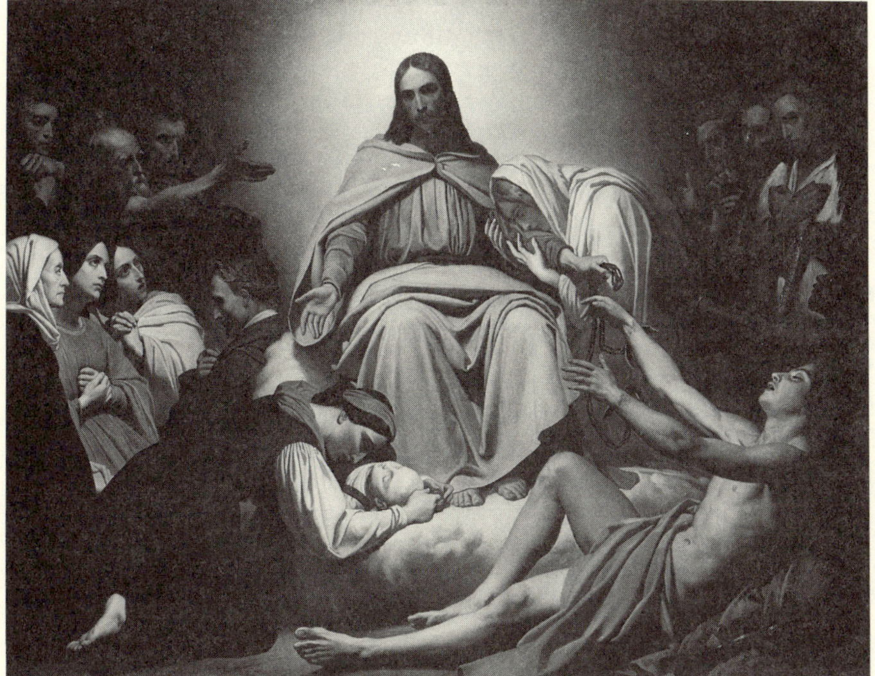

Plate 13. Ary Scheffer: *Le Christ consolateur,* Salon of 1837. Dordrechts Museum, Dordrecht, Holland.

tween faith, morality, and history. Promotion of art as a buttress to confessional and ethical currents in society draws its justification from a philosophy of history that accords a pivotal role to religion and sees ultimate realization of equitable social relations as depending on the fulfillment of the moral imperatives inscribed in faith. In all of this, Buchez's interpretation of history serves as a crucial conceptual foundation, informing his social philosophy at the same time as providing the framework for a particular reading of the history and function of art.

HISTORY OF FAITH AND HISTORY OF ART

Buchez's understanding of the purpose of historical study stood in the tradition of Condorcet and Saint-Simon. From Condorcet, he inherited the belief in history not as an *annalistique* activity,[29] accumulating knowledge of

[29] See M.J.A.N.C. de Condorcet, *Esquisse d'un tableau historique des progrès de l'esprit humain* (1793), ed. M. Himcker and F. Hincker (1966), 253.

past cultures as an end in itself, but adopted instead what was termed a *conclusif* method, more concerned with a synthetic appreciation of the general principles underlying human evolution. Like Condorcet, Buchez maintained that such an approach would provide an understanding of human destiny and offer an insight into the future development of society.[30] The theoretical tools for this task were largely borrowed from Saint-Simon, whose insistence on a shared goal, or *but d'activité*, as an essential basis for sociality profoundly affected Buchez's approach to cultural history.[31] Like Saint-Simon, Buchez looked to the natural sciences as a model for historical method and also followed his predecessor in constructing an understanding of social organization around analogies drawn from individual physiology.[32]

Buchez associates the very coherence of a society with the *but d'activité* derived from universal endorsement of a prevailing faith and identification with the historical goal embedded within it. Without such solidarity, society, in any meaningful sense, ceases to exist.[33] Buchez used his understanding of individual physiology to arrive at a historicist interpretation of the growth and subsequent decline of successive civilizations. Any form of human action was seen as relying on a sequence of psycho-physiological processes beginning with desire (identified with sentiment), mediated by reason, and finally producing muscular activity. Buchez transferred this tripartite sequence to an analysis of historical change, elaborating the Saint-Simonian antithesis of "organic" and "critical" periods into a model that placed greater emphasis on the dynamics of progress working over time.[34] The foundation of religious belief he located in an initial synthetic phase of history, during which sentiment prevailed and the sacred and secular norms within society were universally endorsed. The ensuing critical period was identified with reason and, while conceived in the Saint-Simonian sense as an age of questioning traditional beliefs, took on more positive connotations as an ultimately constructive stage in a long-term process. The outcome of these two antithetical periods occurred in a final era of *exécution*, the

[30] Buchez defines history as "une science dont le but est de prévoir l'avenir social de l'espèce humaine, dans l'ordre de son libre activité," *Science de l'histoire*, 1:60. For a similar notion of historical prevision, see Bazard in *Prod.* 4 (1825): 413.

[31] "On ne saurait trop le répéter, il faut un but d'activité à une société, sans quoi il n'y a pas de système politique" Saint-Simon, *Du système industriel*, in *O.S.S.E.*, 21:14.

[32] See Petri, *Historical Thought*, 25; Isambert, *Politique, religion*, 248–72; F. A. Isambert, "Physiologie sociale et système des sciences chez Buchez," *Cahiers internationaux de sociologie* 36 (January–June 1964): 101–16.

[33] "Or, il n'y a de société que là où il existe un but commun d'activité, qui rallie tous les hommes dans un même désir, un même système et un même acte." Buchez, *Science de l'histoire*, 1:45–46. See also H. Auger, *Moralités* (1834), 1:120: "Dieu et société ne sont . . . qu'une seule idée."

[34] See Buchez, *Science de l'histoire*, 1:251ff.

historical parallel to action in the human body, during which the moral system implicit in the dominant faith received definitive expression and the *but d'activité* was at last fulfilled.

Buchez's schematization of history led him to modify Saint-Simonian periodicity, and prompted a reassessment of past cultures in the light of this revised system. Like the Saint-Simonians, Buchez associated artistic achievement with organic societies in which religion provided the basis for a coherent ideology and securely ordered hierarchy. The instances singled out to exemplify this organicism differed from those chosen by the Saint-Simonians in certain important respects. Perhaps most strikingly, the Buchezians demoted the classical Mediterranean cultures at the expense of those of Egypt, India, and Mexico, all of which they described as monotheistic societies. While Piel attacks "the impure heat of antique art"[35] and condemns contemporary classicism as symptomatic of moral bankruptcy, Auger accuses ancient art of formalism, generated by social and religious fragmentation:

> This crowd of statues contains only figures—gods or heroes—and nowhere does one find a broad, overarching idea from which humanity can draw long-term repose for the people's happiness. With liberty, or more accurately lack of direction, leaving the individual the absolute master of his thoughts and actions, art pursues perfection since there is nothing for it to create.[36]

The materialism of classical statuary was adduced as evidence of the inferiority of Hellenistic civilization. This position contrasts with the Saint-Simonians, who regarded materialism as the antithetical complement of *esprit*, the two together alternating in successive religious systems and awaiting final synthesis in a definitive—pantheistic—conception of God as *esprit* and *matière*. Buchez's opposition to such tendencies explains the demotion of a society identified with materialism in favor of socioreligious systems where spiritual values ostensibly prevailed.

Antimaterialism underlay Buchezian interpretations of the Renaissance, an area where their critical strictures coincided both with the Saint-Simonians and with Catholic revivalists such as Montalembert and Rio.[37] All judged the Renaissance from the perspective of the Middle Ages, and regarded the later period as initiating a critical era of which contemporary

[35] "Cette chaleur impure de l'art antique." Piel, "Déclamation," 267.

[36] "Cette foule de statues ne contient que des personnages, Dieux ou héros, et nulle part on ne trouve une de ces idées larges, unitaires sur lesquelles l'humanité assise se repose longtemps pour le bonheur des peuples. La liberté, ou pour mieux dire l'absence de direction, laissant l'individu maître absolu de ses pensées et de ses actions, l'artiste perfectionne faute d'avoir à créer." H. Auger, "Des beaux-arts considérés comme moyen d'éducation," *Journal officiel de l'instruction publique* 1, no. 61 (31 May 1832): 245.

[37] See P. de Lallemand, *Montalembert et ses amis dans le romantisme 1830–1840* (1927).

society was the inheritor. Buchezian attitudes were uniformly hostile; Louis Piel's remarks of 1839 show them perhaps at their most violent: "For me, the renaissance is the whore of Babylon which has filled the world with the impurity of its fornications. I despise this false art . . . and I will despise it until I have been convinced that to surprise is the same thing as to move, that to seduce is the same as to warm the heart."[38]

In their interpretation of the High Renaissance, the Buchezians diverge from Saint-Simonian assessments of artists such as Raphael and Michelangelo. The attempts made by Barrault and others to explain the coincidence of artistic flowering with religious and ideological crisis depended upon arguments around the prophetic power of art, which Buchez did not share. The Saint-Simonians further elevated the High Renaissance as a brief but fertile fusion of spiritualist and materialist conceptions of divinity, a position inimical to Buchezian theology. The materialist elements discerned in Michelangelo's designs for Saint Peter's or Dante's *Divine Comedy* were rather seen as unfortunate symptoms of an erosion of the spiritualist tradition.[39] Even Raphael did not escape this antipathy, being described as "a young libertine who died of consumption while waiting for the art that issued from his brush . . . to consume the flesh of the artistocrats to whom he had sold himself."[40] Buchezian theorists further equated the decline of organic institutions during the Renaissance with the emergence of formalism and artistic individualism. In losing their social role as auxiliaries to faith, the arts forfeited their popular appeal through a preoccupation with mythology and cultivation of such private patrons as "princes, bankers, and contractors."[41] As a consequence, the period was judged the "starting point of art for art's sake,"[42] driven by an empty display of imitative skill and deprived of any broader sense of social meaning.

The similarity of this diagnosis with remarks on contemporary art derives

[38] "La renaissance est pour moi la prostituée de Babylone qui a rempli la terre de l'impureté de ses fornications. Je méprise ce faux art . . . et je le mépriserai jusqu'à ce qu'on m'ait prouvé qu'étonner c'est émouvoir, que séduire c'est attendrir." L. Piel to G. S. Trébutien, 17 May 1839, in Teyssier, *Notice biographique*, 275.

[39] See P.J.B. Buchez [?], "Des artistes aujourd'hui," *L'Européen* 1, no. 10 (4 February 1832): 150–51. For a historical overview of the period, see A. Ott, *Manuel d'histoire universelle* (1842), 2:378–84.

[40] "Un jeune libertin qui mourut de consomption en attendant que l'art sorti de son pinceau . . . frappât de phtisie la chair aristocratique à laquelle il était vendu." Anonymous, "Peines et récompenses, en matière des beaux-arts," *L'Européen* 2, no. 31 (7 July 1832): 69. For contemporary critiques of Raphael, see B. Foucart, *Le Renouveau de la peinture religieuse en France (1800–1860)* (1987), 38–39, and M. P. Driskell, *Representing Belief: Religion, Art, and Society in Nineteenth Century France* (1992), 74–81.

[41] "Des princes, des banquiers et des fournisseurs." Piel, "Salon de 1837," *L'Européen*, 2d ser., 2 (July 1837): 24.

[42] "Point de départ de l'art pour l'art." D. Gazel, "Travaux de M. H. Flandrin à Saint-Germain-des-Prés," *Revue nationale* 1, no. 5 (September 1847): 141.

from an analysis of current society in which many of the evils of the Renaissance had ostensibly borne fruit.[43] Paralleling the Saint-Simonians in much of his critique of the modern world, Buchez attributes fragmentation and class exploitation to the demise of the organic social structure formerly upheld by religious faith; in particular, the conflict of interests between different classes emerges even more forcefully than in Saint-Simonian texts.[44] To some degree, however, Buchez's concept of historical periodicity leads him to adopt a less negative tone, perceptible also in a more nuanced assessment of contemporary art. Buchez's tripartite historical schema, together with his belief in the continuing viability of Christianity, situates the modern world not at the end of a particular cycle of development, but rather on the brink of a final period of *réalisation*.

This perspective was far from encouraging an indulgent attitude toward the shortcomings of contemporary society or its culture, however. In common with other groups on the left, the Buchezians related deficiencies in the arts to the fragmentation of society, which had its roots in the fifteenth century and had reached crisis point under the restored monarchy. Buchezian critics subscribe to the prevalent radical etiology in approaching contemporary art: lack of social mission, the blight of individualism and consequent preoccupation with form are all associated with the present malaise. The absence of religiosity becomes symptomatic of a broader abdication of responsibility:

> It is so sad to see that we have come to this; all inspiration, if not from religion (that would be called grotesque these days) then at any rate all serious and moral feeling, is completely nonexistent or, if it survives, is so weak and unusual among artists that all of their work is stamped with the most banal egotism and the most shameless indifference.[45]

While echoing radical attacks on official cultural institutions,[46] Buchezian critics were particularly sensitive to art's reduction to commodity status, exchanged on an open market dominated by "these well-off bourgeois who call for . . . the reproduction of their insignificant effigies, the occasional view of the well-sanded avenues in their grounds, and lubricious images to

[43] See P.J.B. Buchez, "Art," in *Encyclopédie du XIXe siècle* (1842), 3:717.

[44] See, for example, Buchez, *Science de l'histoire*, 1:8.

[45] "Il est bien triste de voir que nous en soyons venus là; que toute inspiration, je ne dis pas religieuse, on appelerait cela grotesque aujourd'hui, mais que tout sentiment grave et moral même, n'existe plus nulle part, ou du moins, si faible et si rare chez les artistes que toutes leurs productions portent le cachet de l'égoïsme le plus plat et l'indifférence la plus dévergondée." Anonymous, "Exposition de la Société des amis des arts," *L'Européen* 1, no. 2 (10 December 1831): 25.

[46] See Anonymous, "Concours pour le grand prix," *L'Européen* 2, no. 46 (20 October 1832): 312; Anonymous, "Envois de Rome," ibid. 2, no. 41 (15 September 1832): 230–31; H. Auger, "Les Ecoles," *La Vérité* 12 (10 January 1835).

divert aging libertines."[47] This "commercial typhoid," whose hold is judged symptomatic of "this immovable commercial system which these days has overtaken everything,"[48] represents the individualist tendencies associated with capitalism, responsible for occluding any broader perception of the moral economy within contemporary artistic production. Capitalist economic relations epitomize for Buchez and his followers the demise of an organic conception of society in favor of a regime characterized by the erosion of shared moral values.[49]

In circumstances so hostile to creative enterprise, the Buchezians found only one area—that of caricature—where the arts maintained any social purchase. With the critical nature of contemporary society generating consensus around only negative issues, caricature came to signify a means of harnessing this for socially beneficial ends. Described as "the formula given by painting to Christian revolutionary thought, the formula of equality preached by the painter who wants to spread his own anger to all,"[50] caricature inspired particular enthusiasm in early issues of *L'Européen*, at a time when Buchez's Carbonarist background lent the school an insurrectionary edge blunted by the drift to Catholicism. In singling out satire as evidence of residual artistic vitality—a point shared with the Saint-Simonians—the group effectively underlined the atomized state of contemporary society, where shared doctrines had been eclipsed by critical questioning of the status quo.

Buchez also echoes Saint-Simonian theorists in discovering the strongest antithesis to current critical tendencies in pre-Reformation Europe.[51] In applying his theories to a study of world history, Buchez's disciples Boulland and Ott emphasize the supremacy that medieval art derived from its theological inspiration, with Ott describing the period as one "when sentiment dominates, when every event is clothed in sentimental form, when this form itself reaches its highest expression."[52] The synthesis represented by the

[47] "Ces bourgeois aisés qui demandent . . . la reproduction de leurs insignifiantes effigies, quelques vues des allées bien sablées de leurs parcs, et puis des images lubriques pour amuser de vieux libertinages." J. Bastide, "Salon de 1847," *Revue nationale* 1, no. 1 (May 1847): 25.

[48] "Typhus marchand"; "cet immuable système commercial qui s'est superposé à tout en ce temps." Anonymous, "Salon de 1844," *L'Atelier*, 4th year, 7 (April 1844): 110.

[49] See, for example, H. Auger, *Physiologie du théâtre* (1839), 1:4.

[50] "La formule donnée par la peinture à la pensée révolutionnaire chrétienne, la formule de l'égalité prêchée par la colère du peintre qui veut donner de sa colère à tous." Anonymous review of the *Biographie allégorique et fantastique des illustrations contemporaines*, *L'Européen* 1, no. 8 (21 January 1832): 123.

[51] Buchez's admiration for Northern art during a visit to Holland and Belgium in 1861 did however prompt a questioning of earlier assumptions; as he writes to Ott (Buchez Papers, C.P. 3717, f. 225r., letter dated 28 June 1861): "serait-il donc vrai que le protestantisme est nuisible à l'art? Vous avez été en Prusse, qu'en dites vous?"

[52] "Où le sentiment domine, où toute manifestation se revêt d'une forme sentimentale, où cette forme elle-même arrive à son plus haut point d'expression." Ott, *Manuel d'histoire*, 2:278. See also J.F.A. Boulland, *Essai d'histoire universelle* (1836), 2:232–34.

Gothic cathedral signifies in Buchezian theory the high point of art's social integration; the collaborative labor mobilized in fashioning its monumental form embodies the submission of individual will to a collective goal,[53] while the mass celebrated within its walls represents a supremely organic, unifying experience, in which "the faithful are at once actors and spectators."[54] A further attribute of the cathedral, its combination of varied media in a unified whole, recalls Saint-Simonian preference for art works that solicit all the senses simultaneously. Identifying two artistic modes—the descriptive, primarily associated with language, and the figurative, embodied in music, mime, and the plastic arts—Buchez maintains a fundamental interdependence of both currents in all forms of artistic utterance and relates aesthetic perfection to their combination in a synthetic whole. Arguing that "the absolute synthesis is that which includes all arts in a single display,"[55] Buchez presents the cathedral, animated by the liturgical drama of the mass, as attaining this supreme perfection.

In thus extolling the Middle Ages, Buchez and his followers differed from the Saint-Simonians both in their continuing commitment to the tradition it embodied and in their assessment of the period as encapsulating a complete understanding of the nature of God. While the Saint-Simonians too valued the Middle Ages as an era of organic social relations, their contention that the emphasis on the spiritual character of divinity was fundamentally incomplete flew in the face of Buchezian doctrine.

This unqualified admiration for the Middle Ages informed Buchezian attitudes toward contemporary production. While endorsing works that applied Christian doctrine to topical issues, the group stood apart from many other advocates of *art social* in promoting revivalism rather than modernity. In critical terms, primitivizing currents in the work of Flaxman, Ingres, and Flandrin won the school's approval,[56] while the latter's murals for Saint-Germain-des-Prés were praised as a supreme example of the renewal of religious art in France and Germany.[57] Such work was interpreted as evidence of incipient artistic regeneration and of the Christian tradition's vitality, not only in art but within society itself.

Revivalist sympathies emerge in discussions of Gothic architecture and in the support offered by *L'Européen* for the preservation of medieval buildings.[58] The journal's championship of the Gothic won plaudits from Mon-

[53] See Auger, *Physiologie*, 1:71.

[54] "Les fidèles sont en même temps acteurs et spectateurs." Buchez, "Art," 717.

[55] "La synthèse absolue est celle qui comprend tous [les arts] en une seule manifestation." Buchez, *Science de l'histoire*, 1:401.

[56] See Anonymous, "Concours pour le grand prix," 312.

[57] "Il a . . . réalisé l'alliance de la pensée et de la forme . . . il a renoué avec plus de succès qu'aucun de ses devanciers les traditions de la peinture religieuse dans son expression la plus élevée." Gazel, "Travaux de M. H. Flandrin," 143.

[58] See, for example, Anonymous, "Saint-Germain-l'Auxerrois et St Jacques-la-Boucherie," *L'Européen*, 1, no. 18 (31 March 1832): 279–80.

talembert who, in *Du vandalisme et du catholicisme dans l'art*, described it as containing "several articles on the arts dictated by deep learning and the purest feeling for the demands of Christian thought."[59] His admiration focused on Louis Piel who, like Steinheil and Boileau, was actively involved in the Gothic revival in ecclesiastical architecture.[60] Montalembert was, indeed, associated with Piel's first major project for the church of Saint-Nicolas in Nantes, and later canvassed for his appointment as architect of the parish church at Byans-les-Uziers in the Doubs, a work intended by Piel as "the first page in a portfolio of country churches which I hope to publish."[61]

Piel's construction of the basilique Saint-Nicolas proved a turning point in the Buchezian artistic enterprise, providing not only an unrivaled opportunity to turn theory into practice, but also serving as a catalyst in uniting currents within Christian socialism and liberal Catholicism. Piel won the commission in 1838, as a result of a competition held by the bishop of Nantes, Monseigneur Fournier.[62] His desire to construct a church in thirteenth-century style coincided with the bishop's own preferences, and Piel produced a design intended to emulate French architecture in its highest national and stylistic purity.[63] In its elaborate symbolic program, Piel's work drew not only on his own studies of the Gothic but also on the theoretical explorations of ecclesiastical architecture undertaken by Buchez. Buchez himself enthusiastically endorsed Piel's designs, while regretfully expressing doubts whether the Ecole des beaux-arts would tolerate a similar undertaking in Paris.[64] Unfortunately, Nantes proved no easier to win over. In April 1840 the Conseil des bâtiments civils rejected the plans as an "anachronisme frappant" and questioned both the architect's competence and the costing of the building. Shortly before this, Piel had resigned from the project for personal reasons; in June 1841 his successor, Jean-Baptiste Lassus, submitted a new design, which, while retaining the use of

[59] "Plusieurs articles en matière d'art dictés par une science profonde et le sentiment le plus pur des exigences de la pensée chrétienne." C.F.R. de Montalembert, *Du vandalisme et du catholicisme dans l'art* (1839), 182.

[60] Both Boileau and Steinheil worked with Lassus on the restoration of Saint-Germain-l'Auxerrois. See Darcel, "Louis Steinheil," 65.

[61] "La première page d'un cahier d'églises de campagne que je veux publier." Piel to Montalembert, in Teyssier, *Notice biographique*, 62.

[62] See Abbé Pothier, *Monseigneur Fournier, évêque de Nantes. Sa Vie, ses oeuvres* (1900), 1:403.

[63] For Piel's justification of the architectural sources for his project, see ibid., 412. More generally, see B. Foucart and V. Noël-Bouton, "Saint-Nicolas de Nantes, bataille et triomphe du néo-gothique," *Congrès archéologique de France*, 126th session, Haute-Bretagne (1968), 136–81.

[64] See letter from Buchez to Fournier, 28 September 1838, in Pothier, *Monseigneur Fournier*, 411.

thirteenth-century Gothic, appears less ambitious than Piel's original conception.[65]

Though important for the Buchezian aesthetic program, the Nantes episode also had broader doctrinal implications. During his stay in the city, Piel contacted the young businessman Réquédat and the exiled Italian radical Niccolo Tommaseo, whom he had possibly already encountered in Paris.[66] As a consequence, he became attracted to Thomism and in 1837 formally joined the Catholic church. The following year, Réquédat responded to Lacordaire's call to restore the French Dominican order, and in 1839 accompanied the abbé to Rome. Piel, too, while maintaining his contacts with Buchez, gravitated toward Lacordaire and, in July 1839, founded the Parisian section of the Confrérie de Saint Jean l'Evangéliste, a brotherhood of Catholic artists dedicated to religious revivalism. Instructed by Lacordaire to pursue "the sanctification of art and artists by the Catholic faith, and the propagation of the Catholic faith by art and artists,"[67] the group attracted the Buchezians Duseigneur and Bion, together with figures such as Louis Janmot and Claudius Lavergne.[68]

Piel's close friend, the painter Jean-Baptiste Besson, simultaneously pursued a parallel course: converted to Catholicism in May 1837, he encountered Réquédat the following year[69] and left for Rome soon after. Here, he too came under Lacordaire's influence and, in April 1839, joined the painter Hallez in establishing a branch of the Confrérie, enlisting the sculptor Bonnassieux, and the composer Gounod—both *pensionnaires* at the Villa Medici.[70] This drift toward Catholicism culminated in Piel and Besson taking holy orders—in May 1840 Piel joined Lacordaire at the convent in Bosco, where he died the following year, while in the same month Besson became a Dominican, pursuing his artistic career in monasteries in Italy and France until his death in 1861.[71]

Though the trajectory followed by these artists eventually divided them from Buchez, in 1842 Besson could still extol his former mentor, describing

[65] On Lassus's indebtedness to Piel, see Foucart and Noël-Bouton, "Saint-Nicholas de Nantes," and J.-M. Leniaud, *Jean-Baptiste Lassus (1807–1857) ou le temps retrouvé des cathédrales* (1980), 135ff.

[66] Tommaseo was in direct contact with Buchez during 1834–36; see N. Tommaseo, *Diario intimo*, ed. R. Ciampini (1939), 195ff.

[67] "La sanctification de l'art et des artistes par la foi catholique, et la propagation de la foi catholique par l'art et les artistes." Founding charter of the group, prepared by Lacordaire at the convent of Quercia, dated 21 July 1839, in Teyssier, *Notice biographique*, 58.

[68] See G. Claudius-Lauvergne, *La Corporation des artistes chrétiens en France* (1895), 9.

[69] Le P. Berthier and Le P. Vallée, *Un Peintre dominicain: l'oeuvre artistique du R. P. Besson* (1909), 7.

[70] See Cartier, *Un Religieux dominicain*, 1:73–77.

[71] On this aspect of Besson's career, see Horaist, "L'Oeuvre du R. P. Besson," vol. 2, and Foucart, *Renouveau de la peinture religieuse*, 228–33, 315–16.

his circle as "the most Christian of all our century's socialist schools."[72] Indeed Lacordaire's sympathy for Buchez was such that in 1839 he invited him to join the Dominicans—an invitation that foundered over Buchez's insuperable ambivalence toward the Catholic church.[73] As this episode illustrates, Buchez's attitude toward organized religion prevented any unambiguous rapprochement with Catholicism. For individuals such as Besson and Piel, his school could only go so far in providing a structure for their Christian commitment; beyond a certain point the humanitarianism preached by Buchez was incapable of accommodating individuals for whom Catholicism seemed to offer the most attractive theological option.

HISTORY AS SYNTHESIS AND PREVISION

Buchez's *conclusif* mode of historical analysis encouraged a broad discursive sweep in the presentation of evidence. The conclusions he draws from the history of art rest on a wide-ranging synthesis of material taken from diverse periods and cultures. This may be seen in his progressive interpretation of social development, expressed in the sequence *individu*, *famille*, *tribu*, *nation*, where corroborative evidence is drawn from architectural history. Thus, as the growing sophistication of religious expression matches the increasing complexity of social units, so the mediation between man and God is said to be embodied in monumental forms of ever greater richness.[74] The architectural sequence *autel*, *temple*, *cathédrale* embodying this progression gained wide currency in Buchezian circles, featuring in Boulland and Ott's universal histories and appearing in modified form in Maurisset's frontispiece to Auger's *Moralités* of 1834 (plate 14). This understanding of history in broad, synthetic terms underlines three projects emanating from Buchez and his school. The former Saint-Simonian Roux-Lavergne, who emphasizes Buchez's interest in the arts,[75] describes a monumental column he conceived as a symbolic representation of the sequence altar, temple, cathedral: "For a pedestal, he gave it a majestic altar of the earliest ages, above which was a giant obelisk, decorated with sculptures evoking India and Egypt. At the peak was a sheaf of slim thirteenth-century columns which carried the Christian sign of the cross five-hundred feet into the

[72] "La plus chrétienne de toutes les écoles socialistes de notre siècle." Letter dated 20 February 1842, in J. B. Duroselle, *Les Débuts du catholicisme social en France 1822–1870* (1951), 103.

[73] See R. P. Duval, "Lacordaire et Buchez. Idéalisme révolutionnaire et réveil religieux en 1839," *Revue des sciences philosophiques et théologiques* (July 1961): 422–55.

[74] Buchez, "Art," 713–17.

[75] See P. C. Roux-Lavergne, *Un Sentier à travers le siècle: les idées et les hommes* (1869), 71. On the lectures on art given at the rue des Bons-Enfants in 1830, ibid., 71–72. According to Auger (*Mémoires*, 377), Jeanron and Hauréau regularly attended Buchez's lectures.

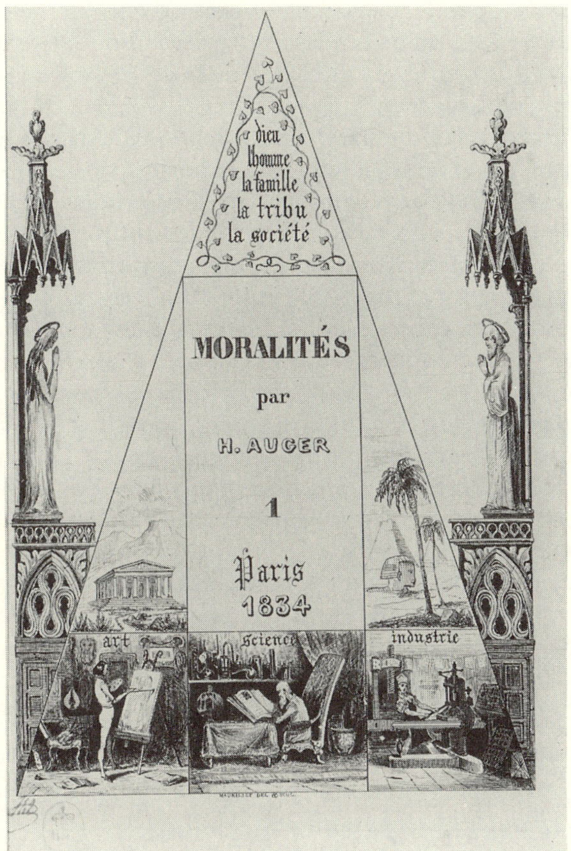

Plate 14. Maurriset: Cover to Hippolyte Auger, *Moralités,* 1834. Bibliothèque nationale, Paris.

air."[76] The teleological schema implicit in the monument's structure, together with the reference to Eastern cultures, makes of this bizarre fabrication a clear illustration of Buchez's theories of historical periodicity. Despite its ambitious scale, Buchez's symbolic column pales into insignificance beside a scheme devised by one of his followers, Théophile Bra, whose projected *Musée de la Paix* aimed at nothing less than a synthetic presentation of world history revealing the future destiny of mankind.

The *Musée*'s intellectual inspiration is virtually impossible to disentangle, forming as it does a bizarre potpourri of utopian and Illuminist currents.

[76] "Il lui donnait: pour piédestal, l'autel grandiose des premiers âges; au-dessus, un obélisque gigantesque, orné de sculptures résumant l'Inde et l'Egypte; au sommet, un faisceau de colonettes en style du XIIIe siècle, portant à 500 pieds dans les airs le signe chrétien: la Croix." Roux-Lavergne, *Um Sentier*, 73.

Bra's involvement with Saint-Simonianism had done nothing to stifle his enthusiasm for somnambulism and he appears also to have had Masonic links[77] as well as contacts with disciples of Swedenborg and the Russian mystic Mme de Krüdener.[78] Though certain elements in his vocabulary suggest interest in Fourierism,[79] Saint-Simon and Buchez apparently had the greatest impact on his thought. Bra seems to have been most attracted toward Saint-Simon's early writing—and, indeed, the *Musée de la Paix* resembles a Christianized version of the Temple of Newton.[80] Like Saint-Simon, he looks to Newtonian physics as an epistemological catalyst, proposing it as a tool for historical analysis.[81] This suggestion relates to Bra's preoccupation with epistemological synthesis as the foundation of a new social order—a theme that again relates most closely to the Saint-Simon of the *Introduction aux travaux scientifiques*.[82] The synthesis of the physical and natural sciences as the basis of a social science—an aspect of Saint-Simonian thought also important for Buchez—emerges strongly in the program for the *Musée*, where Bra argues: "The spirit of union forces us to encyclopedize in the interests of a unity that is self-evident, and to trust the salvation of our era to this great intellectual exercise."[83] The theme of synthesis constantly recurs in Bra's manuscript notes and drawings; describing himself as "mad, sick for unity," he proclaims "I am a synthetist—such is my inclination and my profession" and elaborates the symbol of a winged hermaphrodite emerging from a spiral to represent this supreme value.[84]

[77] See R. Allender, "Les Francs-maçons à l'Orient de Douai (1800–1851): description sociale d'un groupe en mouvement," *Revue du nord* 72, no. 84 (January–March 1990): 66.

[78] Bra was a friend of Emile Broussais, the Swedenborgian author of *Régénération du monde!* (1842), and Helmine Klenke-Chézy, an admirer of Mme de Krüdener; see M. Fargeaud, "Autour de Balzac et de Marceline Desbordes-Valmore," *Revue des sciences humaines* 21, no. 82 (1956): 159–61.

[79] See the use of terms such as *simple*, *composé*, and *analogie* in T. Bra, "Du renouvellement de l'art en France," *Journal des artistes*, 2d ser., 4 (18 July 1847): 19, and T. Bra, *Introduction au Musée de la Paix* (1852), 31–35.

[80] Significantly, Bra describes one feature of the *Musée*—a dungeon containing "tous les crimes qui se trament contre la société" (*Introduction*, 61)—that directly recalls a similar feature in Saint-Simon's temple destined to house Robespierre as a symbol of darkness.

[81] Ibid., 91–94.

[82] See citation of Saint-Simon in ibid., 85–86, and "Du renouvellement" (18 July 1847), 18, where such a synthesis is offered as the basis for artistic renewal.

[83] "L'esprit d'union nous force à encyclopédiser au profit d'une unité qui se démontre, et met notre salut d'époque dans ce grand exercise intellectuel." Bra, *Introduction*, 30.

[84] "Fou, malade d'unité"; "je suis synthétiste—c'est mon penchant et ma profession." Bibliothèque municipal, Douai, Bra Mss. 1674, no. 64 (album 1). See also *Le Concilialisme—Théologie nouvelle* (October 1833) in the same collection and Bra's description of his project as the "Musée pacifique synthétique" (ibid., no. 3, 366). The theme of androgyny is characteristically Saint-Simonian and is found, for example, in the symbolism of the plan for Duveyrier's *Ville nouvelle*.

The obsession with synthesis is supplemented by a number of themes clearly traceable to Buchez. Bra's attraction toward Buchez apparently relates to his Christian commitment—something he had found wanting in Enfantin's version of Saint-Simonianism.[85] Bra maintained a strong faith in Christianity, which he regarded as a dynamic social force whose spirituality provided an essential spur toward synthesis and offered art "GREAT THEOLOGICAL ENCYCLOPEDIAS, INTEGRATED AND ACCEPTED, in which societies evolve."[86] A habitué of Buchez's meetings at the rue de Choiseul in 1830, he appears to have maintained contact with the group for a number of years, despite misgivings over Buchez himself.[87]

The *Musée de la Paix*—"notre Sixtine"[88]—combines a peculiarly heterodox Christianity with a characteristically Buchezian conception of history. Conceived as a huge classical rotunda housing sculpture and painted murals (plates 15 and 16), the *Musée* combines metaphysical allegories with historical panoramas as a means of interpreting the past and displaying man's future. Emphasizing the need for a "perfect understanding of the future and a peaceful, social era, strengthened by the unification of intellectual and moral powers,"[89] Bra regards the *Musée* as a work whose predictive force and persuasive power will facilitate the attainment of social harmony. His theory of historical prevision owes much to Buchez, though some of the projected murals, featuring such abstractions as "l'esprit de toute vérité" and "l'esprit et la vie d'harmonie," suggest Illuminist sources (plate 17). Bra's description of a mural for the *Musée*'s central chamber, depicting the "RENAISSANCE DES IDEES DE L'UNITE," indicates the project's hermetic metaphysical inspiration. The work shows:

> A reappearance of the spirits of uniquely conceived things. The luminous Being contains them in its brightness, dominating them. In such a way he is able to identify the initiating spirit, reestablish truths that which have been hidden or

[85] See the *Essai sur Saint-Simon et son école[. O]riginalité et défaut du maître et des élèves* (n.d., Bra Mss. 1674, no. 1).

[86] "DE GRANDES ENCYCLOPEDIES THEOLOGIQUES, COORDONNEES ET ACCEPTEES, dans laquelle [*sic*] des sociétés se meuvent." "Du renouvellement de l'art en France," *Journal des artistes*, 2d ser., 4 (1 August 1847): 43–44. See also Bra Mss. 1674, box 3 (1–792), containing material from 1846 in which Bra anticipates the "triomphe absolu et prochain de l'église catholique" (339).

[87] See Auger, *Mémoires*, 378, and Balzac to Bra, December 1833, in H. de Balzac, *Correspondance*, ed. R. Pierrot (1962), 2:427–29, on the rue de Choiseul. In Mss. 1674, box l, unnumbered sheet, Bra writes: "Buchez est également dans l'impuissance et veut la place de chef de Convention avec une guillotine dans le présent pour appliquer la peine du crime d'infraternité."

[88] Bra, "Du renouvellement" (11 July 1847), 11. In a more overtly Catholic spirit, Bra also described the project as the "Musée de la pleine lumière de l'homme" (Ms. 1674, no. 3, 418).

[89] "Connaissance parfaite de l'avenir et une ère pacifique, sociale, forte de toutes les puissances intellectuelles et morales unies." Bra, *Introduction*, 40.

Plate 15, right. Théophile Bra: *Musée de la Paix:* front and side elevations, c. 1846. Ms. 1674/3, f. 703, Bibliothèque municipale, Douai.

Plate 16, below left. Théophile Bra: *Musée de la Paix:* ground plan, c. 1846. Ms. 1674/3, f. 702, Bibliothèque municipale, Douai.

Plate 17, below right. Théophile Bra: *Musée de la Paix: Entrée de la Salle des lois. Porte de la Renaissance active de l'Esprit de l'homme,* c. 1846. Ms. 1674/3, f. 713, Bibliothèque municipale, Douai.

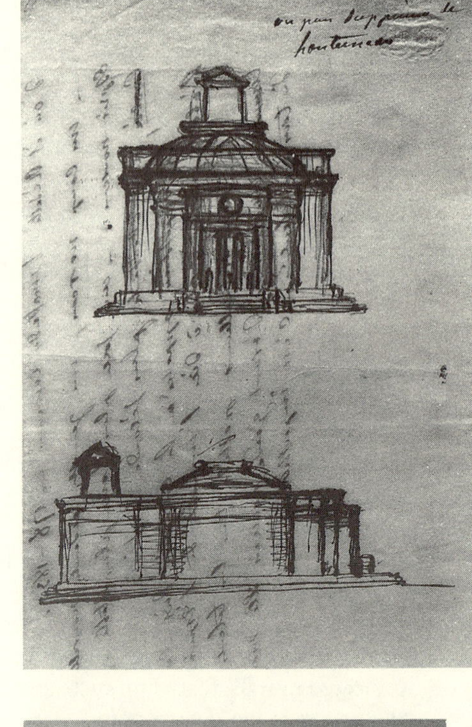

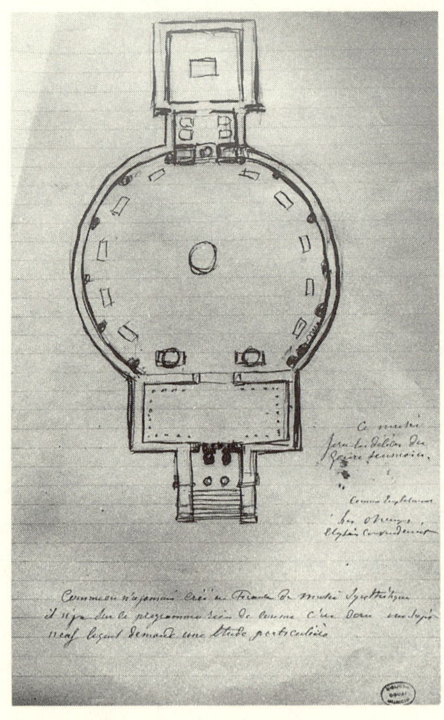

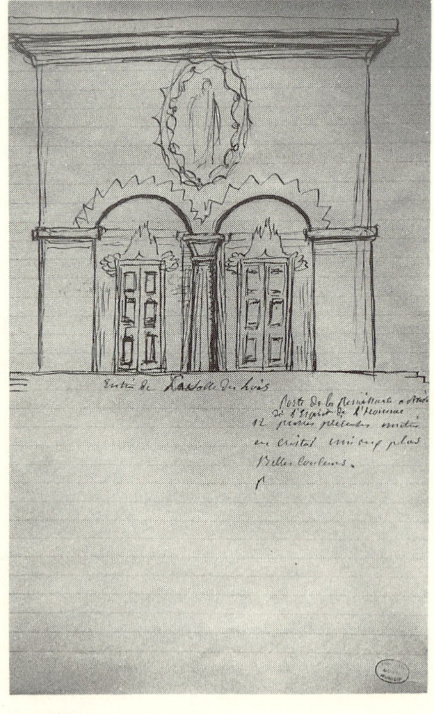

> disputed, and establish the mathematical belief that he promises the world for the day of almost universal doubt when the Church carries all before it.[90]

This abstract presentation is combined with a sequence of historical themes that depict the crisis blighting humanity and outline the growth of Christianity as a harbinger of universality. This latter sequence of statues and drawings ostensibly reveals how faith "opens the way to certain, inevitable conclusions which will establish the final era, that of mathematically enlightened Christianity."[91]

Bra's project—utopian in every sense of the word—recalls Paul Chenavard's palingenetic interpretation of historical development and decline in the 1848 scheme for the Panthéon, though the sculptor's philosophical background leads to a more optimistic conception of progress than is found in the Panthéon murals, with their cyclical conception of history drawn from Ballanche and Vico.[92] Both artists share a sweeping historical vision and partiality for abstraction which aligns them with the romantic tradition of the epic, epitomized by the Illuminist *philosophe inconnu* Saint-Martin and by Ballanche himself, who in 1827 had projected a vast poetical evocation of his *Paligénésie sociale*.[93] Both, too, regarded their work as a vehicle for intellectual synthesis and subordinated formal appeal to a pedagogical concern for art as a form of *écriture*.[94] In philosophical conception, however, Bra's grandiloquent scheme is unique. Its genealogy in Buchezian philosophy—expressed in peculiarly hybrid terms—indicates the breadth of reading that could be applied to Buchez's historical texts, a feature that clearly emerges when the *Musée de la Paix* is juxtaposed with Piel's doctrinal ambitions for the Basilique Saint-Nicolas in Nantes.

This contrast neatly symbolizes the position of history within Buchezian theory, poised as it was between a retrospective evocation of the Middle Ages and a firm conviction in the organic unfolding of the historical process. The complementary nature of these seemingly incompatible initiatives is highlighted by a third—equally abortive—scheme by a member of the

[90] "Une réapparition des esprits des choses de la conception unique. L'Etre lumineux les contient en ses clartés et les domine et c'est par là qu'il peut ressaisir ce que fut l'esprit du commencement, rétablir des vérités obscurcies ou combattues, et fonder la croyance mathématique qu'il promet au monde pour le jour du doute presque universel où l'Eglise pourra porter toutes choses." Ibid., 56.

[91] "Nous ouvre la voie des conclusions certaines, inévitables, qui établiront la période chrétienne mathématiquement éclairée, ou la dernière." T. Bra, *Suite à l'introduction au Musée de la Paix* (1853), 21.

[92] See M. A. Grunewald, "Paul Chenavard (1807–1895). La Palingénésie sociale ou la philosophie de l'histoire 1830?–1852?" *Bulletin des musées et monuments lyonnais* 6, no. 1 (1980): 317–43.

[93] See P. Bénichou, *Le Sacre de l'écrivain 1750–1830*, 105, 169.

[94] On Chenavard's concern to "encyclopédiser" diverse forms of knowledge, see J. Buche, *L'Ecole mystique de Lyon 1776–1847* (1935), 258.

school, the *cathédrale synthétique* of Louis-Auguste Boileau (plate 18). Boileau's absorption of Buchezian philosophy led him to abandon Gothic revivalism and to confront instead the problem of evolving an architectural style more appropriate for contemporary needs and beliefs. In the half century following his discovery of Buchez in the late 1830s,[95] he elaborated a schematization of architectural change constructed around Buchez's theory of historical periodicity.[96] A staunch critic of the Renaissance betrayal of Christian tradition, Boileau opposed contemporary eclecticism as the outcome of a gradual dissociation between architecture and the belief systems it was intended to symbolize. While attacking eclecticism for indiscriminately plundering the past, Boileau argued for a new architecture which would employ past precedent in a historically informed way. He sets out his program in 1853:

> To identify the architectural types that mark the different stages in the progress of monumental art, arrange them in sequence, determine the highest point the art has reached and, from this, reach higher still: —in a word, to summarize tradition and deduce from this undertaking the progress to be accomplished in our own times.[97]

In his synoptic overview of architectural history, begun in 1851 and finally published in 1886, Boileau expanded Buchez's equation between religious eras and monumental forms. His researches informed a style that ostensibly resolved the impasse in contemporary architecture by providing new building types encompassing traditional motifs in a synthesis that adapts the past for the needs of the present. Thus the architecture of the future is conceived as growing organically out of the past in the same way as Bra's predictive vision in the *Musée de la Paix* propels the visitor forward to glimpse a new society whose accuracy is validated by historical precedent. Boileau's amalgamation of past and future, elaborated in several projects of which the *cathédrale synthétique* is the most ambitious, combines technological innovation with forms developed from the Gothic church. Iron enables Boileau to adapt traditional methods in a spectacular system of engaged vaults, which not only gives the new synthetic style a distinctive appearance

[95] According to L. A. Boileau's *Nouvelle Forme architecturale. Exposé. Notes et appréciations* (1853), the architect's stylistic researches began in 1837, the year before he met Louis Piel, to whom he emphasizes his theoretical obligation (40–41). Contact with Buchez can be dated to this period.

[96] In the *Histoire critique de l'invention en architecture* (1886), Boileau remarks "Pour moi, l'hypothèse générale de Buchez sur le progrès est celle qui répond le mieux à la vérité des faits" (33). His own analysis leans heavily on Buchez.

[97] "Déterminer les types architectoniques qui marquent les différents termes de la progression dans l'art monumental, en établir la série, constater le point le plus élevé que cet art ait atteint, de là s'élever plus haut encore; —en un mot, résumer la tradition et déduire de ce travail le progrès à réaliser de nos jours." Boileau, *Nouvelle Forme*, 3.

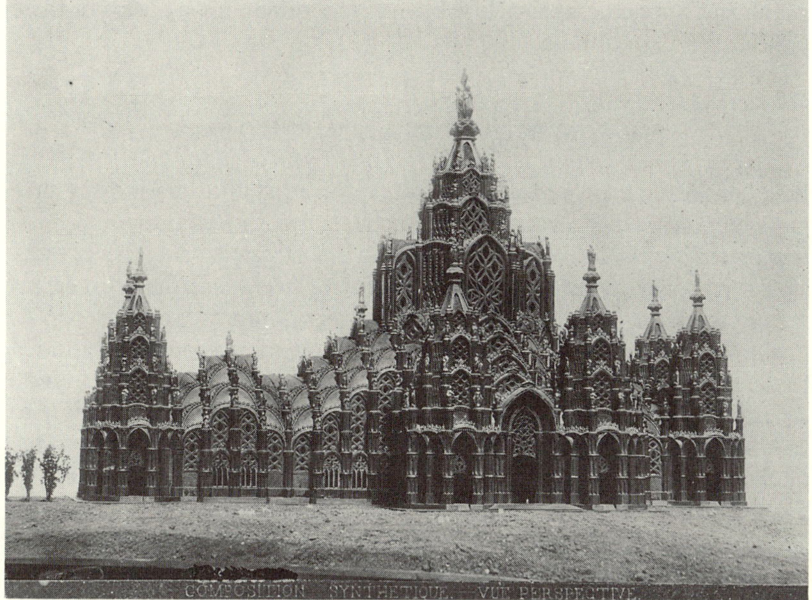

Plate 18. Louis-Auguste Boileau: Model of the *Cathédrale synthétique,* reproduced from the *Nouvelle Forme architecturale,* 1853. Bibliothèque nationale, Paris.

but also allows great play in the use of stained glass to heighten the emotional impact of the internal space. The work's scale, combined with the hostility of the Conseil des bâtiments civils, frustrated Boileau's plans, though in the relatively modest surroundings of the Eglise Saint-Eugène in Paris, completed in 1856, he was able to fulfill an ambition in employing iron as a major structural feature in a Gothic revival setting.[98]

As Bruno Foucart has observed, Buchez's philosophy of history offered "a remarkable liberating power as regards stylistic, geographical, and chronological distinctions."[99] Yet Buchezian projects are more than imaginative stylistic by-products of an arcane philosophy. Rather, their exploration of history evolves out of a political perspective sensitive to the social importance of religious belief and intent on elaborating stylistic solutions as a means of affirming and consolidating faith. In their apparently disparate ways, Piel, Bra, and Boileau all share a belief in *architecture parlante*, with the monument soliciting allegiance to an ideological system through the meanings incorporated within its very structure. In this respect, Buchez's philosophy of history is more than a source of stylistic inspiration; it serves instead

[98] See J. Delbrouck, *L'Eglise Saint-Eugène à Paris. Vues et description* (1856).

[99] "Un remarquable pouvoir libérateur à l'égard des distinctions stylistiques, géographiques et chronologiques." Foucart, "Cathédrale synthétique," 51.

to validate a concept of society which in very different ways each of these projects serves to uphold.

"SENTIMENT," "EDUCATION," AND "ART"

If his philosophy proved a fertile source of artistic inspiration for progressively inclined contemporaries, Buchez himself focused theoretical attention less on the act of creation than on the perceiving subject's psychological response to aesthetic stimuli. Relative neglect of the artist in his mature work marks a retreat from the prophetic authority promised in *Le Producteur* consequent on a perception of culture more thoroughly attuned to the guiding authority of religious belief. Buchez's interest in the mind's capacity to effect attitudinal and behavioral change through responding to sensory stimuli laid the foundations for an aesthetic more attentive to the mechanics of spectatorial cognition than to the origins of creative insight. Though echoed by groups such as the Saint-Simonians and Fourierists, this concern with perception and affect assumes particular significance in Buchez's work, in terms both of its structural integration into his overall philosophy and in its exposure of the tensions fragmenting a system of thought trapped uncomfortably between radical materialism and more conservative spiritualist impulses.

Buchez's extensive investigation of perception and aesthetic response, pursued together with the Italian physiologist Laurent Cerise,[100] directly informs his followers' aesthetic position and draws upon the work of such theorists as Bichat and Cabanis to arrive at an account of human behavior which rehabilitates the status of reason. This repudiation of Saint-Simonian notions of sentiment had important implications for Buchezian attitudes toward art, reinforcing commitment to the fundamentally social nature of the creative act and serving to emphasize the educative potential of the arts as auxiliaries to preexistent religious and moral structures. Yet the careful anatomization of neurological processes through which Buchez and Cerise secured their defense of art's didactic role exposes a theoretical ambivalence over the psycho-physiological nature of man, which interlocks with broader debates in contemporary medical philosophy and exposes a doctrinal inability to reconcile metaphysical convictions with progressive politics.

In embracing Christianity in the late 1820s, Buchez had been obliged to reassess some of the most fundamental beliefs underpinning his attitudes toward physiology and, by extension, toward the major philosophical questions concerning human existence and understanding. The materialism propounded in his contributions to *Le Producteur* had imposed a monist repu-

100 On Cerise, see P. Foissac, "Notice biographique sur le docteur Cerise," introduction to L. Cerise, *Mélanges médico-psychologiques* (1872): i–xii.

diation of belief in an immaterial soul and endorsement of sensationalist claims that ideas were exclusively derived from sense impressions.[101] Such a position was consistent with more advanced medical opinion, associated with political liberals such as Cabanis and François Broussais, which focused on physiological processes of innervation when describing human cognition and dismissed dualist beliefs in the existence of the soul,[102] but was no longer suitable as Buchez gravitated toward Christianity. This new conviction necessarily involved acceptance of dualism and further implied a belief in innate ideas, in line with the teachings of "spiritualist" defenders of traditional notions of the mind's relationship with the body and man's relationship with God. The incompatibility of such premises both with the project for a *science de l'homme* invoked by Saint-Simon and with Buchez's own medical background permanently destabilized his theoretical allegiances as he attempted to reconcile the religious aspects of "spiritualism" with the physiologists' insistence on the material processes mediating the body's transformation of sensations into ideas. Buchez's emphasis on the precise neurological processes of innervation, central to his understanding of aesthetic reception, suggests a monist preoccupation belied in his assertion that "each man is a soul possessing an organism which serves him as an instrument."[103] Propounding what François Isambert has described as "a psychology trapped between physiology and metaphysics,"[104] Buchez sent out contradictory signals on an issue where his theoretical inclinations directly conflicted with his political sympathies.[105] On the associated question of innate ideas, again central to his discussion of the arts, he attempted a similar reconciliation, arguing against established sensationalist and spiritualist positions[106] to propose a theory of knowledge rooted in divine revelation and foregrounding the role of reason in the acquisition of ideas through education.[107] It is this overdetermination of physiological under-

[101] See Isambert, *Politique, religion*, 204–6.

[102] For a lucid exposition of these positions, see J. Goldstein, *Console and Classify: The French Psychiatric Profession in the Nineteenth Century* (1987), 240–63.

[103] "Chaque homme est une âme pourvue d'un organisme qui lui sert d'instrument." P.J.B. Buchez, *Introduction à l'étude des sciences médicales* (1838), 107. See also P. Buchez, "Etudes sur les éléments pathogéniques de la folie," Buchez Papers, C.P. 3716:78r.

[104] "Une psychologie coincée entre la physiologie et la métaphysique." Isambert, *Politique, religion*, 227.

[105] See, for example, the unambiguous assertion of spiritualist sympathies in Buchez, *Sciences médicales*, 155–56, as opposed to the critique of both spiritualist and materialist positions in the "Etudes sur les éléments pathogéniques," Buchez Papers, C.P. 3716:80r–81r. For Cerise's attempted reconciliation of spiritualism and materialism, see his 1843 essay "Que faut-il entendre, en physiologie et en pathologie, par ces mots: 'influence du moral sur le physique, influence du physique sur le moral'?" *Mélanges*, 21.

[106] For rejections of sensationalism, see "Des idées innées—object," Buchez Papers, C.P. 3706:64. On sensationalism, see Buchez, *Sciences médicales*, 120.

[107] See Buchez, *Sciences médicales*, 118–35.

standing by ideological *partis pris* that colors the theoretical premises on which Buchez constructed his notion of art as an agent of individual persuasion and of collective change.

Bichat's identification of three human types, which the Saint-Simonians had used as the basis for their trinity of the *artiste*, *savant*, and *industriel*, takes on a rather different form in Buchez's work. While accepting this social typology,[108] he echoes Pierre Leroux in associating the faculties of *sentiment*, *raison*, and *activité* not with particular temperaments, but with all forms of behavior. For Buchez, every act combines all three faculties sequentially: external stimuli provoke a *sentiment* in the nervous system, which is interpreted by *raison*; this cognitive stage produces a reaction to the initial sensation, manifested in muscular *activité*. Such a perspective promotes reason as a vital intermediary in human response and hence modifies Saint-Simonian assertions of the preeminent role of sentiment in the aesthetic domain.

Concentration on rational mediation also appears in a further terminological distinction adopted from Bichat between *vie organique* and *vie animale*. The former denotes physical needs such as nutrition and reproduction, whereas the latter is equated with reflection, will, and—crucially for Buchez—human relations whereby "[the animal] exists outside of itself."[109] As we shall see, by relating the psycho-physiological mechanisms of the *vie animale* to art's role in reinforcing faith during organic periods, Buchez underlines culture's inherently social function. Such a position further suggests that at such historical conjunctures the aesthetic appeal to sentiment operates as part of a rational process—a position that allows for the intervention of free will consonant with Christian theology.

Buchez presents two distinctive modes of sentiment—the essentially egocentric "unité sentimentale de conservation" ("emotional apparatus of self-preservation"), associated with the physical needs of the *vie organique*, and the "appareil sympathique ou d'imitation" ("sympathetic or imitative mechanism"), rooted in the *vie animale*, whose more altruistic impulses underwrite social relations.[110] In line with his theory of progress, he argued that as improved material conditions increasingly satisfied physical needs, so the *appareil sympathique* grew in influence, fostering a heightened sense of reciprocity in social relations. In advancing such a thesis, he expanded upon Bichat's *Recherches*, relating the instinct of self-preservation to the spontaneous reflex action of the *vie organique* as opposed to the sympathetic mech-

[108] See A. Ott, "Notice sur la vie et les travaux de Buchez," in *Traité de politique et de science sociale*, by P.J.B. Buchez (1866), xc–xcii.

[109] "[L'animal] existe hors de lui." M.F.X. Bichat, *Recherches physiologiques sur la vie et la mort* (1800; reprint, 1844), 420.

[110] See Buchez, *Science de l'histoire*, 1:371–73.

anism's dependence on the mediating influence of reason in transforming sentiment into action.

Through associating reason with the *appareil sympathique*, Buchez emphasized the moral dimension of this form of sentiment. Reason, manifested as *volonté*, was seen as uniquely allowing man to differentiate between emotional stimuli on ethical grounds, subordinating egocentric desire to a socially informed sense of long-term duty. As Cerise remarks in his investigation into the psycho-physiological effect of the arts:

> Through reason, the need and feeling that disturbed us acquire a name, and become a desire whose goal is understood, whose moral complexion is fixed and felt, and toward whose satisfaction the organism's movements are directed, arrested, or modified. In a word, will displays freedom, which is an attribute of reason.[111]

By relating the *appareil sympathique* to the *vie animale*, Buchez and Cerise posit sentiment as physiological proof of human solidarity. Both argue that the nervous system responds to displays of emotion through a process of *innervation imitative*, whereby the affective faculties stimulate muscular activity and simulate the emotional state that had initially excited the *appareil sympathique*.[112] Thus, for example, displays of amusement provoke laughter within the perceiving subject, whereas the sight of pain induces sympathetic facial and muscular contractions. From this, Buchez and Cerise infer a profound sense of human interdependence.[113]

Conceived as an organic need, whose suppression disrupts individual psycho-physiological equilibrium, the process of *innervation imitative* is also presented as a social need, facilitating contact and the transmission of emotion, either by strengthening altruistic feeling or by modifying behavior through an appeal to sentiment. This imitative process had already been identified by Rousseau as fundamental to affective relations,[114] while Cabanis had maintained the necessity of rooting aesthetic theory upon "a methodical understanding of the intelligent and sentient being," asserting that "A man acts on others, or makes them share his ideas or feelings, only by

[111] "Par l'esprit, le besoin et l'impression qui nous agitaient prennent un nom, ils deviennent un désir, le but en est apprécié, la moralité en est déterminée et sentie, les mouvements de l'organisme propres à l'atteindre sont dirigés, arrêtés ou modérés. La volonté en un mot manifeste alors la liberté qui est l'attribut de l'esprit." L. Cerise, "Considérations physiologiques sur les éléments et sur les moyens de l'art," *L'Européen*, n.s., 1, no. 6 (25 March 1836): 174.

[112] See Buchez, *Science de l'histoire*, 1:360–67.

[113] "On peut . . . dire avec rigueur que les hommes ont reçu un organisme qui leur permet de souffrir et de sentir les uns dans les autres." Buchez, "Art," 711.

[114] See J.-J. Rousseau, *Emile, ou l'éducation* (1762), in *Oeuvres complètes*, ed. B. Gagnebin and M. Raymond (1969), 4:505.

joining with them in a state of sympathy that makes his listeners or spectators feel and think in the same way as he does through his use of natural or artificial forms of language."[115] Ironically, while the materialist Cabanis had done no more than point to the need for a neurological explanation of this process, it was the more instinctively spiritualist Buchez and Cerise who elaborated a psycho-physiological model of response and invested in this formulation of *sympathie* their conviction in the power of art and its social effect. Definitions current within the school focus on the transmission of sentiment through sympathy. Cerise, for example, describes art as "the collection of expressive forms through which human feelings are spread sympathetically among men"[116]—and it is this power that provides the basis for its discussion as an educative force within society.

Belief in sentiment's reliance on the mediating influence of reason encouraged a strictly instrumental view of art as a vehicle for soliciting adherence to a specific idea. Such an attitude relates to Buchez's emphasis on the historical goal toward whose achievement each society must work; in the same way, art itself must attract the intellect by proposing a specific *but*. He thus conceives of the imagination as at once "affective et intellectuelle"—the point at which the emotional impact of an external stimulus meets and is galvanized by the power of intellect. Such a process can only occur where the work of art's emotional power is matched by a meaning capable of inspiring intellectual concurrence. As Cerise remarks in 1842:

> For the imagination to be moved by a work of art, the mind must intervene, transforming the sympathetic emotion into a specific desire. Only then, under the impact of ideas that feed this desire, will an intra-cerebral [intellectual] and cerebro-ganglionary [sentimental] innervation supplement the feeling with the various intellectual and affective elements that constitute imagination. Images then form, events are sketched in the mind's eye in a way that differs from their character in the sensory realm, and which corresponds to the desire that gave rise to them in thought.[117]

115 "La connaissance méthodique de la nature intelligente et sensible"; "Un homme n'agit sur les autres, ou ne leur fait partager ses idées et ses sentiments, qu'en se mettant avec eux dans un état de sympathie qui fasse sentir et penser ceux qui écoutent ou regardent, en commun avec celui qui parle ou qui se sert de tout autre langage, soit naturel, soit artificiel." P.J.G. Cabanis, "Lettre à M. T**, sur les poèmes d'Homère," in *Oeuvres complètes* (1825), 5:354.

116 "L'ensemble des formes expressives à l'aide desquelles les sentiments humains se propagent sympathiquement parmi les hommes." L. Cerise, *Des fonctions et des maladies nerveuses dans leurs rapports avec l'éducation sociale et privée, morale et physique* (1842), 144.

117 "Pour que l'imagination soit ébranlée par une oeuvre d'art, il faut que l'esprit intervienne et que l'émotion sympathique soit transformée en un désir déterminé. Alors seulement, sous l'empire des idées qui alimentent ce désir, l'innervation intra-cérébrale [i.e., intellectual] et cérébro-ganglionnaire [i.e., sentimental] viennent apporter au sentiment le cortège des éléments intellectuels et affectifs qui constituent l'imagination. Alors, des images se forment, des événements se dessinent aux yeux de l'esprit, avec un caractère différent de celui qu'ils mani-

Ranging the arts among a complex of institutions devoted to promoting normative moral values, such as the press, the educational system and judiciary, the Buchezians saw them as contributing to the citizen's "continuing education,"[118] soliciting acceptance of "a specific goal, a code of duties, a general rule of behavior."[119]

Emphasis is here placed upon *conservation*, the maintenance of fundamental social values that provide the precondition for fulfilling the *but commun d'activité*, rather than on any advocacy of art as an incitement to change.[120] Such conservative priorities derive not only from Buchez's ambition to realize moral imperatives already implicit in the dominant belief system, but also relate to the school's appreciation of art's dependence on other areas of social practice—most notably religion—for its source of meaning. In this regard, the arts are delegated responsibility for rallying support around values inculcated within other spheres of society and strengthening the bonds of solidarity promoted by faith and the prevalent moral code. Such a perspective suggests an apprehension of the arts as a buttress of dominant ideology, rather than as a weapon to be used against it.[121]

While maintaining a vigorous critique of the July Monarchy and attacking the hardship generated by the emergent capitalist system, the Buchezians were committed to promoting Christian values apparently stifled by the prevailing national climate. It is this moral system that they called upon art to project. Thus, for example, a reviewer in the workers' journal *L'Atelier* can range such seemingly conservative values as "the love of our fathers, charity, gentleness, family concord, chaste and pure love" among those to be promoted, while at the same time asserting that "artists must be revolutionaries." This more dynamic role devolves from the obligation to "maintain us in the path of those duties to be fulfilled in progressing toward the nation's goal," itself identified with "the achievement of liberty, equality, and fraternity."[122] Political and moral imperatives thus coincide through

---

festent dans la sphère sensoriale, avec un caractère tout à fait conforme au désir qui les a fait surgir dans la pensée." Ibid., 156. The interrelationship between reason and sentiment is conceived more loosely by Buchez in his later work. See the posthumous *Traité de politique*, 1:144–45.

[118] "Education continuée"; Buchez, *Traité de politique*, 1:143.

[119] "Un but déterminé, un code de devoirs, une règle générale de conduite." Cerise, *Fonctions et maladies*, 82.

[120] See Buchez, *Traité de politique*, 1:134, where art is described as one of the "moyens de transmettre, d'une génération à une autre, la connaissance, la conviction et l'amour du but commun d'activité, en le tenant constamment présent à l'esprit de tous."

[121] See, for example, Anonymous, "Galerie de tableaux de M. Erard," *L'Européen* 2, no. 35 (4 August 1832): 139.

[122] "L'amour de nos pères, la charité, la douceur, la paix de la famille, l'amour chaste et pur"; "les artistes doivent être révolutionnaires"; "nous entretenir dans la ligne des dévouements à accomplir pour le progrès vers le but national"; "la réalisation de la liberté, de l'égalité et de la fraternité." Anonymous, "Salon de 1841," 55.

their common origin in Buchez's social reading of Christian doctrine. Conservation and change are held in balance, since political transformation becomes the medium for authentic realization of a received ethical code.

The psycho-physiological conceptualization of aesthetic response allows a positivist tone to infiltrate Buchezian theory. Ascribing to art "a moral and even a hygienic value" of cardinal social importance,[123] Buchez argues for a broad identity of response which allows the work of art to achieve a largely foreseeable effect on its audience:

> There are certain sounds, movements, and works of art which, depending on our sensibility, will once encountered more or less inevitably stimulate the complete emotional mechanism of our instinct for preservation, to the extent that we imitate wholly and in every way the emotion that stimulated them.[124]

Such a point is made even more forcibly by Cerise, who ranges art with those auxiliary educative institutions ostensibly having the power to "determine in the nervous system those changes most beneficial for fulfilling duties we have been taught."[125] Beauty itself is defined in ethical terms as "the moral idea clothed in the power of sentiment,"[126] while an insistence on the historical specificity of particular moral systems leads the group to refute formalist assertions of its immutability.[127] Aesthetic pleasure is thus conceived not as a self-sufficient reaction deriving from the disinterested contemplation of formal perfection, but as a catalyst whereby endorsement of particular moral imperatives can be secured.[128] Repeated exposure to the pleasurable experience of art cultivates certain emotional mechanisms, inculcating specific moral values through the force of habit.[129]

Buchez's belief that "the self is formed and develops in the same way as any acquired knowledge"[130] implicitly accords prominence to education

123 "Une valeur morale et même une valeur hygiénique"; Buchez, *Science de l'histoire*, 1:356.

124 "Il est des sons, des gestes, des oeuvres d'art, qui, une fois senties, provoquent, plus ou moins inévitablement, suivant notre sensibilité, l'émotion de l'appareil entier de la vie de conservation, de telle sorte que nous imitons complètement, et dans toutes les variétés, l'émotion qui les a produites." Ibid., 361.

125 "Déterminer dans l'organisme nerveux les modifications les plus favorables à l'accomplissement des devoirs enseignés." Cerise, *Des fonctions*, 140.

126 "L'idée morale revêtue de la puissance sentimentale." Ott, "Notice sur . . . Buchez," lxxxvi. Buchez defines beauty as "ce qui se fait imiter et aimer, ce qui entre dans les sympathies humaines" (*Science de l'histoire*, 1:404), Cerise as "la forme la mieux appropriée à faire aimer le bien" (*Des fonctions*, 146).

127 See A. Ott, "Art," in *Dictionnaire des sciences politiques et sociales* (1854), 1:423: "le mot beau n'est, en réalité, qu'un terme de classification dont la signification n'a rien de précis ni d'absolu. L'idée du beau a souvent changé."

128 See Buchez, *Traité de politique*, 1:144, and *Science de l'histoire*, 1:356.

129 See Buchez, *Traité de politique*, 1:145.

130 "Le moi se forme et se développe à la manière de toute connaissance acquise." P.J.B. Buchez, *Essai d'un traité complet de philosophie, du point de vue du catholicisme et du progrès* (1838–40), 3:467.

and to such auxiliary institutions as the arts in molding individual consciousness and thus—on a broader scale—in directing collective action. It is from such a position that the Buchezians evolved a theory of language and of the sign whose emphasis on their mediating value in social relations further strengthened the group's adherence to a utilitarian aesthetic.

Already, in *Le Producteur*, Buchez had asserted the crucial role of language as a medium for progress, allowing the transmission and enrichment of human knowledge.[131] During the 1830s he and Cerise elaborated this position, arguing for the centrality of language and the exchange of signs as the basis of sociality. Maintaining that "it is the gift of signs which brings us together and makes us human,"[132] Buchez argued that the appearance of language was coeval with human creation and was indispensable as a medium of cognition, conceptualization, and communication.[133] Yet language is not conceived as a purely instrumental medium facilitating individual intellectual development and human interchange; rather Buchez and Cerise both argue that with other semiological codes it plays an active role in constructing consciousness, implanting within the individual "a generating principle for his feelings, his ideas, and his acts."[134] Exploring the psychophysiological mechanisms of this process, Cerise associated the capacity to organize sense impressions, the refinement of affectivity, and development of conscience and understanding with responsiveness to sign systems.[135]

While following Cabanis in emphasizing the importance of signs in the expression and communication of *sympathie morale*,[136] Cerise went further in highlighting the social aspect of this process, affording it even greater influence on the development of individual consciousness than the formative power of the *milieu physique*.[137] Thus he sees the faculties of reasoning and emotion, whose functioning relies upon responsiveness to sign systems, as being dependent upon the particular social milieu in which they are found. In such a way, the sign, as a historically specific phenomenon, constructs individual consciousness in conformity with dominant social and ethical norms.[138] The congruence between the individual and the

[131] See P.J.B. Buchez, "Des termes de passage de la physiologie individuelle à la physiologie sociale," *Prod.* 4 (1826): 83–84.

[132] "C'est le don des signes qui nous associe et nous fait hommes." Buchez, *Science de l'histoire*, 1:417.

[133] See Ott, "Notice sur . . . Buchez" cxxiv.

[134] "Un principe générateur de ses sentiments, de ses conceptions et de ses actes." Cerise, *Des fonctions*, 106.

[135] Ibid., 22.

[136] Cabanis, *Rapports du physique et du moral de l'homme* (1802), ed. F. Thurot (1824), 3:222.

[137] Cerise, *Des fonctions*, 57.

[138] "La mémoire, l'imagination, le raisonnement etc., considérés dans les opérations cérébrales dont ils réclament le concours, sont chez l'individu, l'image fidèle de l'état moral et intellectuel exprimé par le langage de la société dans laquelle il vit." Ibid., 421.

collectivity, attributed to language, thus secures *solidarité* around a *but commun*.

In asserting the crucial role of language in forming consciousness, the Buchezians relied upon a theory of the sign that argued for the universality of its emotional effect on the basis of the identity of the mechanisms of psycho-physiological response. Buchez based this argument on a distinction between two forms of sign: "Those intended simply to transmit thought, and those which, together with thought, transmit passion—in other words, a certain organic or physical emotion accompanying the thought."[139] The diversity of national languages provided evidence for the arbitrariness of the signifying process within the former current, identified with the purely functional aspects of "la parole articulée ou écrite" ("written or spoken language"). The emotional power of the sign, associated with artistic expression, transcends this arbitrariness, since the mechanisms it exploits are apparently common to all men.[140]

Such ideas suggest a universalist theory of form, though Buchez stops just short of this. If his identification of the emotional power of art is based upon a universalist conception of the psychological processes,[141] his understanding of their deployment is strictly historicist. The differences in social and moral complexion he attributes to successive societies presuppose modes of consciousness that are historically specific, since each stage of history is identified with a particular *but*. The concrete forms given to this ideological goal are generated by the belief system they are designed to promote and mold individual consciousness accordingly. Buchez's awareness of the variety of social structures and types of cultural expression prevents any reductive equation between emotional mechanisms and artistic utterance; in all of this, the mediation of particular social circumstances remains paramount. His identification of a fundamental concordance between form and response does, however, leave room for the possibility of isolating, and eventually of influencing, certain behavioral reactions through the strategic use of particular sign systems.

Emphasis on art as a form of *écriture*[142] highlights its function as a vehicle for meaning drawing validity from its responsiveness to contemporary social and ethical imperatives embodied in religion. This notion of artistic

[139] "Ceux destinés à transmettre simplement la pensée; et ceux qui, en même temps que la pensée, transmettent la passion, c'est-à-dire une certaine émotion organique ou charnelle qui accompagne cette pensée." Buchez, *Science de l'histoire*, 1:418.

[140] "Les formes en sont fixes jusqu'à un certain point; elles ressortent de principes qui ne sont pas de convention; les modifications qu'on peut y introduire sont bornées et ne sont nullement arbitraires; en un mot, ces formes ont la fixité des expressions passionnées elles-mêmes." Ibid.

[141] See Buchez, *Science de l'histoire*, 1:404.

[142] Auger applies the term to various art forms in *Moralités*, 1:132–33.

dependence provides the basis for a theoretical distinction between a priori and a posteriori forms of creation, which integrates the Saint-Simonian antitheses "organic" versus "critical," and "synthetic" versus "analytical" within a fundamentally theological framework.

Like Saint-Simon, Buchez identified organic periods of history with an a priori epistemological system grounded in a universal religious belief whose appeal to sentiment provided the basis for a unified social system: "A formula conceived a priori gives a shared vigor and desire to all the energies of the sentimental apparatus, blending individual appetites and achieving a synthesis from them."[143]

Like the Saint-Simonians, Buchez and his followers regarded the social climate provided by faith during these eras as peculiarly conducive to an art matching formal perfection with emotional resonance. At such a time, the artist shared the profound faith that animated society and was moved by its a priori principles in all his works. Identifying creativity during these periods with the predominance of the altruistic *vie animale*, the Buchezians regarded their art as a "spiritual activity dominating organic impulses,"[144] celebrating the solidarity of human life inscribed in faith and subordinating the egocentricity of physical desire.

In the same way as Enfantin's emphasis on love as distinguishing the artist during organic periods underscores his inherent sympathy and understanding of the surrounding world, so the Buchezians conceive his religious devotion as allowing an enhanced sense of identification with society.[145] In this respect, individualism is attenuated as he instinctively responds to the needs of those around him, in a process that mirrors the subordination of self-interest to collective goals.[146] The artist's immersion in society lends the creative act a particular force within Buchezian discourse. Rather than depending on individual motivation, creativity is regarded as being impelled by necessity, the a priori principles of revealed religion implanting a need to express ideas and feelings conducive to the "but collectif de la société." Thus Bion, Besson, and Baptiste describe such an act of creation:

> Through a continual transformation, its action moves from interior to exterior, since its goal is the production of a new sign, a new form of expression, which

[143] "La formule conçue a priori donne à toutes les énergies de l'appareil sentimental une impulsion commune, un désir commun, dans lequel se confondent les appétances particulières, et dans lequel elles trouvent leur synthèse." Buchez, *Science de l'histoire*, 1:377.

[144] "Activité spirituelle dominant les impulsions organiques." Cerise, "Considérations physiologiques," 171.

[145] See Buchez, *Science de l'histoire*, 1:387.

[146] This position derives directly from early writings, where the arts are described as "les créations des sentiments passionnées, c'est à dire de ce qu'il y a de moins individuel dans l'homme" See P.J.B. Buchez, "Quelques Réflexions sur la littérature et les beaux-arts," *Prod.* 4 (1826): 190.

as yet exists only in the mind: in this, it draws upon what already exists, taking what is favorable to it, rejecting what is inimical: it judges everything according to the goal in view, so that it can be said that once man has freely accepted a principle of activity, this principle acts within and through him, so long as his will does not oppose it.[147]

Works inspired by such a priori principles are stamped by their monumental, synthetic character. Applied to a variety of poetic and plastic forms, Buchez's notion of monumentality designates a grandeur of conception unique to those eras during which the arts drew upon faith for their emotive power.[148] Such expressions of belief foster art forms that combine the verbal, the visual, and the architectonic for enhanced emotional effect. Like the Saint-Simonians, Buchez regards the orator as embodying this synthesis and the cathedral as its highest expression. It is through their eloquence and power to command emulation that these forms attain monumentality.[149] Their perfection is contingent on art's grounding in faith, which, as the ultimate verity of existence and human conduct, is "essentiellement encyclopédique." Any artistic utterance that deviates from its inspiration is deemed fragmented and thus inimical to emotive effect:

> One will still encounter thoughts directed at particular feelings, such as love, pity, anger, hatred, devotion, selfishness, etc., but there will no longer be any capable of exciting all of them at once; and from that it will follow that in the end the artist will no longer dominate those listening to him. He will become their slave, obliged, before creating a work, to interrogate his public, producing specifically for them and, finally, falling so low as to lend his brush or his pen to satisfying the basest instincts and most loathsome appetites.[150]

[147] "Son action se fait du dedans au dehors par une transformation continue; car il s'agit de produire un signe nouveau, une expression nouvelle, qui n'existe encore que dans l'esprit: pour cela elle s'aide de ce qui existe déjà, acceptant ce que lui est favorable, rejetant ce que lui est contraire: tout par elle est jugé au point de vue du but à atteindre, de sorte que l'on peut dire que quand l'homme a une fois accepté librement un principe d'activité, ce principe agit en lui et par lui, tant que sa volonté ne s'y oppose pas." Bion, Besson, and Baptiste, "Salon de 1836," 189.

[148] See Buchez, *Science de l'histoire*, 1:393–96.

[149] "Ainsi une synthèse d'art donne toujours, à la pensée, un geste par lequel elle commande l'attention. Ce geste seul est un monument et une enceinte dans laquelle le sentiment se dramatise en se mouvant sous toutes les faces, se répétant dans toutes les expressions possibles. Enfin, ce monument tout entier est doué d'une puissance harmonieuse, qui inspire la pensée morale par imitation ou sympathie, en même temps qu'il est signe pour l'esprit." Ibid., 395–96.

[150] "On rencontrera encore des pensées qui s'adresseront à des sentiments spéciaux, tels que l'amour, la pitié, la colère, la haine, le dévouement, l'égoïsme etc., mais on n'en trouvera plus de capables de les remuer tous à la fois; et il suivra de là, en définitive, que l'artiste cessera d'être le dominateur de ceux qui l'écoutent; il deviendra leur esclave; il sera obligé, avant de faire oeuvre, de s'enquérir de son public; il produira spécialement pour celui-ci, et, de chute en chute, il arrivera enfin à mettre son pinceau et sa plume au service des plus sales instincts et des plus méprisables appétits." Buchez, "Art," 713.

Buchez associates this degenerative process with the usurpation of faith by the a posteriori principles of critical society. Whereas in periods of belief, art's development under the aegis of a comprehensive moral code allowed the integrity of any action or representation to be rationally assessed, in abandoning faith, society sees such moral imperatives eroded, thus compromising individual subordination to collective need. Buchez relates this loss of equilibrium to the eclipse of the rational, altruistic impulses of the *vie animale* by the self-centered, physical impulsions of the *vie organique*; as a consequence, social solidarity and aesthetic integrity are squandered in favor of individual sensory gratification.

The Buchezians explained this promotion of form over content in physiological terms. A posteriori art, in which form predominates, is said to provoke "weakened phenomena of imitative or affective innervation, without eliciting the intelligence and, so to speak, unbeknownst to our moral or intellectual activity."[151] Sentiment and its imitative apparatus may thus still be affected by aesthetic experience but the critical artist's failure to solicit the intellect produces only a superficial, undirected response incapable of stimulating moral action. Such art is deemed to provoke "the instinctive appetites of our animal nature, and translate the senses' impressions"[152] without appealing to the perceiving subject's ethical judgment. Arguing that "art must speak to the intellect by way of the senses, and not to the senses for the senses' sake,"[153] the Buchezians maintained that this short-circuiting of response represented a denial of free will, since its imperious appeal to the senses excluded any arbitrating role for reason. Without foundations in the a priori principles of religious belief, the arts of such a period thus count as little more than impotent diversions or, at worst, provocations to sensual excess.[154]

In terms of production, the Buchezians identify a posteriori formalism with mimesis, in which the artist's "excitation extérieure ou organique"[155] finds satisfaction in nature's appearance without any complementary sense of its moral significance. As a consequence, they dismiss formalism as narrowly materialist, capable of showing only "the instinctual gestures of living things, and the form and color of objects."[156] Buchez further scorned for-

[151] "Des phénomènes affaiblis d'innervation imitative ou affective, sans participation de l'intelligence, et pour ainsi dire, à l'insu de notre activité morale ou intellectuelle." Cerise, *Des fonctions*, 140. See also L. Cerise, *Déterminer l'influence de l'éducation physique et morale sur la production de la sur-excitation du système nerveux* (1841), 148.

[152] "Les appétits instinctifs de la machine animale, et traduire les impressions des sens." Buchez, "Salon de 1834," 127.

[153] "L'art doit parler à l'intelligence par les sens, et non aux sens pour les sens." H. Auger, "Du sentiment dans les arts," *La Vérité* 14 (17 January 1835).

[154] See Cerise's remarks on masturbation in *Déterminer l'influence*, 150.

[155] Cerise, *Des fonctions*, 171.

[156] "Des mouvements automatiques des êtres, de la forme et de la couleur des choses." Piel, "Salon de 1837," 54.

malism as deriving from an alien philosophical tradition and traced its genealogy to a Germanic Protestant current extending from Luther to Mme de Staël. Through repudiating the moral influence of art and identifying creation and reception with a socially exclusive spiritual refinement, French Eclecticism, its latest manifestation, was indicted as elitist and politically reactionary.[157] Such a position negates the Buchezians' conception of art as a universally accessible medium, appealing to a psycho-physiological mechanism operating irrespective of rank and generating moral sentiment as a means of achieving its full resonance. Formalism thus stands as a symptom of contemporary fragmentation, where the public's exclusive concern for pleasure is matched by the artist's solipsistic exploration of subjectivity.[158] In embracing such beliefs in the name of aesthetic liberty, the Buchezians asserted, the artist had fundamentally restricted his freedom, investing his efforts in the reproduction of finite, material objects at the expense of the infinite domain of ethical choice.

While castigating formalism as symptomatic of a critical society, the Buchezians were anxious to emphasize the positive connotations of form as an ingredient in art. Conceived as a vehicle for enhancing the impact of a work's meaning on the *appareil sympathique*, form remains subsidiary to content, while being seen as "a power acting on the impressions, a great force affecting men's hearts, whatever the author's intention. . . . Form is the symbol; it is the outside figuring, the clothing of thought, just as a word is the sign for an idea."[159]

This functional attitude infuses Buchezian criticism. The observation on Duseigneur's *Archange Michel terrasant le démon*, for example, that "the archangel's head, his gesture, and the pose of his body are admirable thoughts,"[160] indicates a responsiveness to form in terms of its perceived amplification of meaning. From such a perspective, stylistic shortcomings are more easily forgiven in a work whose moral intentions are admired than is technical virtuosity at the expense of moral feeling—an accusation leveled against Ingres's *Martyre de St Symphorien* in 1834.[161] By contrast to Ingres's work, where a bravura technical display is seen as uppermost in the artist's

[157] See, for example, Buchez, "Salon de 1834," 124.

[158] "[La forme] n'est plus que l'expression des émotions personnelles d'un homme cherchant un écho dans les émotions individuelles de l'oisivité, cherchant à réveiller et à accroître l'énergie des appétits les plus grossiers de notre nature." Cerise, "Considérations physiologiques," 171.

[159] "Une puissance impressionnelle, une force vive qui agit sur le coeur de l'homme, quel que ait été l'intention de l'auteur. . . . La forme est le symbole; c'est la figure extérieure, le vêtement d'une pensée; tout comme un mot est le signe d'une idée." Anonymous, "Peines et récompenses," 130.

[160] "La tête de l'archange, son geste, la pose de son corps, sont des pensées admirables." Buchez, "Salon de 1834," 130.

[161] Ibid.

mind, Buchez responds favorably to Delaroche's *Jane Grey*, where "the painter . . . has worked in such a way that we forget him and attend only to the subject. Oblivious to the form, we want only what it expresses."[162] This approval of the seemingly transparent rendition of moral significance indicates a more entrenched functionalism than is suggested by the notion of form as "the clothing of thought." The implications of both statements are clear, however: technique is considered a means to an end, and the success or failure of an object must ultimately be judged according to the appropriateness of that end, irrespective of the skill displayed in its production.

In exploring the power of form as a moral signifier, Buchez advanced an associative theory in which aesthetic harmony acted as a metaphor—and a spur—for goodness. Thus the *admirative* mode displayed divine providence by revealing natural harmony, while in *satirique* forms of art the spectator was filled with repulsion for evil through the use of discordant pictorial effects. In describing the psychological impact of ideal beauty—the *mode sublime* found in such works as Robert's *Arrivée des moissonneurs dans les marais pontins* (plate 19)—Buchez emphasizes the moral dimension of response:

> Under the influence of the sublime, the soul is uplifted and extended, susceptible to every sympathy; at the same time, it grasps a broader range of objects, embracing them all with equal pleasure, since it is aware of the bond uniting them and is itself united with them in a great harmony.[163]

Form thus carries ethical associations reminiscent of classical idealism while emphasis on harmony introduces notions of divine providence to a theme central to Fourierist aesthetics. Rather than constituting an autonomous aesthetic domain, form comes to serve art's social function of inculcating faith and persuading man of the divine program for a world where the ordering of social relations matches the harmony of nature.

In all of this—the attitude toward form, the distinction between a priori and a posteriori currents in art, and the notion of the educative function of the aesthetic—primacy is given to art as a vehicle for meaning. Concentration on art's dependence on other social institutions for its source of meaning tends to displace emphasis on the artist as a privileged being, found in Buchez's early Saint-Simonian pronouncements, though elevation of his

[162] "Le peintre . . . a travaillé de telle sorte qu'on l'oublie lui-même, et qu'on est saisi seulement par un sujet. On n'aperçoit point la forme, on ne veut que ce qu'elle exprime." Ibid., 129.

[163] "L'âme s'élève, s'agrandit, s'ouvre à toutes les sympathies, lorsqu'elle est sous l'influence du mode sublime; elle saisit en même temps un plus grand nombre d'objets, qu'elle embrasse avec un égal sentiment de plaisir, parce qu'elle sent leurs rapports et qu'elle-même se trouve liée avec eux dans une grande harmonie." P.J.B. Buchez [?], "Des artistes aujourd'hui," *L'Européen* 1, no. 9 (2 January 1832):131.

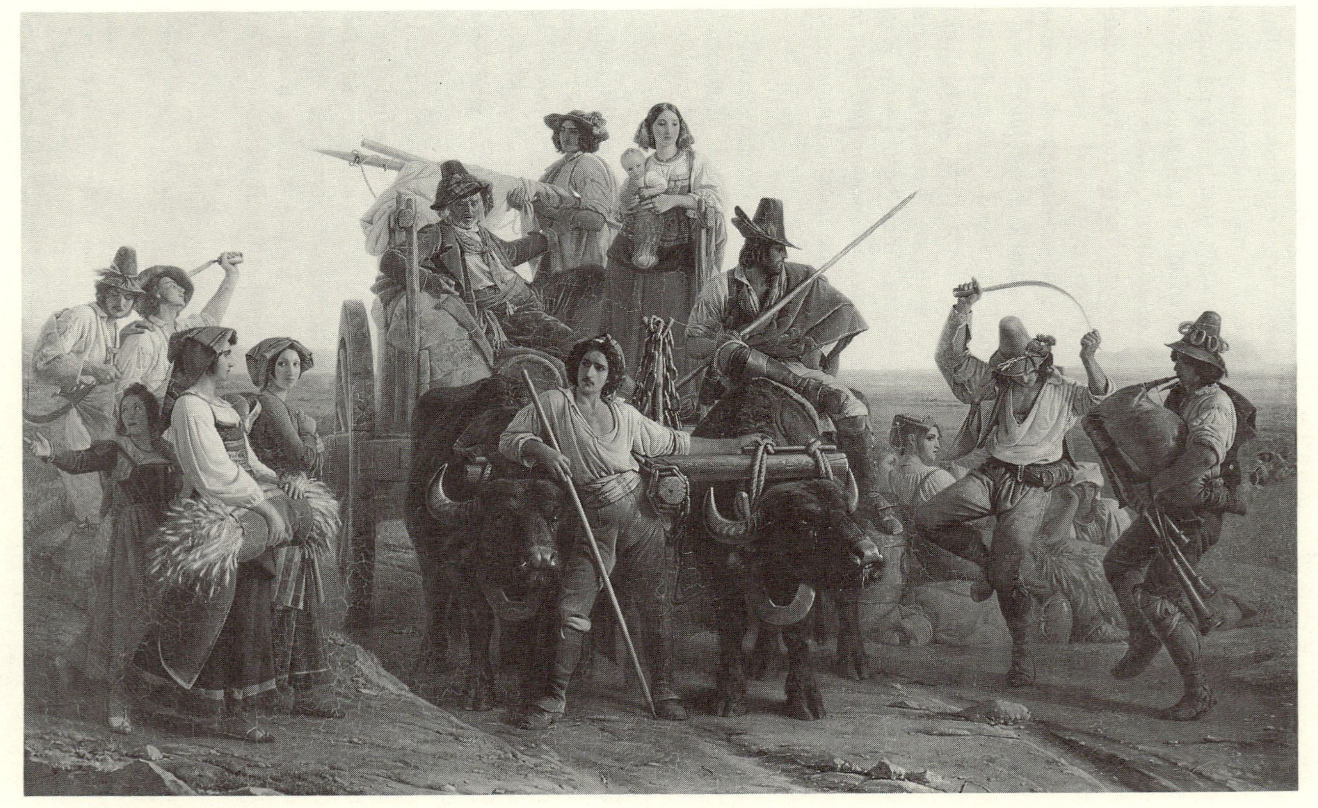

Plate 19. Léopold Robert: *Arrivée des moissonneurs dans les marais pontins,* Salon of 1831. Musée du Louvre, Paris.

superior insight is found in certain doctrinal texts. In asserting that "[sympathy] is capable of a range and power that surpasses the strength of the majority and which only a few are privileged to experience,"[164] Buchez himself included the artist among this minority. An anonymous reviewer in *L'Européen* further describes artists as being able to unveil "the mysteries of this social order which to the incredulous seems . . . impelled by chance," and possessing a "profound insight into the decrees of Providence, allowing them to interpret all phenomena from the viewpoint of the progressive advance of humanity."[165] Attribution of a sacerdotal function to the artist is uncommon in Buchezian discourse, and is held with any consistency only by Hippolyte Auger. This emerges as the one major point of difference between Auger's aesthetic stance and that of his former colleagues after his estrangement from Buchez in the mid 1830s.[166] While the principles guiding such texts as *Moralités* and the *Physiologie du théâtre* are fundamentally Buchezian, on this point he remains closer to a Saint-Simonian position, attributing to the great artist, for example, an equilibrium between sentiment, reason, and action that matches the Saint-Simonian conception of the priest—"The artist par excellence," he remarks in 1839, "is he who feels everything, knows everything, and is capable of everything."[167]

Théophile Bra, too, surpasses Buchezian orthodoxy in his conception of the artist's inherent social power. Foreseeing a pivotal role for art in engineering a future alliance between science's analytical tradition and the synthetic spirit of Christianity in a regenerative "mutual infusion of enlightenment,"[168] Bra imagines the artist elevated to an eminent social position from which he would create works of encyclopedic insight:

> How can we express the delights of the artist of the future?—Can threefold passion and absolute beauty be described? To see and feel everything with enthusiasm, to taste everything wholeheartedly but calmly . . .
>
> . . .The love of goodness always guides him, inspiring his images of greatest beauty, which are soon offered to the nations, whose recognition of their source gladdens the artist.

164 "[La sympathie] est susceptible à un degré d'étendue et de puissance qui est au-dessus des forces du plus grand nombre, et qui est le privilège de quelques-uns." Buchez, *Science de l'histoire*, 1:369.

165 "Les mystères de cet ordre social qui semble aux incrédules . . . marcher au hasard"; "pénétration profonde des décrets de la Providence, qui leur permet d'interpréter tous les phénomènes du point de vue de la marche progressive de l'humanité." Anonymous review of Janin's *Barnave*, *L'Européen* (10 December 1831), cited in Hunt, *Le Socialisme et le romantisme*, 85.

166 See, for example, Auger, *Moralités*, 1:135.

167 "L'artiste par excellence est celui qui sent tout, qui sait tout, qui peut tout." Auger, *Physiologie du théâtre*, 1:13.

168 "Pénétration mutuelle des lumières." Bra, "Du renouvellement" (1 August 1847), 45.

The true artist was always God's elect, and will be for all time.[169]

The more muted tone found in mainstream Buchezian writings derives from the group's philosophical position toward history and religion. The ideological dynamic around a *but commun d'activité* associated with a priori, synthetic phases of history is related to the pervasive influence of religion across all aspects of life. A society's goal is found within its system of belief, the validity of the theses it proposes corroborated by the concordance of reason and sentiment. Within such a structure, art is allotted a substantial though subsidiary role, shared with other regulative institutions and forms of social practice. For Buchez, there is no ambivalence about the relative importance of the artist and the priest. While the artist assumes a significant task in reinforcing the moral and spiritual imperatives of faith, the structuring of Buchezian philosophy denies his autonomous operation as a source of social or ethical values. Moreover, the physiological emphasis on the interplay between reason and sentiment represents a modification of Saint-Simonian ontological conceptions that attenuates the primacy of art as a stimulus to emotional response. The sympathetic mechanisms theorized by Buchez and Cerise require grounding in an a priori system of belief if their activation through the intervention of reason is to occur. Such a conception suggests the need for an appeal to a preexistent ideological structure upon which the perceiving subject can frame a reasoned response to an emotional stimulant; under such circumstances the malleability of the subject, inherent in Saint-Simonian theories of response, is limited by the prevailing system of belief. Art thus takes on a role of reinforcement and of "conservation," its dynamic function as a call to change depending on its presentation of unfulfilled moral imperatives.

This framework governs the insistence on morality and religion in Buchezian aesthetics. Though the less exalted conception of the artist suggests a more limited assessment of the social role of art than is found in Saint-Simonianism, the group nevertheless accords it an important place within the sacred and secular realm. Their identification of art's educative power underlines its status within a constellation of institutions designed to perpetuate an ideology in conformity with the progressive values of faith. As such, its social role becomes paramount and its responsibility in indicating and accelerating man's providential destiny a matter of crucial concern.

169 "Comment exprimer les délices de l'artiste de l'avenir? La passion triplée attachée au beau absolu peut-elle se décrire? Tout voir et tout sentir avec chaleur, tout goûter à plein coeur sans emportement . . .

". . . Toujours l'amour du bien le stimule et lui suggère ses plus belles images, celles-ci bientôt passent aux nations qui en reconnaissent la source, et l'artiste est heureux.

"L'artiste véritable fut toujours l'appelé de Dieu et il le sera dans tous les temps. " Bra, *Introduction*, 97.

CHAPTER 6

Pierre Leroux and the Aesthetics of *Humanité*

ALTHOUGH his adherence to Saint-Simonianism was short-lived, Pierre Leroux's contact with the group represents an important element in a political and philosophical career spanning half a century. A self-taught print worker, Leroux achieved early prominence, establishing the daily paper *Le Globe* in 1824, when he was only twenty-seven, and attracting such figures as Sainte-Beuve, Rémusat, and Lerminier. In relinquishing editorship to the Saint-Simonian Michel Chevalier in November 1830, he not only provided the sect with an invaluable platform, but also demonstrated his disillusionment with the liberal tradition that had triumphed following the July Revolution. His early involvement with the Eclectics Victor Cousin and Théodore Jouffroy, for whom *Le Globe* provided a mouthpiece under the Restoration, had collapsed in the late 1820s as both men showed an increasingly accommodating attitude toward the Bourbon regime. Bourgeois liberalism, too, quickly lost its appeal, as Leroux's initial exaltation after "les Trois Glorieuses" was replaced by realization that Louis-Philippe had no intention of conceding serious social or political reform.[1] It was under such circumstances that the rapprochement with Saint-Simonianism occurred. Throughout his year's involvement with the group, Leroux retained his distinctive democratic republican leanings: it was indeed distaste at the authoritarian implications of Enfantin's doctrine that provoked his departure at the time of the *Père*'s disputes with Bazard.[2]

In the years following his secession, Leroux retained links with a number of former disciples—most notably with Jean Reynaud, with whom he collaborated on the *Revue encyclopédique* and the *Encyclopédie nouvelle*. In common with the Buchezians, Leroux and his colleagues on the *Revue encyclopédique*—taken over by Charton, Fortoul, Carnot, and other dissidents in 1831—claimed Saint-Simon's inheritance and accused Enfantin's circle of doctrinal *lèse-majesté*.[3] During the 1830s, however, Leroux's filia-

[1] On this period, see J.-J. Goblot, *Aux origines du socialisme français: Pierre Leroux et ses premiers écrits (1824–1830)* (1977), 20–23, 59–62.

[2] According to fellow Saint-Simonian Charles Lambert, "Leroux, tout en admettant le dogme en général, avait conservé son caractère républicain. Les formes trouvées pour l'hiérarchie le révoltaient, et le Père et Bazard en sentaient bien le défaut." Arsenal Ms. 7817.

[3] See J.-P. Lacassagne, "Pierre Leroux, Saint-Simon et les Saint-Simoniens," *Economies et sociétés* 7, no. 1 (January 1973): 64–68.

tion with Saint-Simon declined as he developed a distinctive philosophical stance, supplemented with a practical desire to unite oppositional forces around the republican Société des droits de l'homme.[4] With his brother Jules, Leroux established a system of thought which modified Saint-Simonian theories of human psychology, religion, and historical periodicity within a political doctrine designed to reconcile individual liberty with social organization. His work excited considerable interest among artists and intellectuals: both Gustave Courbet and the sculptor David d'Angers appear to have responded to Leroux's ideas,[5] while he and the critic Théophile Thoré enjoyed a long-standing association. Most fruitful of all, however, was the relationship with George Sand, whose novels of the late 1830s and 1840s gave dramatic expression to Leroux's philosophy, and with whom he collaborated on the *Revue indépendante* between 1841 and 1843 and the *Revue sociale* between 1845 and 1850.[6] Though the abstract quality of his thought precluded any broad popular following, and exile condemned him to obscurity under the Second Empire, his impact on French socialism under the July Monarchy should not be underestimated.

Aesthetic investigation figures prominently in Leroux's work. Maintaining that "artistic questions implicitly contain the highest religious and social questions,"[7] Leroux's activities as a critic and aesthetician are integral to his philosophical enterprise. In contrast to other socialist commentators, his perspective on artistic questions is analytical rather than exhortatory. While his democratic convictions prevent assimilation of the arts into a controlling hierarchy and his understanding of the creative act breeds hostility toward overt didacticism, Leroux elaborated a psychological theory as a response to Eclectic rationalism, which identifies the artist with epistemological qualities of greater penetration than discursive forms of thought. Although the implications of this position, with its equation between sentiment and art, superficially resemble Saint-Simonian and Buchezian theory, Leroux's conclusions constitute an implicit critique of these groups' attitudes toward human psychology and social organization. In examining his assessment of the artist's role and his discussion of symbolism within the broader corpus of his thought, the present investigation will highlight the philosopher's

[4] See H. Mougin, *Pierre Leroux* (1938), 37.

[5] See N. McWilliam, " 'Un Enterrement à Paris': Courbet's Political Contacts in 1845," *Burlington Magazine* 125 (1983): 155–57; David d'Angers to Robert David, letter dated 18 July 1852, reprinted in H. Jouin, *David d'Angers et ses relations littéraires* (1890), 303.

[6] On the relationship with Sand, see D. O. Evans, *Le Socialisme romantique: Pierre Leroux et ses contemporains* (1948), 105–31, and J.-P. Lacassagne, ed., *Histoire d'une amitié: Pierre Leroux et George Sand d'après une correspondance inédite* (1973). Editorship of the *Revue indépendante* was assumed by Louis Blanc between 1843 and 1848.

[7] "Les questions de l'art contiennent implicitement les plus hautes questions religieuses et sociales." Introduction to the *Discours sur la situation actuelle de la société et de l'esprit humain*, 1841, quoted by Goblot, *Aux origines*, 90.

importance in extending the conceptual range of *art social* and outline his influence on the critical output of Théophile Thoré during the 1840s.

PSYCHOLOGICAL THEORY AND THE STATUS OF THE ARTIST

Leroux's conception of the individual—and by extension of the psychological origins of artistic utterance—operates as a structural analogy to his notion of humanity. In a very real sense, for Leroux, man is a microcosm of the totality he inhabits, an intermixture of elements mirrored on a larger scale in the realm of social relations. An emphasis on synthesis, not as a desirable goal dependent on attaining suitable forms of social and religious organization but as a quality inherent in nature to be refined and actualized by sacred and secular regeneration, provides a structuring motif in Leroux's exploration of man and his place in the world. The central notion of *humanité* stresses interdependence not simply on a functional level but as a metaphysical belief. For Leroux, men are not isolated individuals sharing a common culture, but exist as constitutive elements of an organic whole—humanity itself. Humanity is thus conceived as a virtual state of harmony whose fulfilment in lived experience can be achieved through appropriate social organization:

> Humanity is a species.
>
> The species Humanity is an ideal being made up of a myriad of real beings, who themselves are the seed of Humanity, Humanity in its virtual state.
>
> Each human being is a real being in whom there lives, in a virtual state, the ideal being named Humanity.
>
> Each human being is Humanity.[8]

At the heart of such a belief lies a perception of God as an omnipresent animating impulse, drawing Humanity toward solidarity. Present "in every creature, without being any of these creatures, nor the sum of all these creatures,"[9] Leroux's God inhabits man and nature without being elided into nature as a vague pantheistic force. In presenting God as a synthesis of spirit and matter, Leroux echoes elements in Saint-Simonianism, and indeed his overall methodological emphasis on synthesis relates to ideas artic-

[8] "L'Humanité est une espèce. / L'espèce Humanité est un être idéal composé d'une multitude d'êtres réels, qui sont eux-mêmes l'Humanité en germe, l'Humanité à l'état virtuel. / Chaque être humain est un être réel, dans lequel vit, à l'état virtuel, l'être idéal appelé Humanité. / Chaque être humain est l'Humanité." P. Leroux, *De l'humanité, de son principe et de son avenir*, (1840), 1:204.

[9] "Dans toutes les créatures, sans être ni aucune de ces créatures, ni toutes ces créatures ensemble." Ibid., 164.

ulated by Enfantin. Though he repudiates the latter's theocratic tendencies, the priority accorded to organicism implies a similar commitment to religion as a bedrock to social organization.

While rejecting Saint-Simonian historical periodicity in favor of a belief in continuing progress, Leroux was acutely aware of the crisis of faith affecting contemporary society. His solution to this depended upon the emergence of a new religious and epistemological synthesis allowing humanity to achieve organic human relations and develop appropriate social institutions. Yet rather than following Saint-Simonian commentators in interpreting the contemporary scene as evidence of a civilization that had run its course, Leroux maintained that current disarray concealed encouraging signs of lasting social change:

> We believe in the need for a new general synthesis of human knowledge; we believe that, without being clearly aware of it, this is the task society is currently accomplishing through politics, science, and art, that this is the hidden cause for all our age's pain, and that it will be the remedy to all this pain; at the same time, we do not believe in the restoration of the former synthesis which was Christianity, and today is in ruins.[10]

Central to his political doctrine, notions of synthesis and interdependence also dominate Leroux's psychological theories, determining an attitude toward the artist which diverges significantly from the Saint-Simonians and Buchez. In the same way as Leroux's social philosophy ruptures Saint-Simonian emphasis on hierarchy and authority, striving instead for a form of organization that manages to "reconcile AUTHORITY with LIBERTY,"[11] so his psychological theory carries with it a modified attitude toward the division of labor, which implicitly involves a more restricted notion of the artist's power. As elaborated during the 1830s, Leroux's psychology signifies a rejection both of Jouffroy's Eclectic rationalism and of the implications drawn from Bichat's psychological typology by the Saint-Simonians. This genealogy thus simultaneously follows the Saint-Simonians in promoting sentiment as an important facet of human makeup while conceiving its operation within the social sphere in a markedly different way.

The route taken to reach this position differed from that followed by

10 "Nous croyons à la nécessité d'une nouvelle synthèse générale de la connaissance humaine; nous croyons que c'est le travail que la société accomplit aujourd'hui par la politique, par la science et par l'art, sans en avoir encore clairement conscience, que c'est là le but caché de toutes les douleurs de notre époque, et que ce sera le remède à toutes ces douleurs; et en même temps nous ne croyons pas à la restauration de l'ancienne synthèse, aujourd'hui ruinée, qui fut le christianisme." P. Leroux, "De la philosophie et du christianisme," *R.E.* 55 (August 1832): 283.

11 "Concilier l'AUTORITE à la LIBERTE." P. Leroux, *D'une religion nationale* (1846), viii.

other contemporaries in its reliance on the work of Leibnitz. In Leroux's estimation, previous philosophical analyses of human psychology had spawned flawed and incomplete conceptions of the state; Plato's emphasis on reason, the sensualism of Hobbes and Machiavelli, Rousseau's elevation of sentiment—all were seen as harboring the potential for despotism. Leibnitz's virtue, in Leroux's eyes, was his insistence on human psychological unity, which countered disproportionate regard for any single faculty.[12]

This synthetic perception provided a fundamental structuring motif in Leroux's work, repeatedly invoked by the formula "In his nature and essence, man is *sensation–sentiment–knowledge* indivisibly united."[13] Furthermore, its implications are developed across a broad field, through analogies around such topics as family relations and the structure of the state. Crucially, Leroux's definition of God as simultaneously "Force–Amour–Intelligence"[14] underlines the identity between the deity and his creations, establishing synthesis as a basic natural law. A symmetrical series of correspondences is thus established, seamlessly connecting the individual with the totality of nature and of God in a progression that relates the interdependence of human faculties to an inherent interdependence on the social level. Leroux adduces neurological evidence to confirm psychological unity, and projects this in turn onto a collective plane through the assertion of a communality of faculties within *humanité* itself: "neither your intelligence, your senses, nor your feelings belong exclusively to you, since you draw them from humanity."[15]

Like the Saint-Simonians, Leroux regarded sentiment as an essential element for achieving the religious and intellectual synthesis that would overcome the anarchic skepticism of the modern world. He condemned the Eclectics' attempts in this direction as handicapped by a narrow rationalism in which a deductive methodology perpetuated an artificial distinction between philosophy and religion. Only by recognizing the value of sentimental modes of perception, embodied in religion, could true synthesis be achieved through the marriage of inductive and deductive thought processes.[16] Similarly, in social relations, Leroux related sentiment to the impulse toward synthesis. Identifying reason with the subjective conscious-

[12] See Leroux, *De l'humanité* 1:126.

[13] "L'homme est, de sa nature et par essence, *sensation–sentiment–connaissance* indivisiblement unis." Ibid., p. 157. Parallels can be seen here with Enfantin's trinitarian structures; see, for example, the "Premier Enseignement," 28 November 1831, in *O.S.S.E.*, 14:5–35. For a discussion of Leroux's notion of sentiment, see A. Le Bras-Chopard, *De l'égalité dans la différence. Le Socialisme de Pierre Leroux* (1986), 29–35.

[14] P. Leroux, *Doctrine de l'humanité. Aphorismes*, ed. L. Desages and A. Desmoulins (1848), 8.

[15] "Ni votre intelligence, ni vos sens, ni vos sentiments ne sont exclusivement à vous, car vous les tenez de l'humanité." P. Leroux, *De l'humanité*, 1:205.

[16] See P. F. Thomas, *Pierre Leroux, sa vie, son oeuvre, sa doctrine* (1904), 180–81.

ness of the *moi* (or self) and sensation with the *non-moi*'s objective consciousness of external reality, Leroux regarded sentiment as the essential bridge enabling the individuals to enter into fraternal relations with their fellows.[17] Thus, his pupil Grégoire Champseix points to the centrality of sentiment in facilitating reciprocity and providing the basis for an ethical code:

> By introducing him into a world of harmony, [sentiment] points man toward a harmoniously regulated life, enabling him so to imagine his relations with all beings, and particularly his fellows, and raising him up, by the beauty revealed to him, to love the good, the beautiful, and the true in all its majesty. Its generic name is *morality*.[18]

Leroux's insistence on psychological unity forestalls categorical identification of specific faculties with particular modes of activity, however. In this respect, his indebtedness to German metaphysics leads to a behavioral model significantly different from that of either Buchez or the Saint-Simonians, with their common grounding in physiological theory. Thus, for example, Leroux regards acts of moral judgment as drawing simultaneously on reason and sentiment and demurs from applying any strict demarcation between the instinctual impulse of passion and the controlling force of willpower, arguing that "man is unified in all of his acts."[19]

This holistic understanding of psychology had a determining influence on Leroux's social model, producing a conception of functional distinctions markedly different from the Saint-Simonians'. On one level, he apparently adopts Saint-Simonian typology, distinguishing three separate characterial and professional groupings within society. Arguing that "man is predominantly manifested as activity, sentiment, or knowledge. He is an *Industriel*, an Artist, or a Thinker,"[20] he seemingly replicates a model inherited from Saint-Simon. Yet such categorical divisions were incompatible with his psychological theory, which conceived the individual as an intermixture of tendencies. He thus explicitly challenges the Saint-Simonians for regarding each social group as being marked by "a difference in their essence or nature."[21] Instead, Leroux proposes a more attenuated inter-

[17] See P. Leroux, *De l'égalité* (1846), 2–4.

[18] "[Le sentiment] indique à l'homme, en l'introduisant dans le monde de l'harmonie, une vie réglée sur cette harmonie, lui fait concevoir ses rapports avec tous les êtres et surtout avec ses semblables, et l'élève, par la beauté qu'il lui découvre, à l'amour du bien, du beau et du vrai dans toute sa grandeur. Son nom générique est *moralité*." G. Champseix, "Exposé sommaire de la doctrine de l'humanité," *Revue sociale* 2 (December 1846): 34.

[19] "L'homme est un dans tous ses actes." P. Leroux, "Activité," *Encyclopédie nouvelle* (1834)1: 78.

[20] "L'homme se manifeste, d'une façon prédominante, ou comme activité, ou comme sentiment, ou comme connaissance. Il est ou Industriel, ou Artiste, ou Savant." P. Leroux, *Projet de constitution démocratique et sociale* (1848), 21.

[21] "Une différence essentielle ou de nature." Leroux, *De l'égalité*, 42.

pretation of social distinctions, which accommodates his insistence on psychological unity within a conceptual framework emphasizing equality and interdependence:

> For all that they are what they are—in other words certain potentialities that are widely varied though whose essence is hidden—thinkers, artists, and *industriels* are no less equal as men. Though within each of them one of the three aspects of our nature dominates, they all nonetheless combine all three aspects, and are thus equal. They transcend this general state of uniformity when fulfilling the special function for which they have been destined and shaped by God: it is then that their special nature emerges. It is in acts that are at once stamped with the triple seal of sentiment, sensation, and intellection, but which arise from a particular innate characteristic that they are revealed as they are, particular and distinct. But, since they themselves, and those with whom they are in contact, distinguish only sensation–sentiment–intellection, they remain our equals, whose natures are similar to our own—human beings, in a word.[22]

This position has far-reaching implications in identifying Leroux with democratic socialism. Crucially, such remarks challenge Saint-Simonian notions of hierarchy, denying as they do any direct equation between psychological propensity and functional ranking. This refutation of inequality carries with it the rejection of an elite charged with directing society. In avoiding the authoritarian implications of Saint-Simonianism, Leroux therefore casts aside any notion of a sacerdotal class enjoying superior insight, and necessarily also denies the artist any ancillary role within a guiding elite. While his awareness of the value of sentiment allows art and its representatives an important place in society, he thus proposes a social model in which acknowledgment of the collective contribution of diverse talents and of the individual's balance of psychological propensities outweighs any inclination to grant privileged authority to particular groups.

This perspective is reinforced by Leroux's insistence that all activities mirror man's psychological unity by simultaneously calling on *sensation*, *sentiment*, and *connaissance*. Such a conviction leads him to elaborate a system of cooperative labor, the *Triade*, which envisages the collaboration on a single task of individuals representing each psychological type. This

[22] "Pour être ce qu'ils sont, c'est-à-dire certaines virtualités bien diverses, mais cachées dans leur essence, les savants, les artistes ou les industriels, ne sont pas moins tous égaux, en tant qu'hommes. Parce qu'il y a prédominance chez eux de l'un de ces trois aspects de notre nature, ils n'en réunissent pas moins ces trois aspects, et voilà pourquoi ils sont égaux. Ils sortent de cet état général d'uniformité quand la fonction spéciale à laquelle Dieu les a destinés et rendus propres commence: alors leur particularité se révèle. Des actes empreintes à la fois du triple cachet de la sensation, du sentiment, et de la connaissance, mais qui ont leur source dans une innéité particulière, les révèlent ce qu'ils sont, les particularisent et les distinguent. Mais, ne saisissant eux-mêmes en eux et ne communiquant aux autres hommes que sensation–sentiment–connaissance, ils restent par là même nos égaux, des natures pareilles aux nôtres, des personnes humaines en un mot." Ibid.

pooling of talents is seen as fulfilling "the true moral law," since "it corrects everybody's tendencies to develop one faculty excessively, and brings them back to the unity of their being, their true personality."[23] The concept of the *Triade* receives broad application in Leroux's work: not only does he propose a constitution incorporating elected representatives of art, science, and industry in equal proportions,[24] he further suggests the system's application in scientific research and artistic creation.[25]

All of this places the artist in a significantly different position from that envisaged by Leroux's contemporaries. The concept of the *Triade* embodies a belief in psychological unity that implicitly attenuates the notion of artistic particularity. Though still recognized as a predominantly "sentimental" being, the artist no longer monopolizes sentiment in as categorical a way as the Saint-Simonians had suggested. In his most pronounced refutation of artistic messianism toward the end of his career, Leroux emphasizes that the poet simply concentrates propensities shared by all, and should not be elevated as possessing transcendent powers: "So you wish the Poet to enjoy a special privilege among mortals. But what a strange pretension! since the Poet is a man and, at bottom, every man is to some degree a poet."[26]

If such a statement appears little more than the logical outcome of Leroux's psychological theories, it must be set against a persistent current suggesting a far more sympathetic assessment of the artist and his place within society. This countervailing tendency produces a tension in Leroux's work, as he attempts to reconcile his inclination toward artistic progressivism with the broader implications of his theoretical position.

Interest in art's progressive potential predates Leroux's involvement with the Saint-Simonians and indeed anticipates the prophetic status allotted to the artist by such commentators as Barrault. As early as 1827, as Jouffroy's political maneuverings placed their relationship under increasing strain, Leroux began to question the primacy of rationalism and to explore the apparently more audacious possibilities of inductive thought. Defining the "artist" with a breadth common to his generation, Leroux investigated the mechanisms whereby imaginative thinkers such as More, Fénelon, and the Abbé de Saint-Pierre could outflank "commonsense" reason and envisage daringly new possibilities of human organization. He identifies this

[23] "La véritable loi morale"; "elle corrige les tendances de chacun vers le développement excessif d'une de ses facultés, elle ramène chacun vers l'unité de son être, vers sa véritable personnalité." P. Leroux, *Réfutation de l'éclecticisme* (1839), 45.

[24] See Leroux, *Projet de constitution*, 37–39.

[25] See P. Leroux, "Suite de la lettre au docteur Deville," *L'Espérance* (January 1859): 188–89. See M. Abensour, "Pierre Leroux et l'utopie socialiste," *Economies et sociétés* 6, no. 12 (December 1972): 2201–47.

[26] "Tu veux donc que le Poète ait, parmi les mortels, un privilège particulier. Une telle prétention est tout de même singulière! car le Poète est un homme et, au fond, tout homme est un poète dans un certain mesure." P. Leroux, *La Grève de Samarez* (1863), ed. J. P. Lacassagne (1972), 2:552.

breadth of thought with the artistic mentality, whose prophetic vision penetrates existing conditions and grants a privileged freedom denied the more inhibited rationalist: "Excessively daring ideas are the province of adventurous, imaginative, or infinitely inventive minds, who succeed in imposing them only if they are artists."[27]

Such notions infiltrate much of Leroux's aesthetic writing during the 1830s and 1840s. In particular, he displays an abiding preoccupation with the lyrical pessimism of Byron and Goethe, which he relates to despair at the modern world's moral confusion. While stringent in condemning figures such as Hugo and Lamartine, whose preoccupation with the past he interprets as a refusal to grapple with the present, Leroux sees in romantic spleen the artist's frustration with the present and his aspiration for a solution to the contemporary crisis.[28] This sympathy for lyrical introspection contrasts sharply with many Saint-Simonian commentators, who invariably dismiss such self-indulgence and advise a good dose of utopian theory as a suitable corrective. Leroux, however, is much more positive, glimpsing a prophetic message beneath this "great veil of melancholy."[29] The expression of discontent takes on a more vital, exhortatory gloss; the poet's despair points to its own solution, and so inspires broader aspiration for change. Thus Leroux regards artists as "heralds of the new religion,"[30] whose elegies for a dying civilization unconsciously carry within them the germ of social rebirth. "The funeral chorus of the old social order," artists simultaneously become "rousing fanfares who call to a new life, and anticipate the promised destiny of humanity, without themselves seeing the dawn."[31]

The artist's projective capacity forms a recurrent theme in Leroux's writings during the 1830s: art, "which has always been prophetic, even in its grief,"[32] reveals "what seed of progress humanity harbors in its bosom,"[33]

[27] "Les principes trop avancés tombent dans le domaine des esprits aventureux, romanesques, ou infiniment inventeurs; et ceux-ci ne réussissent à les faire valoir qu'à la condition d'être artistes." P. Leroux, "De l'union européenne," *Le Globe* 6, no. 1 (24 November 1827).

[28] "Le poète est le représentant du sentiment dans l'humanité. Tandis que l'homme de la sensation et de l'activité se satisfait de ce monde misérablement ébauché qu'il a devant les yeux, et que l'homme de l'intelligence cherche à le perfectionner, le poète s'indigne de ces lenteurs, et finit par n'avoir plus que des paroles d'ironie et des chants du désespoir." P. Leroux, "Considérations sur Werther, et en général sur la poésie de notre époque," preface to second edition of Leroux's translation of *Werther* (1839), xxii.

[29] "Grand voile de mélancolie." Ibid., xxxiii.

[30] "Annonciateurs de la religion nouvelle." P. Leroux, "Religion. Aux philosophes," *R.E.* 51 (September 1831): 516.

[31] "Chantres de mort de l'ancien ordre social"; "fanfares éclatantes, qui appele[nt] la vie nouvelle, et prélude[nt], sans en voir [elles]-mêmes l'aurore, aux destinées promises de l'humanité." Ibid.

[32] "Qui a toujours été prophète, même dans sa douleur." [P. Leroux], "Tendance nouvelle des idées," *R.E.* 53 (January 1832): 6.

[33] "Quel germe de progrès l'humanité porte actuellement dans son sein." P. Leroux, "De la poésie de notre époque," *R.E.* 52 (November 1831): 413.

and in so doing is able to "excite men's feelings in favor of association."[34] This construct is facilitated by Leroux's abandonment of the Saint-Simonians' cyclical philosophy of history in favor of a doctrine of continuous perfectibility, a perspective that no longer equates artistic pessimism with the terminal decline of a historical epoch, but resituates it as part of an uneven but essentially unidirectional process of social regeneration. Rather than a remnant of the past, the artist thus becomes an augury of the future, inspired in his resentment of the present by his presentiments of human destiny. As a fragment of *humanité* he is immersed in his own society, so that "the slightest work of art reflects an entire civilization."[35] At the same time he stands on the brink of a world that still eludes his contemporaries, but which his enhanced sentiment enables him to see. As Leroux remarks in relation to Goethe, "as ever, the flight of sentiment anticipated what was possible in the world."[36]

In some respects, this exalted view sits uncomfortably with Leroux's psychological theory, which, in emphasizing the unified nature of the human subject significantly dilutes any sense of artistic exceptionality. Moreover, his appropriation of the "law of continuity" from Leibnitz's *Monadology* further implies that prophetic power is not exclusive to the artist, but is implicit in man's position within the overall historical process. As Leroux argues in the *Réfutation de l'éclecticisme*: "Not in vain did Leibnitz say: 'The present, born of the past, is pregnant with the future.' This formula is the very law of humanity and the world."[37] The artist thus stands for Leroux not as a uniquely privileged visionary, but rather as someone concentrating within himself propensities found in a more diffuse state among other members of society.

This conception of the artist and his relationship to progressive historical development underlies the almost total absence within Leroux's work of the sort of appeal for direct support mounted by other radical theorists. Rather than predicating change on a radical break with the present or on a revivification of ailing belief systems, Leroux sees it as a long-term process whose course is inevitable and whose form is instinctively discerned by all. This obviates the necessity for the artist to act as a catalyst for progress, spurring the masses' repudiation of present conditions in favor of a better future. By

[34] "Exciter les sentiments des hommes vers l'association." P. Leroux, "De la philosophie," 304.

[35] "Dans la moindre oeuvre d'art [il y a] le reflet de toute une civilisation." P. Leroux, *Réfutation de l'éclecticisme*, quoted in Thomas, *Pierre Leroux*, 204.

[36] "[L]'élan du sentiment a devancé, comme toujours, les possibilités du monde." Leroux, "Considérations sur Werther," quoted in Evans, *Le Socialisme romantique*, 164.

[37] "Leibniz n'a pas dit vainement: Le présent, engendré du passé, est gros de l'avenir. Cette formule est la loi de l'humanité même et du monde." Leroux, *Réfutation*, 17–18. Leroux further credited Leibnitz with overcoming the incompleteness of Cartesian rationalism and Locke's sensationalism through his emphasis on sentiment; *De l'humanité*, 1:126.

extension, Leroux's liberal egalitarianism has no place for the artist as an agent of ideological control acting in concert with the ruling elite, as the Saint-Simonians had proposed. These considerations fundamentally affect the way he approaches cultural commentary: rather than focusing his energies on winning over the artist as an active apostle, he is more concerned with diagnosing the state of contemporary art and using the evidence to clarify an understanding of broader changes. For Leroux, in art, as in society itself, "the present . . . is pregnant with the future."

Such an attitude promotes emotional authenticity as a criterion of judgment surpassing considerations of either beauty or utility. Centrally for Leroux, "art is life communicating with life";[38] its creator must therefore speak a language comprehensible and emotionally accessible to a contemporary audience. Explicit didacticism contravenes such desiderata, since it allegedly derives from a misconceived notion of art where content usurps the rightful place of emotion. For Leroux, rather than advancing a particular thesis, the artist's role involves the deployment of sentiment to establish a bridge between the *moi* and the *non-moi*. This concrete realization of human solidarity entails a transcription of internal emotion into a palpable language drawn from nature: "[Man] will draw images capable of transmitting to us those sensations, feelings, and even judgments which he wishes to express from the outside world, from the common store of impressions, from the ocean of life in which we all swim."[39]

This communicative act allows the artist to speak to the present and, more implicitly, to speak of the future. However, Leroux sees a danger in short-circuiting this process through a solipsistic regard for the creative act itself and fiercely condemns formalism as a dereliction of the artist's duty as a member of *humanité*. In cultivating form as a self-sufficient goal, Leroux regards the artist as dissociating his work from the world around him, and hence of forfeiting any claims to prophetic status.[40] Uneasiness at this tendency, exemplified for Leroux in the work of Victor Hugo, reaches a climax in the prose poem *La Grève de Samarez* of 1863, prompting a radical reassessment of the value of art. Here, self-consciousness is seen as having entirely overtaken the modern artist, sapping his sense of solidarity with his fellows and reducing him to narcissistic impotence:

> At first, Art is separated from the totality of human knowledge, and we have *Art for Art's sake*. But then we no longer have a guide, a beacon. What is Art?

[38] "L'art, c'est la vie qui s'adresse à la vie." Leroux, "De la poésie," 410. See also H. Fortoul, "De l'art actuel," *R.E.* 59 (July–August 1833): 108.

[39] "[L'homme] ira puiser dans le monde extérieur, à la source commune des impressions, dans l'océan de vie où tous nous sommes plongés, des images capables de donner par elles-mêmes les sensations, les sentiments, et jusqu'aux jugements qu'il veut exprimer." Leroux, "De la poésie," 407.

[40] Ibid., 413.

> Nobody knows. So we necessarily arrive at the conclusion that "Art is fantasy." . . . But we can't stop there; we must go still further. Since fantasy is the fantasy of somebody, so, in the end Art is *the Artist*.[41]

At the same time as accusing the arts of moral vacuity, Leroux asserts their redundancy as a viable expression of human ideas. Now it is the great imaginative thinker—Saint-Simon, Owen, Fourier—whom he sees as "the true seer of our age."[42] In a process strangely reminiscent of the rebellion against Jouffroy in 1827, when Leroux turned to More, Fénelon, and Saint-Pierre as exemplifying a way of seeing the world capable of breaking through the pusilanimity of rationalism, so now he turns to their spiritual heirs, the masters of contemporary utopianism next to whose far-sightedness and audacity the artist appears sterile and self-indulgent.

In expressing this disenchantment, inspired by distaste for art's abdication of social responsibility, Leroux pronounces its marginal status. Exhausted as a meaningful vehicle for man's hopes and aspirations, the arts are judged to have entered a fallow period from which they can only be saved through the realization of the great socialist thinkers' message:

> Today there is no longer a place for art. . . . I do not believe that artists are capable of leading Humanity any further; for the moment, their essential work is done and, for good or ill, they will not produce anything more until the onset of Socialism, which will need them to establish its cult.[43]

The wheel has come full circle. If Leroux's initial interest in sentiment had been sparked by frustration at the limitations of reason, so now the debasement of sentiment in the self-regarding realms of art provokes a similar reaction. At both points of crisis, separated by almost forty years, Leroux turns to a radically different form of reason, whose infusion of the mercurial, uninhibited values of sentiment generates a boldness of vision capable of stripping away rationalism's mundanities. More, Fénelon, Saint-Simon, and Fourier—all combine reason and sentiment in an epistemological and psychological synthesis that reaches beyond the limitations of art and science. "*Sensation–sentiment–connaissance* indivisiblement unis," they exemplify the potentiality of synthesis in a way art alone had revealed itself

[41] "On commence par séparer l'Art du faisceau de la Connaissance humaine, et on a *l'Art pour l'Art*. Mais alors plus de guide, plus de fanal. Qu'est-ce que l'Art? On n'en sait rien. On arrive donc nécessairement à cette conclusion: 'L'Art, c'est la fantaisie.' . . . Mais on ne peut pas s'arrêter là; il faut aller plus loin encore. Car la fantaisie, c'est la fantaisie de celui qui l'a. Donc, en définitive, l'Art c'est *l'Artiste*." Leroux, *La Grève*, 2:545.

[42] "Le vrai Vates de notre époque." Leroux, "Suite de la lettre au docteur Deville," 196.

[43] "L'art aujourd'hui n'a plus de lieu. . . . Suivant moi, les artistes ne sont pas capables de guider plus loin l'Humanité: leur oeuvre capitale pour le présent est achevée, et, bon gré mal gré, ils ne produiront plus rien jusqu'à l'avènement complet du Socialisme, qui aura besoin d'eux pour instaurer son culte." Ibid., 188–89.

incapable of achieving. In a sense, then, this final demotion of the artist, this questioning of his prophetic insight, resolves the tension that had surfaced in the 1830s by reasserting the priority of synthesis on an epistemological level and firmly reinstating its centrality as a psychological concept.

NATURE, ART, AND THE SYMBOL

Leroux's analysis of the mechanisms of artistic creation and reception, focusing on his theory of the symbol, is firmly embedded in his general aesthetic and political philosophy. Discussion of this aspect of his work has habitually concentrated on questions of sources and influence and thus failed to account for its place within his thought.[44] In attempting to restore unity, it becomes clear that Leroux's preoccupation with the symbol as the "fundamental principle of art"[45] closely relates to his conviction that art is "an expression of life at different periods as well as an aspiration toward a better world,"[46] and is integral to his overall philosophical enterprise.

Leroux's initial exploration of symbolism, contained in a discussion of Victor Hugo and contemporary poetry in 1830,[47] approaches metaphor within the framework of his heightened regard for inductive thought. Identifying its use as the outstanding characteristic of the romantic school, Leroux argues that metaphor is integral to all poetic utterance, in whatever medium.[48] This process he defines as the substitution of a concrete image for an abstract idea, a device that goes beyond simple comparison by displacing explicit reference to the underlying concept altogether. Metaphor thus depends on the poet's ability to make analogies, to "[discover] relationships of every sort through all the powers of his soul."[49] This essentially inductive embodiment of ideas in images is at once spiritual and rational,

[44] See, for example, B. Juden, *Traditions orphiques et tendances mystiques dans le romantisme français (1800–1855)* (1971), 317–22., 497–99.; M. Forcina, *I diritti dell'esistente. La filosofia della "Encyclopédie nouvelle" (1833–1847)* (1987), 111–31, and the commentary provided for the reprint of "Du style symbolique" in M. Bonfantini, "Pierre Leroux e le origini del simbolismo in Francia," in *Studi in onore di Italo Siciliano, Bibliotheca dell'Archivum Romanicum*, ser. 1, 86, no. 1 (1966): 85–96. Goblot, *Aux origines*, 62–64, provides a notable exception to this current.

[45] "Principe même de l'art." Leroux, "De la poésie," 404.

[46] "Une expression de la vie à diverses époques, en même temps qu'une aspiration vers un monde meilleur." Introduction to *Oeuvres* (1850), quoted by Evans, *Le Socialisme romantique*, 55.

[47] P. Leroux, "Du style symbolique," *Le Globe* 7, no. 28 (8 April 1829).

[48] Leroux uses the term *métaphore* generally to denote "la comparaison, l'emblème, le symbole, l'allégorie," though he indulges in a terminological lattitude that allows the interchangeable use of these terms.

[49] "[Saisir] des rapports de tout genre par toutes les puissances de son âme." Leroux, "Du style symbolique."

drawing upon the "soul" while recalling the analytical methodology of the geometer:

> What does the poet do—what indeed do all artists and men in general do—but continually exchange the purely conceptual for the concrete, or in other words seize on connections and exchange them with identical connections drawn from another register of ideas, exactly as the geometer substitutes at will numbers for planes, and planes for numbers?[50]

Not only does this allusion to mathematical techniques refute suggestions that the artist's ability carries mystical connotations, but reference to the universality of such relational skills further prevents his elevation as an exceptional being. Where the artist does differ from others is in the nature of the connections he draws, which are not concrete and deductive in the mathematical sense but imaginative and enigmatic in their conflation of reason and sentiment. Leroux highlights the "mystery" of metaphor, arguing that the symbol is "comprehensive and poetic, precisely because it is at once indefinite, vague, and obscure."[51] Metaphor is thus valued as a device that at once opens up and closes down possibilities, allowing the imagination to proliferate meaning in decoding the image, while at the same time protecting meaning from those incapable of deciphering the artist's figurative language. Provoking flights of the imagination free from the constraints of "commonsense" rationalism, metaphor simultaneously acts as a guardian shielding the wisdom it encapsulates from those unable to make such a leap.

This concept is developed in "De la poésie de notre époque," later partially republished as the *Encyclopédie nouvelle* definition of "art."[52] Here, Leroux distinguishes between industry and art, identifying the former with man's adaptation of nature for his physical needs, and the latter with his exploration of external reality to express inner life, a definition that implicitly accords a central place to metaphor. As an example of this association of ideas, Leroux describes how man drew upon natural forms in constructing temples to the creator, a process that has subsequently molded perception of these forms:

> The forest and mountain were monuments of nature; the temple, inspired by nature, is a monument of man. And thus a new harmony was established in the world: man can no longer see the forests' colonnades and the mountains' altars

[50] "Que fait le poète, en effet, que fait tout artiste, et que font en général tous les hommes, sinon substituer continuellement le sensible aux conceptions pures, ou en d'autres termes saisir des rapports et leur substituer des rapports identiques pris dans un autre ordre d'idées, de même que le géomètre substitue à volonté des nombres aux surfaces, des surfaces aux nombres?" Ibid.

[51] "Compréhensive, poétique, précisément parce qu'elle est indéfinie, mais en même temps vague et obscure." Ibid.

[52] See P. Leroux, "Art," *Encyclopédie nouvelle* (1836), 2:82–84.

> without recalling the temple to the Eternal. It is in such a way that the entire world, including *art* which forms part of it as do the natural monuments which it supplements, becomes a *symbol.*[53]

To see here, as previous commentators have done, endorsement of a Swedenborgian notion of *correspondances*—and an anticipation of Baudelaire—is fundamentally to misrepresent the train of argument. Rather than affirming any inherent symbolism in nature accessible to man through observation of the world around him, Leroux rather conceives the process operating in reverse. Man draws upon natural forms, in this instance to create buildings to worship God, and subsequently—through association of ideas—spontaneously recalls the temple when confronting those forms that served as its initial inspiration. Perceiving nature, he projects back cultural associations that infuse the landscape with symbolic connotations. The initial process governing the appropriation of these forms implies no inherent symmetry between their appearance and specific metaphysical associations. Leroux thus remains at some distance from Baudelaire's more spiritually charged perception of *correspondances*; claims for any direct filiation between the two not only misread Leroux's ideas, but also overlook the prevalence of such concepts during the July Monarchy.[54]

Just as Leroux's notion of the symbol derives from an associational theory of perception, rather than from any belief in a mystical vocabulary buried within nature itself, so his sense of synesthesia has firm perceptual foundations. Such ideas are rooted in his theory of psychology and should not be confused with a broader notion of phenomenological interpenetration where, for example, colors and sounds are thought to possess a specific and inherent equivalence. Thus he writes in 1831:

> Poetry is that mysterious wing that glides at will in the entire world of the soul, in that infinite sphere of which one part is colors, another sounds, another movements, another judgments etc., but which all vibrate in unison in accordance with the same laws, so that a vibration in one area is conveyed to another. It is art's privilege to feel and express these relationships, which are deeply

[53] "La forêt, la montagne étaient des monuments de la nature: le temple, inspiré par elle, est un monument de l'homme. Et alors s'établit dans le monde une nouvelle harmonie: l'homme ne peut plus voir les colonnades des forêts et les autels des montagnes, sans que l'idée d'un temple à l'Eternel lui revienne en mémoire. C'est ainsi que le monde tout entier, en y comprenant *l'art*, qui en fait partie au même titre que les monuments naturels auxquels il s'ajoute, devient *symbole*." Leroux, "De la poésie," 404.

[54] See C. Pichois, "Baudelaire en 1847. Petit Essai de sociologie littéraire," in *Baudelaire. Etudes et témoignages* (1967), 114–16. While emphasizing the breadth of such ideas, which are found in the work of Quinet, the Abbé Constant, Rochery, Esquiros, and others, Pichois does attempt to connect Baudelaire and Leroux. See also P. Bénichou, *Le Temps des prophètes. Doctrines de l'âge romantique* (1977), 339–40. A. Zielonka, *Alphonse Esquiros (1812–1876): A Study of His Works* (1985), 210–11, argues for Leroux's influence on the younger writer.

hidden in the very unity of life. For out of these vibrations in the different regions of the soul there results an *accord*, and this accord is life; and when this accord is expressed, that is art; so, the expression of this accord is the symbol, and the form of its expression is rhythm, which itself is part of the symbol: this is why art is the expression of life, and life itself.[55]

It is thus within man, whose unified psychological makeup is conceived of as a seamless and coherent spectrum of thoughts and feelings, that different forms of sensual experience set up resonances that produce a harmonious sense of experiential unity. Art is deemed capable both of provoking such sensations and of embodying them in a formal *accord* that gives external expression to internal harmony. It is here that all types of art converge, each in its particular way translating inner emotion into tangible forms and evolving a vocabulary that finds in the natural world phenomena capable of symbolizing particular psychological states and hence of evoking them in the perceiving subject.

Such an understanding of aesthetic experience underpins Leroux's distaste for formalism, which abandons concern for the affective potential of art. At the same time, his notions of the symbol and aesthetic response obviate the need for overt didacticism. As "the expression of life . . . life itself," art is of its essence social. Enhancing consciousness of personal harmony, it simultaneously confirms a sense of social *solidarité* by celebrating the harmony of nature and the universality of human emotion. In this way, art becomes "one strand in the cluster of human knowledge" operating in concert with other facets of experience. In maintaining that "the aim of politics, science, and art is to proclaim the related truths that infuse the human soul with harmony,"[56] Leroux at once insists on the social nature of art while asserting that all aspects of human action are interrelated because of the psychological unity of man and the inherent solidarity of social relations.

At the same time as emerging naturally from his more general preoccupations, Leroux's theory of the symbol structurally relates to his overall philo-

55 "La poésie est cette aile mystérieuse qui plane à volonté dans le monde entier de l'âme, dans cette sphère infinie dont une partie est couleurs, une autre sons, une autre mouvements, une autre jugements etc., mais qui toutes vibrent en même temps suivant certaines lois, en sorte qu'une vibration dans une région se communique à une autre région, et que le privilège de l'art est de sentir et d'exprimer ces rapports, profondément cachés dans l'unité même de la vie. Car de ces vibrations harmoniques des diverses régions de l'âme il résulte un *accord*, et cet accord, c'est la vie; et quand cet accord est exprimé, c'est l'art; or, cet accord exprimé, c'est le symbole; et la forme de son expression, c'est le rhythme, qui participe lui-même du symbole: voilà pourquoi l'art est l'expression de la vie, et la vie elle-même." Leroux, "De la poésie," 407–8.

56 "Un rayon du faisceau de la connaissance humaine"; "Le but de la politique, de la science et de l'art, c'est de proclamer des vérités liées qui mettent de l'harmonie dans l'âme humaine." Leroux, "De la philosophie," 284.

sophical method. Much of his work suggests a series of metaphors between man, nature, and God, with each level of creation embodying the same elements on differing scales. This equivalence is underpinned by God's pervasiveness in man and nature, which secures the harmony of creation. As a microcosm of divine qualities, man reflects the *force*, *amour*, and *intelligence* of God in his own combination of *sensation*, *sentiment*, and *connaissance*, and finds a similar equilibrium in nature. This harmony allows the artist to discern connections—"saisir des rapports"—and discover suitable metaphors in the world around him. Far from suggesting any pregiven concordance between particular feelings and specific associations in nature, this process is much more fluid, arising from man's generalized perception of his affinity with his environment. It is for this reason that Leroux describes metaphor as comprehensive and indefinite. Examined in this light, then, the theory of symbolism can be seen not as a peripheral interest, but as an organic part of the metaphysics underpinning Leroux's political philosophy.

PIERRE LEROUX AND THÉOPHILE THORÉ

Much of Leroux's aesthetic speculation remains on an abstract level, or is applied to literature rather than the visual arts. Though his colleagues on the *Revue encyclopédique* demonstrate similar preoccupations when writing on art, their attitude owes most to a common Saint-Simonian heritage. Only Reynaud, whose association with Leroux was to prove relatively long-standing, shows a deeper affinity with his ideas—though where parallels do occur they invariably become coarsened in translation.[57] It was not until the 1840s that the critic Théophile Thoré emerged as a practical exponent of Leroux's critical method, the philosopher's ideas providing him with much of the theoretical background for the reviews he produced during the last years of the July Monarchy. Though historians have noted the close personal and political relationship between the two men,[58] their aesthetic affiliation has received less attention. This specific aspect of Thoré's work will occupy us here.

The origins of Thoré's relationship with Leroux are obscure. As early as

[57] See J. Reynaud, "Coup d'oeil sur l'exposition de sculpture," *R.E.* 57 (March 1833): 576, 583, where Reynaud discusses the emblematic power of art. A more committed advocate of social didacticism, he argues that art should appeal primarily to the spectator's intelligence (571).

[58] On personal and theoretical affiliations between the two men, see P. Grate, *Deux Critiques d'art à l'époque romantique: Gustave Planche et Théophile Thoré* (1959), 140–41, Lacassagne, *Histoire d'une amitié*, 107–8; and F. S. Jowell, *Thoré-Bürger and the Art of the Past* (1977), 23–92.

1834 he claimed to have been offered the editorship of the *Revue encyclopédique*,[59] while his remark the following year that he was involved with "ideas spawned by Saint-Simonianism" may refer to Leroux's circle,[60] though at this stage Thoré's political convictions were still in a state of flux. While beginning to contribute regularly to republican journals, his commitment to a didactic aesthetic and his interpretation of history retain vestiges of youthful involvement with Saint-Simonianism as late as 1837,[61] while much in his *Dictionnaire de phrénologie* of 1836 suggests Fourierist leanings. By the end of the decade, however, the two men had established close contact. In 1838 Thoré secured Leroux's support for his abortive journal *La Démocratie*, whose prospectus is heavily indebted to the philosopher. Thoré in turn was closely involved with Leroux on the *Encyclopédie nouvelle*, the *Revue sociale*, and the *Revue indepéndante*, contributing articles on the arts as well as a "Chronique politique" under the pseudonym Jacques Dupré.[62] He could now declare that Leroux's work provided "the seed of the religious, political, and moral doctrine of the future"[63] and backed up his support under the Second Republic by promoting Leroux's ideas in his journal *La Vraie République*. Nor did the two men's association flounder with the destruction of their political hopes in 1849—in exile in London in 1852, both lent support to the *Union socialiste*, an organization designed to unite the opposition in an effective campaign against the imperial regime.

Thoré shared Leroux's belief in the need for a political system reconciling individual interest with social solidarity. Saint-Simonianism, Babouvism, and the "dictatorial pretensions" of Cabet's Icarianism all stood accused in Thoré's eyes of sacrificing personal liberty to collective cohesion,[64] a failing not perceived in Leroux's vision of "the Holy Family of Humanity, equal and united."[65] Concern with this balance between the individual and society forms a leitmotif not only in Thoré's political writings, but also in his aesthetic philosophy, surfacing most consistently in his discussion of nature. Exploration of this question in the Salon reviews of the late 1840s, generally interpreted as a recantation of his earlier commitment to social art, relates closely to many of Leroux's preoccupations; when examined from this per-

[59] T. Thoré to his mother, letter dated 17 April 1834, in *Thoré-Burger peint par lui-même*, ed. P. Cottin, (1900), 16.

[60] "Des idées enfantées par le saint-simonisme." Ibid., 21.

[61] See particularly "L'Art social et progressif," *L'Artiste* 1st ser., 7 (1834): 38–42, and "L'Art dans mille ans," *Le Don-Quichotte* 8 (19 February 1837).

[62] Cottin, *Thoré-Burger*, 74.

[63] "Le germe de la doctrine religieuse, politique et morale de l'avenir." T. Thoré, review of *De l'humanité* in *J. P.* (6 December 1840).

[64] "Prétention à la dictature." On Saint-Simonianism, see *Le Réformateur* (16 October 1834); on Babeuf, see "Babouvisme," *J. P.* (24 November 1839); on Cabet, see "Du communisme en France," *Revue indépendante* 1 (1841): 337–48.

[65] "La Sainte Famille de l'Humanité, égale et solidaire." T. Thoré, *Salon de 1844, précédé d'une lettre à Théodore Rousseau* (1844), 89.

spective they reveal the assimilation of a body of ideas that allowed the critic to develop a more flexible understanding of the social influence of art.

Significantly, it is in a work dedicated to Leroux, the novella *La Recherche de la liberté* of 1845, that Thoré sets out his ideas concerning man's relationship with nature most graphically. His theme emerges in the prefatory remarks to the philosopher: "Man needs man, even to understand nature and love God"[66]—human solidarity is a fundamental truth whose neglect leads to isolation from society and consequent disillusionment with nature. In demonstrating this thesis, Thoré tells the tale of Georges Derval, a young Parisian who abandons the city for the forest near Pierrefonds, hoping to escape the corruption of modern life and discover himself through the contemplation of nature. Settling with a simple peasant girl, Georges is at first blissfully happy, but gradually realizes his appalling error and resorts to suicide, leaving a note in which he confesses his mistake:

> Life is not repose but struggle. Happiness is not sterile contemplation but the fulfillment of duty. Liberty lies in the use of strength and our God-given faculties.
>
> This is what I have learned from a year's isolation, meditation, and pain! It is impossible to flee the world. Our destiny ties us invincibly to the destiny of our fellows.[67]

Thoré had provided theoretical justification for his hero's tragic revelation the previous year, in the letter to Théodore Rousseau prefacing his 1844 Salon review. In the gentle reproof leveled at the landscapist, it is possible to see Rousseau as the model for Derval, since he ostensibly shares the young Parisian's tendency to seek in nature a refuge from the world. For Thoré, who cites approvingly Leroux's aspiration for "l'homme complet dans la société complète,"[68] the polarity between nature and civilization implied by Rousseau's stance is a false one. This scission is attributed to the impoverished mentality fostered by industrialization, with its obsessive "exploitation of dead things";[69] disgust with such alienation has provoked Rousseau's self-imposed exile from society and led to a distorted investment in the natural world as a unique source of value. As a consequence, Thoré claims that the landscapist has imprisoned himself in an introspective

[66] "Il faut l'homme à l'homme, même pour comprendre la nature et pour aimer Dieu." T. Thoré, *La Recherche de la liberté* (1845), 2.

[67] "La vie n'est pas le repos, mais la lutte. Le bonheur n'est pas une contemplation stérile, mais l'accomplissement du devoir. La liberté, c'est l'exercise de la force et des facultés que nous tenons de Dieu.

"Voilà donc ce que j'ai appris dans une année de retraite, de méditation et de douleur! Il est impossible de se sauver hors du monde. Notre destinée nous attache invinciblement à la destinée de nos semblables." Ibid., 64.

[68] Thoré, *Salon de 1844*, xiv. The phrase is also used to define the egalitarian society to which "la jeune démocratie" aspires: see T. Thoré, *La Vérité sur le parti démocratique* (1840), 37.

[69] "Exploitation des choses mortes." Ibid.

"paradis cérébral" from which concern for society has been banished.[70] For Thoré, the exploration of nature is meaningful only if the artist regards his work as a "true dialogue with the outside world,"[71] and he follows Leroux in arguing that the artist should treat nature as a vehicle for communicating inner emotion. Drawing on Leroux's distinction between poets who cultivate nature as a self-sufficient source of formal inspiration and those able to "ally a feeling for nature with an equally strong feeling for the destiny of humanity,"[72] Thoré encourages Rousseau to realize its potential as a privileged means to "contribute directly in perfecting other creatures through a holy communion of our feelings and thoughts."[73] Such an appeal does not intend to constrain the artist's liberty; rather, Thoré postulates an equilibrium between subjective emotional authenticity and a sense of broader social responsibility, replicating in the aesthetic domain the reconciliation between the individual and the collectivity integral to his social philosophy. Understood as a lexicon of potential meaning, nature thus offers a foil for experiential exploration whose implications surpass introspective gratification.

This perspective allows Thoré to moderate his advocacy of explicit didacticism, while continuing to promote a humanitarian aesthetic. In adapting Leroux's apprehension of nature as a source of meaning whose resonance is ultimately social, Thoré sees in it a lesson of harmony vital for perfecting human relations. Important in this shift is Thore's development of an understanding of symbolism, which is again indebted to Leroux. In certain respects, he surpasses his mentor in discussions of synesthesia and allegory, suggesting both a more unambiguously pantheistic conception of nature and an inclination toward Fourierist readings of the material environment as part of an *analogie universelle*.

From the early 1840s, Thoré subscribes to Leroux's definition of the symbol as "the fusion of a moral idea with a physical image," and stresses its central importance for the history of art.[74] This emphasis allowed the incorporation of genres such as landscape into his social aesthetic, by proposing a metaphorical reading of nonnarrative themes. Through investing a wealth of immanent meaning in the material world, to be liberated by the artist's imagination, communion with nature could be accorded broader significance, though Thoré argues that access to this realm is confined to those

[70] Ibid., xxi.

[71] "Véritable entretien avec le monde extérieur." Ibid., x.

[72] "Joindre au sentiment de la nature un sentiment également vif des destinées de l'humanité." Leroux, "Considérations sur Werther," xlv.

[73] "Contribuer directement au perfectionnement des autres créatures par une sainte communion de nos sentiments et de nos pensées." Thoré, *Salon de 1844*, xxii.

[74] "La fusion de l'idée morale dans l'image physique." See, for example, Thoré's remarks in his entry "Sculpture" for the *Encyclopédie nouvelle* 8 (1841): 68, which clearly echo Leroux on nature and the origins of the temple in "De la poésie."

who recognize that interpretation of exterior reality is an imaginative, rather than a dryly mimetic, process.[75] Emphasis again falls on the intervention of the artist as a subjective agent, inspired by emotion rather than reason. Thus he describes poetry as "the manifest sign of a particular impression. Poetry is not nature, but the feeling that nature inspires in the artist. It is nature reflected by the human spirit"[76]—a definition that explains his indifference toward the painstaking naturalism of the landscapists Delaberge and Brascassat.[77] In their attention to surface appearance, such artists are seen as blind to the symbolic significance of the objects they so laboriously copy.

Thoré's opposition to realism and his emphasis on the harmony of nature relates to a conception of divine presence in creation, which again owes much to Leroux. His insistence that "God is everywhere and in all things, marvelous in every way"[78] facilitates a move away from a utilitarian aesthetic; by the mid 1840s Thoré could maintain that any form of representation contains potential ethical value, since the universe is a coherent body informed by overriding moral laws. Through imaginative insight, the artist is able to penetrate this truth and to express "life in anything and everything";[79] form, irrespective of content, carries implicit moral force, stirring within the spectator an understanding of God, of nature and, by extension, of man's preordained unity with his fellows and with the world he inhabits.

Thoré's speculations on synesthesia posit a fundamental identity of all art forms around a belief in the harmony of the phenomena they portray. Thus he suggests an equivalence between the chromatic spectrum and the musical scale,[80] and compares the mood evoked by Rousseau's canvases with the work of Beethoven. The emergence of these ideas in such texts of the mid 1830s as the *Dictionnaire de phrénologie* and the article "L'Art des parfums,"[81] apparently written under Fourierist influence, helps to explain

[75] As an example of this process, which Thoré emphasizes is not always a result of the artist's conscious intentions, see his remarks on Rousseau's *Allée de châtaigniers*, in the *Salon de 1845*, xvii.

[76] "Le signe manifeste d'une impression particulière. La poésie n'est pas la nature, mais le sentiment que la nature inspire à l'artiste. C'est la nature reflétée par l'esprit humain." Thoré, *Salon de 1844*, 3.

[77] See, for example, remarks on Brascassat in *Salon de 1845, précédé d'une lettre à Béranger* (1845), 88–89.

[78] "Dieu est en tout et partout, merveilleux à tous les degrés." T. Thoré, *Salon de 1847, précédé d'une lettre à Firmin Barrion* (1847), 65.

[79] "La vie dans n'importe quoi." T. Thoré, *Salon de 1846, précédé d'une lettre à George Sand* (1846), 118. This position allows Thoré to assert in *Salon de 1847*, 64, "le sujet est absolument indifférent dans les arts."

[80] T. Thoré, "Salon de 1842," *La Revue indépendante* 3 (1842): 528–29.

[81] See *L'Ariel* 13 (April 1836). See also the article "De l'analogie dans l'art," *Revue française et étrangère* 6 (May–June 1838), signed "T. T." and almost certainly by Thoré; the following remarks suggest strong Fourierist connections: "La fable, c'est à dire l'analogie, c'est à dire les tropes, la métaphore, l'allégorie, sont installés éternellement et partout dans la nature pour qui sait les déchiffrer. . . . La langue analogique est la véritable langue de l'art" (227).

Thoré's gravitation toward Leroux at the end of the decade. These works share with the Salon reviews of the 1840s an insistence on natural harmony, couched in terms of outright pantheism,[82] and extrapolate laws of social organization from this belief.[83] In transferring his allegiance to Leroux, Thoré discovered a theoretical bedrock compatible with his earlier position. As with the Fourierists, and in common with theorists such as Louis Blanc, Leroux stressed the harmonious identity of human interests, while aspects of his aesthetic, most notably relating to nature and the symbolic function of art, also display affinities with Phalansterian thinking. In abandoning his apparently short-lived interest in Fourierism, Thoré discovered in Leroux ideas more closely suited to his political perspective, which also enabled him to amplify the redefinition of social aesthetics begun under the aegis of Fourier's philosophy.

Integral to this was a revised understanding of artistic creation and response which could explain the moral influence of art in more nuanced terms than those offered by orthodox utilitarianism. Here Leroux's psychological theory allowed Thoré to develop an understanding of creativity which consolidated his belief in the ameliorative potential of exposure to nature. His discussion of the creative process exploits Leroux's notion of man's psychological unity to secure an understanding of art that overcomes the polarity between form and content. In 1842, for example, he draws upon Leroux for a definition of art where moral intention and practical execution become inseparable aspects of a single process:

> If one now asks what painting consists of other than color, we would reply that color is the means of execution but that there are two other essential terms in painting: composition, which corresponds to *intelligence*, as color, form, or technique correspond to *sensation*, and finally feeling. It is thus not enough to be a technician or a colorist; one must also have the poet's feelings, and the thinker's sense of composition.[84]

The image's intermixture of constitutive elements mirrors the psychological equilibrium of its individual creator, becoming a microcosm of man, who is himself a fragment of God. Through such a chain, art is deemed capable of

[82] "L'avenir est au panthéisme." T. Thoré, *Dictionnaire de phrénologie et de physionomie* . . . (1836), 325.

[83] See ibid., 133.

[84] "Si l'on demande maintenant ce qui constitue le peintre outre la couleur, nous répondrons que la couleur est le moyen d'exécution, mais qu'il y a, en peinture, deux autres termes essentiels: la composition, qui correspond à *l'intelligence*, comme la couleur, ou la forme, ou l'exécution, correspond à *la sensation*; et enfin le sentiment. Il ne suffit donc pas, assurément, d'être praticien ou coloriste; il faut encore être poète ou avoir du sentiment, être penseur ou avoir de la composition." Thoré, "Salon de 1842," 530. See also the description of the artist's prerequisites as "un oeil perspicace, une raison droite, un sentiment convaincu" in *Salon de 1847*, 7.

conveying the essence of nature's harmony to the spectator. Such a process corresponds to the concept of art elaborated by Leroux in the early 1830s, focusing as it does on the interplay between subjective emotion, external nature, and the material forms evolved to capture this relationship. In the same way as Leroux identifies sentiment as a bridge between the *moi* and the *non-moi*, so Thoré emphasizes that "creation results from love";[85] the material domain, regulated by *intelligence* and *sensation*, receives its vivifying impulse from sentiment's generous perception of man and nature existing within a harmonious totality. In this respect, sentiment acts as a motor, animating the other faculties through the need to exteriorize inner emotion. Echoing Leroux, Thoré writes in 1846: "The arts are nothing other than the expression of the interior life that swells in the human breast in order to be conveyed to other men."[86]

Although Thoré's earlier promotion of overt didacticism periodically resurfaces during the 1840s,[87] his allegiance to Leroux enables him to respond to the moral value of a broader spectrum of artistic forms. Throughout, his commitment to a humanitarian aesthetic remains intact. If in 1847 he acknowledges the relative failure of *art social* and bitterly indicts the sterility of contemporary art,[88] his verdict does not imply diminished enthusiasm for an *art pour l'homme*. The formalist current, for which he shared a distaste as sharp as Leroux's, left Thoré disillusioned before the proliferation of artists who "no longer even try to interpret the life of man and nature."[89] It is this act of penetration that Thoré had come to expect of art. This, rather than any programmatic exhortation for social change, epitomizes the critical ambitions he had drawn from Leroux. In the same way as the philosopher proposed an aesthetic maintaining profoundly social aims while repudiating explicit didacticism, so too Thoré in the 1840s evolved a critical system that sought out social implications in diverse branches of art and developed a strong sense of the moral value of beauty. The modifications implicit in this position, whose roots lay in the late 1830s and Thoré's encounters with Fourier and Leroux, do not represent a retreat from the ambitions of *art social*. Rather they must be seen as a coherent philosophical realignment that accompanies Thoré's commitment to the democratic socialist doctrine of *humanité*.

[85] "La création résulte de l'amour." Thoré, "Salon de 1842," 525.

[86] "Les arts ne sont que l'expression de la vie intérieure qui s'agite au sein de l'homme pour se communiquer aux autres hommes." Thoré, *Salon de 1846*, 44.

[87] See, for example, *Salon de 1844*, 26–27 and *Salon de 1847*, 134–35.

[88] *Salon de 1847*, 154–55.

[89] "Ne cherchent même plus à interpréter la vie humaine et la vie de la nature." Thoré, "Salon de 1842," 525.

CHAPTER 7

The Beauty of Happiness: *Art Social* and Fourierist Criticism

IN THE year that saw the dispersal of the Saint-Simonians' convent at Ménilmontant and the imprisonment of the group's leaders, a new journal appeared devoted to the ideas of one of the most vociferous rivals of Enfantin and his sect, Charles Fourier. The publication of *Le Phalanstère* in 1832 initiated the growth of Fourierism as a radical force, a position it maintained until the early years of the Second Empire. Unlike Saint-Simon, who enjoyed only a posthumous notoriety, Fourier was able to witness the growth of a small but avid group of devotees before his death in 1837. Recognition had not come easily, however. He had published his first major work, the *Théorie des quatre mouvements*, in 1808, and had to wait some twenty years until his earliest disciples, Juste Muiron and Clarisse Vigoureux, began to proselytize on his behalf. Decisive in promoting Fourier's ideas was the young polytechnicien Victor Considerant, who emerged as leader of the movement in the late 1830s. Under his guidance, the Fourierists reached a national following, largely drawn from the prosperous middle class. Much more loosely structured than the Saint-Simonians, the group established its own publishing house and disseminated its ideas through a series of journals and reviews. The Fourierists' commitment to the pacific adoption of radical social and economic change, organized around the foundation of semi-autonomous communities collectively housed in large-scale *phalanstères*, left them confused and indecisive in the face of political upheaval in 1848. Failure to seize any initiative during the Second Republic, coupled with official hostility under Napoleon III, led to a dramatic decline in fortunes. Though Considerant led an abortive attempt to establish a Fourierist community in Texas during the 1850s, support dwindled rapidly, leaving only an isolated band of adherents at the end of the century.

Fourier himself was the most unambiguously utopian of nineteenth-century French thinkers. His blueprint for change was based upon an ostensibly scientific anatomization of human passion. Claiming that physical and psychological impulsions were the product of inherently benign desires whose misguided repression generated crime and social antagonism, Fourier presented a vision of the future in which such constraints had been abolished and universal harmony achieved. For Fourier, insight into passion would transform labor into a pleasure, liberate sexual instincts, eradicate

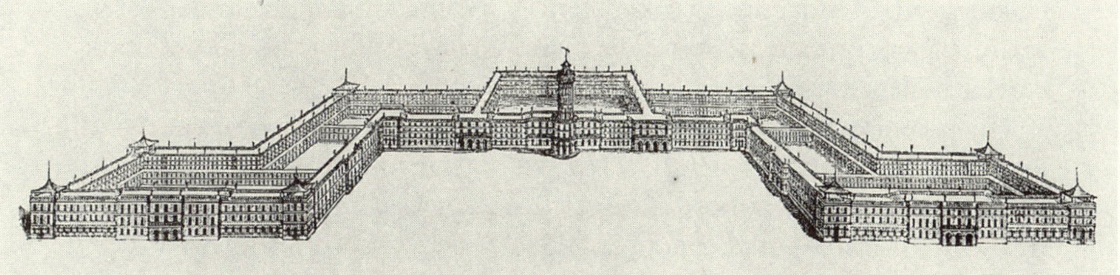

Plate 20. Anonymous: *Idée d'un Phalanstère,* reproduced from Victor Considerant, *Destinée sociale,* volume 1, 2d edition, 1847. University of East Anglia, Norwich.

poverty, foster fraternal relations, and promote individual and collective happiness. The setting for this wonderous transformation, the Phalanstère (plate 20), was described with a painstaking detail characteristic of Fourier's obsessive imagination, which ranges broadly from the culinary arrangements of collective life to speculations on cosmogony and metempsychosis. In describing the role enjoyed by the artist in the luxurious surroundings of the Phalanstère, however, Fourier is surprisingly restrained.

Commitment to the liberation of human passion excludes consideration of the arts as a moralizing medium, since Fourier associates such external restraints with the suppression of instinct underlying contemporary social dislocation. Explicitly repudiating the sacerdotal role of moral leadership accorded to the artist by the Saint-Simonians, he warns that in reality the group's authoritarian tendencies promise "a sorry future of subjection to theocrats, to whom the artist will be shamefully obligated in assisting their Machiavellian schemes."[1]

Fourier's own attitude toward art emphasizes sensual rather than intellectual appeal, echoing Rousseau's evocation of the unalienated culture of the Golden Age in his regard for music and dance as physical embodiments of spiritual harmony.[2] While cultivation of these arts carries utilitarian overtones, through instilling enhanced grace, taste is identified less with personal refinement than with the development of such sensory faculties as a discriminating palate. Nonetheless, Fourier argues that in his "nouveau monde industriel et sociétaire," "every child born within the *Séries passionnelles* will become as polite as are today the offspring of the wealthy, as educated as are those of the intellectuals." In becoming "presentable to the affluent classes" through their new-found culture, the people would enjoy more fraternal relations with their superiors and social harmony would be

[1] "Un triste avenir de soumission à des théocrates, à qui l'artiste devrait de viles complaisances pour aider leur machiavélisme." C. Fourier, *Pièges et charlatanisme des deux sectes Saint-Simon et Owen, qui promettent l'association et le progrès* (1831), 56.

[2] On Rousseau and dance, see P.E.J. Robinson, *Jean-Jacques Rousseau's Doctrine of the Arts* (1984), 81–82.

encouraged.[3] Under such circumstances, Fourier maintains, the artist will address a vastly increased audience and achieve the wealth and eminence currently denied him.

The promise of fame and fortune lies at the heart of Fourier's appeal to the artist. Castigating the belief that creativity thrives on poverty and neglect, he argues that financial subordination effectively constrains the artist's talent by throwing him upon the mercy of the market, compromising his independence, and dissuading criticism of the prevailing social order. As an enticing contrast, Fourier holds out the prospect of wealth and renown, which he regards as the true, if unacknowledged, spurs to artistic and intellectual endeavor.[4] Various means are proposed for achieving this goal, principally the establishment of an international system of awards, whereby each Phalanstère would vote for those works they most admired, contributing to a cash prize levied in every community throughout the world. The enormous sum thus accumulated would be distributed among those artists receiving greatest acclaim, the electorate's cultivation guaranteeing that true merit would be appropriately awarded. This financial inducement is supplemented by formal recognition, with outstanding artists being declared *magnats du globe*.[5] The visual artist enjoys similar fortune in embellishing the surroundings of the Phalanstère and producing monuments commemorating "leaders of the sect, individuals who have excelled in its endeavors and usefully contributed to its enrichment."[6]

Despite such inducements, there is little to suggest that Fourier had a particularly highly developed sense of the artist's value in Societarian society. Claims in the *Théorie des quatre mouvements* that his ideas had far-reaching implications for cultural production[7] were explored by a series of critics in the 1830s and 1840s, however; individuals such as Eugène d'Izalguier, François Cantagrel, Désiré Laverdant, and François Sabatier, all closely

[3] "Tout enfant né et élevé dans les Séries passionnelles y devient aussi poli que le sont aujourd'hui ceux des grands, aussi instruit que le sont ceux des savants"; "présentables aux classes riches." C. Fourier, *Cités ouvrières. Des modifications à introduire dans l'architecture des villes* (1849), 31; *Théorie de l'unité universelle*, in *Oeuvres complètes de Fourier* (1841), 3:433. On Fourier's regard for music, see *Le Nouveau Monde industriel et sociétaire* (1829; reprint, 1974), 267; on the supremacy of culinary over aesthetic taste, see ibid., 303.

[4] "Gloire et fortune, tel est le but commun des savants et artistes: on pourrait dire 'fortune et gloire,' pour s'exprimer plus exactement, pour classer au premier rang l'objet le plus désiré. Mais en Civilisation il n'est pas d'usage de parler comme on pense; de là vient que les auteurs civilisés feignent et doivent affecter de préférer la gloire; au moins avoueront-ils qu'il serait bon d'y joindre la fortune, car, selon certain adage, 'l'argent ne gâte rien.' " Fourier, *Theorie de l'unite universelle*, 3:362.

[5] See ibid., 354.

[6] "Des patrons de la secte, des individus qui ont excellé dans ses travaux et l'ont enrichie de quelques méthodes utiles." Fourier, *Nouveau Monde* , 165, n. 1.

[7] See C. Fourier, *Théorie des quatre mouvements et des destinées générales* (1808), ed. S. Debout (1967), 79–80.

involved with the movement, did much to adapt the master's theoretical precepts to an analysis of the visual arts. While Fourier's theory was substantially diluted under Considerant's leadership in an attempt to win broader public support, application of his philosophy in art criticism displays a striking fidelity to doctrinal issues increasingly neglected in the group's political program during the 1840s.

This cross-fertilization of theory and critical analysis had far-reaching effects on Fourierist appreciation of the social influence of art, allowing the elaboration of an aesthetic highly sensitive to the ameliorative potential of beauty and form. In common with other radical groups of the period, the Fourierists aimed to provide a totalizing explanation not only of the workings of human society but, beyond this, of man's relationship with nature and, indeed, with God. Fourier's idiosyncratic, all-encompassing vision provided fertile foundations upon which an understanding of aesthetic experience as a form of self-realization could be elaborated. His claim to have discovered the key to harmonizing individual psychology with the uncorrupted forces of nature pointed toward the achievement of a heightened state of personal and social equilibrium, from which all sources of potential conflict or repression had been eliminated. At its most refined, such harmony implied the aestheticization of every aspect of human experience, though in the interim traditional cultural forms could be understood as embodying a perfection that reflected this privileged state, however feebly, and thus contributed to its eventual achievement. While abjuring the overt didacticism embraced by other radical groupings, Fourierist critics thus regarded art as fulfilling an exhortatory role. To this end, they evolved a complex understanding of its capacity to modify the individual's attitudes and behavior, compromising a theoretical commitment to unconstrained emotional freedom central to Fourier's claims to mastery over the secrets of man's *économie passionnelle*.

In the second half of the chapter, discussion of the artists and critics involved with the movement will reveal differences in theoretical approach and practical application of Fourier's ideas; initially, however, precedence will be given to examining the conceptual range of the group's aesthetic. In line with their preeminence in Phalansterian political theory, this investigation will begin with a discussion of the notions of harmony and happiness in Fourierist criticism.

HARMONY, BEAUTY, AND HAPPINESS

The centrality of the notion of *bonheur* within Fourier's philosophy is paralleled by the importance accorded to happiness as the fulfillment of human destiny in the aesthetic system developed by his disciples. As expressed by the group's leading theorist, Désiré Laverdant, the arts reveal and thus hasten the achievement of this destiny by exposing the deficiencies of man's present state and evoking an ideal attainable through the adoption of a sociopolitical system consonant with human needs and impulses:

> The aim of art is . . . to make us imagine and love our true destiny while distancing us from those conditions of life which are false and disordered. Art's mission is thus to reveal to us, in its most general sense, the idea of happiness, which is the ultimate goal and divine consecration of true destiny.[8]

For Fourier and his followers, happiness surpasses a simple sense of well-being or physical ease; rather, it signifies a social environment in which desire receives unrestricted satisfaction. Fourier had been able to provide the blueprint for just such an environment since he believed that his discovery of the mechanisms of human passion allowed exact formulation of a socio-political structure in which individual desire and the needs of society would be in absolute harmony. Claiming that deviant behavior occurred only because of the repression of passion, he argued that in a society where no restrictions were placed upon emotional liberty an ideal equilibrium would obtain in which the pursuit of personal happiness would have an optimum social effect. Society's coercive nature was regarded as the root cause of individual discontent and collective dislocation; only in a world that represented and indulged the natural urges of all could harmony be achieved.[9]

Just as classical commentary had elevated harmony as "the soul of the fine arts"[10] within an overall belief in God's providential governance of nature, so theorists such as Laverdant adopted the term as the aesthetic expression of individual and collective ideals articulated in Fourier's political writings. Art gains its importance in Fourierist theory both as an ideated expression of harmony and as a stimulant to its attainment, inducing a harmonious sensation in the spectator carrying ultimately political ramifications. Fourierist conceptions of beauty thus elide sensual gratification and utilitarianism, since arousal of the individual's sense of harmony through aesthetic

[8] "Le but de l'art est . . . de nous faire concevoir et aimer la destinée vraie et de nous éloigner de conditions de vie fausses et désordonnées. L'art a donc pour mission de nous révéler, dans son expression la plus générale, l'idée du bonheur, dernière fin et consécration divine de la vraie destinée." D. Laverdant, "L'Art et sa mission," *D.P.*. 1, no. 2 (2 August 1843).

[9] Laverdant emphazises this interdependence in his definition of human destiny in 1845: "L'homme a le bonheur, qui porte en soi la destinée, lorsqu'il y a pour lui accord et harmonie entre le désir et l'acte, dans ses sens, dans ses affections, dans ses idées; quand il n'a plus à lutter, au nom de la raison, contre la matière, contre la passion, contre l'imagination, en d'autres termes, quand il est en unité avec la nature, avec son semblable, avec l'univers." D. Laverdant, *De la mission de l'art et du rôle des artistes. Salon de 1845* (1845), 5.

[10] The term is from the Abbé Batteux, *Les Beaux-Arts réduits à un même principe* (1746), 169, cited in R. G. Saisselin, *The Rule of Reason and the Ruses of the Heart* (1970), 101–2.

experience ostensibly provokes questioning of the discordant nature of actual social relations and encourages aspiration for change.

Within Fourierist theory beauty and harmony are virtually synonymous. The harmony of nature that constitutes ideal beauty in the aesthetic realm is simultaneously the expression of an exemplary political regime in which the individual's natural propensities are given free rein. Eugène d'Izalguier, the group's first aesthetic theorist, identifies beauty both in terms of the traditional Platonic equation with goodness and also with the unhindered fulfillment of innate function, arguing that

> the nearer something is to its fundamental utility, the nearer it approaches its perfect form; that its utilitarian and its aesthetic modalities progress simultaneously toward their archetype; and finally that when both have attained their apogee, so the thing itself has reached the ultimate expression of its perfectibility and purpose.[11]

Izalguier thus equates formal perfection with the uninhibited development and deployment of all the faculties—the fulfillment of *destinée* in *bonheur*. The repressive mechanisms preventing such fulfillment in contemporary society (dismissed by Fourier with the disparaging epithet *civilisation*) distort nature's inherent harmony of form and function, producing ugliness in the aesthetic domain and discord within society. The notion of the ideal thus carries political connotations, since attainment of perfect beauty depends on a social framework free from the constraints on freedom which produce ugliness. Under such circumstances, the ideal comes to signify not simply an abstract combination of forms found dispersed in reality, but a perfection supposedly attainable under a social regime attentive to the laws of nature revealed by Fourier. Laverdant captures the hypothetical, projective character of the ideal in his definition of its presence in works "that express, either in portrayals of nature or human relations, harmonies, beauties, and pleasures of the soul the immediate model for which the artist does not possess, but which already exist in his imagination."[12] The temporal implications of such remarks reveal the prophetic connotations attached to this notion of the ideal: perfect form is conceived as

[11] "Plus une chose est près de son utilité radicale, plus aussi elle est près de sa forme parfaite; que sa modalité utilitaire et sa modalité esthétique progressent simultanément vers leur archétype; et qu'enfin, lorsque toutes deux elles ont atteint leur maximum, la *Chose* est aussi arrivée à son point culminant de perfectionnement et de fonction." E. d'Izalguier, "Loi de la corrélation de la forme sociale et de la forme esthétique," in *Trois Discours prononcés à l'Hôtel de ville, faisant complement à la publication du Congrès historique*, ed. Dain, V. Considerant, and E. d'Izalguier (1836), 113.

[12] "Qui expriment, soit dans les tableaux de la Nature, soit dans les relations des hommes, des harmonies, des beautés, des jouissances de l'âme, dont l'artiste n'a pas le modèle autour de lui, qui n'existent encore que dans son imagination." D. Laverdant, "Salon de 1843," *Phal.* (30 April 1843): col. 2137.

occurring only in a perfect society—and Laverdant indeed suggests that the members of Societarian society would far surpass in beauty their emotionally and physically constrained predecessors in *civilisation.*[13]

In the eyes Baudet-Dulary, a physiologist with Fourierist leanings, the divinely ordained harmony of the body and its metabolic functions testify to man's innate propensity for happiness and indicate that physical and psychological deviations from this original idea result from the perverting effect of restrictive moral codes and aberrant social institutions.[14] The human form thus possesses the potential for realizing the ideal, though only within a moral order uncontaminated by psychic and physical repression. Such a notion of beauty rejects any normative system of physical attributes; Fourier's insistence on global harmony as the free play of individual capacities means that ideal beauty is conceived inside this framework of unity within diversity. Symmetry between form and function thus exists on an individual level and, rather than producing a homogeneous notion of perfection, is achieved through the self-realization of fundamentally diverse personalities—a point emphasized by Théophile Thoré, in a monograph on phrenology suffused with Fourierist terminology:

> Each individual nature is good in itself since it is suited to its relative function and fulfills its special purpose. . . . In relation to humanity, individuals resemble notes of differing pitch, each contributing to the great concert of life. Furthermore, individuals are more or less harmonious when considered in their own right.[15]

Fourierist critics extended this understanding of the ideal beyond the consideration of beauty: Laverdant, in particular, argues for a *laideur idéale*—a quintessential expression of evil—which again relates physical appearance to moral character.[16] Looking to Fourier for theoretical justi-

[13] D. Laverdant, "Envois de Rome," *D.P.* 3, no. 92 (30 September 1844).

[14] A. Baudet-Dulary, *Essai sur les harmonies physiologiques* (1844), chap. 12, "Economie et harmonie des fonctions."

[15] "Toutes les natures différentes départies aux individus sont bonnes en elles-mêmes parce qu'elles conviennent à leur destination relative, et qu'elles accomplissent leur mission spéciale, . . . les individus, par rapport à l'humanité, sont des notes de valeurs diverses, qui concourent toutes au grand concert de la vie. Mais en outre, les individualités considérées par rapport à elles-mêmes, sont plus ou moins harmonieuses." T. Thoré, *Dictionnaire de phrénologie et de physionomie* . . . (1836), 199.

[16] Laverdant here parts company with Baudet-Dulary and Thoré, who both display different theoretical priorities in approaching this question. Thoré argues that the concept of beauty is socially determined and that "il n'y a rien de laid dans la nature; car toute forme est appropriée à sa destination" (*Dictionnaire*, 228), an assertion that allows him to remain close to Fourier's belief in the innate goodness of all forms of life. Baudet-Dulary, on the other hand, repudiates any direct correspondence between ugliness and evil in an attempt to avoid the determinist implications of physiognomic theory, which, if carried to their logical extreme, would invalidate Fourierist pretensions for social reform through instinctual liberation (*Essai*, 319–22).

fication, he elaborates ideas first developed by Eugène d'Izalguier who, in 1836, had formulated a precise equation between form and function, regarding ugliness as the moral antithesis of beauty: "Throughout creation, beauty is the formula and embodiment of goodness and truth, ugliness the formula and embodiment of evil and falsehood; in all things, there is coexistence and harmony between the mathematical, or rational, mode, and the formulatory, or aesthetic."[17]

A direct symmetry is thus established between an object's physical appearance and the fulfillment of its destiny. From such a perspective, ugliness represents a disharmony proportionate to the deviation from this destiny and provides the tools for an exact etiology of social malaise. It is this signifying power of aesthetic disharmony which Laverdant develops in his concept of *laideur idéale*, a representational strategy he regards as a potent weapon in indicting *civilisation*. If ideal beauty reveals nature restored to a state of true harmony and happiness, so its antithesis exposes the corruption of nature within a social regime that has generated discord and discontent.

These two opposing conceptions of the ideal provide a vehicle for Fourierist discussion of artistic production, allowing an ostensibly objective analysis of formal properties within a discursive framework intent on pointing up the political potential of visual imagery. Each of the contrasting ideals is related to a mode of vision of ultimately social import. Characterized respectively as "critical" and "prophetic," these antithetical categories parallel similar oppositions elaborated by other advocates of *art social*, yet remain distinct through emphasizing form rather than content as a repository of meaning. Social and aesthetic harmony thus become virtual homologues and lend formal analysis directly political ramifications.

Fourierist attitudes toward critical art balance this emphasis on form with more direct calls for the artist to expose contemporary injustice. Condemning modern painters' preoccupation with anachronistic subject matter, the critic Delrieu counsels more active social engagement, proposing a spectrum of topics that connect directly with Fourierist critiques, particularly relating to the oppressive relationship between the sexes:

> Show me marriage with its shocking anomalies, its scandalous behavior, its mysterious suffering and self-denial, its appalling tortures of servitude and perpetual bondage . . . show me love as it exists in our exhausted civilization, suffering, melancholy, asphyxiating, deprived of well-being, independence, and physical power; show me the corruption that takes place in political life, at the cost of individual happiness, which it claims to satisfy while increasing its

[17] "Partout dans la création, le beau est la formule, la manifestation du bon et du vrai; le laid, la formule, la manifestation du mauvais ou du faux; partout coexistence, accord harmonique du mode mathématique ou rationnel et du mode formulateur ou esthétique." Izalguier, "Loi de la corrélation," 113.

price and undermining its quality . . . in a word, show me our society, however ugly or beautiful it might appear to your eyes, and then, without suspecting it, your art will naturally take on meaning, faith, and purpose.[18]

Apart from its distinctive litany of civilization's ills, such an exhortation is virtually indistinguishable from many similar calls for a militantly critical art made at the period. Its explicit didacticism is gradually displaced, however, as the analogy between social dislocation and the disruption of natural harmony is extended into the aesthetic sphere. Laverdant broadens the critical category in the 1840s to embrace artists as diverse as Salvator Rosa, Ribera, Caravaggio, Rembrandt, Delacroix, Charlet, and Ary Scheffer.[19] What apparently unites this otherwise disparate group is an ability to portray either human suffering or the disorder of nature consequent on man's infringement of the laws of harmony. In a state of *civilisation*, the shortcomings of social organization are seen as having direct repercussions on nature, whose innate harmony is disrupted through man's ignorance of the true path to happiness. Maintaining that the spectacle of such disharmony exerts a powerful effect, Laverdant enjoins the artist to produce uncompromising work that will provoke a violent reaction against the evils *civilisation* has spawned: "Since we have to make a stand against evil, the artist must show the circumstances in which it is produced so that our soul is more firmly aroused to oppose it."[20]

For Laverdant, the critical artist must strive after complete honesty; he repudiates attempts to attenuate the spectacle of human suffering and natural disharmony through recourse to the picturesque and calls instead for unflinching realism.[21] Such an attitude prompts criticism of artists whose work ostensibly indulges rather than disturbs by their sentimental or pictur-

[18] "Rendez-moi le mariage avec ses anomolies choquantes, ses déportements scandaleux, ses mystères de souffrance et d'abnégation, ses effroyables tortures de servage, d'enchaînement et de perpétuité . . . rendez-moi l'amour tel que notre civilisation épuisée nous le dispose, l'amour souffreteux, mélancolique, manquant d'air, de bien-être, d'indépendance et de force physique; rendez-moi la corruption qui s'exerce dans nos moeurs politiques, au détriment des jouissances individuelles, qu'elle prétend satisfaire et dont elle augmente le coût en diminuant la qualité . . . rendez-moi dans un mot, notre société si belle ou si laide qu'elle soit à vos yeux, et sans que vous vous en doutiez, l'art sous vos doigts trouvera naturellement une pensée, une foi, un but." Delrieu, "Du désordre dans la peinture," *Phal.* 1 (1 September 1836): col. 196.

[19] D. Laverdant, "Souvenir du Salon de 1846," *Phal.*, 1st ser., 3: (1846) 561.

[20] "Nous avons besoin de prendre parti contre le mal—l'artiste devra donc le représenter dans les conditions où il se produit, afin que votre âme irritée mette plus de soin à le combattre et, par une réaction vive, s'attache à réaliser le bien." D. Laverdant, "Salon de 1842," *Phal.*, 3d ser., 5 (10 April 1842): col. 698.

[21] On the artist's obligation to represent the consequences of disharmony in a direct, unmediated way, Laverdant writes in 1842 (ibid., col. 699): "Au lieu d'arranger coquettement les scènes de la misère et de la laideur, chargez le tableau, s'il est possible. Montrez-nous les plaies et les déformations du corps de la classe indigente. . . . Comme le poète dont le vers ardent et généreux pleure sur le sort des pauvres, artistes, retracez-nous le tableau du malheur pour exciter la pitié de l'âme. Voilà l'emploi juste et utile du laid dans les arts."

esque approach. At a time when peasant painters such as Hédouin and Adolphe and Armand Leleux were noted by other commentators—often with some distaste—for their realistic portrayals of the countryside, Laverdant repeatedly decries the ruralists' "prettification of ugliness."[22] Attacking those artists who, "whenever they encounter the poor, living in hardship, bent over difficult and tedious labors . . . contrive to group them attractively in an atmosphere of ease and enjoyment,"[23] he accuses figures such as Adolphe Leleux of moral dishonesty and regularly judges them harshly.

This hostility to the picturesque finds an echo only in the critical position adopted by François Sabatier in his *Salon* of 1851, where both Jules Breton and Octave Tassaert are rebuked for their recourse to melodrama,[24] while Antigna and Millet, whose *Le Semeur* attracts particular praise for its rendition of the hardship of labor,[25] are congratulated for apparently avoiding similar pitfalls. Few other Fourierist critics distinguish between *art critique* and sentimentalism in this way—Eugène Pelletan and Charles Brunier, for example, both express unqualified admiration for Adolphe Leleux,[26] while Louis Ménard's remarks on Garnerey's landscapes in 1847 show a complacency quite at odds with Laverdant's strictures:

> M. Hippolyte Garnerey has devised his own genre in which for the moment he remains unrivaled; his paintings are poems of ugliness. His requirements are stinking ponds, surrounded by ruined walls, and old houses with delapidated beams on the verge of collapse. Well! he finds a way of making charming pictures out of this, as pleasing in their appearance as they are astonishing in their truth. One would not wish to spend five minutes in the country he portrays, though one could remain for hours in front of his paintings. I will no longer be able to see ruined old hovels, standing by filthy streams and dank lanes, without conjuring up a charming picture by M. Garnerey.[27]

[22] "Enjolivement de la laideur." *Phal.*, 3d ser., 5 (8 May 1842): col. 903.

[23] "S'ils rencontrent de pauvres gens du peuple, vivant dans la gêne, courbés à un travail dur et fastidieux, . . . s'ingénient à les grouper agréablement, à leur donner un air d'aisance et de fête." D. Laverdant, "Salon de 1844," *D.P.* 2, no. 116 (25 April 1844).

[24] See comments on Breton's *La Faim*, for example, in F. Sabatier-Ungher, *Salon de 1851* (1851), 59.

[25] Ibid., 39.

[26] See E. Pelletan, "Salon de 1845," *D.P.* 4, no. 97 (7 April 1845) and Charles Brunier, "Salon de 1846," *D P.* 6, no. 97 (7 April 1846).

[27] "M. Hippolyte Garnerey s'est créé un genre à lui dans lequel il se trouve, jusqu'ici, sans rivaux; ses tableaux sont la poésie du laid. Ce qu'il lui faut, à lui, ce sont des mares puantes, au milieu de murs en ruines, de vieilles maisons qui vont crouler, et dont la charpente détraque. Eh bien! il trouve moyen de faire avec cela de charmants tableaux, qui plaisent par leur aspect autant qu'ils étonnent par leur vérité. On ne voudrait pas passer cinq minutes dans le pays qu'il représente, et on resterait des heures devant ses tableaux; je ne pourrais plus voir de vieilles masures dégradées, bordant des ruisseaux sales et d'obscures impasses sans me figurer une charmante peinture de M. Garnerey." Louis Ménard and René Ménard [d'Arnem], "Salon de 1847," *D.P.* 8, no. 92 (17 April 1847).

In terms of Laverdant's position, such an attitude is not only aesthetically unacceptable but theoretically inconceivable through its implicit reconciliation with the shortcomings of *civilisation*. Ménard repudiates art's function as a stimulant to change through a critical stance that seemingly endorses inertia—and even delectation—before the prevailing disharmony of the natural world. By contrast, Laverdant proposes a more interventionist role in which, rather than cultivating a "poésie du laid," the artist is enjoined to "corriger la nature," revealing its suppressed harmony. He recommends this prophetic role to the landscapist in 1842:

> To work, to work, young souls who aspire to the great and the divine, correct the ugliness and impoverishment of nature in those lands which are so poorly cultivated under Barbarism and even under Civilization. To work, then! overturn the peasant's hideous hut, drain the marshes, eradicate our countryside's disarray; provide divine examples of harmonious distribution so that Enchanted Gardens can soon be realized.[28]

The artist is thus empowered to see beyond the contingent flaws of nature, revealing the latent harmony that will achieve full realization in a state of human happiness. In this respect, he apparently possesses prophetic powers, though as examination of this predictive capacity will suggest, Fourierist conceptions of such an ability are not limited to explicit evocations of future felicity but embrace a wide repertoire of moods and formal devices seen as inherent in the harmonious work of art.

PROPHECY, LUXURY, AND NATURE

The artist as prophet—revealing the enchantment of a harmoniously ordered society—supplements the function of his critical counterpart's anatomization of *civilisation*'s discontents. Endowed with a peculiarly privileged status, such artists are described by François Cantagrel as *hommes d'élite*, "who already paint man as he should be, as one day he will be, and not as he now is."[29] This ability to anticipate the future and give formal expression to harmony is not simply equated with unqualified acceptance of Fourier's teachings—though continual recommendations of the master's work make clear the desirability of such a step. Rather, the prophetic artist's insights

[28] "Allez, allez jeunes âmes qui aspirez vers le grand et le divin, corrigez-nous cette vilaine et mesquine nature des pays si pauvrement cultivés par la Barbarie et même par la Civilisation. . . . Allez, donc! renversez la hideuse cabane du paysan, déssechez les mares, effacez le désordre de nos campagnes; donnez de divins modèles de distribution harmonique, afin que soient bientôt réalisés les Jardins Enchantés." D. Laverdant, "Salon de 1842," *Phal.* 3d ser., 5 (29 May 1842): cols. 1042–43.

[29] "Qui peignent déjà l'homme tel qu'il devrait être, tel qu'il sera un jour, et non tel qu'il est." F. Cantagrel, "Salon de 1841," *Phal.*, 3d. ser., 3 no. 6 (14 May 1841): col. 92.

derive from his particular psychological qualities. In the same way as the future inhabitants of Societarian society are conceived of as attaining happiness through the harmonious development of their faculties and emotions, so the artist in *civilisation* enjoys a similar equilibrium, distinguishing him from his contemporaries and infusing his work with an instinctive harmony. Fourierist critics do not perceive such harmony exclusively in terms of explicitly predictive works, but as being manifested in a more diffuse approach to representation, closer to Laverdant's notion of the *correction* of nature.

If this latter approach enabled Fourierist critics to incorporate a wide variety of works—most notably landscapes—within the category of *peinture prophétique*, it did not exclude agitation for a prophetic art more nearly attuned to Fourierist teaching. In 1842, when confronting Papety's apparent response to such a call in the *Rêve de bonheur*, Laverdant outlined how such a vision of future happiness might appear:

> In the *measured* satisfaction of all his desires, and the perfect harmony of his earthly happiness, man will imagine the true God, will glimpse the celestial lands and, through aspiring to them, rise up to this blessed world where he in turn must one day live. Thus, as the expression of Humanity's highest happiness, we would place religious feeling in our painting's center, where, to the sound of heavenly harps, priests' and vestals' invocations bring Earth into communion with the Divinity. At the altar's base we would group study and science, who enlighten and teach the faith. Slightly below, we would place glorious ambition, the contented smile of motherhood and the benefits of family life, the charms of friendship and the pure reflections of love. Finally would come productive labor, industrial activity, and, in the favorably discreet half-light toward each corner, joyful sensuality. Everywhere, man's genius would shine forth in sublime monuments and fertile landscapes, artistic masterpieces and rich products of the earth, fruit and flowers, while incense would rise from the altar toward the God of eternal goodness.[30]

[30] "L'homme, dans la satisfaction *mesurée* de tous ses désirs, dans l'harmonie parfaite de sa félicité terrestre, concevra le vrai Dieu, entreverra les célestes demeures, et s'élevera par son aspiration vers ces mondes bienheureux qu'il doit habiter à son tour. Aussi, comme expression la plus haute du bonheur de l'Humanité, nous placerions au centre de notre tableau le sentiment religieux, les prêtres et les véstales mettant par leurs invocations la terre en communion avec la Divinité, aux accords des harpes saintes. Au pied de l'autel se grouperaient l'étude et la science qui éclairent, qui enseignent la foi. Un peu plus bas, nous placerions l'ambition glorieuse, le suave sourire de la maternité et les bienfaits de la famille, les charmes de l'amitié et les pures contemplations de l'amour. Enfin, viendraient les travaux productifs, l'activité industrielle, et vers les deux extrémités, dans la demi-teinte favorable et pudique, de riantes sensualités. Partout éclaterait le génie de l'homme, monuments sublimes et campagnes plantureuses, chefs-d'oeuvre des arts et riches produits de la terre, fruits et fleurs, et, de l'autel, l'encens monterait vers le Dieu d'éternelle bonté." D. Laverdant, "Ecole des beaux-arts. Envois de Rome. M. Papety," *Phal.*, 3d ser., 6 (2 October 1842): cols. 677–78.

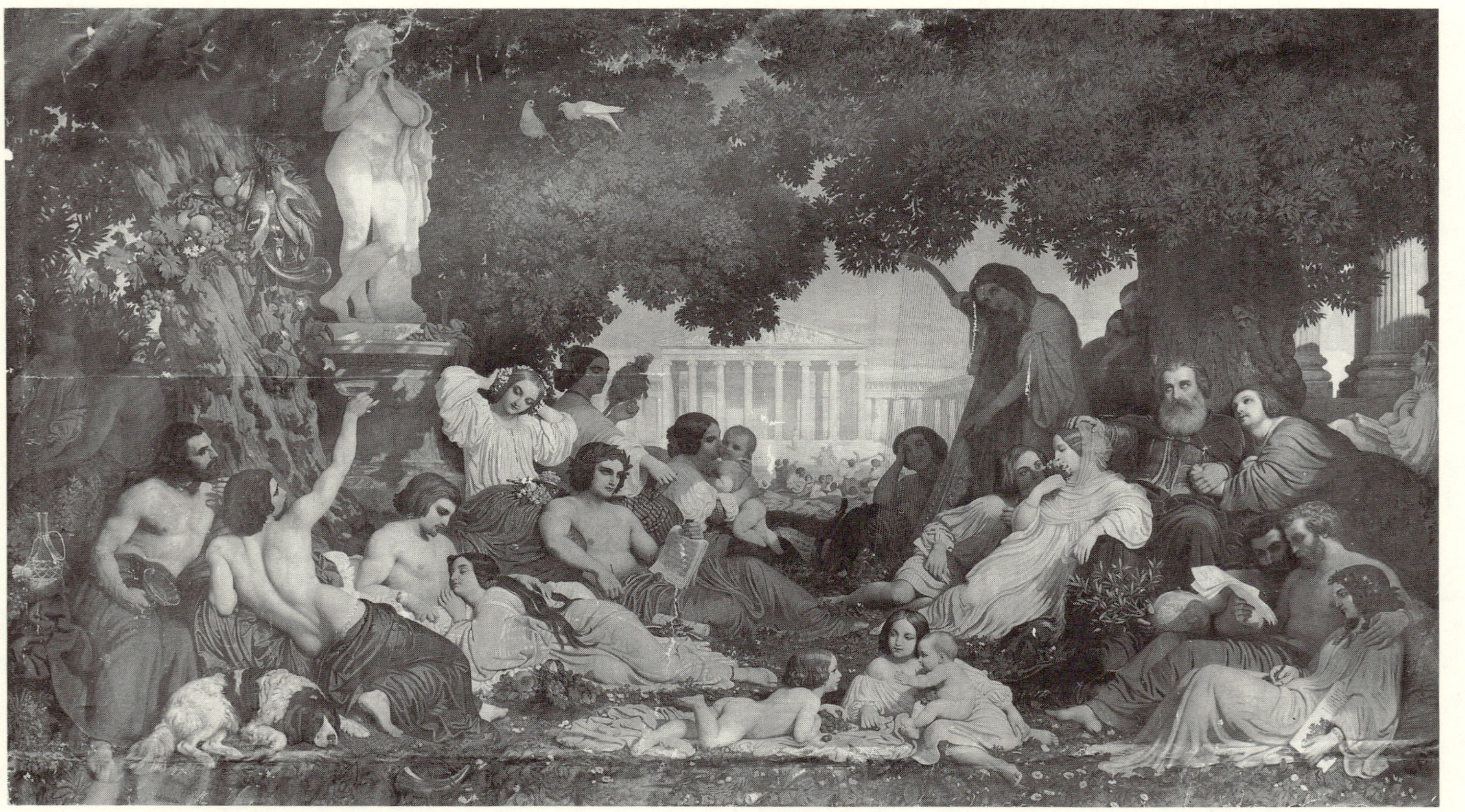

Plate 21. Dominique Papety: *Un Rêve de bonheur,* Salon of 1843. Musée Vivenel, Compiègne.

Though in some ways merely paraphrasing Papety's composition, Laverdant's comments provide an indication of the elements sought in a prophetic work and help to illuminate the rationale behind the term's application to several paintings exhibited at the period. Crucially, Laverdant evokes a world where man is in harmony with self, with nature, and with God, the ultimate expression of harmony. This perfect felicity has been attained through the "*measured* satisfaction" of human desire—namely, through observation of the hierarchy of passions discovered and enumerated by Fourier. Examples of the four affective passions—*amour*, *amitié*, *ambition*, and *familisme* (love, friendship, ambition, family feeling)[31]—figure prominently within Laverdant's description, while labor, transformed from hardship into pleasure through Fourier's discovery of *attraction industrielle*, and sensual gratification, liberated by the overthrow of sexual prohibitions, both form part of this comprehensive evocation of potential *bonheur*. The juxtaposition of industry and agriculture, "sublime monuments" and "fertile landscapes," corresponds to the balance of economic activity envisaged by Fourier for the inhabitants of the *Phalanstère*. Laverdant thus sketches a paradigmatic rendition of an ideal society, designed to inspire commitment to change and allegiance to the movement best able to secure it: Fourierism itself.

The *Rêve de bonheur* (plate 21), by the Fourierist convert and pupil of Ingres, Dominique Papety, stands as the most complete response to this call for a prophetic evocation of harmonian society. Both in his account of its first showing in 1842 and in his review of the 1843 Salon, Laverdant clearly sees Papety as having produced a programmatic picture of ideal happiness. He describes the work as portraying "the idea of happiness in all its guises and under every type of harmony"[32] and emphasizes its compatibility with

[31] On the affective passions, see Fourier, *Théorie des quatre mouvements*, 114–16, and S. Debout, "La Théorie des quatre mouvements ou le dessein d'un 'grand oeuvre,' " in ibid., 34–44.

[32] "L'idée du bonheur sous tous les faces où il se manifeste, dans tous les accords où il se produit" The following discussion disputes the conclusion of N. A. Finlay, "Fourierist Art Criticism and the 'Rêve de Bonheur' of Dominique Papety," *Art History* 2, no. 3 (September 1979): 327–38. Finlay asserts that the picture's reputation as a Fourierist allegory largely relies on Laverdant's description and that overt doctrinal details—the inscription "Harmonie" on the base of a statue of a satyr, and the title "Unité universelle" on the book read by the young scholars—are "obviously superficial . . . and late addition[s]" (331). Not only does she base this assertion on an incomplete examination of the preparatory sketches (see J. Claparède, *Inventaire des collections publiques françaises vol. 6. Montpellier, Musée Fabre. Dessins de la collection Alfred Bruyas et autres dessins des 19e et 20e siècles*, [Paris, 1962]), she also misconstrues the implications of Laverdant's remarks, explored here. In addition, she dates Papety's acquaintance with Sabatier firmly to 1840, while a letter from the sculptor Auguste Ottin to his mother, dated 2 June 1840 (Archives du Louvre, Mss. 9HH7), suggests that the relationship was already well developed at this stage.

Finlay further overlooks the circle of Fourierists with whom Papety was acquainted at the

the Fourierist ideal. Rather than isolating superficial details, Laverdant argues that the very structure of the work embodies a series of antinomies between left and right which articulate precise prophetic intent. He identifies a deliberate, harmoniously balanced contrast between sensual pleasure—love and courtship signified by the voluptuous couple, the drinkers saluting the statue of Harmony, and the young girl tressing garlands—and spirituality, represented by the "noble old man," the group engaged in study, and the woman absorbed in rapt devotion. This antithesis is supplemented by a structural contrast between courtship on the left, married love on the right, and the pleasures of family life, symbolized by the children playing in the foreground.[33] Laverdant further alludes to the affective passions, seen as integral to a portrayal of *bonheur idéal*, in enumerating the work's presentation of "maternal tenderness," "the graceful friendship of childhood," and "the pure and gentle love of the betrothed."[34] The background, altered by Papety following adverse critical comment, is detailed by Laverdant in terms that allude not only to the conflation of agriculture and industry in the Phalanstère, but also to the artist's evocation of *travail attrayant*:

> On the bank, impatient friends bid their farewells and greet the travelers who come and go. A lighthouse has guided them along the coast, and the arms of a telegraph transmitter send news through the air to heads of state and to the jetties to direct the unloading of cargoes from ships' holds. At the bay's edge, all is work and festivities. The inhabitants of this new world dance across the plain, bringing back the treasures of Ceres, like Léopold Robert's Harvesters; soon, as night falls, they will gather at the temple, the majestic precincts of which you can see, to adore and bless God, who has made this happy land.[35]

Villa Medici (see further discussion here and F. Tamisier, "Dominique Papety: sa vie et ses oeuvres," *Tribune artistique et littéraire du midi* 1 [1857]: 51; R. Hanoune, "De Douai à Rome et Athènes: un architecte oublié, Florimonde Boulanger [1807–1875]," *Revue du nord* 61 [April–June 1979]: 427–37; and C. Brunier, "Mort de Dominique Papety," *D.P.* 14, no. 194 [25 September 1849], in which the critic mentions his own contacts with the artist at this period). A letter of 28 August 1840 from Papety to Hippolyte Flandrin, reprinted in F.-X. Amprimoz, "Lettres de Dominique Papety à ses parents et ses amis, Rome 1837–1842," *Archives de l'art français*, n.s., 28 (1986): 260–61, implies that the painter's conversion to Fourier had recently occurred at this date. Finlay further minimizes the artist's subsequent contacts with the group, discussed later.

[33] Laverdant, "Salon de 1843," *Phal.* (14 May 1843): cols. 2243–44.

[34] "La tendresse maternelle"; "l'amitié sous les grâces de l'enfance"; "l'amour pur et doux des fiancés." Laverdant, "Envois de Rome," col. 683.

[35] "Sur le rivage, les amis impatients font des adieux de bon revoir ou des saluts de bien venue à ceux que les embarcations emportent ou ramènent. Un phare a guidé les voyageurs sur la côte, et les bras d'un télégraphe transmettent par les airs les nouvelles aux chefs des Etats, aux débarcadères pour enlever aux flancs des navires leurs cargaisons. Au bord du golfe, ce n'est que travail et fête. Les habitants de ce nouveau monde dansent, par la plaine, en rapportant les

Laverdant's account thus locates Papety's work firmly within the domain of *peinture prophétique* and accords it specifically Fourierist overtones. The juxtaposition of telegraph lines and steamships with the classically draped figures confirms that, rather than a retrospective Golden Age, the work projects the Golden Age into an ideal future. Yet the very ambivalence of Papety's vision, uncomfortably suspended between a clichéd Arcadianism and a timid glimpse of technological innovation, underscores the limitations both of the available visual idioms and of Fourierism's capacity to confront the challenges of industrialization. Rather than offering a distinctively modern evocation of a world transformed by human mastery over the physical environment and the attainment of individual and collective harmony, Papety apparently finds in academic classicism a vocabulary entirely suited to displaying the promised benefits of Societarian society. So attenuated is his vision of the future that elimination of intrusive signs of the modern world, already relegated to the middle distance, simply involves substituting a classical portico for a commercial port. The superficiality of the gesture, calmly restoring an Arcadian harmony disturbed by an anachronistic glimpse of the present, inadvertently reveals Fourierism's broader incapacity to envision the future as anything more than a pallid repetition of a mythical past.

Though subjected to considerable ridicule in 1843 and frowned upon by the Académie, the *Rêve de bonheur* established Papety's reputation as a propagandist for the Ecole sociétaire, allowing a columnist to remark in 1847 "Each of M. Papety's paintings is a page of the *Démocratie pacifique* rendered in color."[36] However overstated, the artist's standing within Fourierist circles is clear.[37]

While providing an example of "the supreme limit of the ideal" with his

---

trésors cueillis de Cérès, comme les Moissonneurs de Léopold Robert, et bientôt, quand tombera le jour, ils se rendront au temple dont vous apercevez les majestueux parvis, pour adorer et bénir Dieu qui fait la terre heureuse." Laverdant, "Salon de 1843," *Phal.* (14 May 1843): col. 2243. A similar description in the account of the "Envois de Rome" demonstrates that this prophetic element was integral to the work as originally conceived and was not simply tacked on in response to Laverdant's promptings.

[36] "Chaque tableau de M. Papety est une page de la *Démocratie pacifique* mise en couleur." Anonymous, "Paris le soir: le Café des arts," *La Silhouette* 4 (16 May 1847): 3.

[37] However, his Salon exhibits failed always to elicit praise in the Fourierist press: Laverdant regretted the unsuitability of the *Vierge consolatrice* in 1846 ("Salon de 1846," 583), while Brunier was unenthusiastic about his *Solon dictant ses lois* (C. Brunier, "Salon de 1846," *D.P.* 6, no. 97 [7 April 1846]). Papety's reputation in Fourierist circles can be gauged from Brunier's obituary of the artist ("Mort") where he writes: "Jeune et déjà célèbre, Papety avait trouvé dans l'étude de la théorie de Fourier un aliment à sa vaste intelligence. . . . Depuis longtemps il appartenait par ses convictions à l'Ecole Phalanstérienne, dont il était un des apôtres les plus dévoués." See also the remarks in E. Pelletan, "Compiègne. Ses Souvenirs historiques, son Musée Vivenel," *L'Echo de l'Oise* (12 July 1850).

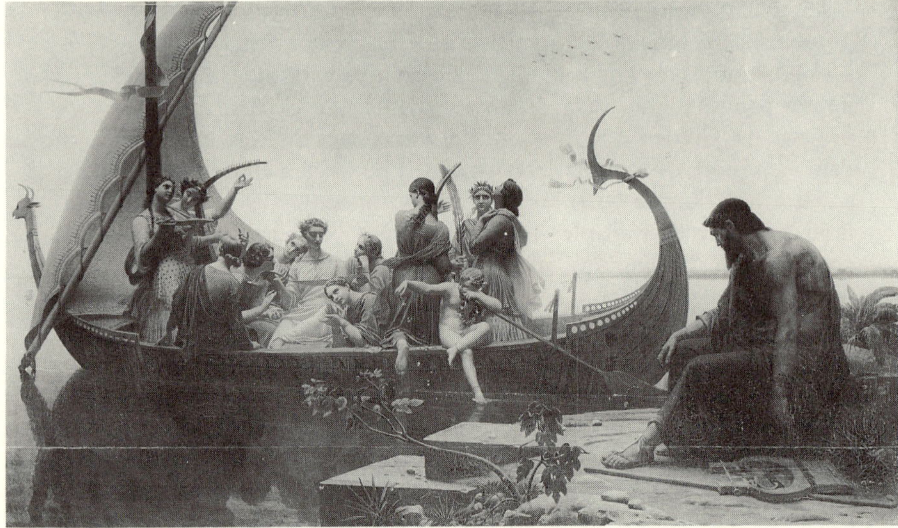

Plate 22. Charles Gleyre: *Le Soir,* Salon of 1843. Musée du Louvre, Paris.

"immense utopia,"[38] Papety was not alone in satisfying demands for a prophetic art. In the same Salon as the *Rêve de bonheur*, Gleyre's classical allegory *Le Soir* (plate 22) was warmly praised by Laverdant and given a Fourierist gloss. He interprets the old man on the shoreline as "some mournful inhabitant of civilization who watches, like us, and listens to the divine concert, and regrets that in the world where we vegetate he is not surrounded by these happy festivities which pass in a dream." The young women in the boat are described in terms that elide their beauty with the physical perfection enjoyed by the inhabitants of a Phalanstère—"this beauty grown up in affluence, safe from care, in the open air at the festivities of attractive labor"[39]—and Laverdant speculates that their journey will end in an amorous encounter. Both in his language and in the positioning of his remarks in the text, Laverdant presents *Le Soir* as effectively forming one half of a diptych with Papety's work—Gleyre portraying the aspiration for happiness in *civilisation*, Papety showing its consummation in harmony.

Fourierist critics classified similar scenes of social or sexual concord as corresponding to the prophetic ideal, and often supplemented the literal

[38] "La limite suprême de l'idéal"; "immense utopie." Laverdant, "Salon de 1843," *Phal.* (14 May 1843): col. 2246.

[39] "Quelque civilisé chagrin, qui regarde, comme nous, et écoute le divin concert, et s'afflige de ne point voir autour de lui, sur la terre où nous végétons, cette fête heureuse qui passe dans un rêve"; "cette beauté dévelopée dans la richesse, à l'abri des soucis, au grand air, dans les fêtes du travail attrayant." *Phal.* (30 April 1843): col. 2145.

description of a painting with a reading that highlights elements in its composition consonant with Fourierist thought. On several occasions, for example, Laverdant refers to Léopold Robert as providing vivid evocations of *travail attrayant*. The critic interprets his Italian peasant scenes not as idealized representations of contemporary labor, vulnerable to accusations of picturesque obfuscation, but as prophetic indications of the pleasures of association, where solidarity and cooperation have supplanted alienation and subservience. It is such a strategy that, in 1845, allows him to read the *Retour des vendanges* as a programmatic statement of the advantages of *attraction industrielle*:

> Do you know any book that makes a more poetic call to work, to *attractive work*, than the *Return from the Grape Harvest*? We have here a large band of people in which young and old, beautiful girls and young lovers, joyfully help each other; festive dress, luxury and dignity, dancing and music, beneath a pure and brilliant sky. Standing before this picture, do you have any notion of servility? Do you see the exploitative master and the harassed, miserable pauper? No, what we have here are groups united in brotherhood, with happiness in their midst. And who would not wish to join them and share in this joyful festival of labor?[40]

Similarly, in 1841 Cantagrel groups works by Winterhalter, Roqueplan, and Maréchal under the prophetic category. In the case of the former's *Decameron*, such a designation is consistent with remarks by other Fourierist critics on similar scenes carrying overtones of the *fête champêtre*, such as Müller's *Primavera*.[41] Maréchal's exhibits—two pastels portraying a young student and a gypsy boy—present a rather different notion of *peinture prophétique*. As opposed to a scene of ideal social relations, Maréchal's compositions allegedly portray corporeal and psychological harmony, explicitly associated with "the inhabitants of harmony in that admirable world prepared by Fourier." Cantagrel's description of the student emphasizes such well-being:

[40] "Connaissez-vous un livre qui convie plus poétiquement au travail, au *travail attrayant* que le *Retour des vendanges*? Réunion nombreuse, où s'aident en souriant enfants et vieillards, belles femmes et jeunes amants; habits de fête, luxe et solennité, danses et musique, sous un ciel pur et resplendissant. Avez-vous, devant ce tableau, l'idée des conditions serviles? Apercevez-vous le maître exploitant et le pauvre harassé et misérable? Non, ce sont bien là des groupes fraternellement unis, le bonheur est au milieu d'eux. Et qui ne voudrait en être? Qui ne souhaiterait prendre part a cette fête joyeuse du travail?" Laverdant, *Salon de 1845* (1845), 17. See Laverdant's 1842 Salon, *Phal.*, 3d ser., 5 (15 May 1842): col. 953, and Pelletan, "Salon de 1845," *D.P.* 4, no. 97 (7 April 1845). Laverdant seems here to be conflating several works by Robert, who did not produce anything bearing this title. In all probability, the description confuses elements from the *Arrivée des moissonneurs* (plate 19) and the *Retour des pélerins*.

[41] See Laverdant on Müller in "Salon de 1846," 582.

> What grace and distinction in all his being! How happy and carefree he is! How free and independent he feels! His eye reveals his intelligence, and we feel that he is right to trust to it. His soul is open and guileless; benevolent and pure, it knows neither pain nor hindrance; it has no inkling of wrongdoing; it is oblivious to envy, pride, fear, and even modesty; it does not even suspect the existence of sadness; it knows nothing of our vices or prejudices; in a word, it is as God made it.[42]

Form, rather than content, thus determines Cantagrel's assessment of Maréchal's work as prophetic, allowing him to associate a composition carrying contemporary connotations with a putative future state. This derives from the critic's declared response to the work as a harmonious composition—harmony here being identified as much with the artist's representation of the subject as with the subject itself. The physical becomes a metaphor and a symptom of the moral, in line with the school's strictures on the moral connotations of the ideal.

The importance accorded to sensual well-being both within Fourier's social model and in conceptions of *peinture prophétique* finds further expression in the emphasis on *luxe* as an attribute of the ideal society. In contrast to the egalitarianism of Cabet and the Icarians with their elevation of utility over beauty,[43] Fourierism presents luxury both as a spur to social change and as a benefit to be enjoyed by all under a regime in which "good taste is universal, and people are sufficiently wealthy to afford their common luxury."[44] As a fundamental aspect of *bonheur*, luxury represents a means not only of consolidating social interdependence, but also of impelling man to a deeper love of God by developing heightened sensual regard for nature.[45] Such a perspective indicts the communist philosophy represented by Cabet both as an anathema to art and as incompatible with a well-balanced society. The rarity value accorded to objects prized for their beauty is presented as fostering a beneficial social dynamic by encouraging those lower in the hierarchy to greater efforts in order to acquire the luxuries they desire.

[42] "Les populations harmoniennes dans cet admirable milieu social que Fourier a préparé"; "Que de grâce, que de distinction dans toute sa personne! Comme il est heureux et insouciant! Comme il se sent libre et indépendant! Que son oeil a d'intelligence, et on sent qu'il a raison d'y compter. Son âme s'ouvre sans défiance; elle est bienveillante et pure, elle ne connaît ni la douleur ni les entraves; elle n'a pas l'idée du crime, elle ignore l'envie, l'orgueil, la crainte, la modéstie même; elle ne soupçonne pas que le malheur soit possible; elle ne sait rien de nos vices, rien de nos préjugés; elle est enfin telle que Dieu l'a faite." Cantagrel, "Salon de 1841," *Phal.*, 3d ser., 3, no. 6 (14 May 1841): col. 93.

[43] Cabet's rejection of private property leads him to outline a society in which individual habitations are entirely standardized and all art works are confined to the public domain. See E. Cabet, *Voyage en Icarie* (1840; 2d ed., 1842 ed.), 69.

[44] "Le bon goût est général, et les peuples sont assez riches pour payer leur luxe collectif." M. Briancourt, *Visite au Phalanstère* (1848), 290.

[45] See Laverdant, "L'Art et sa mission," and Sabatier, *Salon de 1851*, v.

While a communist regime achieves "the generalization of a sort of pleasant but vulgar comfort, served up on the table of equality," under Fourierism, luxury stands as "the ideal placed at the highest limits, eternally attracting the human soul, the motive of our ceaseless aspiration toward the source of absolute beauty."[46] Rather than an aestheticist aberration, such anti-egalitarianism entirely matches Fourier's own work, with its emphasis on a productive social hierarchy of functions and benefits, given concrete expression in the unequal distribution of accommodation within the Phalanstère itself.

Art's obligation to "glorifier le luxe" is not confined to the depiction of scenes of collective contentment or opulence. Rather, the notion is broadly cast to embrace such aspects as *luxe interne*—the physical well-being discerned in Maréchal's student—and the richness of nature. Laverdant's inclusion of figures as diverse as Gros, Dedreux, Robert, Ingres, Géricault, Delaroche, and Vernet within the category of painters of *luxe* indicates the term's elasticity.[47] A notable feature within his listing is the predominance of landscape artists—Corot, Huet, Français, Dupré, Aligny, Marilhat—an indication of the priority accorded to nature both as a manifestation of *luxe* and as a privileged vehicle for *peinture prophétique*.

The centrality of nature in Fourier's work, both as an ontological and social model and as an environment the "harmonious management" of which would release new splendors, parallels the precedence accorded landscape as a medium for *peinture prophétique*. Fourier had argued that abandoning civilization's abuse of nature would produce an earthly paradise, fertile and benign in its responsiveness to human need. While ignoring Fourier's more extravagant speculations, Laverdant presents nature in a state of harmony as surpassing in luxuriance anything experienced by the inhabitants of civilization and predicts an enhanced sensibility to natural phenomena consequent on human self-realization as unobstructed "natural" beings.[48] While deeming such accord contingent on fundamental social transformation, Fourierist critics argue that the landscapist's evocation of potential harmony serves to accelerate such a process. Landscape thus acquires a privileged role as a prophetic medium, and the proliferation of the genre is welcomed as a symptom of growing artistic sensitivity to the beauty of nature.[49] The emphasis on landscape as the representation of a harmonious

[46] "L'universalisation d'un certain confortable, agréable et vulgaire, servi sur la table de l'égalité"; "L'idéal placé à la limite suprême, éternel attrait de l'âme humaine, mobile de notre incessante aspiration vers la source de l'absolue beauté." Laverdant, *Salon de 1845*, 10–11.

[47] Ibid., 11. Fourier places "le luxisme, ou désir de luxe" as the first of the "centres d'attraction" in his "arbre passionnel" and draws the distinction, found in critical discourse, between "luxe interne" and "luxe externe." The former is identified with "santé" (physical well-being), the latter with "richesse." See Fourier, *Théorie des quatre mouvements*, 116–17.

[48] See Laverdant, "Salon de 1844," *D.P.*, 2, no. 120 (29 April 1844).

[49] See Sabatier, *Salon de 1851*, 2.

ideal provokes some criticism over naturalism,[50] with Laverdant in particular counseling an idealized rendering of nature and exhorting the artist:

> Ah! make us hear the fertile, happy land's great murmurings; show us its hidden grace; reveal its treasures and spread them before us so that, by contemplating this divine mother's beauties, we are inspired with renewed enthusiasm to cover her breast with adornments and that, in its delight, our soul should send up blessings to the celestial Powers![51]

Such idealism has nothing in common with the classical scenes of Aligny and Paul Flandrin, of whom Laverdant is particularly critical. Rather than imposing a preconceived aesthetic model on nature—analogous to its deformation by the social conventions of civilization—he encourages landscapists to develop a notion of the ideal immanent in nature through direct observation. Thus Fourierist critics express greater enthusiasm for painters associated with the romantic movement—Huet, Diaz, Français—and with Corot, all of whom they regard as placing personal experience above pictorial formulas.[52]

This emphasis on subjectivity relates to landscape's perceived capacity to induce a vivid sense of nature's potential harmony in the spectator. In highlighting his subjectivity, the landscapist is presented as part of an instinctive social vanguard, particularly attuned to the inherent harmony of nature through the enhanced harmony of his own personality. Thus François Sabatier maintains that the genre's popularity forms part of a providential plan to restore man's links with nature, a process described in terms clearly suggesting the Fourierist inspiration behind such a move:

> Whether we want to or not, we must think about abandoning the cities. Providence seems to have charged landscapists with preparing us for this event by familiarizing and reconciling us with the countryside, man's natural home. You can be sure that this is why there are so many capable landscapists today. Landscape itself is becoming socialist; don't laugh: it is just that socialism is nothing but the enhancement of the power of nature by reason, and its harmonious ordering by science and love.[53]

[50] See, for example, Laverdant's condemnation of naturalism in 1842 ("Salon de 1842," *Phal.*, 3d ser., 5 [29 May 1842]: col. 1041) and 1843 ("Salon de 1843," *Phal.* [21 May 1843]: col. 2304). By contrast, Sabatier expresses no such misgivings, writing sympathetically of Troyon's "réalisme objectif" in 1851 *(Salon de 1851*, 17).

[51] "Ah! faites-nous entendre les grands murmures de la terre féconde et souriante; révélez-nous ses grâces voilées; découvrez ses trésors et les étalez devant nous, afin que, dans la contemplation des beautés de cette mère sainte nous puisions une ardeur nouvelle à couvrir son sein de parure, afin que notre âme ravie élève ses bénédictions vers les célestes Puissances!" Laverdant, "Salon de 1843," *Phal.* (21 May 1843): col. 2304.

[52] On Diaz, see Sabatier, *Salon de 1851*, 21, and on Corot, Pelletan, "Salon de 1845," *D.P.* 4, no. 111 (21 April 1845).

[53] "Qu'on le veuille ou non, il faudra bien qu'on songe à déménager des cités. Les paysagistes semblent avoir été chargés par la Providence de nous préparer, eux aussi, à cet événe-

It is the harmonious rendition of nature, rather than overtly didactic subject matter, which Fourierist critics associate with the progressive potential of landscape. Diaz, for example, "carries us away to imaginary worlds,"[54] while Huet and Corot impress through their ability to induce an enhanced awareness of natural harmony. Like Baudelaire, Laverdant hankers after romantic escapism, regretting the passing of the days when "M. Paul Huet invented fantastic parks, enchanted lakes, fairy-tale palaces and pavillions."[55] In the more prosaic climate of the 1840s, he values Corot's pastoral scenes for evoking a harmonious ideal whose particular strength derives from the artist's exploration of his own subjectivity: rather than copying the flaws of nature under *civilisation*, he creates a personal microcosm of pristine perfection.[56]

The landscapist as prophet and *rêveur*[57] draws the spectator into the image, ostensibly suspending awareness of time and momentarily inserting the viewer into another, more perfect world; he thus exploits the imagination's response to sensual attraction as a means of operating the *écart absolu*—the leap required in the social sphere to attain a state of harmony. As a *rêve de bonheur*, the image reveals new perspectives, promises untold pleasures, and stimulates the will to realize in social practice the transience of prophetic insight:

> To make us dream is to transport us through time and space, to carry us into the unknown. Such a work, indeed, solicits hope and desire. In this way, Pleasure forms and proliferates. Art thus rises up as its effect broadens and continues, the artist sees deeper into the heart and further into the unfolding of existence, as in some sense he sees into the individual's fate.[58]

---

ment; ils nous familiarisent et nous réconcilient avec la campagne, demeure naturelle de l'homme; c'est pour cela, soyez-en sûr, qu'il y a tant d'habiles paysagistes aujourd'hui. Le paysage lui-même se fait socialiste; ne riez pas: c'est que le socialisme n'est autre chose que la nature élevée en puissance par la raison, et organisée harmoniquement par la science et l'amour." Sabatier, *Salon de 1851*, 26.

[54] "Nous emporte dans les mondes imaginaires." Laverdant, "Salon de 1846," 569.

[55] "M. Paul Huet inventait des parcs fantastiques, des lacs enchantés, des palais et des kioskes féeriques." Ibid., 568.

[56] "Quand il veut s'égayer et nous réjouir l'âme, M. Corot cherche, dans les chants des poëtes ou dans son imagination, un ciel pur, des campagnes sereines, des eaux limpides, les ombrages fraîchissants des tièdes climats où l'homme n'est pas réduit à s'engoncer et s'étouffer sous ces matelas de laine que nous appelons des habits." Laverdant, "Salon de 1843," *Phal.* (30 April 1843): col. 2139.

[57] The term is applied to Diaz by Brunier in 1846 ("Salon de 1846," *D.P.*, 6, no. 97 [7 April 1846]).

[58] "Faire rêver, c'est transporter dans l'espace et le temps, c'est entraîner au-delà du connu. Telle oeuvre, en effet, engage à désirer, à espérer. La Jouissance, ainsi, se compose et se multiplie. L'art s'élève donc à mesure que son action s'étend et se prolonge, à mesure que l'artiste voit plus au fond des coeurs et plus au loin dans le cours de l'existence, à mesure qu'il pénètre en quelque sorte la destinée de l'individu." Laverdant, *Salon de 1845*, 10. This encouragement of "rêverie" as possessing inherently beneficial effects is, however, modified by Laver-

While the *rêverie* demanded of aesthetic experience by Baudelaire is essentially introverted, Laverdant's concept of *jouissance* is social in its implications. The dynamic of desire is not contained by introspective delectation, but rather ruptures a sense of the inevitability of the present and opens up new horizons where revelation stimulates a will for change. Thus, in expressing his disappointment at the shortcomings of the Fourierist landscapist Français in 1846,[59] Laverdant enjoins the artist to exploit his talent for reproducing nature's harmony in works that will inspire the spectator: "Full of passion, emotion, and tenderness, the crowd must one day stop before his canvases and cry out: 'There is the promised land! Hail, fields of paradise! Hail, man's royal home in the midst of the royal home of God!' "[60]

This identification of *rêverie* with a progressive impulse for change draws upon Fourierist conceptions of emotional response which form part of a broader interest in the mechanisms of human psychology. The group's investigations of aesthetic reception molded their perception of the conflict between formalists and advocates of *art social* and contributed to the development of a vocabulary of form ostensibly capable of resolving this antithesis through investing social meaning in visual phenomena. As the following discussion will show, commentators looked to Fourier's theories of psychology and of the analogies between physical objects and abstract emotions to understand the process of aesthetic response and forge a theory of art sensitive to the implicit social significance of line and color.

RECEPTION AND THE MEANING OF FORM

The claims of Fourier's *économie passionnelle* to provide a social model consonant with individual psychic and physical needs established a framework within which aesthetic response could be explored. As with Saint-Simonianism during its positivist phase, and in common with Buchez and his followers, early Fourierist commentators were confident that the arts could be transformed into finely tuned triggers, manipulating the perceiv-

---

dant in comments provoked by Diaz in 1844 ("Salon de 1844," *D.P.* 2, no. 137 [16 May 1844]), where he writes: "nous vivons dans un temps où il faut être sobre d'encouragements pour la fantaisie, par cette raison qu'elle trône en souveraine, et où les critiques considérables doivent employer leur autorité à recommander particulièrement à l'inspiration des artistes les sujets d'un caractère déterminé et élevé."

[59] On Français' adherence to Fourierism, see A. Dubuisson, *Les Echos du bois sacré. Souvenirs d'un artiste. De Rome à Barbizon* (1924), 205. Français was a friend of Papety (ibid., p. 80) and in 1834 developed associations with Célestin Nanteuil, another Fourierist sympathizer, sharing an apartment with him around 1843 (see P. Burty, *L'Age du romantisme: Célestin Nanteuil* [1887], 18).

[60] "Il faut qu'un jour, la foule émue, passionnée, attendrie, s'arrête devant ses toiles en s'écriant: La voilà, la terre promise! Salut, champs du paradis! Salut, domaine royale de l'homme au sein du royaume de Dieu." Laverdant, "Salon de 1846," 569.

ing subject's emotions with scientifically foreseeable results.[61] In predicting a correspondence between the *loi sociale* and the *loi esthétique*, Izalguier in particular envisaged the extension of Fourier's psychological principles in an aesthetic system capable of stimulating response in a precise and socially beneficial way:

> If, indeed, through his profound knowledge of the demands of human nature, [Fourier] was able precisely to calculate the social conditions most appropriate to that nature and most propitious for satisfying its demands, by building on his work on human passions it will also be possible to calculate the *artistic* conditions most in harmony with those passions and best capable of satisfying or directing them according to the artist's intentions. Every aesthetic combination will thus have its laws and rationale, as will every musical, pictorial, or numerical combination, and the new science will be established.[62]

Though later theorists mitigated such positivistic claims, figures such as Sabatier and Laverdant continued to draw upon Fourier's psychological theory in asserting the arts' superiority as stimulants to social sensibility. In so doing, they employ a tripartite division of human response, in which categories of sense, emotion, and intellect parallel the Saint-Simonians' social trinity of *industriels*, *artistes*, and *savants*. Each of these faculties is seen as operating within the individual, with art's sensual appeal possessing greater resonance the more effectively it is able to stimulate both the intellectual and emotional faculties. As Laverdant argues in 1842, outlining a theory of response where emphasis on this equilibrium contrasts with the precedence accorded to *sentiment* by the Saint-Simonians:

> Art's aim is simultaneously to satisfy all the feelings that go to make up man. The broader the appeal to the soul's impulses, the greater the interest produced. Pleasure is made complete by the sympathetic emotion of the heart and the harmonious complicity of the intelligence. For a work to be perfect, it must therefore appeal at once to the eye, to the affective soul, and to the mind.[63]

[61] Thus Delrieu ("Du désordre dans la peinture," col. 195) promises that in the future the spectator's response will accord precisely with the artist's wishes: "Le spectateur sentirait naître en lui, à la vue d'une belle toile, des idées correspondant à l'idée du peintre, et ressentirait une disposition involontaire, spontanée, curieuse, d'accomplir l'acte dont le spectacle peint l'aurait frappée." See also Miget, "De la peinture," *Phal.* 1 (20 November 1836): col. 455.

[62] "Si, en effet, connaissant à fond les exigences de la nature humaine, [Fourier] a pu calculer avec précision les conditions *sociales* les mieux appropriées à cette nature, les plus favorables à la satisfaction de ces exigences, —il sera possible aussi, profitant de ses travaux sur les passions de l'homme, de calculer les conditions *d'art* les mieux en harmonie avec ces passions et les plus capables de les satisfaire ou de les diriger selon le but de l'artiste. Dès lors toute combinaison esthétique aura sa loi et sa raison, comme toute combinaison musicale, comme toute combinaison picturale, comme toute combinaison de nombres, et la science sera fondée." Izalguier, "Loi de la corrélation," 127.

[63] "L'objet de l'art, c'est la satisfaction combinée de tous les sentiments qui font l'homme. Plus il y a de forces de l'âme solicitées, plus il y a d'intérêt produit. La jouissance se complète par

In advancing such a theory of response, Fourierist commentators imagine art enhancing awareness of harmony and exploiting its effect in order to act on the subject in more than a superficially gratifying way. The appeal through the senses to emotion and intellect stimulates the imagination, inducing either distaste before the critical spectacle of disharmony or *rêverie* in response to a prophetic image of ideal harmony. The reaction described by Laverdant before the landscapes of Corot and Huet combines an emotional attraction toward the ideal world they portray with a concomitant intellectual conviction in its superiority over the discordant chaos of *civilisation*. Their capacity to "impel one toward the unknown" derives from the combined appeal of these reactions on the imagination, whose empathetic mechanisms transport the viewer out of the imperfect present and grant unique access to nature purified of conflict and contradiction.

The mechanisms of imagination and their implicitly didactic effect receive more systematic exploration in the physiological treatise, the *Traité élémentaire de l'homme considéré sous tous ses rapports*, published by the Fourierist Gabriel Gabet in 1842. Pointing to the imagination's projective capacity, Gabet argues that it not only enables man to anticipate future events through extrapolation from the present but further allows the elaboration of hypothetical models of existence, ostensibly more compatible with innate human needs:

> Becoming the interpreter and organ for the eternal laws of truth, the imagination traces an image of things as they should be; it forms every idea of what we call laws; it forms the notion of the principles of society, based on elements provided by our faculties, needs, and inclinations; it marks out man's destiny, the purpose and use of every object, the means of realizing every talent.[64]

Gabet argues that the arts can serve within this process to stimulate the imagination, reinforcing its natural tendency to prefigure the ideal by giving it concrete expression in verbal or visual form. The sensual experience he describes carries emotional and intellectual connotations in its stimulation

l'émotion sympathique du coeur et par l'accord harmonique de l'intelligence. Pour qu'une oeuvre soit parfaite, il faut donc qu'elle s'adresse à la fois à l'oeil, à l'âme affective et à l'esprit." Laverdant, "Salon de 1842," *Phal.*, ser., 5 (3 April 1842): col. 646. A similar point is made by Sabatier in 1851 (*Salon de 1851*, v), where he argues that art appeals to "l'homme intégral" and is thus "l'expression la plus haute et la plus complète du microcosme humain, la plus sublime création de l'homme social."

[64] "L'imagination, devenant l'interprète et l'organe des lois éternelles du vrai, trace le tableau de ce qui devrait être; elle forme toutes les idées de ce que nous appelons les lois; elle forme la notion des principes sociaux, sur les éléments qui résultent de nos facultés, de nos besoins, de nos penchants; elle marque à l'homme sa destinée, à chaque objet sa fin et son emploi, aux talents leurs méthodes." G. Gabet, *Traité élémentaire de l'homme considéré sous tous ses rapports* (1842), 1:155.

of desire for unrealized perfection and its ability to implant moral imperatives consonant with achieving an enhanced state of being:

> Poetry produces these great effects only because it draws its images from the realm of the ideal; through them, the soul is as if transported to heights from where it sees things formerly unknown, and the lessons it draws from them later serve as rules of behavior. Poetry thus not only serves for our pleasures; rather, the lessons it gives, the inspirations it conveys, bring into play the soul's deepest powers, and through their eloquence move the most insensitive hearts.[65]

Such a theory of reception combines Fourier's psychological doctrine with the tenets of neo-Platonic aesthetics in a model of response that surmounts habitual distinctions between form and utility. While the Saint-Simonians' differentiation between intellect and passion provoked initial reluctance to abandon an overtly didactic art, Fourierist commentators draw on theoretical distinctions between modes designated as *simple* and *composé* to describe response as simultaneously engaging emotional and intellectual perceptions. Fourier's preference, in the psychological domain, for pleasures appealing to a combination of faculties rather than one alone, extends in aesthetic commentary to the elevation of the *mode composé* in artistic response—the appeal to *l'homme intégral*, identified by Sabatier as the distinguishing attribute of art. This conflation of sensory reaction, intellection, and empathy as the paradigm of aesthetic reception thus draws on Fourier's model of *économie passionnelle* to secure a definition of response that negates standard contrasts between form and utility.[66] The neo-Platonic equation between beauty and truth can be incorporated into such a scheme through the theoretical identification of formal harmony with the fulfillment of *destination*, a strategy also made viable through application of Fourier's concept of nature.

The model of response outlined here predominates in Fourierist aesthetic discourse, but nonetheless meets with some variations within the overall critical corpus. Brunier, for example, describes aesthetic experience as "this blessed consolation, this sure haven against pain and sadness," offering a respite from disharmony and social dislocation out of which the perceiving subject emerges better disposed toward those whose less favored circum-

[65] "La poésie ne produit ces grands effets que parce qu'elle puise ses tableaux dans l'idéal: par eux l'âme est comme transportée à une hauteur d'où elle voit des choses inconnues jusqu'alors, et les leçons qu'elle y puise servent ensuite de règles de conduite. Ainsi la poésie ne sert pas seulement à nos plaisirs; mais les leçons qu'elle donne, les inspirations qu'elle transmet, mettent en jeu les plus profondes puissances de l'âme, et remuent éloquemment les plus insensibles coeurs." Ibid., 2:292.

[66] On the appeal to the three faculties considered in the context of reconciliation of form and utility, see Izalguier, "Loi de la corrélation", particularly 134 and 143.

stances do not allow such moments of repose.[67] This rather indulgent position contrasts with the theoretical posture elaborated by Izalguier and Laverdant. Emotion, for Brunier, is a supplement to aesthetic experience, a warm afterglow outlasting the instant of perception. The nature of the act itself, and the responses it activates, remain undefined and the value of art is invested entirely in its "otherness" from life. Such an attitude conflicts with Laverdant's condemnation of bourgeois preference for undifferentiated emotion in art. Attacking the popularity of sentimentalized genre painting he observes, in line with Izalguier's remarks on the *loi esthétique*, that "an ill-defined emotion is inadequate . . . it is a question of precisely defining the emotion's law."[68]

This interest in the precise triggers of response extends within Fourierist critical theory to the emotional power of form. Though reminiscent of Saint-Simonian investigations in the *Livre nouveau* and certain pronouncements by such republicans as Thoré and Charles Blanc in the 1840s, Fourierist attitudes depart from more exclusively didactic currents on the left, and display a qualified tolerance of formalism unusual among advocates of *art social*. For members of the group, the disjunction between form and utility—whose theoretical interdependence derives from the preoccupation with the harmony of form and function—diminishes art both as a sensual experience and as a social force. Izalguier relates formalism to the disequilibrium between the individual and society, manifested in the predominance of the egotistic passion of *favoritisme* over the altruistic impulse of *unitéisme*,[69] and argues that the emergence of conflicting aesthetic doctrines is mutually impoverishing:

> For of the two things, the USEFUL and the BEAUTIFUL, each is by divine creation the unavoidable and inevitable vivifying condition of the other. There is between them a correlation as intimate as that of the basic notes in a musical chord . . . for their isolation leads to their weakness, and their failure to contribute to a common action inevitably leads them to wither and die.[70]

[67] "Cette consolation sainte, ce refuge assuré contre les chagrins et les peines"; "Lorsqu'on vient, en compagnie des grands artistes, se reposer des fatigues morales de la vie, loin des bruits discordants, des hommes et des luttes impies, on se prend à penser à ceux qui souffrent dans leur corps et dans l'intelligence, à ces déshérités pour lesquels il n'est pas de compensation, et, devenu meilleur par l'influence du beau, on rêve de charité et de justice." C. Brunier, "M. Eugène Delacroix. Peintures de la bibliothèque de la Chambre des députés," *D.P.* 10, no. 26 (30 January 1848).

[68] "Une émotion quelconque ne suffit pas . . . c'est précisément la loi de l'émotion qu'il s'agit de déterminer." Laverdant, "Salon de 1842," *Phal.*, 3d ser., 5 (3 April 1842): col. 651.

[69] Izalguier, "Loi de la corrélation," 112.

[70] "Car des deux choses L'UTILE et le BEAU, chacune est, de création divine, la condition vivifiante de l'autre, condition inéluctable et *sine qua NON*; car entre elles il y a une corrélation aussi intime qu'entre les notes élémentaires d'un accord musical . . . car leur isolement produit leur faiblesse, et de la non participation à l'activité d'ensemble résulte nécessairement leur dépérissement et leur mort." Ibid., 113.

Far from signifying an unreserved contempt for formal questions, Izalguier's hostility toward *l'art pour l'art*—"never was immorality brazened out so impudently"[71]—relates to his belief in the necessary interdependence of form and utility. His comments on the ideal correspondence between form and function derive from Fourierist identification of physical beauty with fulfillment of destination. Thus the portrayal of perfect form carries for Izalguier its own utility, the denial of which by formalist commentators excites his disapproval. His assertion of the fundamental identity of interest between formalism and *art social* is shared by Laverdant, who shows a more accommodating attitude toward *l'art pour l'art*, qualified by a belief in the doctrine's imperfect partiality. While acknowledging the utility inherent in the depiction and contemplation of beauty,[72] Laverdant qualifies such abstracted activities as *actions simples*, inferior in value to the more complex appeal to the senses and intellect found in art forms which unite the *beau* with the *bien*. Indiscriminate attraction toward beauty as an end in itself is thus regarded as a misconception of the fundamental identity of beauty with utility, summed up in the oft-quoted adage "beauty is the splendor of truth."

Any misgivings expressed over the validity of formalism are more than equaled in Fourierist aesthetics by rejection of utilitarianism. Though Victor Schoelcher and, to some extent, Charles Brunier share the language and perceptions of more orthodox adherents to *art social*, other Fourierist commentators judge overt didacticism and its proponents harshly. Both François Cantagrel and Louis Ménard express opposition to utilitarianism,[73] but it is Laverdant who mounts the most sustained repudiation of the values advanced in the republican press.

Laverdant expresses distaste for "writers of the Democratic school, advocates of the principle of interpretation,"[74] arguing that their inability to appreciate the potential social value of genres lacking explicit didactic overtones seriously restricts their capacity to acknowledge the possibility of art possessing any but the most literal-minded ethical value. The "incomplete theory of Moralism"[75] further stands accused of being inextricably bound up with a perspective on morality incompatible with the ethical liberation postulated by Fourier. An aesthetic endorsing art as a medium for the

[71] "Jamais immoralité ne s'afficha avec plus d'impudeur." Ibid., 112.

[72] In 1844, for example, Laverdant comments ("Salon de 1844," *D.P.* 2, no. 116 [25 April 1844]): "A lui [l'artiste] permis, jusqu'à un certain point, de copier au hasard le beau, de faire de l'art pour l'art dans les régions heureuses, puisque de son oeuvre résulte une jouissance quelconque. C'est toujours agir dans le sens de la destinée, qui est le bonheur."

[73] Ménard's most direct condemnation of utilitarianism is in "Salon de 1847," *D.P.* 8, no. 89 (14 April 1847).

[74] "Des écrivains de l'Ecole démocratique, promoteurs du principe de l'interprétation." Laverdant, "Salon de 1844," *D.P.* 2, no. 116 (25 April 1844).

[75] "Théorie incomplète du Moralisme." Laverdant, "Salon de 1843," *Phal.* (21 May 1843): col. 2307.

projection and dissemination of exemplary acts runs counter to Fourierist emphasis on happiness as the sole moral absolute, since it inhabits an ethical system still bound by prescriptive and—in Fourierist terms—oppressive notions of good and evil.[76]

This antimoralism, together with its aesthetic ramifications, is rooted in Fourier's philosophy of nature. His assertion of the fundamental goodness of all human passions, and his indictment of constraints on individual freedom, contrast sharply with the ethical position held by many radical thinkers. While Fourier and his followers imagine an ideal society as enjoying perfect, self-regulating moral equilibrium through the free play of the *économie passionnelle*, others on the left fail to associate social reformation with moral perfectibility. The function they ascribe to the artist is thus essentially directive in character, instilling socially desirable traits, discouraging deviancy, and eliciting support for government initiatives. Within Fourierist behavioral models, such functions would not only be redundant in a properly ordered society, their prescriptive connotations would seem positively harmful. Rather than teaching lessons and helping to modify comportment, art's function is related to promoting a state of harmony where the regulation of morality no longer has a meaningful role in social relations.[77]

Though certain analogies can be seen here with Saint-Simonian aspirations to eliminate coercion from social relations, significant differences nonetheless remain. Saint-Simonianism does not regard social transformation as bringing about an ontological revolution. For Fourier, coercion is redundant, since all potential conflict between individual and collectivity has been eradicated. By contrast, Saint-Simonianism stops short of such optimism, while arguing that the advisibility of governmental initiatives would be transparent to those enjoying full command over the powers of reason. For the others, the arts intervene as one means of eliminating social friction, eliciting universal acquiescence by an appeal to passion. Despite this ostensible repudiation of coercion, the more instrumental role conceived for the arts within certain Saint-Simonian currents retains some commitment to overt didacticism largely absent from Fourierist aesthetics. For Saint-Simon and his followers, the artist justifies his status through an ability to make precise and socially decisive interventions over particular issues, something quite foreign to Fourierist critics.

[76] Discriminating between the Fourierist position and traditional moralism, Laverdant writes: "On disait: 'Il faut rendre l'homme meilleur'; nous disons: 'Il s'agit de rendre l'homme heureux.' Et nous déclarons que le plus sûr et le seul moyen de rendre l'espèce humaine meilleure, c'est de la rendre d'abord plus heureuse." Laverdant, "Salon de 1844," *D.P.* 2, no. 116 (25 April 1844).

[77] See comments in A. Colin, "De la moralisation," *Le Nouveau Monde* (21 September 1839).

The pronounced ideological distinction between Fourierist libertarianism and the more centralized, directive notion of power pervading rival leftist philosophies underlines differences in attitude toward the social function of art. The interventionist role ascribed to the artist by a republican such as Decamps is replaced in Fourierist theory by a more abstracted notion of the pervasive social benefits accruing from the spectacle of natural harmony. Though not entirely usurping advocacy of thematic didacticism,[78] this aesthetic dominated Fourierist critical discussion in the 1840s and helped to project the group as extending an essentially unhindered freedom to the artist, contrasting with the more committed attitude demanded elsewhere on the left. The extent of this apparent freedom was limited, however. While elaborating a model capable of assimilating a broader range of aesthetic options and identifying socially beneficial elements in works containing no manifest social content, Fourierists were uncompromising in condemning images apparently inspired by exclusively formal preoccupations and lacking any explicit or unconscious social ramifications.[79]

The preoccupation with mechanisms of response to verbal and visual stimuli demonstrates the Fourierists' interest in elaborating a formal vocabulary whose effectiveness would be assured and whose attainment would ostensibly eliminate redundancies and herald an art amalgamating formal beauty with social force. Acceptance of such a vocabulary evidently compromises unrestrained creative independence and also attenuates notions of art as a source of unmediated *jouissance*. In a situation where the artist's work is modulated according to a functional conception of form and where response is conceived as blending aesthetic stimulation with social receptivity, the Fourierists' proclaimed libertarianism is evidently somewhat qualified. Not only is the artist limited in the range ultimately at his disposal, but the purpose to which his work contributes in stimulating certain attitudes and discouraging others dilutes any sense of unlimited emotional and instinctual autonomy in Fourierist society.

In pursuing the notion of the social influence of form, several Fourierist commentators went to some length in elaborating a complex series of analogies between pictorial structure and social meaning, thus following Izalguier's call for a *loi esthétique* capable of overcoming the disjuncture

[78] See, for example, Sabatier's definition of the "mission de l'art," *Salon de 1851*, 54.

[79] "Nous resterons indifférents à l'égard des artistes indifférents, à l'égard des hommes dont le coeur n'a pas de chants pieux pour la souffrance, pas d'hymnes pour le bonheur. . . . Vous nous vanterez telle oeuvre insouciante et sans idée, pour l'habilité du faire, pour le bien rendu des chairs, pour l'éclat et harmonie des couleurs: que nous importe! Pouvons-nous saluer de nos applaudissements un artiste auquel Dieu a donné la force et la puissance, et qui ne sait employer cette force et cette puissance qu'à des inutilités, au lieu de les consacrer au bonheur de ses semblables, à l'oeuvre du salut du monde!" Laverdant, "Salon de 1844," *D.P.* 2, no. 117 (26 April 1844).

between form and utility. In so doing, they drew upon Fourier's concept of nature and his system of analogies, evolving a pictorial vocabulary that conceives of form as having precise connotative value capable of being used with foreseeable consequences on the spectator.

Although attracting some interest among contemporaries, Fourier's legacy of the system of analogies remained largely unexploited by his disciples. With the exception of Alphonse Toussenel, whose *zoologie passionnelle*, developed on the basis of Fourier's ideas, ostensibly offered new insights into the natural world,[80] it is perhaps critical attempts to establish a codification of pictorial form on analogical foundations that provide the clearest extension of Fourier's speculations. Writing in 1841, the architectural journalist César Daly claimed that "the study of analogies between the physical and moral world offers the artist a precious source," arguing that their exploration would extend "the domain of symbolism in art and create an expressive language of great richness and variety, accessible to every century and to all peoples."[81] Baudet-Dulary points to this infallible, if enigmatic, relationship between the physical and moral spheres in his *Essai sur les harmonies physiologiques*, where he argues:

> If particular colors and shapes please us independently of any sense of their usefulness and without our understanding why, this is because they express analogies and relationships that are no less real for not yet being understood. There is always a moral idea in those things that are apparently freest of them.[82]

The pursuit of the precise mechanisms of visual analogy forms a recurrent theme in Fourierist aesthetics. Both Laverdant and Cantagrel speculate on the symbolic connotations of pictorial structure,[83] while color and synesthesia provoke considerable attention. In all of this, the image's internal

[80] Toussenel's work on the moral significance of animals and plants, set out in such studies as *L'Esprit des bêtes* (1847), led to his contributing a number of articles on still lifes and animal studies to Salon reviews published in *La Democratie pacifique* during the 1840s.

[81] "L'étude des analogies du monde physique et du monde moral offre une mine précieuse à l'artiste"; "le domaine de la symbolique dans l'art et créerait une langue d'une expression, d'une richesse et d'une variété immenses, compréhensible dans tous les siècles, à tous les peuples." C. Daly, "Monument de juillet élevé sur la Place de la Bastille," *Phal.*, 3d ser., 1 (5 February 1841): col. 270. Daly's article is reprinted from the *Revue générale de l'architecture et des travaux publics*, which he had founded in 1839. On Daly, see H. Lipstadt, *Architecte et ingénieur dans la presse: polémique, débat, conflit* (1980), 135–97, 233–91; R. Becherer, *Science plus Sentiment: César Daly's Formula for Modern Architecture* (1984); and M. Saboya, *Presse et architecture au XIXe siècle. César Daly et la 'Revue générale de l'architecture et des travaux publics'* (1991).

[82] "Si certaines couleurs, certaines formes nous plaisent indépendamment de toute idée d'utilité et sans que nous puissions rendre compte du pourquoi, c'est parce qu'elles expriment des analogies, des rapports, non encore compris, il est vrai, mais réels. Dans ce qui en paraît le plus dégagé, il y a toujours une idée morale." Baudet-Dulary, *Essai sur les harmonies*, 317.

[83] See Cantagrel's remarks on Gué's *Le Jugement dernier* in "Salon de 1841," *Phal.*, 3d ser., 3, no. 6 (14 May 1841): col. 90, and his application of Fourier's *géométrie passionnelle* in "Concours d'architecture," *D.P.* 3, no. 82 (20 September 1844).

ordering is judged according to criteria adapted from social analysis, with the moral connotations implicit in such language carrying the same weight as in its initial usage. Thus, in his critique of Delaroche's hemicycle at the Ecole des beaux-arts, Laverdant focuses on the work's lack of compositional unity, interpreting the passivity and isolation of the masters assembled in the frieze in terms of the atomized individualism characterizing contemporary society. In Delaroche's composition, "everyone lives within themselves and for themselves"; Laverdant reads the artist's failure to achieve a unified and coherent structure as symptomatic of the vitiated social environment in which he works.[84]

Laverdant amplifies this social analogy in applying Fourier's *série passionnelle* to compositional structure. The three *distributive*, or intellectual, passions are isolated as contributing the most fundamental ingredients to pictorial composition; their moral characteristics suggest certain figurative qualities whose balanced integration he deems essential to formal cohesion. The interplay of the three passions—*cabaliste* (cooperative or conspiratorial), *papillonne* (capricious, loving change), and *composite* (balancing the particular with the general)—allows the reconciliation of centrifugal and centripetal emotional tendencies in a harmonious social equipoise that incorporates the values of unity in diversity.[85] Successful pictorial composition is similarly identified with the judicious coordination of these three elements, which together ensure an aesthetic totality the internal harmony of which mirrors the equilibrium of an ideal social structure:

> All of the painter's work—the marriage and contrast of tones, the opposition and symmetry of groups and masses, the necessary variety of color, movement, and line, the organization and execution—in fact the entire pictorial work, depends on laws of *concord*, *discord*, and *variety*, on the coordination of elements within the painting according to the demand of the three passions known as *composite*, *cabalistic*, and *butterfly*.[86]

Failure to achieve such an effect leads to displeasing work which "is not amusing" in the same way as collective failure to satisfy the demands of the distributive passions produces a "society that is not amusing."[87]

This social analogy takes on further resonance through identification of

[84] "Chacun vit en soi-même et pour soi." D. Laverdant, "L'Assemblée des artistes par Paul Delaroche," *Phal.*, 3d. ser., 4 (29 December 1841): col. 854.

[85] For a discussion of *passions distributives*, see S. Debout's introduction to the *Théorie des quatre mouvements*, 44–47.

[86] "Tout le travail du peintre, mariage et contraste des tons, opposition et symétrie des groupes et des masses, variété nécessaire dans les couleurs, les mouvements et les lignes, ordonnance et exécution, toute l'oeuvre picturale enfin repose sur les lois de l'*accord*, du *discord* et de la *variété*, sur la co-ordination des éléments du tableau suivant les exigences des trois passions *composite*, *cabaliste* et *papillon*." Laverdant, *Salon de 1845*, 6.

[87] Ibid.

the act of aesthetic creation with principles underlying the form of the natural world as created by divine providence. Here again, the distributive passions give implicit theoretical underpinning to the conceptual analogies brought to bear. The three principles of composition advanced by Laverdant conflate divine attributes with each of the three passions in an analysis of the fundamental aspects of pictorial construction. Most important, Laverdant argues, a composition must be conceived as a coherent, harmoniously balanced whole. This principle, analogous to the *composite* in the distributive passions, he associates with the *universalité de providence* of divine power. The second law of composition, paralleling the *papillon* in its reconciliation of varied elements in a totalizing hierarchy, recalls the *justice distributive* of God. Finally, compositional clarity and avoidance of distracting detail, a function of the *cabaliste* passion, is likened to the *économie de ressorts* testified by divine creation. In drawing such analogies, Laverdant imagines the fabricated image as a microcosm of the natural world, operating according to the same principles and generated by similar impulsions. At its most perfect, therefore, the painting attains a formal harmony reminiscent of nature in a state of grace. Instinctively respecting the laws of divine creation, the artist becomes analogous to God, shaping in miniature a perfection that in actuality has been destroyed by man: "The artist has a recollection of heaven; he too is a creator and organizer; he shares divine faculties, and would be incapable of creating anything beautiful that failed to conform to the pattern of the work of God himself, since there is a unity in the laws of universal life."[88]

These compositional analogies take on further precision through reference to Fourier's *géometrie passionnelle*—the equation between particular passions and specific geometrical forms—which Laverdant contends allows the formulation of precise compositional rules for depicting various emotions.[89] A study of great art is advanced as infallible proof for the validity of Fourier's analogical systematization, and Laverdant argues for its extension into all areas of representation, remarking that "there must be as many types of disposition as there are types of passion and principal forms of grouping."[90] Although only Cantagrel matches this interest in the use of analogies

[88] "L'artiste se souvient du ciel; il est, lui aussi, créateur, organisateur; il participe aux facultés divines, et il ne saurait rien faire de beau qui ne soit conforme au type des oeuvres de Dieu lui-même, car il y a unité dans les lois de la vie universelle." Laverdant, "Salon de 1844," *D.P.* 2, no. 123 (2 May 1844); the analogy between the artist and God is drawn by Miget, "De la peinture," *Phal.* 1 (10 December 1836): col. 513.

[89] See Laverdant's analysis of Champmartin's *Christ aux enfants* in "Salon de 1844," *D.P.* 128 (7 May 1844). See also his application of *géométrie passionelle* as an analytical tool in his articles "Concours de sculpture. L'Eglise de St Vincent-de-Paul. M. Maréchal. M. Eugène Farochon," *D.P.* 3, no. 74 (12 September 1844), and "Envois de Rome."

[90] "Il devait y avoir autant de types généraux d'ordonnance qu'il y a de types passionnels et d'espèces principales de groupes." Laverdant, "Salon de 1844," *D.P.* 2, no. 128 (7 May 1844).

in practical problems of composition, other commentators expanded upon similar indications provided by Fourier. Victor Hennequin, for example, ostensibly under the influence of the *âme de la terre*, conjured up at spiritualist séances in the early 1850s, established a systematic table aligning each of the passions not only with a particular geometrical form, but also with specific colors and notes from the musical scale,[91] while the writer Léon Gozlan, an adherent to Fourierism in the 1840s, evokes the following correspondences: "For me, piety is a gentle blue, resignation pale grey, joy is apple green, satiety is the color of milky coffee, pleasure velvet pink; sleep is the color of tobacco smoke, thought is orange, pain is the color of soot, boredom is chocolate."[92]

Extrapolation of compositional rules founded on Fourier's analogies displays an attempt to overcome the antinomy of *forme* and *pensée* attacked by Izalguier. Such an initiative recalls Saint-Simonian efforts in *Le Livre nouveau* to develop a formal vocabulary capable of evoking a precise emotional response, and indeed echoes comparable ambitions nurtured by Buchezian commentators. Confirmation of the accuracy of these cardinal rules in the art of the past apparently demonstrates the degree to which they have been neglected by contemporary artists, stultified by academicism and isolated from nature by *civilisation*. Yet, though ostensibly underwritten by nature, this insistence on the infallibility of a set of formal principles extrapolated from Fourier's analogical investigations compromises assurances both of creative independence and of the wider freedoms to be enjoyed by the citizen in Societarian society. While the formulas offered as the bedrock of a rejuvenated artistic practice threaten to be as constrictive as any previous disciplining of the autonomous imagination, so their effect on the perceiving subject implies a channeling of desire incompatible with promises of instinctual liberation. The very aspiration to equip the artist with the means of manipulating—and even of conditioning—the emotional reflexes of his fellows presupposes a degree of affective alienation at odds with the unconstrained self-mastery Fourier's psychological theories apparently allow.

[91] See V. Hennequin to V. Considerant, 20 September 1853, Archives nationales, Paris, Archives sociétaires 10 AS 39(2). Hennequin published two doctrinal works, *Sauvons le genre humain* (1853) and *Religion* (1854), both apparently dictated by the "âme de la terre." He was committed to a mental asylum in 1854. See A. Erdan, *La France mystique* (1858), 2:163–73, and E. Nus, *Choses de l'autre monde* (1880), 135–40. Hennequin's list of analogies is founded on ideas already provided by Fourier; see B. Malon, *Histoire du socialisme* (1879), 115–17. Izalguier points to the artistic potential of this series of correspondences in "Loi de la corrélation," 125.

[92] "Pour moi, la piété est bleue tendre, la résignation gris perle, la joie est vert-pomme, la satiété est café au lait, le plaisir, rose velouté; le sommeil est fumée de tabac, la réflexion est orange, la douleur est couleur de suie, l'ennui est chocolat." Fragment dated 9 May 1849, reprinted in *L'Autographe* 1 (5 December 1863). Gozlan is listed as a supporter of the movement in the *Almanach social* (1840): 184–87.

Even in its most libertarian guise, therefore, radical philosophy conceals a bid to control the collective will beneath a proclaimed commitment to individual freedom.

If Fourier's analogies apparently provided the artist with a *loi esthétique*, they could also be vaunted as analytical tools capable of replacing subjective appreciation with a precise grammar of composition and form. In applying such a system, Laverdant thus responds to the calls made by Izalguier in 1836. Significantly, however, his theoretical pronouncements receive only limited practical application and compositional analysis tends to remain largely divorced from more general concerns. In one area, though, it is possible to discern greater critical consensus: Fourierist discussions of linearism versus colorism, which dovetail into perceptions of the contrasting significance of romantic and classical aesthetic principles, display a merging of formal and conceptual concerns operating within a framework drawn from Fourierist notions of harmony and passion.

LINE, COLOR, AND THE PRINCIPLES OF HARMONY

With the exception of Louis Ménard, Fourierist critics express an unqualified preference for colorism rooted in a doctrinal analogy between colorist composition and the harmonious unity of diverse elements. Within nature, harmony is said to result from the ambient effect of light, whose irradiation dissolves the contours that bound individual bodies and blends the varied colors of organic and inorganic forms in a perfect tonal consonance.[93]

The visual cohesion produced by light ostensibly acts in concert with an internal irradiation inherent in bodies whose energy generates an impalpable physical nimbus, attenuating outlines through the impulsions of its ectoplasmic force.[94] According to Laverdant, sensitivity to this irradiation distinguishes such exemplary colorists as Correggio, Murillo, and Rembrandt, whose formal superiority permits a spiritual penetration surpassing the mere transcription of external reality. Among contemporaries, Delacroix continues this tradition. Laverdant attributes popular disregard for his work to a general tendency to apprehend nature through the mediationof pictorial convention; Delacroix's more authentic rendition of atmospheric effect

[93] "Dans la réalité, la ligne du contour se modifie, se combine, se diversifie par tout ce qui l'enveloppe, la limite; par le fluide ambiant, par le mouvement qu'elle subit ou qu'elle communique, par cette réciprocité d'échanges qui vont, qui viennent d'un ton à un autre, d'un objet à un autre, d'un plan à un autre plan." Pelletan, "Salon de 1845," *D.P.* 4, no. 83 (24 March 1845).

[94] "Il y a en nous comme un second corps qui dépasse l'autre; c'est que l'être humain a un rayonnement à lui propre, et ces fluides irradiants sont sensibles même au travers des vêtements." Laverdant, *Salon de 1845*, 48.

breaks with this formalized vision, challenging spectatorial preconceptions. The artist's juxtaposition of contrasting colors—also identified in works by Troyon, Diaz, Géricault, and Gros—comes to signify not only an exemplary rendition of "the dramatic expression of atmosphere, the harmony between the painting's lighting effect and its subject,"[95] but also carries a crucial symbolic connotation. Pictorial representation of the harmony of nature gives palpable form to the fundamental natural—and social—law of unity in diversity; thus, in Delacroix's art, "every color, every nuance is carefully mixed, fused, and combined, so that at a distance there emerges from this confusion and variety a tonal unity which is truth itself."[96]

Like Baudelaire, Pelletan attributes the power of Delacroix's art to its mnemonic quality; rather than attempting a literal transcription of nature, the artist allows memory to strip away contingent detail, producing a peculiarly evocative sense of atmosphere, which embodies a perfect symmetry between form and compositional mood.[97] Thus the "dramatic tone" of the *Dernières Paroles de Marc-Aurèle*,[98] the "sharpness and brilliance" of the *Combat du Giaour*, and the "clear and laughing" atmosphere of the *Femmes d'Alger* all amplify the meaning of the works. In certain instances, atmosphere is interpreted as integral to dramatic effect, as in the Saint Denis *Piéta* where the desolate landscape intimates that "supernatural beings join in the boundless sorrow of Mary and the Magdalen."[99]

Although, like other critics, Fourierist commentators do express some misgivings over his *défauts*,[100] Delacroix nonetheless consistently emerges in their writings as the period's supreme artist. His standing demonstrates the degree to which the school's aesthetic philosophy allowed the abandonment of a strictly utilitarian position—though Laverdant does suggest that his shortcomings would vanish if he were to undertake such socially meaningful themes as "the abolition of poverty and the organization of world peace."[101] Yet it is primarily for his formal qualities that Delacroix wins

[95] "L'expression dramatique de l'atmosphère, l'harmonie entre l'effet lumineux et le sujet du tableau." Ibid., 50.

[96] "Toutes les couleurs, toutes les nuances sont mêlées, confondues, combinées savamment, et de cette confusion, de cette variété, résulte, à distance, l'unité de ton, la vérité même." Ibid., 49.

[97] Pelletan, "Salon de 1845," *D.P.* 4, no. 83 (24 March 1845). This notion has evident parallels with Baudelaire's concept of "l'art mnémonique" in *Le Peintre de la vie moderne*.

[98] "Drame du ton." Ibid.

[99] "Air . . . vif et ardent"; "limpide et riant"; "les êtres supramondains s'associent à la douleur immense de Marie et de Madeleine." Laverdant, *Salon de 1845*, 50 and 51.

[100] See ibid., 53, "Les Défauts du peintre"; Brunier ("Salon de 1846," *D.P.* 6, no. 88 bis [29 March 1846]) describes Delacroix as "cette grande individualité puissante et originale, mais incomplète et bizarre." Of Fourierist critics, only Lemarant in 1837 expresses fundamental reservations over his work: E. Lemarant, "Salon de 1837," *Phal.* 1 (20 March 1837): col. 845.

[101] "L'abolition du paupérisme et l'organisation de la paix du monde." Laverdant, *Salon de 1845*, 54.

praise. The analogical significance attached to color allowed the Fourierists to transform his entire technique into an implicit confirmation of a position the progressive ramifications of which extended far beyond the aesthetic domain. In 1845, Pelletan underlines this association in claiming that his art combines the tenebrism of Rembrandt with the harmony of Titian and the color of Veronese; he remarks on this stylistic reconciliation that "M. Delacroix, who has understood that the tendency of our era is to be comprehensive and synthetic, has developed in parallel all the strengths of other schools."[102]

In such a way, style is explicitly related to social consciousness. As an artist, Delacroix represents the vanguard of a movement overturning the idealized, antinaturalistic conception of *beauté* with a more vital and harmonious rendition of nature identified with *vie*. This *école de vie*, in its rehabilitation of the direct perception of nature over an aesthetic tradition wedded to the antique, represents one facet of "a magnificent palingenesis," of which social renovation provides the most important thrust.[103]

As an antithesis to this progressive tendency, linearity carries connotations of "immobility" and "absolute subjection to the past."[104] Whereas colorism expresses the innate harmony of nature, Fourierist critics associate line with a repudiation of natural organicism; the bounding contour—condemned as a mannerism learned from artistic tradition rather than through observation of perceived reality—violates harmony and leads to a fragmented and sterile rendition of form as an end in itself:

> If it is exclusively concerned with technique, art loses its greater sense of harmony, scarcely conceives of things as a whole, strays off in search of minutiae, and loses itself in detail with an unhealthy enthusiasm. This is the source of the special characteristic and essential fault of contemporary work—Mannerism.[105]

Within Laverdant's critical vocabulary, *mannerism* serves as the strongest term of condemnation. In the same way as *civilisation* has destroyed man's harmony with nature through disregard for its fundamental laws, so the mannerist's preoccupation with tradition and style induces a similar isolation.

Among contemporary artists, it is Ingres and his pupils who are most

[102] "M. Delacroix, qui a compris que la tendance de notre époque est d'être compréhensive et unitaire, a développé parallèlement tous les mérites des autres écoles." Pelletan, "Salon de 1845," *D.P.* 4, no. 83 (24 March 1845).

[103] "Une palingénésie magnifique." Ibid.

[104] "Immobilisme"; "la soumission absolue au passé." *D.P.* 4, no. 84 (25 March 1845).

[105] "L'art, exclusivement préoccupé du faire, perd le sentiment des grandes harmonies, conçoit à peine une ensemble, s'égare dans de recherches minutieuses, se perd dans le détail avec une ardeur maladive. De là vient le caractère particulier, le vice capital des oeuvres de notre temps, le Maniérisme." Laverdant, "Salon de 1842," *Phal.*, 3d ser., 5 (3 April 1842): col. 643.

frequently condemned for mannerism. Lehmann and Chassériau suffer repeated attacks—the latter in particular consistently attracts Laverdant's harshest critical strictures.[106] Similarly, the current of historical landscape associated with Paul Flandrin stands accused of having "bent nature to a discipline and regularity it does not possess."[107] Only Louis Ménard adopts a more sympathetic tone toward the Ingristes, a position determined by his preference for line as appealing to more ideated sentiments in the spectator. Regarding linearism as calling on "that higher register of feeling the idea of which is achieved only through meditation and reflection,"[108] he writes admiringly of Hippolyte Flandrin and Chassériau, and praises the Ingristes for having "rejected the seductions of color to devote themselves to the cult of ideal forms."[109] Significantly, Ménard's defense of the idealist tradition is accompanied by an elitist insistence on the intellectual character of art unique among Fourierist critics and a consistent contempt for what he regards as the debasement of contemporary production by populist tendencies.[110]

Ménard's admiration for such works as Flandrin's murals at Saint-Germain-des-Prés is also at odds with Fourierist attitudes toward stylistic archaism and its theoretical ramifications. In condemning the Ingristes for attempting to "restore the coarseness of primitive techniques,"[111] Laverdant rejects pre-Raphaelite revivalism as carrying unacceptable ideological implications. In the work of the Primitives, "the figures' stillness and stiffness . . . confirm man's subjection to matter";[112] as such, their style embodies both the theologically repressive tradition of the Old Testament and a politically repressive tradition associated, for example, with the Byzantine Empire. Rehabilitation of such masters as Fra Angelico and Cimabue, and renewed interest in "Byzantine daubings of the eleventh century," are interpreted as disquieting evidence of the reassertion of the puritan spirit, which

[106] On Lehmann see, for example, Lemarant, "Salon de 1837," *Phal.* (1 April 1837): col. 873. Amongst Laverdant's attacks on Chassériau see "Salon de 1842," *Phal.*, 3d ser., 5 (8 May 1842): col. 895, and "Salon de 1844," *D.P.* 2, no. 128 (7 May 1844).

[107] "Pli[é] la nature à une discipline et une régularité qu'elle n'observe pas." Pelletan, "Salon de 1845," *D.P.* 4, no. 111 (21 April 1845).

[108] "Cette région supérieure du sentiment de l'idée à laquelle on n'arrive que par la méditation et le recueillement." L. Ménard, "Peinture murale—M. Hippolyte Flandrin," *D.P.* 8, no. 131 (2 June 1847).

[109] "Repoussé[s] les séductions de la couleur pour se consacrer au culte des formes idéales." Ibid. For Ménard's assessments of Chassériau, see "Peinture murale—Mm. Chassériau et Delacroix," *D.P.* 9, no. 67 (17 September 1847).

[110] See, for example, his remarks on the proliferation of genre painting in "Peinture murale—M. Hippolyte Flandrin."

[111] "Renouveler la grossièreté des procédés primitifs." Laverdant, "Salon de 1842," *Phal.* (1 May 1842): col. 853.

[112] "La fixité et la raideur des figures . . . constatent l'asservissement de l'homme à la matière." Ibid., col. 859.

aims to discredit the celebration of physicality associated with such colorists as Titian, Correggio, and Rubens.[113]

In an analysis of Western art owing much to Saint-Simonian historiography, Miget traces the contemporary scission between formalism and utilitarianism to Christian roots. Within the early church, he argues, the assertion of "the law that mortifies the flesh, extinguishes the senses, stifles and represses the passions" gave rise to an art whose hieratic forms proclaimed spirituality at the expense of sensitivity toward "the spectacle of nature over which a veil of malediction was thrown."[114] Only in the transformed political and theological climate of the Renaissance was spirituality finally reconciled with the physical plenitude of nature, though such groups as the Ingristes and persistent debates concerning the primacy of *forme* over *pensée* demonstrate that a definitive synthesis is still to be achieved. Within this continuing polarization, linearity and archaism signify an antimaterialism inimical to Fourierist commitment to physicality as a fundamental attribute of *bonheur*. The ontological division between spirit and matter, embraced by both Saint-Simonians and Fourierists, together with their common ambition to transcend this historical antinomy, thus informs not only their conception of Western artistic tradition but further inflects critical preferences toward contemporary art. The division between color and line is inserted within a broader historical framework and imbued with moral implications, which receive direct application in assessing particular canvases in the Salon.

Parallel to this debate, and drawing upon the same theoretical premises, is a valorization of romantic *passion* over the discipline and reason exemplified by classicism. Sabatier, in particular, equates romantic preoccupations with the rehabilitation of human passion in Fourierist political philosophy. Whereas classicism stands for the suppression of instinct by reason, through a misguided commitment to self-mastery, romanticism is presented as an exploration—and vindication—of the full gamut of human emotion. As such, Delacroix stands as the instinctive harbinger of a new order, in whose work "passion is of the very essence,"[115] while romanticism denotes the repudiation of moral repression and man's reconciliation with the fundamental springs of human nature.[116]

113 "Les croûtes byzantins du lle siècle." *Phal.*, 3d ser., 5 (10 April 1842): cols. 694–95.

114 "La loi qui mortifie la chair, éteint les sens, étouffe et comprime les passions"; "le spectacle de la nature sur laquelle une voile de malédiction était jetté." Miget, "De la peinture," *Phal.* 1 (20 December 1836): col. 548.

115 "La passion est l'essence même." Sabatier, *Salon de 1851*, 64.

116 "Dans son amour aveugle pour les passions extrêmes, à force de chercher des phénomènes psychologiques nouveaux, le romantisme est entré dans l'analyse de l'âme et a fait faire un grand pas à la connaissance de l'homme. L'incompressibilité, l'excellence même des passions est ressortie clairement de cette étude; des gens se sont pris à douter à leur insu de cette loi sociale qui ne pouvait se concilier avec elles, et faisait tourner les plus nobles et les plus légitimes en autant de sources de malheur. . . . Le romantisme a été aussi un instrument de révolution

This rehabilitation of passion allows romanticism to be represented as a paradigm of the artistic enterprise, embodying the distinctive characteristics of the creative personality. Here again, close similarities with Saint-Simonian typology appear, both in the value ascribed to romanticism within the broader historical process and in the conception of the artist's emotional attributes. Yet if Saint-Simonianism sees these as capable of reconciling divergent characterial groupings in a progressive social equilibrium, the centrality of passion as a universal, if repressed, human impulse in Fourierist thought elevates the artist into a portent of the human personality liberated from the constraints of *civilisation*.

This promotion of passion has broad implications for perspectives on subject matter, notably as regards religious themes and history painting. In line with his distinction between the repressive ideology of the Old Testament and the humanitarian teachings of Christ, Laverdant discriminates between scenes of divine wrath punishing human transgression and the representation of happiness through the unconstrained liberation of passion.[117] Accordingly, his conception of religious painting rests more on the emotions portrayed than on any explicitly sacred subject—thus, in 1844, Dedreux's *Cheval abandonné sur le champ de bataille* can be embraced within the religious category.[118] The concept of passion plays an equally decisive role in Laverdant's attitude toward history painting and contemporaneity. While rejecting academic elevation of the past as a matter of principle, he counsels a broad eclecticism, defining contemporaneity less in terms of setting than in the relevance of the passions portrayed. He advises the history painter: "Faithfully reproduce passionate feelings, active life, and, beneath whatever the costume, show us the living body and the heart with its sufferings, ambitions, and radiant pleasures. In such a way, you will always produce historical painting."[119]

Laverdant attributes republican critics' emphasis on modernity to the movement's political naïveté, where "the problem of social reform remains on the surface of things."[120] In the same way as republican political aspirations stop short at superficial tinkering with the system, so their artistic *parti pris* over contemporaneity is condemned as similarly cosmetic. Laverdant

---

sociale." Ibid., 63. By contrast, Izalguier regards the introverted concerns of romanticism as symptomatic of the repression of passion in contemporary society; "Loi de la corrélation," 146.

117 See his remarks in "Salon de 1842," *Phal.* 3d ser., 5 (24 April 1842): cols. 787–88.

118 Laverdant, "Salon de 1844," *D.P.* 2, no. 120 (29 April 1844).

119 "Retracez avec fidélité les mouvements passionnés, la vie active et, sous l'habit, quel qu'il soit, montrez-nous le corps vivant, le coeur dans ses souffrances, ses aspirations et ses jouissances rayonnantes. Ainsi vous ferez toujours de la peinture historique." Laverdant, "Salon de 1842," *Phal.* 3d ser., 5 (17 April 1842): col. 746.

120 "Le problème de la réforme sociale tient à la surface des choses." *Phal.* 3d ser., 5 (10 April 1842): col. 691.

follows Miget's assertion that "man, organized in the same way irrespective of time or place, feels, thinks, and acts under the same conditions" in claiming that "man is the same in every age."[121] This notion of transcendent human essence, which obviates the need for contemporaneity, underlies the Fourierists' more far-reaching political program and is predicated on an analysis of the passions as human constants surviving the vagaries of historical change. Within such a problematic, consciousness is contingent on social formation only to the degree that social forces form ideology and deform innate potentialities. Such potentialities—and, in a "critical" context the past abuses they have suffered—furnish the subject for the history painter, while their liberation under a harmonious *économie passionnelle* is the object of Fourierist social transformation.

Fourierist critics regard the suppression of *passion* by *civilisation* as fundamentally debilitating for the arts: not only is their potentially revivifying effect denied to the spectator, but social and institutional limitations frustrate realization of the artist's passionate nature, spawning either arid academicism or introverted individualism. Appealing to an audience whose emotions have been systematically suppressed, and denied any profound insight into the mechanisms of *passion*, the artist produces work in an affective void, while the public responds in a tentative and confused fashion: "One is moved, without knowing why, how, or to what ends."[122] Laverdant's persistent irritation at Salon exhibits "thoroughly lacking in specific expression"[123] is fired by an insistence on the need for art to elicit a specific emotional response. Yet the achievement of such a response eludes the artist because of his inability to manipulate passion through an ignorance of its authentic nature. [124]

As an underlying factor in this sterility, commentators again have recourse to Fourier's notion of *économie passionnelle* and its apparent abuse in current social practice and institutions. In the arts, critics diagnose a damaging polarity between the complementary passions of *favoritisme* and *unitéisme* (or individualism, conceived in a positive sense, and the associative instinct). On the one hand, academicism represents a travesty of the associative spirit, while on the other, individualism has degenerated into isolated introspec-

121 "L'homme, organisé de même partout et dans tous les temps, sent, pense, agit sous les mêmes conditions"; "l'homme à toutes les époques est le même." Miget, "De la peinture," *Phal.* 1 (20 December 1836): col. 551, and Laverdant, "Salon de 1842," *Phal.*, 3d ser., 5 (10 April 1842): col. 691.

122 "On est ému, mais on ne sait ni pourquoi, ni comment, ni à quoi bon." Delrieu, "Du désordre dans la peinture," col. 195.

123 "Absolument dénuées de toute expression déterminée." Laverdant, *Salon de 1845*, 23.

124 Izalguier blames this situation for the prevalence of meritricious and misguided work: "Ne pouvant remplir leur rôle d'expansion réelle, [les artistes] se refoulent en des expansions fictives; offrant à l'humanité pour la distraire de ses souffrances, des tableaux illusoires de passion, de bonheur, d'harmonie, faisant écho à ses plaintes, à ses désirs, à ses espérances, trop souvent à ses fureurs." Izalguier, "Loi de la corrélation," 146.

tion. The meaninglessness of much contemporary art and the artist's social isolation are blamed on this debilitating scission, which gives rise either to academic mannerism or formalist solipsism.

Fourierist responses to artistic individualism are far from clear-cut. Izalguier, who regards individualism as a primary cause for the emergence of *l'art pour l'art*, associates such egocentricity with broader fragmentation in a society where "each individual abstracts himself from the social whole, draws up a private circle, [and] poses questions unattached to any outside consideration."[125] Though early commentators are particularly scathing at the artist's abnegation of social responsibility,[126] the pluralism consequent on individual experimentation could be more positively interpreted as a prelude to a historical sea change in which society would no longer repress instinct. From such a perspective, individualist tendencies in contemporary art were often understood as presaging positive social transformation. Thus Considerant welcomes the abandonment of "conventionalized beauties" in literature as an assertion of independent thought and individual imagination,[127] while Sabatier regards individualist currents as a necessary prelude to association, allowing the artist to explore the full range of personal potential.[128]

By asserting individual creative instinct, and favoring direct observation of nature over deference to artistic tradition, romanticism finds itself assimilated into this process. In applauding the movement's rejection of mannerism, Laverdant extols individual inspiration, advising artists "above all, be yourself,"[129] and tries to dispel fears that Fourierist theory restricts creative freedom:

> Artists, do not presume that our doctrines contain any idea that could disturb your free and independent spirit. Despite the inadequacy of our words, if you have understood our thought, if you have responded to the feeling in our heart, you must already realize that in our New World your freedom will not be restrained nor your soul oppressed; we will always speak to you of Charity, Hope, and Faith.[130]

[125] "Chacun s'abstrait du *tout* social, se fait un cercle individuel, [et] se pose des problèmes indépendants de toute considération extérieure." Ibid., 112.

[126] See A. de la Tour du Pin, "Sur la position qu'ont prise depuis la révolution de juillet les savants et les littérateurs français," *Le Phalanstère* 1 (1832): 176.

[127] "Les beautés conventionnelles." V. Considerant, "Des tendances actuelles de la littérature," *Le Phalanstère* 2 (8 January 1833): 62.

[128] See Sabatier, *Salon de 1851*, 7. But see also his more negative remarks in ibid., 55.

[129] "Avant tout soyez vous-mêmes." Laverdant, "Salon de 1846," 566.

[130] "Artistes, ne cherchez pas dans nos doctrines une idée qui puisse inquiéter votre génie libre et indépendant. Sous la faiblesse de notre parole, si vous avez compris notre pensée, si vous avez entendu le sentiment de nos coeurs, vous devez savoir déjà que, dans notre Nouveau Monde, votre essor ne sera point gênée ni votre âme opprimée; nous vous parlerons toujours de Charité, d'Espérance et de Foi." Laverdant, *Salon de 1845*, 22.

This qualified attitude, while partially echoing Saint-Simonian critiques of contemporary artistic fragmentation, nonetheless highlights sympathy toward individualism derived from Fourierist psychological theory. What is being attacked by critics such as Izalguier in his repudiation of formalism is not so much individualism per se as the damaging tendencies perceived in contemporary art resulting from a collective imbalance where individual propensities work against, rather than in concert with, society itself. As a fundamental tenet of Fourierist doctrine, the fulfillment of individual desire is essential to social harmony. As such, guarantees of artistic liberty have a theoretical consonance—and thus a credibility—far greater than pledges made by Saint-Simonian commentators.

Regard for individualism informs distaste for the institutional and pedagogical structures reinforcing aesthetic orthodoxy. Within Fourierist discourse, the influence of the Académie and the atelier system represents a debilitating parody of the values of *unitéisme*, securing cohesion through proscriptive dictates rather than any measured coordination of diverse talents.[131] Misgivings over training methods most frequently recur in relation to the Ecole des beaux-arts and the Ecole de Rome, institutions in which the individual voice is encouraged to "efface itself completely."[132] The very notion of learning artistic skills through a transmitted body of rules entirely contravenes the doctrine's psychological theories and its conception of education.[133] While Fourier founds his educational system on *attraction passionnelle*—the unconstrained fulfillment of individual propensities—academic teaching exemplifies *civilisation*'s despotic regimentation of personality.

Such disaffection is in tune with Fourierist misgivings over the state of modern art, though their attitudes are not as comprehensively dismissive as among other advocates of *art social*. Landscape painting and currents within romanticism encourage some optimism, while both Ménard and Brunier explicitly justify their belief in the superiority of modern art through reference to the doctrine of perfectibility.[134] Yet this optimism is heavily outweighed by a more sober diagnosis that rests on an appreciation of the profound structural flaws within present-day society and their impact on cultural life. Social and artistic concerns thus intersect in critiques of the inadequacies in contemporary production. Analysis of these perceived fail-

[131] See C. Brunier and Monchovet, "Beaux-Arts. Considérations générales," *D.P.* 6, no. 38 (7 February 1846).

[132] "S'effacer absolument." D. Laverdant, "Concours de peinture," *D.P.* 3, no. 88 (26 September 1844). See also, on Ingres's domination of students such as Flandrin, E. d'Izalguier, "Exposition des envois de l'Ecole de Rome," *Phal.* 1 (1 September 1836): cols. 197–98.

[133] On educational theory, see D. Zeldin, *The Educational Ideas of Charles Fourier (1772–1837)* (1969).

[134] See Ménard, "Peinture murale—M. Hippolyte Flandrin," *D.P.* (2 June 1847), and C. Brunier, "Beaux-Arts," *D.P.* 9, no. 105 (31 October 1847).

ings, seen in the light of the alternative critical modes advanced by Fourierist commentators, provides some insight into the group's vision of the articulation between the social and the aesthetic under a Societarian regime.

THE FAILINGS OF ART AND THE TASK OF THE CRITIC

The elements in the group's diagnosis of the state of culture are already familiar, their litany of the symptoms and origins of artistic malaise broadly echoing attitudes expressed by the Saint-Simonians and by many republican critics. In common with them, Fourierist commentators relate artistic sterility to the disorientation of the contemporary world. In a society "without beliefs or faith," artists have become confused and marginalized, "given over to the fatal and chaotic risks of a changing world, having no other guide than fantasy—in other words, individual spontaneity."[135] The artist is thus portrayed as a victim of a social system that "misdirects impulses, paralyzes progressive tendencies,"[136] and prevents the arts from realizing their true potential.

From such a perspective, the Salon becomes a microcosm of the outside world, blighted by the same "failure of order and classification, the same lack of regularity."[137] Like the Saint-Simonians, Fourierist commentators argue that the disintegration of shared systems of belief prevents the artist from articulating ideas possessing any broad social resonance.[138] Yet the corollary drawn from this argument by Saint-Simonian commentators, with their condemnation of the indulgence and elitism of contemporary art as appealing to *oisifs*, is only rarely voiced in the Fourierist press. Significantly, it is in *Le Nouveau Monde*, the journal founded in 1839 by Gatti de Gamond and Jean Czynski as a means of proselytizing to the working class, that such ideas receive most explicit expression. Though the journal largely ignores cultural matters as irrelevant to their intended readership, the sculptor Arthur Guillot did contribute two articles on the present sterility and future possibilities

[135] "Livrés aux chances fatales de ce chaos d'un monde qui se transforme, n'ayant guère d'autre boussole que la fantaisie, c'est-à-dire la spontanéité individuelle." Edouard de Pompéry, "Le Salon de 1843," *La Revue synthétique* 2 (1843): 172. See also Guillemon, "Sur un caractère de notre époque: ambition et ennui," *Le Phalanstère* 1 (1832): 96–97.

[136] "Fausse les essors, paralyse les tendances progressives." C. Brunier, "Beaux-Arts," *D.P.* 6, no. 69 (10 March 1846).

[137] "Défaut d'ordre et de classement, la même absence de régularité." Cantagrel, "Salon de 1841," *Phal.*, 3d ser., 2, no. 39 (31 March 1841): col. 635.

[138] "Il n'y a véritablement pas de sujet pour la peinture. Il n'y a pas de sujet, parce qu'il n'y a pas de croyance vivante commune, pas de passion collective avec laquelle le peintre puisse se mettre en contact, par laquelle il puisse aller saisir, élever les imaginations des spectateurs." Pelletan, "Salon de 1845," *D.P.* 4, no. 97 (7 April 1845).

of the visual arts. Here, he attacks the arts' status as luxury goods, accessible only to those who "enjoy a certain ease," and denied to "the man who survives by his labor." Given such disparity, together with the more fundamental injustices in contemporary society, Guillot maintains that art's position has become untenable: "In our current malaise, our way of using [art] seems, despite ourselves, almost an insult to the misery of the poor."[139]

The chaos and injustices of the market form a central theme in Fourierist discourse and gave rise to a number of concrete initiatives for reform. Although relatively commonplace in contemporary criticism, the appearance of such proposals takes on an added dimension in Fourierist writings through their integration within the movement's broader program, with its advocacy of collective associations as an alternative to capitalist exploitation.[140] Support for institutional change draws upon a doctrinal critique of the oppressive hierarchy of labor in contemporary society and a belief in *travail attrayant*, where every individual engages in forms of work suited to his tastes and aptitudes. Institutional reform feeds into this movement, liberating the artist from commercial pressures and overcoming the debilitating isolation in which he currently works. Such change thus becomes a precondition to art fulfilling its social potential.[141]

To this end, the Fourierists sponsored a number of initiatives to rectify shortcomings in artistic education and administration. Experiments in tuitional reform pioneered at the Ecole royale du dessin during the 1840s by Horace Lecoq de Boisbaudran drew on Fourier's exploration of mnemonics and notions of *travail attrayant* to foster a spontaneous perception of nature ostensibly unmediated by extraneous cultural reference. Inspired by a desire to promote the decorative arts through the union of art and industry, Lecoq's association of a refined visual memory with an enhanced understanding of nature implicitly positions artistic education within a broader agenda carrying ultimately political ramifications.[142] More predictably, per-

[139] "Possesseur[s] d'une certaine aisance"; "l'homme qui vit de son travail"; "Dans l'état de marasme où nous sommes, notre manière d'employer [l'art] se trouve être, malgré nous, presque une insulte à la misère du pauvre." A. Guillot, "Des arts dans la société présente," *Le Nouveau Monde* (1 September 1839).

[140] Such initiatives as the cooperative Boulangerie véridique were founded before 1848, though the school was most active in launching associative schemes—among such diverse professions as tailors, doctors, butchers, carpenters, and architects—under the Second Republic; see A. Chabosseau, *De Babeuf à la Commune* (1911), 38–39.

[141] See J. Lechevalier, "Questions politiques dans l'intérêt de l'art et des artistes," *Revue du progrès social* 1 (May 1834): 454.

[142] Published in 1848 by the Fourierists' own press—the Librairie phalanstérienne—Lecoq de Boisbaudran's *Education de la mémoire pittoresque* carried Considerant's endorsement. On memory, see p. 4; on spontaneity in tuition, see p. 6; on the unmediated perception of nature, see pp. 13–14. Lecoq also contributed an article, "Prélude à l'unité religieuse," *D.P.* 8, no. 93 (18 April 1847), subsequently reissued in pamphlet form.

haps, administrative reform was a topic repeatedly broached by Fourierist commentators. Both Brunier and Pelletan outlined schemes for bypassing the Salon through a permanent exhibition sponsored by an independent artists' association,[143] while the alliance between architects and engineers provided one of the guiding principles for Daly's *Revue générale de l'architecture et des travaux publics*.[144] In March 1843 Pelletan presented a paper on alternatives to the Salon at a meeting of artists held in the offices of *La Phalange*;[145] five years later, under the Second Republic, the Fourierist composer and music critic Allyre Bureau worked for the foundation of a musicians' cooperative, and the school played a leading role in convening a meeting at the Salle Valentino to establish an association of artists.[146]

Such initiatives were seen only as a prelude to a broader reorientation of artists' working practices. Participative work was counseled as fulfilling Fourier's principle of *travail attrayant* and as a means of rejuvenating monumental art. In this context, a number of Fourierist critics were sympathetic to the concept of "schools" of artists, working under the beneficent guidance of an acknowledged master. This ideal departed from contemporary studio practice in emphasizing participative labor on quasi-medieval lines: instead of disciplining individual creativity through dogmatic training, the master was to work with his pupils, orchestrating their efforts in ambitious large-scale projects.[147] More far-reaching, in an *Appel aux artistes* issued in 1850, Joseph Brémond (de Guérin) outlined a radical realignment of working methods and economic relations focusing on the establishment of a network of "Artistères."[148] Prototypical cultural centers facilitating broad popular access, the Artistères spearhead Brémond's scheme for securing social regeneration through an appeal to the imagination. At the heart of

[143] See Pelletan, "Salon de 1845," *D.P.* 4, no. 75 (16 March 1845), and Brunier, "Beaux-Arts," *D.P.* 6, no. 69 (10 March 1846). See also the Ménards' endorsement of Clément de Ris's scheme for a permanent exhibition in "Salon de 1847," *D.P.* 8, no. 67 (19 March 1847), and Breton's proposals for a decentralized selection scheme for the Salon set out in Cantagrel, "Salon de 1841," *Phal.*, 3d series, 2, no. 39 (31 March 1841): cols. 640–42.

[144] See Daly's "Prospectus" in the *Revue générale de l'architecture et des travaux publics* 1 (1840): cols. 2–3.

[145] See the account in A. Fillioux, "Salon de 1843," *La Revue critique* (23 March 1843): 37.

[146] See A. Bureau, *L'Art dans la République. Aux artistes musiciens* (1848), and G. Rey, *Le Fouriériste Allyre Bureau (1810–1859)* (1962), 197–210. On the Salle Valentino meeting, see J. Ziegler, "Des sociétés en général et de la Société héliographique en particulier," *La Lumière* 1, no. 1 (9 February 1851): 3.

[147] For advocacy of monumental art, see, for example, A. Meray, "Un Rêve d'harmonie dans l'atelier de M. Ottin," *D.P.* 15, no. 131 (13 May 1850).

[148] J. Brémond (de Guérin), *Appel aux artistes. Rénovation sociale par les arts* (1850). Though no explicit reference is made to Fourier, the tenor of Brémond's ideas is predominantly Fourierist in tone. The author of a guide to French participles in 1837, Brémond's identity remains a mystery. A promised sequel, on the organization of a "Société artistérienne" and the foundation of an "Artistère," failed to appear.

these palatial institutions, comprising a series of amphitheaters, libraries, exhibition halls, commercial galleries, and *jardins d'hiver*, Brémond envisages workshops for artists and intellectuals, in which collective projects will flourish and "an artistic flowering will develop, as great as the world that it must decorate with its works."[149]

In proposing that the various artistic professions unite their efforts, Fourierist critics advanced a system of work appropriate for decorating the public spaces of the Phalanstère. Cooperative labor not only provides the resources for such ambitious undertakings but also enhances quality through the collaboration of diverse talents:

> I am convinced that from the moment when a few artists of goodwill and differing attitudes get together to work, attempt an enterprise in which emulation redoubles each participant's talents, and common supervision corrects individual defects, then the results would surpass expectations. . . . The transition from individual to collective painting will bring about an immense revolution. But when?[150]

From all of this it is clear that the Fourierists accord the artist a vital role in society. Yet in the absence of any clear division of forces within that society—such as the Saint-Simonians established through their tripartite distinction between *artistes*, *savants*, and *industriels*—the precise articulation between the artist and the surrounding world remains unclear. Although hints of such a division, and such characteristically Saint-Simonian terms as *sacerdoce*, occasionally appear,[151] the more fluid conception of society implicit in Fourierist thought prevents such categorical distinctions from emerging.

The implications of such guiding principles as *économie passionnelle* and *travail attrayant* abolish strict functional demarcation in future society, encouraging a chameleon-like obedience to instinct, rather than any more regimented insertion within an organized hierarchy. The professional distinctions upholding art as a discrete activity are attenuated, and creative impulses within the population as a whole are encouraged to bloom. Yet the artistic temperament is nonetheless identifiable through certain characteristics—the dominance of *passion*, for example—whose primacy

[149] "L'essor artistique se développera, immense comme le monde qu'il doit embellir de ses oeuvres." Ibid., 15.

[150] "Je suis convaincu que du moment où quelques artistes de bonne volonté, d'attitudes diverses, se mettraient un jour à l'oeuvre, essaieraient un travail où l'émulation viendrait doubler les forces de chacun, la surveillance commune rectifierait les erreurs individuelles, le résultat dépasserait les espérances. . . . Le passage de la peinture individuelle à la peinture collective amènera une immense révolution. Mais quand?" Pelletan, "Salon de 1845," *D.P.* 4, no. 111 (21 April 1845).

[151] See, for example, Miget, "De la peinture," *Phal.* 1 (20 December 1836): col. 545.

will incline individuals toward certain directions. Within this schema, artists assume three distinctive though overlapping roles: a barometer of the prevailing ideological climate, they simultaneously prefigure the emergence of shifts within society, while facilitating the achievement of change through their inspiring effect. Certain texts emphasize differing elements in this equation—in some instances, the arts seem predominantly passive, simply mirroring currents in the contemporary world, yet typically this etiological function is supplemented by a sensitivity to progressive trends still nascent in society. Thus Sabatier can reconcile the reflexive and the predictive by seeing art as part of a historical present which holds within itself the seeds of future growth:

> Art is the expression of the moral and intellectual development of nations. Everything in nature interconnects: the present is always *pregnant* with the future. We, who see prophetic signs in every aspect of the present day, can and must discover in art symptoms of the event which we await—the birth of a new world. It will often give us a much truer sense of a period than any number of mighty tomes of so-called political economy. As is a people, so will be its art.[152]

Given art's innate tendency to reveal progressive shifts within society, the Fourierists stress the need to sharpen artists' consciousness, and to transform their implicit receptivity to advanced ideas into explicit endorsement. Laverdant sees art as a natural ally of the Fourierist movement through its traditionally meliorist sympathies—"divine art has always guided humanity toward the eternal light, toward the very sources of happiness."[153] Both he and La Tour du Pin call upon artists to form an "avant-garde," in the socially progressive sense mooted by the Saint-Simonians, with the former appealing for a "sacred battalion, made up of the elite" from the intellectual classes to serve as an "avant-garde and . . . rallying point."[154]

On an immediate level, harnessing this potential force is associated with converting artists to the movement itself, and exhortations regularly punctuate Fourierist commentary. Yet, unlike many Saint-Simonian and republi-

[152] "L'art est l'expression du développement intellectuel et moral des nations. Tout se tient dans la nature: le présent est toujours *gros* de l'avenir; et nous qui voyons dans tous les faits contemporains des signes précurseurs de la rénovation sociale, nous pouvons et devons trouver dans l'art des symptômes de l'événement que nous attendons; la naissance du monde nouveau. Il nous donnera souvent une idée plus vraie d'une époque que bien des gros livres d'économie soi-disant politique. Tel art, tel peuple." Sabatier, *Salon de 1851*, vi.

[153] "L'art divin guida toujours l'humanité vers l'éternelle lumière, vers les sources mêmes du bonheur." Laverdant, "L'Art et sa mission," *D.P.* 1, no. 2 (2 August 1843); see also, for example, the notion of artists as "les sublimes révélateurs, les chercheurs d'harmonie" in Brunier, "M. Eugène Delacroix."

[154] "Bataillon sacré, formé de tous les gens d'élite"; "avant-garde et . . . centre de ralliement." La Tour du Pin, "Sur la position," 176. Laverdant identifies the artist as a prophet who should be "bien à l'avant-garde" in *Salon de 1845*, 4.

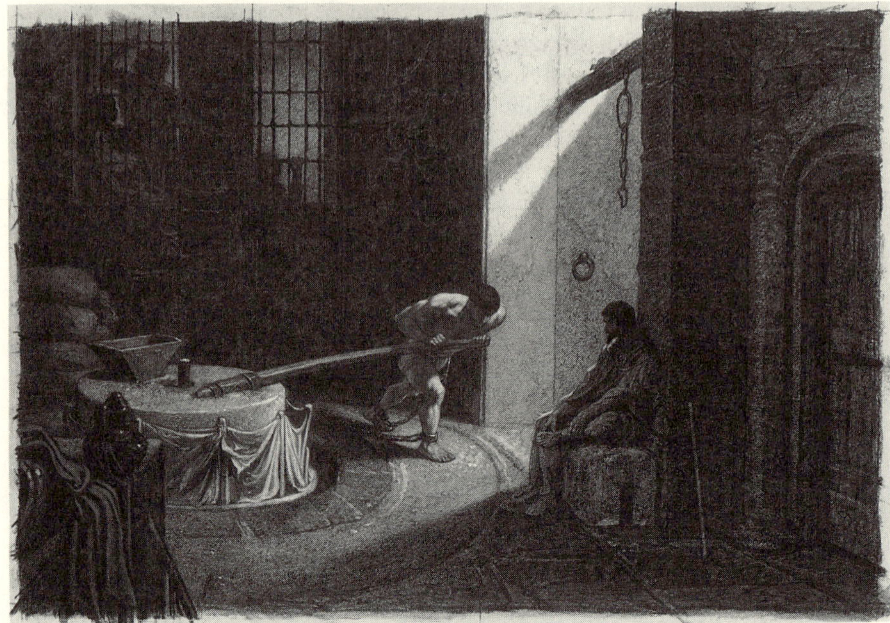

Plate 23. Alexandre-Gabriel Decamps: *Samson tournant la meule,* Salon of 1845. Musée des beaux-arts, Lyons.

can critics, the group appears less concerned with propagating explicitly doctrinal or socially conscious works than with fostering an attitude toward art consonant with the ambitions of the movement itself. This relatively undogmatic approach relates on one level to a critical flexibility toward artistic intentionality. The breadth invested in such notions as "prophetic" and "critical" art, and the elaboration of tools for the political interpretation of style, allow a critic such as Laverdant to escape any restrictive notion of *art social* and to read meanings off from works whose implicit presence apparently owes more to the emotional complexion of the artist than to any conscious *parti pris.*[155] This involves the critic in a process of thematic extrapolation or metaphoric interpretation, as in Pelletan's reading of Decamps's *Samson at the wheel* (plate 23) as an allegory of working-class sufferings.[156]

155 Thus Laverdant argues that Léopold Robert's ostensible intuition of *travail attrayant* originates in characterial disposition, rather than overt doctrinal sympathy: "Robert avait l'âme haute, naive, généreuse, et son inspiration a concordé avec les calculs du penseur," *Salon de 1845*, 17.

156 Pelletan, "Salon de 1845," *D.P.* 4, no. 84 (25 March 1845). See also Laverdant on the same artist's *Sortie d'école*, in "Salon de 1842," *Phal.*, 3d ser., 5 (8 May 1842): col. 900. By contrast, the Ménards reject any departure from the consideration of artistic intentionality; see "Salon de 1847," *D.P.* 8, no. 67 (19 March 1847). For a similar strategy in the republican

Rather than making utility dependent on the artist's explicit endorsement of a particular ideology, the Fourierists thus tend to see the progressive potential of his work arising out of his innate propensities. A harmonious personality and a perception unclouded by academicism predispose him toward a vision of nature inherently compatible with Fourierist teaching. Though recommending certain themes relating to precise doctrinal concerns, figures such as Laverdant lay greater emphasis on artistic spontaneity and receptivity to nature.[157] In encouraging such an attitude, Fourierist critics thus uphold their mentor's insistence on instinctual freedom while elaborating a conceptual apparatus capable of opening up broad areas of contemporary production to a politically progressive interpretation. With theories of pictorial construction and analogies, the movement ostensibly reconciles radical commitment with a high degree of artistic independence: the exploitation of such formal devices apparently allows the artist to harness his work for social change while continuing within the traditional repertoire of subjects.

The latitude offered to the artist within Fourierist aesthetics places considerable emphasis on the critic. As a theoretician and observer, he takes on the crucial role both of refining a set of practical principles aimed at enhancing the emotional force of art and of extrapolating conceptual trends from the diversity of contemporary production. Fourierist commentators largely agree on the gravity of the critic's task and on his responsibility to develop a *loi esthétique* capable of effectively articulating with the *loi sociale*. Such a process involved the elaboration of a *science*, a set of objective criteria to supersede the impressionistic subjectivity of current writing. A critical *science* hence opens up a collaborative role for the commentator, who offers the artist practical advice while generating a more responsive and socially alert attitude among his public.[158] Drawing upon an objectively constituted body of theory, the Fourierist critic thus presents himself as drawing out meanings or discerning trends obscure to the artist himself. In fulfilling such a function, he enlightens the artist and amplifies his progressive commitment.[159]

This *science* of forms draws sustenance from an apparently irrefutable

---

press, see the reading of Delaroche's *Jane Grey* as an allegory of Russian oppression in Poland or the destruction of art by materialism in T[horé?], "L'Art," *Le Polonais* 5 (December 1835): 362–63.

[157] "Laissez-vous aller librement, naïvement, au sentiment intime et pur de l'âme, et la leçon juste et féconde va s'imprimer par elle-même sur votre toile, parce qu'il y a une harmonie essentielle entre l'attrait de votre âme et la destinée vraie." Laverdant, *Salon de 1845*, 17.

[158] See E. d'Izalguier, "De la critique dans les oeuvres d'art," *Phal.* 1 (10 August 1836): cols. 130–31.

[159] "C'est . . . à la science, à la critique qu'il appartient de découvrir le sens profond dans l'oeuvre de l'artiste, et de lui signaler de plus en plus clairement le but vers lequel il est poussé par l'instinct du génie, le but auquel il doit tendre avec énergie." Laverdant, "L'Art et sa mission."

science sociale, facilitating the development of an art in perfect accord with the emotional needs of the individual and the collectivity. The group's scientistic ambitions fuel a desire to clarify aesthetic vocabulary and to systematize the classification of the arts. Thus Laverdant attempts to elaborate a more precise critical terminology for analyzing individual works[160] and proposes the reclassification of genres according to emotional categories found within Fourierist psychological theory. Though other commentators share similar ambitions,[161] only Laverdant regularly adopts the *série passionnelle* as the basis for his critical practice,[162] presenting his reordering of the genres as a significant contribution to the school's ambition to apply the *loi sériaire* to all aspects of human life. Since "the mission of the Societarian school . . . is to classify everything, to establish for everything the serial type which distributes harmony,"[163] the critic's function involves extending this principle to the arts in order to facilitate their contribution to social progress.

Laverdant takes a relatively interventionist stance, at odds with his endorsement of creative independence and the school's theoretical commitment to instinctual freedom, reinterpreting works or suggesting fundamental "improvements" to them. Though Izalguier shares his highly developed sense of the critic's status, other Fourierists have more limited pretensions. While figures such as Brunier, Pelletan, and Cantagrel all assume directive responsibilities and maintain the importance of a clear grasp of theory, others are less categorical. Lemarant vaunts a pragmatism in keeping with the banal and undertheorized tenor of his remarks. Sabatier, on the other hand, insists that the democratic climate following 1848 dictates that the critic should serve as the "artist's companion and friend" rather than adopting a more prescriptive role.[164] Although posing as a simple mediator between artist and public, Sabatier nonetheless displays a theoretical awareness absent in Fourierist criticism following Laverdant's retirement in 1846.

The energy invested in elaborating analytical tools for assessing Salon painting and encouraging artistic reform had the long-term aim of exploding the whole notion of art as it was understood in contemporary society—as elitist, as private, as individualist in conception and circumscribed in consumption. Rather, the Fourierists envisage the art of the future as a

[160] See, for example, the use of such terms as *goût*, *style*, and *couleur* in D. Laverdant, "Ecole des beaux-arts. Concours de sculpture," *Phal.*, 3d ser., 4 (10 September 1841): cols. 84–85 and the article on the "Concours de peinture" in ibid. (26 September 1841): cols. 193–94.

[161] See, for example, F. M. Foisy and O.-A. Barbier, "Exposition de tableaux du Musée royal du Louvre. Mode d'indication du placement des ouvrages de peinture, sculpture etc. . . ," *Phal.* 1, no. 25 (10 March 1837) (also issued in pamphlet form).

[162] See, for example, his article on the "Classification des genres dans la peinture," "Salon de 1842," *Phal.* 3d ser. 5, 46 (17 April 1842): cols. 739–50.

[163] "La mission de l'école sociétaire . . . est de *tout classer*, de produire en toutes choses le type sériaire qui distribue les harmonies." Laverdant, "Salon de 1846," 558.

[164] "Compagnon et ami de l'artiste." Sabatier, *Salon de 1851*, ii.

totalizing experience more ambitious in scope and all-embracing in effect than can be conceived within the divided realms of *civilisation*. Culture as luxury commodity gives place to a democratization of pleasure, where "art is a universal right, like air or labor,"[165] and beauty forms an integral part of the material environment. No longer confined to the museum or the amateur's *cabinet*, the arts enter into everyday life; the *Phalanstère* itself, with its shaded parks and towering halls, constantly solicits the eye and provokes the imagination. In evoking this popular Versailles, Guillot promises unprecedented beauty freely accessible to all:

> Once it is no longer individual but shared, luxury will be rehabilitated in all eyes. It will be palaces belonging to society as a whole, its roads, parks, and manufactories, that artists will decorate with their finest masterpieces. There, great rooms will demand great subjects, the brush will play easily across surfaces designed to satisfy the painter's imagination and proportionate to the nobility of art and the dignity of homes destined for a free, intelligent people.[166]

More radically than this, however, Fourier's philosophy of happiness imagines a conflation of the aesthetic and the utilitarian which will transform every aspect of human life into pleasurable experience. For a society regulated by "pleasure on every level and for every faculty, pleasure for each and every one,"[167] the demarcations that regulate a discrete notion of the aesthetic cease to exist. As beauty is identified with happiness and labor loses its oppressive character, the aesthetic subsumes all forms of activity and experience, transforming the world itself into an all-encompassing *Gesamtkunstwerk*.[168] The liberation of instinct allows continual gratification and becomes an unceasing source of delight.[169]

165 "L'art est de droit commun aussi bien que l'air et le travail." Ibid., 93.

166 "Le luxe, devenu social, après avoir été individuel, sera réhabilité aux yeux de tous. Ce seront les palais de la société entière, ses routes, ses parcs, ses manufactures que les artistes décoreront de leurs plus beaux chefs-d'oeuvre. Là de vastes salles réclameront de vastes sujets, là le pinceau pourra jouer à l'aise sur des espaces faites pour servir à l'imagination des peintres et proportionnés à la noblesse de l'art comme à la dignité des habitations destinées à des êtres intelligents et libres." A. Guillot, "Des arts dans la société future," *Le Nouveau Monde* (11 September 1839).

167 "La jouissance dans tous les ordres et pour toutes les facultés, la jouissance pour tous et pour chacun." Miget, "De la peinture," *Phal.* 1 (20 December 1836).

168 R. Schérer ("L'Esthétique passionnelle de Charles Fourier," *Pari sur l'impossible. Etudes fouriéristes* [1989], 92–93) has described this, in relation to Fourier's own philosophy, as "une esthétique du mouvement, qui rompt avec toutes les esthétiques contemplatives." The theme of the *Gesamtkunstwerk* is pursued in relation to Fourier's interest in opera in C. Morilhat, *Charles Fourier, imaginaire et critique sociale* (1991), 147–202.

169 "Le Beau et le Vrai se composent et convergent incessamment dans un ralliement absolu. Le travail et le plaisir coincident, et jusque dans les moindres accidents de la fonction de l'homme se trouvent coexistants le mode Utilitaire et le mode Esthétique." Izalguier, "Loi de la corrélation," 146.

This hedonistic vision lies at the heart of Fourierist philosophy and is characteristic of its ambitions as a political creed. Like Saint-Simonianism, Fourierism aspires to eradicate conflict within society. Its notion of harmony is at once social and ontological: friction between individuals and groups is eliminated by removing its apparent root cause—the psychological disequilibrium within the individual, generated by the repressive structures of society itself. In advancing a notion of a transcendent human essence, the harmony of which survives the deformations wrought by aberrant social organization, Fourier held out the prospect of a completely integrated society attainable through realization of his theoretical proposals. The "nouveau monde industriel et sociétaire" would enjoy absolute concord, since its structure was carefully designed to give free play to the broad spectrum of human passion and promote happiness and plenty.

Just as a harmonious, pacific society was the goal, so the means of attaining such a regime were to be peaceful. Abjuring any violent overthrow of the present order, the Fourierists favored persuasion rather than force—Fourier himself recommended the establishment of a prototype *Phalanstère*, whose unqualified success would advertise the merits of rapid social transformation. Though, in common with the Saint-Simonians, the Fourierists deplored current social inequality, their overtures to the working class inculcated respect for property and avoided any sense of class antagonism. Regarding inequality as symptomatic of a social order incompatible with the needs of human nature rather than as a source of social antagonism in itself, the group sought its remedy in psychosocial transformation and repudiated any frontal assault on class society. In the same way as the Saint-Simonians promised the peaceful eradication of injustice by reconciling such structural antinomies as spirit and matter, science and industry, thought and action, through the synthetic force of love, religion, and art, so the psychological theories underpinning Fourierism promised an era of harmony through resolving a comparable range of ontological and epistemological antitheses. Healing such rifts, experienced individually within each human subject and reified in the social organization of *civilisation*, would allow the liberation of passion and ensure the achievement of universal harmony.

As an end in itself, harmony signifies the elimination of conflict. In achieving this end, the visual image ideally stands as a solicitation and an analogy. In its demonstration of current disharmony and its vision of potential future harmony, it induces awareness of present shortcomings and stimulates desire for change. As an analogy, the ideal pictorial composition renders harmony tangible through its disposition of colors and shapes, and thus provokes an equivalent emotional state within the spectator. The image's exhortatory effect not only serves to represent harmony as the antithesis of conflict—the concert of color, the elimination of compositional redundancies, the absence of jarring tones—but also helps to develop a psychological disposition for nonconflictual change.

Within a Societarian regime the image stands as a microcosm, an analogy of the harmony that pervades society. Yet, despite persistent suggestions that art might play a more directly manipulative role, the aesthetic effect seems relatively dissipated. While in Saint-Simonian society the image serves an essentially instrumental purpose, rallying the masses behind administrative decisions, for the Fourierists the arts act as a magnificent embellishment rather than intervening in social practice. This differing conception of the function of art has two sources. On the one hand, the Fourierists conceive human behavior in Harmony as self-regulatory: the free play of passions secures a social order that effectively runs itself and thus renders directive intervention redundant. On the other hand, the universal attainment of *jouissance* transfers aesthetic experience from the circumscribed domain of cultural consumption to the very texture of life itself. Art enhances a sense of harmony through beautifying the environment, yet in some degree it remains only a simulacrum of a harmony experienced far more intensely in lived relations. A nonconflictual society, where repression of the passions gives place to their celebration, where class fragmentation is superseded by association, and where man and nature are in complete accord, actualizes the harmonious power of art and becomes an aesthetic experience in itself.

CRITICAL POSITIONS AND ARTISTIC PRODUCTION: PROBLEMS OF PRACTICE

So far, our discussion of Fourierist art criticism has been concerned with guiding principles rather than with identifying variations in voice or isolating particular critical profiles. As a body of writing, Fourierist criticism straddles a number of discursive forms, drawing upon the language and conceptual repertoire not only of artistic commentary but also of political theory. It is the integration of these two languages which stands as the central ambition of many critics contributing to the Fourierist press. This is conceived not merely as resulting from adherence to superficial economic and institutional change but is rather predicated on a radical reappraisal of the nature of man and the responsiveness of the social domain to a range of ostensibly fundamental human needs. In its most highly developed form, therefore, Fourierist commentary aspires to a far-reaching redefinition of art compatible with this reappraisal of human psychology, a redefinition that breaks with those perspectives on *art social* which remain primarily concerned with issues of social responsibility and evangelization.

Yet it is clear that the body of artistic commentary generated within the movement, and indeed the works produced by sympathetic artists, are marked by a heterogeneity that suggests differing degrees of investment in this theoretical exercise. While figures such as Izalguier and Laverdant evidently regard elaboration of a critical science rooted in Fourier's philosophy as a central priority, others display a more or less epidermal commitment to such an enterprise, a discrepancy that seems to depend on a number of factors. Although by the early 1840s a conceptual framework had been elaborated which allowed the assimilation of widely differing areas of artistic production within an explicitly doctrinal position, another language continued to present itself as a countervailing force—the language of art itself. Together with many others apparently committed to overturning current artistic priorities and openly hostile to formalist tendencies within critical writing, the dominance of this discourse exercised a more or less insidious influence on Fourierist aesthetics. In the practical business of criticism, formal considerations and their associated terminology provided a means of address and a set of conventions from which it was virtually impossible to make a clean break.

In large measure, the possible range of utterances and conceptual references which preceded the individual act of writing exerted a powerful influence in framing the parameters of the text. Such limitations permeate the work even of a critic such as Laverdant, who explicitly repudiates traditional discursive strategies in pursuing a critical science founded on an alternative hierarchy of values. Yet, however sustained the attempt, critical conventions embodied in the language of art penetrate the surface. This frequently leads to the discussion of form not as an integral part of a coherent alternative philosophy of art but simply as an end in itself—an indicator of artistic excellence autonomous from broader philosophical concerns. This tendency is, to some degree, held in check by scientistic ambitions that consciously attempt to demote critical subjectivity in favor of an "objective" perspective on artistic production. Yet, in large measure, contemporary critics relied on the assertion of subjectivity as a means of establishing their authority as professional arbiters of artistic value. Enhanced personal sensibility, rather than any systematic evaluative method, informs much of the critical self-projection that allows the writer to speak as a competent judge.

This interpenetration of subjectivism and the formal language of art lies behind the position adopted by such Fourierist critics as Lemarant and Ménard. Cantagrel, too, despite his greater doctrinal commitment and somewhat contrary to his actual practice, also proclaims a degree of pragmatism that respects artistic intentionality and asserts the critic's essentially subjective role.[170] This flexibility allows greater space for independent judg-

170 Cantagrel, "Salon de 1841," *Phal.* 3d ser., 2, no. 44 (11 April 1841): col. 725. For Lemarant's repudiation of a systematic approach to criticism, see "Salon de 1837," *Phal.* 1, no. 26 (20 March 1837): col. 843.

ment, articulated in a formal language only occasionally diluted by doctrinal reference or allusions to the social responsibilities of art. While more committed critics such as Laverdant and Sabatier continually struggle to master the received language of art, to appropriate it in a modified form in developing a radically new critical position, other Fourierist commentators remain largely within the conceptual domain serviced by this language, drawing away only infrequently to append a pronouncement on the artist's duties toward society. In more theoretically informed texts, this infusion of the language of art appears not as acquiescence, but as tension. Doctrinal imperatives snap beneath the pressure of a dominant mode of discourse which offers itself as the natural way of speaking of art, and the critic almost involuntarily returns to a language apparently at odds with his theoretical commitments. Such tensions also operate within the range of positions open to Fourierist commentators as critics on the left: the highly theorized assimilation of form in an understanding of the social function of art, for example, occasionally yields to a more orthodox—and doctrinally inconsistent—defense of social didacticism, akin to the position held by many republican writers.[171] The prevalence of such tensions and contradictions highlights the difficulty in arriving at an essential synthesis of the two opposing currents in contemporary discourse—a synthesis, moreover, that relied on the language of these currents while fundamentally questioning the conceptual grounds on which they were based.

These difficulties account for some of the limitations of the Fourierist enterprise. Yet this alone does not explain the dramatic discrepancies within the school's critical corpus. Of vital consideration in deciphering its differing levels is individual critics' varying commitment to the movement itself. Not all were, in fact, adherents to the group, and even among those more closely involved a broad range of doctrinal positions emerges. At least one cultural commentator, Victor Schoelcher, seems to have had no sustained contact with Fourierism. More closely identified with liberal republican currents under the July Monarchy,[172] he apparently owed his contribution to *La Phalange* in 1838 to his broader journalistic career, during which he also reviewed for the *Revue de Paris* and *L'Artiste*. As with the previous year's reviewer, Lemarant, Schoelcher's identification with Fourierist principles seems to have gone no further than a general belief in aesthetic utilitarianism, a position already effectively rejected by Eugène d'Izalguier in 1836. It is Izalguier's secession from the group which probably explains the recourse to Lemarant and Schoelcher at a stage when *La Phalange* had yet to arrive at a consistent policy on artistic questions.

Similar ambiguity also underscores the positions of Eugène Pelletan and

[171] Compare, for example, Sabatier's remarks on beauty, *Salon de 1851*, v–vi, with his more conventional defense of didacticism, ibid., 54.

[172] See L. Bougenot, *Victor Schoelcher* (1921), 23–29.

Louis Ménard. Though internal evidence suggests that both were more than superficially involved with the school, in neither case is it possible to argue for complete allegiance. A republican for most of his career, Pelletan's possible flirtation with Saint-Simonianism and his sustained period with *La Démocratie pacifique*[173] suggests a broader range of political interests. His involvement with the Fourierist journal was apparently instigated by his mentor Lamartine, but his participation in an anthology of doctrinal writings in 1844, and in Fourierist agitation for reform of artistic institutions, points to more than a merely professional relationship with the group. A frequent contributor to *La Presse*, *Le Siècle*, the *Revue de Paris*, and *L'Artiste*, Pelletan nonetheless displays certain characteristic doctrinal preoccupations, his remarks on nature and the symbolic significance of color in particular echoing the ideas of Désiré Laverdant. Evidence of Ménard's attraction to Fourierism is more circumstantial and his writing displays only sporadic signs of sympathy for the group and its aesthetic position. His own political views in the mid 1840s seem to have owed far more to Cabet and Leroux,[174] suggesting that participation on *La Démocratie pacifique* was inspired by his association with the radical publicist Paul de Flotte and the poet Leconte de Lisle, a friend of Laverdant who published verse in the journal in 1845.[175] Both Ménard and Leconte shared an interest in classical civilization—a preference that informs Ménard's sympathy for Ingres and his pupils. This enthusiasm brought the two men into contact with Thalès Bernard, with whom they established a clandestine group combining radical politics with an interest in Greek mysticism. Though at least one established Fourierist, Eugène Maron, was attracted to this circle, the participation of such left-wing sympathizers as Lacaussade, the Spaniard Bermudez de Castro, and the painters Jacquemard, Jobbé-Duval, and Jules Breton implies no direct Fourierist connections.[176]

With the partial exception of Pelletan, none of the critics discussed so far added to the group's theoretical repertoire, and to a significant degree their work either ignores or implicitly repudiates the fundamental tenets of Fourierist criticism, embracing either a narrow utilitarianism or a broadly formalist position.

In the same way as variations emerge through examination of the political allegiances of individual critics, so confirmed adherents display differing

173 The Saint-Simonian connection is asserted by Vapereau. Pelletan wrote for *La Démocratie pacifique* between 1841 and 1845. See E. Petit, *Eugène Pelletan (1813–1884). L'Homme et l'oeuvre d'après des documents inédits* (1913), and Erdan, *La France mystique*, 2:234–47.

174 See H. Peyre, *Louis Ménard (1822–1901)* (1932), 31, and P. Valkhoff, "Louis Ménard (1822–1901)," *Néophilologus* 1 (1915–16): 88–100.

175 See A. Colocci, *Paulo de Flotte (1817–1860)* (1912), 30–32, and F. Calmettes, *Leconte de Lisle et ses amis* (1902).

176 See Peyre, *Louis Ménard*, 52–53.

responses to the problems of elaborating a coherent aesthetic program. While adopting a characteristically doctrinal stance, neither François Cantagrel,[177] writing in the wake of Izalguier's theoretical pronouncements, nor Laverdant's successor, Charles Brunier, develop a Fourierist aesthetic with the same single-mindedness that characterizes both these writers and their methodological heir, François Sabatier. Although much in Cantagrel's review of the 1841 exhibition points in directions later explored by Laverdant, doctrinal commitment frequently remains extrinsic to pictorial analysis. Works are examined largely according to familiar stylistic criteria and a Fourierist moral appended as a by-product of subject matter, rather than being integrated within a more nuanced consideration of the mechanics of representation. Nonetheless, Cantagrel's work does mark the first practical application of certain indications elaborated by Izalguier and demonstrates a significant inflection of the critical stance he had adopted when writing for *L'Artiste* in the mid 1830s. Joining the editorial group of *La Phalange* in 1838, he seems to have maintained close contact with the director of *L'Artiste*, Achille Ricourt, himself a supporter of the Fourierist cause. Ricourt had published several articles highly sympathetic to the Fourierists and employed a number of commentators with firm radical credentials.[178] Although he seems never to have contributed directly to the Fourierist press, Ricourt was asked for help by Cantagrel in composing the 1841 review, which possibly combines views held by both men.[179]

Cantagrel's apparent difficulty in sustaining an integrated Fourierist perspective on the arts emerges again in the writing of Charles Brunier, appointed to fill the vacancy left by Laverdant in 1846. Himself an amateur landscapist, Brunier was closely involved in Fourierist journalism and retained his contacts with the group well into the 1850s.[180] His critical reviews and theoretical pieces substantiate his commitment, with their advo-

[177] See J. P. Thomas, "L'Oeuvre dialogique de François Cantagrel," *Corpus* 2 (January 1986): 149–55.

[178] See, for example, the review of Considerant's *Destinée sociale* in *L'Artiste*, 2d ser., 2 (1839): 114. Considerant himself contributed to the journal on several occasions, most notably in 1833, when "Des tendances actuelles de la littérature" was partially reprinted from *Le Phalanstère* 2 (8 January 1833): 61–63. Charles Villagre's obituary of Fourier for the journal (21 November 1837) was reprinted, with a sympathetic preface, in *La Phalange*. Ricourt employed such former Saint-Simonians as Villagre and Saint-Chéron, together with the Fourierist Arthur Guillot. On Ricourt's Fourierist allegiance, see the letter dated 14 October 1837 from J. Manesca to "M. Becour [*sic*], rédacteur du journal 'L'Artiste' à Paris," Archives nationales, Paris, Archives sociétaires 10 AS 40(1).

[179] For Cantagrel's solicitation of Ricourt's help, see Cantagrel to Ricourt, 12 March 1841, Bibliothèque d'art et d'archéologie, Fondation Jacques Doucet, Papiers Achille Ricourt, Dossier 43 (Amateurs).

[180] Nus, *Choses de l'autre monde*, 123, describes Brunier as a leading protagonist in the spiritualist séances held in the former offices of *La Démocratie pacifique* in 1853.

cacy of association, their belief in the perfectibility of art under a Societarian regime, and their evocation of a reformed world where art and labor exist in total harmony. Such priorities inform his critical pronouncements to a significant degree, notably in his assessment of such colorists as Delacroix and Decamps, yet despite the complex critical apparatus bequeathed by Laverdant, Brunier fails to elaborate any equivalent ideological perspective on the question of form.

This apparent retreat from a comprehensive assimilation of Fourier's political and psychological doctrine into the aesthetic domain does not seem to have been fortuitous. Rather, the more restrained tone of Brunier and Ménard in the late 1840s appears to result from shifts of attitude within the school which coincide with Laverdant's growing alienation from the editorial group of *La Démocratie pacifique* and his eventual estrangement from the Fourierist leadership.

In order to understand the evolution of Laverdant's involvement with the movement, a brief outline of his personal circumstances and intellectual formation is necessary. Born in Port-Louis, capital of the French colony of Mauritius, on 21 November 1809,[181] Laverdant left for France at the age of nine and entered the law after studying at the Collège de Sainte-Barbe and the Ecole polytechnique. Attracted to Fourierism as early as 1832, he had already established firm contacts with the group at the time of his return to Mauritius in 1836.[182] While pursuing his legal practice and initiating a journalistic career, Laverdant proselytized and gave practical expression to his beliefs with the foundation of an *asile rurale*.[183] Soon after his definitive return to France in 1840, he joined the editorial board of *La Phalange* and began his association with *La Démocratie pacifique*, for which he wrote not only on the arts but also on colonial affairs and horse racing. Described as grave and sententious in a hostile profile published in *La Silhouette*,[184] Laverdant's prominence in the pages of *La Démocratie pacifique* during the early 1840s suggests close involvement in the movement. By 1844, however, tensions were beginning to surface—during a tour of provincial groups, Cantagrel reported that his writing was thought "occasionally alarming for the paterfamilias," containing "excessively audacious ideas on free love, which means that not all the issues of D.P. in which these ideas are

[181] The principal biographical sources on Laverdant are A. Toussaint's entry in the *Dictionnaire de biographie mauricienne: Société de l'histoire de l'Ile Maurice* 2, no. 14 (July 1944), 435, together with the addendum in ibid., 2, no. 32 ("Mutanda and Addenda," no. 5), January 1970; G. Baschet's note in *L'Intermédiaire des chercheurs et curieux* 69 (10 February 1914): cols. 166–67, and the entry in J. Maitron's *Dictionnaire biographique du mouvement ouvrier français (1789–1864)* (1965), 2:449–50.

[182] On his early contacts with the group, see Laverdant's letter to the editors of *La Science sociale*, 3d year, 17 (16 September 1869): 248.

[183] See *Le Bulletin phalanstérien* (15 February 1847).

[184] Anonymous, "Tableaux d'intérieur: les boutiques de journaux. *La Démocratie pacifique*," *La Silhouette* 2 (31 May 1846): 1013.

found can be lent out."[185] If such an assault on bourgeois propriety caused some discomfort among the Fourierist hierarchy, the development of Laverdant's position over the next five years stretched his relationship with the movement to breaking point.

The issue that precipitated this rupture was Laverdant's increasing sympathy for Catholicism, which resulted in his formal conversion around 1848.[186] In itself, this development need not have precipitated direct conflict with the group—several Fourierists, including the painter Dominique Papety, combined their political convictions with a strong Catholic commitment, and Papety's cover for the *Almanach phalanstérien* (plate 24), with its juxtaposition of Christ, Socrates, Moses, and Fourier, apparently proclaims a perfect consonance between the two movements.[187] Yet the timing of Laverdant's conversion, together with the irrascible and dogmatic nature of his belief, made conflict inevitable. Though during the mid 1840s the group had become increasingly conciliatory toward the church, this attitude changed to outright hostility in 1848. By this time, partially under the influence of his wife,[188] Laverdant had become an avid supporter of Lacordaire and Ozanam. The trenchantly anti-Catholic tone cultivated in *La Démocratie pacifique* provoked a furious correspondence from Laverdant, who seems to have spent much of the Second Republic divided between Clermont-Ferrand, where he was editor of *L'Auvergne démocratique* and an unsuccessful candidate for the National Assembly, and southern health resorts, where he battled with illness and nervous lassitude.

Laverdant's irritation at his colleagues' anti-Catholicism formed only one facet of his disenchantment with Fourierist politics after 1848. His pacifism provoked condemnation of the school's attitude toward the unstable European situation, while overtures toward the new republican regime led to accusations of an opportunistic abandonment of principle. Arguing that "we have become party hacks,"[189] Laverdant condemned any gradualist flirtations with such "revolutionaries" as Ledru-Rollin, Michel de Bourges, "et les autres Titis de la Montagne,"[190] and attempted to persuade his

[185] "Effrayant quelquefois pour les pères de famille"; "des thèses de liberté amoureuse trop pressée, qui font qu'on ne peut pas prêter tous les nos. de la D.P. où ces thèses se trouvent." Cantagrel to Bureau, letter from Dijon, 5 November 1844, and from Lons-le-Saulnier, 15 November 1844, Archives sociétaires 10 AS 37.

[186] On Laverdant's Catholic phase, see J.-B. Duroselle, *Les Débuts du catholicisme social en France (1822–1870)* (1951), particularly 379–81.

[187] Tamisier, "Dominique Papety," 64, describes Papety as a "chrétien fervent"; see also the artist's own comments on religious painting in ibid., 54. The vignette shows Fourier as "l'élu du Christ," who has "trouvé la loi du royaume de Dieu promis à la terre." It is this discovery that Diogenes (seated at bottom left) acknowledges by extinguishing his lantern.

[188] See Laverdant to Considerant, 19 October [1849], Archives sociétaires 10 AS 39(8).

[189] "Nous sommes devenus des *hommes de parti*." Laverdant to Brunier, undated [1849]; ibid.

[190] Laverdant to the Conseil de rédaction de *La Démocratie pacifique*, letter from Nice dated 2 December 1849; ibid.

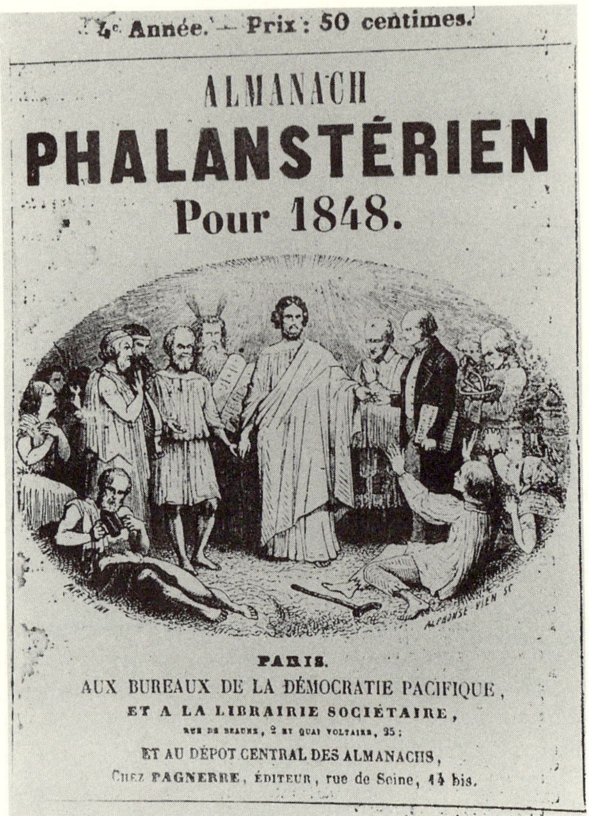

Plate 24. Dominique Papety: Cover illustration to the *Almanach phalanstérien pour 1848*. Goldsmith Library, University of London.

colleagues of the incompatibility of such a stance with the principles enunciated by Fourier. Asserting that the revolution presented an opportunity for an ambitious program of *réalisation*, Laverdant claimed to be remaining true to the spirit of Fourier's philosophy at a time when those who proclaimed themselves his most faithful disciples were compromising their principles: "Is it by speaking thus, my brothers, that I seem *backward*, are you going to think me a utopian? Ah! therein lies all our strength, in being described as *utopians*, and let us not forget it."[191]

Laverdant's disaffection did not provoke a complete rupture with the group, however. Though he complained that "my leader and colleagues on

[191] "Est-ce [qu']en parlant ainsi, mes frères, je vous semblerais *arriéré*, est-ce que vous allez me traiter d'Utopiste! Ah! toute notre force est là, dans ce titre d'*utopistes*, ne l'oublions pas." Laverdant to Brunier, letter from Nice, undated (1849); ibid.

the Council tell me nothing of plans, attitudes, or the state of the school,"[192] and maintained regular contact only with Charles Brunier, in 1852 he collaborated with Auguste Saverdan on a project for a "children's colony" at Condé-sur-Vesgres. His uncompromising position over religious questions quickly soured relations with Saverdan, however, and in October 1852 he abandoned the scheme, taking with him a ten thousand franc pledge he had offered to help in its establishment.[193] As this episode symbolized his definitive estrangement from Fourierist circles, so Laverdant developed his contacts with Catholic socialists. His involvement with Arnaud de l'Ariège had led to the foundation of the short-lived Cercle de la démocratie catholique in 1851, and the following year he joined Louis Guérin on the *Mémorial catholique*, a journal with which he was associated for the next eighteen years.

It would appear from these events that it was Laverdant who had deviated from Fourierist orthodoxy. If his subsequent evolution does mark an increasing ambivalence toward his former allegiances, it is nonetheless clear that, until the early 1850s at least, he considered his Catholicism entirely compatible with his Fourierist convictions. In correspondence with Considerant and others, Laverdant argues for an amalgamation of the two doctrines, which he regards as entirely consistent with Fourier's own teaching. In 1850, for example, he writes to Brunier: "I remain a Phalansterian to my fingertips and work to reconcile the science developed specially by Fourier with his solemn and intimate affirmation: *Jesus is the Messiah*."[194]

It is in this sustained commitment to the philosophy of Fourier, rather than to the interpretation of his doctrine advanced by the Ecole sociétaire, that the key both to Laverdant's aesthetic position and to his estrangement from the school can be found.

Under Considerant's leadership, the group had quietly jettisoned much of Fourier's teaching, developing a cooperatist philosophy less exalted in tone and more pragmatic in intent than the doctrine inherited from the master himself. It seems clear that Laverdant had little sympathy for such moves. His repudiation of political compromise and his defense of utopian commitment appear less as the rear-guard action of a figure aware of his isolation than as the consistent outcome of an ideological *parti pris* evident in his writing from the early 1840s. Throughout this period, his reviews display an ambition to extend even the most arcane ideas into the aesthetic

[192] "Mon chef et mes collègues du Conseil ne m'apprennent rien des projets, des vues, de l'état de l'Ecole." Laverdant to Brunier, letter from Nice, undated (1849); ibid.

[193] See Saverdan to Bureau, 30 October 1852 and, for a retrospective assessment of the project, his letter to an unknown correspondent of 7 October 1853; Archives sociétaires 10 AS 41 (14).

[194] "Je reste phalanstérien jusqu'au bout des ongles, et je travaille à accorder la science spécialement élaborée par Fourier avec cette affirmation solennelle et intime de Fourier: *Jésus est le Méssie*." Laverdant to Brunier, January 1850, Archives sociétaires 10 AS 39 (8).

domain, at a time when his colleagues were busily temporizing. Laverdant's evocation of Fourier's controversial sexual libertarianism, his exploration of the theory of analogies, and his emphasis on *attraction passionnelle* coincide with a general move away from the speculative to the more concrete aspects of Fourier's philosophy. Paradoxically, it is through his orthodoxy that Laverdant became marginalized within the movement. From his own perspective, it was Considerant and his allies who were the schismatics, since they repudiated so much established doctrine. As a disciple of Fourier rather than as an adherent to this modified philosophy, Laverdant was bound to come into conflict with his colleagues on *La Démocratie pacifique*. In this respect, his commitment to an idiosyncratic anti-Gallican Catholicism merely exacerbated tensions that were already in play, and which seem to have focused on criticism of his aesthetic speculations. In a long letter of December 1849 to the editorial board of *La Démocratie pacifique* some indication of these tensions and his attitude toward subsequent modifications of the Fourierist aesthetic clearly emerge:

> I seem to remember that four years ago it became the fashion in our office to tear apart my work on the fine arts. I lost no time in relinquishing my place to others. It is undeniable that since then the *Démocratie*'s theatrical and artistic columns have been more amusing than mine, but I don't quite see what intellectual *fertility* has replaced my sterility. I at least tried to extrapolate theoretical deductions from the central body of theory. Our friends have abandoned this and so we have had more or less skillful performances and any number of tendencies (in Fleury's work, for example) to imitate J. Janin. We have virtually lost what I attempted to do within the limits of my abilities, to give the School's *feuilleton* gravity, dignity, and some sense of originality and benevolence. Let's say I wasn't very good; at least I was full of goodwill, so that one felt that any lack of knowledge was made up for by love. Apart from Brunier's occasional and belated efforts . . . I swear to God, my friends, that my benevolence has perished without any benefit to knowledge.[195]

[195] "J'ai souvenance qu'il devint, il y a quatre ans, le *ton* dans nos bureaux de me démolir sur le terrain des *beaux-arts*. Je m'empressai de céder la place tout entière à d'autres. Il est incontestable que la *Démocratie* a eu, depuis, des feuilletons théâtre et arts plastiques beaucoup plus amusants que les miens, mais je ne vois pas trop quelle fécondité *d'idées* a remplacé ma stérilité. J'avais du moins essayé à tirer des déductions théoriques de la théorie-mère. Nos amis y ont renoncé et nous avons eu de la technie plus ou moins heureuse et forces tendances (dans Fleury par exemple) aux allures J. Janin. Nous avons à peu près perdu ce que j'avais cherché dans la mesure de mes moyens, à donner au feuilleton de l'Ecole, du sérieux, de la dignité, un air de recherches et de bienveillance. Mettons que je n'ai pas été fort; j'ai été bienveillant; on sentait alors qu'à défaut de science, il y avait de l'amour. Sauf les efforts interrompus et tardifs de Brunier . . . j'en atteste les Dieux, mes bons amis, la bienveillance a tourné au sec, sans profit pour la science." Laverdant to the Conseil de rédaction de *La Démocratie pacifique*, letter from Nice, 2 December 1849; ibid.

If one allows for a measure of injured self-justification, it seems clear from Laverdant's remarks that the tone of his aesthetic writings had strained relations with the school. While his colleagues were busily asserting that "Fourier does not want man to give his passions free rein,"[196] Laverdant was maintaining precisely this. In some respects, dominant currents within the movement, in diluting the implication of the *économie passionnelle*, seem to have regarded aesthetic gratification as providing a form of transference for the erotic notion of pleasure set out by Fourier. Aesthetic pleasure, extended to all domains of human activity, satisfies desire through solicitation of the senses, and hence demotes sexuality as a form of gratification. For Laverdant, the arts supplement rather than supplant sexuality as a source of emotional release. The force of such an argument, embodied in a prose style in itself given to unrestrained evocations of physicality,[197] set Laverdant at odds with the more cautious moralism of Considerant and his allies.

It is tempting to parallel Laverdant's marginalization and eventual disaffection with the apparent experiences of Eugène d'Izalguier in the previous decade. Izalguier's seminal role in developing a Fourierist theory of art was abruptly curtailed in 1837 and he seems subsequently to have severed all connections with the movement.[198] Though remarks on his secession imply allegiance to a possibilist position at odds with dominant currents within the school in the late 1830s, the question of the group's attitude toward his aesthetic theories remains open—particularly in view of the emergence of such moderate figures as Lemarant and Schoelcher as his successors. In the case of Laverdant, temporization after his 1846 Salon is clear: Brunier, despite his commitment to a distinctively Fourierist aesthetic line, abjures

[196] "Fourier ne veut pas que l'homme lâche la bride à ses passions." "Préface des éditeurs (lecture obligée)," *Théorie des quatre mouvements*, 327.,

[197] See, for example, the highly charged description of Glaize's *Les Baigneuses du séjour d'Armide* in "Salon de 1843," *Phal.* (30 April 1843): col. 2141. Laverdant's extremely critical treatment of erotic themes in reviews for *Le Mémorial catholique* during the 1860s frequently employs violently sexual language; see, for example, "Esprit du Salon de 1863. Bilan de l'art après dix-huit siècles d'évangalisation," *Le Mémorial catholique*, n.s., 4 (October 1863): 392–95.

[198] Cantagrel mentions an encounter with Izalguier at the agrarian colony of Mettray, near Tours, in 1841. He remarks "J'ai vu là d'Izalguier qui m'a reçu assez froidement et d'un air gêné. Il ne lit jamais *La Phalange*, bien qu'on la reçoive à Mettray. Il semble être tout à fait étranger à l'idée sociétaire, et quand on lui donne des nouvelles de son progrès, il semble revenir de l'autre monde. Evidemment, ce jeune homme n'a pas compté sur la puissance de la découverte, et maintenant . . . il paraît être hostile aux idées qu'il a soutenues autrefois. Cependant, il ne les renie pas; je l'ai mis au pied du mur à cet égard; il s'est retranché dans l'impossibilité du succès d'un essai; il pense, dit-il, qu'il fallait se borner à faire un journal, et pousse tous les chefs des industries à faire des applications de détail (telle a été, ajoute-t-il, la cause de sa rupture avec *La Phalange*)." Cantagrel to X, letter from Amboise, 7 March 1841, Archives sociétaires 10 AS 37(2). This is apparently the only surviving mention of Izalguier.

more speculative ideas, while the doctrinal convictions of the drama critic Jules Fleury were openly questioned by his predecessor.[199] Only with the emergence of François Sabatier in 1850 was any attempt made to reassert a more integrated aesthetic grounded in Fourierist theory.

Though a long-standing adherent to the movement, Sabatier's contacts with the central council in Paris appear to have been relatively slight before the February Revolution.[200] A native of Montpellier, where he was born into a family of wealthy landowners in 1818, he spent much of his early life outside France, traveling to Italy with the painters Auguste Bouquet and Edmond Wagrez in 1838. Following marriage to the singer Caroline Ungher in March 1841, Sabatier established himself at his wife's country house La Concezione, near Florence, and at their home in the Palazzo Renai in the city itself. Sabatier's literary interests and Caroline Ungher's professional engagements led the couple to Austria and Germany in 1841–42, before returning to Montpellier at the end of 1842. Sabatier remained in France until 1845, when he left for Austria with Bouquet and Papety, continuing to Greece with Papety in 1846. Following the February Revolution, he returned to France, remaining in Paris until the December 1851 coup, when his political associations forced him to leave once more for Italy.

Throughout this period, Sabatier combined his cosmopolitan life-style with a scholarly interest in the history of art and European literature, and a firm commitment to Fourierist politics. His wealth contrasts with the more modest circumstances enjoyed by most members of the group, as do his cultural connections, something in which he is rivaled only by Désiré Laverdant. A friend of such figures as Vigny, Ledru-Rollin, Lamartine, and the painters Eugène Devéria and Ricard, Sabatier hosted a fashionable salon in his home on the rue Bonaparte during the Second Republic. His journalistic career with *La Démocratie pacifique* was short-lived, and is largely confined to his review of the 1850–51 Salon, issued in volume form in March 1851.[201] While reviving a number of theoretical preoccupations articulated by Laverdant and Izalguier, Sabatier significantly avoids any reference to the more speculative aspects of Fourier's thought, which had apparently brought Laverdant into disfavor. Most conspicuously, his remarks testify an awareness of recent political events, prompting endorsement of such artists as Courbet, Millet, and Antigna for their portrayal of popular life, and

[199] In his letter of 2 December 1849, Laverdant describes Fleury as an "esprit étroit, civilisé." See also Laverdant to Brunier, 9 October 1849, Archives sociétaires 10 AS 39/8.

[200] The main biographical sources on François Sabatier are F.-X. Amprimoz, "Un Décor 'fouriériste' à Florence," *Revue de l'art* 48 (1980): 57–67; J. Claparede, "Le Séjour de Courbet à la Tour de Farges," *Bulletin des Amis de Gustave Courbet* 7 (1950): 9–12; O. Hartwig, "François Sabatier und Caroline Sabatier-Ungher," *Deutsche Rundschau* (May 1897): 227–43, and the anonymous introduction to J. W. von Goethe, *Faust*, trans. F. Sabatier (1893), vi–xvii.

[201] Sabatier's only other contribution to the journal is a review of Etex's *Cours élémentaire du dessin*, *D.P.* 16, no. 18 (1 December 1850).

emphasis on the need for artists to respond to the social conditions of the modern world. Sabatier thus emerges as a firm advocate of contemporaneity, which he equates with representation of the new progressive political class—the people themselves. As he remarks in an evaluation of Courbet that projects the artist as the first to react to the changed political climate, "having entered into politics, the people also wishes to enter into art."[202]

The populist emphasis in Sabatier's work introduces a positivist tone which inflects his interpretation of Fourierist theory more toward the functionalism of republican advocates of *art social* than toward the metaphysical speculations of Laverdant. Yet such speculative flights are not entirely absent, as his comments on landscape and Delacroix demonstrate. Remarks in a letter to the Montpellier collector Alfred Bruyas further suggest that the 1850 review represents only a limited application of Fourierist doctrine in a field Sabatier regarded as holding out far greater theoretical possibilities:

> Since everything in the world is logically connected, it was not without some value properly to set out the relation between artistic matters and social questions, drawing on the theory of passions. That is what I tried to do, very briefly it is true, but clearly enough to be understood by those familiar with this theory. But I had to resist going any further and plunging into the abstract depths of the subject; I thus left to one side the transcendental aspect of art. If I had continued to write Salon reviews for the same journal, I would gradually have reached it, or at least attempted to do so.[203]

Perhaps as significant as his contribution to critical theory was Sabatier's role as a patron of Fourierist artists. Though Papety's *Rêve de bonheur* was produced without such financial support, thanks to the facilities he enjoyed as a pupil of the Villa Medici, the importance of Sabatier in his subsequent career, and in that of his fellow *pensionnaire*, the sculptor Auguste Ottin, indicates how significant sympathetic patronage could have been in helping to produce an alternative doctrinal art form.

Papety, encountered together with Ottin during the visit to Rome in 1838, was the greatest beneficiary of Sabatier's largesse, and produced a number of Fourierist allegories at his behest. *Le Passé, le présent et l'avenir*

[202] "Le peuple, entré dans la politique, veut aussi entrer dans l'art." Sabatier, *Salon de 1851*, 27.

[203] "Comme tout se tient logiquement dans le monde, il n'était pas sans utilité de bien présenter les questions d'art dans leur rapport avec les questions sociales, et en s'appuyant sur la théorie des passions. C'est ce que j'ai essayé de faire, très en abrégé, il est vrai, mais assez clairement pour être compris des gens à qui cette théorie est familière. Mais j'ai dû m'abstenir d'aller plus loin et de m'enfoncer dans les profondeurs abstraites du sujet; j'ai donc laissé de côté la partie transcendentale de l'art. Si j'avais continué dans ce même journal de faire les salons, j'y serais arrivé par degrés, j'aurais tâché du moins." Letter dated October 1854 in A. Bruyas, *Explication des ouvrages de peinture du cabinet de peinture de M. Alfred Bruyas* (1854), 209.

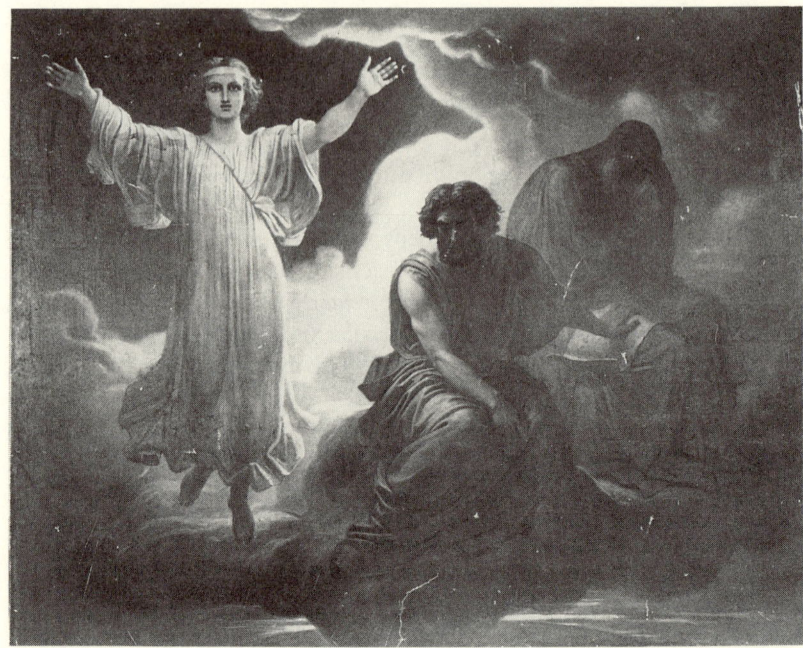

Plate 25. Dominique Papety: *Le Passé, le présent et l'avenir,* Salon of 1847. Musée des beaux-arts, Marseilles.

(plate 25), exhibited in the 1847 Salon and subsequently displayed in Sabatier's Florentine residence, provides a synoptic allegory of Fourierist historiography, though its abstract character failed to impress Ménard at the time of its Paris showing.[204] Allegory is used in *Le Dernier Soir de l'esclavage* (plate 26), a sketch produced around 1848, which possibly reflects Sabatier's optimistic expectations of the new republic.[205] As with the *Rêve de bonheur*, neither work is explicitly contemporary in conception, though in his emblematic representation of the overthrow of *civilisation* Papety incorporates the figures of Mirabeau and Voltaire, and such anonymous protagonists as an "ouvrier abattu, malade" and "un banquier roi de l'argent boycotteur." Portraying as it does the dynamic movement from present to future, the *Dernier Soir* serves almost as a prologue to the *Rêve de bonheur*. Yet, as with the earlier work, Papety seems to encounter difficulties in couching political allegory in a contemporary visual language, and largely

[204] Ménard, "Salon de 1847," *D.P.* 8, no. 83 (7 April 1847).

[205] The sketch was donated to the Musée Fabre, Montpellier by Sabatier, though Amprimoz ("Lettres de Dominique Papety," 203) speculates that it may relate to an unidentified commission awarded to the artist under the Second Republic.

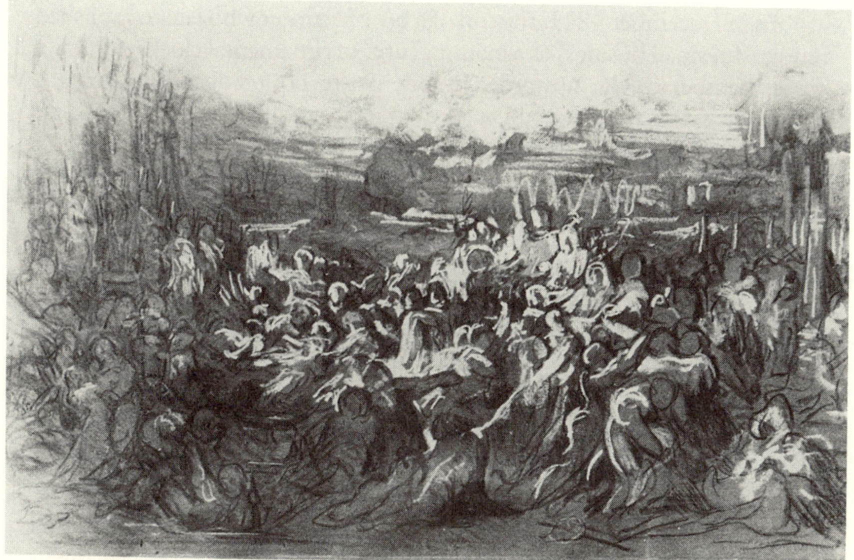

Plage 26. Dominique Papety: *Le Dernier Soir de l'esclavage*, c. 1848. Musée Fabre, Montpellier.

relies on the classical vocabulary acquired during his academic training. The hold of this tradition surfaces again in the artist's attempt at contemporary Christian allegory in the *Consolatrix Afflictorum*, and its persistency during the 1840s was to provoke some misgivings among Fourierist commentators.

As well as providing Papety with an opportunity to explore Fourierist allegory, Sabatier also patronized the artist more generally, commissioning family portraits and purchasing several drawings.[206] He also offered financial support and enabled Papety to develop an interest in Byzantine art with a visit to Greece, during which he copied the mosaics in the monastery on Mount Athos.[207] Perhaps most importantly, Sabatier presented his protégé with a major commission during his period at the Ecole de Rome—the decorative scheme for the Palazzo Renai in Florence. This major undertaking involved three other figures—the painter Auguste Bouquet, together with two *pensionnaires* at the Villa Medici, the architect Lefuel and the sculptor Ottin.

[206] See Amprimoz, "Un Décor 'fouriériste,' " n. 116, and Claparède, *Inventaire*, nos. 188, 211–17.

[207] On Sabatier's financial assistance, see Papety to Ottin, letter of 10 November 1841, Archives du Louvre Mss. 9HH7. On the visit to Greece, see E. A. Thouvenal, *La Grèce du roi Othon* (1890), 67.

Born in December 1811, the son of a bronze turner who later established a successful small business as a manufacturer of ornamental clocks,[208] Ottin was a member of the upwardly mobile petite bourgeoisie. Following a private education, he entered David d'Angers's studio as the sculptor's first student, and began to frequent the atelier of Célestin Nanteuil around 1835. Nanteuil was himself a Fourierist,[209] and Ottin's adherence to the movement probably dates from this period.[210] At the time of his departure for Rome in 1836, he had developed a wide circle of friends among young artists and writers, including Gautier, Nerval, Petrus Borel, Armand Leleux, and the Fourierist musician Allyre Bureau.[211] In Rome itself, the Villa Medici contained a remarkable number of Fourierist sympathizers. Apart from Papety, the sculptor Farochon, the architect Florimonde Boulanger, and the musician Besozzi were all supporters of the school.[212]

It was into this environment that François Sabatier was introduced in 1838. His personal friendship and doctrinal sympathy for Ottin and Papety were to pay practical dividends for the artists two years later, when he approached the students with proposals for a major decorative scheme. In advance of his marriage, Sabatier intended renovating his fiancée's townhouse in Florence. The architect Lefuel was commissioned to undertake structural modifications, while Ottin and Papety, together with Auguste Bouquet, were engaged to provide a large-scale decorative scheme.[213] Papety's initial project for murals showing "Dieu, l'univers et l'homme" was rejected in favor of a series of great artists from the past. Raphael, Michelangelo, Goethe, and Molière were portrayed by Bouquet, while Papety took on Shakespeare, Dante, and Mozart (plate 27), apparently finishing work on the scheme by the mid 1840s.[214] Ottin took rather longer, since his contribution was the most ambitious of the three. Sabatier's commission of a monumental fireplace (plate 28), complete with bust of Fourier, allegorical figures, and scenes of Societarian life, was eventually shown at the Salon of 1850, though the bust had been refused three years earlier, when the entire

208 See the manuscript *Biographie d'Ottin (Auguste-Louis-Marie) sculpteur par son fils* (i.e., Léon-Auguste Ottin), which incorporates extracts from a personal memoir by Ottin himself, in Archives du Louvre Mss. 9HH7, pp. 2–8.

209 See Malon, *Histoire du socialisme*, 106, and the *Biographie*, 11–14 and 21.

210 Meray, "Un Rêve d'harmonie."

211 Loubens to Ottin, 1835, in Archives du Louvre Mss. 9HH7. For letters from the period in Rome, together with details of Ottin's student career, see A. Le Normand, *La Tradition classique et l'esprit romantique: les sculpteurs de l'Académie de France à Rome de 1824 à 1840* (1981).

212 On Boulanger, see Hanoune, "De Douai à Rome." On Farochon and Besozzi, see the *Biographie*, 21.

213 Full details of the scheme's genesis are given in Amprimoz, "Un Décor 'fouriériste.' "

214 On 8 March 1842 he writes to Ottin: "Je termine tous les travaux de François dans un ou deux ans" (Louvre Mss. 9HH7).

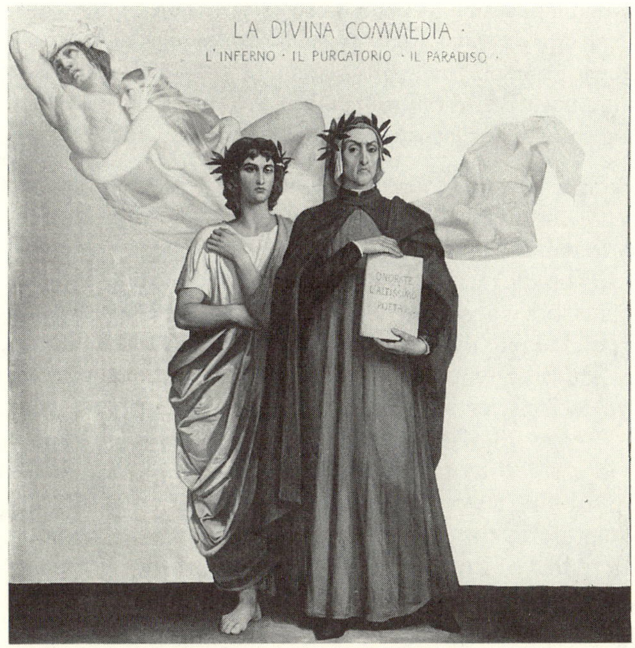

Plate 27. Dominique Papety: *La Divina Commedia,* 1842–47. Palazzo Renai, Florence.

scheme was supposedly already near completion.[215] Based upon Gigoux's portrait of 1836 and Fourier's death mask, versions of the bust (plate 29) enjoyed a prominent place in the school's visual propaganda. Initially displayed at a banquet of *ouvriers phalanstériens* in April 1847,[216] a copy was subsequently placed on Fourier's tomb in the cemetery of Montmartre, while plaster replicas were sold by the Librairie Phalanstérienne.

In the definitive scheme for the fireplace, the bust was placed upon a base inscribed with the Christian injunction "Vos omnes fratres estis" and flanked by two allegorical figures of Justice and Truth. Personified respectively by naked male and female adolescents, equipped with emblems of a balance and a tulip, a mirror and a lily, the symbolism of these two figures was interpreted in Fourierist circles as a significant innovation. Meray argued that the identification of Justice with the male was consonant with the "firm" and "inflexible" qualities of the masculine character, while the exploitation of accessories also expanded symbolic meaning:

[215] See Ménard, "Salon de 1847," *D.P.* 8, no. 67 (19 March 1847), and C. Brunier, "Beaux-Arts," *D.P.* 9, no. 105 (31 October 1847).

[216] See account of the banquet in *D.P.* 8, no. 97 (23 April 1847).

> There is nothing classical about these two figures. The scales, placed calmly on the ground under a young woman's hand, seem to show that in the world to which the artist-prophet transports us, equity is so innured in people's lives, the sense of justice exists so naturally in their hearts, that the material need for weighing things up in commerce or the law has become virtually redundant.[217]

The fireplace surround incorporates both allegory, in its depiction of two groups representing the *petites bandes* and the *petites hordes* on either side of the grate, together with more direct representation of Fourierist society in the bas-relief on the mantlepiece. A further symbolic reference, in the form of two candelabra whose thirty-two branches alluded to a *série mesurée*, was not incorporated into the finished work.[218] The bas-relief, like the allegorical figures, directs attention toward Fourier's educational philosophy with such scenes as "l'instruction sollicitée," "le damoisselat," and "l'éclosion des vocations" (plate 30). As with Papety's *Rêve de bonheur*, future felicity is couched in classical terms; the various protagonists wear loosely fitting drapery, inhabiting a world reminiscent of a lost Golden Age. Discussions of the sculpture in the Fourierist press accord it a significance virtually equivalent to that of Papety's painting. Describing the fireplace as "a hymn of praise to Fourier's great idea; . . . the first stone of the monument humanity will raise to him," the work's patron regarded it less as a didactic "comprehensive exposé of the Phalansterian doctrine" capable of winning new converts than as a "series of elegant scenes which are entirely intelligible and universally interesting."[219] Indeed, in this respect, the chimneypiece corresponds to the general tenor of the room for which it was intended. Rather than embodying any overtly programmatic message, such as Papety's initial proposal suggests, the decorative panels combine references to the Sabatiers' personal interests in European literature and grand opera[220] with a pantheon of great men in which Fourier is given pride of place. The room in the Palazzo Renai thus serves as an intellectual biography of its owners, incorporating the personal and the political in a monumental domestic setting.

Sabatier provided Ottin with his only opportunity to give unambiguous

[217] "Ces deux figures n'ont rien de classique. Les balances, tranquillement posées à terre sous la main du jeune homme, semblent indiquer que dans le monde où l'artiste prophète nous transporte, l'équité est tellement incarnée dans la vie des peuples, le sentiment de la justice existe si naturellement dans les coeurs, que la nécessité matérielle de la pesée sur les comptoirs ou devant les tribunaux est devenue à peu pres inutile." Meray, "Un Rêve d'harmonie.

[218] Brunier, "Beaux-Arts," *D.P.* 9, no. 105 (31 October 1847).

[219] "Un hymne de louange à la grande idée de Fourier; . . . la première pierre du monument que lui élevera l'humanité"; "exposé complet de la doctrine phalanstérienne"; "série de scènes gracieuses parfaitement intelligibles et intéressantes pour tous." Sabatier, *Salon de 1851*, 75–76.

[220] Papety's mural of Mozart and figures from *Don Giovanni* incorporates a portrait of Caroline Ungher in the guise of Donna Anna, a role for which she was particularly renowned.

form to his Fourierist convictions. In October 1848, however, he was to receive an official commission from Charles Blanc for a bas-relief depicting the *Marche triomphale de la République*, in which his democratic internationalism gave a particular inflection to the official ideology of the Second Republic. Though the work remained in the artist's studio following the coup d'état and was later sent to New York, a second—possibly modified—version was ordered in 1882, and subsequently figured in the 1885 Salon and the Exposition universelle of 1889 (plate 31).[221] Its complex iconography is elucidated in a poem by the sculptor's friend Eugène Pottier, published following the relief's appearance in 1885. A bizarre juxtaposition of races and historical periods, ranging from China and ancient Greece to Brittany and Alsace, the bas-relief juxtaposes allegorical personifications with contemporary figures to preach the virtues of education, international concord, and industrial expansion under the guidance of a matriarchal Republic crowned by a figure representing universal suffrage. As interpreted by Pottier, the bas-relief points the way toward universal freedom and association:

> Tu viens de l'ombre et vas au jour;
> Tu viens de la haine à l'amour
> Sur la planète fédérée.
> Tu conduis, ordre fraternel,
> Vers le bien-être universel
> L'humanité transfigurée.[222]

The figures discarding their chains at the feet of "la République" signify for Pottier not merely the abolition of slavery, but the overthrow of wage labor itself:

> L'esclavage est mort, mort son plagiat,
> Son moule dernier, le Salariat![223]

The work's internationalist implications are driven home by the Pantheon before which the parade passes. Surmounted by the motto "Aux hommes utiles, l'humanité reconnaissante," its pillars are inscribed with the names of

[221] The work's complex history is set out in the *Biographie*. The first version was sent to the United States for the Universal Exhibition of 1853. Problems over freight charges for the return voyage led the sculptor to donate the relief to the "musée de géographie" in New York. This subsequently involved Ottin in difficulties with the artistic administration under the Third Republic, since he had been paid for the original relief in 1848. Neither the 1885 replica nor the original relief are traceable today, though the plaster is held in storage at Ivry by the Ville de Paris.

[222] "You move from darkness to day, / From hatred to love / In the planetary federation. / Fraternal order, you guide / Transfigured humanity / To universal well-being." E. Pottier, "Marche triomphale de la République," *Revue socialiste* 1, no. 6 (1885): 538; reprinted in *Oeuvres complètes d'Eugène Pottier*, ed. P. Brochon (1966), 163–64.

[223] "Slavery is dead, dead too its imitation / Its final form, wage labor!"

Plate 28, near right. Auguste-Louis-Marie Ottin: Decorative Fireplace, Salon of 1850–51. Palazzo Renai, Florence.

Plate 29, far right. Auguste-Louis-Marie Ottin: *Charles Fourier*, Salon of 1850–51. Palazzo Renai, Florence.

Plate 30, below left and right. Auguste-Louis-Marie Ottin: *Eclosion des vocations* and *Instruction sollicitée:* details from bas-relief, monumental fireplace, Salon of 1850–51. Palazzo Renai, Florence.

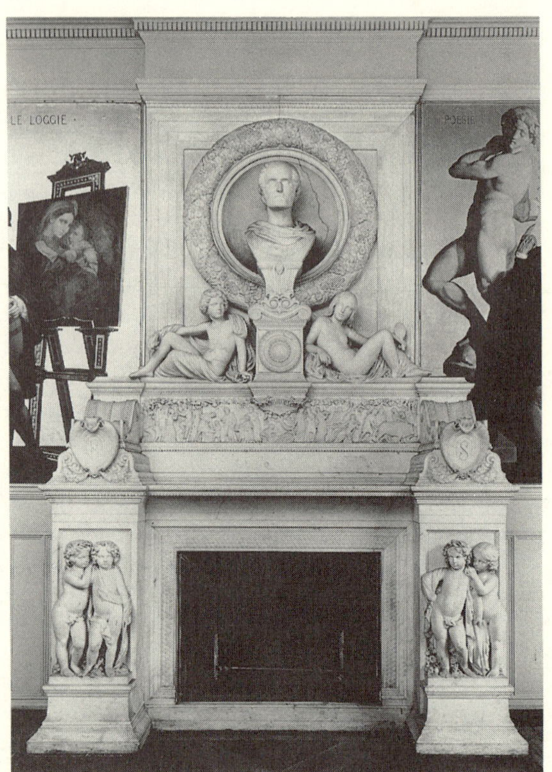

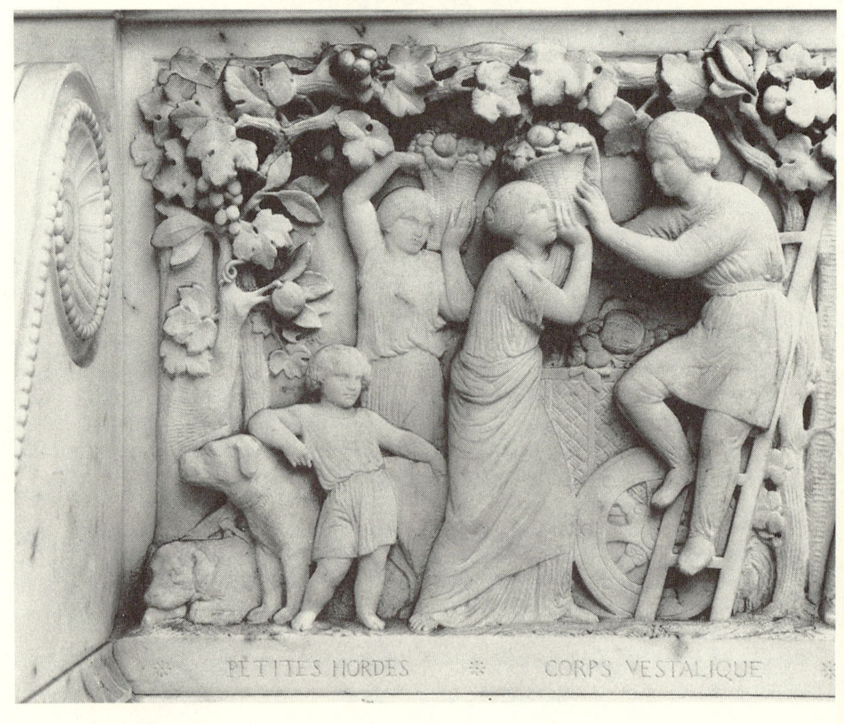

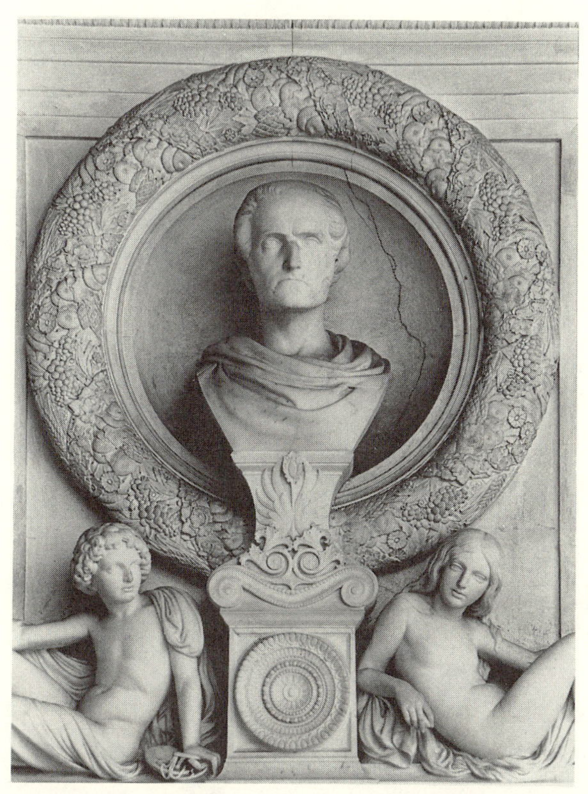

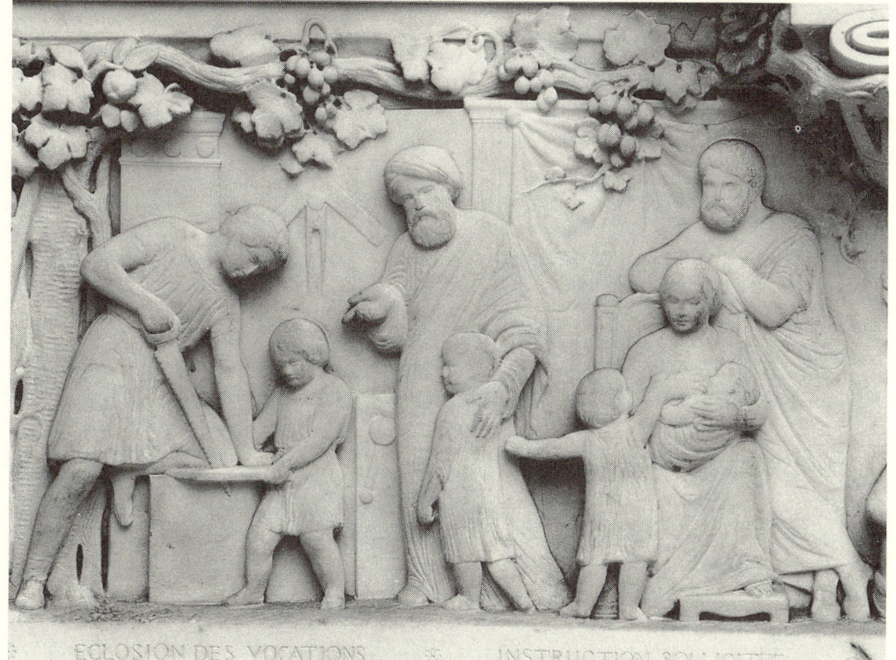
ECLOSION DES VOCATIONS
INSTRUCTION SOLLICITEE

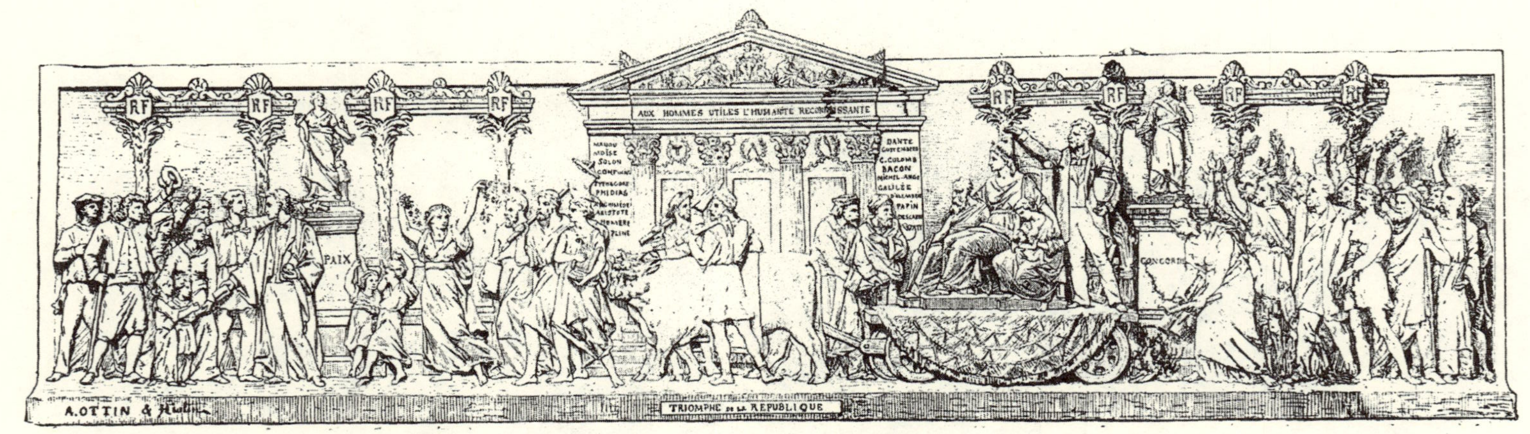

Plate 31. Auguste-Louis-Marie Ottin: *Marche triomphale de la République,* Salon of 1885. Reproduced from F.-G. Dumas, *Catalogue illustré du Salon de 1885*.

artists, scientists, and philosophers of the ancient and modern world. Although similar in tone to certain republican socialist currents prevalent in 1848—and the images generated by these tendencies—the political connotations of Ottin's bas-relief are unusually radical for an official commission. Despite the absence of any explicit reference to Fourier, his interpretation of republican ideology seems closer to *La Démocratie pacifique* than to *Le National.*

Ottin's Fourierist convictions survived imprisonment in June 1848[224] and dispersal of the movement under the Second Empire. Still proclaiming his allegiance to Fourier, he participated in the defense of the 18e arrondissement under the Commune and, together with his son Léon, was appointed to the Fédération des artistes. With the repression of the Commune, Ottin helped the socialist Benoît Malon escape to Switzerland, spending time in Basel, Geneva, and Neuchâtel before returning to France.[225] Several practical initiatives undertaken by the sculptor under the Third Republic demonstrate a commitment to mutualist politics. In 1872 he approached the Chambre syndicale with proposals for a drawing school owned and run as a workers' cooperative, and in May of that year joined Chabert in founding the mutualist Union syndicale ouvrière, a body repressed by the government five months later. From this perspective, Ottin's participation in the 1874 exhibition of the "Artistes indépendants" suggests endorsement of a cooperatist venture within the artistic professions, rather than any aesthetic sympathy with the other participants.

Ottin's interventions in working-class politics inform his interest in educational questions. The author of a drawing manual, the sculptor was appointed to the Inspectorat de l'enseignement du dessin by Viollet-le-Duc after 1870. His manual on sculpture, published in 1864, demonstrates a continuing commitment to Fourierism, both in its vocabulary and conceptual framework. Describing art as generated by a need for communication, itself "one of the thousand consequences of the principle of solidarity that unites men," Ottin elaborates a trinitarian notion of aesthetic response, based upon the interplay of *sentiment*, *sensation*, and *activité*, reminiscent of Izalguier and Laverdant.[226] Though his output after 1850 was almost entirely determined by official demands for decorative and commemorative statuary,[227] Ottin's pedagogical and political activities allowed the sculptor to apply his Fourierist beliefs in a practical way long after the organizational demise of the movement itself.

224 Ottin, *Biographie*, 27.

225 See entry on Ottin in Maitron's *Dictionnaire biographique du mouvement ouvrier français (1864–1871)*, 2:68–69, and Malon's obituary of the sculptor in the *Revue socialiste* (December 1890): 756–57.

226 "Une des milles conséquences du principe de solidarité qui relie les hommes entre eux." A. Ottin, *Esquisse d'une méthode applicable à l'art de la sculpture* (1864), 3, 5.

227 See the manuscript list of "oeuvres d'Auguste-Louis-Marie Ottin, statuaire" by Léon Ottin, Archives du Louvre Mss. 9HH7.

Of the group of Fourierists resident in the Villa Medici in the late 1830s, only the architect Florimonde Boulanger matches Ottin in the persistency of his beliefs. Like Ottin, Boulanger seems to have directed his efforts to practical questions concerned with associative schemes. Such a proposal was made to the Greek government in 1847, and appears to have been an abiding preoccupation, emerging both in his study *Ambélakia, ou les associations et les municipalités helléniques* of 1875 and in his bequest to the "maison rurale d'expérimentation sociétaire" at Ry following his death in the same year.[228] Farochon, too, retained ties with Fourierism well into the 1840s, though his practical involvement seems to have been limited.

Like Saint-Simonianism, the Fourierists attracted a number of more or less obscure figures engaged in the artistic professions—the architects Gay and Laplanche, Fugère the engraver, Louis Guémied, a pupil of Ingres during the 1840s, and the Toulousain sculptor Dorval and his compatriot Constantin Prévost, who was a regular participant in the Salon during the July Monarchy and professor of drawing at the Ecole des beaux-arts in Toulouse.[229] A list of artistic adherents appended to the 1840 edition of the *Almanach social* provides a number of equally obscure names, though it is significant that the former Saint-Simonian Jules Laure, then involved with Flora Tristan, appears in this context.[230] Gautier's association with the movement has given rise to speculation, while it appears clear that Théophile Thoré was attracted to Fourier's philosophy in the mid 1830s.[231] The painter Jean Gigoux, a close friend of Cantagrel and Considerant, was undoubtedly well disposed toward the group, though nothing suggests any more formal commitment.[232]

228 See Hanoune, "De Douai à Rome," 430, and the anonymous introduction to *Ambélakia, ou les associations et les municipalités helléniques avec documents confirmatifs* (1875), xvi.

229 On Gay, see J. L. Gay to X, 13 August [1832], Archives sociétaires 10 AS 38 (8); on Laplanche, see F. Laplanche to X, 31 July 1837, ibid., 10 AS 39 (7); on Fugère, see Raibaud l'Ange to Considerant, 15 August 1836, ibid., 10 AS 41 (11); on Guémied, see Guémied to the Direction, 17 July 1837, ibid., 10 AS 38 (16); on Dorval, see X to Considerant, 11 August 1836, ibid., 10 AS 41 (9); on Prevost, see G. Dorval to Considerant, 4 August 1836, ibid., 10 AS 38 (14) .

230 On Laure and Tristan, see J. Baelen, *La Vie de Flora Tristan* (1972), 81, n. 21, and 230.

231 On Gautier, see P. S. Hambly, "Théophile Gautier et le Fouriérisme," *Australian Journal of French Studies*, 2, no. 3 (September–December 1974): 237–52. On Thoré, see the *Dictionnaire de phrénologie*, and "L'Art des parfums," *L'Ariel* (March 1836).

232 The Archives sociétaires 10 AS 38 (11) contain four letters from Gigoux to Cantagrel, dated 1846–47, one to Considerant of 28 March 1848, and five letters to M. and Mme Considerant dating from the 1870s. On 30 December 1846 Gigoux writes to Cantagrel: "Je ne puis, ni ne veux, recevoir de l'argent de tout ce que je ferai pour les phalanstériens; malheureusement je suis si petit dans ce monde que je ne peux rien—voilà la seule raison qui fait que vous n'avez pas entendu parler de moi plus souvent; mais permettez-moi toujours, en attendant, toutes les fois que l'occasion s'en présentera, de vous apporter *ma pierre* pour ce monument que vous construisez."

None of this amounts to very much. With the exception of Papety and Ottin, Fourierist intervention in the arts appears to have been as limited as that of the Saint-Simonians. What is surprising is the extent to which those attracted to the group in Rome depart from the profile of the *artiste manqué* observed among Saint-Simonian adherents. The interest aroused among figures such as Gautier, Gigoux, Gozlan, and Ricourt also suggests a slightly different constituency from Saint-Simonian converts. This somewhat broader appeal relates perhaps to the looser structure and more conventionally bourgeois image of the Ecole sociétaire; though its ideas may have shocked middle-class sensibilities, its image in the 1840s grew progressively more respectable, while its philosophy and organizational hierarchy was far removed from the apostolic fervor of Enfantin's *église*. It was precisely the ability to tap support among individuals enjoying institutional protection, such as Papety at the Ecole de Rome, or financial power, such as Sabatier in Florence, that allowed the Fourierists to make their limited, if undeniably spectacular, interventions in the visual arts during the 1840s.

Yet the stereotype of the Fourierist painter, exemplified by the figure of Dubourdieu in Balzac's *Les Comédiens sans le savoir* of 1845, inhabits the marginal world of bohemian Paris rather than these more substantial circles of the middle class. In its syncretism of Fourierist and republican ideals and its absurdly recondite potpourri of allegorical devices, Dubourdieu's "figure allégorique de l'Harmonie" points to popular preconceptions of the innate weakness of any art inspired by the *humanitaires*—at once ridiculously complex and comically clumsy:

> With one's first glance, the planet's destiny can be guessed. In one hand, the queen holds the pastoral wand, symbolizing the growth of those races useful to mankind; she wears a liberty bonnet on her head and has six breasts, in Egyptian style, since the Egyptians anticipated Fourier; her feet rest on two clasped hands which embrace the globe in a sign of fraternity between races, she tramples destroyed cannons underfoot to signify the abolition of war, and I have attempted to make her express the triumph of agriculture. . . . What's more, next to her I have put an enormous curly cabbage, which, according to our master, symbolizes concord.[233]

[233] "Au premier coup d'oeil qu'on y jette, on devine la destinée du globe. La reine tient le baton pastoral d'une main, symbole de l'aggrandissement des races utiles à l'homme; elle est coiffée du bonnet de la liberté, ses mamelles sont sextuples, à la façon égyptienne, car les Egyptiens avaient pressenti Fourier; ses pieds reposent sur deux mains jointes qui embrassent le globe en signe de la fraternité des races humaines, elle foule des canons détruits pour signifier l'abolition de la guerre, et j'ai tâché de lui faire exprimer l'agriculture triomphante. . . . J'ai d'ailleurs mis près d'elle un enorme chou frisé qui, selon notre maître, est l'image de la concorde." H. de Balzac, *Les Comédiens sans le savoir* (1845), in *Oeuvres complètes*, ed. M. Bouteron (1936), 7:46. L. Rosenthal identifies Dubourdieu with the painter Chenavard (*Du romantisme au réalisme* [1914], 365), though the description seems to have more in common with Balzac's friend Théophile Bra.

Dubourdieu's potential talent is seen as having been squandered as a result of his political affiliations. Léon de Lora, the story's central character, acts as a mouthpiece for much contemporary critical opinion in equating doctrinal involvement with a misguided thirst for public recognition. Rather than aiding the artist, political engagement becomes a fatal handicap:

> All too often in Paris, desiring to win more rapidly than by legitimate means the fame which for them means fortune, artists borrow the wings of opportunism. Believing that their stature will grow through allying themselves to a particular position and becoming the exponents of a system, they hope to transform a small coterie into a broad following. One becomes a Republican, another a Saint-Simonian, yet others are Aristocrats, Catholics, Juste-Milieu, Medievalists, or Germans through deliberate choice. But not only do such opinions fail to endow the artist with talent, they almost always destroy whatever he has, as the poor boy you have just seen demonstrates.[234]

Balzac's unfavorable diagnosis of artistic *parti pris* articulates in satirical form a number of truisms circulated in critical discourse. The often mocking responses to the *Rêve de bonheur* and Ottin's fireplace testify not only to mistrust for Fourierism as a doctrine, but to also contempt for the broader enterprise of an *art humanitaire*. While perfectly willing to encourage, and indeed counsel, an element of *pensée*—or "thought"—in art, the majority of commentators regarded the infiltration of direct Fourierist subject matter into the Salon as both politically distasteful and aesthetically unviable. If the rather awkward iconographic mixture served up by the Fourierists fueled critical resistance, what was ultimately at stake was a conflict over the legitimate functions of art. Dubourdieu, and his nonfictional counterparts, stood accused of exploiting a medium traditionally regarded in terms of pleasure or edification for didactic ends, which stood outside the accepted ideological spectrum of the middle class. Though Laverdant and his colleagues in the Fourierist press might attempt to resolve this impasse by standing the argument on its head and appropriating a formal vocabulary for ideological ends, such a process could easily be interpreted as a sign of defeat. In contemporary eyes, the failure of Dubourdieu and his like to excite anything other than ridicule stood as firm proof of the Fourierists' failure to harness the visual arts as a stimulant for social change.

234 "Trop souvent à Paris, dans le désir d'arriver plus promptement que par la voie naturelle à cette célebrité qui pour eux est la fortune, les artistes empruntent les ailes de la circonstance, ils croient se grandir en se faisant les hommes d'une chose, en devenant les souteneurs d'un système, et ils espèrent changer une coterie en public. Tel est Républicain, tel autre était Saint-Simonien, tel est Aristocrate, tel Catholique, tel Juste-Milieu, tel Moyen-Age ou Allemand par parti pris. Mais si l'opinion ne donne pas le talent, elle le gâte toujours, témoin le pauvre garçon que vous venez de voir." Balzac, *Les Comédiens*, 47.

CHAPTER 8

Vision and Virtue: The Aesthetics of Republicanism

THE YEARS bounded by the revolutions of June 1830 and February 1848 witnessed the reassertion of a vigorous republican tradition in France, firmly opposed to the Orléanist monarch whose constitutional regime had emerged from the struggle against the Bourbons. Less a coherent movement than a fluctuating alliance, republicanism covered a broad ideological spectrum from moderate reformists seeking limited political change to revolutionary socialists committed to a comprehensive reordering of the nation's economic institutions in the interests of the laboring poor.[1] The volatility of political life under the July Monarchy, punctuated by insurrectionary explosions and abortive attempts on the king's life, owed less to formal opposition forces than to grass-roots frustration at Orléanism's imputed betrayal of its origins in popular revolt. The republican leadership nonetheless suffered unrelieved repression, intensified following the 1834 uprisings in Paris and Lyons, which handicapped attempts at organizing extraparliamentary association and agitation through the newspaper and periodical press.[2] With the exception of a militant wing dominated by Blanqui, most prominent republicans advocated peaceful reform and, despite the intensification of their campaign against the regime with the 1847 banquet movement, were scarcely prepared for the popular violence unleashed during the February Days.[3] To some degree, this unreadiness testifies to the predominantly bourgeois complexion of a movement that made only limited inroads among the urban working class, and which remained ambivalent toward those groups whose social and economic interests they sought to advance.

Other than the various political associations, such as the Jacobin inspired Amis du peuple or the more gradualist Société des droits de l'homme, the republicans' main forum and source of identity was provided by their publications. Particularly following the draconian reform to the Association Laws in March 1834, the press was to prove crucial in sustaining opposi-

[1] See G. Weill, *Histoire du parti républicain en France (1814–1870)* (1928), particularly chaps. 2–8.

[2] On the role of the radical press under the July Monarchy, see C. Ledré, *La Presse à l'assaut de la monarchie 1815–1848* (1960), 125–95.

[3] See Weill, *Histoire du parti républicain*, 202–9.

tional momentum. Though constant prosecution stifled more radical voices and sapped journals' human and material resources, the republican press did survive, however tenuously, throughout the eighteen years of Orléanist rule. Dominated by the opposition's leading ideologues and polemicists—Carrel and Marrast at *Le National*, Ledru-Rollin at *La Réforme*, Cavaignac and Louis Blanc at the *Journal du peuple*—the press addressed an essentially middle-class readership and tended to promote more moderate currents on the left. Though the social question took on increasing prominence, particularly after 1834 with the establishment of such publications as Raspail's *Réformateur* and Dupont's *Revue républicaine*, emerging socialist trends maintained often strained relations with the powerful bourgeois reformist wing centered on *Le National*.

These tensions, and the ideological diversity from which they arose, not only weakened republican opposition but also frustrate retrospective attempts to identify a coherent and unified political "movement." By the same token, aesthetic discourse tends to be more varied and diffuse than is the case within more ideologically focused groups, such as Saint-Simonianism or Christian socialism. Even within a single journal, positions fluctuated quite dramatically: *Le National*, for example, could successively employ the relatively conservative figures Désiré Nisard and Louis Peisse in the early 1830s, and the committed radical Alexandre Decamps at the end of the decade, before entrusting artistic commentary to a disciple of Buchez's, Henri-Robert Feugueray, and a moderate republican, Prosper Haussard, during the 1840s. Similar diversity characterizes differences within the ideological spectrum of the republican press. Yet, despite this heterogeneity, a distinctive "republican aesthetic" can still be discerned, privileging themes that echo the movement's characteristic preoccupations. In focusing on the issues of morality, nature, truth, and modernity, our investigation aims to highlight the ideological resonance of an aesthetic whose limitations reveal the political difficulties encountered in challenging the founding values of a regime the republicans were dedicated to overthrowing.

THE NECESSITY OF VIRTUE

"In a popular state, an additional stimulus is required: that of VIRTUE."[4] Montesquieu's identification of democracy as nothing less than a state of mind demanding the active moral participation of all members of the polis serves as a leitmotif that echoes through French republican thought. In common with their eighteenth-century antecedents, republicans of all

[4] "Dans un état populaire, il faut un ressort de plus, qui est la VERTU." C. de Secondat de Montesquieu, *De l'esprit des lois* (1748), in *Oeuvres complètes* (1950), 1:26.

shades under the July Monarchy insisted on the seamless interdependence between private virtue and the vitality of the public realm. Of formative importance in shaping much republican aesthetic discourse, this concern with personal behavior bore the traces of a secular rationalism bequeathed by the Enlightenment and mobilized in civic and educational programs after 1789. Common to this tradition was a desire to subordinate individual will and action to the needs and interests of the collectivity, a process to be achieved not by coercion but through the citizen's internalization of ethical codes compatible with the general good. For Montesquieu, it was in "love of laws and nation" that the citizen sublimated any temptation to indulge self-interest, seeking personal realization instead in altruistic service to an egalitarian community.[5] As elaborated by republican theorists later in the century, this relationship with the state increasingly implied the colonization of individual consciousness, as moral choice was conceived less as an autonomous process of reflection and judgment than as an automatic reflex programmed by external stimuli. Though given fullest expression during the 1790s, particularly in discussions of education and the arts, this instrumental perception of morality as integral to citizenship was to prove fundamental to republican perspectives on *art social* in the succeeding century.

Enlightenment theories of natural rights, predicated on utilitarian rather than transcendental foundations, defined the individual moral agent first and foremost as citizen. The transparent relationship with an omniscient deity, formerly regulating the believer's transactions with his fellows, was supplanted by an equally intimate and pervasive conception of the state, whose surveillance operated less as an external constraint than as an integral aspect of ethical discrimination. For Rousseau, statecraft consisted in forging institutions facilitating the individual's immersion into the collectivity, a transformative process intended to "change man's nature, deprive him of his absolute existence in favor of a relative one, and insert the *self* into the unified community."[6] Frequently reiterated during the Revolution,[7] this aspiration toward a social organicism actualized in the ethical protocols of everyday life

[5] "L'amour des lois et de la patrie." Ibid., 46, 55.

[6] "Dénaturer l'homme, lui ôter son existence absolue pour lui en donner une relative, et transporter le *moi* dans l'unité commune." J.-J. Rousseau, *Emile, ou l'éducation* (1762), in *Oeuvres complètes*, ed. B. Gagnebin and M. Raymond (1969), 4:586. See also "Du législateur," *Du contrat social* (1762), ibid. (1964), 3:381–84.

[7] See, for example, Rabaut-Saint-Etienne's remark, reported in the *Moniteur* (22 December 1792): "L'enfant qui n'est pas né appartient déjà à la patrie. Elle s'empare de tout l'homme sans le quitter jamais." Quoted in A. Sicard, *L'Education morale et civique avant et pendant la Révolution (1700–1808)* (1884), 250. See also F. A. de Boissy d'Anglas, *Essai sur les fêtes nationales suivi de quelques idées sur les arts; et la nécessité de les encourager* (an II), 75. For an exemplary discussion of Rousseau's impact on revolutionary notions of virtue, see Carol Blum, *Rousseau and the Republic of Virtue: The Language of Politics in The French Revolution* (1986), chaps. 8–14.

attenuated all distinction between public and private. As the state increasingly abrogated a jurisdiction over individual action formerly claimed by the church, so a new gospel of enlightened self-interest, founded on a symmetry between public duty and private benefit, offered a more secular incitement to virtue. The advance of reason, it was claimed, would guarantee the consolidation of a social morality of infallible efficacy. As Lakanal argued in 1794, in the future, "The moral sciences, so necessary to peoples governed by their own virtue, will be subject to proofs as rigorous as those for physics and the exact sciences."[8]

This faith in reason, perpetuated by the Idéologues and seen by some commentators as characteristic of republican thought,[9] envisages a positivist theory of ethics. Its realization in lived experience, however, calls upon other mechanisms, solicits compliance through an appeal to other faculties. In line with what Bronislaw Baczko has described as "an entire anthropological and pedagogical tradition within the Enlightenment,"[10] it was to the more responsive emotional triggers associated with sentiment that theorists looked in order to inculcate virtue in the population at large. As the cult of *sensibilité* disrupted the traditional dichotomy between reason and passion, so eighteenth-century commentators increasingly emphasized the benefits to be derived from cultivating moral feeling. Rooted in experience rather than intellection, sentiment came to be closely identified with the emotionally vivid representation of edifying actions. Though this preoccupation with civic instruction shaped discussion of education during the Revolution,[11] the inculcation of morality was not to be confined to the classroom. Rather, all aspects of life would strengthen the citizen's commitment to the common good as "the entire French nation" became an immense forcing ground of public virtue. "Circuses, gymnasia, armed displays, public games, national festivals"[12]—all would be exploited in the pursuit of a moral sense so profoundly inscribed within individual consciousness as to become "an emotion, a source of happiness, and thus a deeply rooted habit."[13]

[8] "Les sciences morales, si nécessaires aux peuples qui se gouvernent par leurs propres vertus, vont être soumises à des démonstrations aussi rigoureuses que les sciences exactes et physiques." Reported in the *Moniteur* (28 November 1794), cited by Sicard, *Education morale*, 326–27.

[9] See C. Nicolet, *L'Idée républicaine en France. Essai d'histoire critique* (1982), 33–34.

[10] "Toute une tradition anthropologique et pédagogique des Lumières." B. Baczko, *Une Education pour la démocratie. Textes et projets de l'époque réevolutionnaire* (1982), 31.

[11] On educational theory and practice during the Revolution, see R. R. Palmer, *The Improvement of Humanity: Education and the French Revolution* (1985).

[12] "Des cirques, des gymnases, des armes, des jeux publics, des fêtes nationales." J.-P. Rabaut-Saint-Etienne, reported in the *Moniteur* (22 December 1792), and cited by Sicard, *Education morale*, 360.

[13] "Un sentiment, un bonheur et par conséquent une forte habitude." C. M. de Talleyrand-Périgord, *Rapport sur l'instruction publique* (September 1791), reprinted in C. Hippeau, ed., *L'Instruction publique en France pendant la Révolution* (1881), 158.

Some half a century after the Revolution, the issue of public virtue remained central to republican discourse. Though Louis Blanc refuted Montesquieu's celebrated formula on virtue and democracy,[14] the language of radicalism during the 1830s and 1840s reveals an unyielding sense of politics as the practical realization of ethical imperatives. In celebrating popular probity and attacking the bourgeoisie as an exploitative class, theorists such as Blanc and Marrast established a symbiosis between political analysis and moral critique,[15] with the latter asserting that the ethical implications of citizenship surpassed in importance the formal organization of power:

> In the end, the form of government will no longer be important enough to arouse passions, since the legislators' first concern will be to use education, the press, the theater, games, festivals, every heuristic device, and every propaganda technique to instill general habits of probity, liberty, and fraternity. These will be the laws' best guarantors, if not the only ones capable of overcoming those feelings of monopoly and usurpation which pride instills in all rulers.[16]

The institutional network envisaged here typifies a preoccupation with *éducation morale* inherited from Rousseau and his revolutionary successors. Radiating out of formal educational initiatives, in which many republicans took an active interest in the early 1830s,[17] civic instruction was conceived as an integral aspect of cultural life, transcending arbitrary distinctions between public and private. In the same way as Rousseau had projected education as one facet of a didactic continuum to fashion "patriots by choice, passion, and need,"[18] so radicals such as the neo-Babouvist Albert Laponneraye, writing in 1835, could forsee a day when young citizens would behave virtuously "mechanically and instinctively, as they eat and drink."[19]

[14] L. Blanc, "De la vertu considérée comme principe de gouvernement," *R.R.* 4 (1835): 5.

[15] See, for example, "La Bourgeoisie—La République," in Marrast's *Vingt Jours de secret ou le complot d'avril* (1834), and Louis Blanc on social inequality in *De l'organisation du travail* (1839), 24ff.

[16] "Les formes du gouvernement finiront par n'être plus assez importantes pour qu'on se passionne pour elles, car le premier soin des législateurs aura été de former par l'éducation, par la presse, par le théâtre, par les jeux, par les fêtes, par tous les moyens d'enseignement, par tous les stimulants de la publicité, des moeurs générales de probité, de liberté, de fraternité, qui seront la meilleure sanction des lois, la seule même qui puisse paralyser cet esprit d'accaparement et d'usurpation que l'orgueil infiltre à quiconque est armé du pouvoir." Marrast, *Vingt Jours*, 38.

[17] See, for example, on Raspail and the activities of the Association libre pour l'éducation du peuple, of which the painter Jeanron was a member, Weill, *Histoire du parti républicain*, 77.

[18] "Patriotes par inclination, par passion, par nécessité." J.-J. Rousseau, *Considérations sur le gouvernement de Pologne* (1771), in *Oeuvres complètes*, ed. B. Gagnebin and M. Raymond (1964), 3:966.

[19] "Machinalement, instinctivement, comme ils boivent et mangent." A. Laponneraye, "De l'éducation morale," *Mélanges d'économie sociale, de littérature et de morale* (1835), 1:370.

Understood according to such priorities, art was less a *sacerdoce* than an *enseignement*, the artist treated less in the exalted role of priest interceding with humanity than as a teacher imparting lessons of civic duty to his fellow men. Though increasingly attenuated by concern for the emotional impact of form, the didactic bias of republican aesthetics owed much to this essentially pragmatic concern with art as a medium for moral instruction, a primary function of which was to inculcate particular social values through the power of example. Like the schoolmaster—an ideological folk hero of a later generation of republicans—the artist was deemed capable of transforming individual behavior, working as an "éducateur du sentiment"[20] to consolidate desirable moral reflexes through the immediacy of representation. For Etienne Arago, writing in 1835, a new secular mythology, rooted in the cardinal principles of republicanism, offered the artist a thematic repertoire as dramatically engaging and morally inspiring as the Christian narrative it superseded:

> What more brilliant theogony than one in which the spirit is presented with divine versions of *liberty*, *equality*, and *fraternity*, that holy trinity around which would be arrayed *devotion*, *resignation*, and *patience*—all virtues of *labor*. Such are the gods of Goodness; the gods of Evil will be *egotism*, *ambition*, *indifference*, *self-interest*—all the selfish passions of *leisure*.[21]

Regarding art as "a propaganda mission,"[22] Arago and commentators like him were most sensitive to the portrayal of themes directly affecting the individual's perceptions of his duties and allegiances as a Frenchman. At the same time as exalting values associated with the republican trinity, they thus reveal a nationalist impulse largely absent amongst other radical critics.[23] Republican susceptibility to patriotic and military themes, which found its quintessential voice in the verse of Béranger, fostered admiration for such battle painters as Charlet and Raffet,[24] at the same time as encouraging

20 J. F. Dupont, "Introduction," *R.R.* 1 (April 1834): 20.

21 "Quelle théogonie plus brillante que celle qui présenterait à l'esprit, en les divinisant, *la liberté*, *l'égalité*, *la fraternité*, cette trinité sainte autour de laquelle se grouperaient *le dévouement*, *la résignation*, *la patience*, toutes les vertus du *travail*. Les dieux du Bien vous sont donnés; les dieux du Mal seront *l'égoïsme*, *l'ambition*, *l'indifférence*, *l'intérêt matériel*, toutes les passions cupides du *loisir*." E. Arago, "La République et les artistes," *R.R.* 2 (10 July 1834), 25.

22 "Une mission de propagande." Ibid., 28.

23 The trait is also found in Buchezian artistic commentary, and is particularly conspicuous in the work of Henri-Robert Feugueray, a Christian socialist contributing to *Le National* as Henri Robert. In 1842, he calls for artists to become "les prêtres de la nationalité, chargés de faire aimer la patrie et de réveiller dans les âmes appesanties les sentiments patriotiques qui y sommeillent," "Salon de 1842," *Nat.* (15 April 1842).

24 See, for example, remarks on Bellangé by Henri Robert, "Salon de 1842," *Nat.* (24 April 1842). On Béranger, and comparisons with the populism of Charlet, see A. Decamps, "Les Arts et l'industrie au dix-neuvième siècle," *R.R.* 3 (10 October 1834): 43. See P. Bénichou, *Le Temps des prophètes. Doctrines de l'âge romantique* (1977), 387–95, on Béranger's social themes.

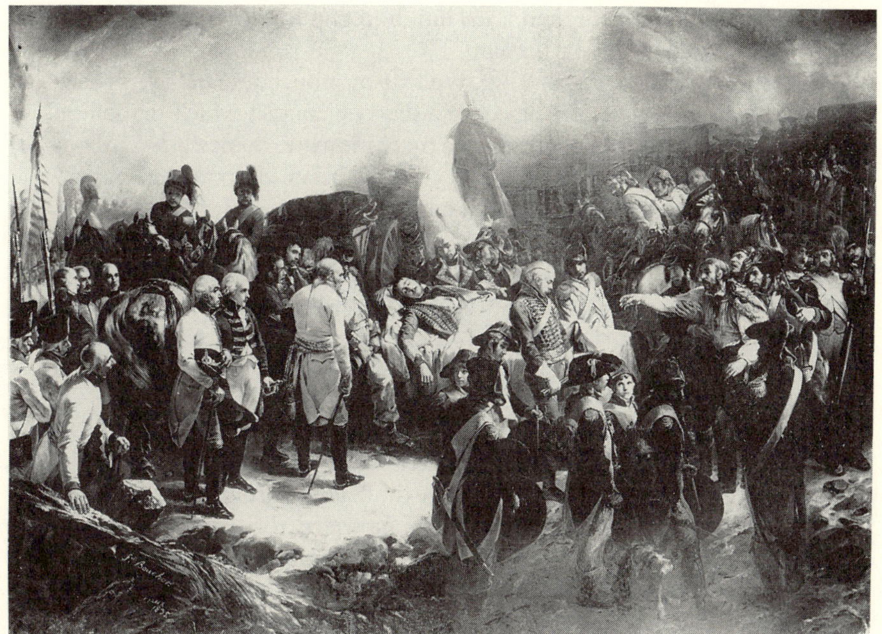

Plate 32. François Bouchot: *Les Funérailles du Général Marceau,* Salon of 1835. Hôtel de ville, Chartres.

favorable evaluations of works such as Bouchot's *Funérailles du Général Marceau* (plate 32), exhibited at the Salon of 1835, and Leullier's *Nauffrage du "Vengeur"* of 1841.[25] The association of such episodes with periods of recent history admired for their military audacity and success provoked unflattering parallels with France's current international standing. Writing in the *Journal du peuple*, for example, the critic Jules Baget described Leullier's evocation of a 1794 naval combat with the English as "a protest against France's humiliation and our government's cowardice before other nations."[26] Yet such scenes also promoted a more generalized jingoism, which lies beneath the surface of much republican aesthetic discourse. Official commissions recording the Algerian campaign thus more typically aroused a bellicose patriotism than any anticolonialist sentiments—for Buchez's disciple Henri-Robert Feugueray, writing in the republican *Le National*, Bellangé's *Prise du Col de Téniah* of 1841 "awakens within the spectator the

[25] On Bouchot, see, for example, A. Decamps, "Salon de 1835," *R.R.* 5, no. 14 (10 May 1835): 164–65, where the painting is described as "l'une des oeuvres les plus complètes qu'ait vu naître la peinture depuis la *Méduse* de Géricault."

[26] "Une protestation contre l'abaissement de la France et contre les lâchetés de notre gouvernement en face de l'étranger." J. Baget, "Salon de 1841," *J.P.* (21 March 1841).

slumbering military spirit, and leads him to regret not having fired on the Arabs and shared in the day's events."[27]

Contemporary history painting, typified by Bouchot, Leullier, or Bellangé, corresponded to one aspect of a didactic couplet which republican critics also envisaged as operating on a more intimate, domestic level. Thus Alexandre Decamps, writing in 1836, could associate *art social* with a monumental public art, exemplified in the major canvases of figures such as David, Géricault, and Gros, and contrasting with a more private *art familier*, in which past masters such as Cellini, Ghiberti, Palissy, and Rembrandt had excelled.[28] These complementary forms, previously unified in the less segregated social environment of classical antiquity, were said to engage the spectator both as active citizen and as affective individual, inculcating ethical responses appropriate to these contiguous levels of existence.[29]

While alert to the dangers posed by naive sentimentality,[30] republican critics' conception of *art familier* promoted some sympathy for the moralizing genre painting that proliferated in the Salon during the 1830s and 1840s. Although some commentators interpreted the eclipse of history painting by genre works as symptomatic of the pervasive individualism and fragmentation within contemporary society,[31] the majority echoed Decamps's belief in their capacity to extend moral instruction into the private sphere. Here, the increasing accessibility of cheap reproductions met with particular approval, as a means of inculcating "heroic examples, moral instruction, lessons of equality,"[32] and addressing sections of society habitually excluded by the protocols of high culture. The publication in 1839 of Prévost's engravings after Léopold Robert elicited particular approval from both Decamps and Charles Blanc, for whom *Les Moissonneurs* (plate 19) was inspired by "a deeply plebeian idea" capable of fostering popular self-respect by celebrating "the majesty, grace, and energy" of ordinary working people.

27 "Réveille chez le spectateur l'esprit militaire endormi, et lui fait regretter de n'avoir pas tiré des coups de fusil aux Arabes et prendre sa part de la journée." Henri Robert, "Salon de 1841," *Nat.* (23 March 1841).

28 A. Decamps, "Salon de 1836," *Nat.* (4 March 1836).

29 "L'art monumental nous rappelle la pratique des vertus publiques, l'amour de la patrie, la morale, la religion, le culte des grands hommes; l'art des foyers embellit et charme notre demeure, nous attache à ce qui nous entoure, et développe en nous les sentiments de sympathie généreuse qui ne sont jamais étouffés complètement par l'abrutissement de l'égoïsme et de l'ignorance." A. Decamps, "Salon de 1837," *Nat.* (27 April 1837).

30 See Robert's remarks on the *sensiblerie niaise* of the Greuzian tradition in his 1841 review, *Nat.* (15 April 1841).

31 See, for example, B. Hauréau, "Coup d'oeil cynique sur l'exposition," *Mercure de France au XIXe siècle*, 33 (1831): 485.

32 "Les héroïques exemples, les leçons de morale, les enseignements d'égalité"; "les plus beaux types de la nature humaine." C. Blanc, "Beaux-Arts: gravure," *R.P.* 1 (15 February 1839): 145.

For Blanc, Robert's elevation of an ostensibly realistic scene through the portrayal of "human nature at its most beautiful"[33] revealed the nobility of labor and helped refine popular consciousness through exposure to beauty.

Such an initiative could be construed as ultimately furthering political emancipation by contributing to the subordinate classes' liberation from their ethically debilitating environment.[34] At the same time, however, republicans were unable to confront—let alone overcome—the contradictions inherent in promoting a range of values integral to the subordination of those groups whose emancipation they sought. The strict moralism of republican ideologues such as Marrast and Blanc, though intended to demonstrate that the popular classes possessed an integrity that legitimized their political claims, ran the risk of merely endorsing a system of values which underwrote the status quo, rather than calling it into question.

This investment of the visual arts with ethical and ideological responsibilities encouraged a number of republican commentators to proclaim an exclusive concern with content in evaluating contemporary production. Though rarely maintained with any consistency in practice, this stance implied a predominantly instrumental notion of art reminiscent of Buchezian theory. Thus, for example, in 1839 the *Journal du peuple*'s critic Jules Baget—himself paradoxically a professional flower painter—could denigrate art as a source of sensual pleasure and pronounce himself sympathetic only toward work that was "good, useful, moral, and national."[35] Similar priorities inform Prosper Haussard's credo prefacing his 1843 review in *Le National*, where he promises "to demand first of every work an underlying idea, and only afterward technique; to prefer the thinking artist to the 'naturalist,' feeling to imitation, the soul to the hand."[36] Such critics imposed upon the artist a burden of moral responsibility more appropriate to the pedagogue than the prophet, and often judged harshly apparent deviations from the lofty standards with which they approached the Salon exhibition. At the same time as endorsing radical antipathy toward formalism, at least on a theoretical level, many republican commentators were alert to artists' betrayal of their responsibilities as active citizens, particularly when this entailed collusion with the despised Orléanist regime. Condemnation of figures such as Gérard, Heim, and Vernet for opportunistic *courtisanne-*

[33] "Une pensée profondément plébeienne"; "la majesté, la grâce, l'énergie"; Ibid., p. 146. See also, A. Decamps, "Salon de 1839," *Nat.* (9 April 1839).

[34] See, for example, E. Hervé, "De l'art," *L'Intelligence* (July 1838): 14, who argues "Enlever le peuple aux plaisirs grossiers qui seuls lui sont accessibles, c'est lui donner le sentiment de sa vie morale et intellectuelle, c'est développer l'élément progressif."

[35] "Bon, utile, moral, national." J. Baget, "Salon de 1839," *J.P.* (14 April 1839).

[36] "Dans toute oeuvre, exiger d'abord l'idée, l'exécution après; préférer l'artiste penseur au 'naturaliste,' le sentiment à l'imitation, l'âme à la main." P. Haussard, "Salon de 1843," *Nat.* (15 April 1843).

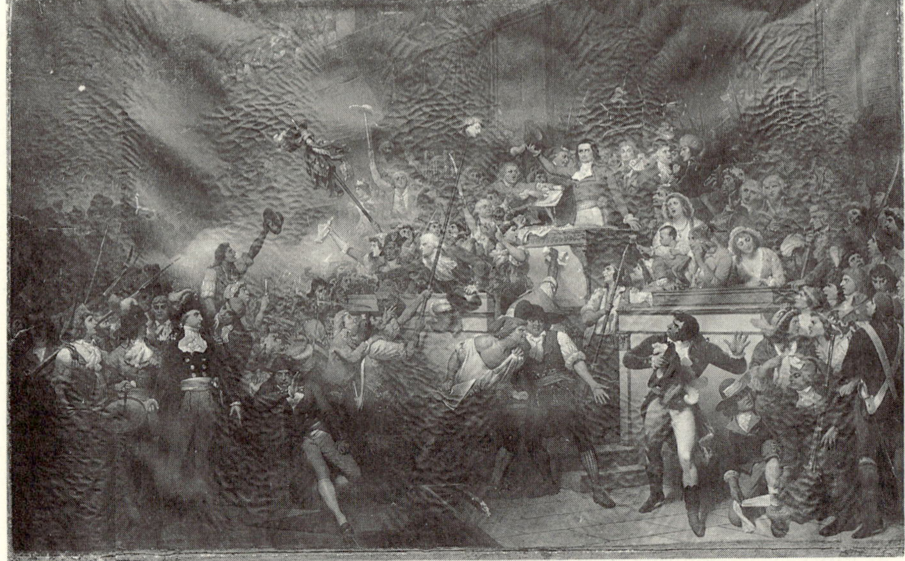

Plate 33. Joseph-Désiré Court: *Boissy d'Anglas, présidant la Convention nationale, journée du 1er prairial An III,* Salon of 1833. Musée des beaux-arts, Rouen.

rie[37] could, on occasion, inspire virulent *ad hominem* polemic, most spectacularly in 1833 when Jean-Barthélémy Hauréau attacked Court for displaying his "haine contre le peuple et les révolutions" in his *Boissy d'Anglas, présidant la Convention nationale, journée du 1er prairial An III* (plate 33), a particularly gory scene of popular revolt in 1795. Reminding the artist of his humble origins as a wigmaker's son, the critic disdained his work as "the most lucrative form of flattery he could offer those in power," a cynical insult toward the people motivated by greed and ambition.[38]

The cultural and political bankruptcy of the present contrasted in republican mythology with the Revolution's mobilization of the arts in the national interest. Standing as a paradigm of art's capacity to engage directly with a mass audience and elaborate a pictorial and monumental vocabulary of public forms stamped with "the mark of the people,"[39] the First Republic

[37] The term is J. B. Hauréau's, in relation to Vernet, in his "Salon [de 1833]," *La Tribune politique et littéraire* (11 March 1833). On Heim, see Hauréau, "Salon de 1834," ibid. (3 March 1834).

[38] "La plus lucrative flatterie qu'il pût faire au pouvoir." Hauréau, "Salon," *La Tribune politique et littéraire* (9 March 1833). See also T. Thoré, "Exposition ambulante de tableaux contre-révolutionnaires et Salon de 1835," *Le Réformateur* (11 March 1835).

[39] "Le cachet du peuple." G. Cavaignac, "Monuments révolutionnaires," *R.R.* 3 (November 1834): 150. On the Revolution, see, for example, A. Decamps, "Les Arts et l'industrie au dix-neuvième siècle," *R.R.* 3 (10 October 1834): 36, and B. Hauréau, "De la politique et des arts," *L.A.* 1 (August 1832): 29–30.

served to demonstrate a productive alliance between painters and politicians, which had allowed artists to serve the state without becoming subservient to it. This dynamic integration of culture into the public realm, ostensibly realized in the wake of 1789 and anticipated once again after 1830,[40] represented an ideal of cultural production in which the artist participated in the unfolding process of history as commentator and guide rather than standing outside it in the guise of a *vates* signaling toward a promised utopia. Thus conceived, art's value accrued primarily from its ability to speak to the citizen of the present, whether in the exalted tones of David's revolutionary canvases or in the more intimate language of contemporary genre works, with their lessons of personal probity and social equity.

Yet, in common with other proponents of *art social*, republican commentators more frequently express frustration than satisfaction when assessing the ideological tenor of current production. Crediting only a tiny handful of figures, such as the painters Jeanron, Charlet, and Latil or the sculptors Maindron, Préault, and David d'Angers, with any sustained social commitment, they regularly lament the cultural vacuity displayed at the Salon and castigate the majority of exhibitors for their studied indifference to art's moral potential. In common with the priority accorded by republican theorists to the eradication of poverty in society,[41] critics sharing such an ideological perspective showed themselves particularly receptive to images exposing the material hardship endured by the popular classes. Consistent with their perception of art's primarily instructional status, critics valued such work as sensitizing the viewer to social injustice and prompting a questioning of the laissez-faire capitalism promoted by the Orléanist regime. Though embracing such generalized representations as Préault's *La Mendicité* of 1833, it was to the more specific and ostensibly naturalistic work of figures such as Jeanron, Trimolet, and Latil that attention primarily turned. Preeminent among this group, Jeanron attracted consistent praise during the 1830s, notably for the *Scène de Paris* (plate 34) exhibited in 1833, which consolidated the artist's reputation for sympathetic portrayals of popular life established with *Les Petits Patriotes* the previous year.[42] The implicit political critique signaled by the juxtaposition of the impoverished veteran of the July Days with the Chamber of Deputies—"the palace where every day men who claim to represent the French people pass laws for the privileged which

[40] According to E. Arago, "Le Théâtre considéré comme moyen révolutionnaire," *Paris révolutionnaire* 1 (1833): 61, following the July Revolution "les artistes . . . croyaient à l'émancipation complète de la pensée."

[41] As stated, for example, by Garnier-Pagès during the "Procès des quinze" in 1832: "tout gouvernement, quand il n'existerait que quinze jours, devrait trouver le temps de s'occuper des classes malheureuses"; cited in Weill, *Histoire du parti républicain*, 51.

[42] On the *Scène de Paris*, see M.-C. Chaudonneret, "Jeanron et 'l'art social': *Une Scène de Paris*," *Revue du Louvre* 4–5 (October 1986): 317–19, and G. P. Weisberg, "Early Realism," in *The Art of the July Monarchy. France 1830–1848*, ed. G. P. Weisberg (1990), 105–7.

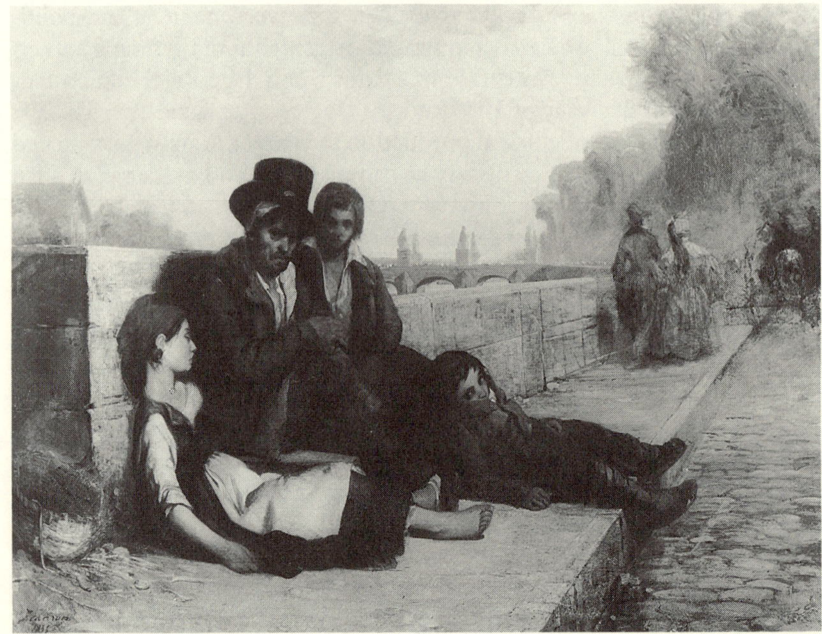

Plate 34. Philippe-Auguste Jeanron: *Une Scène de Paris,* Salon of 1833. Musée des beaux-arts, Chartres.

steal the last crumb of bread out of the mouth of the proletarian's children"[43]—served to enhance the work's appeal for radical opponents of the regime. For Hauréau, who saw in Jeanron's canvas the eloquence of "two volumes of contemporary history," the artist's work demonstrated a commitment to restoring dignity to a class deprived of moral and material independence by capitalist exploitation:

> What dominates throughout is the love and intelligence of the people, and particularly the people of Paris, impoverished and made ugly by the hunger that sucks their veins and hollows their cheeks, this Caliban cursed by evil masters, dragging their bodies through the mud bent, like Shakespeare's monster, beneath heavy burdens.[44]

As transposed into the language of republican critical discourse, such a work generated moral meaning through a form of reading intent on extrap-

[43] "Le palais où des hommes, qui se prétendent les mandataires du peuple français, stipulent tous les jours des lois de privilège qui ôtent le dernier morceau de pain à la bouche des enfants du prolétaire"; "deux tomes d'histoire contemporaine." G. Laviron and B. Galbaccio [*sic*], *Salon de 1833* (1833), 257.

[44] "Ce qui domine partout, c'est l'amour et l'intelligence du peuple, et surtout de ce peuple de Paris pauvre et enlaidi par la faim qui lui suce la veine et lui creuse les joues, ce Caliban maudit par de méchants maîtres, et comme le monstre de Shakespeare, traînant misérablement

olating extrinsic anecdotal content from intrinsic detail. Speculation on the character ("a great and generous soul") and material circumstances of the indigent father ("a laborer who has worked every day of his life"),[45] or the social identity of those indifferent to his plight ("the son of a banker, made rich by his father's crimes, trotting away in the background in his open carriage"),[46] repositioned works such as Jeanron's as the first link in a hermeneutic chain using the fictive and particular to advance a broader critique of a pervasive social malaise. In many instances, such images' recourse to empathetic identification with the central protagonists arguably undercuts such a process, while their habitual passivity positions the poor as objects for pity and philanthropic relief rather than as active agents capable of challenging their own subservience. Of reputed polemical value in questioning the human cost of laissez-faire liberalism, such works were further admired as a suitable reproach to those whose affluence depended on the exploitation of the poor and vulnerable. Thus, in 1839, for example, Alexandre Decamps asserts that Trimolet's *Maison de secours*, a scene of the impoverished receiving alms, could exert a salutary influence if acquired for a prestigious private collection: "It would have more effect on rich visitors' souls than a sermon and would perhaps be more useful than a charitable collection authorized by one of the archbishop's pastoral letters."[47] Yet republicans shared other radical critics' awareness that it was precisely this market structure, sustained by the taste and susceptibilities of an affluent clientele, that most inhibited initiatives to temper art's critical edge. Though the sculptor David d'Angers could conceive of art as a formidable popular tribunal serving as "the sanctuary that preserves the annals of virtue and of tyrants' crimes,"[48] others realized that prevailing circumstances dictated a more anodyne formula. As Thoré noted contemptuously in 1835, "Satin, roses, dancing and festivities, a great tapestry good enough to conceal the tears of thirty million proletarians, that is what our patrons require, since our patrons are bankers and parvenus."[49]

---

dans la fange son corps ployé sous les lourds fardeaux." Hauréau, "Salon," *La Tribune politique et littéraire* (9 March 1833).

[45] "Une âme grande et généreuse"; "un ouvrier qui a travaillé tous les jours de sa vie." Laviron and Galbaccio, *Salon de 1833*, 256.

[46] "C'est le fils d'un banquier, enrichi par les crimes de son père, qui court dans le fond sur sa calèche ouverte." Hauréau, "Salon," *La Tribune politique et littéraire* (11 March 1833). For a similar descriptive strategy, see Baget on Mascré's *Bal au profit des pauvres* in his "Salon de 1839," *J.P.* (21 April 1839).

[47] "Il y produirait plus d'effet qu'un sermon sur l'âme des riches visiteurs, et serait peut-être plus utile qu'une quête à domicile en vertu d'une lettre pastorale de l'archevêque." Decamps, "Salon de 1839," *Nat.* (25 April 1839).

[48] "Le sanctuaire conservateur des annales de la vertu et des crimes des tyrans." P.J. David d'Angers in E. Duclerc and L. A. Pagnerre's *Dictionnaire politique* (1842).

[49] "Du satin, de velours, des roses, des danses, des festins, grande tapisserie tout au plus bonne à cacher les pleurs de 30 million de prolétaires; voilà ce qu'il faut à nos Mécènes; car nos Mécènes sont des banquiers et des parvenus." Thoré, "Exposition ambulante."

Repeated complaints from republican critics, who lamented the scarcity of Salon exhibits directly confronting the moral and political issues of the day, gradually moderated during the 1840s as new conceptions of the ethical and social implications of physical beauty, manifested in nature and reproduced in art, began to displace agitation for overtly didactic imagery. Yet rather than implying the abandonment of concern with art's public responsibilities, this evolution—reminiscent in its broad trajectory of the Saint-Simonians' reinterpretation of form—testifies a new understanding of the aesthetic process and its operation on the perceiving subject. In all of this, it is the potential of nature to embody ethical imperatives, and of art to transmute and intensify the experience of nature, which underwrites the emergence of new concerns in republican critical theory in the years leading up to 1848.

THE MORALIZATION OF NATURE

The shift in theoretical paradigm during the 1840s has been noted by previous historians, who have remarked on a growing preoccupation with nature among critics on the left.[50] Such accounts demand some qualification, since they tend not only to establish an artificial polarity with the ostensibly more reductive utilitarianism of the Saint-Simonians and Fourierists,[51] but also fail adequately to comprehend the ideological connotations of the changes they describe. Though David Kelley has pointed to "a close correspondence between the social ideal and the aesthetic ideal,"[52] his incorporation of differing theoretical currents under the catchall term *humanitaire* obscures significant variations in the sense ascribed both to nature and to art by contending radical groups. The 1840s marked the culmination of what might be described as a politicization of nature; working from distinctive premises, a republican such as Charles Blanc could foster an aesthetic in which it played as prominent a role as in the critical language of Pierre Leroux's disciple Théophile Thoré or the Fourierist Désiré Laverdant. In each instance, the theoretical inflection of nature as an ideological

[50] See L. Nochlin, *Gustave Courbet: A Study of Style and Society* (1976), 88: "Little by little the direction of the best left-wing criticism turns from a mere demand for didactic, moralizing or allegorical painting, to a praise for simple, unpretentious art, endowed with deep attachment to nature and the natural man and faithful to external reality." The observation was first made by P. Grate, *Deux Critiques d'art à l'époque romantique: Gustave Planche et Théophile Thoré* (1959), 182–84, and is explored by D. Kelley, *Baudelaire. Salon de 1846* (1975), 73–84.

[51] See Nochlin, *Gustave Courbet*, 86. This is not the case with Kelley, particularly as set out in "L'Art: l'harmonie du beau et de l'utile," *Romantisme* 5 (1973): 18–36.

[52] "Une correspondance intime entre l'idéal social et l'idéal esthétique." Kelley, *Baudelaire*, 74.

construct affected its status within the aesthetic domain.[53] In republican discourse, pantheistic connotations proved seminal, particularly for Blanc, whose progressive repudiation of overt didacticism invoked a philosophy of nature ultimately political in tone. This reformulation of aesthetic priorities on the republican left was far from comprehensive, however; not only did relatively unsophisticated commentators such as Baget and Haussard continue to dilute an explicit commitment to didacticism with an untheorized weakness for formal analysis, but new critical voices that emerged in 1848 frequently advocated an unreconstructed utilitarianism oblivious to more abstract stylistic preoccupations.

It is perhaps Charles Blanc, brother of the radical publicist and politician Louis, and himself destined for administrative eminence in 1848, who best epitomizes the often tentative and contradictory accommodation of nature in republican critical language of the 1840s. His first Salon review, published in his brother's *Revue du progrès* in 1839, reveals Blanc a qualified opponent of formalism, convinced that only assimilation of "the tendencies and teachings of democracy"[54] can restore the nation's former artistic supremacy. Confronted by an exhibition in which only the work of a foreigner—Ary Scheffer's *Paolo and Francesca*—testified proper concern for the role of *pensée* in art, Blanc pointed to the betrayal of a long-standing tradition of prioritizing content in favor of a preoccupation with technique meaningful only to a privileged minority.[55]

Sharing unease toward this "artistic sensualism" with other contributors to the review,[56] Blanc's antiformalism can be related to his brother's critique of Lockean sensationalism, a philosophy he regarded as inimical to altruistic impulse through its positioning of the sentient individual as the "point of convergence at the center of the universe."[57] Yet in Blanc's 1839 review this valorization of reason over sensation is counterbalanced by an inherent attraction toward form and the "sublimes palettes" of figures such as Delacroix, Brune, Ziegler, and Decamps. While regarding them as having

[53] On competing notions of nature at this period, see N. Green, *The Spectacle of Nature: Landscape and Bourgeois Culture in Nineteenth-Century France* (1990).

[54] "Les tendances et les enseignements démocratiques." C. Blanc, "Salon de 1839," *R.P.* 1, no. 8 (1 May 1839): 478.

[55] "Les merveilles de la plastique sont incomprises de la multitude; n'espérez pas à l'initier à tous ces mystères égoïstes qui font la joie des grands-prêtres de l'art; conservez-les dans un coin du sanctuaire; mais la foule rassemblée aux portes du temple veut qu'on lui parle un autre langage." *R.P.* 1, no. 5 (15 March 1839): 271.

[56] "Sensualisme de l'art." See H. Fortoul, "De la littérature sensualiste," *R.P.* (1 February 1839), a review of Emile Barrault's novel *Eugène*, cited in Hunt, *Le socialisme et le romantisme en France* (1935), 167.

[57] "Point de convergence au milieu de l'univers." L. Blanc, *Histoire de la Révolution française* Paris, (1869), 1:362. See L. A. Loubère, *Louis Blanc: His Life and Contribution to French Jacobin-Socialism* (1961), 23.

"abandoned the French principle," he nonetheless expresses indulgence toward these "exceptional personalities, impatient of rules and restraints."[58] Though it is Gigoux whose apparent subordination of technique to meaning is presented as exemplary, and Delacroix and Brune whom he chastises as materialists receptive only to "pagan beauties,"[59] in the final reckoning, Blanc's own receptivity to formal bravura destabilizes his proclaimed theoretical priorities.

It is, perhaps, landscape painting that most effectively exposes Blanc's ambivalent position. The critic diagnoses the genre's current strengths as evidence of the eclipse of signification by sensation, though regrets the investment of poetic sentiment in "the simple fidelity of imitation," and points to the essentially limited range of subjective feeling the landscapist can convey. At the same time, though, he recognizes a universal moral resonance in the portrayal of nature capable of reconciling artistic individualism with the public's emotional needs:

> The thought that escapes from the landscapist's soul to animate his canvas is doubtless vague, intimate, drawn from the deepest recesses of his heart, selfish in its love of unknown retreats and inaccessible places, searching out the forests' mystery and fathomless solitude. But this individual feeling that infuses landscape is capable of moving the masses, since in every one of us it sets heartstrings vibrating with joy and sadness, feelings that are shared by all.[60]

In embracing pantheism, Blanc discovered a mediating term capable of reconciling form and *pensée*. Formerly ambivalent toward nature as overwhelmingly material, and thus of limited ethical value, Blanc was now able to regard it as infused with a moral meaning that the artist could articulate through the celebration of physicality. Arguing that "love of form is an aspect of wisdom," he temporized earlier misgivings over beauty's general accessibility and pronounced its rendition in art "necessary to the world's existence, for without it we would be plunged into barbarism."[61] From such a perspective, the antithesis between form and *pensée* loses its edge, though traces of Blanc's moralism subsist. Now, ideal beauty—understood as em-

[58] "Abandonné le principe français"; "natures exceptionnelles, impatientes du frein et de la règle." Blanc, "Salon de 1839," *R.P.* 1, no. 5 (15 March 1839): 271.

[59] "Beautés paiennes." *R.P.* 1, no. 6 (1 April 1839): 345, 341.

[60] "La simple fidélité de l'imitation"; "Sans doute, la pensée qui s'échappe de l'âme du paysagiste pour faire vivre sa toile est une pensée vague, intime, venue des sources les plus reculées du coeur, une pensée égoïste qui aime les retraites inconnues et les lieux inaccessibles, qui recherche le mystère des forêts et les solitudes où l'on se perd. Mais ce sentiment individuel qui s'épanche dans un paysage est de nature à émouvoir la foule, car il fait vibrer dans chacun de nos cordes de la joie et de la mélancolie qui sont les mêmes chez tous les hommes." *R.P.* 1, no. 8 (1 May 1839): 473.

[61] "L'amour de la forme est une portion de la sagesse"; "nécessaire à l'existence du monde, car son absence nous laisserait plongé dans la barbarie." C. Blanc, "Salon de 1845," *La Réforme* (16 April 1845).

bracing the spectrum of natural phenomena, from the humblest to the most refined—incorporates inherent moral meaning through the interpretative intervention of the artist's imagination. Arguing that "if the painter has been able to represent the body's perfection, it may be that every viewer can generously infuse it with a soul,"[62] Blanc now denigrates Scheffer's attenuation of pictorial values in the pursuit of spirituality as misguided and self-defeating, and instead regards the interpretation of nature as integral to art's edifying effect. Earlier misgivings over "pagan beauties" are abandoned, for example, in his assessment of the sculptor James Pradier, "a thoroughbred pagan," whose love of beauty as a self-sufficient value capable of elevating the spectator he applauds. The idealism of the *Phyrné* (plate 35), admired for its refinement and the "intimate initiation into the mysteries of beauty, seduction, and grace" it affords,[63] epitomizes for Blanc sculpture's ability to "magnify the soul, and raise it to the ideal, thus maintaining among men a vision of beauty, and above all of the cult it merits."[64]

This apparently orthodox reiteration of classical idealism acquires broader resonance when extended to a figure such as Decamps, whose vision of nature Blanc regards as revealing the immanence of the divine within creation. As with Pradier, an artist for whom "form . . . is the very substance,"[65] so with Decamps style *is* signification, investing meaning in the facticity of paint and in the interpretative process accompanying its application. Unlike naturalism, which Blanc repudiates as prosaically materialistic in its superficial preoccupation with surface appearance, Decamps's art is praised for actively transmuting the real through subjective perception, revealing spiritual depth in the least elevated of natural forms:

> Modern pantheism has discovered its painter, and that painter is Decamps. He finds the ideal everywhere—in fields and woods, in the canyons' loneliness, and in the sadness of the miserable lichen growing on the rocks. He pursues and betrothes the divine in nature's breast, and, if he notices tall trees on the horizon tormented by the wind, thinks he has discovered the soul of the world in the tempest's roar.[66]

[62] "Si le peintre a su atteindre la perfection du corps, il peut arriver que chacun vienne généreusement y souffler une âme." C. Blanc, "Salon de 1846," *La Réforme* (4 April 1846).

[63] "Un païen de pur sang"; "intime initiation aux mystères de la beauté, de la séduction et de la grâce." Blanc, "Salon de 1845," *La Réforme* (16 April 1845).

[64] "Agrandir l'âme, de l'élever jusqu'à l'idéal, de conserver chez les hommes le type de beauté, mais surtout le culte dont elle est digne." *La Réforme* (26 April 1845).

[65] "La forme . . . , c'est le fond même." *La Réforme* (16 April 1845).

[66] "Le panthéisme moderne a trouvé son peintre, et ce peintre, c'est Decamps. Pour lui, l'idéal est partout, dans les champs, dans les bois, dans la solitude des ravins, dans la tristesse du misérable lichen qui pousse sur les rochers. C'est au sein de la nature qu'il poursuit et qu'il épouse la divinité, et s'il aperçoit à l'horizon de grands arbres tourmentés par le vent, c'est l'âme du monde qu'il croit deviner dans le souffle de la tempête." Blanc, "Salon de 1846," *La Réforme* (25 March 1846).

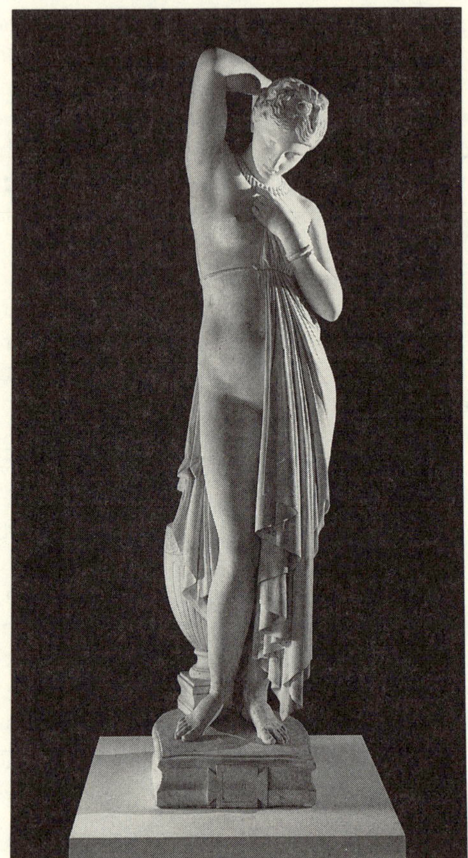

Plate 35. James Pradier: *Phyrné,* Salon of 1845. Musée de Grenoble.

No longer equating form with sensualism, and its celebration with self-gratification, Blanc recognizes in Decamps, as in painters such as Delacroix, Rousseau, Dupré, and Troyon,[67] the capacity to transmit nature's inherent moral sense through their mastery over the medium of paint. Investing this morality in his understanding of nature as an "emanation of the divine,"[68] Blanc uses pantheism as a point of reconciliation between aesthetics and politics. Because pantheism is democratic in ideological terms, through its nonhierarchical perception of God, whose authority is understood as suffused throughout creation, from an aesthetic point of view it rehabilitates form as the material manifestation of divine presence. Thus, Blanc maintains, love of beauty carries socially beneficial ramifications in the harmony

[67] See *La Réforme* (10 April 1846).

[68] "Emanation de la divinité." Blanc, "Salon de 1845," *La Réforme* (16 April 1845).

of thought and action it instills, a perspective that inclines him toward the classicism of David as the supreme expression of formal perfection and provokes misgivings over romantic rehabilitation of the grotesque.[69]

Despite such reservations, Blanc extols Delacroix for the "skillful harmony" of his technique and for the fusion of form and meaning in works such as the Saint Denis *Piéta*[70] and the *Justice de Trajan*.[71] Here, and in his sympathy toward Decamps, Corot, and Rousseau, the critic responds to a vision of nature ostensibly rooted in individual perception and unmediated by tradition. Equating originality with the naïveté of a figure such as Corot, whose art "derives only from himself,"[72] Blanc increasingly refutes obedience to stylistic authority as isolating the artist from nature and compromising his individuality. Thus, in 1845 he attacks Lehmann's *Océanides* (plate 36) for confusing the superior truth of ideal beauty with the hollowness of borrowed convention. Whereas attainment of the ideal demands the active interpretation of nature by the artist's unique sensibility, Blanc accuses such a work of exemplifying the effacement of nature in the abdication of creative autonomy it displays: "Style is a convention substituted for nature. Painting with style thus means imprinting things with a character compatible with tradition."[73]

The premium placed on creative authenticity and independence from tradition echoes an antiacademicism characteristic of republican critical discourse. Blanc's understanding of form and the morally inspiring value of beauty recalls comments by such radicals as Victor Schoelcher or Jules de Caudin, who in 1848 could describe the art of Delacroix and Rousseau as an "an act of faith in the brotherhood of all things, in the eternal fusion of goodness and beauty."[74] At a period, too, when other commentators could variously perceive nature as the embodiment of "solidarity," "harmony," or "the order and unity of life,"[75] Blanc's pantheism exemplifies a tendency to

[69] Ibid., where Blanc argues that "En attaquant David, le romantisme commit une faute énorme, un contre-sens monstrueux; car il allait ainsi directement contre son principe, qui était le panthéisme, c'est-à-dire l'adoration de la matière." He continues with an attack on Hugo's exaltation of ugliness in the form of Quasimodo.

[70] "Savante harmonie." *La Réforme* (16 March 1845).

[71] C. Blanc, "Salon de 1840," *R.P.* 3, no. 5 (31 March 1840): 217.

[72] "Ne procède que de lui-même." *R.P.* 3, no. 8 (1 May 1840): 358.

[73] "Le style, c'est une convention substituée à la nature. Faire du style, c'est donc imprimer aux choses un caractère conforme à la tradition." Blanc, "Salon de 1846," *La Réforme* (4 April 1846).

[74] "Acte de foi dans la fraternité de toutes choses, dans l'éternelle fusion du bon avec le beau." Jules de Caudin, "Salon de 1848," *La Réforme* (21 May 1848). See V. Schoelcher, "Salon de 1835," *Revue de Paris*, n.s., 16 (1835): 55, where he qualifies advocacy of overt didacticism by remarking "Le beau porte en soi sa vertu, il a la propriété d'exalter l'imagination et de nous remuer noblement."

[75] "L'ordre et l'unité de la vie." P. de Flotte, *La Souveraineté du peuple: essai sur l'espirit de la révolution* (1851), 285. Flotte's discussion of aesthetics in this work is built upon a pantheist viewpoint.

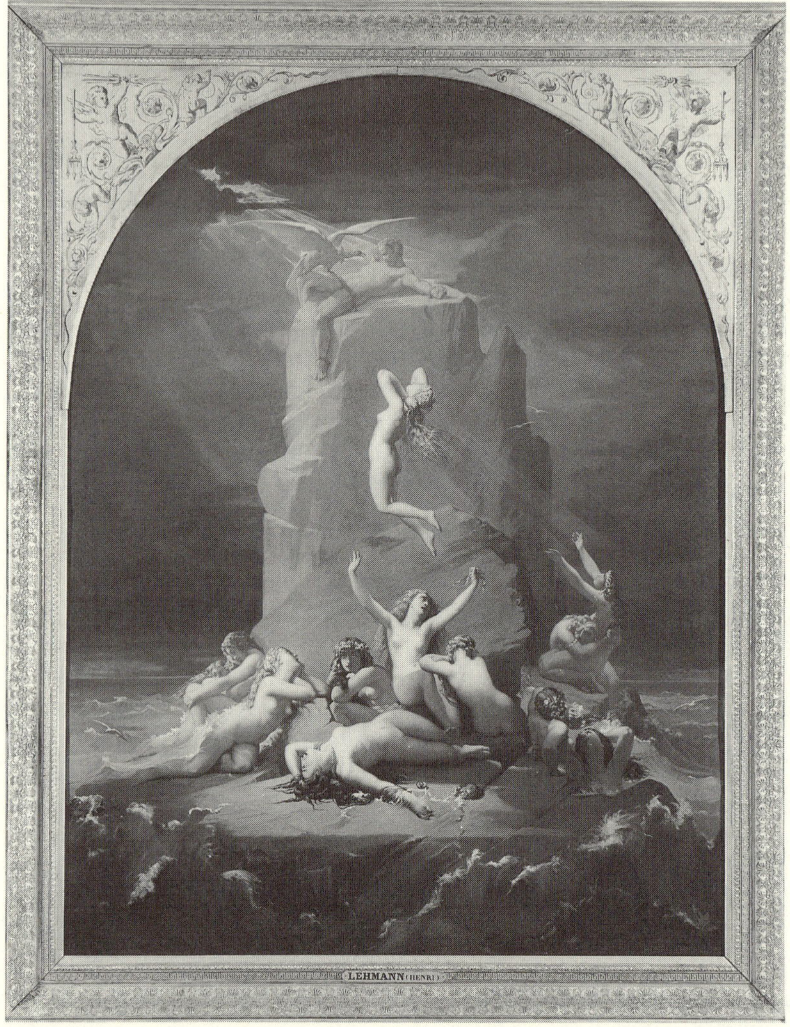

Plate 36. Henri Lehmann: *Les Océanides,* Salon of 1845. Musée départemental, Gap.

ground social philosophy upon an understanding of the material world. Within the critical system he develops during the 1840s, nature becomes a metaphor for the ideal society; balanced and harmonious, distributing moral authority equitably across all of its elements, nature provides a model and solicitation for a democratic order capable of guaranteeing universal self-fulfillment.

This critical model did not wholly eclipse Blanc's earlier commitment to explicit didacticism. Though in 1845 he could dismiss Victor Robert's elaborate allegory *La Religion, la philosophie, les sciences et les arts éclairant l'Europe* as "une lourde dissertation" in which literalism defied the expressive potentialities of paint,[76] he nonetheless welcomed Robert-Fleury's *Un Auto-da-fé* for its indictment of religious fanaticism, and remarked approvingly: "What admirable power painting possesses! It speaks to the illiterate, gives form to thought, endows history with a second life, colors the ideal, and thus strikes home with greater effectiveness than philosophy itself, for it enchants men and moralizes them into the bargain."[77]

Such a formulaic justification of painting's social role, reminiscent of Enlightenment moralism in its emphasis on instruction through pleasure, reveals a persistent attraction toward art as a vehicle for clearly articulated ethical positions. Disdainful of the contrived and ultimately inarticulate codes in Robert's "six hundred horsepower monumental and palingenetic allegory,"[78] Blanc responds to Robert-Fleury for the legibility and immediacy with which his depiction of the past addresses the present. Yet this apparent preference for narrative and conceptual clarity, which compromises Blanc's less instrumental aesthetic position in the 1840s, coexists with a countervailing attraction toward hermeneutic openness, inviting the spectator to elaborate meaning with the minimum of authorial restraint. It is this quality that particularly appeals in Decamps's *Samson* series in 1845.[79] Though, like Eugène Pelletan, he sees parallels with popular oppression in the biblical hero's humiliation at the wheel (plate 23), Blanc reads the sequence of nine scenes less as a retelling of the Old Testament story than as a richly allusive dialogue with the epic tradition, invoking meanings of universal significance: "[Decamps] seems deliberately to have mixed up all the ancient epics into a single meaning, and to have discovered their true sense: that of humanity. We are constantly presented with man and his passions, his love, his courage, and his eternal weakness and majesty."[80]

The preference displayed here toward open narrative, susceptible to interpretation on multiple levels, echoes Blanc's attitude toward nature as a medium for meaning. In both instances, the oblique and allusive carry

[76] Blanc, "Salon de 1845," *La Réforme* (26 March 1845).

[77] "Admirable puissance de la peinture! Elle parle à ceux qui ne savent pas lire, elle prête un corps à la pensée, elle donne une seconde vie à l'histoire, elle colore l'idéal, et frappe ainsi des coups plus sûrs que la philosophie elle-même, car elle enchante les hommes, et, par-dessus le marché, les moralise." Ibid.

[78] "Allégorie monumentale et palingénésique de la force de six cents chevaux." Ibid.

[79] On criticism of the series more generally, see D. F. Mosby, *Alexandre-Gabriel Decamps 1803–1860* (1977), 1:186–201.

[80] "[Decamps] semble avoir voulu confondre à dessein, dans une même signification, toutes les épopées antiques, et en avoir trouvé le vrai sens, le sens de l'humanité. C'est constamment la mise en scène de l'homme avec ses passions, son amour, son courage, et son éternelle faiblesse et sa grandeur." Blanc, "Salon de 1845," *La Réforme* (9 April 1845).

greater force than the explicit and univocal—a principle that holds good for the act of creation as surely as for the process of reception. Thus, Blanc resists the attempts of a figure such as Laverdant to hedge the artist with directives and proscriptions; rather than looking for "the copy of my feelings, the replica of my thought," the critic counsels the artist, "express your own feelings and make your paintings speak the language of your heart."[81]

This sentiment provides the touchstone for an aesthetic that, far from renouncing art's social dimension or attenuating its moral responsibility, transfers these concerns to a different register. Though constantly threatened by tensions and internal contradictions, symptomatic of much radical critical discourse, which strain toward antithetical poles of form and *pensée*, Blanc seeks resolution in the interpretative act of creation. Regarding the artist as deprived of an organic ideology allowing him directly to address his audience as a coherent constituency of shared interests and beliefs, Blanc encourages him to appeal to different impulses, communicate by different means. The rehabilitation of matter, central to romanticism, provided just such a means. Though romantic materialism had allegedly limited the artist to passive imitation, Blanc maintains that radical aesthetics dignify him with the responsibility of interpreting nature, thus simultaneously elevating his social role and reinvigorating the traditionally intellectual bias of the French school:

> As we await the moment when the French school produces the masterpieces of which it is capable, as we wait for heroes, let us recognize that it is to the democratic school that the honor falls of having introduced the principle of interpretation, which is now generally accepted. A fruitful and generous principle, it should be taught to painters of every school, since it magnifies the artist's individuality by allowing him to express his personal feelings, and enhances the dignity of art by according it an important purpose, elevating it to the regions of the mind, and directing it toward poetry.[82]

Though in some respects conceived as a stopgap solution necessitated by the prevailing ideological vacuum, the political motivation underlying Blanc's emphasis on artistic interpretation is nonetheless real enough. His

[81] "La copie de mes sentiments, le pléonasme de ma pensée"; "sentez à votre manière et faites parler à vos tableaux le langage de votre coeur." C. Blanc, "Etat de la sculpture en France," *La Réforme* (16 May 1844), where Laverdant's strictures on "interprétation" are explicitly rejected.

[82] "Nous, en attendant que l'école française trouve des occasions aux chefs d'oeuvre qu'elle est en état de produire, en attendant les héros, reconnaissons que l'école démocratique a eu l'honneur d'inaugurer le principe de l'interprétation, désormais incontesté; principe fécond et généreux qu'il faut enseigner aux peintres de toutes les écoles, parce qu'il ennoblit l'individualité de l'artiste en lui donnant à exprimer ses passions personnelles, et rehausse la dignité de l'art en lui assignant un grand but, en l'élevant aux régions de la pensée, en lui conseillant la poésie." C. Blanc, *Histoire des peintres français au dix-neuvième siècle* (1845), 46.

commitment toward individualism as the source of artistic inspiration and moral insight identifies subjectivity not with material gratification but with an expansive, outward-looking impulse founded on self-knowledge. In affording political significance to these freedoms, ontological and aesthetic, Blanc echoes a more generalized defense of creative autonomy central to radical agitation for institutional reform under the July Monarchy. Spearheaded by a number of young artists and critics, united in their opposition to the *monarchie censitaire* and its cultural placemen, this campaign highlights the centrality of artistic freedom within republican discourse, both as a philosophical ideal and as a practical commitment.

ANTIACADEMICISM AND THE POLITICS OF TRUTH

"Mort à l'Institut! Mort au professorat!"—the battle cry emblazoned on the masthead of *La Liberté*, the trenchantly iconoclastic art journal that enjoyed a brief but vigorous existence in the early 1830s,[83] condenses radical antipathy toward the state's cultural institutions and their accredited representatives with characteristic economy and force. Though misgivings over the Academy were voiced across the political spectrum,[84] republican critiques carry added ideological coherence, both as specific instances of a more comprehensive indictment of the Orléanist regime and as the polemical foundation for asserting the necessity of unmediated truth in the visual arts. Despite concern over the Academy's material impact on the artistic community—its tuitional control over the Ecole des beaux-arts, its restriction on professional access to the public through the Salon jury, its members' disproportionate share of official purchases and commissions—republican attacks ultimately form part of a broader philosophical agenda, which repudiated oppressive state control as an impediment to art communicating an authentic perception of nature capable of enlightening a mass public.

On a more immediate level, art journalism offered relatively effective cover for sniping at those in power. *La Liberté* itself became the training ground of a new generation of writers and artists, including Hauréau, Decamps, Laviron, Galbacio, Jeanron, and Duseigneur, whose republican politics, tempered by the disillusionment that succeeded the July Days, found an outlet in scathing attacks on the nation's rulers. Outdistancing

[83] On *La Liberté*, see M. Rousseau, "P.-A. Jeanron 1808–1877. Peintre. Écrivain. Directeur des Musées nationaux" (1935), 35–50. Established in August 1832, the journal published nineteen issues before closing in February 1833.

[84] On agitation for Salon reform and resistance to the Academy, see M. Ivens, "La Liberté guidant les artistes," *Les Révoltes logiques* 10 (1979): 52–94.

more moderate claims for organizational reform, voiced by groups such as the Société libre des beaux-arts, their militant campaign showed little readiness for compromise and displayed an acute awareness of the imbrication of cultural institutions in the broader nexus of power.[85] The pages of *La Liberté* abound with political metaphors, which revive the language of the Academy's opponents in the 1790s and highlight its collusion in upholding an inequitable social system. Likening the Institut to the Bastille, embodying "nothing less than an aristocracy in the arts," the journal presented itself as an "enemy of bourgeois and aristocratic oppression"[86] whose antipathy to cultural exploitation informed a deeper democratic commitment.

Such a stance became the hallmark of republican criticism throughout the 1830s. The irreverent, mocking tone used to deflate academicians' pretensions and to deride the cowed obedience of their students[87] provided the model for an acerbic language of political subversion developed in response to draconian censorship restrictions imposed in 1835. Unflattering descriptions of royal portraits, burlesque accounts ridiculing the regime's self-glorification in scenes of the July Days, and pointed meditations on the inherent cultural deficiencies of constitutional monarchy,[88] all formed part of the armory at the republican critic's disposal. The regular display of canvases specially commissioned for the Musée historique at Versailles offered a particular hostage to fortune as commentators disparaged their inferior quality and exposed their tendentious political inspiration. Accusing Louis-Philippe of manipulating history for callow dynastic advantage, critics highlighted the scheme's bankruptcy by accusing the regime of employing second-rate artists as a means of saving money.[89] Alexandre Decamps further charged that the museum's deficiencies displayed the reassertion of academic influence over commissioning policy, after a brief liberal interlude following the July Revolution. Angered by the challenge to their former supremacy, Decamps maintained that the Academy had pressurized the government, which had readily abandoned a policy whose openness increasingly compromised broader ideological commitments. The moral drawn from this retrenchment was clear enough and typifies republican

[85] See, for example, Hauréau, "De la politique et des arts," 26–30.

[86] "Aristocratie dans les arts, rien de plus"; "ennemi de l'oppression bourgeoise et nobiliaire." J. Raimbaud, "Union et liberté," *L.A.* 2 (August 1832): 14, 16; P.-A. Jeanron, "Journaux, feuilletons, revues," ibid., 15 (December 1832): 60.

[87] See, for example, the attack on David d'Angers in P. Borel, "Les Fourberies de Scapin," *L.A.* 3 (August 1832): 13–16, and 7 (September 1832): 109–12. See also the defense of the journal's iconoclastic style in G. Laviron, "De ceux à qui notre allure ne convient pas," ibid., 6 (September 1832): 90–96.

[88] For a typical example, see B. Hauréau's article "De l'art dynastique," in his "Salon de 1837," *J.P.* (19 March 1837).

[89] On Versailles, see, for example, Decamps, "Salon de 1836," *Nat.* (19 March and 4 April 1836); B. Hauréau, "Le Musée de Versailles," *J.P.* (2 and 30 July 1837).

alertness to the political connotations of cultural policy: "Everything in society is connected. Our rulers are so well aware of this that they no more want competitions, juries, or elections in artistic matters than they do anywhere else."[90]

Republican critics proved indefatigable in pursuing the beneficiaries of this cultural autocracy—the Academicians whose work they deprecated for the redundancy of its conception and the mediocrity of its execution. While they were frequently well disposed toward the more socially responsive art of David,[91] and sympathetic to his vigorous campaign for institutional reform, the Davidian cohort dominating the Academy provoked only contemptuous allegations of betraying their master's legacy.[92] Classicism's apparent deterioration from a visual language rich in contemporary resonance to a sterile recycling of moribund formulas offered a versatile polemical weapon with which to attack exhibiting academicians. It was used to full effect by critics such as Decamps, Hauréau, Galbacio, and Laviron, whose derisive appraisal of Blondel's *Le Triomphe de la religion sur l'athéisme* (plate 37) captures the tone:

> Seriously, what are we supposed to make of this drivel? what could it possibly have in common with contemporary ideas? At least if it were properly drawn and painted we could look for form and color in the absence of thought; but there's nothing, absolutely nothing; just finish, finish, finish—enough to drive a miniaturist mad—and that's all.[93]

Indignant reports of unjust exclusions from the Salon exhibition served to highlight the Academy's factional attempts to silence those who challenged its precepts, though—in the eyes of Thoré, at least—such ambitions were ultimately doomed, since "the revolution has impinged upon painting, as on everything else, and the old regime is in ruins."[94] Pointing to a rising generation of talented artists consistently frustrated by the Academy's vendetta, republican critics asserted that the establishment had resorted to crude revenge as control began to slip from their grasp. Thus challenged,

[90] "Tout se tient dans la société; et les hommes qui la gouvernent le savent si bien, qu'ils ne veulent pas plus de concours, ni de jurés, ni d'élections dans les questions d'arts, qu'ils n'en voudraient voir partout ailleurs." Decamps, "Salon de 1837," *Nat.* (25 March 1837).

[91] See, for example, the chapter on David in B. Hauréau, *La Montagne. Notices historiques et philosophiques sur les principaux membres de la Montagne* (1834), 65–80.

[92] See, for example, Laviron and Galbaccio, *Salon de 1833*, 10; P.-A. Jeanron, "De l'anarchie dans les arts," *L.A.* 11 (November 1832): 162–65.

[93] "Sérieusement, qu'est-ce qu'on nous veut avec tout ce fatras? qu'est-ce que cela peut avoir de commun avec les idées de notre temps? Encore si cela était convenablement peint et dessiné, à défaut de pensée on y chercherait de la forme et de la couleur; mais rien, absolument rien; du fini, fini, fini à désepérer un miniaturiste, et voilà tout." G. Laviron, *Salon de 1834* (1834), 108.

[94] "La révolution a débordé en peinture comme partout, et l'ancien régime est en ruines." Thoré, "Salon de 1838," *J.P.* 15 (15 April 1838).

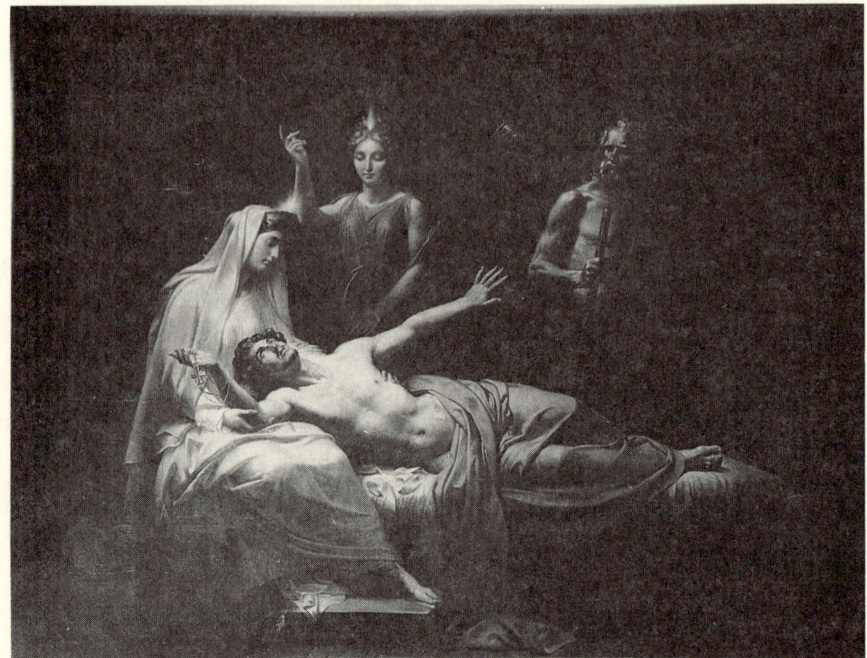

Plate 37. Méry-Joseph Blondel: *Le Triomphe de la religion sur l'athéisme,* 1828. Musée Crozatier, Le Puy-en-Velay.

their only response was to impose unthinking obedience by playing upon artists' material interests; as a consequence, what Laviron and Galbacio described as "our military government of the fine arts"[95] hoped to reassert its threadbare authority by starving opponents into submission.

Resentful at the Academy's perceived intolerance toward signs of creative independence, republicans regarded moves against artistic spontaneity and innovation as symptomatic of a regime determined to eradicate all forms of effective opposition. It was "this power that paralyzes, chains thought, and lulls consciences"[96] whose authority lent institutional legitimacy to the Academy itself. Though prudence—and the September Laws—made it impossible to say out loud, there was tacit consensus that only by overthrowing the regime itself could cultural oppression be defeated.[97]

Liberating the artist from institutional restraints stood as a goal not

[95] "Notre gouvernement militaire des beaux-arts." Laviron and Galbaccio, *Salon de 1833*, 10.

[96] "Ce pouvoir qui paralyse, enchaîne la pensée, assoupit les consciences." Anonymous letter from an artist, printed in *J.P.* (18 March 1838), in response to Anonymous, "De la condition sociale des artistes. A propos de l'exposition et du jury," ibid. (11 March 1838).

[97] The point is made by the artist cited in the previous note.

merely because it promised such practical benefits as unrestricted access to the marketplace, but more ambitiously because of the prospect it offered of fundamental cultural renewal. As the Academy had become a byword for the regulation of individuality and the imposition of stylistic convention inimical to an understanding of nature, so its eradication could be presented as reinvigorating and cleansing, freeing the artist from the burden of tradition. Proclaiming "we must bring anarchy to art if we are to save it," the painter Jeanron—who had played a leading role in petitioning for change following the 1830 revolution[98]—called for a complete *tabula rasa*.[99] As a disciple of the neo-Babouvist Filippo Buonarotti,[100] his remedy entails provoking a crisis from which the arts will emerge better equipped to confront the present:

> Out of the anarchy we support, the arts will emerge as if from a crucible, purified of the corrosive alloy of prejudice, academic tradition, and compromise with modern fads which are here today and gone tomorrow. Out of anarchy strong men will emerge who, having mastered their individual talents in solitude, will join hands to revive an art that has fallen so low that we now ask what use it is, and how and why it still survives.[101]

Such a formula for cultural regeneration, privileging the unhindered exploration of individual imagination, commanded wide support. Analogous to the political conception of the republic as a state of equal, sovereign individuals, shielded from tyranny and freely working for the collective good, the antiacademic discourse resisted incursions on artistic independence as compromising the autonomy upon which creative insight and ideological commitment were said to depend. The restraint of the sovereign imagination, enshrined in academic protocols, diminished the individual and debilitated the artist. Its liberation, by contrast, heralded a future in which "the poet, musician, and sculptor will invent an art of their own, which is unexpected, gripping, sublime, and deeply touched by the mood of contemporary society and the unique personality of each artist."[102] Pre-

[98] See Rousseau, "Jeanron," 24.

[99] "On doit anarchiser l'art si on veut le sauver"; "table rase." Jeanron, "De l'anarchie," 166.

[100] See M. Rousseau, "Filippo Buonarotti et les artistes français sous la Monarchie de juillet," *Revue des études italiennes* 3 (1938): 159–69.

[101] "De l'anarchie où nous voulons qu'ils passent, les arts sortiront comme d'un creuset, épurés de l'alliage corrosif des préjugés, des traditions d'écoles et des concessions aux modes éphémères de nos jours, sans veille et sans lendemain.—De l'anarchie il naîtra des hommes forts qui, après avoir conquis solitairement leurs talents individuels, se donneront la main pour relever l'art aujourd'hui tellement tombé, qu'on lui demande à quoi il est bon, et comment et pourquoi il vit encore." Jeanron, "De l'anarchie dans les arts," *L.A.* 8 (September 1832): 115.

[102] "Le poète, le musicien, le sculpteur inventeront un art à eux, imprévu, saisissant, sublime et profondément empreint du caractère actuel de la société et de l'humeur particulière de chaque artiste." G. Laviron, "Rembrandt," *L.A.* 16 (December 1832): 78.

cisely how such impulses would be accommodated within the structure of a market economy remained tellingly vague, however.

This assumption of creative autonomy was equated with the victory of truth, embodied in the unconstrained perception of nature, over the false and alienated vision imposed by rule and convention. Carrying ultimately political connotations, this valorization of truth empowered the individual through the premium it placed on the unmediated interpretation of reality. Artistic convention stood accused of obscuring the truth immanent in nature, impeding the imaginative penetration of the artist's gaze and stifling its revelatory power. Realization of art's progressive potential thus depended on casting aside received beliefs. As Laviron and Galbacio declared in 1833, "a conventionalized art, born in an era of prejudice, no longer suits a society which is freeing itself and has elsewhere advanced from traditional falsehood to positive knowledge."[103] For Laviron and Galbacio, naturalism stood as the goal of artistic emancipation, representing as it did the only pictorial idiom capable of embodying truths about the modern world. In associating "contemporaneity and the social tendency of art" with "truth in representation,"[104] the two critics offered a formula frequently reiterated in the republican press. Yet, here as elsewhere, the notion of truth explicitly excludes mimetic objectivity and denotes instead the refraction of external reality through the artist's imagination.[105] Naturalism thus privileges subjectivity, rather than subordinating it to the purely mechanical process of recording physical likeness. As Thoré points out in 1842, "Art is not imitation, but creation. A true work of art is not the material reproduction of nature, but the artist's own substance and the embodiment of his being."[106]

While departing from the normative perception of beauty inherent to classical idealism, naturalism's insistence on the artist's expressive investment in the representation of truth allows moral meaning to be distilled from the transcription of reality. A certain essentialism thus underwrites a philosophy of art in which the interpretation of nature is simultaneously a process of revelation and edification. This moral subtext proves central to Laviron and Galbacio's promotion of naturalism, as emerges clearly in their description of the school's adepts as artists who "in [their] study of nature,

[103] "Un art de convention, né dans une époque de préjugés, ne peut plus convenir à une société qui s'émancipe et qui, sur d'autres points, a passé du faux traditionnel à l'éducation positive." Laviron and Galbaccio, *Salon de 1833*, 392.

[104] "L'actualité et la tendance sociale de l'art"; "la vérité de la représentation." Ibid., 30.

[105] "L'art ne consiste pas à faire des trompe-l'oeil, mais bien à rendre le caractère particulier de chaque chose que l'on veut représenter." Ibid., 25.

[106] "L'art n'est pas l'imitation, mais la création. Une véritable oeuvre d'art n'est pas une reproduction matérielle de la nature, mais bien la substance de l'artiste et l'incarnation de sa vie." T. Thoré [George Dupré], "Salon de 1842," *R.P.* 7, no. 4 (1 May 1842): 231.

seek out the secret of human passions, to play out their drama on canvas or in marble, thus using art as a civilizing force."[107]

What is being canvassed here could, perhaps, more appropriately be described as an "ideal naturalism," which, in common with Charles Blanc's openly pantheistic vision, invests in the artist's encounter with reality the capacity to distill immanent meaning from contingent appearance. Curiously reminiscent of Victor Cousin's reformulation of the *beau idéal* and his definition of art as "the expression of Spirit—and not [the] imitation of nature,"[108] republican naturalism elevates artistic truth as an "essential truth,"[109] perceptible only when subjective vision is unclouded by externally imposed preconceptions. Such a stipulation underpins the modification to overtly utilitarian demands during the 1840s. In 1841, for example, Laviron dissociates naturalism from the ostensibly incomplete doctrines of formalism and utilitarianism, counseling instead a fidelity to experience unmediated by aesthetic *parti pris*. By protecting clarity of vision, Laviron postulates a higher truth attainable through art: "The truth of art is truer than the truth of nature: it is the eternal truth of everything, truth in its most sublime manifestations."[110]

By qualifying calls for naturalism in such a way, republican critics equate truth with the revelation of harmony, a process of ultimately political import through the insight it offers of a potential concord between men and the world whose bounty they share. This inherently idealist inflection to the "truth" of naturalism explains the widespread preference for an attenuated portrayal of the hardships of labor. Exemplified in the popularity of Léopold Robert's Italianate scenes, or in Haussard's call for the peasant painter Adolphe Leleux to "elevate and enlarge truth to the level of poetry,"[111] resistance to the uncompromising portrayal of work and poverty should not be read simply as political squeamishness. Though apparently aestheticizing in implication, demands that scenes of popular life should elevate their subjects rather than dwelling on ugliness and misery do not contravene the logic of naturalism as understood in republican circles. Approached from such a perspective, the artist's task is to see through the

[107] "Cherche[nt] dans l'étude de la nature le secret des passions humaines, pour les dérouler en drame sur la toile ou sur le marbre, et faire ainsi de l'art un moyen civilisateur." Laviron and Galbaccio, *Salon de 1833*, 343.

[108] "L'expression de l'Esprit—et non [l']imitation de la nature." Manuscript note (Bibliothèque Victor Cousin, feuillet 26) cited in M. Iknayan, *The Concave Mirror: From Imitation to Expression in French Esthetic Theory 1800–1830* (1983), 104.

[109] "Vrai essentiel." G. Laviron, *Salon de 1841* (1841), 4.

[110] "La vérité de l'art est plus vraie que la vérité de la nature: c'est la vérité éternelle de chaque chose, c'est le beau dans ses plus sublimes manifestations." Ibid., 5.

[111] "Hausser et de grandir la vérité jusqu'à la poésie." P. Haussard, "Salon de 1844," *Nat.* (31 March 1844).

material degradation that isolates the poor as an object of distaste, and to reveal instead their inherent dignity, the realization of which depends upon political emancipation and the achievement of social justice. Though overdetermined by an inhibiting regard for aesthetic *bienséances*, temporization of the "real" in the interests of a higher "truth" is integral to republican cultural politics, rather than signaling a deviation from it.

At issue here, as more generally in republican assessments of style, is the notion of emotional truth depending on form following content, rather than being systematically imposed according to formulaic precept. Prioritizing an unmediated communication of emotion between artist and spectator, republicans understand style as a ductile medium for creative *tempérament*,[112] modified in accordance with the dramatic implications of the scene portrayed. Disqualifying the more laconic visual rhetoric of such figures as Delaroche and Ingres, such demands favored instead an artist like Préault, in whose *Tuerie* of 1834 (plate 38) Galbacio could discern a perfect concordance between meaning and means of expression: "His art develops out of the moral ideas he sees as basic to his subject. Not only is his bas-relief . . . full of energy, power, variety, and animation, it also contains characters and feelings that are forcefully expressed."[113]

Similar priorities helped sensitize republican critics to landscape as a privileged medium for exploring subjective feeling and communicating truth. Largely endorsing Charles Blanc's contention that "the great landscapists have always been those who have seen nature with emotion and stamped it with the mark of their own character,"[114] republicans generally favored the rising naturalist school, embracing figures such as Diaz, Aligny, Cabat, Flers, Benouville, Marilhat, and Desgoffe. The hallmark of such painters, understood as a "naïve sincerity"[115] responsive to the moral meaning of nature, placed them at the very center of a broader current discerned in contemporary art, the penetration of whose vision promised to eclipse the unrealized ambitions of the romantic generation.

First identified by Laviron and Galbacio in 1833, this "école des naturalistes" comprised what in retrospect appears a remarkably mixed bag. Defined in opposition to a rather older romantic group, including Delacroix, Champmartin, Boulanger, and Orsel, the naturalists were distinguished by their commitment toward "truth and contemporaneity."[116] Em-

[112] See P.-A. Jeanron, "Salon de 1845," *La Pandore* 1 (1 April 1845): 187.

[113] "Chez lui l'art procède par les idées morales déduites du fond du sujet. Son bas-relief . . . est non seulement plein de verve, de puissance, de relief et d'animation; mais il renferme encore des caractères et des passions largement exprimés." B. Galbacio, "Salon de 1834," *Le Locateur*, no. 25 (March 1834).

[114] "Les grands paysagistes ont toujours été ceux qui ont vu la nature avec émotion et lui ont imprimé le cachet de leur caractère personnel." Blanc, "Salon de 1845," *La Réforme* (17 May 1845).

[115] Robert [H. R. Feugueray], "Salon de 1841," *Nat.* (6 April 1841).

[116] "Du vrai et de l'actualité." Laviron and Galbaccio, *Salon de 1833*, 124.

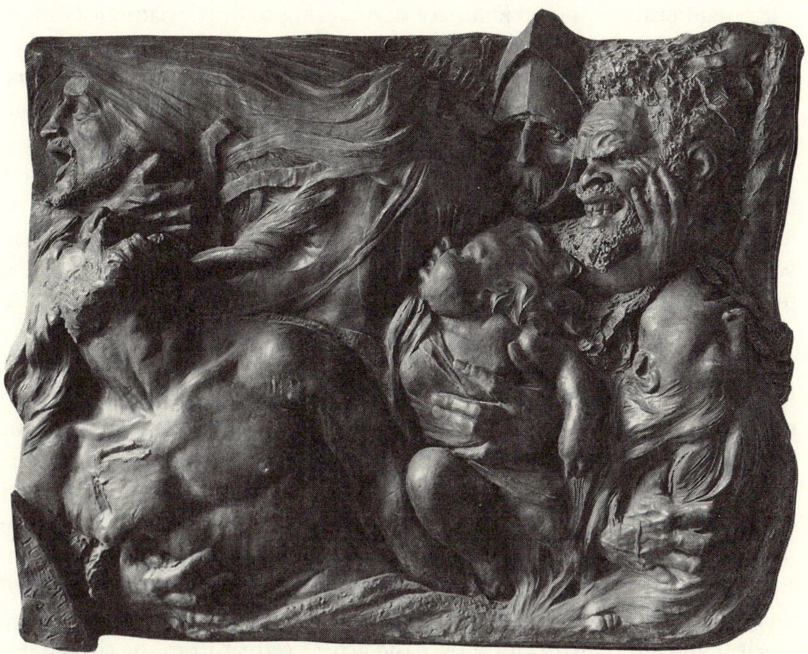

Plate 38. Antoine-Augustin Préault: *Scène de tuerie,* Salon of 1834. Musée des beaux-arts, Chartres.

bracing such figures as Jeanron and Gigoux, habitually well received in republican circles, the critics' listing also features the names of Sigalon, Scheffer, and Vernet, all of whom later provoked severe reproof in the radical press, as well as painters generally treated with indifference or disdain, such as Larivière, Couder, and Guichard.[117] Despite its heterogenous character, this putative "school" includes artists often singled out by republican critics during the 1830s, and throws into relief a pervasive ambivalence toward romanticism. The younger artists' independence, contemporaneity, and ostensibly direct perception of nature contrasted, not only for Laviron and Galbacio but also for fellow critics on the left, with romanticism's retreat from the challenge it had posed only a decade earlier. Equally dismissive of the visual pyrotechnics of a Boulanger as of the archaizing precision of an Orsel, they taxed Delacroix with debilitating self-doubt,[118] and the movement as a whole with pusillanimity.[119]

117 Ibid., 69.

118 Ibid., 108, 114, 96.

119 "C'est la vigueur et la confiance en eux-mêmes qui ont le plus manqué aux opposants de cette époque; car, s'ils avaient eu parmi eux, nous ne disons pas un homme de génie, mais seulement un homme d'audace, ils auraient fait capituler l'Institut, et nous aurions aujourd'hui un art quasi-académique, comme nous avons un gouvernement quasi-légitime." Ibid., 100.

Romanticism's imputed failure of nerve, eclipsed by the naturalists' more comprehensive challenge to the orthodoxies of pictorial convention, generally diminished the movement's significance for radical commentators. The largely pejorative connotations with which it was associated in republican discourse—medievalism, theatricality, formalism, stylistic facility—reduced romanticism to the level of just another set of factitious visual mannerisms, an academicism more liberal in scope, though ultimately no less pernicious in effect, than the pictorial establishment whose codes it had sought to overthrow. Expressions of admiration for the movement's leading protagonists, Decamps and Delacroix, focus on their essential independence rather than on any restrictive stylistic allegiance. Thus, whatever misgivings they provoke,[120] the two painters appeal through their allegedly spontaneous perception of nature, untainted by tradition or aesthetic *parti pris*. Arguing in 1834 that the originality displayed by Decamps in the *Défaite des Cimbres* could thrive only while the artist maintained his independence, Bruno Galbacio saw allegiance to any preconceived system as compromising the "two levers essential for poetry," "innocence and freshness of brush," and extolled the artist for disregarding stylistic convention.[121] Similarly, it was as the "complete expression of an original sentiment, of a particular taste"[122] that Delacroix attracted radical sympathies, albeit tempered by frustration over the artist's retreat from the contemporary inspiration displayed in the *Massacre de Scio* and *La Liberté guidant le peuple*.[123] Thus Decamps writes in 1835: "There is nothing borrowed in his work, no studying past masters, no concession to particular demands or contemporary opinion; his work is entirely his own, wholly personal and original."[124]

As the physical manifestation of interior emotion, style was read as a signature the integrity of which could only be diminished by compromise with pictorial tradition or popular taste. To see the world through another's eyes was to abdicate creative autonomy and to deprive art of its capacity to

[120] See, for example, Laviron's attack on Delacroix for his indifference towards subject matter in the *Salon de 1834*, 92.

[121] "Deux léviers indispensables à la poésie"; "la virginité, la verdeur du pinceau." B. Galbacio, "Salon de 1834," *Journal des gens du monde* 1 (1834): 155.

[122] "Expression complète d'un sentiment original, d'un goût particulier." P.-A. Jeanron, "De l'exposition de 1838, et du résultat des expositions," *Revue du nord*, 3d ser., 4, no. 2 (April 1838): 48.

[123] See P. Le Nouëne, "Représentation du peuple dans les tableaux d'histoire exposés aux Salons entre 1831 et 1848," in *Exigences de réalisme dans la peinture française entre 1830 et 1870* (1983), 18.

[124] "Il n'y a en lui ni recherche, ni étude de tel ou tel maître, ni concession à telle exigence ou telle opinion de ses contemporains; son oeuvre est la sienne en propre tout entière, tout originale, tout personnelle." Decamps, "Salon," *R.R.* 5, no. 13 (10 April 1835): 74. See also Laviron, *Salon de 1841*, 46.

convey authentic meaning to the spectator. Rallying artists in 1833 with the cry "Young men, beware! get out of the schools, if there is still time," Hauréau expressed particular distaste for Ingres's pupils and their systematic imitation of the master's style: "We declare this school . . . false and harmful because it is a school and artistic form can never be taught."[125] Ingres's own reliance on tradition as a source of personal inspiration and cultural legitimation provoked similar complaints of artificiality, as did Delaroche's apparent readiness to assume an anodyne anecdotalism in the pursuit of public favor.[126]

In every instance, critical disapproval focuses on occluded vision, associated with the alienation of personal independence to outside control. The communicative value of art becomes indistinguishable from the uncorrupted gaze of its creator. Positing an ideal, unmediated transparency between the artist and the natural world, critics such as Laviron and Decamps regard truth in art as the reward only of those whose strength and integrity keep alive an absolute autonomy. Exclusivity—the restriction of freedom by factional affiliation or stylistic imitation—connotes abdication of individual will to an external authority. Aesthetic truth thus depends on protecting in art that liberty on which, within the political realm, democracy depends.

That this association could stand as more than a vague though suggestive metaphor is confirmed in the significance accorded to artistic convention as an instrument of political repression and the emphasis on the emancipatory power of authentic vision. Equating *mensonge*—lies—with the governing classes, whose oppressive denial of truth in all spheres relied on the substitution of *forme* for *idée*, Auguste de Gasperini in 1850 directly imputes the denial of creative freedom to an appropriation of the arts by those in power. Obscuring truth, convention thus becomes a tool for perpetuating existing social relations and the false consciousness on which they depend. Language itself falls victim to a distortion of meaning, which serves to naturalize the prevailing distribution of force and deprive its opponents of a voice:

[125] "Jeunes gens, alerte! hors des écoles, s'il en est encore temps"; "Nous déclarons cette école . . . fausse et mauvaise, parce qu'elle est école et que la forme dans l'art ne s'enseigne jamais." Hauréau, "Salon," *La Tribune politique et littéraire* (20 March 1833). See also Galbacio, "Salon de 1834," *Journal des gens du monde* 1 (1834): 154: "Les écoles les plus brillantes n'inventent rien, elles répetent. L'histoire est là pour dire que chaque invention est un fait isolé."

[126] On Delaroche, see particularly Decamps, *Le Musée. Revue du Salon de 1834* (n.d.), 31, where the artist is accused of cultivating "un ensemble d'effets raisonnables au milieu desquels rien ne doit choquer la susceptibilité du public; il ne hasarde rien parce qu'il préfère les applaudissements donnés à sa belle parole, aux émotions violentes d'une expression vraie comme la nature, mais souvent aussi douloureuse ou repoussante comme elle."

> It is society's rulers who created words to correspond to ideas and who, by substituting the particular and conventionalized ideas of a minority for ideas that are total, universal, and necessary, everywhere diverted words, those figurative signs of thought, from their real and absolute sense.[127]

Assertion of the redemptive power of truth in the face of art's manipulation by hostile ideological pressures echoes ideas that had been articulated by figures such as Thoré and Baget during the 1830s,[128] and which were reiterated with striking vehemence in the wake of the February Revolution by the former Saint-Simonian Pierre Hawke. Proclaiming the need for "truth in all and over all," Hawke asserted that the "sterile rules of the past" impeding art's attainment of truth were symptomatic of a more pervasive social mendacity buttressing the unequal distribution of power.[129] Both he and Gasperini linked artistic renewal to the elimination of those forces which conventional beauty served to uphold, and invested in social emancipation the promise of an art whose unmediated vision of nature would articulate absolute truth. Thus, in a unified society, Gasperini predicts that "words made by all and for all would return to their original and necessary sense,"[130] and that the transparency of social relations will foster an art whose access to reality allows the elaboration of ostensibly verifiable, positivistic forms.[131] For Gasperini, realism is absolute presence; no longer distorted by convention, which obscures nature from artist and public alike, truth is guaranteed by the unimpeded encounter between subjectivity and the material world. The real is thus the prize of political transformation, won by defeating oppressive ideological forces and their attendant regime of representation. Just as the citizens of Rousseau's ideal republic enjoy absolute transparency in the realm of social relations, so Gasperini's notion of truth projects a seamlessness between object and perception which releases unrealized powers of artistic expression and interpretation. This idealist glorification of natural plenitude seeks ultimate sanction in liberal theology, identifying Christ with the promotion of human solidarity and the rehabilitation of every aspect of nature. Truth as nature and as ideal thus become one and the same, embraced in the totality of truth which is God:

[127] "C'est cette partie de la société gouvernante qui a créée les mots correspondants aux idées, et qui, substituant partout l'idée d'un petit nombre, l'idée particulière, l'idée conventionnelle, à l'idée totale, universelle, nécessaire, a partout détourné les mots, signes figuratifs de la pensée, de leur sens réel et absolu." A. de Gasperini, *De l'art dans ses rapports avec le milieu social* (1850), 1:9.

[128] See, for example, Thoré, "Exposition de 1835," *Le Réformateur*, no. 144 (2 March 1835), and Baget, "Salon de 1839," *J.P.* (7 April 1839).

[129] "Vérité en tout et partout"; "règles stériles du passé." P. Hawke, "Quelques Mots sur le Salon de peinture au Louvre—1848," *Le Représentant du peuple* (5 April 1848).

[130] "Les mots faits par tous et pour tous retourneraient à leur sens primitif et nécessaire." Gasperini, *De l'art*, 1:9.

[131] Ibid., 1:19ff.

"Unity! unity! Such is truth, such is life. Each man for all; all men in God: such is the foundation, the support, the sovereign law."[132]

Gasperini's conflation of realism and religion points to the complex genealogy of republican naturalism. For him, as for earlier commentators such as Laviron and Hawke, the artist's encounter with nature was a moment charged with political consequence, not merely in terms of the immediate "truths" he chose to represent or ignore, but more fundamentally in terms of the epistemological resonance of art as a vehicle for meaning. Inherent to this exaltation of artistic truth, subjectivity stands as the cornerstone and guarantor of naturalist aesthetics. Far from implying the effacement or attenuation of the creative personality, republican naturalism anchors the interpretative process in the particularity of the perceiving subject. Individualism, conceived as sovereign independence from convention and tradition, provides the grounding for authenticity, rather than a distorting lens obscuring clarity of vision. It is in this sense that we might understand the later remarks of Gustave Courbet, an artist whom in 1848 Hawke extolled as an exponent of *vérité*.[133] The painter's frequent denial of his indebtedness to any master other than nature and his identification of realism as the "negation of the ideal"[134] assert a resistance to artistic convention in favor of an ostensibly unmediated contact with the material world. The centrality of individual experience to such a process is clearly articulated in the celebrated manifesto of 1855, where tradition is acknowledged only as a reference point to be explored at will and adapted for the materialization of subjective inspiration:

> I have wished simply to draw from a complete knowledge of tradition the reasoned sense of my own individuality.
>
> To know in order to be capable, such was my idea. To be in a position to translate the habits, ideas, and appearance of my era, according to my own judgment, to be not only a painter but also a man, in a word to produce living art—such is my goal.[135]

[132] "Unité! Unité! Voilà la vérité, voilà la vie. Chaque homme pour tous les hommes; tous les hommes en Dieu: voilà la base, l'appui, la loi souveraine." Ibid., 2:14.

[133] Hawke, "Quelques Mots sur le Salon de peinture au Louvre—1848," *Le Représentant du peuple* (16 April 1848). See also his "Salon de 1848," *La Voix des femmes* 21 (12 April 1848).

[134] "Négation de l'idéal." G. Courbet, speech quoted in *Le Précurseur*, Antwerp (22 August 1861). On Courbet's notion of the ideal, see P. B. Crapo, "Disjuncture on the Left: Proudhon, Courbet and the Antwerp Conference of 1861," *Art History* 14, no. 1 (March 1991): 67–91, and J. H. Rubin, *Realism and Social Vision in Courbet and Proudhon* (1980).

[135] "J'ai voulu tout simplement puiser dans l'entière connaissance de la tradition le sentiment raisonné de ma propre individualité.

"Savoir pour pouvoir, telle fut ma pensée. Etre à même de traduire les moeurs, les idées, l'aspect de mon époque, selon mon appréciation, être non seulement un peintre, mais encore un homme, en un mot, faire de l'art vivant, tel est mon but." G. Courbet, "Le Réalisme," preface to *Exhibition et vente de 40 tableaux et 4 dessins de M. Gustave Courbet* (1855).

Such criteria legitimized representation only insofar as it flowed directly from experience. It was the present toward which the artist was directed, rather than the evocation of an intangible past or a metaphysical other, since in venturing beyond the material and familiar, he was said to forfeit both autonomy and authenticity.

Courbet's insistence on experiential immediacy echoes a commitment toward modernity which republican commentators of the 1830s had inherited and adapted from romantic polemicists of a previous generation. While endorsing the negative appraisal of the present common to radical ideologies of the period, their espousal of naturalism and moralism dictated artistic engagement with the contemporary world. Yet, despite its centrality in republican aesthetics, the call for modernity exposes an incapacity to articulate a distinctive social vision and reveals the difficulty of evolving visual codes rooted in the present rather than tainted by the past. Though mid-century realism owed much to the theoretical debates of the July Monarchy, the elaboration of a new visual language proved tentative and uncertain, as was thrown into sharp relief by developments in cultural policy after 1848.

MEANING AND MODERNITY

The call for modernity is perhaps the most distinctive characteristic of republican critical discourse during the 1830s. Though contemporaneity was a key ingredient within competing radical programs of the period, and had indeed emerged as a theme in artistic commentary as early as the 1760s,[136] in the writings of figures such as Decamps and Laviron it constituted an essential prerequisite to art's fulfillment of its moral responsibilities and to the artist's unhindered perception of the material world. Integral to the struggle against the Academy as well as to aspirations for more genuinely accessible cultural idioms, modernity focused the yearning for an art whose rootedness within experience would allow the artist to speak with clarity and emotional power to a mass public. At the same time, however, it revealed the occluded vision of the future characteristic of much contemporary republican thought. Ambivalent toward the encroaching industrial culture of high capitalism and its disruption of the subordinate classes' traditional ethical and social systems, many republican theorists were incapable of breaking with dominant values, to which they appealed in attempting to discredit prevailing injustices and promote a more equitable distribution of political and economic power. This hesitancy characterizes the

[136] See K. Herding, "Utopie concrète à l'échelle mondiale: l'art de la Révolution," in *La Révolution française et l'Europe* (1989), 1:xxi.

ethical connotations of republican calls for modernity. The conservative values subtending the group's moral philosophy frustrated the emergence of a coherent and persuasive vision of the future as anything more than a renovated and reformed variation on the past. While calling upon the artist to engage with the contemporary world, disillusionment with the present, coupled with a tentative appreciation of radical moral alternatives, limited the republicans' capacity to exploit modernity as a stimulant for change.

For critics and polemicists under the Restoration, modernity had stood as a central goal in artistic reform. Deschamps's assertion in 1828 that "first and foremost, one must be of one's own time"[137] echoed figures such as Stendhal and Hugo in repudiating dependence on themes and forms inherited from the distant past. Not only in literature, but in the visual arts too, innovation came to be associated with enhanced naturalism and contemporary relevance, features discerned in the work of such emerging masters as Delacroix, Vernet, and Delaroche. Despite the predominantly stylistic inspiration sustaining these calls for modernity, moral and political imperatives were also invoked, notably by the republican critics Ferdinand Flocon and Marie Aycard, whose enthusiasm for Delacroix's *Massacre de Scio* in 1824 centered on its polemical force.[138] Their indictment of the Academy's classical repertoire as foreign to contemporary sentiments and concerns took on added bite after the July Revolution in the pages of *La Liberté*, which declared uncompromisingly: "We are French in our habits, dress and language, opinions and beliefs; we demand to be so in art as well."[139] The implications of this position were elaborated during the succeeding decade by a broad range of critics, many of whom had participated in *La Liberté*'s campaign against the Institut and regarded modernity as integral to developing more socially responsive art forms. In surveying contemporary output, however, many commentators were most acutely aware of a pervasive crisis in representation, which disabled art as a medium for engaging with the present and sustained a range of outmoded stylistic references, accessible only to a cultivated minority.

The crisis of meaning in the arts was not imputed solely to the Academy and its tenacious promotion of classicism, though it did figure as a leading culprit and prime symptom in diagnoses of the broader malaise. More insidious was art's alleged inability to elaborate authentically contemporary forms and its retreat into the past as an escape from more urgent responsibilities. While the Revolution had recognized in the ancient world a

[137] "Avant tout et en tout, il faut être de son temps." E. Deschamps, *La Préface des Etudes françaises et étrangères*, ed. H. Girard (1923), 17.

[138] F. Flocon and M. Aycard, *Salon de 1824* (1824), 14–15.

[139] "Nous sommes français de moeurs, d'habits et de langage, d'opinions et de croyances, nous demandons de l'être d'art aussi." Didron, "Nous sommes français," *L.A.* 1 (August 1832): 20.

sounding board for current concerns and had forged a serviceable symbolic repertoire out of inherited codes, such procedures no longer carried conviction for radicals in the 1830s and 1840s. Though hard pressed to describe what contemporaneity in art might mean in anything other than general terms, republican critics concurred in judging prevailing stylistic options uniformly ill-suited to the demands of the present. Defining beauty as historically contingent rather than as an immutable, transcendent essence,[140] commentators insisted on the impracticality of reviving the formal languages of earlier cultures. Where such attempts were made—most conspicuously in pre-Raphaelite interpretations of sacred themes—recourse to past idioms was read as confirmation of the outmoded nature of the ideologies that underlay such works. Thus in 1833 Hauréau rebuked the Lyonnais painter Victor Orsel for failing to recognize that the Renaissance masters inspiring his religious homily *Le Bien et le mal* (plate 39) had grappled with contemporary problems in a way he seemed incapable of doing. Transforming Perugino and his contemporaries somewhat improbably into social crusaders attacking vice and oppression—represented by "handsome fifteenth-century feudal knights oppressing the people with their arms" and "debauchery in leather jerkins as well as black cassocks, filling the poor dishonored serf's family with scandal"[141]—Hauréau argued that a contemporary such as Jeanron would provide a more appropriate model to emulate, since in style and subject his work confronted current abuses, as Perugino had formerly done.

Similar considerations fostered hostility toward the vogue for illustrating episodes from national history, characteristic both of the romantics and of eclectics such as Delaroche. Less inclined than earlier critics to welcome the portrayal of medieval and Renaissance themes as a decisive break with academic protocols, republican critics of the 1830s demanded that any evocation of the past address issues of direct consequence for the present. Dismissed as "inhabile à suivre le mouvement de la société, à la défendre, à la glorifier,"[142] romanticism stood accused of withdrawing from the present to conceal its lack of critical perspective on the conflicts shaping the nation's future. In an address to romantic artists in *La Liberté*, Gabriel Laviron dismisses their fixation with past history as meaningless to a society making its own history in its continuing struggle against the Orléanist regime:

> When society is shaken to its foundations; when rebellion spreads screaming through the streets and squares; when bullets fly and the cannon roars; when

[140] See, for example, E. Pelletan, "Salon de 1841," *La Presse* (16 March 1841), on the historically relative nature of beauty.

[141] "Les beaux chevaliers seigneurs du quinzième siècle, opprimant le peuple avec le fer"; "La débauche en juste-au-corps de buffle comme en soutane noire, remplissant de scandale la famille du pauvre serf déshonoré." Hauréau, "Salon," *La Tribune politique et littéraire* (11 March 1833).

[142] H. Fortoul, "Souvenirs romantiques," *R.E.*, 60 (October–December 1833): 268.

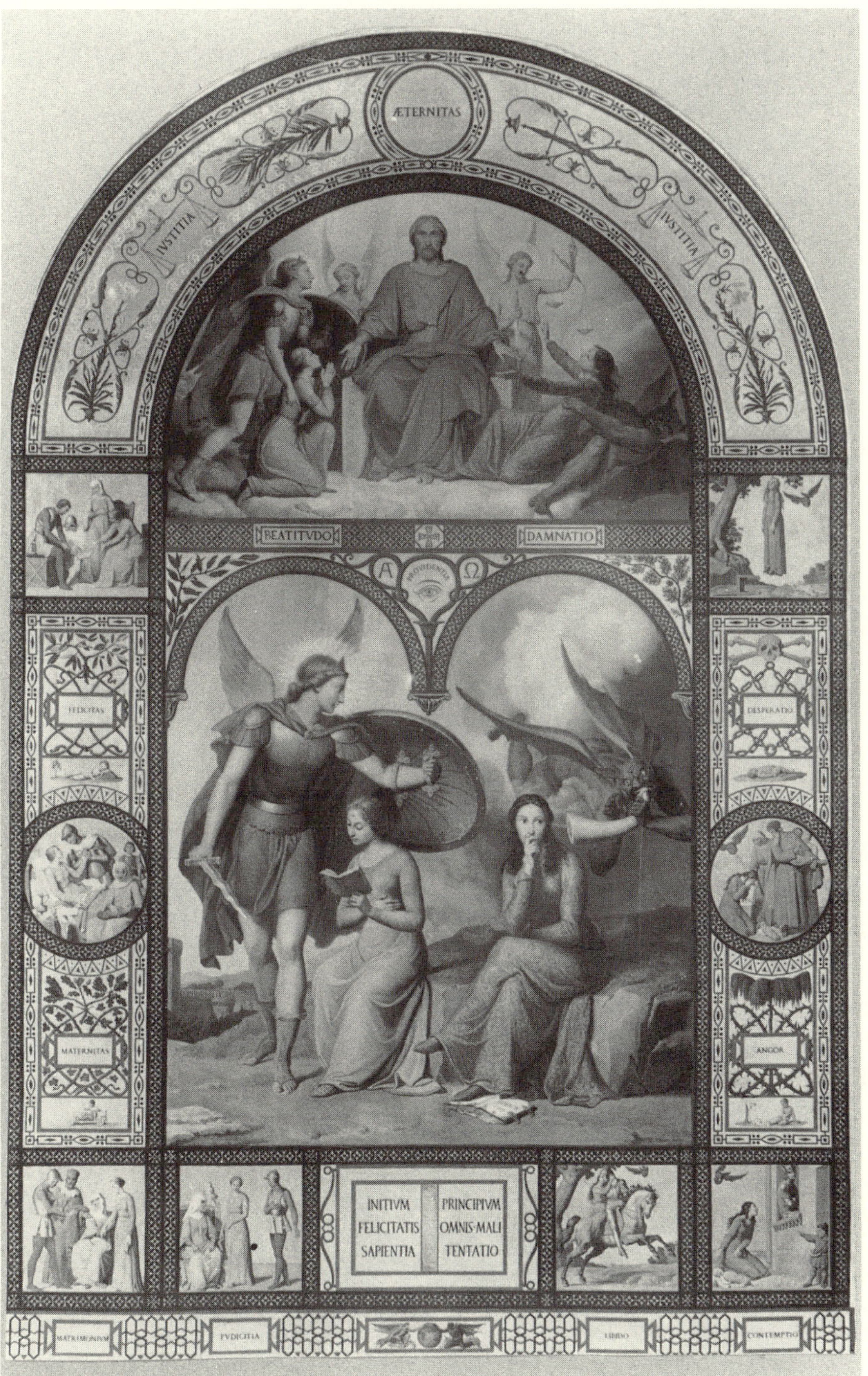

Plate 39. Victor Orsel: *Le Bien et le mal,* Salon of 1833. Musée des beaux-arts, Lyons.

> political passions litter the streets with corpses, you find nothing better to present to people who still have the taste of powder in their mouths and the *tocsin*'s ring in their ears than some insignificant chronicle from past times, and since you are incapable of lending it interest, you try to stimulate curiosity by exaggerating some shocking details. And you have the nerve to complain of the public's indifference![143]

The sense that the artist was adrift from the vital forces shaping society and that an impasse had been reached in the languages at his disposal, frustrating the transmission of meaning, frequently resurfaced throughout the 1830s and 1840s. Allegorical codes were deemed incapable of articulating contemporary experience and prompted calls for renovation.[144] The republican sculptor David d'Angers devoted particular attention to the problem, elaborating a vast range of emblematic groupings in sketches and notebook entries, and attempting, in works such as *La Jeune Grecque au tombeau de Marco Botzaris* (plate 40), to forge a visual language whose independence from established convention would enhance accessibility for the culturally disenfranchised. Commenting on the monument to the Greek patriot, first exhibited in 1827, Thoré interprets the young girl's symbolic connotations as residing in the formal and expressive aspects of the figure itself rather than in the decoding of extraneous detail meaningful only to a lettered minority. Empathetic association, rather than emblematic allusion, becomes the key to meaning:

> Why is this simple composition so moving? Because of a glorious death for the people's freedom. And then, what a gracious and touching symbol is this personification of Greece's rebirth as a charming young girl! And how admirably supple is her body! How simple and natural this young girl is, with her powerful head, so full of the future, great and childlike, its brow radiating intelligence and poetry, with a sad yet animated expression on her face. For if she feels pain and regret, there is also hope and courage which the future will not deceive.[145]

[143] "Quand la société est ébranlée jusque dans ses fondements; quand l'émeute roule en hurlant dans les rues et sur les places; quand les balles sifflent, et que le canon gronde; quand les passions politiques jonchent les rues de cadavres, vous ne trouvez rien de mieux à raconter à des gens qui ont encore le saveur de la poudre à la bouche et le bruit du tocsin aux oreilles, que quelque insignifiante chronique du temps passé, et faute d'y pouvoir mettre de l'intérêt, vous essayez de piquer la curiosité en exagérant quelques atroces détails. Et vous avez l'effronterie de vous plaindre de l'indifférence du public!" G. Laviron, "Progrès de nos doctrines," *L.A.* 18 (January 1833): 135.

[144] See, for example, A. Guillot, "De l'allégorie et des attributs au temps moderne," *L'Artiste*, 2d ser., 1 (1838): 290–93, a critique of Pradier's allegories of French cities in the Place de la Concorde. Guillot's call for new emblems, exemplified in his—extremely traditional—description of a female personification of War, apparently had little resonance in his own sculptural practice.

[145] "Pourquoi donc êtes-vous ému en regardant cette composition simple? C'est qu'il y a là une mort glorieuse pour l'affranchissement du peuple! Et puis quel gracieux et touchant

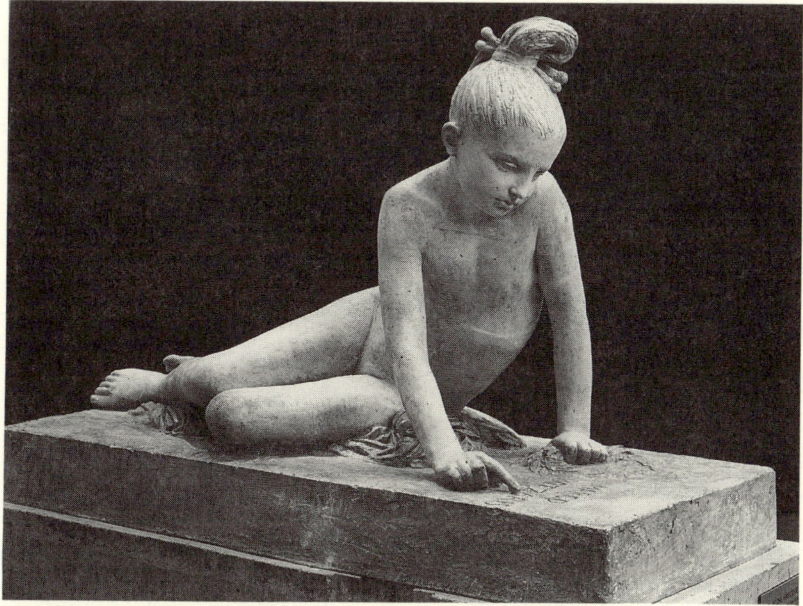

Plate 40. Pierre-Jean David d'Angers: *La Jeune Grecque au tombeau de Marco Botzaris*, 1827–34. Musée d'Angers.

Yet such examples—and their favorable critical reception—are less characteristic than the storm of contemptuous abuse that greeted the 1848 competition for a symbol of the new Republic, an episode whose ostentatious failure to refurbish the language of political allegory apparently corroborated prevailing suspicions.[146] It was such instances, echoing and amplifying strictures lodged against academic codes throughout the 1830s and 1840s, that focused a sense of art's more deeply rooted aphasia. As visual forms inherited from the past were accounted incommensurate with the social forms of the present, so a sense of the need for urgent iconographic renewal emerged. Calls for change, though, were trapped in a paradox: if previous cultures' meaning and viability were anchored in the

symbole que la personnification de la Grèce renaissante dans cette charmante jeune fille! Et puis, cette torse est si admirablement souple! Il y a tant de naturel et de simplicité dans cette jeune fille! et puis, sa tête est si puissante, si pleine d'avenir, sa grosse tête d'enfant avec son front rayonnant d'intelligence et de poésie, avec son expression de visage si triste et si énergique; car, s'il y a là de la douleur et des regrets, il y a aussi une espérance et un courage que l'avenir ne trompera pas." T. Thoré, "Revue des beaux-arts," *R.R.* 2 (1834): 400. David exhibited the figure in his studio in 1834. On the artist's symbolic language, see J. de Caso, *David d'Angers. L'Avenir de la mémoire* (1988).

[146] See M.-C. Chaudonneret, *La Figure de la République. Concours de 1848* (1987), and A. Boime, "The Second Republic's Competition for the Figure of the Republic," *Art Bulletin* 53 (March 1971): 68–83.

organic social philosophies from which they had drawn substance, how might a distinctive language of modernity be constructed in a world ostensibly characterized by fragmentation and crisis?

In common with other radicals, republican critics were profoundly struck by the antiheroism of modern life. The crisis seen as disabling "a century of doubt, disintegration, and ruins"[147] impacted directly on contemporary culture, since republicans dismissed any notion of transcendence comparable with the Saint-Simonians' belief in the artist's prophetic insight. A product of society, the artist was considered bound by its limitations, impaired by the ideological dispersal diagnosed as the most conspicuous feature of the modern world. Modernity was thus constituted as a lack or absence: of faith, of social organicism, of integrity, of a sense of the future. The past—as for other progressive critics—signified a wholeness forfeited in the present day, which had embraced the artist and his work in a community of sentiment, transforming the image into a materialization of shared meaning. As Alexandre Decamps remarked in 1834, in an argument apparently indebted to the Saint-Simonians' cyclical philosophy of history, in the past "works were adopted unanimously, accepted with admiration, since they resumed ideas held by every individual within society."[148] The prevailing climate foreclosed such possibilities: Decamps's sense of the transitional nature of contemporary society suspended the artist in a creative vacuum, deprived of a voice and a message for it to convey:

> Caught today between a faith whose tenets are all exhausted and powerless and a new belief that has not yet been formulated for the simple and the ignorant, the arts languish and drag themselves painfully through a society that denies the past and is obviously looking for a future of which it is still unaware.[149]

This, Decamps claimed, fostered the retrograde resuscitation of the past, which drew on a sense of despair at present ills and a desperate search for answers in previous experience.[150]

For the rest, republicans reiterated the same litany of evils we have encountered elsewhere: government commissioning policy, academic authoritarianism, the deficiencies of the market, and the narrowly materialist outlook of private patrons were all evoked as contributing to art's incapacity to

[147] "Un siècle de doute, de dissolution et de ruines." Anonymous, "Salon de 1833," *L'Artiste*, 1st ser., 5, no. 6 (1833): 70.

[148] "Les oeuvres étaient adoptées unaniment, acceptées avec admiration, parce qu'elles résumaient les idées que chaque individu nourissait dans la société." A. Decamps, "Les Arts et l'industrie," *R.R.* 3 (10 October 1834): 34.

[149] "Aujourd'hui, entre une croyance dont toutes les formules sont épuisées et impuissantes, et une croyance nouvelle qui n'est pas encore formulée pour les simples et les ignorants, les arts languissent et se traînent avec peine au milieu des tiraillements d'une société qui répudie le passé et cherche évidemment un avenir qu'elle ne connaît pas encore." Ibid., 33.

[150] See Decamps, "Salon de 1839," *Nat.* (7 March 1839).

communicate with the modern world. As Charles Blanc lamented in 1845, noting the preoccupation with technique displayed in contemporary art: "We don't know what to teach, so how should we know what to paint?"[151]

Blanc's question encapsulated the dilemma of modernity. The injunction to engage with the present presupposed distinctive characteristics capable of arousing artists' enthusiasm, though by common admission contemporary life offered little enough to fire the imagination. It was primarily as critics of social injustice and spiritual alienation that they were to be enlisted to the republican cause, exposing the moral bankruptcy of those in power and the consequences of their imputed misrule. Thus, in 1834, Arago enjoined the artist: "Take your inspiration from the intimate feelings of the day, plumb the moral and material suffering of a society that is falling apart in order to regenerate,"[152] a role consistent with the "propaganda mission"[153] he envisaged for culture. Significantly qualifying the artist's role in present and future society as an "apostolate," Arago conceives of modernity as a functional extension of the republicans' ideological critique of prevailing social institutions. Here, as elsewhere, modernity functions as exposé rather than as celebration, arraigning the present rather than displaying the future.

Whether anything more than this was possible was questioned by a number of critics, who maintained that the development of new artistic idioms must ultimately depend on prior social change. For Hauréau, who dismissed the capacity of dominant culture to engage meaningfully with the diversity of contemporary life, the agents and institutions regulating artistic output were identified with the political and aesthetic ideologies of the past. While demanding that "every artistic thought should henceforth be inspired by the present, with its passions and misery, and every artistic fantasy should have a goal, a will, and an action in the real world,"[154] he acknowledged that such radical reorientation faced considerable obstacles. Not only was modernity evasive and contradictory as a progressive value, the attainment of "a new language for a new feeling"[155] necessitated comprehensive social change, comparable with the "renewal" out of which medieval culture had emerged. Both here and elsewhere,[156] then, true modernity—the artistic

[151] "Nous ne savons pas ce qu'il faut enseigner, comment saurions-nous ce qu'il faut peindre?" Blanc, "Salon de 1845," *La Réforme* (16 March 1845).

[152] "Inspirez-vous des sentiments intimes de l'époque, initiez-vous aux souffances morales et matérielles d'une société qui se dissout pour se régénérer." Arago, "La République et les artistes," 26.

[153] "Mission de propagande." Ibid., 28.

[154] "Toute pensée d'art soit désormais inspirée du présent, de ses passions, de ses misères, que toute fantaisie d'art ait son but, sa volonté, son action dans ce monde actif." Hauréau, "Salon de 1834," *Tribune politique et littéraire* (15 March 1834).

[155] "Une langue nouvelle pour un sentiment nouveau." Ibid. (24 March 1834).

[156] See, for example Thoré, "Salon de 1838," *J.P.*, no. 17 (29 April 1838): "Il ne faut . . . pas nous flatter d'une révolution en fait d'art avant la rénovation politique qui se prépare."

assimilation and articulation of an organic social ideology rooted in the needs and opportunities of a democratic industrial culture—is situated in the future, its emergence made contingent on developments in which the arts themselves were imagined to play only a peripheral role.

Only rarely within the republican press is this essentially passive construction of culture's relationship to social change called into question. The visionary insight accorded to the artist by such groups as the Saint-Simonians was out of key with the more circumspect assessment of art's transformative effects upheld by most republicans. On the rare occasions when this prophetic image was invoked, as by an anonymous reviewer for *Le Réformateur* in 1835, it is still as a propagandist retailing a formulaic picture of enhanced social relations that the artist operates, rather than as a *vates* indulging in more metaphysical flights:

> The romantic would be that painter or sculptor who made himself not only the organ of the present but also the prophet of the future, who broke through the cloud shrouding our everyday intelligence in order to familiarize us with a general reform in our habits and social relations, who made us love and respect this reform through his elegant compositions, whose energy encouraged us to aspire toward it, and who instilled sublime feelings in the people by drawing inspiration from the midst of his children.[157]

The revelatory quality evoked here is explicitly associated with a small elite comprising David, Gros, Géricault, and—perhaps more surprisingly—Gérard, all of whom apparently spoke directly to their contemporaries. Yet the juxtaposition of such sentiments with a preference for anecdotal, moralizing work—the critic shows a particular weakness for Gallait's *Musiciens ambulants* and Latil's *Moralité du peuple*—indicates some of the contradictions in republican notions of modernity. These are further highlighted in the selection of artists and works most often nominated as responding to current needs. For the *Liberté* group in particular, Géricault epitomized the strong artist whose originality and independence were so gravely missed in the wake of romanticism's imputed failure of nerve.[158] Regarded as a forerunner and source of inspiration, his art stood as a model in the work of such critics as Laviron, Galbacio, and Decamps, who extolled the deceased

[157] "Le romantique serait le peintre ou le statuaire, qui se constituerait non seulement l'organe du présent, mais encore le prophète de l'avenir; qui, du bout de son pinceau, percerait la nue dont se couvre notre intelligence routinière, et nous familiariserait avec les idées d'une réforme générale dans les moeurs et les rapports sociaux, qui nous la ferait aimer cette réforme, par la suavité de son dessin, qui nous la ferait respecter, et ambitionner par l'énergie de sa composition, et qui formerait le peuple aux sentiments sublimes en s'inspirant au sein de ses enfants." W., "Exposition de 1835," *Le Réformateur*, no. 157 (15 March 1835).

[158] "Cet homme fort nous manque, il nous aurait été en aide, lui qui préparait la guerre que nous avons engagé." Jeanron, "De l'anarchie," 163. See also the "Premier Extrait d'un manuscrit de Géricault," ibid., 167–68, and Laviron, "Progrès de nos doctrines," 136.

painter for pursuing "the true and original expression of the present day."[159] Yet it was Decamps too who credited the anecdotal military painter Charlet and his literary counterpart Béranger with being "the first to have revealed the sources of modern art," addressing a broad popular audience through a vernacular idiom in which "the people were able to recognize themselves and their fellows."[160] The artist's nostalgic chauvinism, together with that of fellow Bonapartists Raffet and Vernet, won admiration for glorifying "the unaffected heroism of our old campaigners,"[161] and was credited with hastening the fall of Charles X—an accolade far surpassing any recognition extended toward Daumier and his fellow satirists in the comic press.[162] Rather than popular caricature, with its increasingly refined political range, republicans showed themselves more susceptible to the consecrated languages of high art, singling out a royal commission—Foyatier's monument to Spartacus, leader of a slaves' revolt in pre-Christian Rome—as an outstanding example of "proletarian art," "infused with contemporary feeling."[163]

What seems to be missing from this heterogenous selection is any coherent sense of the specificity of modern experience. Support for naturalism apparently provides one consistent thread, though here again what subject matter might prove appropriate for its exponents remains elusive, and is hemmed in by a prevailing regard for traditional moral and aesthetic values. It is this which might ultimately be seen as the most insidious and inhibiting check to the republicans' project for modernity, as indeed to more general ambitions for a social art. Despite their proclaimed disillusionment with contemporary society and its cultural institutions, the republicans found it difficult, if not impossible, to break free from a fundamental belief in the particularity (and, in some respects, the superiority) of the aesthetic domain. Such an attitude colored their basic address to the arts, both as an abstract object of theoretical inquiry and as a more tangible and localized subject of evaluation in the Salon exhibition. This attitude allowed radicals

159 "L'expression vraie et originale de l'époque contemporaine"; "le peuple a su se reconnaître et reconnaître ses contemporains." Decamps, "Salon de 1837," *Nat.* (7 April 1837). See also, for example, Laviron and Galbaccio, *Salon de 1833*, 107; B. Galbacio, "Salon de 1834," *Le Locateur* 24 (March 1834).

160 "Les premiers [qui ont] révélé les sources de l'art moderne." Decamps, "Les Arts et l'industrie," 43.

161 "L'héroïsme sans façon de nos vieux grognards." Arago, "La République et les artistes," 23.

162 On Daumier's meager reputation at this period, see M. Melot, "Daumier and Art History. Aesthetic Judgement/Political Judgement," *Oxford Art Journal* 11, no. 1 (1988): 3–4.

163 "Art prolétaire"; "empreinte de l'idée présente." G. Cavaignac, "Monuments révolutionnaires," 173. Foyatier's work was similarly praised in, for example, Thoré, "Revue des beaux-arts," 399, and in the artisans' journal *L'Atelier*: Anonymous, "Salon de 1841," *L'Atelier* 1 (March 1841): 55, and Anonymous, "Causes du peu de popularité de la statuaire en France," ibid., 5th year, 10 (July 1845).

of virtually every ideological hue to equivocate constantly, proclaiming allegiance to essentially functionalist aesthetic principles while repeatedly contravening—or simply forgetting—them in their subjective encounter with the work of art. It was an attitude, too, that tended to hold the work of art aloof from the world, despite all conscious efforts to rupture its privileged isolation, and worked against any contrary impulse to forge an aesthetic that attenuated the very distinction between the cultural and the quotidian. This residual idealism was perfectly compatible with commitment toward art's edifying potential, an issue on which virtually all critics concurred, and could easily accommodate the instructive tableaux of popular probity to which republicans as well as other radicals proved so responsive. Greater difficulty was encountered in developing a more far-reaching strategy that involved questioning not only the basic presuppositions sustaining dominant notions of the aesthetic, but also those which helped to fashion fundamental social perceptions of the meanings of modernity.

Symptomatic of this constrained and ambivalent position is the paucity of references to industry in descriptions of what the artist might embrace in his survey of modern experience. Decamps, in 1834, calling for an "art positif et industriel" reminiscent of early Saint-Simonian ideals, evokes such feats as the construction of a suspension bridge or the manufacture of a steam engine as equaling the triumphs of the ancient world,[164] while in 1850 Pierre Vinçard, a disciple of Louis Blanc, exhorts artists to confront the spectacle of labor:

> Workshops, factories, mines, construction sites, manufacturies—these thousand cogs of wood or iron creating machines which seem to have been invented by God alone, and yet which are only the work of men—all of this marvelous and sometimes somber side of modern industry should reveal a vast horizon to them and lend their works originality.[165]

While moderating his paëan to the industrial sublime with some reference to popular "perseverance" and "abnégation," there is little in Vinçard's description to suggest that the workplace might ever be the site of class antagonism rather than social concord—a particularly telling oversight in the wake of the crisis of the National Workshops and the bitter struggle of the June Days.

Such occlusion is characteristic of an ideology that habitually interpreted

[164] Decamps. "Les Arts et l'industrie," 36–37.

[165] "Les ateliers, les usines, les mines, les chantiers, les fabriques, ces mille rouages de fer ou de bois créant des machines qui ont l'air d'être inventées par dieu seul, et ne sont pourtant que l'ouvrage des hommes, tout ce merveilleux et parfois si sombre aspect que l'industrie présente, devrait leur faire entrevoir un immense horizon, et donner à leurs oeuvres un caractère original." P. Vinçard, *Les Artistes et le peuple* (1850), 8.

inequality as a moral as much as a social problem, attributable to the *égoïsme* of *oisifs* intent on self-gratification at the expense of the poor but honest worker. Despite the revolutionary wing centered on the Société des saisons under Barbès and Blanqui, republican factions, from the reformists associated with *Le National* through what in 1840 Thoré described as "la Jeune Démocratie,"[166] sought reconciliation between classes. Such an attitude tended to foster an idealized perception of the people as the upright but stoical victims of corrupt masters, who sought less revenge for their repression than acceptance as equals in a morally cleansed nation of brothers. Though occasionally conceding that subordinate groups might not have remained immune to the perceived crisis of values afflicting society, commentators more usually projected the laboring population as the nation's moral examplar, and its potential source of salvation.[167] Thus conceived, the working poor were introduced into the discourse of modernity as a force through which the prevailing crisis could be resolved. This essentialized class, in whose sanitized guise the traditional ethical values of the bourgeoisie were paradoxically incorporated and amplified, could be mobilized by republican commentators to make fundamental social change seem less like a violent repudiation of inherited beliefs than as their reaffirmation and realization.

It was this construction of the people which informed the populist bias in republican notions of modernity. The people were the voice of the future—even if, as articulated by their spokesmen, its sound seemed strangely disembodied and archaic in its reiteration of familiar moral injunctions. Populism, too, meant less the elaboration of new artistic codes or the exploration of unfamiliar media more appropriate for groups largely excluded by the conventions of high art, but rather the induction and incorporation of those groups into a preexisting culture. Though commentators occasionally denounced the social segregation implicit in institutions such as the Salon,[168] only sporadically was there any sense that a new constituency might be most effectively addressed in forms more closely related to their everyday experience. Indeed, when Vinçard speaks to the artist on behalf of the working poor, it is to solicit initiation to the established languages of culture, which he extols for their capacity to reconcile the disadvantaged with their impoverishment, rather than for their power to stimulate change: "You accuse me of ignorance, yet you refuse to enlighten me! Instead of condemning me,

[166] In his pamphlet *La Vérité sur le parti démocratique*, cited in Weill, *Histoire du parti républicain*, 139.

[167] The classic statement of this position is J. Michelet, *Le Peuple* (1846). See A. Pessin, *Le Mythe du peuple et la société française du XIXe siècle* (1992), particularly 99–125.

[168] See, for example, E. Delacroix, "Exposition.—Ceux qui en veulent et ceux qui n'en veulent pas," *L.A.* 18 (January 1833): 130.

initiate me, become my guide, teach me to admire what is beautiful, just, and good. Console me, so that my poverty seems less of a burden by being made poetic through your works."[169]

This singularly compromised vision is entirely consistent with calls made on the republican left throughout the 1830s and 1840s for an *art du peuple*, since this demand habitually carried connotations which, by eliding the moral and the social, anchored the term firmly within the values of high culture. In all of this, *le peuple* signified not so much a class defined in economic and social terms as a more or less ineffable moral entity constituted as a gauge of artistic integrity. As an anonymous commentator remarked in 1835: "The more art becomes isolated from the people, the more it becomes false and impoverished, so the more it becomes common and vulgar"[170]—a reversal of epithets based on an identification of the common people with the universal values of nature. The republican ideal, encapsulated in Hauréau's observation that "inspiration for great things has taken refuge among the people: the artist soon will draw from it,"[171] conceived the art of the future as drawing moral regeneration from a class identified with values rooted in the past.

Such representations of the laboring poor and their culture focused a series of contradictions, moral and aesthetic, inherent to republican ideology. The transformative ambitions it harbored, whether for political and economic change or for artistic renewal, depended on a vision of the people that simultaneously projected them as inheritors of the future and guardians of the past. The role played by *le peuple* in republican notions of modernity highlights the ideological limitations of the movement both in thinking through the aesthetic implications of *art social* and the social consequences of challenging the effects of nascent high capitalism. In both spheres, these limitations were fatally exposed in 1848, a moment that revealed the contradictions and equivocations embedded in the uneasy coalition of forces that had made up the republican movement under the July Monarchy.

[169] "Vous m'accusez d'ignorance, et vous vous refusez à m'instruire! Au lieu de me condamner, faites-vous mes initiateurs; devenez mon guide; apprenez-moi à admirer ce qui est beau, juste et bon. Consolez-moi, faites que ma pauvreté me semble moins pesante, en la poétisant par vos oeuvres." Vinçard, *Les Artistes et le peuple*, 7.

[170] "Plus l'art se retire du peuple, et plus il se fausse et s'appauvrit, plus il devient commun et vulgaire." Thoré[?], "L'Art," *Le Polonais* 5 (December 1835): 370.

[171] "L'inspiration des grandes choses s'est réfugiée chez le peuple:—l'artiste y puisera bientôt." Hauréau, "Salon," *La Tribune politique et littéraire* (3 March 1833).

CHAPTER 9

Conclusion

CLASS AND THE SNARE OF CULTURE

In an unfinished account of the cooperative associations that sprang up in Paris following the February Revolution, the locksmith and people's deputy Jérôme-Pierre Gilland offers a glimpse of the ideological work of the work of art in a mass democracy.[1] Describing a visit to a tailors' collective in the faubourg Saint-Denis, he recalls the sight of three popular prints decorating the workshop's walls: a portrait of the radical leader Armand Barbès, an image of Christ trampling the demon of pride flanked by allegories of Liberty and Equality, and a personification of the Republic—one of many such—whose emblematic trappings focus on the balance she holds before her brow.[2] In the company of a young worker—attracted by Gilland's spontaneous exclamation of pity at the sight of the recently imprisoned Barbès—the erstwhile artisan explores the images as a form of social catechism, dramatizing the citizen's allegiances and obligations within the new regime. His expression of admiration for Barbès—"a friend and model to us all"—provokes the apprentice tailor to assert Christ's superior claim as a model for emulation, a qualification the older man readily conceeds, describing him as "the most beautiful social model offered to man." Their conversation unfolds beneath the tutelary gaze of the Republic, whose balance Gilland particularly notes as resuming a fundamental moral truth: "This balance is a symbol, telling men: raise yourselves through work, intelligence, and virtue; and when you are great, remain humble and remember that modest folk are your brothers; serve them, love them, do all you can to raise them up to you."[3]

The inspiration Gilland draws from "these poor, darkened little images

[1] See J.-P. Gilland, *Revue anecdotique des associations ouvrières* (1850), 11–17.

[2] Gilland's description of Christ approximates to the Buchezian *Prenez et lisez* (plate 13). The portrait of Barbès may be Traviès's depiction of the revolutionary leader in jail, based on his painting *Un Détenu politique*, refused at the 1835 Salon. The figure of the Republic cannot be identified.

[3] "Notre ami, notre modèle à tous"; "le plus beau type social qui soit offert à l'homme"; "Ce niveau est un symbole; il veut dire aux hommes: élevez-vous par le travail, l'intelligence et la vertu; et quand vous serez grands, restez humbles, rappelez-vous que les petits sont vos frères; servez-les, aimez-les, faites tous vos efforts pour qu'ils puissent venir jusqu'à vous." Gilland, *Revue anecdotique*, 14.

. . . so badly drawn, yet lofty and moral in conception"[4] reminds him of a recent visit to a wealthy household where two artworks of a very different stamp—a pair of statuettes depicting "Leda and the Swan" and "Sara la baigneuse"—had caught his eye. Though he admits their formal perfection, the ornaments' immodesty repels the locksmith, who sees in their contrast with the humble workshop a metaphor for the ethical antitheses subtending class divisions:

> On the one hand, comfort, sweet restfulness, discreet debauchery, petty concerns, petty frivolities, petty vices, and boredom: the boredom of a life which is useless and insipid when it is not shameful and criminal.
>
> On the other hand, profound poverty after strenuous labor; a vital faith revealed through action; absolute dedication, the sacrifice of all harmful passions to selfless ideals; love of others elevated to the most sublime self-denial; and, for unique reward and worldly consolation, the hope of a better tomorrow to bequeath to future generations![5]

The story's moral symmetry is made complete when Gilland learns of the young tailor's recent arrival in Paris, his impoverishment after discovering an elder brother near death, his recuperation by the tailors, and his hard-working, altruistic nature. Touched by the tale of this exemplary worker, Gilland reflects: "Yet these are . . . the men treated as enemies of the family, religion, and property. In truth, there are some uncaring, cruel people in this world!"[6]

This brief episode serves as an ideal representation of the tonic effect that advocates of a social aesthetic anticipated from art's integration into the gestures and rituals of daily life. The contrasting preferences of worker and bourgeois become signifiers of broader oppositions in outlook: while the former devotes his scant resources to imagery whose public resonance reaffirms his civic dedication, the latter treats art as a provocation to introverted indulgence. The hardships of labor are compensated through a visual rhetoric preaching the moral nobility that redeems a life of privation; the corrosive effect of luxury imprints itself in the libidinous tastes of the *grand*

[4] "Ces pauvres petites images noires . . . d'une exécution si incorrecte, mais conçu[es] dans une pensée haute et morale." Ibid.

[5] "D'un côté, le confort, les doux loisirs, la débauche discrète, les petits intérêts, les petites frivolités, les petits vices et l'ennui; l'ennui d'une vie inutile et fade quand elle n'est pas honteuse et criminelle.

"De l'autre côté, un dénuement profond après des labeurs acharnés; la foi vive se révélant par des oeuvres; le dévouement absolu, l'immolation de toutes les passions mauvaises à une idée généreuse; l'amour du prochain porté jusqu'aux sacrifices les plus sublimes; et, pour tout bien, pour toute consolation dans le monde, l'espérance d'un avenir meilleur à léguer aux générations futures!" Ibid., 15.

[6] "Voilà pourtant . . . ces hommes qu'on traite d'ennemis de la famille, de la religion, de la propriété. En vérité, il y a dans ce monde des êtres bien légers, bien cruels!" Ibid., 17.

monde. And yet . . . Gilland finds it hard to suppress a hint of admiration for the statuettes' artistry—"it is true that the modeling was superb!"[7]—which betrays the worker-poet, a veteran of *L'Atelier* and *La Ruche populaire*, who prided himself on the elegance of his written style.[8]

The tension is one which Jacques Rancière has argued is implicit in the divided identity of a proletarian intellectual such as Gilland, trapped between days of prose, spent at the workbench or in the field, and nights of poetry, inspired by an "individualizing impulse" offering respite from the everyday. Embarking on this "journey of apprenticeship in the land of the other's culture,"[9] figures such as Gilland inclined less toward the vernacular of the *veillée* or the *goguette* than to the lyric refinement of high poetry—verse, in fact, like Hugo's *Sara la baigneuse*, a subject Gilland has no difficulty recognizing even as he snorts disapproval. Rather than marking a betrayal of class allegiances, Rancière has argued for the ultimately progressive implications of this assimilation of the language and protocols of high art by the culturally dispossessed. For Gilland, as for other artisanal aspirants to artistic legitimation, transcending the socially determined oxymoron of worker-poet in terms of the ordained conventions of dominant culture rather than the rough music of the street constitutes a subversive, destabilizing claim to "aestheticize the life of the people,"[10] a liberating refusal to assume the exclusions and constraints of working-class life as preordained and inevitable.

Yet laying claim to a cultural identity was no easy matter and no one strategy could be pursued without paying a price. Throughout the 1830s and 1840s bourgeois commentators increasingly probed the working-class *habitus* for evidence of a collective moral being, and inclined to treat alleged cultural preferences as elements in a broader social etiology. For some, increasing literacy brought with it the threat of insubordination provoked by lurid and immoral works through whose corrupt appeal the people became "insolent, cavilling, impudent, blasphemously cynical, rebellious, unruly, mad on debauchery, and consumed by every impious fever."[11] For others, the emergence of a pleiad of cultivated artisans such as Gilland suggested that, far from compromising social stability through congenital weak-mindedness, the worker could act as an exemplar to his reputed supe-

[7] "Il est vrai que le modelé était superbe!" Ibid., 15.

[8] "Doué de beaucoup d'amour-propre, Gilland s'efforce d'atteindre la beauté, l'élégance du style," M. Nadaud, *Les Mémoires de Léonard, ancien garçon maçon*, ed. J. Follain (1948), 170.

[9] "Mouvement d'individualisation"; "voyage d'apprentissage au pays de la culture de l'autre." J. Rancière, "Ronds de fumée (les poètes ouvriers dans la France de Louis-Philippe)," *Revue des sciences humaines* 61, no. 190 (April–June 1983): 34.

[10] "Esthétiser la vie du peuple." Ibid., 46.

[11] "Insolent, ergoteur, effronté, sacrilègement cynique, révolté, mutin, avide de débauches, et dévoré par toutes les fièvres impies." Fortunat, "Du colportage des mauvais livres," *L'Ange gardien* 1 (1848): 467.

riors. Extolling the people as "the providential, inevitable, necessary, and imminent initiator to the principles of equality against which the old world still struggles," George Sand calls on the worker-poet to "sing your hymns of truth"[12] to a middle class that needs reminding of its common bonds with a group it now shuns: "The same blood flows in your veins; interests alone only apparently divide you. Find, then, the religious, social, and political law that will unite all interests in one, and which will remix the blood of every race in a single family."[13]

This messianic role precluded any militant challenge to the established order, however. For bourgeois liberals such as Sand, social conciliation, inaugurating a new, more equitable regime, would be won through moral precedent rather than physical force. Stoical contentment or martyrdom was thus integral to the worker-poets' exemplary role, signifying a majesty of spirit capable of transcending the material oppression of poverty and physical hardship.[14] To repudiate class and calling, to inspire dissent rather than social harmony, was to infringe the terms on which the plebeian could lay claim to validation by the liberal intelligentsia as an authentic representative of a mythical *peuple*. Yet the poetry of self-sacrifice could seem less enticing to those for whom labor was a daily reality rather than a pathetic ideal. For the joiner Gauny, the romantic sufferings of a René or an Obermann paled in comparison to the miseries of the anonymous worker:

> Sublime unfortunates! You have not known the sorrow of sorrows, the vulgar sorrow of the lion caught in a trap, of the plebeian subjected to the horrible sessions in the workshop; the penitentiary expedient gnawing at spirit and body through boredom and the madness of long labor. Ah! old Dante, you never traveled to the *real hell*, the *hell without poetry*, farewell!![15]

Conscious of his suffering, yet equally sensitive to dominant culture's unwillingness to recognize how deadening manual labor could be, a prole-

[12] "L'initiateur providentiel, fatal, nécessaire et prochain, aux principes d'égalité contre lesquels le vieux monde lutte encore"; "chantez vos hymnes de vérité." G. Sand, "Préface du *Chantier* par Poncy," in *Questions d'art et de littérature*, in *Oeuvres complètes* 30 (1878; reprint, 1980), 166.

[13] "Le même sang coule dans vos veines, les intérêts seuls vous divisent en apparence. Trouvez-la donc, cette loi religieuse, sociale et politique, qui réunira tous les intérêts en un seul, et qui mêlera de nouveau le sang de toutes les races dans une seule famille." Ibid., 171–72.

[14] For a discussion of bourgeois reception of worker-poets, see E. Thomas, *Voix d'en bas* (1979), 56–68. The theme of social conciliation is particularly striking in the preface to the anthology of workers' verse compiled by the former Saint-Simonian, Olinde Rodrigues, *Poésies sociales des ouvriers* (1841), where he extols the "idées d'ordre et de paix" they convey.

[15] "Sublimes malheureux! vous n'avez pas connu la douleur des douleurs, la douleur vulgaire, celle du lion pris au piège, celle du plébéien en proie aux horribles séances de l'atelier; cette ressource pénitentiaire qui ronge l'esprit et le corps par l'ennui et la folie de son long travail. Ah! vieux Dante, tu n'as pas voyagé dans l'*Enfer réel*, dans l'*Enfer sans poésie*, adieu!!" *Louis Gabriel Gauny. Le Philosophe plébéien*, ed. J. Rancière (1983), 37. On this phenomenon, see J. Rancière, *La Nuit des prolétaires* (1981), 25–30.

tarian intellectual such as Gilland or Gauny was caught in a trap. Investment of personal identity in art or literature attenuated bonds with his peers, yet placed him in an ambivalent, unstable relationship with a class whose language he used but whose validation was made conditional on maintaining social distance. Elite culture too served simultaneously as a lure and an object of distaste. While Gilland's admiring aside betrays a covert assimilation of the connoisseur's vocabulary, many artisan polemicists expressed their sense of exclusion from a culture they regarded as foreign to their interests and indifferent, if not openly hostile, to their class. Journals explicitly directed at a working-class readership, such as the Christian socialist *L'Atelier* or Cabet's *Le Populaire*, either ignored events such as the Salon altogether or framed their comments from an explicitly populist perspective.[16]

Particular resentment was expressed at misrepresentations of the worker as dissipated and ignorant, notably in the boulevard theaters where popular audiences could easily be subborned into applauding their own grotesque caricatures.[17] Yet the punctiliousness that indicted bourgeois immorality masquerading as art was equally harsh on the rough pleasures of the people at the carnival or *barrière*.[18] Such distaste insidiously colluded with bourgeois commentators in identifying a *classe dangereuse* in need of moral rehabilitation rather than political liberation through militant action. It pointed the way toward a redemptive discourse, which invested faith in the capacity of family love, civic pride, and the ennobling power of unalienated labor to elevate a regenerate working class above a decadent and self-centered bourgeoisie. In the words of the communist *La Fraternité de 1845*:

> Workers, how many things we need to change in ourselves. Let each of us seriously examine his conscience and ask what needs reforming in his tastes, his pleasures, his relationships, and in the way he uses his time. Let us dedicate everything we eliminate from our present behavior which is idle, useless, or vicious to the life of the mind. . . . Are you resigned to living forever the brutalizing life that the world offers you today? Do you renounce, then, the complete development of your being? . . . Learn at last how to raise yourselves from your intellectual lethargy, your shameful degradation.[19]

[16] See, for example, Anonymous, "Causes du peu de popularité de la statuaire en France," *L'Atelier*, 5th year, 10 (July 1845).

[17] See Rancière, *La Nuit*, 269. For a similar critique by a middle-class radical, see E. Arago, "Les Beaux-Arts et la littérature du peuple," *Almanach du Nouveau Monde pour 1850*, (1849): 145–46.

[18] Rancière, *La Nuit*, 266–68.

[19] "Ouvriers, que de choses à réformer en nous; que chacun se fasse subir un sérieux examen, qu'il se demande en conscience ce qu'il a à réformer dans ses goûts, dans ses plaisirs, dans ses relations, dans l'emploi de son temps; que tout ce que nous retrancherons d'oiseux, d'inutile ou de vicieux dans notre manière d'être actuelle soit destiné à la vie de l'esprit. . . . Consentez-vous à vivre éternellement de la vie abrutissante que vous fait le monde actuel? Renoncez-vous enfin au développement complet de votre être? . . . Sachez enfin vous relever de cette léthargie intellectuelle, de cet abaissement honteux." Ibid., 276.

The sentiments are not so very different from the bourgeois moralists' vision of the proletarian as delinquent, or, indeed, from the Saint-Simonians' ideal of reeducating the people through contact with the spiritually refined culture of their betters. Underscoring such remarks is the insidious conviction that in some sense it is the worker himself who is answerable for his abasement, rather than the oppressive material circumstances that govern his life. The mechanics of social change thus come to depend less on the worker's struggle against those forces sustaining his oppression from above than on an internal struggle against moral failings ostensibly responsible for his degradation. The message Gilland reads in the Republic's symbolic balance embodies this insistence on an ethical revolution in which labor, intelligence, and virtue are weapons enough in a battle that respects family, faith, and property rather than challenging the system they uphold. This occluded vision of power and class identity encourages an artisan intellectual such as Gilland to regard the transcendental values he invests in art as an instrument of popular liberation and impedes any more radical questioning of its possible collusion in naturalizing the ideological foundations of social inequality.

The conflicted identity of a figure such as Gilland concentrates broader tensions in radicals' definitions of the class whose material liberation they sought. From the Saint-Simonians' barely suppressed anxieties at the potentially explosive power of popular energies to their containment in the Republicans' totemic ideal of a morally pristine class, the laboring poor were essentialized in such a way as to immobilize them as an autonomous force. No matter how intransigent toward accepted convention—as in the Saint-Simonians' sexual politics—radical movements failed to break free from a paternalistic vision of the proletariat, which rendered them passive even when confering them with the exemplary role of social regeneration. What is, then, perhaps most striking about *art social* and the politics within which it was framed, is the difficulty faced by middle-class radicals, as well as by artisan intellectuals, in staking out an authentically different moral terrain on which to construct a progressive sociocultural practice.

This failure to forge a distinctive ethical identity through which an independently empowered working class could assume responsibility for its own social transformation characterizes much radical discourse in the 1830s and 1840s. Saint-Simon's rigid sense of hierarchical organization, Enfantin's desire for conciliation, Buchez's moral traditionalism, Considerant's bowdlerization of Fourier's instinctual liberation—all point to an implicit accommodation of prevailing social norms. In their understanding of art, too, radical commentators reveal the difficulty of turning forms of expression so thoroughly embedded in prevailing socioeconomic structures against the very foundations of these structures themselves. As a constant counterpoint to their proclaimed investment in art as a spur to social change, commentators across the left display an insurmountable attraction toward aesthetic gratification as an end in itself. Though qualified by a sustained effort to explore the transformatory power of artistic form, this pervasive tendency points up the tacit pressures sustaining dominant conventions of reception and understanding. Reluctance, too, to question the centrality of a cultural tradition founded in the socially overdetermined media showcased at the Salon, and to promote idioms more in keeping with popular experience, further testifies to the structural constraints limiting radical reassessment of the arts. The contradictions that dogged the attempts of a worker such as Gilland to conscript the languages of high art to the popular cause thus proved ultimately as debilitating to middle-class radicals who viewed the aesthetic as a powerful catalyst for social change.

This process of containment and recuperation confirms Richard Terdiman's observation on "how deeply implicated in the structures of dominant discourse even the most concerted strategies of resistance cannot fail to find themselves."[20] Terdiman's identification of "counter-discourses," which challenge and subvert dominant ideologies' investment of the contingent principles sustaining them with a sense of natural inevitability, stresses the strategic importance of form: "their object," he argues, "is to represent the world *differently*."[21] Terdiman detects this provocative defamiliarization at work in the writings of Baudelaire, Flaubert, and Mallarmé, and, in the visual arts, in Daumier's anatomization of bourgeois mores. Common to these instances of subversion, Terdiman claims, is a "struggle over the paradigms of social representation themselves."[22] It is this struggle that proved so elusive to the proponents of *art social*. Though in Fourier the left had one of the most authentically irrepressible counter-discursive voices of the period, outflanking received wisdom at every turn in a language whose excess constantly disorientates and incites, his followers and their contemporaries more typically defer to moral conventions, even while contesting their social consequences. Preoccupation with form failed properly to transcend this inhibition: while the Saint-Simonians' exploration of new artistic languages worked to promote an inegalitarianism even more rigid than that currently dividing society, Fourierist understanding of the ameliorative effect of sensual experience discreetly neutralized the sexual implications central to the founder's teachings. In this regard, the repudiation of the most overtly utopian of Fourierist critics, Désiré Laverdant, by colleagues disconcerted at his assault on domestic propriety neatly symbolizes the doctrinal temporization of the 1840s.

Such ideological constraints crucially enfeebled the clarity of vision upon

[20] R. Terdiman, *Discourse/Counter-Discourse. The Theory and Practice of Symbolic Resistance in Nineteenth-Century France* (1985), 190.

[21] Ibid., 149.

[22] Ibid.

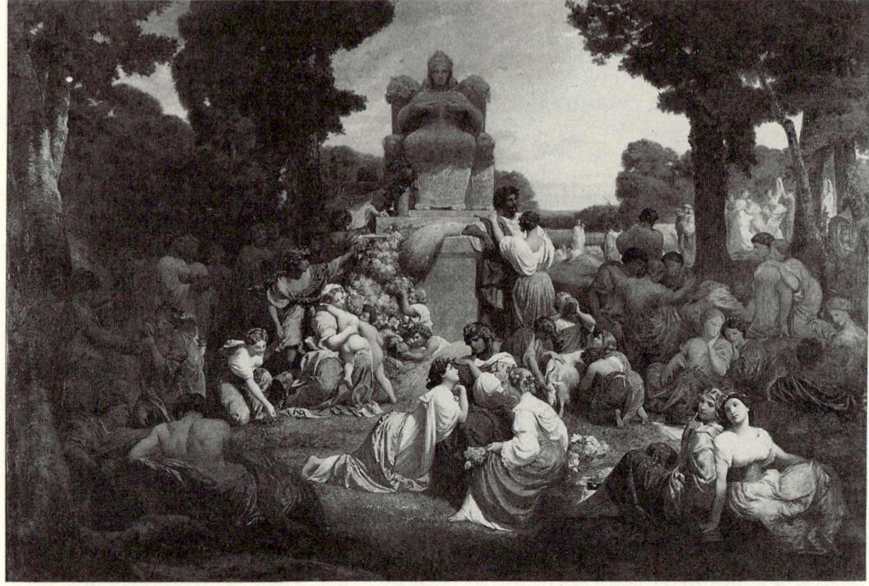

Plate 41. Henri-Pierre Picou: *Fête à la Nature,* Salon of 1850–51. Musée des beaux-arts, Nantes.

which a distinctive radical art practice could be founded. The prophetic mode—vigorously promoted by both Saint-Simonians and Fourierists as a stimulant to social transformation compensating for the lack of any more convincing blueprint for achieving change—failed conspicuously to conjure up a distinctive model of future existence. Fourier's endlessly garrulous descriptions of the Phalanstère, the minutest detail of whose form and function he obsessively noted, could inspire only Papety's pallid reworking of standard-issue Arcadianism, a striking testimony to the doctrine's inherent failure to confront the impact of industrial expansion on social organization. Comparable myopia characterizes the left's general enthusiasm for Léopold Robert's *Moissonneurs* (plate 19), a work whose evocation of an exotic, untroubled agrarian society fostered a nostalgic yearning for a mythically spontaneous organicism apparently lost in the alienated regime of industrial labor. This escapism can be seen as a more general feature of the period, with its incipient rococo revival and its fondness for Arcadian scenes such as Haussoullier's *Fontaine de Jouvence* and Picou's *Fête à la Nature*[23] (plate 41). This projection of the Golden Age into a more or less identifiable

[23] See also comments on Gleyre's location of an ideal society in his vision of the ancient world, in A. Boime, "The Instruction of Charles Gleyre and the Evolution of Painting in the Nineteenth Century," in Winterthur, Kunstmuseum, *Charles Gleyre, ou les illusions perdues* (1974), 102.

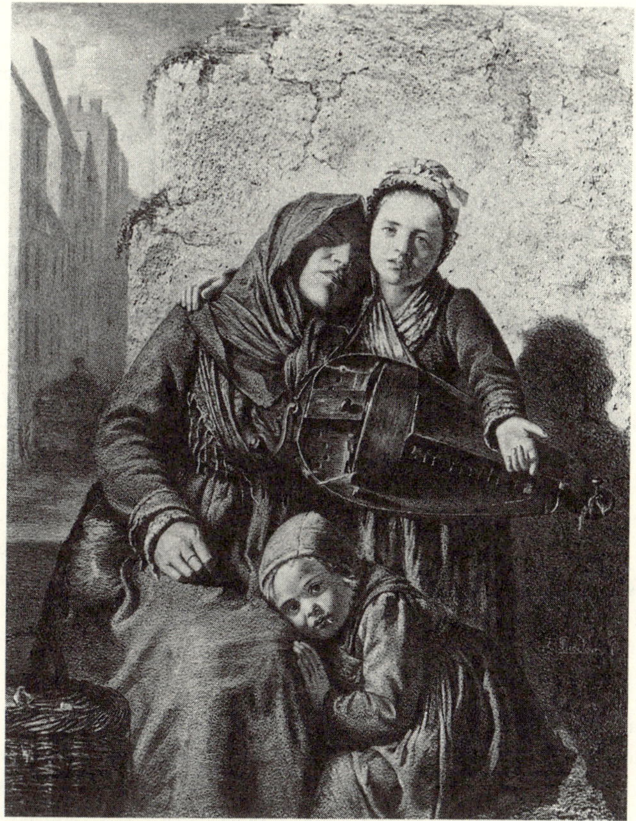

Plate 42. Engraving after Jean-Pierre-Alexandre Antigna: *Pauvre Famille,* Salon of 1847. Cabinet des estampes, Bibliothèque nationale, Paris.

past suggests an implicit unease at the advance of industrial capitalism, spawning a regressive fantasy of prelapsarian innocence and community. It is some measure of the left's limitations that it was able only to collude in such a fantasy, rather than offering its own, more convincing vision of the future.

Radical attempts to indict the injustices of contemporary society in a "critical" art were similarly thwarted by ideological and cultural restrictions. Though portrayal of poverty by figures such as Jeanron and Antigna (plate 42) highlighted the plight of the poor, they depicted them as an essentially passive class, soliciting compassion in a situation they themselves appeared powerless to change. The mechanisms of empathy on which such works relied abstracted out larger questions of social causation and left the idiom they evolved vulnerable to exploitation from a contrary political perspective. Albert Boime's identification of an "Official Realism" under the Second Empire[24] demonstrates just such a process of recuperation, as a conservative regime seeking popular support adapted the formulas of "critical" naturalism to extol values congenial to those in power. The relative similarity of such work to canvases praised by radical commentators in the 1830s and 1840s—and the Empire's sponsorship of figures such as Breton and Antigna previously admired for their oppositional stance—indicates how qualified *art social*'s break with dominant values and modes of representation had in fact been.

These limitations emerge all the more vividly when measured against conservative initiatives to deploy the arts in consolidating popular acquiescence to dominant values. Perhaps even more instinctively than their opponents on the left, supporters of the established order understood how formative an effect culture could have in shaping ideological positions, a realization given added urgency as educational reform and a broadening consumer economy extended previously inaccessible cultural products to subordinate groups. The need to pacify apparently innate tendencies toward disobedience and immorality and to foster respect for authority encouraged close and critical inspection of working-class leisure and inspired a vocal reform campaign.[25] Pointing to the high stakes invested in cultural control, the poet Anne Bignan argued in 1838:

> Give a moral purpose to art, which is humanity's highest expression, enlighten people as to the true nature of their rights and duties, and you will inspire within them an enthusiasm for work and a love of order; no longer will society need to fear brutal attacks or the blind rebellions of misery and ignorance against wealth and knowledge.[26]

Though hostile toward attempts to conscript art to promote radical politics, critics across a broad ideological spectrum enthusiastically endorsed a functional aesthetic designed to instill normative moral values and secure harmony between classes. In common with the Saint-Simonians, many conservative commentators extolled art's refining influence on vitiated pro-

[24] A. Boime, "Le Réalisme officiel du Second Empire," in *Exigences de réalisme dans la peinture française entre 1830 et 1870* (1983–84), 100–33.

[25] See, for example, E. Bères, *Les Classes ouvrières. Moyens d'améliorer leur sort sous le rapport du bien-être matériel et du perfectionnement moral* (1836), 234ff., and H. A. Frégier, *Des classes dangereuses de la population dans les grandes villes et des moyens de leur rendre meilleurs* (1840), 359–66, 405–16.

[26] "Donnez un but moral à l'art qui est la formule la plus haute de l'humanité, éclairez les peuples sur la véritable nature de leurs droits et leurs devoirs, et vous leur inspirerez le désir du travail, l'amour de l'ordre; la société n'aura plus à craindre ces attaques brutales, ces aveugles insurrections de la misère et de l'ignorance contre la richesse et le savoir." A. Bignan, *Essai sur l'influence morale de la poésie* (1838), 340.

letarian sensibilities, rerouting traditional idealist associations with spirituality and restraint to the practical needs of social hygiene. Signs of growing interest in events such as the Salon attracted favorable comment as evidence of a gradual transformation in the popular temperament. Thus, Ulysse Ladet takes heart from working-class frequentation of the Louvre, charting an osmotic process of acculturation touching even the most recalcitrant:

> These lessons, picked up haphazardly and by chance, ripen in the shadows; they give the people a gentler tone; they spread mysteriously from one person to another, seeping into even the most rebellious personalities until one finds their beneficial signs even where one would least expect such a discovery.[27]

Understanding of art's social benefits was not confined to the edifying effects of beauty but also embraced an interest in didactic subject matter, mirroring radical priorities and often foregrounding similar themes. Conservative diffidence toward the subordination of art to an extraneous cause exempted what was described as a need for *pensée*—a notion habitually denoting portrayal of an explicit moral theme deemed to carry universal rather than factional significance. Valuing subject matter as a spur to emulation, advocates of *pensée* opposed formalism with an emphasis on the artist's obligation to produce works that "speak to the soul and the moral aim of which is to depict an error, a vice, a scene of everyday life."[28] The predominantly domestic nature of the imagery identified under this rubric[29] sustained a myth of ideological neutrality—often explicitly contrasted with radical critics' ostensible devaluation of artistic integrity for tendentious ends—though the values it upheld disseminated an overwhelmingly middle-class view of behavioral norms.

The anecdotalism of such works, which perpetuated a Greuzian concern for familial relations, appealed across a broad social spectrum, though the idiom lent itself to more pointed proselytization of the working class. Inculcation of dominant values inspired such patrician initiatives as the Prix Montyon, an annual bequest administered by the Académie française to reward outstanding acts of popular virtue and to promote improving liter-

[27] "Eh bien! ces enseignements recueillis au hasard et sans suite fructifient dans l'ombre; ils jettent sur le peuple une teinte plus douce; ils se transmettent mystérieusement de l'un à l'autre, s'infiltrent dans les natures les plus rebelles, et l'on en retrouve les heureuses traces là où l'on devait le moins s'attendre à une découverte de ce genre." U. Ladet, "De l'influence des beaux-arts sur la civilisation," *L'Artiste*, 3d ser., 1 (1842): 83.

[28] "Parlent à l'âme et dont le but moral est de retracer une erreur, un vice, une scène de la vie habituelle." Mme. A. Aragon, "Salon de 1833," *Journal des femmes* 4 (2 March 1833): 69.

[29] See, for example, the list of suitable subjects offered by the artist Victor Orsel: "Duel, nourrice étouffant l'enfant; Enfant seul, périssant dans le feu; Fils maudit (de Greuze); Testament déchiré; Lecture de la Bible." From the lecture notes "Les Arts sont-ils utiles?" (1837), in *Oeuvres diverses de Victor Orsel*, ed. by A. Perin (1852), 2:57. The scene of a wet nurse suffocating a child derives from Pierre Vigneron's 1833 Salon exhibit *Avis aux mères*.

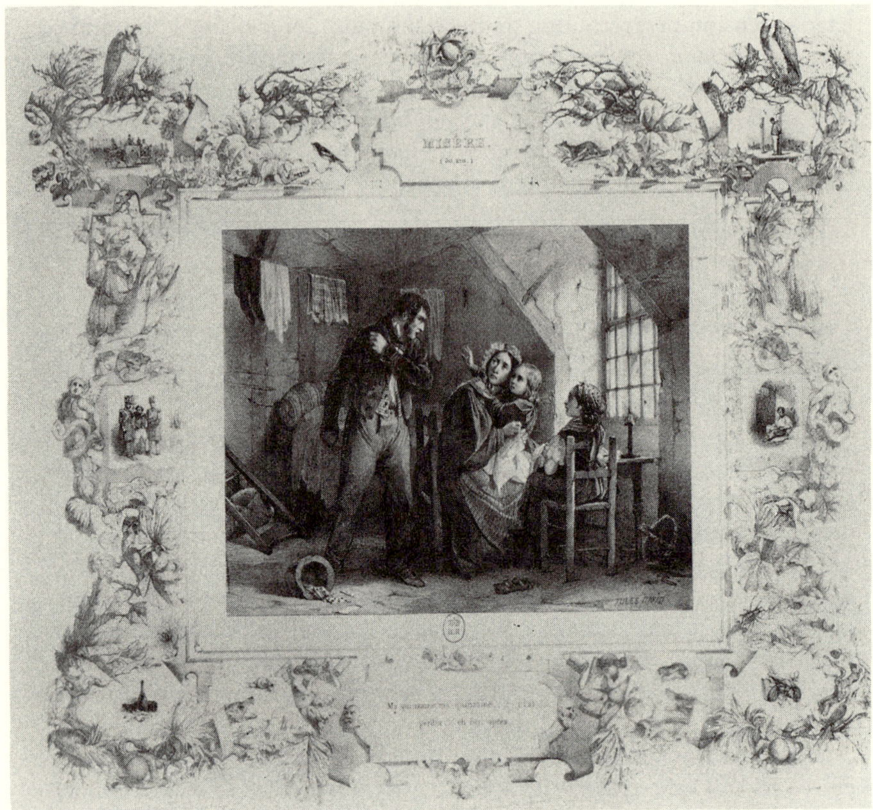

Plate 43. Jules David: *Misère (30 ans)* from *Vice et vertu,* 1836. Cabinet des estampes, Bibliothèque nationale, Paris.

ary works,[30] as well as the prize competition mounted in 1836 by Benjamin Delessert, president of the Paris savings bank, to encourage moralizing imagery. The winning project, a sequence of twelve lithographs by Jules David entitled *Vice et vertu*, transposes the Hogarthian homily of the Idle and Industrious Apprentices to the workshops of modern Paris.[31] The story

[30] See the *Testament de M. le Baron Auget de Montyon et pièces relatives aux legs par lui faits aux indigens de la ville de Paris et aux Académies* (1823), 5–8. Tales of prize-winning virtue provided a staple for the column "Vertu et dévouement du peuple" in the republican *Journal du peuple*.

[31] See J. David, *Vice et vertu. Album moral représentant en action les suites inévitables de la bonne et de la mauvaise conduite* (1836) in Cabinet des estampes, Bibliothèque nationale: DC 204 t.2. This contains an additional six scenes showing feminine virtue. David produced a number of similarly "improving" works for periodicals such as the *Journal des demoiselles* and the *Musée chrétien*, as well as illustrating *La Morale en action*, a compendium of improving tales, many based on Prix Montyon winners, published by Benjamin Delessert in 1842. On the 1836 competition, for which Delessert offered a two thousand franc prize, see J. Janin, "Salon de 1839," *L'Artiste*, 2d ser.,: 2, no. 24 (1839): 339.

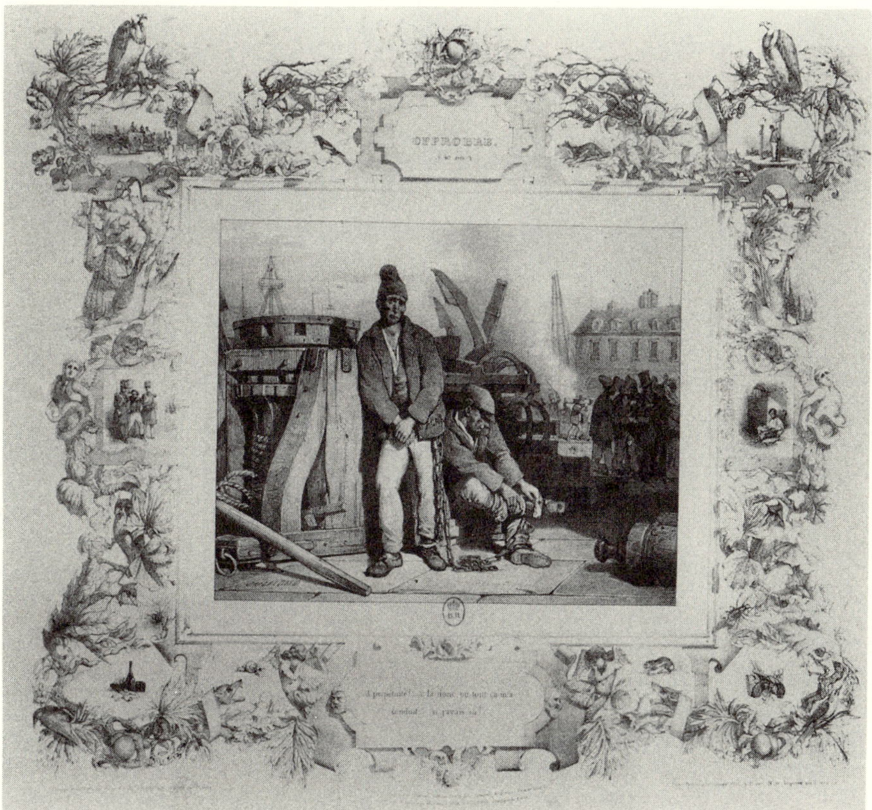

Plate 44. Jules David: *Opprobre (40 ans)* from *Vice et vertu,* 1836. Cabinet des estampes, Bibliothèque nationale, Paris.

is a familiar one: Tom Idle's gallic nephew, initially shown shirking his duties to play dice, sacrifices wife and family to drink and dissipation before violent larceny brings retribution (plates 43 and 44); his exemplary counterpart meanwhile ensures a brilliant career by investing his savings in the bank, perfects his craft while his workmates go drinking at the *barrière*, marries the boss's daughter, and reaps his rewards through wealth and public esteem (plates 45 and 46). Explicitly designed for the "worker's home and the manufacturer's office,"[32] David's prints contrast the archetype of popular probity with the mythological embodiment of the *classes dangereuses*, whose savage outline haunted bourgeois dreams of industrial progress. The inexorable logic that drags the idle apprentice to his doom reveals fears of the vulnerability of established hierarchies as the worker-turned-thief menaces a sleeping female victim; by the same token, their relative impregnability is

32 "Demeure de l'ouvrier et le cabinet du fabricant."

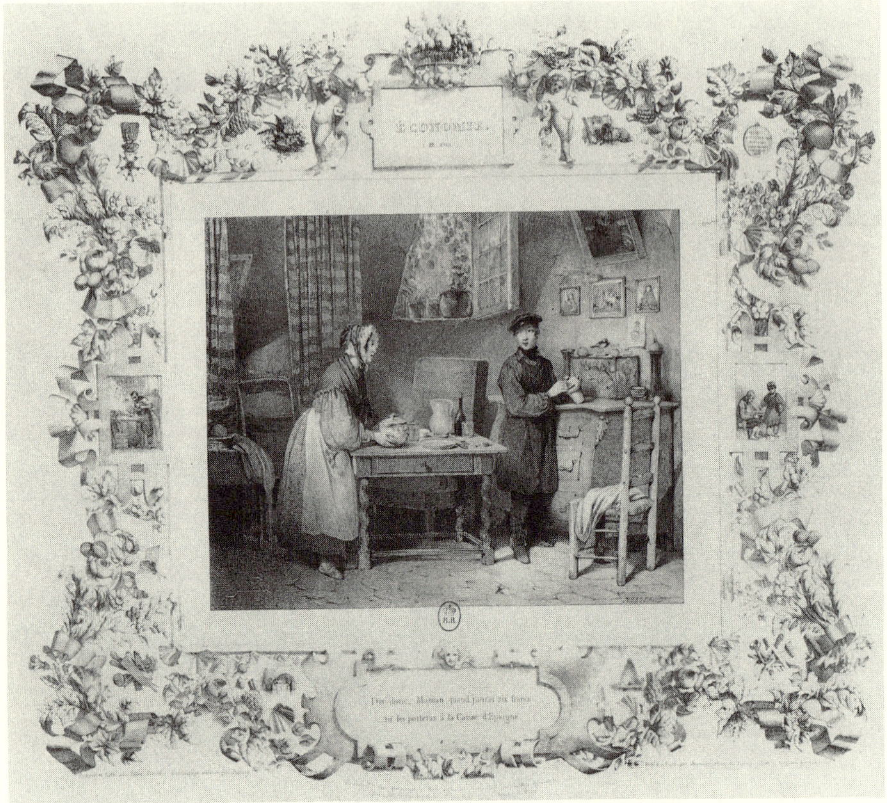

Plate 45. Jules David: *Economie (12 ans)* from *Vice et vertu,* 1836. Cabinet des estampes, Bibliothèque nationale, Paris.

tacitly acknowledged through the extraneous narrative device of marriage, used to infiltrate the virtuous worker into a social rank credibly inaccessible to him by his independent endeavors. His conscription into polite society, rather than a direct consequence of self-realization through labor, depends on an exogamous alliance conferring upon him a status he is denied in his own right. Subtended by an emphasis on familial devotion and philanthropic duty, David's narrative equates success with an *embourgeoisement* that, predictably enough, evades any awkward interrogation of class divisions.

What is, perhaps, most striking here is not the radical difference between the sentiments extolled by a pillar of Orléanist finance capital such as Delessert and those endorsed by the regime's most uncompromising opponents, but their fundamental resemblance. The goals, of course, stand in

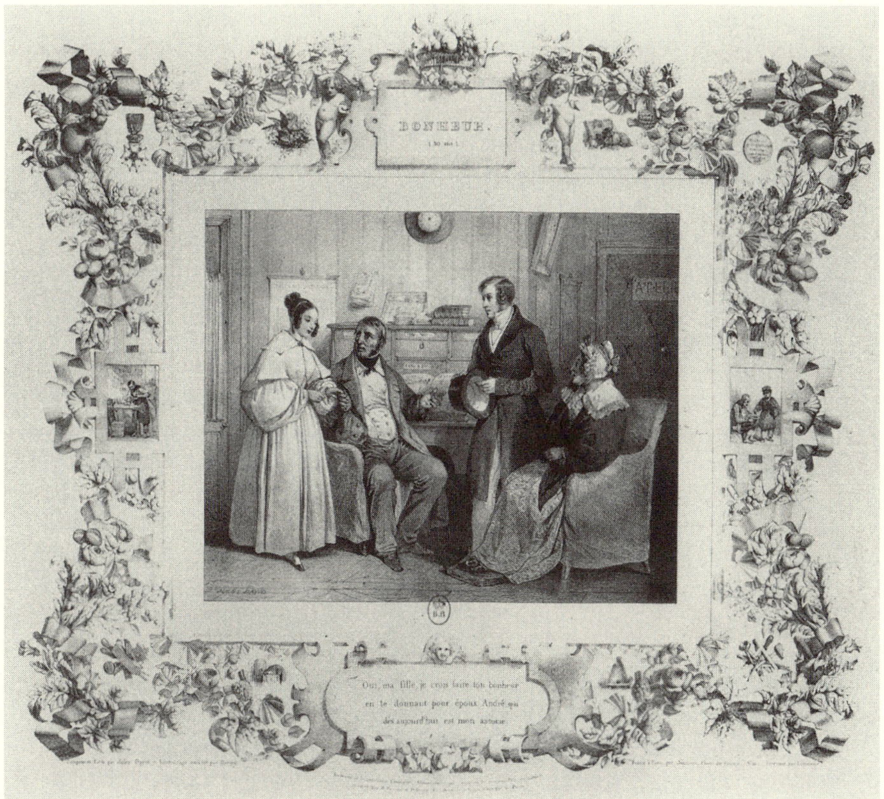

Plate 46. Jules David: *Bonheur (30 ans)* from *Vice et vertu,* 1836. Cabinet des estampes, Bibliothèque nationale, Paris.

vivid contrast; material comfort as an individual incentive and reward versus the promised land of harmony and universal brotherhood. The means, however—frugality, domesticity, respect for hard work—are virtually identical and reveal the inherent constraints frustrating radical overthrow of the prevailing order.

The tragic consequences of this ambivalence were played out in the troubled months separating Louis-Philippe's overthrow by popular revolt in February 1848 from Louis Napoléon's seizure of power in December 1851. The shortlived Second Republic, racked by sporadic conflict and disabled by political indecision, exposed the fragmentation of radical forces and revealed too how elusive were hopes of harnessing the arts to progressive social change. Following a regime that, with such dynastic projects as the historical museum at Versailles, had cultivated a shrewd understanding of art's propagandist role,[33] the republicans evidently anticipated the dawning of a new culture, informed theoretically by the previous twenty years' critical debate and working practically to rally popular opinion.

The story of this project's frustration has been frequently told,[34] and historians have carefully anatomized such abortive undertakings as the competition for an allegorical figure of the Republic and Paul Chenavard's controversial commission for a panorama of world history to cover the walls of the Panthéon.[35] Commentators such as Clark and Vaisse have pointed to the administrative shortcomings of the Direction des beaux-arts under Charles Blanc's leadership, overwhelmed by artists' demands for financial assistance following a collapse of the market. They have detailed the muddled pragmatism of cultural policy, its vulnerability to ingrained patterns of political influence and to more recent tensions within an increasingly unstable interplay of ideological forces. Historians have noted, too, the failure to revivify an artistic vocabulary, which all too often offered nothing more than a pallid and unconvincing reprise of shopworn motifs from the 1790s. The universally ridiculed competition for a republican emblem announced in March 1848, the Fête de la Concorde, whose timing less than a week after the 15 May coup attempt highlighted the hollowness of its sentiments as well as its form, the various plans by figures such as David d'Angers and Etex to transform Paris into a monumental mnemonic of republican virtues[36]—all were overburdened by reference to a tradition that failed to conceal the ideological and creative confusion of the present. Charles Blanc, in a policy document published in October 1848, could conjur up a republican renaissance enriching city streets, public edifices, and railway stations with morally inspiring works of art, reaching out to the village school and the peasant's cottage with lithographs and engravings, eradicating individualism

[33] See M. Marrinan, *Painting Politics for Louis-Philippe. Art and Ideology in Orléanist France, 1830–1848* (1988). In his *Le Roi Louis-Philippe: liste civile* (1851) the former Intendant de la liste civile, Montalivet, describes the king's instrumental attitude toward art: "l'art, comme le style, comme la parole, n'était pas pour Louis-Philippe un but, mais un moyen, un instrument subordonné. Il dédaignait un peu la forme, quand elle ne s'attachait pas à traduire une pensée pratique, une idée vraie, un souvenir exact. . . . la constante préoccupation de Louis-Philippe fut de donner à l'art une direction exclusivement historique et nationale" (115–16; 117).

[34] See T. J. Clark, *The Absolute Bourgeois: Artists and Politics in France 1848–1851* (1973); P. Vaisse, "Considérations sur la Seconde République et les beaux-arts," *1848. Révolutions et mutations au XIXe siècle* (1985): 59–85; M.-C. Chaudonneret, "1848: La République des arts," *Oxford Art Journal* 10, no. 1 (1987): 59–70; N. McWilliam, "Art, Labour and Mass Democracy: Debates on the Status of the Artist in France around 1848," *Art History* 11, no. 1 (March 1988): 64–87.

[35] See J. C. Sloane, *Paul-Marc Chenavard, Artist of 1848* (1962) and M.-C. Chaudonneret, *La Figure de la République. Concours de 1848* (1987).

[36] On Etex's project, see the *Moniteur universel* (13 May 1848): 1022; see also "Note adressé à M. le ministre de l'Intérieur par le comité de l'Intérieur, sur la proposition de M. David d'Angers," ibid. (27 July 1848): 1777.

and heralding a truly popular art. The regime's legacy, consisting overwhelmingly of abandoned projects, such as Chenavard's murals, and a random accumulation of landscapes, genre, and history paintings purchased to forestall outright crisis in the cultural economy, fell far short of these ambitions. Rather than challenging established boundaries, the Republic's art largely remained within the museums. Rather than using art to voice a clear and unambiguous alternative to the moral codes of early industrial capitalism, its ideology remained enmeshed in values frustrating any clean break with the past. Though artists themselves militated for enhanced social recognition and greater say in coordinating cultural policy,[37] those in power had learned enough from proponents of *art social* to recognize the need to maintain official controls. What they were unable to achieve, in the face of ideological dispersal and archaic cultural forms, was a true galvanization of art by the energizing force of political renewal.

The exceptions to this rule are either curiously marginal—Daumier's minimalist *République*, admired by radicals like Haussard and Thoré, though ranked in competition well below more orthodox allegorical performances;[38] Courbet's *Après-Dîner à Ornans*, at once monumental and introspective, treating rural life with a new seriousness and respect—or they are virulently reactionary. The bitterness and conflict of the June Days, which so searingly exposed the tensions implicit in the French radical movement, inspired a counter-revolutionary vision sharpened by the fear of unrestrained popular force. It is a vision that inspires Meissonier's gruesome miniature, *La Barricade* (plate 47), whose forensic, antiheroic description of the aftermath of revolt bluntly warns against proletarian insurrection. It informs, too, *Les Deux Fléaux* (plate 48), a chilling, apocalyptic allegory by Horace Vernet—erstwhile Bonapartist, liberal enemy of the Bourbon Restoration, intimate of Louis-Philippe. With a violence of almost pornographic intensity, Vernet casts aside the stiff, po-faced personifications of the Republic to reveal socialism as a threat to civilization as fatally insidious and alien as the oriental demon of cholera with whom he consorts. In its corrosive directness, Vernet's work makes a play on the emotions—on *sentiment*—at once more involving and uncompromising than any of the exhortations to patriotism and probity sponsored by the Republic's artistic program. While official art mitigates social effect through its reluctance to break with cultural forms validated by the very structures of power that radicals wished to overturn, Vernet uses a popular graphic medium and a simple, idiomatic language to discredit the left and demand a return to order.

This contrast points to a larger failure—implicit in the project of *art social*

[37] See McWilliam, "Art, Labour," 72–80.

[38] See Clark, *Absolute Bourgeois*, 107–8.

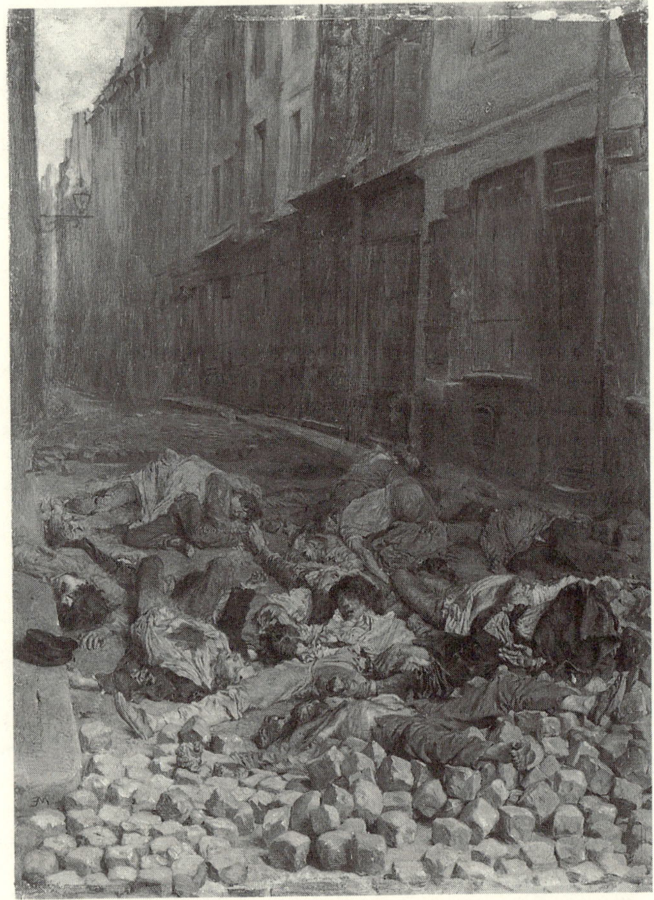

Plate 47. Jean-Louis-Ernest Meissonier: *La Barricade,* 1849, Musée du Louvre, Paris.

as elaborated under the July Monarchy and made apparent in the Republic's inability effectively to harness the arts in promoting a progressive politics. It is a failure to understand how deeply dominant notions of the aesthetic—to which most radical critics ultimately deferred—were implicated in the ideological underpinning of bourgeois society. Beauty, harmony, the real and ideal, high and low—all had come to share in particular definitions of the state of the world, to naturalize certain values, neutralize certain choices, preclude certain forms of action. Instead of attempting to work with these values, reshape them as weapons against the order they had come to serve—as Rancière sees in the worker-poets' sonnets and hexameters—a radical aesthetic had to see through them, rather than attempting vainly to see with

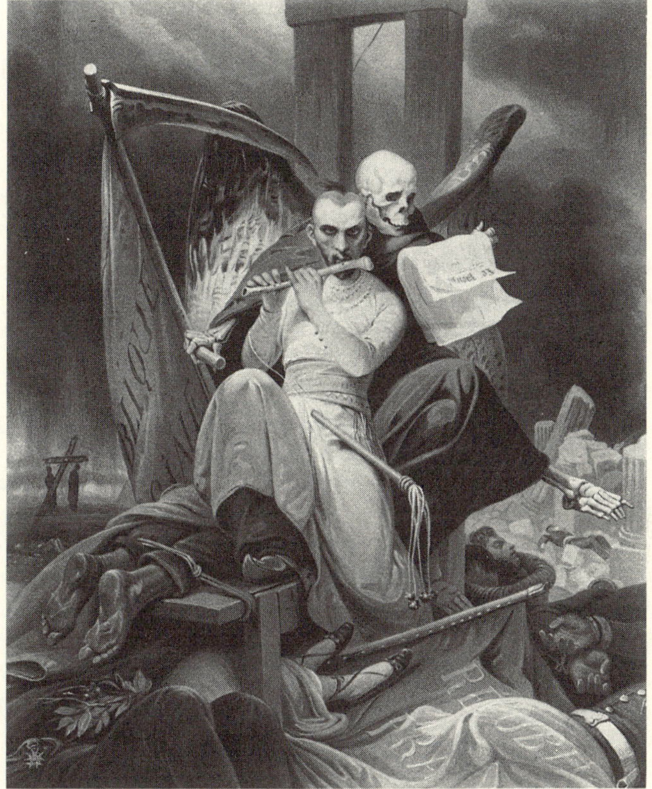

Plate 48. Horace Vernet: *Les Deux Fléaux,* 1850. Cabinet des estampes, Bibliothèque nationale, Paris.

them. It was in 1849, barely a year before he scandalized critical opinion with the *Enterrement*, that Courbet summed the situation up. For him there was no room for compromise—"il faut encanailler l'art."[39]

FROM SOCIAL ART TO SOCIALIST REALISM

Louis Napoléon's coup d'etat of December 1851 not only brought the state's faltering attempts to nurture a social art to an abrupt end, but also confirmed an authoritarianism increasingly apparent since Bonaparte's

[39] The full meaning of the phrase, drawing on the noun *canaille*—mob, or rabble—escapes adequate translation, though its gist is that "Art must be dragged into the gutter." Courbet to Francis Wey, 26 November 1849, in P. Courthion, ed., *Courbet raconté par lui-même et par ses amis* (1950), 2:76.

presidential victory three years earlier. The left's retreat had gathered pace as many prominent leaders—including Louis Blanc, Ledru-Rollin, and Théophile Thoré—had fled into exile following demonstrations against French intervention in Italy in June 1849. The December coup finished the rout. Rapid introduction of draconian controls, together with the flight of many outspoken radical journalists, stifled the opposition press. The tentative cultural experiment begun in 1848 was put to an end as Charles Blanc was dismissed as Directeur des beaux-arts and Jeanron removed from control at the Louvre. Major commissions—Couture's *Enrolement des volontaires*, Ottin's *Triomphe de la République*, Chenavard's Panthéon murals—were cancelled; indeed, the Panthéon itself was hastily restored to the Catholic church to cement a new alliance with those in power.

Eighteen forty-eight had proved a watershed as much for *art social* as for the political groupings committed to its support. As these groupings were repressed in the name of social stability, so agitation for militant cultural intervention was muted, if not silenced altogether. Yet, despite the setbacks of 1848 and the frustration previously experienced in devising workable formulas for artistic mobilization, early agitation for a social art was to prove seminal in the development of radical aesthetic programs well into the twentieth century. Though inflected by changing ideological commitments and evolving historical circumstance, two alternative conceptions of art's social function survived the crisis of the French left to organize subsequent theoretical debate. More directive notions of the artist's responsibility to undertake overtly didactic projects at the behest of radical opposition or progressive government derived principally from early Saint-Simonianism and currents within the Republican movement, while a countervailing insistence on individual creativity and its extension to all aspects of practical existence owed most to Fourier. Echoing an ideological divide between collectivist and individualist commitments in French politics both before and after 1848, this dichotomy is occasionally obscured to reveal a tension between libertarian and more interventionist assessments of state power. While the prominence of anarchist thought from Proudhon to the fin-de-siècle initially favored an aesthetic model most reminiscent of Fourier, longer-term developments, culminating in the Soviet Union's adoption of socialist realism in the 1930s, shared more authoritarian priorities. Though caution is required in attributing direct influence to such developments, what is of most immediate interest is the persistence and adaptability of discursive frameworks for conceptualizing the operation of culture in socialist societies.

Though explicitly indebted to the German idealist tradition,[40] the aes-

[40] On the sources of Proudhon's aesthetic, see K. Herding, "Proudhon's *Carnets intimes* and Courbet's *Portrait of Proudhon*," in *Courbet: To Venture Independence* (1991), 102.

thetic philosophy of the anarchist thinker Pierre-Joseph Proudhon works within—and against—understandings of art's social role elaborated on the French left. From his earliest public pronouncement in 1843 to the posthumously published *Du principe de l'art et de sa déstination sociale*, Proudhon developed an aesthetic whose inherent contradictions reveal debts toward contrasting formulations of *art social*. Support for a positivist art in his early writing—in which Proudhon anticipated a day when "painting, architecture, and sculpture would be treated like exact sciences, so that artistic composition will resemble the construction of a ship, the integration of a mathematical curve, or the calculation of stress and strain"[41]—echoes the Saint-Simonianism of *Le Producteur*. Such expectations imply an instrumental role for art as an expository medium, the rational foundations of which confer a degree of social authority on the artist. Though stopping short of the Saint-Simonians' hopes for a formal language capable of exerting a predictable psychological effect on the spectator, and emphasizing art's role in representing contrasting opinions, Proudhon qualifies this apparent openness by anticipating its value in embodying ideals deemed "eminently transcendental." Though never as strongly committed to art's capacity to modify collective opinion as many of his predecessors, Proudhon nonetheless retained a sense of its ideological effectivity essentially at odds with the antiauthoritarian tenor of his politics. This tension, to some degree inherent in the moralizing undercurrent common to more libertarian variants of *art social*, emerges most clearly in the contrasting notions of art as individual self-realization and as embodiment of the ideal, outlined in the *Philosophie de la misère* and the *Philosophie du progrès*, and amplified in *Du principe de l'art*.

On one level, Proudhon echoed Fourier in subordinating art to lived experience. Regarding a commodified culture, pursued by professional artists for material gain, as a poor substitute for the spontaneous, unmediated apprehension of beauty in everyday life, he focused instead on art as a process of self-discovery, enacted in man's transformation of the physical world through labor and in his spiritual growth through political and philosophical endeavor. This expanded notion of the aesthetic, valuing as it did the moral benefits inherent in the act of making over the ameliorative effect of any finished product designated as "art," identified the ideal not with a bloodless abstraction remote from nature but with an idea of perfection distilled from direct experience of reality. This redefinition eclipsed notions of art as a discrete, formalized activity entrusted to a spiritual elite with a more expansive sense of its intervention in all aspects of human existence:

[41] "La peinture, l'architecture et la statuaire seraient traitées comme des sciences exactes, et la composition artistique assimilée à la construction d'un navire, à l'intégration d'une courbe, à un calcul des forces et de résistances." P.-J. Proudhon, *De la création de l'ordre dans l'humanité* (1843; reprint, 1927), 216.

"Throughout our lives we are all artists and we all have the task of erecting a statue to BEAUTY in our persons, our bodies, and our souls. Our model lies within us; those gods of marble and bronze adored by the vulgar masses serve merely as reference points."[42]

The conversion of labor into an unalienated, individually enriching aesthetic experience would enable man to fulfill his instinct for self-esteem, as mastery over the physical world enhanced moral insight.[43] Though contemptuous of Fourier's advocacy of *travail attrayant*, with its insistence on occupational variety as a cure for alienation, Proudhon shared his commitment toward transforming work into a source of self-mastery and wellbeing. In this regard, for both thinkers art represents a pallid substitute for experience, the need for which will diminish as the intrinsic richness of life itself is realized.

In anticipation of this social revolution, Proudhon envisaged the continuation of traditional artistic forms, albeit in directions that marked a clear break with recent production. While the philosopher's general distrust of individual leaders extended to rejection of the artist's claims to guide society, his understanding of the ideal in a strictly cultural context left open both moralistic and prophetic functions, while emphasizing art's primary role as a critical weapon in hastening radical change. Though common to earlier formulations of *art social*, this dichotomy most closely resembles Fourierist distinctions between art as a visionary medium, presenting the individual in perfect accord with society, and its role in inspiring discontent with the current abuses of *civilisation*. This is most apparent in the similiarity between Proudhon's notion of the ideal and the Fourierists' understanding of *harmonie*. His modification of the term's Platonic sense to indicate a perfection immanent in nature rather than a purely disembodied idea, projected art—man's attempt to translate the ideal into sensual form—both as evidence of humanity's own potential for perfection and as a spur to its achievement. Yet, just as the Fourierists argued for a countervailing *laideur idéale*, so Proudhon maintained that the artist should also cultivate an *idéalisme critique*,[44] whose analytical exposure of social disequilibrium would stimulate the revolutionary process.

This perspective framed Proudhon's evaluation of cultural history, en-

[42] "Tous tant que nous vivons nous sommes artistes, et notre métier à tous est d'élever en nos personnes, dans nos corps et dans nos âmes, une statue à la BEAUTE. Notre modèle est en nous-mêmes; ces dieux de marbre et de bronze que le vulgaire adore, n'en sont que des étalons." P.-J. Proudhon, *Philosophie du progrès* (1853; reprint, 1946), 93. For a discussion of this aspect of Proudhon's thought, see J. H. Rubin, *Realism and Social Vision in Courbet and Proudhon* (1980), 88–90.

[43] See the *Système des contradictions économiques ou Philosophie de la misère* (1846), II, chap. XIII, part 3, section 2 (1850 reprint), 342–74.

[44] P.-J. Proudhon, *Du principe de l'art et de sa déstination sociale* (1865), 232. For a sustained critique of this text, see M. Raphael, *Proudhon, Marx, Picasso* (1980), 21–75.

couraging an ambivalence toward the abstract perfection of classical and Renaissance art, and fostering sympathy for the naturalism and contemporaneity of the Dutch. In the same way as Revolutionary classicism—dismissed as "clumsy, pedantic, and rhetorical"[45]—and the decadent irrationalism of the romantics[46] were judged to replicate art's historical tendency to elevate aesthetic formulas over the direct observation of nature, so Proudhon praised contemporary realism as a worthy successor to the Dutch masters. This judgment—which demanded of art an inclusive embrace of all aspects of life, however apparently distasteful[47]—nonetheless insisted on a clear commitment to interpretation quite distinct from any unmediated transcription of the real. Art should thus pursue the ideal not as a veil concealing reality but as a rational, analytical tool offering insights into its fundamental nature.[48]

In common with the Fourierists, such a position implied rejection of overt didacticism, since the very act of portraying the ideal—positive or negative—was deemed instructive in itself. Yet Proudhon's highly literal interpretation of the work of Courbet, his preference for "the CONTENT rather than the *container*,"[49] and his persistent moralism set up a tension in which art is seen in more orthodox terms as aiming at "the deification of men, sometimes through the celebration of their virtues and beauties, sometimes through the condemnation of their ugliness and crimes."[50]

Once more, art and morality are inextricably related and, under present conditions, Proudhon regards criticism as its immediate priority. Only with the achievement of a higher form of social organization—when, by his own admission, art will anyway be surpassed as a discrete activity as its principles inform all areas of being—will conditions exist for a new synthesis that not only transcends the limitations of current practice[51] but also heralds a new integration of art into the fabric of everyday life. Though such ambitions recall aspects of Fourierist aesthetics, the more obstinate moralism in Proudhon's thinking imposes a demand for rationalism, responsibility, and common sense[52] hostile to any assertion of unrestricted creative independence. This familiar qualification, with its resultant hostility toward artists

[45] "Gauche, pédantesque et déclamatoire." Proudhon, *Du principe*, 94.

[46] Ibid., 104–5.

[47] See ibid., 200.

[48] "Notre idéalisme, à nous, consiste à nous apprendre nous-mêmes, à nous amender jour par jour, non d'après des types conçus *à priori* et plus ou moins ingénieusement figurés, mais d'après les données que fournissent incessamment l'expérience et l'observation philosophique." Ibid., 199–200.

[49] "Le CONTENU avant le *contenant*." Ibid., 371.

[50] "La déification des hommes, tantôt par la célébration de leurs vertus et de leurs beautés, tantôt par l'exécration de leurs laideurs et de leurs crimes." Proudhon, *Philosophie du progrès*, 94.

[51] See Proudhon, *Du principe*, 103.

[52] See, for example, ibid., 144.

judged negligent of the social meaning of their work, pits interpretative content against expressive form while apparently surpassing any meaningful distinction between the two through the notion of the ideal. Proudhon's insistence on *pensée* and the need for popular *instruction*[53] thus undermines any intrinsic value attributed to the ideal and compromises the freedom of artistic vision that the term implies.

These tensions, whose roots extend back to the 1830s and 1840s, characterize the recrudescence of radical cultural debate under the early Third Republic. The vitality of the left, embracing a complex spectrum of anarchists, communists, radical socialists, and syndicalists, refocused attention on the artist's potential contribution to expediting change and offering guidance in a regenerate society. As new ideological configurations emerged, asserting the individual's autonomy from central control, so the theoretical divide between more directive understandings of art's political function and a libertarian emphasis on independent vision gradually intensified. While the left was united in its antipathy toward the formalist excesses of the symbolists and initiatives such as Josephin Péladan's *Salon de la Rose + Croix*,[54] there was little agreement over the precise obligations artists should assume in rallying to the progressive cause.

Anarchist and communist circles proved most resistant to prescriptive definitions, maintaining that "art is essentially individualist, essentially anarchist. There is no banner beneath which it can be regimented, no formula that can contain it, no symbol before which it bows down."[55] This apprehension of art as the quintessential expression of unalienated being, the inherent value of which could only be compromised by programmatic constraints, won support from such leading theorists as Elisée Reclus as well as from artistic adherents like Signac and Lucien Pissarro.[56] It was a viewpoint that fostered resistance to stylistic *parti pris* and credited groups such as the impressionists with achieving an independence of vision of ultimately social import.[57] This defense of creative autonomy, reminiscent of antiacademic discourse of the 1830s and 1840s, upheld the intrinsic moral value of nature, echoing the pantheism of a figure such as Charles Blanc, and encouraging a striking sympathy for the work of Puvis de Chavannes. Identified by

[53] Ibid., 357.

[54] See the hostile remarks on the *Salon de la Rose + Croix* in Gervaise, "Salons 1892–1er mai," *Revue socialiste* (May 1892): 628.

[55] "L'art est essentiellement individualiste, essentiellement anarchiste. Il ne s'enregimente sous aucune bannière, il ne s'enferme en aucune formule, il ne s'incline sous aucun symbole." A. Girard, "L'Art du peuple," *Les Temps nouveaux*, 4th year, 10 (2–8 July 1898): 1.

[56] On Reclus and Signac, see J. G. Hutton, "A Blow of the Pick: Science, Anarchism, and the Neo-Impressionist Movement" (1987), 115, 111–12. See also L. Pissarro's response to Charles-Albert, "Art et société," *Les Temps nouveaux* 32 (7–13 December 1895): 1–2.

[57] See Pissarro, "Art et société," 2, and A. Germain, "Salon de 1886," *Le Coup de feu* 12 (August 1886): 23.

the republican socialist Alphonse Germain in 1885 as a leading exponent of an *art humain*,[58] fifteen years later Puvis could be extolled by Jaurès for instinctively evoking a new Golden Age:

> Here humanity is happy and fraternal in an image that anticipates what tomorrow's society will be. Puvis de Chavannes had only to dream of peaceful and harmonious crowds to imagine our dreams in advance. It is as though the communist ideal touched him with one of its rays even before its dawning.[59]

The evocation by Germain and Jaurès of Proudhon's call for an *art humain*[60] indicates the philosopher's enduring influence on aesthetic debate in the fin-de-siècle, both in his calls for a synthesis of the ideal and the real, and in his vision of the aestheticization of labor. As Miriam Levin has pointed out, demands that artists should inflect their portrayal of the contemporary world with a regard for the ideal were commonplace under the Third Republic.[61] Dissatisfaction with what was seen as the documentary passivity of the naturalists emerges particularly strongly in Kropotkin's critique of their "simple anatomization of society" and his characteristically Proudhonian call for the subordination of "realist description" to "an idealist goal."[62] Though challenged, as we shall see, by advocates of a more uncompromisingly veristic exposé of inequality and oppression, this defense of idealism offered both artist and critic a degree of latitude in defining limits to the project for a social art.

It was the revolutionary syndicalist Georges Sorel who emerged as one of the most prominent advocates of labor's transformation into a source of individual self-realization, with his vision of a day when the worker, having assumed control of the means of production, would see an end to the distinction between art and industry. Unalienated labor, in which the individual artisan invests pride, ingenuity, and a sense of self-worth, becomes a

[58] Germain, "Salon de 1886," 22. For a more hostile assessment, see E. Chatelain, "Profession de foi," *Le Coup de feu* 1 (September 1885): 2. Chatelain's misgivings prompted an editorial note disassociating the journal from the opinions expressed by Germain.

[59] "C'est l'humanité heureuse, fraternelle: c'est l'image anticipé de ce que sera la société de demain. Et il a suffi à Puvis de Chavannes de rêver de vastes ensembles apaisés et harmonieux pour deviner d'avance ce que nous rêvons. On dirait que l'idéal communiste l'a effleuré de son rayon avant même de s'être levé." J. Jaurès, "L'Art et le socialisme," *Le Mouvement socialiste* (15 May 1900): 587.

[60] For Jaurès' use of the term, see ibid., 584.

[61] M. R. Levin, *Republican Art and Ideology in Late Nineteenth-Century France* (1986), 190–94. An artist such as Puvis de Chavannes, admired by certain currents on the left, was widely praised for fulfilling such a criterion. As John Hutton remarks ("Blow of the Pick," 118), the political inflection of the notion of harmony remains a pervasive theme in late nineteenth-century radical criticism. Evident parallels can be drawn with Fourierist use of the term.

[62] "Simple anatomie de la société"; "la description réaliste"; "un but idéaliste." Cited in A. Reszler, *L'Esthétique anarchiste* (1973), 49.

source of moral liberation as a consciousness of creative power extends to all sectors of society. In the interim, Sorel regards the artist as embodying an individualism whose realization by all he foresees as a major social advance: "The artist is really only an artist to the extent that he has an energetic sense of his spiritual independence; if all men become workers and work with art, we can hope that the aesthetic education they receive will develop individualism in the world—and that is a good thing."[63]

Such aspirations were accompanied by calls for the cultural enfranchisement of the masses, to be achieved through developing more active, participatory forms of art at the expense of genres appealing to isolated introspection.[64] Yet awareness of the proletariat's lack of responsiveness to contemporary culture encouraged a cautionary emphasis on the prior need to adopt forms of economic organization which would allow the liberation of instincts atrophied by the burden of alienated labor. Under present conditions, figures such as Lucien Pissarro questioned the viability of cultivating explicitly populist forms, arguing instead for the benefits to be derived from protecting artistic autonomy.[65]

Such appeals were made in the face of agitation for more prescriptive control over artistic production, focusing on the promotion of explicitly didactic works targeted at a popular audience. For the syndicalist leader Fernand Pelloutier, the task ahead was clear: "Art must make rebels."[66] Displaying an unusually developed sense of culture's subterranean influence in sustaining existing power relations,[67] he asserted that art could potentially adopt a subversive role as an unrivaled force for change. Its exploitation, however, demanded the abandonment of any pretensions to creative independence in favor of a comprehensive assault on the ideological pillars of bourgeois society: "Expose society's lies, tell how and why religions were created, the cult of patriotism devised, the family set up on government lines, the need for masters inspired: this must be the goal of revolutionary Art."[68] Brushing aside earlier radicals' accommodation with the founding

[63] "L'artiste n'est vraiment artiste que dans la mesure où il sent l'énergie de son indépendance spirituelle; si tous les hommes deviennent travailleurs et travaillent avec art, on peut espérer que l'éducation esthétique qui leur sera donnée, aura pour effet de développer l'individualisme dans le monde;—et cela est bon." G. Sorel, "La Valeur sociale de l'art," *Revue de métaphysique et de morale* 9 (1901): 276.

[64] See, for example, Jean Grave's proposals for participatory forms of theater in Reszler, *L'Esthétique anarchiste*, 54.

[65] "Ne vaut-il pas mieux produire ce qui est la vérité pour soi, quitte à n'être compris que de dix individus qui aideront la compréhension des autres, et ainsi de suite? N'est-ce pas ainsi que s'accomplit le progrès?" L. Pissarro, "Art et société," 1.

[66] "L'art doit faire des révoltés." F. Pelloutier, *L'Art et la révolte* (1896), 7.

[67] "L'art bourgeois fait plus pour le maintien du régime capitaliste que toutes les autres forces sociales réunies: gouvernement, armée, police, magistrature . . . " Ibid., 26.

[68] "Dévoiler les mensonges sociaux, dire comment et pourquoi ont été créées les religions, imaginé le culte patriotique, construite la famille sur le modèle du gouvernement, inspiré le besoin de maîtres: tel doit être le but de l'Art révolutionnaire." Ibid., 7.

institutions of civil society, Pelloutier forecloses any possibility of art negotiating with a moral regime whose basic predicates he rejects absolutely. In this refutation of normative values, Pelloutier reveals his anarchist sympathies, though this is an anarchism that is uncompromising in subordinating the creative imagination to the imperatives of social revolution.

This authoritarianism is echoed in the pages of *L'Art social*—the mouthpiece of the Club de l'Art social, founded in 1889 by a group of writers and theorists with anarchist and republican socialist sympathies.[69] Riven by internal dissent after barely a year, this short-lived initiative in many respects sums up the abiding tensions setting those committed to a prescriptive aesthetic against advocates of intellectual independence. For those sharing Pelloutier's belief in the artist's responsibility to demystify contemporary social relations, naturalism became an inescapable stylistic option. Providing "a sure guarantee against any movement of social reaction,"[70] its clinical analysis of capitalism's collective pathology was judged to offer an unambiguous statement of creative commitment. In the words of the communist Georges Diamandy: "Artists must become conscious and informed of their surroundings and of the interests of their class in order to put art at the disposal of that class."[71]

This endorsement of naturalism's superior claims as a critical form looked to the natural and social sciences to provide a positive grounding for the artist's exploitation of his medium as a diagnostic tool.[72] Yet calls for reason and discipline were qualified by a libertarian current within the group hostile to stylistic constraints on the "infinite aesthetic consciousness."[73] This more inclusive perception fostered a particularly sympathetic assessment of works, such as Charles de Groux's *Le Christ aux outrages* or Pierre Fritel's antimilitarist allegory *Les Conquérants* (plate 49), which were deemed to address contemporary issues through an allusive, though accessible, use of symbol.[74] What was not negotiable, however, was an overt commitment to progressive politics, though the implications of this for creative autonomy

69 On the Club de l'Art social, see A. Tabarant, "Le Club de l'Art social," *La Revue socialiste* (January 1890): 101–6, and Hutton, "Blow of the Pick," 106–9.

70 "Une garantie certaine contre tout mouvement de réaction sociale." M. Batilliat, "Le Naturalisme et l'art social," *L'Art social* 4 (February 1892): 85.

71 "Les artistes doivent devenir conscients et instruits de leur milieu et des intérêts de la classe à laquelle ils appartiennent, afin de mettre l'art à la disposition de cette classe." G. Diamandy, "Le Matérialisme dans l'art," *L'Art social* 7 (July 1892): 186.

72 The club's statutes included the commitment to "suivre en commun les travaux scientifiques se rapportant à la biologie et à la sociologie." Tabarant, "Le Club de l'Art social," 104. See also, E. Couret, "Oeuvre à faire," *L'Art social* 1 (November 1891): 16–17.

73 "Infinie conscience esthétique." A. Viedaux, "L'Art individualiste," *L'Art social* 5 (March 1892): 101.

74 See G. Le Rouge, "Le Christ aux outrages. Tableau de M. de Groux," *L'Art social* 6 (June 1892): 145–47; E. Museux, "Les Conquérants au Salon des Champs-Elysées," ibid., 153–55. See also, E. Museux, "Un Triptyche au Salon du 'Champ de Mars,'" ibid., 7 (July 1892): 189–90, on Léon Frédéric's *Le Peuple verra un jour le lever du soleil*.

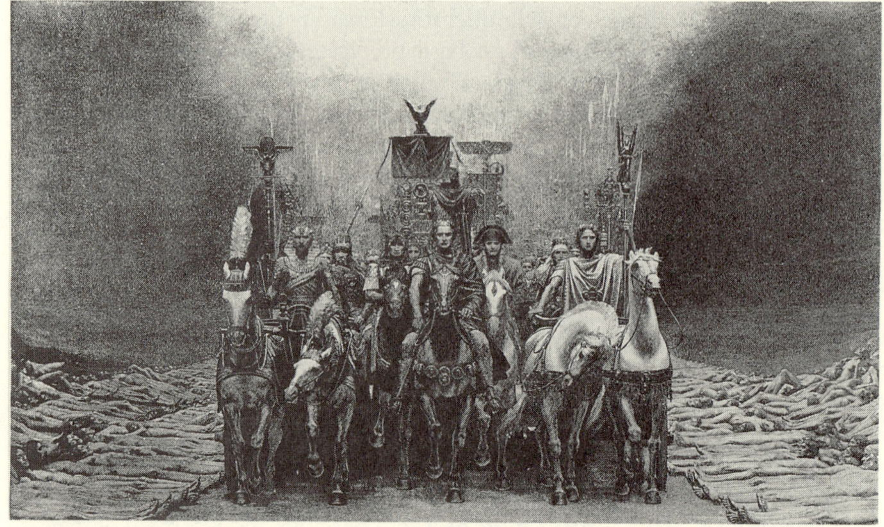

Plate 49. Pierre Fritel: *Les Conquérants,* Salon of 1892. Reproduced from *European Pictures of the Year, 1892.*

were minimized. Asserting that "we must attempt to produce artists who are aware," the club's spokesperson Adolphe Tabarant denied any ambitions to direct their work, arguing that "We simply say to them: draw from the springs of truth, refresh yourself from life, search out the people's future. Slowly, by a process of organic change, the social ideal will come of its own accord, and the work will bear the sign."[75]

Beneath this pragmatic response, Tabarant is attempting to square the circle, reconciling essentially incompatible philosophies of social aesthetics. His own words betray the difficulty of such a task since, beneath the rhetorical abstractions in which he distills the artist's relationship with the contemporary world, there remains the lingering question as to the nature of the life, the truth, and the future the artist is to explore in achieving consciousness. In the end, his demand that "the artist must force himself to study the social environment"[76] indicates a necessary channeling of creativity which compromises guarantees of independence. Half a century on, the dilemma confronted by the Saint-Simonians, with their assurance that the artist could follow unhindered "his vocation, his taste, his inclination," while expressing in his work "the revelation of progress," remains stubbornly unresolved.

[75] "Nous devons tendre à la production d'artistes conscients"; "Nous leur disons seulement: puisez aux sources de la vérité, abreuvez-vous de vie, cherchez l'avenir dans le peuple. Lentement, par un phénomène de transformation cellulaire, l'idée sociale viendra d'elle-même, et l'oeuvre en sera marquée." Tabarant, "Le Club de l'Art social," 103–4.

[76] "L'artiste doit s'efforcer d'étudier le milieu social." Ibid., 102.

Many commentators have identified this contradiction as inherent to the cultural initiatives sponsored by socialist regimes during the twentieth century.[77] Investigations of socialist realism's emergence as the approved style in the Soviet Union, for example, have pointed to the discrepancy between Lenin's and Trotsky's relatively open attitude toward expressive freedom and the regimented control of the artist under Stalin.[78] Claims that a direct genealogy can be traced linking Saint-Simon with Marx and developments in postrevolutionary Russia have tended to map out a seamless theoretical narrative that, while pointing to some suggestive analogies between early French theory and later Soviet practice, misleadingly situates Marx as a proponent of a so-called productivist aesthetic indebted to Saint-Simon's classification of the artist as an ally of the *industriel*.[79] Though there is an undeniable affinity between Saint-Simon's highly instrumental notion of art and the commitment to social didacticism advanced by such mid-nineteenth-century Russian theorists as Belínsky, Chernyshevsky, and Pisarev,[80] Margaret Rose's claims for a "latent Saint-Simonian aesthetic" in Marx's work are much more problematic.[81]

Central to the difficulties with such an assertion is the disproportionate emphasis Rose accords to Saint-Simon's theories "on the need for art to be both technically avant-garde and economically productive."[82] The first claim is, as we have seen, founded on a defective reading of the connotations accorded by the French thinker to the notion of the "avant-garde,"[83] while the second promotes a relatively peripheral aspect of his thought to theoretical pride of place. Saint-Simon's identification of the artist as a *producteur*, as distinct from such nonproductive *oisifs* as usurers and landowners, secures his inclusion amongst the progressive forces in society but does so—crucially—on the basis of his serving as a mouthpiece for the ruling elite.[84] By contrast, in their relatively brief and allusive discussions of culture, both

[77] See, for example, A. Flaker, "Presuppositions of Socialist Realism," in *The Culture of the Stalin Period*, ed. H. Günther (1990), 97–109, and I. Golomstock, *Totalitarian Art* (1990). Golomstock emphasizes parallels between understandings of art's social function in communist societies (the Soviet Union, China) and fascist states (Nazi Germany, Italy).

[78] See T. Eagleton, *Marxism and Literary Criticism* (1976), 37–43.

[79] See M. A. Rose, *Marx's Lost Aesthetic: Karl Marx and the Visual Arts* (1984).

[80] See R. Robin, *Le Réalisme socialiste. Une Esthétique impossible* (1986), 120–39.

[81] Ibid., 34.

[82] Ibid., 123.

[83] See our discussion of Egbert's misreading of Saint-Simon in Chapter 2. For a discussion of Saint-Simon's concept of the *producteur* that demonstrates the breadth accorded the term, see A. Cuvillier, "Les Antagonismes de classe dans la littérature sociale française de Saint-Simon à 1848," *International Review of Social History* 1, no. 3 (1958): 436–37.

[84] A decisive contrast must also be noted with Marx's materialist conception of class, which operates with a distinctively different theoretical model of the relationship between culture and the economy. Marx's materialist understanding of consciousness also stands in sharp contradistinction to Saint-Simon's essentially idealist notion of religious belief as the foundation of collective consciousness.

Marx and Engels largely reject the politically prescriptive role accorded to art by Saint-Simon.[85] Indeed, both point to the possibility of artworks articulating a political progressivism foreign to the conscious intentions of its creator. In contrasting the manifest content of the writings of a conservative such as Balzac with the ideologically disruptive meanings they conceal, Marx and Engels echo a hermeneutic familiar from Laverdant's interpretation of a painter such as Léopold Robert.[86]

Affinities with Fourier rather than Saint-Simon emerge quite explicitly in Marx's and Engels' discussion of artistic production and the division of labor. Distinguishing between "directly productive labor" and "labor that is not directly productive" (such as cultural production), they evoke Fourier's notion of *travail attrayant* in asserting that "In a communist society there are no painters but at most people who engage in painting among other activities."[87] Such a position grows out of Marx's reworking of Feuerbach's theory of alienated consciousness in the *Economic and Philosophic Manuscripts* of 1844, where he credits the abolition of private property with ushering in "the complete emancipation of all human senses and aptitudes"[88] and transforming unalienated labor into a creative act. Such elements in early Marxist aesthetics thus indicate a utopian-libertarian inclination quite foreign to Saint-Simon's positivist ambitions for art as an instrument of social control.

Art's strict subordination to political imperative under socialist realism marks a reversion to a Saint-Simonian conception of culture after a brief post-Revolutionary interlude of pluralism and experimentation.[89] While Lenin had argued in the 1920s that "a rather large field of action for thought and imagination, for form and content" was essential to aesthetic creation,[90] calls for the state to organize culture as part of a broader program of ideological control had been voiced within the artistic community soon after the Revolution.[91] Evoking a society in which the individual had been completely absorbed by the collectivity, theorists such as Sergei Tretiakov echoed the Jacobins in anticipating a world in which "Everything known as 'private affairs' or 'personal interest' comes under the control of the collec-

[85] See, for example, Engels's letter to Minna Kautsky of 1885 in K. Marx and F. Engels, *On Literature and Art* (1976), 87–89.

[86] See Engels's remarks on Balzac in his letter to Margaret Harkness of 1888 in ibid., 89–92. See also Marx's reading of Sue's *Les Mystères de Paris* in *The Holy Family*, in *Collected Works* by K. Marx and F. Engels, (1975), 4:55–76.

[87] K. Marx and F. Engels, *The German Ideology* (1846), ed. C. J. Arthur (1977), 108–9.

[88] Cited in Rose, *Marx's Lost Aesthetic*, 72.

[89] Rose incorrectly distinguishes between the Stalinist organization of culture and the system outlined by Saint-Simon in arguing that the latter "had separated the avant-garde from the bureaucratic maintenance of order" (139).

[90] V. I. Lenin, *On Art and Literature*, cited in Eagleton, *Marxism and Literary Criticism*, 41.

[91] See Golomstock, *Totalitarian Art*, 22–23.

tive."[92] Under such a regime, art would no longer serve as a space for subjective gratification, but would be modulated by "psycho-engineers" as "a means for emotionally organizing the psyche in connection with the tasks of the class struggle."[93] Once again, a scientistic ambition to discover objective rules of creation and response impelled a collectivist understanding of culture as a branch of "social engineering."[94]

The doctrine of socialist realism, initiated by Stalin at the Seventeenth Party Congress in 1932, was intended to satisfy calls for artistic forms that would help transform consciousness and thus engage in transforming the reality they purported to represent. Demanding that "the truthfulness and historical concreteness of the artistic portrayal should be combined with the ideological remolding and education of the toiling people in the spirit of socialism,"[95] its founding theorist Andrei Zhdanov called not merely for a record of "objective reality" but for the depiction of "reality in its revolutionary development."[96] It is in this sense that the historian Boris Groys has argued that, rather than being mimetic, socialist realism is essentially an idealist projection of the hypothetical future formulated by the ruling elite.[97] Seen in this light, a clear continuity of purpose can be traced between the social function attributed by Saint-Simon to prophetic scenes of future happiness and the exhortatory effect invested in depictions of the "New Socialist Man" under Stalin. Just as the artist had been elected mouthpiece of the *savant* and *industriel* in Saint-Simon's later works, so now he serves as an agent of the vanguard Communist Party, whose vision of social emancipation he makes vivid and accessible to the mass proletariat.

Stalin's celebrated description of the writer as an "engineer of the human soul"—ironically echoing the avant-gardist Tretiakov,[98] and resonant of ambitions extending back to the Enlightenment—represents one facet of a theoretical couplet whose more libertarian trajectory embraces such twentieth-century thinkers as Marcuse and Bloch, and whose practical effects have been felt most nearly in the revolutionary art of a Latin American nation such as Nicaragua[99] or in the countercultural movements of the 1960s and 1970s. The monolithic, authoritarian management of culture by the centralized regimes of Asia and Eastern Europe has, until recently,

[92] Ibid., 26.

[93] Tretiakov, cited in ibid.

[94] The term was first coined by Aleksei Gastev, a leading figure in the Proletkult movement, which repudiated all bourgeois forms in favor of a distinctively proletarian art.

[95] A. A. Zhdanov, "Soviet Literature—The Richest in Ideas, the Most Advanced Literature," in *Soviet Writers' Congress 1934*, ed. M. Gorky et al. (1977), 21.

[96] Ibid.

[97] See B. Groys, "The Birth of Socialist Realism from the Spirit of the Russian Avant-Garde," in Günther, *Culture of the Stalin Period*, 125–26.

[98] See Golomstock, *Totalitarian Art*, 26.

[99] See D. Craven and J. Ryder, *Art of the New Nicaragua* (1983), 10–18.

overshadowed the more open, ludic, and protean forms that have been fashioned to address new constituencies and respond to changing ideological demands. Yet, as the monuments forged as icons of authority are cast down, and the end of history is pronounced as the obituary of socialism, the need for new dreams of happiness is perhaps greater than ever before.

Bibliography

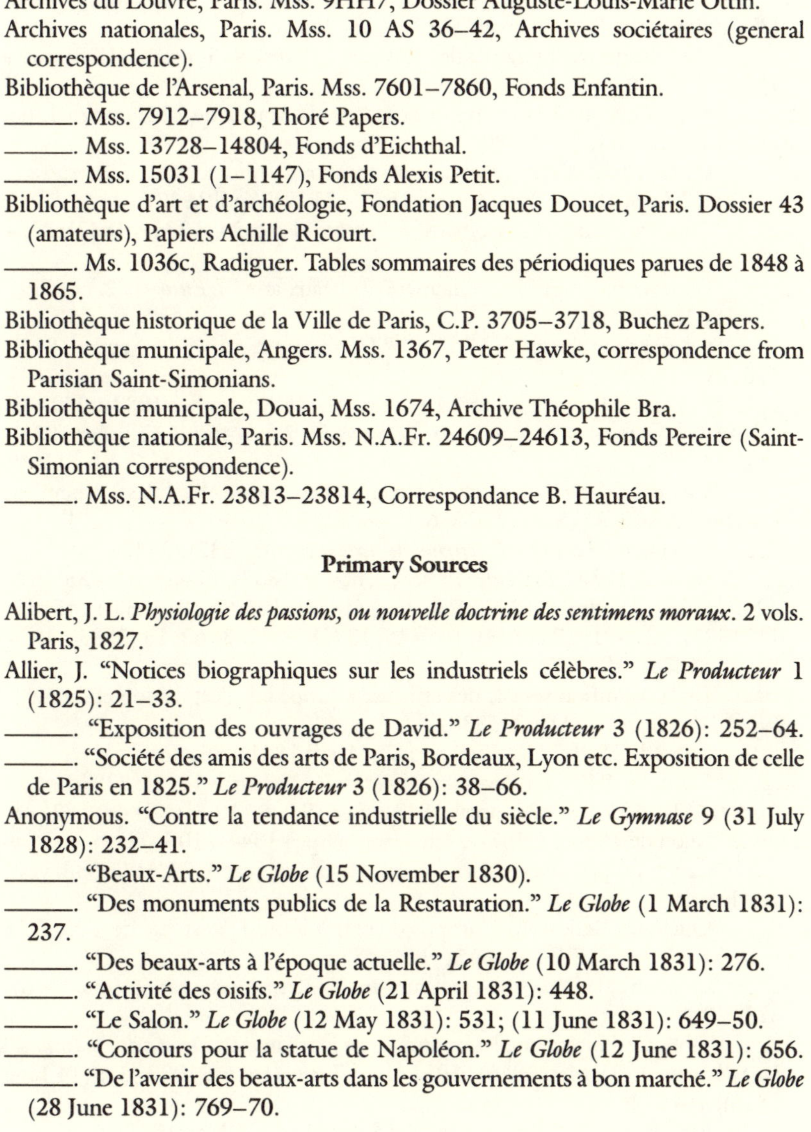

Archival Sources

Archives du Louvre, Paris. Mss. 9HH7, Dossier Auguste-Louis-Marie Ottin.

Archives nationales, Paris. Mss. 10 AS 36–42, Archives sociétaires (general correspondence).

Bibliothèque de l'Arsenal, Paris. Mss. 7601–7860, Fonds Enfantin.

______. Mss. 7912–7918, Thoré Papers.

______. Mss. 13728–14804, Fonds d'Eichthal.

______. Mss. 15031 (1–1147), Fonds Alexis Petit.

Bibliothèque d'art et d'archéologie, Fondation Jacques Doucet, Paris. Dossier 43 (amateurs), Papiers Achille Ricourt.

______. Ms. 1036c, Radiguer. Tables sommaires des périodiques parues de 1848 à 1865.

Bibliothèque historique de la Ville de Paris, C.P. 3705–3718, Buchez Papers.

Bibliothèque municipale, Angers. Mss. 1367, Peter Hawke, correspondence from Parisian Saint-Simonians.

Bibliothèque municipale, Douai, Mss. 1674, Archive Théophile Bra.

Bibliothèque nationale, Paris. Mss. N.A.Fr. 24609–24613, Fonds Pereire (Saint-Simonian correspondence).

______. Mss. N.A.Fr. 23813–23814, Correspondance B. Hauréau.

Primary Sources

Alibert, J. L. *Physiologie des passions, ou nouvelle doctrine des sentimens moraux*. 2 vols. Paris, 1827.

Allier, J. "Notices biographiques sur les industriels célèbres." *Le Producteur* 1 (1825): 21–33.

______. "Exposition des ouvrages de David." *Le Producteur* 3 (1826): 252–64.

______. "Société des amis des arts de Paris, Bordeaux, Lyon etc. Exposition de celle de Paris en 1825." *Le Producteur* 3 (1826): 38–66.

Anonymous. "Contre la tendance industrielle du siècle." *Le Gymnase* 9 (31 July 1828): 232–41.

______. "Beaux-Arts." *Le Globe* (15 November 1830).

______. "Des monuments publics de la Restauration." *Le Globe* (1 March 1831): 237.

______. "Des beaux-arts à l'époque actuelle." *Le Globe* (10 March 1831): 276.

______. "Activité des oisifs." *Le Globe* (21 April 1831): 448.

______. "Le Salon." *Le Globe* (12 May 1831): 531; (11 June 1831): 649–50.

______. "Concours pour la statue de Napoléon." *Le Globe* (12 June 1831): 656.

______. "De l'avenir des beaux-arts dans les gouvernements à bon marché." *Le Globe* (28 June 1831): 769–70.

———. "Saint-Germain-l'Auxerrois." *Le Globe* (18 July 1831): 800.
———. "Politique et beaux-arts." *Le Globe* (30 August 1831): 967.
———. "La Liste civile et les beaux-arts." *Le Globe* (14 October 1831): 1148.
———. "Exposition de la Société des amis des arts." *L'Européen* 1, nos. 2 (10 December): 25–26; 3 (17 December 1831): 41–42.
———. Review of "*Gemaeldaustellung in Paris* (*Salon de 1831* etc.) par M. Heine; extrait de plusieurs articles du *Morgenblatt*." *Le Globe* (2 January 1832): 8.
———. Review of *Biographie allégorique et fantastique des illustrations contemporaines*. *L'Européen* 1, no. 8 (21 January 1832): 123–24.
———. "De deux nouvelles statues des Tuileries." *L'Européen* 1, no. 12 (18 February 1832): 189–90.
———. "Saint-Germain-l'Auxerrois et St Jacques-la Boucherie." *L'Européen* 1, no. 18 (31 March 1832): 279–80.
———. "De l'art théâtral considéré dans ses moyens d'utilité sociale." *L'Européen* 1, nos. 19 (7 April 1832); 20 (14 April 1832); 21 (21 April 1832).
———. "Exposition du Musée Colbert." *L'Européen* 1, no. 24 (12 May 1832): 377–78.
———. "Peines et récompenses, en matière des beaux-arts." *L'Européen* 2, no. 31 (7 July 1832): 67–69.
———. "Galerie de tableaux de M. Erard." *L'Européen* 2, no. 35 (4 August 1832): 138–39.
———. "Envois de Rome." *L'Européen* 2, no. 41 (15 September 1832): 230–31.
———. "Concours pour le grand prix." *L'Européen* 2, no. 46 (20 October 1832): 312.
———. Review of *Cinq Leçons sur l'art d'associer les hommes* by Jules Lechevalier. *L'Artiste*, 1st ser., 3 (1832): 173–76.
———. "Specimen." *La Liberté. Journal des arts* (August 1832): 3–15.
———. "Salon de 1833." *L'Artiste*, 1st ser., 5, nos. 5 (1833): 57–58; 6 (1833): 69–72; 7 (1833): 81–85; 8 (1833): 93–97; 9 (1833): 105–7; 10 (1833): 117–19; 11 (1833): 129–31; 12 (1833): 141–46; 13 (1833): 153–62; 15 (1833): 181–84; 16 (1833): 193–95.
———. "De la condition sociale des artistes. A propos de l'exposition et du jury." *Journal du peuple* (11 March 1838).
———. "Salon de 1841." *L'Atelier* 1, no. 7 (March 1841): 55–56.
———. "Salon de 1843." *La Revue indépendante* 7 (25 March 1843): 228–43; (10 April 1843): 402–15; (25 April 1843): 583–93; 8 (10 May 1843): 72–88.
———. "Salon de 1844." *L'Atelier*, 4th year, 7 (April 1844): 109–11.
———. "Causes du peu de popularité de la statuaire en France." *L'Atelier*, 5th year, 10 (July 1845).
———. "Quelques Réflexions à propos de l'exposition de la statue de Viala." *La Fraternité de 1845* 17 (May 1846): 144–45.
———. "Le Salon et la Direction des beaux-arts." *L'Atelier*, 6th year, 9 (June 1846): 328–29.
———. "Tableaux d'intérieurs: les boutiques de journaux. *La Démocratie pacifique*." *La Silhouette* 2 (31 May 1846): 1011–14; (7 June 1846): 1029–31; (14 June 1846): 1045–46.
———. "Paris le soir: le Café des arts." *La Silhouette* 4 (16 May 1847): 3–5.

______. "Salon de 1848." *La Revue nationale* 1, no. 14 (23 March 1848): 345–46.
______. "François Sabatier." In *Faust* by J. W. von Goethe translated by F. Sabatier. Paris, 1893.
Arago, E. "Le Théâtre considéré comme moyen révolutionnaire." *Paris révolutionnaire.* 1 (1833): 59–89.
______. "La République et les artistes." *Revue républicaine* 2 (10 July 1834): 14–29.
______. "Les Beaux-Arts et la littérature du peuple." *Almanach du Nouveau Monde pour 1850* (1849): 141–46.
Aragon, Mme A. "Salon de 1833." *Journal des femmes* 4 (2 March 1833): 67–71; (9 March 1833): 88–91; (23 March 1833): 127–31; (30 March 1833): 146–49; (6 April 1833): 168–71; (27 April 1833): 230–34.
Auger, H. [anonymous]. "Des beaux-arts considérés comme moyen d'éducation." *Journal officiel de l'instruction publique* 1, nos. 48 (15 April 1832): 193–94; 51 (26 April 1832): 206–7; 53 (3 May 1832): 212–13; 57 (17 May 1832): 229–30; 59 (24 May 1832): 238–39; 61 (31 May 1832): 245–46; 67 (21 June 1832): 279–80; 69 (28 June 1832): 287–88; 72 (8 July 1832): 300–302; 76 (22 July 1832); 315–16; 87 (30 August 1832): 355.
______. *Moralités.* 2 vols. Paris, 1834.
______. [anonymous]. "Les Ecoles." *La Vérité* 12 (10 January 1835).
______ [anonymous]. "Du sentiment dans les arts." *La Vérité* 14 (17 January 1835).
______. *Physiologie du théâtre.* 3 vols. Paris, 1839–41.
______. *Mémoires (1810–1859).* Edited by P. Cottin. Paris, 1891.
Bacon, F. *New Atlantis.* Edited by A. Johnston. Oxford, 1974.
Baget, J. [J.B.]. "Salon de 1839." *Journal du peuple* (7, 14, 21, 28 April 1839).
______. "Salon de 1840." *Journal du peuple* (15, 22, 29 March; 12 April; 3 May 1840).
Baget, J., and E. P. "Salon de 1841." *Journal du peuple* (18, 21, 28 March; 27 April; 6 May).
Ballanche, P. S. *Du sentiment considéré dans ses rapports avec la littérature et les arts.* Paris, 1801.
Balzac, H. de. "Des artistes." *La Silhouette* 1, nos. 10 (25 February 1830): 73–74; 12 (11 March 1830): 89–92; 2, no. 5 (22 April 1830): 33–35.
______. de [?]. Review of *Aux artistes* by Emile Barrault. *Le Feuilleton des journaux politiques* (March 1830).
______. *Les Comédiens sans le savoir.* In *Oeuvres complètes*, edited by M. Bouteron, 7:11–67. Paris, 1936.
______. *Correspondance.* Edited by R. Pierrot. 5 vols. Paris, 1960–69.
Barbier, A. *Salon de 1836.* Paris, 1836.
Barrault, E. *Aux artistes. Du passé et de l'avenir des beaux-arts.* Paris, 1830.
______. "Prédication du ler mai: l'art." *Le Globe* (2 May 1831): 491–92.
______. "Prédication du 27 novembre." In *Religion saint-simonienne. Cérémonie du 27 novembre.* Paris, 1831.
Bastide, J. "Salon de 1847." *Revue nationale* 1, no. 1 (May 1847): 24–27.
Battiliat, M. "Le Naturalisme et l'art social." *L'Art social* 4 (February 1892): 84–86.
Baudelaire, C. *Curiosités esthétiques, l'Art romantique et autres oeuvres critiques.* Edited by H. Lemaitre. Paris, 1962.
Baudet-Dulary, A. *Essai sur les harmonies physiologiques.* Paris, 1844.

Bazard, S.-A. *Doctrine de Saint-Simon. Exposition de la deuxième année (1829–1830).* In *Oeuvres de Saint-Simon et d'Enfantin*, 42:149–432. Paris, 1877.

Beaumont, G. de. *Marie, ou l'esclavage aux Etats-unis. Tableau de moeurs américaines.* 2 vols. Paris, 1835.

Bères, E. *Les Classes ouvrières. Moyens d'améliorer leur sort sous le rapport du bien-être matériel et du perfectionnement moral.* Paris, 1836.

Berlioz, H. *Correspondance générale. Volume 1 (1803–1832).* Edited by P. Citron. Paris, 1972.

Bichat, M.F.X. *Recherches physiologiques sur la vie et la mort.* 1800. Reprint. Paris, 1844.

Bignan, A. *Essai sur l'influence morale de la poésie.* Paris, 1838.

Bion, E., J.-B. Besson, and Baptiste. "Du Salon de 1836." *L'Européen*, 2d ser., 1, no. 6 (25 March 1836): 189–94.

Blanc, C. "Beaux-Arts: gravure." *Revue du progrès* 1 (15 February 1839): 144–50.

———. "Salon de 1839." *Revue du progrès* 1, nos. 5 (15 March 1839): 268–73; 6 (1 April 1839): 341–49; 8 (1 May 1839): 468–78.

———. "Salon de 1840." *Revue du progrès* 3, nos. 5 (15 March 1840): 217–25; 6 (1 April 1840): 269–77; 8 (1 May 1840): 356–66.

———. "Etat de la peinture en France." *La Réforme* (18 April 1844).

———. "Etat de la sculpture en France." *La Réforme* (16 May 1844).

———. "Salon de 1845." *La Réforme* (16, 26, 31 March; 9, 16, 26 April, 17 May, 4 June 1845).

———. *Histoire des peintres français au dix-neuvième siècle.* Paris, 1845.

———. "Salon de 1846." *La Réforme* (25 March; 4, 10, 19 April; 1, 12, 27 May 1846).

Blanc, L. "De la vertu considérée comme principe de gouvernement." *Revue républicaine* 4 (1835): 3–18.

———. *De l'organisation du travail.* 1839.

Boileau, L. A. *Nouvelle Forme architecturale. Exposé. Notes et appréciations.* Paris, 1853.

———. *Histoire critique de l'invention en architecture.* Paris, 1886.

Boissy d'Anglas, F.-A. *Essai sur les fêtes nationales suivi de quelques idées sur les arts; et la nécessité de les encourager.* Paris, an II.

Bonald, L.G. de. *Réflexions sur les questions de l'indépendence des gens de lettres, et de l'influence du théâtre sur les moeurs et le goût.* 1805. In *Oeuvres*, 10:65–103. Paris, 1819.

———. *Oeuvres complètes.* 3d ed. 12 vols. Paris, 1838.

Borel, P. "Les Fourberies de Scapin." *La Liberté. Journal des arts.* 3 (August 1832): 13–16; 7 (September 1832): 109–12.

———. "Des artistes penseurs et des artistes creux." *L'Artiste*, 1st ser., 5 (1833): 53–59.

Bouglé, C., and E. Halévy, eds. *Doctrine de Saint-Simon. Exposition. Première année, 1829.* Paris, 1924.

Boulanger, F. *Ambélakia, ou les associations et les municipalités helléniques avec documents confirmatifs.* Paris, 1875.

Boulland, J.F.A. *Essai d'histoire universelle.* 2 vols. Paris, 1836.

———. *Doctrine politique du christianisme.* Paris, 1845.

———. *Mission morale de l'art*. Paris, 1852.

Bra, T. "Du renouvellement de l'art en France." *Journal des artistes*, 2d ser., 4 (20 June 1847): 222–23; (27 June 1847): 229–31; 5 (4 July 1847): 3–4; (11 July 1847): 9–11; (18 July 1847): 17–20; (1 August 1847): 43–45.

———. *Introduction au Musée de la Paix*. Douai, 1852.

———. *Suite à l'introduction au Musée de la Paix*. Douai, 1853.

Brémond (de Guérin), J. *Appel aux artistes. Rénovation sociale par les arts*. Paris, 1850.

Briancourt, M. *Visite au phalanstère*. Paris, 1848.

Brunier, C. "Beaux-Arts." *La Démocratie pacifique* 6, no. 69 (10 March 1846).

———. "Salon de 1846." *La Démocratie pacifique* 6, nos. 80 (21 March 1846); 88 bis (29 March 1846); 97 (7 April 1846); 108 (18 April 1846); 126 (7 May 1846); 130 [*sic*] (21 May 1846).

———. "Concours de peinture." *La Démocratie pacifique* 9, no. 73 (24 September 1847).

———. "Beaux-Arts." *La Démocratie pacifique* 9, no. 105 (31 October 1847).

———. "Exposition de l'Association des artistes." *La Démocratie pacifique* 10, no. 8 (9 January 1848).

———. "M. Eugène Delacroix. Peintures de la bibliothèque de la Chambre des députés." *La Démocratie pacifique* 10, no. 26 (30 January 1848).

———. "Mort de Dominique Papety." *La Démocratie pacifique* 14, no. 194 (25 September 1849).

Brunier, C. and Monchovet. "Exposition de tableaux au profit de la caisse de secours de la Société des artistes." *La Démocratie pacifique* 6, no. 15 (15 January 1846).

———. "Beaux-Arts. Considérations générales." *La Démocratie pacifique* 6, no. 38 (7 February 1846).

Bruyas, A. *Explication des ouvrages de peinture du cabinet de peinture de M. Alfred Bruyas*. Paris, 1854.

Buchez, P.J.B. "De la physiologie." *Le Producteur* 3 (1826): 122–34, 264–81, 459–79.

———. "Des termes de passage de la physiologie individuelle à la physiologie sociale." *Le Producteur* 4 (1826): 68–86, 416–33.

———. "Quelques Réflexions sur la littérature et les beaux-arts." *Le Producteur* 4 (1826): 189–211.

———. [?]. "Des artistes aujourd'hui." *L'Européen* 1, nos. 9 (2 January 1832): 130–34; 10 (4 February 1832): 148–52.

———. [anonymous]. "Le Salon." *Revue républicaine* 1, no. 1 (10 April 1834): 123–32.

———. "Salon de 1836." *L'Européen*, n.s., 1, no. 7 (May 1836): 218–25.

———. *Introduction à l'étude des sciences médicales*. Paris, 1838.

———. *Essai d'un traité complet de philosophie, du point de vue du catholicisme et du progrès*. 3 vols. Paris, 1838–40.

———. "Art." In *Encyclopédie du XIXe siècle*, 3: 707–18. Paris, 1842.

———. *Introduction à la science de l'histoire*. 2d ed. 2 vols. Paris, 1842.

———. "Notice sur la vie et les ouvrages de H. R. Feugueray." In *Essai sur les doctrines politiques de Saint Thomas d'Aquin*, by H. R. Feugueray, i–xxii. Paris, 1857.

———. *Traité de politique et de science sociale*. 2 vols. Paris, 1866.

Bureau, A. *L'Art dans la République. Aux artistes musiciens*. Paris, 1848.

Cabanis, P.J.G. [anonymous]. "Travail sur l'éducation publique trouvé dans les papiers de Mirabeau, fait et publié par Cabanis." In *Oeuvres complètes*, 2:363–581. Paris, 1823.

______. *Rapports du physique et du moral de l'homme*. 1802. Edited by F. Thurot. 3 vols. Paris, 1824.

______. *Lettre à M. T**, sur les poèmes d'Homère*. In *Oeuvres complètes*, 5:277–374. Paris, 1825.

Cabet, G. *Voyage en Icarie*. 1840. 2d ed., Paris, 1842.

Camp, M. du. *Souvenirs littéraires*. 2 vols. Paris, 1882–83.

Campanella, T. *La città del sole: dialogo poetico*. 1623. Translated and edited by D. J. Donno. Berkeley, 1981.

Cantagrel, F. "Salon de 1841" *La Phalange*, 3d ser., 2, nos. 39 (31 March 1841): cols. 635–47; 44 (11 April 1841): cols. 723–30; 50 (25 April 1841): cols. 819–27; 3, nos. 6 (14 May 1841): cols. 83–95; 13 (30 May 1841): cols. 203–13; 17 (9 June 1841): cols. 267–78.

______. *Le Fou du Palais-royal*. Paris, 1841.

______. "Concours d'architecture." *La Démocratie pacifique* 3, no. 82 (20 September 1844).

Carnot, H. [anonymous]. "Discours sur les beaux-arts." *L'Organisateur* (25 December 1830): 145–50.

______. *Sur le Saint-Simonisme*. Paris, 1887.

Caudin, J. de. "Salon de 1848." *La Réforme* (8, 21 March; 21 May 1848).

Cavaignac, G. "Monuments révolutionnaires." *Revue républicaine* 3 (November 1834): 129–75.

Cavel. "Portrait lithographié de P. Enfantin." *Le Globe* (27 March 1832): 345.

Cazavan, G. "Monsieur Mayeux." *Le Globe* (8 January 1832): 32.

Cerclet, A. "Considérations philosophiques sur la littérature." *Le Producteur* 1 (1825): 49–61.

Cerise, L. "Considérations physiologiques sur les éléments et sur les moyens de l'art." *L'Européen*, n.s., 1, no. 6 (25 March 1836): 171–78.

______. *Déterminer l'influence de l'éducation physique et morale sur la production de la sur-excitation du système nerveux*. Paris, 1841.

______. *Des fonctions et des maladies nerveuses dans leurs rapports avec l'éducation sociale et privée, morale et physique*. Paris, 1842.

______. *Mélanges médico-psychologiques*. Paris, 1872.

Champseix, G. "Exposé sommaire de la doctrine de l'humanité." *Revue sociale* 2 (December 1846): 33–35, 69–72; 3 (January 1847): 49–57; (February 1847): 65–76; (March 1847): 81–85.

Charles-Albert. "Art et société." *Les Temps nouveaux* 30 (23–29 November 1895): 1–2; 32 (7–13 December 1895): 1–2.

Charton, E. "Le Feu du ciel, par Louis Boulanger. Causeries critiques. Fragmens d'Hoffmann." *Revue encyclopédique* 53 (February 1832): 341–62.

Chateaubriand, F. de. *Le Génie du christianisme*. 1802. 2 vols. Reprint. Paris, 1966.

Chatelain, E. "Profession de foi," *Le Coup de feu* 1 (September 1885): 1–2.

Colin, A. "De la moralisation." *Le Nouveau Monde* (21 September 1839).

Comte, A. *Cours de philosophie positive*. 6 vols. Paris, 1842.

Condorcet, M.J.A.N.C. de. *Fragment sur l'Atlantide*. In *Oeuvres*, 6:597–660. Paris, 1847.

______. *Esquisse d'un tableau historique des progrès de l'esprit humain*. 1793. Edited by M. Hincker and F. Hincker. Paris, 1966.

Considerant, V. "Des tendances actuelles de la littérature." *Le Phalanstère* 2 (8 January 1833): 61–63.

Cottin, P., ed. *Thoré-Burger peint par lui-même. Lettres et notes intimes*. 1900.

Courbet, G. "Le Réalisme." In *Exhibition et vente de 40 tableaux et 4 dessins de M. Gustave Courbet*. Paris, 1855.

Couret, E. "Oeuvre à faire." *L'Art social* 1 (November 1891): 16–17.

Courthion, P., ed. *Courbet raconté par lui-même et par ses amis*. 2 vols. Geneva, 1948–50.

Couder, A. *L'Architecture et l'industrie comme moyen de perfection sociale*. Paris, 1840.

Daly, C. "Monument de juillet élevé sur la Place de la Bastille." *La Phalange*, 3d ser., 1 (3 January 1841): cols. 237–42; (5 February 1841): cols. 267–70.

Decamps, A. [A.D.]. *Le Musée. Revue du Salon de 1834*. Paris, n.d.

______. "Les Arts et l'industrie au dix-neuvième siècle." *Revue républicaine* 3 (10 October 1834): 27–52; 4 (10 February 1835): 175–94.

______. "Salon de 1835." *Revue républicaine* 4 (10 March 1835): 262–78; 5 (10 April 1835): 69–86; (10 May 1835): 164–82.

______. [A.Ds.]. "Salon de 1836." *Le National de 1834* (16 January; 4, 13, 19 March; 4, 19 April; 1, 13, 19 May 1836).

______. [A.Dps.]. "Salon de 1837." *Le National de 1834* (5, 14, 25, 26 March; 7, 27, 30 April; 3 May 1837).

______. [A.Dps.]. "Salon de 1838." *Le National* (5, 18 March; 7 April; 1 May 1838).

______. [A.Dps.]. "Salon de 1839." *Le National* (7, 16, 22, 29 March; 9, 25 April; 13 May 1839).

Delacroix, E. "Influence du commerce et du gouvernement dans les arts." *La Liberté. Journal des arts* 16 (December 1832): 65–68.

______. "Exposition.—Ceux qui en veulent et ceux qui n'en veulent pas." *La Liberté. Journal des arts*, 18 (January 1833): 129–31.

Delbrouck, J. *L'Eglise Saint-Eugène à Paris. Vues et description*. Paris, 1856.

Delécluze, E.-J. *Louis David, son école et son temps*. Paris, 1855.

Delrieu. "Du désordre dans la peinture." *La Phalange* 1 (1 September 1836): cols. 194–96.

Desages, L., and A. Desmoulins. *Doctrine de l'Humanité. Aphorismes*. Boussac, 1848.

Descartes, R. *Oeuvres de Descartes*. Edited by S. S. de Sacy. 2 vols. Paris, 1966.

Deschamps, E. *La Préface des Etudes françaises et étrangères*. Edited by H. Girard. Paris, 1923.

Desnoyers, L. "Les Beaux-Arts et les socialistes." *La Semaine* 51 (29 October 1848): 665–66.

Diamandy, G. "Le Matérialisme dans l'art." *L'Art social* 7 (July 1892): 182–86.

Didron. "Nous sommes français," *La Liberté. Journal des arts*. 1 (August 1832): 20–26.

Diderot, D. *Oeuvres complètes*. Edited by H. Dieckmann, J. Fabre, J. Proust, and J. Varloot. 25 vols. to date. Paris, 1975–.

Doin, G. T., and E. Charton. *Lettres sur Paris*. Paris, 1830.

Dubuisson, A. *Les Echos du bois sacré. Souvenirs d'un artiste. De Rome à Barbizon*. Paris, 1924.

Duclerc, E., and L. A. Pagnerre, eds. *Dictionnaire politique*. Paris, 1842.

Dupont, J. F. "Introduction." *Revue républicaine* 1 (April 1834): 1–52.

Dussieux, L. *L'Art considéré comme le symbole de l'état social, ou Tableau historique et synoptique du développement des beaux-arts en France*. Paris, 1838.

Duveyrier, C. "Travaux publics—Fêtes." *Le Globe* (11 April 1832): 407–8; (16 April 1832); 425.

Enfantin, P. "De l'influence des fêtes publiques sur le bien-être de la société." *Le Producteur* 1 (1825): 168–79.

______. "Avertissement." *Le Producteur* 2 (April 1826): 628–29.

______. "Notice biographique sur Augustin Enfantin." In *Catalogue des tableaux, études peintes à l'huile, aquarelles, dessins et croquis de feu M. A. Enfantin*. Paris, 1828.

______. "Les Enseignements." (28 November 1831–18 February 1832). In *Oeuvres de Saint-Simon et d'Enfantin*, vols. 14, 16, and 17. Paris, 1868.

______. "Les Mémoires d'un industriel de l'année 2240." In *Oeuvres de Saint-Simon et d'Enfantin*, 17: 143–214. Paris, 1868.

______. "Correspondance inédite d'Enfantin." In *Oeuvres de Saint-Simon et d'Enfantin*, vols. 24–30. Paris, 1868.

Engels, F. *Socialism: Utopian and Scientific*. 1880. Reprint. Peking, 1975.

Etex, A. *Souvenirs d'un artiste*. Paris, 1877.

Feugueray, H.-R. *See* Robert, H.

Fillioux, A. "Salon de 1843" *La Revue critique* (9 March 1843): 6–10; (16 March 1843): 24–26; (23 March 1843): 36–40; (30 March 1843): 49–54; (6 April 1843): 69–72; (13 April 1843): 81–85; (10 May 1843): 6–10.

Flocon, F., and M. Aycard. *Salon de 1824*. Paris, 1824.

Flotte, P. de. *La Souveraineté du peuple: essais sur l'esprit de la révolution*. Paris, 1851.

Foisy, F. M., and O.-A. Barbier. *Exposition des tableaux au musée royal du Louvre*. Paris, 1837.

Fortoul, H. "De l'art actuel." *Revue encyclopédique* 59 (July–August 1833): 107–53.

______. "Souvenirs romantiques." *Revue encyclopédique* 60 (October–December 1833): 264–98.

Fortunat. "Du colportage des mauvais livres." *L'Ange gardien* 1 (1848): 466–69.

Fourier, C. *Théorie des quatre mouvements et des destinées générales*. 1808. Edited by S. Debout. Paris, 1967.

______. *Le Nouveau Monde industriel et sociétaire*. 1829. Reprint. Paris, 1974.

______. *Pièges et charlatanisme des deux sectes Saint-Simon et Owen, qui promettent l'association et le progrès*. Paris, 1831.

______. *Théorie de l'unité universelle*. In *Oeuvres complètes de Fourier*, vols. 2–5. Paris, 1841.

______. *Cités ouvrières. Des modifications à introduire dans l'architecture des villes*. Paris, 1849.

Fournel, H. *Bibliographie saint-simonienne*. Paris, 1833.

Frégier, H. A. *Des classes dangereuses de la population dans les grandes villes et des moyens de leur rendre meilleur*. 2d ed. Paris, 1840.

G., Marie-Camille de. "Salon de 1834." *La Femme nouvelle. Tribune des femmes* 2 (April 1834): 158–64.

Gabet, G. *Traité élémentaire de l'homme considéré sous tous ses rapports*. 3 vols. Paris, 1842.

Galbacio, B. "Salon de 1834." *Journal des gens du monde* 1 (1834): 145–46; 153–55.

Galbacio, B. [B.G.]. "Salon de 1834." *Le Locateur*; *Gazette des travaux publics*, nos. 22 (March 1834): 1; 23 (March 1834): 1–2; 24 (March 1834): 1–2; 25 (March 1834): 1–2; 26 (April 1834): 1–2; 27 (April 1834): 1–2; 28 (April 1834): 1–2; 29 (April 1834): 1–2; 30 (April 1834): 2–3; 31 (May 1834): 1–2; 33 (May 1834): 1–2.

______ [B.G.]. "Quelques Mots sur l'art en général." *Gazette des travaux publics* 43 (20–25 July 1834).

Garnier, A. "Le Salon des industriels." *Le Producteur* 1 (1825): 507–25.

______. "Des fêtes du carnaval," *Le Producteur* 2 (1826): 330–36.

______. "Du beau dans la nature sauvage et du beau dans la société." *Le Producteur* 3 (1826): 500–507.

Gasperini, A. de. *De l'art dans ses rapports avec le milieu social*. 2 vols. Paris, 1850.

Gauny, L. G. *Le Philosophe plébéian*. Edited by J. Rancière. Paris, 1983.

Gautier, T. *L'Art moderne*. Paris, 1856.

Gazel, D. "Travaux de M. H. Flandrin à Saint-Germain-des-Prés." *Revue nationale* 1, no. 5 (September 1847): 140–43.

Germain, A. "Salon de 1886." *Le Coup de feu*, 10 (June 1886): 18–23; 11 (July 1886): 20–22; 12 (August 1886): 22–23; 13 (September 1886): 21–23.

Gervaise. "Salons 1892—1er mai." *Revue socialiste* (May 1892): 619–28.

Gilland, J.-P. *Revue anecdotique des associations ouvrières*. Paris, 1850.

Girard, A. "L'Art du peuple." *Les Temps nouveaux*, 4th year, 10 (2–8 July 1898): 1.

Gorky, M. et al. *Soviet Writers' Congress 1934*. London, 1977.

Grégoire, Abbé H. [G]. *Plan d'association générale entre les savans, gens de lettres et artistes pour accelérer les progrès des bonnes moeurs et des lumières*. Paris, n.d. [c. 1816].

Guillemon. "Sur un caractère de notre époque: ambition et ennui." *Le Phalanstère* 1 (9 August 1832): 96–97.

Guillot, A.? [A.G.]. "Salon de 1836." *Journal du peuple* 5 (May 1836): 156–59.

______. "De l'allégorie et des attributs au temps moderne." *L'Artiste*, 2d ser., 1 (1838): 290–93.

______. "Des arts dans la société présente." *Le Nouveau Monde* (1 September 1839).

______. "Des arts dans la société future." *Le Nouveau Monde* (11 September 1839).

______. "Salon de 1845." *La Revue indépendante* 19 (25 March 1845): 230–41; (10 April 1845): 380–98; (25 April 1845): 504–20; 20 (10 May 1845): 53–81.

______. "Salon de 1846." *La Revue indépendante*, 2d ser., 2 (25 March 1846): 176–87; (10 April 1846): 296–315; (25 April 1846): 427–53.

______. "Exposition annuelle des beaux-arts." *La Revue indépendante*, 2d ser., 8 (25 March 1847): 237–47; (10 April 1847): 380–88; (25 April 1847): 523–33.

Halévy, L. Review of *Les Martyrs de Souli* by Népomucène Lemercier. *Le Producteur* 1 (1825): 74–86.

———. "Souvenirs de Saint-Simon." Edited by G. Brunet. *Revue d'histoire économique et sociale* 13 (1925): 166–76.

Hauréau, B. [B.H.]. "Coup d'oeil cynique sur l'exposition." *Mercure de France au XIXe siècle* 33 (1831): 480–86.

———. "De la politique et des arts." *La Liberté. Journal des arts* 1 (August 1832): 26–30.

———. [anonymous]. "Salon." *La Tribune politique et littéraire* (3, 9, 11, 20, 25 March; 2, 27 April; 3 May 1833).

———. *La Montagne. Notices historiques et philosophiques sur les principaux membres de la Montagne*. Paris, 1834.

———. [B.H.]. "Salon de 1834." *La Tribune politique et littéraire* (3, 10, 15, 24, 31 March; 12 April 1834).

———. "Salon de 1837." *Journal du peuple* (5, 19 March; 9, 23 April 1837).

———. "Le Musée de Versailles." *Journal du peuple* (2, 30 July 1837).

Haussard, P. [P.H.]. "Salon de 1843." *Le National* (15, 24, 29 March; 6, 21, 29 April; 14, 23 May 1843).

———. [P.H.]. "Salon de 1844." *Le National* (15, 23, 31 March; 12, 23 April; 4, 12 May 1844).

———. [P.H.]. "Salon de 1845." *Le National* (23 March; 1, 6, 13, 24 April; 4, 11 May 1845).

———. [P.H.]. "Salon de 1846." *Le National* (27 March; 10, 28 April; 12, 19 May 1846).

———. [P.H.]. "Salon de 1847." *Le National* (16, 28 March; 8, 18, 25 April; 9, 13, 23 May 1847).

Hawke, P. "Quelques Mots sur le Salon de peinture au Louvre—1848," *Le Représentant du peuple* (5, 16, 28 April; 1, 29 May 1848).

———. "Salon de 1848." *La Voix des femmes* 21 (12 April 1848).

———. "Arts plastiques." *Le Lucifer* 1 (16 January 1849); 4 (23 January 1849); 6 (27 January 1849); 8 (3 February 1849).

Heine, H. *De la France*. Paris, 1833.

———. *Allemands et Français*. Paris, 1868.

Hervé, E. "De l'art." *L'Intelligence* (July 1838): 14.

Institut historique. *Congrès historique européen. Discours et compte-rendu des séances*. 2 vols. Paris, 1836.

Izalguier, E. d'. "Exposition des envois de l'Ecole de Rome." *La Phalange* 1 (1 September 1836): 197–98.

———. "Loi de la corrélation de la forme sociale et de la forme esthétique." In *Trois Discours prononcés à l'Hôtel de ville, faisant complément à la publication du Congrès historique*, edited by Dain, V. Considerant, and E. d'Izalguier, 111–48. Paris, 1836.

———. "De la critique dans les oeuvres d'art." *La Phalange* 1 (10 August 1836): cols. 130–35.

———. "De la poétique dans ses rapports avec la science sociale" *La Phalange* 1 (20 August 1836): cols. 169–72.

———. "Les Oeuvres, la critique et le public." *La Phalange* 1 (1 January 1837): cols. 686–87.

Jal, A. *Salon de 1833. Les Causeries du Louvre*. Paris, 1833.

Janin, J. "Salon de 1839." *L'Artiste*, 2d ser., 2, nos. 16 (1839): 213–17; 17 (1839): 225–34; 18 (1839): 237–45; 19 (1839): 253–64; 20 (1839): 269–76; 21 (1839): 285–93; 22 (1839): 301–10; 23 (1839): 321–26; 24 (1839): 337–45.

Jaurès, J. "L'Art et le socialisme." *Le Mouvement socialiste* (1 May 1900): 513–25; (15 May 1900): 582–90.

Jeanron, P.-A. "De l'anarchie dans les arts." *La Liberté. Journal des arts* 8 (September 1832): 113–19.

______. "Journaux, feuilletons, revues." *La Liberté. Journal des arts* 15 (December 1832): 60–62.

______. "De l'exposition de 1838, et du résultat des expositions." *Revue du nord*, 3d ser., 4, no. 2 (April 1838): 28–57.

______. "Salon de 1845." *La Pandore* 1 (1 April 1845): 186–88; (15 April 1845): 201–5; (1 May 1845): 218–20; (15 May 1845): 236–37; (15 June 1845): 265–67.

Joncières, X. "De l'art, à propos de la liste civile." *Le Globe* (6 January 1832): 21.

______. "De la critique littéraire." *Le Globe* (8 April 1832): 396.

______. "Avenir de la littérature." *Le Globe* (19 April 1832): 439–40.

Jouffroy, T. *Mélanges philosophiques*. Paris, 1833.

______. *Cours d'esthétique*. Paris, 1843.

Justus, P. *Vie et liberté ! Pol, apôtre, artiste de l'individualité à ses frères et soeurs en Siant-Simon* [*sic*]. Paris, 1834.

______. *Fêtes publiques, appel à tous les artistes*. Paris, 1848.

______. *Cinq Lettres sur le congrès universel*. Paris, 1849.

______. *Congrès universel: ce que n'a pas fait celui de 1849, ce qu'il aurait dû faire*. Paris, 1849.

______. *Discours prononcé à la séance d'inauguration des salons de la Société internationale des artistes le 13 mai 1850*. Paris, 1850.

______. "Un Mot sur l'utilité de l'art." *La Voix des artistes* 10 (5 July 1850): 73–74; 11 (1 August 1850): 83–84; 12 (4 September 1850): 92–94; 13 (3 October 1850): 100–1; 14 (12 November 1850): 107–8.

Karr, A. [anonymous]. "Les Saint-Simoniens: appel aux poètes." *Le Figaro* (9 April 1832).

______. "Les Saint-Simoniens: les arts," *Le Figaro* (17 April 1832).

Kropotkin, P. *Paroles d'un révolté*. 1885. Reprint. Paris, 1978.

Ladet, U. "De l'influence des beaux-arts sur la civilisation." *L'Artiste*, 3d ser., 1 (1842): 82–83.

Lamennais, F. de. *De l'art et du beau*. Paris, 1865.

Laponneraye, A. *Mélanges d'économie sociale, de littérature et de morale*. 2 vols. Paris, 1835.

La Tour du Pin, A. de. "Sur la position qu'ont prise depuis la révolution de juillet les savants et les littérateurs français." *Le Phalanstère* 1 (11 October 1832): 175–76; (18 October 1832): 182–84.

Laverdant, D. "Ecole des beaux-arts. Concours de paysage historique." *La Phalange*, 3d ser., 4 (3 October 1841): cols. 35–43.

______. "Ecole des beaux-arts. Concours de sculpture." *La Phalange*, 3d ser., 4 (10 September 1841): cols. 75–86.

______. "Ecole des beaux-arts. Concours de peinture." *La Phalange*, 3d ser., 4, (26 September 1841): cols. 187–94.

______. "L'Assemblée des artistes par M. Paul Delaroche." *La Phalange*, 3d ser., 4 (29 December 1841): cols. 851–56; 5 (2 January 1842): cols. 11–16.

______. "Salon de 1842." *La Phalange*, 3d ser., 5 (3 April 1842): cols. 643–54; (10 April 1842): cols. 691–700; (17 April 1842): cols. 739–50; (24 April 1842): cols. 787–97; (1 May 1842): cols. 851–64; (8 May 1842): cols. 895–906; (15 May 1842): cols. 943–56; (22 May 1842): cols. 989–1001; (29 May 1842): cols. 1035–48.

______. "Ecole des beaux-arts. Concours de peinture." *La Phalange*, 3d ser., 6 (25 September 1842): cols. 627–38.

______. "Ecole des beaux-arts. Envois de Rome. M. Papety." *La Phalange*, 3d ser., 6 (2 October 1842): cols. 675–87.

______. "Salon de 1843." *La Phalange* (17 March 1843): cols. 1823–32; (14 April 1843): cols. 2023–32; (23 April 1843): cols. 2087–96; (30 April 1843): cols. 2137–47; (14 May 1843): cols. 2239–53; (21 May 1843): cols. 2295–308; (28 May 1843): cols. 2343–53; (4 June 1843): cols. 2391–404.

______. "L'art et sa mission." *La Démocratie pacifique* 1, no. 2 (2 August 1843).

______. "Salon de 1844." *La Démocratie pacifique*, 2, nos. 90 (30 March 1844); 116 (25 April 1844); 117 (26 April 1844); 120 (29 April 1844); 123 (2 May 1844); 127 (6 May 1844); 128 (7 May 1844); 132 (11 May 1844); 134 (13 May 1844); 137 (16 May 1844); 138 (17 May 1844).

______. "Concours de sculpture. L'Eglise de St Vincent-de-Paul. M. Maréchal. M. Eugène Farochon." *La Démocratie pacifique* 3, no. 74 (12 September 1844).

______. "Concours de peinture." *La Démocratie pacifique* 3, no. 88 (26 September 1844).

______. "Envois de Rome." *La Démocratie pacifique* 3, no. 92 (30 September 1844).

______. *De la mission de l'art et du rôle des artistes. Salon de 1845*. Paris, 1845.

______. "Souvenir du Salon de 1846." *La Phalange*, 1st ser., 3 (1846): 558–88.

______. "Salon de 1853." *Revue générale de l'architecture et des travaux publics* 10 (1853): cols. 253–63.

______. "Esprit du Salon de 1863. Bilan de l'art après dix-huit siècles d'évangélisation." *Mémorial catholique*, n.s., 4 (August 1863): 311–16; (September 1863): 354–57; (October 1863): 392–95; (November 1863): 428–34.

______. "Salon de 1865." *Mémorial catholique*, n.s., 6 (July 1865): 265–69.

______. "Le Salon de 1868. Un Souvenir de l'Exposition universelle. De l'état de l'architecture au 19e siècle." *Mémorial catholique*, n.s., 9 (July 1868): 256–60; (August 1868): 291–95; (September 1868): 381–85.

Laviron, G. "De ceux à qui notre allure ne convient pas." *La Liberté. Journal des arts*. 6 (September 1832): 90–96.

______. "Rembrandt." *La Liberté. Journal des arts* 16 (December 1832): 77–89.

______. "Progrès de nos doctrines." *La Liberté. Journal des arts* 18 (January 1833): 132–37.

______. *Le Salon de 1834*. Paris, 1834.

______. "Concours pour le Grand Prix de Rome." *La Phalange* 1 (10 October 1836): cols. 312–18.

______. *Le Salon de 1841*. Paris, 1841.

Laviron, G., and B. Galbaccio [*sic*]. *Salon de 1833*. Paris, 1833.

Lechevalier, J. [anonymous]. "De l'art comme élément de la vie sociale." *L'Europe littéraire* (22 March 1833).

______. [anonymous]. "Du patronage aristocratique dans les arts.'" *L'Europe littéraire* (7 June 1833).

______. [anonymous[. "Doctrines de la *Revue encyclopédique*." *L'Europe littéraire* (26 June 1833).

______. "Situation et avenir social de la France." *Revue du progrès social* 1 (January 1834): 1–45.

______. "Questions politiques dans l'intérêt de l'art et des artistes." *Revue du progrès social* 1 (May 1834): 453–58.

Lecoq de Boisbaudran, H. *Education de la mémoire pittoresque*. Paris, 1848.

Lemarant, E. "Salon de 1837." *La Phalange* 1 (20 March 1837): cols. 842–48; (1 April 1837): cols. 872–77; (May 1837): cols. 905–10; (June 1837): cols. 937–40.

Le Rouge, G. "Le Christ aux outrages. Tableau de M. de Groux" *L'Art social* 6 (June 1892): 145–47.

Leroux, P. "De l'union européenne." *Le Globe* 6, no. 1 (24 November 1827).

______. "Du style symbolique." *Le Globe* 7, no. 28 (8 April 1829).

______. "Aux philosophes: de la religion." *Revue encyclopédique* 51 (September 1831): 499–516.

______. "De la poésie de notre époque." *Revue encyclopédique* 52 (November 1831): 399–415; (December 1831): 627–48.

______. [anonymous]. "Tendance nouvelle des idées." *Revue encyclopédique* 53 (January 1832): 1–8.

______. "De la philosophie et du christianisme." *Revue encyclopédique* 55 (August 1832): 281–340.

______. "Allégorie." In *Encyclopédie nouvelle*, l:327. Paris, 1836.

______. "Activité." In *Encyclopédie nouvelle*, 1:78–79. Paris, 1836.

______. "Art." In *Encyclopédie nouvelle*, 2:82–84. Paris, 1836.

______. *Réfutation de l'éclecticisme*. Paris, 1839.

______. *De l'humanité, de son principe et de son avenir*. 2 vols. Paris, 1840.

______. "Aux philosophes: de la situation actuelle de l'esprit humain." *La Revue indépendante* 1 (1841): 1–59.

______. "Considérations sur Werther et en général sur la poésie de notre époque." In *Werther de Goethe*, translated by P. Leroux, xv–lii. Paris, 1845.

______. *De l'égalité*. Boussac, 1846.

______. *D'une religion nationale ou du culte*. Boussac, 1846.

______. *Doctrine de l'humanité. Aphorismes*. Edited by L. Desages and A. Desmoulins. Boussac, 1848.

______. *Projet d'une constitution démocratique et sociale*. Paris, 1848.

______. "De la fable." In *Fables de P. Lachambeaudie*. Paris, 1851.

______. "Comment délivrer la France de la tyrannie? ou de la constitution qui convient aujourd'hui à la France. A Auguste Deville, Alfred Talandier, Félix Pyat." *L'Espérance* (October 1858): 163–76.

______. "Suite de la lettre au docteur Deville." *L'Espérance* (January 1859): 177–99.

______. *La Grève de Samarez*. 1863. Edited by J. P. Lacassagne. 2 vols. 1979.

Livre des actes, publié par les femmes 1–11. Paris, 1833–34.

Luchet, A. "A propos du Salon de 1847." *La Réforme* (27 April; 4, 11 May 1847).

Machereau, P.-J. "Profession de foi." *L'Organisateur*, 2d year, 29 (5 March 1831): 227–28.

Marrast, A. *Vingt Jours de secret ou le complot d'avril*. Paris, 1834.

Mars, L. de. "Salon de 1838." *L'Intelligence* (April 1838): 14–16.

Marx, K. *The Holy Family*. In *Collected Works*, by K. Marx and F. Engels, vol. 4. London, 1975.

Marx, K., and F. Engels. *The German Ideology*. 1846. Edited by C. J. Arthur. London, 1977.

______. *Manifesto of the Communist Party*. 1848. Reprint. Peking, 1968.

______. *On Literature and Art*. Moscow, 1976.

Ménard, L. "Peinture murale—M. Hippolyte Flandrin." *La Démocratie pacifique* 8, no. 131 (2 June 1847).

______. "Peinture murale—Mm. Chassériau et Delacroix." *La Démocratie pacifique* 9, no. 67 (17 September 1847).

Ménard, L., and R. Ménard. [d'Arnem]. "Salon de 1847." *La Démocratie pacifique* 8, nos. 67 (19 March 1847); 74 (27 March 1847); 80 (3 April 1847); 83 (7 April 1847); 86 (10 April 1847); 89 (14 April 1847); 92 (17 April 1847); 98 (24 April 1847).

Meray, A. "Un Rêve d'harmonie dans l'atelier d'Ottin." *La Démocratie pacifique* 15, no. 131 (13 May 1850).

Mercier, V. "De la beauté." *Le Globe* (2 March 1832): 245–46.

Michelet, J. *Le Peuple*. Paris, 1846.

Miget. "De la peinture." *La Phalange* 1 (20 November 1836): cols. 455–57; (10 December 1836): cols. 511–15; (20 December 1836): cols. 545–51; (1 January 1837): cols. 575–580.

Montalembert, C.F.R. de. *Du vandalisme et du catholicisme dans l'art*. Paris, 1839.

______. *Mélanges d'art et de littérature*. In *Oeuvres*, vol. 6. Paris, 1861.

Montalivet, M. C. de. *Le Roi Louis-Philippe: liste civile*. 2d ed. Paris, 1851.

Montesquieu, C. de Secondat de. *Oeuvres complètes*. 9 vols. Edited by A. Masson. Paris, 1950–55.

Montyon, A. de. *Testament de M. le Baron Auget de Montyon et pièces relatives aux legs par lui faits aux indigens de la ville de Paris et aux Académies*. Paris, 1823.

Möy, C.-A. de. *Des fêtes, ou quelques idées d'un c[en] français, relativement aux fêtes publiques et à un culte national*. Paris, an VII.

Museux, E. "Les Conquérants au Salon des Champs-Elysées." *L'Art social* 6 (June 1892): 153–55.

______. "Un Triptyche au Salon du 'Champ de Mars.'" *L'Art social* 7 (July 1892): 189–90.

Nadaud, M. *Les Mémoires de Léonard, ancien garçon maçon*. Edited by J. Follain. Paris, 1948.

Nus, E. *Choses de l'autre monde*. Paris, 1880.

Olivier, J. *Paris en 1830*. Edited by A. Delattre and M. Denkinger. Paris, 1951.

Orsel, V. "Les Arts sont-ils utiles?" In *Oeuvres diverses de Victor Orsel*, edited by A. Perin, 2:55–59. Paris, 1878.

Ott, A. *Manuel d'histoire universelle*. 2 vols. Paris, 1840–42.

———. "Art." In *Dictionnaire des sciences politiques et sociales*, 1:421–29. Paris, 1854.

———. "La Doctrine de Buchez sur le système nerveux et sur les rapports de l'esprit avec l'organisme." *Annales médico-psychologiques*, 4th ser., 7 (January 1866): 1–24.

———. "Notice sur la vie et les travaux de Buchez." Preface to *Traité de politique et de science sociale* by P.J.B. Buchez. Paris, 1866.

Ottin, A. *Esquisse d'une méthode applicable à l'art de la sculpture*. Paris, 1864.

Pellarin, C. *Souvenirs anecdotiques: médecine navale—saint-simonisme—chouannerie*. Paris, 1868.

Pelletan, E. "Salon de 1841." *La Presse* (16 March; 4, 14 April; 5, 27 May; 3 June 1841).

———. "Salon de 1845." *La Démocratie pacifique* 4, nos. 55 (24 February 1845); 75 (16 March 1845); 83 (24 March 1845); 84 (25 March 1845); 90 (31 March 1845); 97 (7 April 1845); lll (21 April 1845); 120 (30 April 1845).

———. "Compiègne. Ses Souvenirs historiques, son Musée Vivenel." *L'Echo de l'Oise* (12 July 1850).

Pelloutier, F. *L'Art et la révolte*. Paris, 1896.

Piel, L.A. "Revue des nouvelles églises de Paris: la Madeleine." *L'Européen*, 2d ser., 1, no. 12 (February 1837): 383–92.

———. "Salon de 1837." *L'Européen*, 2d ser., 2 (July 1837): 24–32; (August 1837): 50–64.

Pissarro, L. Untitled letter in Charles-Albert, "Art et société." *Les Temps nouveaux* 32 (7–13 December 1895): 1–2.

Pompéry, E. de [E. de P.]. "Le Salon de 1843." *La Revue synthétique* 2 (1843): 171–75.

Pottier, E. *Oeuvres complètes*. Edited by P. Bronchon. Paris, 1966.

Proudhon, P.-J. *De la création de l'ordre dans l'humanité*. 1843. Reprint. Paris, 1927.

———. *Système des contradictions économiques ou Philosophie de la misère*. 1846. Reprint. Paris, 1850.

———. *Philosophie du progrès*. 1853. Reprint. Paris, 1946.

———. *Du principe de l'art et de sa déstination sociale*. Paris, 1865.

Quatremère de Quincy, A. C. *Considérations sur les arts du dessin en France*. Paris, 1791.

———. *Considérations morales sur la destination des ouvrages de l'art*. Paris, 1815.

Raimbaud, J. "Union et liberté." *La Liberté. Journal des arts* 2 (August 1832): 13–16.

Raymond, G.-M. *De la peinture considérée dans ses effets sur les hommes en général et de son influence sur les moeurs et le gouvernement des peuples*. Paris, 1798.

Religion saint-simonienne; correspondance. Articles extraits du "Globe." Paris, 1831.

Reynaud, J. "De la société saint-simonienne." *Revue encyclopédique* 53 (January 1832): 9–36.

———. "Coup d'oeil sur l'exposition de sculpture." *Revue encyclopédique* 57 (March 1833): 567–97.

Robert, H. "Salon de 1841." *Le National* (16, 23, 30 March; 6, 15, 20, 30 April 1841).

———. "Salon de 1842." *Le National* (17, 28–29 March; 8, 15, 24 April; 8, 17 May 1842).

Rochette, P. "Quelques Mots sur l'art." *Le Globe* (18 April 1832): 435.

Rodrigues, O. *Poésies sociales des ouvriers*. Paris, 1841.

— —. [anonymous]. "L'Artiste, le savant et l'industriel. Dialogue." In *Oeuvres de Saint-Simon et d'Enfantin*, 39: 199–258. Paris, 1875.

Rousseau, J.-J. *Lettre à M. d'Alembert sur les spectacles*. 1758. Edited by M. Fuchs. Lille and Geneva, 1948.

——. *Oeuvres complètes*. Edited by B. Gagnebin and M. Raymond. 4 vols. 1961–69.

Roux-Lavergne, P. C. [P. C. R . . . x]. *Science nouvelle. Lettre d'un disciple de la science nouvelle aux religionnaires prétendus Saint-Simoniens*. Paris, 1831.

——. *Un Sentier à travers le siècle: les idées et les hommes*. Rennes, 1869.

Sabatier-Ungher, F. *Salon de 1851*. Paris, 1851.

Saint-Chéron, A. de [A. de Saint-C.]. "De la position sociale des artistes." *L'Artiste*, 1st ser., 4 (1832): 50–53.

——. "De la poésie et des beaux-arts dans notre époque." *L'Artiste*, 1st ser., 4 (1832): 165–67; 177–79; 221–24; 269–71; 302–4.

——. "De la direction actuelle des beaux-arts et de leur avenir." *L'Artiste*, 1st ser., 10 (1835): 269–73.

Saint-Simon, C.-H. de. *Oeuvres de Saint-Simon et d'Enfantin*. 47 vols. Paris, 1865–78.

——. *Oeuvres de Claude-Henri de Saint-Simon*. 6 vols. Paris, 1966. Partial reprint of the *Oeuvres de Saint-Simon et d'Enfantin*. 47 vols. Paris, 1865–78.

Salles, J. *Mémoires d'un vieil artiste*. Nîmes, 1896.

Salmson, J. *L'Institut devant le suffrage universel*. Paris, 1850.

Sand, G. *Questions d'art et de littérature*. In *Oeuvres complètes*, vol. 30. 1878. Reprint. Geneva, 1980.

Say, J.-B. *Olbie, ou essai sur les moyens d'améliorer les moeurs d'une nation*. 1800. In *Oeuvres diverses*, edited by C. Comte, E. Dairet, and H. Say, 581–615. Paris, 1848.

Schoelcher, V. "Salon de 1835." *Revue de Paris*, n.s., 15 (1835): 325–36; 16 (1835): 44–61, 116–31, 263–75; 17 (1835): 164–94.

——. "Salon de 1838." *La Phalange* 2 (15 April 1838): cols. 123–27; (1 May 1838): cols. 137–42; (15 May 1838): cols. 153–59.

Société de gens de lettres. *Supplément à l'Encyclopédie, ou Dictionnaire raisonné des sciences, des arts et des métiers*. 4 vols. Amsterdam, 1776–77.

Sorel, G. "La Valeur sociale de l'art." *Revue de métaphysique et de morale* 9 (1901): 251–78.

Souvestre, E. *Des arts comme puissance gouvernementale, et de la nouvelle constitution à donner aux théâtres*. Nantes, 1832.

Staël, G. de. *Oeuvres complètes*. 17 vols. Paris, 1821.

——. *Des circonstances actuelles qui peuvent terminer la Révolution et des principes qui doivent fonder la république en France*. 1798–99. Edited by J. Viénot. Paris, 1906.

——. *De l'Allemagne*. 1813. Edited by J. de Pagne. Paris, 1959.

Tabarant, A. "Le Club de l'Art social." *La Revue socialiste* (January 1890): 101–6.

Tajan-Rogé, D. *Les Beaux-Arts aux Etats-unis d'Amérique*. Paris, 1857.

Tessié du Motay, C. M. "Nos Monuments industriels." *La Démocratie pacifique* 5, no. 34 (3 August 1845).

Thoré, T. "De la phrénologie dans ses rapports avec l'art." *L'Artiste*, 1st ser., 6 (1833): 122–25; 259–61.
______. "L'Art social et progressif." *L'Artiste*, 1st ser., 7 (1834): 38–42.
______. "Revue des beaux-arts." *Revue républicaine* 2 (1834): 399–405.
______. [T]. "Exposition de 1835." *Le Réformateur*, nos. 144 (2 March 1835); 147 (5 March 1835); 149 (7 March 1835).
______. [?] [T]. "L'Art." *Le Polonais* 5 (December 1835): 362–74.
______. *Dictionnaire de phrénologie et de physionomie* . . . Paris, 1836.
______. "L'Art dans mille ans." *Le Don-Quichotte* 8 (19 February 1837).
______. [T]."Salon de 1838." *Le Journal du peuple*, nos. 13 (1 April 1838); 15 (15 April 1838); 17 (29 April 1838).
______. *La Vérité sur le parti démocratique*. Paris, 1840.
______. "Du communisme en France." *Revue indépendante* 1 (1841): 337–48.
______. "Sculpture." *Encyclopédie nouvelle* 8 (1841): 67–72.
______. [George Dupré]. "Salon de 1842." *La Revue du progrès* 7, no. 4 (1 May 1842): 224–32.
______. "Salon de 1842." *La Revue indépendante* 3 (May 1842): 525–32.
______. *Le Salon de 1844, précédé d'une lettre à Théodore Rousseau*. Paris, 1844.
______. *La Recherche de la liberté*. Paris, 1845.
______. *Le Salon de 1845, précédé d'une lettre à Béranger*. Paris, 1845.
______. *Le Salon de 1846, précédé d'une lettre à George Sand*. Paris, 1846.
______. *Le Salon de 1847, précédé d'une lettre à Firmin Barrion*. Paris, 1847.
______. "Le Salon de 1848." *Le Constitutionnel* (17 March 1848).
______. *Liberté*. Brussels, 1850.
Tocqueville, A. de. *Oeuvres complètes*. 9 vols. Paris, 1864.
Tommaseo, N. *Diario intimo*. Edited by R. Ciampini. Turin, 1939.
Toussenel, A. "Les Bêtes du Salon." *La Démocratie pacifique* 4, no. 104 (4 April 1845).
______. "Gavarni." *La Démocratie pacifique* 5, no. 15 (15 July 1845).
______. "Salon de 1846"; "Des fleurs du Salon de 1846 et de la botanique passionnelle." *La Démocratie pacifique* 6, nos. 111 (22 April 1846); 118 (29 April 1846).
Viedaux, A. "L'Art individualiste." *L'Art social* 5 (March 1892): 100–101.
Vigny, A. de. *Journal d'un poète*. Edited by J. Baldensperger. London, 1928.
Vinçard, J. *Mémoires épisodiques d'un vieux chansonnier saint-simonien*. Paris, 1878.
Vinçard, P. *Les Artistes et le peuple*. Paris, 1850.
Voilquin, S. *Souvenirs d'une fille du peuple ou la Saint-Simonienne en Egypte*. Paris, 1866.
W.***. "Exposition de 1835." *Le Réformateur*, nos. 157 (15 March 1835); 162 (20 March 1835); 164 (22 March 1835); 169 (27 March 1835); 197 (24 April 1835).
Ziegler, J. "Des sociétés en général et de la Société héliographique en particulier." *La Lumière* 1, no. 1 (9 February 1851): 3.

Secondary sources

Abensour, M. "Pierre Leroux et l'utopie socialiste." *Economies et sociétés* 6, no. 12 (December 1972): 2201–47.

Agulhon, M. *Marianne into Battle: Republican Imagery and Symbolism in France 1789–1880*. Cambridge, 1981.

Allemagne, H. R. d'. *Les Saint-Simoniens. 1827–1837*. Paris, 1930.

———. *Prosper Enfantin et les grandes entreprises du XIXe siècle*. Paris, 1935.

Allender, R. "Les Francs-maçons à l'Orient de Douai (1800–1851): description sociale d'un groupe en mouvement." *Revue du nord* 72, no. 84 (January–March 1990): 49–70.

Ambrière, F. *Le Siècle des Valmore. Marceline Desbordes-Valmore et les siens*. 2 vols. Paris, 1987.

Amprimoz, F.-X. "Un Décor 'fouriériste' à Florence." *Revue de l'art* 48 (1980): 57–67.

———. "Lettres de Dominique Papety à ses parents et amis, Rome 1837–1842." *Archives de l'art français*, n.s., 28 (1986): 201–67.

Anonymous. *Relation de la fête donnée à M. Théophile Bra, sculpteur, et précédée de sa biographie*. Douai, 1852.

Ansart, P. *Sociologie de Saint-Simon*. Paris, 1970.

Armagnac, L. *Bonnassieux. Statuaire. Membre de l'Institut 1810–1892. Sa Vie et son oeuvre*. Paris, 1897.

Armand, F. *Les Fouriéristes et les luttes révolutionnaires de 1848 à 1851*. Paris, 1948.

Baczko, B. *Lumières de l'utopie*. Paris, 1978.

———. *Une Education pour la démocratie. Textes et projets de l'époque révolutionnaire*. Paris, 1982.

Baelen, J. *La Vie de Flora Tristan*. Paris, 1972.

Baker, K. M. *Condorcet: From Natural Philosophy to Social Mathematics*. Chicago, 1975.

Barbéris, P. *Balzac et le mal du siècle. Contribution à une physiologie du monde moderne*. 2 vols. Paris, 1970.

Barthes, R. *Sade, Fourier, Loyola*. Paris, 1971.

Becherer, R. *Science plus Sentiment: César Daly's Formula for Modern Architecture*. Ann Arbor, 1984.

Becq, A. *Genèse de l'esthétique française moderne. De la raison classique à l'imagination créatrice*. 2 vols. Pisa, 1984.

Beecher, J. *Charles Fourier. The Visionary and His World*. Berkeley, 1986.

Bénichou, P. *Le Sacre de l'écrivain 1750–1830*. Paris, 1973.

———. *Le Temps des prophètes. Doctrines de l'âge romantique*. Paris, 1977.

Berenson, E. *Populist Religion and Left-Wing Politics in France, 1830–1852*. Princeton, 1984.

Berthier, le Pere and le Pere Vallée. *Un Peintre dominicain: l'oeuvre artistique du R. P. Besson*. Paris, 1909.

Bibliothèque nationale, Paris. *La Révolution de 1848*. Paris, 1948.

Biermann, K. "Die Anfänge der früsozialistischen Kunst- und Literaturkrik: *Le Globe* (1830–1832)." *Lendemains* 37 (1985): 9–17.

Bigotte, A. "La Sculpture Bra. Eléments d'approche." *Amis de Douai* 9, no. 2 (April–June 1983): 20–27.

Blum, C. *Rousseau and the Republic of Virtue: The Language of Politics in the French Revolution*. Ithaca, 1986.

Boas, G. " 'Il faut être de son temps.' " *Journal of Aesthetics and Art Criticism* 1 (1941): 52–65.

Boime, A. "The Second Republic's Competition for the Figure of the Republic." *Art Bulletin* 53 (March 1971): 68–83.

Bonfantini, M. "Pierre Leroux e le origini del simbolismo in Francia." In *Studi in onore di Italo Siciliano. Bibliotheca dell'Archivum Romanicum*, ser. 1, 86, no. 1 (1966): 85–96.

Bonnefon, P. "Une Famille d'artistes: Raimond Bonheur et Rosa Bonheur." *L'Art*, 3d ser., 3 (1901): 419–31, 464–69, 541–59.

———. "Maxime du Camp et les Saint-Simoniens." *Revue d'histoire littéraire de la France* 17 (1910): 709–835.

Borrell, J. *L'Artiste-roi. Essai sur les représentations*. Paris, 1990.

Bougenot, L. *Victor Schoelcher*. Paris, 1921.

Bourgin, H. *Fourier, contribution à l'étude du socialisme français*. Paris, 1905.

Bouton, V. *Profils révolutionnaires par un crayon rouge*. Paris, 1848–49.

Bovetti Pichetto, M. T. "L'influenza di Joseph de Maistre sul pensiero di Saint-Simon." In *Joseph de Maistre tra illuminismo e restaurazione*, edited by L. Marino, 102–13. Turin, 1975.

Bowman, F. P. *Le Christ des barricades 1789–1848*. Paris, 1987.

Briquet, J. *Agricole Perdiguier: correspondance inédite avec George Sand et ses amis*. Paris, 1966.

Bronchon, P., ed. *Le Pamphlet du pauvre. Du socialisme utopique à la révolution de 1848*. Paris, 1957.

Brookner, A. *Greuze: The Rise and Fall of an Eighteenth-Century Phenomenon*. London, 1972.

Brunet, G. *Le Mysticisme social de Saint-Simon*. Paris, 1925.

Brunius, T. *Alexis de Tocqueville: The Sociological Aesthetician*. Upsala, 1960.

Buche, J. *L'Ecole mystique de Lyon 1776–1847*. Paris, 1935.

Burty, P. *L'Age du romantisme: Célestin Nanteuil*. Paris, 1887.

Cahier, A. *Famille Bra. Notice historique sur une famille d'artistes douassiens*. Paris, 1863.

Calmettes, F. *Leconte de Lisle et ses amis*. Paris, 1902.

Carré, J.M. *Voyageurs et écrivains français en Egypte*. 2 vols. Recherches d'archéologie, de philologie et d'histoire de l'Institut français d'archéologie orientale, vols. 4–5. Cairo, 1932.

Cartier, E. *Un Religieux dominicain: le R. P. Hyacinthe Besson. Sa Vie et ses lettres*. 2 vols. Paris, 1865.

Caso, J. de. *David d'Angers. L'Avenir de la mémoire*. Paris, 1988.

Cassagne, A. *La Théorie de l' art pour l' art*. Paris, 1906.

Chabosseau, A. *De Babeuf à la Commune*. Paris, 1911.

Charlton, D. G. *Secular Religions in France 1815–1870*. Oxford, 1963.

Charléty, S. *Histoire du Saint-Simonisme (1825–1864)*. 1896. Reprint. Paris, 1965.

Chartres, Musée des beaux-arts. *Exigences de réalisme dans la peinture française entre 1830 et 1870*. Exhibition catalog, Chartres, 1983.

Chaudonneret, M.-C. "Jeanron et 'l'art social': *Une Scène de Paris*." *Revue du Louvre* 4–5 (October 1986): 317–19.

______. *La Figure de la République. Concours de 1848*. Paris, 1987.

______. "1848: La République des arts," *Oxford Art Journal* 10, no. 1 (1987): 59–70.

Chojecki, C. E. [C. Edmond]. *Zephyrin Cazavan en Egypte*. Paris, 1880.

Claparède, J. "Le Séjour de Courbet à la Tour de Farges." *Bulletin des Amis de Gustave Courbet* 7 (1950): 9–12.

______. *Inventaire des collections publiques françaises, vol. 6. Montpellier, Musée Fabre. Dessins de la collection Alfred Bruyas et autres dessins des 19e et 20e siècles*. Paris, 1962.

Clark, T. J. *The Absolute Bourgeois. Artists and Politics in France 1848–1851*. London, 1973.

Claudius-Lavergne, G. *La Corporation des artistes chrétiens en France*. Paris, 1895.

Clément, C. *Gleyre. Etude biographique et critique, avec le catalogue raisonné de l'oeuvre du maître*. Paris, 1878.

Collinet, M. "A propos de l'idée du progrès au XIXe siècle." *Diogène* 33 (January–March 1961): 105–21.

Collard, P. *Victor Considerant (1808–1893); sa vie, ses oeuvres*. Dijon, 1910.

Colocci, A. *Paulo de Flotte (1817–1860)*. Turin, 1912.

Colloque de Cérisy. *Le Discours utopique*. Paris, 1978.

Crapo, P. B. "Disjuncture on the Left: Proudhon, Courbet and the Antwerp Conference of 1861." *Art History* 14, no. 1 (March 1991): 67–91.

Craven, D., and J. Ryder. *Art of the New Nicaragua*. New York, 1983.

Cuvillier, A. *P.J.B. Buchez et les origines du socialisme chrétien*. Paris, 1948.

______. *Un Journal d'ouvriers: "L'Atelier" (1840–1850)*. Paris, 1954.

______. "Les Antagonismes de classe dans la littérature sociale française de Saint-Simon à 1848." *International Review of Social History*, 1, no. 3 (1956): 433–63.

______. *Hommes et idéologies de 1840*. Paris, 1956.

Darcel, A. "Louis Steinheil." *Gazette des beaux-arts*, 2d period, 32 (1885): 61–73.

Dautry, J. "Nouveau Christianisme ou nouvelle théophilanthropie? Contribution à une sociologie religieuse de Saint-Simon." *Archives de sociologie des religions* 20 (July–December 1965): 7–29.

Debout, S. "La Théorie des quatre mouvements ou le dessein d'un 'grand oeuvre.' " In *Théorie des quatre mouvements et des destinées générales*, by C. Fourier, 1808. 19–68. Edited by S. Debout. Paris, 1967.

Del Bo, G. *Socialismo utopistico 1. Charles Fourier e la scuola societeria (1801–1922)*. Milan, 1957.

Delmas, G. [anonymous]. *Curiosités révolutionnaires: les affiches rouges*. Paris, 1851.

Delpit, M. J. "Biographie de Raymond Bonheur." *Archives historiques de la Gironde* 3 (1861): 267.

Delveau, A. *Les Murailles révolutionnaires*. Paris, 1852.

Derré, J. R. *Lamennais, ses amis et le mouvement des idées à l'époque romantique (1824–1834)*. Paris, 1962.

Derré, J. R., ed. *Regards sur le Saint-Simonisme et les Saint-Simoniens*. Lyons, 1986.

Desroche, H. *La Société festive: du Fouriérisme écrit aux Fouriérismes pratiqués*. Paris, 1975.

Dijkastra, S. K. "Flora Tristan and the Aesthetics of Social Change." Ph.D. diss., University of California, San Diego, 1976.

Dowd, D. L. *Pageant-Master of the Republic: Jacques-Louis David and the French Revolution*. University of Nebraska Studies, n.s., 3 (June 1948).

Driskell, M. P. *Representing Belief: Religion, Art, and Society in Nineteenth-Century France*. University Park, Penn. 1992.

Drost, W. "Das neue Selbstbewußtsein der Arbeiterklasse und ihr Kampf für das Beau social. Zer Kunstkritik in 'L'Atelier' (1841–1846)." *Lendemains* 37 (1985): 27–36.

Durkheim, E. *Le Socialisme. Sa Définition—ses débuts. La Doctrine saint-simonienne*. 1928. Edited by M. Mauss. Paris, 1978.

Duroselle, J.-B. *Les Débuts du catholicisme social en France 1822–1870*. Paris, 1951.

Duval, R. P. "Lacordaire et Buchez. Idéalisme révolutionnaire et réveil religieux en 1839." *Revue des sciences philosophiques et théologiques* (July 1961): 422–55.

Eagleton, T. *Marxism and Literary Criticism*. Berkeley, 1976.

______. *The Ideology of the Aesthetic*. Oxford, 1990.

Easton, M. *Artists and Writers in Paris: The Bohemian Idea 1803–1867*. London, 1964.

Egbert, D. D. "The Idea of 'Avant-Garde' in Art and Politics." *American Historical Review* 73 (December 1967): 339–66.

______. *Social Radicalism and the Arts. Western Europe. A Cultural History from the French Revolution to 1968*. London, 1970.

Elhadad, L. "Femmes prénommées: les prolétaires saint-simoniennes rédactrices de 'La Femme Libre.' " *Les Révoltes logiques* 4 (1977): 62–88; 5 (1977): 29–60.

Erdan, A. [A. A. Jacob]. *La France mystique. Tableau des excentricités religieuses de ce temps*. 2d ed. 2 vols., Amsterdam, 1858.

Evans, D. O. *Le Socialisme romantique: Pierre Leroux et ses contemporains*. Paris, 1948.

______. *Social Romanticism in France*. Oxford, 1951.

Fakkar, R. *Sociologie, socialisme et internationalisme pré-marxistes: l'influence de Saint-Simon*. Neuchâtel, 1968.

Fargeaud, M. "Autour de Balzac et de Marceline Desbordes-Valmore." *Revue des sciences humaines* 21, no. 82 (1956): 153–74.

Finlay, N. A. "Fourierist Art Criticism and the 'Rêve de Bonheur' of Dominique Papety." *Art History* 2, no. 3 (September 1979): 327–38.

Fleury, E. *Les Cartes à jouer du Comte de Saint-Simon*. Saint-Quentin, 1874.

Forcina, M. *I diritti dell'esistente. La filosofia della "Encyclopédie nouvelle" (1833–1847)*. Lecce, 1987.

Foucart, B. "La 'Cathédrale synthétique' de Louis-Auguste Boileau." *Revue de l'art* 3 (1969): 49–66.

______. *Le Renouveau de la peinture religieuse en France (1800–1860)*. Paris, 1987.

Foucart, B., and V. Noël-Bouton. "Saint-Nicolas de Nantes, bataille et triomphe du néo-gothique." In *Congrès archéologique de France*, 126th session, 136–81. Haute-Bretagne, 1968.

Gaulmier, J. "Fouriérisme et littérature." Introduction to *Ode à Charles Fourier*, by A. Breton, Paris, 1961.

Gay, P. *The Enlightenment: An Interpretation*. 2 vols. London, 1970.

Gentile, F. "La festa nell'invenzione saint-simoniana." *Nuova antologia* (August 1975): 479–93.

Gerits, A. *Additions and Corrections to Giuseppe del Bo's Bibliography 'Charles Fourier e la scuola societaria'*. Hilversum, 1983.

———. *Additions and Corrections to Jean Walch "Bibliographie du Saint-Simonisme."* Amsterdam, 1986.

Goblot, J. J. *Aux origines du socialisme français: Pierre Leroux et ses premiers écrits (1824–1830)*. Lyons, 1977.

Goldstein, J. *Console and Classify: The French Psychiatric Profession in the Nineteenth Century*. Cambridge, 1987.

Golomstock, I. *Totalitarian Art*. London, 1990.

Goodwin, B. *Social Science and Utopia*. Hassocks, Sussex, 1978.

Goodwin, B., and K. Taylor. *The Politics of Utopia: A Study in Theory and Practice*. London, 1982.

Gouhier, H. *La Jeunesse d'Auguste Comte et la formation du Positivisme*. 3 vols. 1933–41.

Graña, C. *Bohemian versus Bourgeois: French Society and the Man of Letters in the Nineteenth Century*. London, 1964.

Granal, P. "Choubrah et le buste du Pacha." *Le Temps* (31 January 1838): cols. 48625–27.

Grate, P. *Deux Critiques d'art à l'époque romantique: Gustave Planche et Théophile Thoré*. Stockholm, 1959.

Green, N. *The Spectacle of Nature: Landscape and Bourgeois Culture in Nineteenth-Century France*. Manchester, 1990.

Griffiths, D. A. *Jean Reynaud, encyclopédiste de l'époque romantique*. Paris, 1965.

Gruner, S. "The Revolution of July 1830 and the Expression 'Bourgeois.'" *The Historical Journal* 11, no. 3 (1968): 462–71.

Grunewald, M. A. "Paul Chenavard (1807–1895). La Palingénésie sociale ou la philosophie de l'histoire 1830?–1852?" *Bulletin des musées et monuments lyonnais* 6, no. 1 (1980): 317–43.

Günther, H., ed. *The Culture of the Stalin Period*. London, 1990.

Guyon, B. "Une Revue romantique inconnue: 'Le Gymnase.' Etude sur les rapports du Saint-Simonisme et de la littérature étrangère." *Revue de la littérature comparée* 11 (1931): 314–21, 489–511.

Hadjinicolaou, N. "L'Exigence de 'Réalisme' au Salon de 1831." *Histoire et critique des arts* 4–5 (May–June 1978): 21–33.

———. "Sur l'idéologie de l'avant-gardisme." *Histoire et critique des arts* 6 (July 1978): 49–76.

———. "Art in a Period of Social Upheaval: French Art Criticism and Problems of Change in 1831." *Oxford Art Journal* 6, no. 2 (1983): 29–37.

Hagan, D. V. *Félicien David, 1810–1876: A Composer and a Cause*. Syracuse, 1985.

Haines, B. "Henri de Saint-Simon and the Idea of Organism." Ph.D. diss., University College of Wales, Aberystwyth, 1969.

———. "Social, Biological and Medical Thought in Saint-Simon and Comte." *British Journal for the History of Science* 11, no. 1 (March 1978): 19–35.

Hambly, P. S. "Théophile Gautier et le Fouriérisme." *Australian Journal of French Studies* 12, no. 3 (September–December 1974): 237–52.

Hanoune, R. "De Douai à Rome et Athènes. Un Architecte oublié, Florimond Boulanger (1807–1875)." *Revue du nord* 61 (April–June 1979): 427–37.

Hart, D. K. "Saint-Simon and the Role of the Elite." *Western Political Quarterly* 17 (September 1964): 423–31.

Hartwig, O. "François Sabatier und Caroline Sabatier-Ungher." *Deutsche Rundschau* (May 1897): 227–43.

Hayek, F. A. von. *The Counter-Revolution of Science*. Glencoe, Ill., 1952.

Hazard, P. "Saint-Simonisme et littérature." *Néophilologus* 33 (1937–38): 129–34.

Head, B. W. *Ideology and Social Science. Destutt de Tracy and French Liberalism*. Dordrecht, 1985.

Herding, K. "Décadence und Progrès als kunsttheoretische Begriffe bei Barrault, Baudelaire und Proudhon." *Wissenschaftliche Zeitschrift der Humboldt-Universität zu Berlin* 34, nos. 1–2 (1985): 35–54.

———. "Fortschritt und Niedergang in der bildenden Kunst: Nachträge zu Barrault, Baudelaire und Proudhon." In *Fortschrittsglaube und Dekadenzbewußtsein im Europa des 19. Jahrhunderts. Literatur—Kunst—Kulturgeschichte*, edited by W. Drost. Heidelberg, 1986.

———. "Utopie concrète à l'échelle mondiale: l'art de la Révolution." In *La Révolution française et l'Europe*, 1:xxii–l. Paris, 1989.

———. *Courbet: To Venture Independence*. New Haven, 1991.

Himelblau, J. "Reflections on Claude-Henri, Comte de Saint-Simon, on the Artist and His Art." *Romance Notes* 19, no. 1 (1967): 75–76.

Hipeau, C., ed. *L'Instruction publique en France pendant la Révolution*. Paris, 1881.

Hoeges, D. "Saint-Simon und die Theorie der Avant-Garde." *Lendemains* 37 (1985): 37–43.

Horaist, B. "L'Oeuvre peint du R. P. Besson O.P. (1816–1861)." 2 vols. Thèse de 3e cycle, Université de Paris X, 1982.

Hôtel de Sully, Paris. *Le "Gothique" retrouvé avant Viollet-le-Duc*. Exhibition catalog. Paris, 1979.

Hubbard, G. *Saint-Simon, sa vie et ses travaux*. Paris, 1857.

Hunt, H. J. *Le Socialisme et le romantisme en France: étude de la presse socialiste de 1830 à 1848*. Oxford, 1935.

Hutton, J. "A Blow of the Pick: Science, Anarchism, and the Neo-Impressionist Movement." Ph.D. diss., Northwestern University, 1987.

Iggers, G. G. *The Cult of Authority. The Political Philosophy of the Saint-Simonians. A Chapter in the Intellectual History of Totalitarianism*. The Hague, 1958.

———. "Henri Heine and the Saint-Simonians: A Re-examination." *Comparative Literature* 10, no. 4 (Fall 1958): 289–308.

Iknayan, M. *The Concave Mirror: From Imitation to Expression in French Esthetic Theory 1800–1830*. Saratoga, Calif., 1983.

Isambert, F. A. "Epoques critiques et époques organiques. Une contribution de Buchez à l'élaboration de la théorie sociale des Saint-Simoniens." *Cahiers internationaux de sociologie* 27 (1959): 131–52.

———. "Physiologie sociale et système des sciences chez Buchez." *Cahiers internationaux de sociologie* 36 (January–June 1964): 101–16.

———. *De la Charbonnerie au Saint-Simonisme. Etude sur la jeunesse de Buchez*. Paris, 1966.

———. *Politique, religion et science de l'homme chez Philippe Buchez (1796–1865)*. Paris, 1967.

Isambert, G. *Les Idées socialistes en France de 1815 à 1848*. Paris, 1905.

Ivens, M. "La Liberté guidant les artistes." *Les Révoltes logiques* 10 (1979): 52–94.

Jacyna, L. S. "Medical Science and Moral Science: The Cultural Relations of Physiology in Restoration France." *History of Science* 25 (1987): 111–46.

Jardin, A. *Histoire du libéralisme politique. De la crise de l'absolutisme à la constitution de 1875*. Paris, 1985.

Jouin, H. *David d'Angers et ses relations littéraires*. Paris, 1890.

———. *Lettres inédites des artistes français du 19e siècle*. Macon, 1901.

Jowell, F. S. *Thoré-Bürger and the Art of the Past*. New York, 1977.

Juden, B. *Traditions orphiques et tendances mystiques dans le romantisme français (1800–1855)*. Paris, 1971.

———. "L'Esthétique: 'l'harmonie immense qui dit tout.' " *Romantisme* 5 (1973): 4–17.

Kelder, D. *Aspects of "Official" Painting and Philosophic Art 1789–1799*. New York, 1976.

Kelley, D. "L'Art: l'harmonie du beau et de l'utile." *Romantisme* 5 (1973): 18–36.

Kelley, D., ed. *Baudelaire: Salon de 1846*. Oxford, 1975.

Kennedy, E. *A "Philosophe" in the Age of Revolution. Destutt de Tracy and the Origins of "Ideology."* Philadelphia, 1978.

Klare, J. "L'Elaboration du vocabulaire politico-social en France dans la première moitié du 19e siècle." *Beitrage zur Romanischen Philologie* 13 (1974): 259–69.

Klumpke, A. *Rosa Bonheur, sa vie, son oeuvre*. Paris, 1908.

Lacassagne, J.-P. "Pierre Leroux, Saint-Simon et les Saint-Simoniens." *Economies et sociétés* 7, no. 1 (January 1973): 57–91.

———. ed. *Histoire d'une amitié; Pierre Leroux et George Sand d'après une correspondance inédite*. Paris, 1973.

Lacroix, J. "Les Idées religieuses et esthétiques de Saint-Simon." *Economies et sociétés* 4 (April 1970): 693–713.

Lallemand, P. de. *Montalembert et ses amis dans le romantisme. 1830–1840*. Paris, 1927.

Larat, J. *La Tradition de l'exotisme dans l'oeuvre de Charles Nodier (1780–1844)*. Paris, 1923.

Larizza, M. "Studi Fourieriani." *Rivista internationale de filosofia del diritto*, 4th ser., 45, no. 1 (1968): 125–47.

———. "L'influenza di Maistre sulla dottrina della scuola sansimoniana." In *Joseph de Maistre tra illuminismo e restaurazione*, edited by L. Marino. Turin, 1975.

Larizza-Lolli, M. " 'Socialisme' et 'utopisme': deux catégories à méditer? Quelques considérations à partir du cas du saint-simonisme." In *Romantismes et socialismes en Europe (1800–1848)*, edited by A. Billaz and U. Ricken. Etudes de littérature étrangère et comparée, 82:137–50. Paris, 1987.

Laubriet, P. "Balzac et la sculpture." *Gazette des beaux-arts*, 6th ser., 57 (June 1961): 331–58.

La Varenne, C. de. *Les Rouges peints par eux-mêmes*. Paris, 1850.

Le Bras-Chopard, A. *De l'égalité dans la différence. Le Socialisme de Pierre Leroux*. Paris, 1986.

Lebrun, R. A. *Throne and Altar: The Political and Religious Thought of Joseph de Maistre*. Ottowa, 1965.

Ledré, C. *La Presse à l'assaut de la monarchie 1815–1848*. Paris, 1960.

Leduc-Fayette, D. *Jean-Jacques Rousseau et le mythe de l'antiquité*. Paris, 1974.

Lehouck, E. *Fourier, aujourd'hui*. Paris, 1966.

———. "Fourier et la liberté." *Revue des études cooperatives*, 48th year, 157 (1969): 267–76.

———. "Un Disciple hérétique de Fourier: Alphonse Toussenel (1803–1885)." *Les Lettres nouvelles* (May 1971): 133–47.

Leith, J. A. *The Idea of Art as Propaganda in France, 1750–1799: A Study in the History of Ideas*. Toronto, 1965.

———. "Nationalism and the Fine Arts in France, 1750–1789." In *Studies on Voltaire and the Eighteenth Century*, vol. 89. *Transactions of the Third International Congress on the Enlightenment* 3 (1972): 919–37.

Leniaud, J. M. *Jean-Baptiste Lassus (1807–1857) ou le temps retrouvé des cathédrales*. Paris, 1980.

Lenoir, H. *Contribution à l'étude des sources de l'oeuvre de Charles Fourier*. Sainte-Geneviève-des-Bois, 1982.

Le Normand, A. *La Tradition classique et l'esprit romantique: les sculpteurs de l'Académie de France à Rome de 1824 à 1840*. Paris, 1981.

Le Normand-Romain, A. "Le Séjour d'Etex à Rome en 1831–1832. Un Carnet de dessins inédit." *Bulletin de la Société de l'histoire de l'art français* (1981, pub. 1983): 175–88.

Le Nouëne, P. "'Les Soldats de l'industrie' de François Bonhommé: l'idéologie d'un projet." *Histoire et critique des arts* 4–5 (May 1978): 35–61.

———. "Représentation du peuple dans les tableaux d'histoire exposés aux Salons entre 1831 et 1848." In *Exigences de réalisme dans la peinture française de 1830 à 1870*, 14–33. Chartres, Musée des beaux-arts, 1983.

Levin, M. R. *Republican Art and Ideology in Late Nineteenth-Century France*. Ann Arbor, 1986.

Levitine, G. *The Dawn of Bohemianism: The "Barbu" Rebellion and Primitivism in Neoclassical France*. University Park, Penn., 1978.

Lipstadt, H. *Architecte et ingénieur dans la presse: polémique, débat, conflit*. Paris, 1980.

———. "César Daly; Revolutionary Architect?" *Architectural Design Profiles 17: The Beaux-Arts* (n.d.): 18–29.

Lloyd, R. "Un Peintre et ses critiques: Dominique Papety." *Romantisme* 50 (1985): 105–10.

Locke, R. P. *Music, Musicians, and the Saint-Simonians*. Chicago, 1986.

Lodewijk de Liefde, C. *Le Saint-Simonisme dans la poésie française entre 1825 et 1865*. Haarlem, 1927.

Loubère, L. A. *Louis Blanc. His Life and Contribution to French Jacobin-Socialism*. Evanston, 1961.

Lukes, S. "The Meaning of 'Individualism.'" *Journal of the History of Ideas* 32, no. 1 (1971): 45–66.

McWilliam, N. "'Un Enterrement à Paris': Courbet's Political Contacts in 1845." *Burlington Magazine* 125 (1983): 155–57.

———. "Art, Labour and Mass Democracy: Debates on the Status of the Artist in France around 1848." *Art History* 11, no. 1 (March 1988): 64–87.

______. *A Bibliography of Salon Criticism in Paris from the July Monarchy to the Second Republic 1831–1851*. Cambridge, 1991.

______. "Opinions professionnelles: critique d'art et économie de la culture sous la Monarchie de juillet." *Romantisme* 71 (1991): 19–30.

Maitron, J., ed. *Dictionnaire biographique du mouvement ouvrier français (1789–1864)*. 3 vols. Paris, 1964–66.

______. *Dictionnaire biographique du mouvement ouvrier français (1864–1871)*. 5 vols. Paris, 1967–71.

Malon, B. *Histoire du socialisme*. Lugano, 1879.

______. "A. Ottin—article nécrologique." *La Revue socialiste* (December 1890): 756–57.

Manuel, F. E. "From Equality to Organicism." *Journal of the History of Ideas* 17 (1956): 54–69.

______. *The New World of Henri Saint-Simon*. Cambridge, Mass., 1956.

______. "The Role of the Scientist in Saint-Simon." *Revue internationale de philosophie* 14 (1960): 345–56.

______. *The Prophets of Paris*. Cambridge, Mass., 1962.

Manuel, F. E., and F. P. Manuel. *A History of Western Utopian Thought*. Oxford, 1979.

Marrinan, M. *Painting Politics for Louis-Philippe: Art and Ideology in Orléanist France, 1830–1848*. New Haven, 1988.

Matoré, G. "Les Notions d'art et d'artiste à l'époque romantique." *Revue des sciences humaines* 16, nos. 62–63 (April–September 1951): 120–37.

______. *Le Vocabulaire et la société sous Louis-Philippe*. Geneva, 1951.

______. ed. *Théophile Gautier: La Préface de Mademoiselle de Maupin*. Paris, 1946.

Matoré, G., and A. J. Greimas. "La Naissance du 'Génie' au dix-huitième siècle. Etude lexicologique." *Le Français moderne* 25 (1957): 256–72.

Melot, M. "Daumier and Art History. Aesthetic Judgement/Political Judgement." *Oxford Art Journal* 11, no. 1 (1988): 3–24.

Morilhat, C. *Charles Fourier, imaginaire et critique sociale*. Paris, 1991.

Mosby, D. F. *Alexandre-Gabriel Decamps 1803–1860*. 2 vols. New York, 1977.

Mougin, H. *Pierre Leroux*. Paris, 1938.

Mustoxidi, T. N. *Histoire de l'esthétique française 1700–1900*. Paris, 1920.

Nathan, M. *Le Ciel des Fouriéristes: habitants des étoiles et réincarnations de l'âme*. Lyons, 1981.

Needham, H. A. *Le Développement de l'esthétique sociologique en France et en Angleterre au 19e siècle*. Paris, 1926.

Nicolet, C. *L'Idée républicaine en France. Essai d'histoire critique*. Paris, 1982.

Nochlin, L. "The Invention of the Avant-Garde: France 1830–1880." *Art News Annual* 34 (1968): 11–18.

______. *Gustave Courbet: A Study of Style and Society*. New York, 1976.

Olander, W. "'Pour transmettre à la postérité': French Painting and Revolution, 1774–1795." Ph.D. diss., New York University, 1983.

Ozouf, M. *La Fête révolutionnaire: 1789–1799*. Paris, 1976.

Palfrey, T. R. *"L'Europe littéraire" 1833–1834, un essai de périodique cosmopolite*. Paris, 1927.

Palmer, R. R. *The Improvement of Humanity. Education and the French Revolution*. Princeton, 1985.

Pauly, A. "Théophile Bra." *Revue artistique et littéraire* 5 (1863): 234–37.

Pellarin, C. *Charles Fourier, sa vie et sa théorie*. 2d ed. 1843.

Pessin, A. *Le Mythe du peuple et la société française du XIXe siècle*. Paris, 1992.

Petit, E. *Eugène Pelletan (1813–1844). L'Homme et l'oeuvre d'après des documents inédits*. Paris, 1913.

Petri, B. P. *The Historical Thought of P.J.B. Buchez*. Washington, D.C., 1958.

Petroz, P. *Un Critique d'art au XIXe siècle. Théophile Thoré*. Paris, 1884.

Peyre, H. *Louis Ménard (1822–1901)*. New Haven, 1932.

Pfeiffer, H. *Der soziale Nutzen der Kunst. Kunsttheoretische Aspekte der frühen Gesellschaftstheorie in Frankreich*. Munich, 1988.

Pfeiffer, H., H. R. Jauss, F. Gaillard, eds. *Art social und Art industriel. Funktionen der Kunst im Zeitalter des Industrialismus*. Munich, 1987.

Pichois, C. "Baudelaire en 1847. Petit Essai de sociologie littéraire." In *Baudelaire. Etudes et témoignages*, edited by C. Pichois, 95–121. Neuchâtel, 1967.

Pommier, E. *L'Art de la liberté. Doctrines et débats de la Révolution française*. Paris, 1991.

Pothier, Abbé. *Monseigneur Fournier, évêque de Nantes. Sa Vie, ses oeuvres*. 2 vols. Nantes, 1900.

Puech, J. L. *La Vie et l'oeuvre de Flora Tristan (1803–1844)*. Paris, 1925.

Ragon, M. *Histoire de la littérature prolétarienne en France*. Paris, 1974.

Rancière, J. *La Nuit des prolétaires*. Paris, 1981.

______. "Ronds de fumée (les poètes ouvriers dans la France de Louis-Philippe)." *Revue des sciences humaines* 61, no. 190 (April–June 1983): 31–47.

Raphael, M. *Proudhon, Marx, Picasso*. London, 1980.

Reardon, M. "The Reconciliation of Christianity with Progress: Philippe Buchez." *Review of Politics* 33, no. 4 (1971): 512–37.

Régnier, P. "Les Idées et les opinions littéraires des Saint-Simoniens (1825–1835)." 3 vols. Thèse de 3e cycle, Université de Paris III, 1983.

______. "Les Saint-Simoniens et le mouvement romantique." In *Romantismes et socialismes en Europe (1800–1848)*, edited by A. Billaz and U. Ricken, 207–23. Etudes de littérature étrangère et comparée, 82. Paris, 1987.

______. *Les Saint-Simoniens en Egypte 1833–1851*. Cairo, 1989.

______. "Les Saint-Simoniens, le prêtre et l'artiste," *Romantisme* 67 (1990): 31–45.

______. ed. *Le Livre nouveau des Saint-Simoniens*. Tusson, 1991.

Reszler, A. *L'Esthétique anarchiste*. Paris, 1973.

Rey, G. *Le Fouriériste Allyre Bureau (1810–1859)*. Publications des annales de la Faculté des lettres—Travaux et mémoires, 21. Aix-en-Provence, 1962.

Roberts, W. *Morality and Social Class in Eighteenth-Century French Literature and Painting*. Toronto, 1974.

Robin, R. *Le Réalisme socialiste. Une Esthétique impossible*. Paris, 1986.

Robinson, P.E.J. *Jean-Jacques Rousseau's Doctrine of the Arts*. Bern, 1984.

Rose, M. *Marx's Lost Aesthetic. Karl Marx and the Visual Arts*. Cambridge, 1984.

Rosenblum, R. *Transformations in Late Eighteenth Century Art*. Princeton, 1967.

Rosenthal, L. *Du romantisme au réalisme*. Paris, 1914.

Rousseau, M. "Une Pétition nationale adressée à la Chambre des députés en septembre 1830 et redigé par Jeanron." *Bulletin de la Société de l'histoire de l'art français* (1934): 186–95.

———. "P.-A. Jeanron 1808–1877. Peintre. Ecrivain. Directeur des musées nationaux." Thesis, Ecole du Louvre, Paris, 1935.

———. "Filippo Buonarroti et les artistes français sous la Monarchie de juillet." *Revue des études italiennes* 3 (1938): 159–69.

Rubin, J. H. *Realism and Social Vision in Courbet and Proudhon*. Princeton, 1980.

Saboya, M. *Presse et architecture au XIXe siècle. César Daly et la "Revue générale de l'architecture et des travaux publics."* Paris, 1991.

Saisselin, R.G. *The Rule of Reason and the Ruses of the Heart: A Philosophical Dictionary of Classical French Criticism, Critics, and Aesthetic Issues*. Cleveland, 1970.

Schérer, R. *Pari sur l'impossible. Etudes fouriéristes*. Vincennes, 1989.

Schiefenbusch, E. "L'Influence de Jean-Jacques Rousseau sur les beaux-arts en France." *Annales de la Société Jean-Jacques Rousseau* 19 (1929–30): 1–212.

Schlanger, J. E. "Bonheur et musique chez Fourier," *Revue de métaphysique et de morale* 70, no. 2 (1965): 226–39.

Seigel, J. *Bohemian Paris. Politics and the Boundaries of Bourgeois Life, 1830–1930*. New York, 1986.

Seigneur, J. du. "Théophile Bra, statuaire." *Revue universelle des arts* 18 (1863): 97–102.

Shroder, M. Z. *Icarus: The Image of the Artist in French Romanticism*. Cambridge, Mass., 1961.

Sicard, A. *L'Education morale et civique avant et pendant la Révolution (1700–1808)*. Paris, 1884.

Silberling, E. *Dictionnaire de sociologie phalanstérienne. Guide des oeuvres complètes de Charles Fourier*. Paris, 1911.

Simon, W. M. "History for Utopia: Saint-Simon and the Idea of Progress." *Journal of the History of Ideas* 17, no. 3 (1956): 311–31.

Singer, I. "The Aesthetics of Art for Art's Sake." *Journal of Aesthetics and Art Criticism* 12 (March 1954): 343–59.

Sloane, J. C. *Paul-Marc Chenavard, Artist of 1848*. Chapel Hill, N.C., 1962.

Société d'histoire de la révolution de 1848 et des révolutions du XIXe siècle. *1848: les utopismes sociaux*. Paris, 1981.

Société de l'histoire de l'Ile Maurice. *Dictionnaire de biographie mauricienne*. Port Louis, 1944.

Sonn, R. D. *Anarchism and Cultural Politics in Fin de Siècle France*. Lincoln, Neb., 1989.

Spencer, M. *The Art Criticism of Théophile Gautier*. Geneva, 1969.

———. "A(na)logie de Fourier." *Romantisme* 34 (1981): 31–46.

Spitzer, A. B. *The French Generation of 1820*. Princeton, 1987.

Stanton, T. *Reminiscences of Rosa Bonheur*. London, 1910.

Starobinski, J. *Jean-Jacques Rousseau. La Transparence et l'obstacle*. Paris, 1971.

Staum, M. S. *Cabanis: Enlightenment and Medical Philosophy in the French Revolution*. Princeton, 1980.

Steinwachs, B. *Epochenbewusstein und Kunsterfahrung. Studien zur geschichtphiloso-*

phischen Ästhetik an der Wende vom 18. zum 19. Jahrhundert in Frankreich und Deutschland. Munich, 1986.

Stenzel, H. "Les Ecrivains et l'évolution idéologique de la bourgeoisie." *Romantisme* 17–18 (1977): 79–91.

———. "Evolution et fonction du concept de la nature dans la littérature romantique et dans le socialisme utopique." *Romantisme* 30 (1980): 29–38.

———. "Ein Ästhetik des 'Vorscheins' Grundpositionen der Literatur- und Kunstkritik der fourieristischen 'Ecole sociétaire.' " *Lendemains* 37 (1985): 18–26.

Swart, K. W. " 'Individualism' in the mid nineteenth century. 1826–1860." *Journal of the History of Ideas* 23 (1962): 77–90.

———. *The Sense of Decadence in Nineteenth-Century France*. The Hague, 1964.

Talmon, J. L. *Political Messianism: The Romantic Phase*. London, 1960.

Tamisier, F. "Dominique Papety: sa vie et ses oeuvres." *Tribune artistique et littéraire du midi* 1 (1857): 47–66.

Temkin, O. "The Philosophical Background to Magendie's *Physiologie*." In *The Double Face of Janus*, edited by O. Temkin, 317–39. Baltimore, 1977.

Terdiman, R. *Discourse/Counter-Discourse: The Theory and Practice of Symbolic Resistance in Nineteeenth-Century France*. Ithaca, N.Y., 1985.

Teysssier, A. *Notice biographique sur Louis-Alexandre Piel, architecte*. Paris, 1843.

Thibert, M. *Le Rôle social de l'art d'après les Saint-Simoniens*. Paris, 1927.

Thomas, E. *Voix d'en bas. La Poésie ouvrière du XIXe siècle*. Paris, 1979.

Thomas, J. P. *Libération instinctuelle, libération politique*. Paris, 1980.

———. "L'Oeuvre dialogique de François Cantagrel." *Corpus* 2 (January 1986): 149–55.

Thomas, P. F. *Pierre Leroux, sa vie, son oeuvre, sa doctrine*. Paris, 1904.

Thouvenal, E. A. *La Grèce du roi Othon*. Paris, 1890.

Tolley, B. "The Social Role of Art and Literature according to the Saint-Simonians 1825–1833." D.Phil. diss., University of Oxford, 1968.

———. "A Saint-Simonian Writer: Hippolyte Auger (1797–1881)." *Australian Journal of French Studies* ll (1974): 288–306.

Vaisse, P. "Considérations sur la Seconde République et les beaux-arts." *1848. Révolutions et mutations au XIXe siècle* (1985): 59–85.

Valkhoff, P. "Louis Ménard (1822–1901)." *Neophilologus* 1 (1915–16): 88–100.

Van Zanten, A. L. "The Palace and the Temple: Two Utopian Architectural Visions of the 1830s." *Art History* 2, no. 2 (June 1979): 179–200.

Viatte, A. *Les Sources occultes du romantisme*. Paris, 1928.

Vidalenc, J. "Les Techniques de la propagande saint-simonienne à la fin de 1831." *Archives de sociologie des religions* 10 (July–December 1960): 3–20.

Vincent-Buffault, A. *Histoire des larmes*. Paris, 1986.

Walch, J. *Bibliographie du Saint-Simonisme*. Paris, 1967.

Wallon, H. "Notice historique sur la vie et les travaux de Jean-Barthélémy Hauréau." In *Institut de France. Académie des inscriptions et belles-lettres. Séance publique annuelle du 12 novembre 1897*, 53–110. Paris, 1897.

Wallon, J. *La Presse de 1848, ou revue critique des journaux publiés à Paris depuis la révolution de février jusqu'à la fin de decembre*. Paris, 1849.

Weill, G. *Saint-Simon et son oeuvre*. Paris, 1894.

______. *L'Ecole saint-simonienne, son histoire, son influence jusqu'à nos jours*. Paris, 1896.

______. *Histoire du parti républicain en France (1814–1870)*. 2d ed. Paris, 1928.

Weisberg, G. P. "The Realist Tradition: Critical Theory and the Evolution of Social Themes." In *The Realist Tradition* edited by G. P. Weisberg, 1–20. Cleveland, 1980.

______, ed. *The Art of the July Monarchy. France 1830–1848*. Columbia, Mo., 1990.

Welch, C. B. *Liberty and Utility: The French Idéologues and the Transformation of Liberalism*. New York, 1984.

Wilcox, J. "La Genèse de la théorie de l'art pour l'art en France." *Revue d'esthétique* 6 (1953): 1–26.

Will, F. *Flumen Historicum. Victor Cousin's Aesthetic and Its Sources*. Chapel Hill, N.C., 1965.

Winterthur, Kunstmuseum, *Charles Gleyre, ou les illusions perdues*. Exhibition catalog. 1974–75.

Zeldin, D. *The Educational Ideas of Charles Fourier (1772–1837)*. London, 1969.

Zielonka, A. *Alphonse Esquiros (1812–1876): A Study of His Works*. Geneva, 1985.

Zilberfarb, J. *Sotsialnaia filosofia Sharlia Fure i ee mesto v istoni sotsialisticheskoi mysli pervoi poloviny XIX veka*. Moscow, 1964.

______. "L'Imagination et la réalité dans l'oeuvre de Fourier." *Mouvement social* 60 (1967): 5–21.

Index